China's Growing Role in World Trade

**A National Bureau
of Economic Research
Conference Report**

China's Growing Role in World Trade

Edited by **Robert C. Feenstra and Shang-Jin Wei**

The University of Chicago Press

Chicago and London

The University of Chicago Press, Chicago 60637
The University of Chicago Press, Ltd., London
© 2010 by the National Bureau of Economic Research
All rights reserved. Published 2010.
Paperback edition 2012
Printed in the United States of America

21 20 19 18 17 16 15 14 13 12   2 3 4 5 6

ISBN-13: 978-0-226-23971-2 (cloth)
ISBN-13: 978-0-226-23974-3 (paper)
ISBN-10: 0-226-23971-3 (cloth)
ISBN-10: 0-226-23974-8 (paper)

Library of Congress Cataloging-in-Publication Data

China's growing role in world trade / edited by Robert C. Feenstra and Shang-jin Wei.
    p. cm.— (National Bureau of Economic Research conference report)
    Includes bibliographical references and index.
    ISBN-13: 978-0-226-23971-2 (alk. paper)
    ISBN-10: 0-226-23971-3 (alk. paper)
    1. International trade. 2. China—Commerce. I. Feenstra, Robert C. II. Wei, Shang-Jin.
  III. Series: National Bureau of Economic Research conference report.
    HF3838.C455 2010
    382.0951—dc22

2009016356

Relation of the Directors to the
Work and Publications of the
National Bureau of Economic Research

1. The object of the NBER is to ascertain and present to the economics profession, and to the public more generally, important economic facts and their interpretation in a scientific manner without policy recommendations. The Board of Directors is charged with the responsibility of ensuring that the work of the NBER is carried on in strict conformity with this object.

2. The President shall establish an internal review process to ensure that book manuscripts proposed for publication DO NOT contain policy recommendations. This shall apply both to the proceedings of conferences and to manuscripts by a single author or by one or more co-authors but shall not apply to authors of comments at NBER conferences who are not NBER affiliates.

3. No book manuscript reporting research shall be published by the NBER until the President has sent to each member of the Board a notice that a manuscript is recommended for publication and that in the President's opinion it is suitable for publication in accordance with the above principles of the NBER. Such notification will include a table of contents and an abstract or summary of the manuscript's content, a list of contributors if applicable, and a response form for use by Directors who desire a copy of the manuscript for review. Each manuscript shall contain a summary drawing attention to the nature and treatment of the problem studied and the main conclusions reached.

4. No volume shall be published until forty-five days have elapsed from the above notification of intention to publish it. During this period a copy shall be sent to any Director requesting it, and if any Director objects to publication on the grounds that the manuscript contains policy recommendations, the objection will be presented to the author(s) or editor(s). In case of dispute, all members of the Board shall be notified, and the President shall appoint an ad hoc committee of the Board to decide the matter; thirty days additional shall be granted for this purpose.

5. The President shall present annually to the Board a report describing the internal manuscript review process, any objections made by Directors before publication or by anyone after publication, any disputes about such matters, and how they were handled.

6. Publications of the NBER issued for informational purposes concerning the work of the Bureau, or issued to inform the public of the activities at the Bureau, including but not limited to the NBER Digest and Reporter, shall be consistent with the object stated in paragraph 1. They shall contain a specific disclaimer noting that they have not passed through the review procedures required in this resolution. The Executive Committee of the Board is charged with the review of all such publications from time to time.

7. NBER working papers and manuscripts distributed on the Bureau's web site are not deemed to be publications for the purpose of this resolution, but they shall be consistent with the object stated in paragraph 1. Working papers shall contain a specific disclaimer noting that they have not passed through the review procedures required in this resolution. The NBER's web site shall contain a similar disclaimer. The President shall establish an internal review process to ensure that the working papers and the web site do not contain policy recommendations, and shall report annually to the Board on this process and any concerns raised in connection with it.

8. Unless otherwise determined by the Board or exempted by the terms of paragraphs 6 and 7, a copy of this resolution shall be printed in each NBER publication as described in paragraph 2 above.

Contents

Introduction

Robert C. Feenstra and Shang-Jin Wei

In less than three decades, China has grown from having a negligible role in world trade to being one of the world's largest exporters, as well as a substantial importer of raw materials, intermediate inputs, and other goods. This tremendous growth is seen by some observers as posing a threat to China's trading partners.[1] But because trade is a positive-sum rather than a zero-sum game, this growth must bring opportunities as well. For industrial countries, China presents the opportunity of a low-cost labor force. Whether the goods are simple toys sold by Mattel, or personal computers sold by Lenovo (the Chinese owner of what used to be IBM's PC division), or sophisticated components for the European Airbus, a large part of Chinese exports involves contracting manufacturing in China for goods that are designed elsewhere. This phenomenon is known as "processing trade," and involves importing inputs into China, which are assembled there and then exported again. This role that China plays in contract manufacturing means that its own success is intricately tied to the fortunes of its trading partners.

Even while China acts as a manufacturing base for firms worldwide, its sheer size and rapid growth also creates challenges for many countries. On the export side, China is a formidable competitor in many markets, overlapping in its export composition with other countries such as India, Malaysia, Mexico, Pakistan, The Philippines, and Thailand. These countries often at-

Robert C. Feenstra is a professor of economics at the University of California, Davis, and a research associate of the National Bureau of Economic Research. Shang-Jin Wei is the N. T. Wang Professor of Chinese Business and Economy at Columbia Business School, and a research associate of the National Bureau of Economic Research.

1. Even Samuelson (2002) presents a case where the United States could be harmed by growth in China if this growth occurs in products where the United States has a comparative advantage.

tribute declines in their own export demand to competition from China. And on the import side, too, China's impact is felt worldwide. Its demand for raw materials, especially to fuel the investment boom of recent years (including the 2008 Olympics), creates market pressure and higher prices for building materials. Likewise, the slowdown in China's industrial production in the midst of the 2008 to 2009 global crisis has contributed to a dramatic fall in commodity prices. The industrial production in China is also believed to have led to pollution in the country, which can spill over international borders, too. So the challenges created by China's rapid growth and expanding trade are both domestic and international in scope. The goal of this volume is to investigate these issues raised by China's growing role in world trade.

Some of the major trends in China's exports and imports are summarized in tables I.1 to I.10. In table I.1, we list the nominal value (in billions of U.S. dollars) of exports and imports attributed to "ordinary" versus "processing" trade, along with the share of export and import values in these categories. As their names suggests, ordinary trade includes imports that enter the country and are not destined to be incorporated into exported goods, or exports that did not rely specifically on imported inputs. Conversely, processing trade includes imports that enter the country duty-free and will be incorporated into exported goods, and exports that rely on these processing imports. These two categories do not exhaust the value of trade: besides ordinary and processing trade, there are also international aid flows, contracting projects, goods on lease, barter trade, and other categories of trade flows. But ordinary and processing trade make up the vast majority of trade flows and together account for over 95 percent of exports and over 80 percent of imports.

As shown in table I.1, the nominal value of exports and imports has risen by roughly ten times over 1992 to 2006 in both the ordinary and processing trade categories. That growth is especially rapid in the later years, however: the value of trade roughly doubled in the first seven years, to 1999, and then grew by nearly five times over the next seven years, to 2006, for a remarkable twenty-five percent annual growth rate in the last seven years. Despite this very rapid growth, the share of processing trade does not change that much. On the export side, the share of processing trade rose from 47 percent in 1992 to a high of 57 percent in 1999 and then fell back to 53 percent by 2006. Likewise, on the import side, the share of processing trade rose from 39 percent in 1992 to a high of 49 percent in 1998 and then returned to 41 percent by 2006. These results show that the very rapid growth in both exports and imports is roughly balanced between ordinary and processing trade, and both of these categories will be important in the chapters that follow.[2]

2. The chapters by Amiti and Freund, Wang and Wei, Deng and Harrigan, Feenstra and Hong, and Blonigen and Ma all make use of detailed trade statistics from China Customs Statistics (various years), which include a breakdown by ordinary versus processing trade. These

Table I.1 China's exports and imports, by ordinary and processing trade (billions of U.S. dollars, share of total value)

Year	Billions of U.S. dollars				Share of total export or import value			
	Export		Import		Export		Import	
	Ordinary	Processing	Ordinary	Processing	Ordinary	Processing	Ordinary	Processing
1992	43.7	39.6	33.6	31.5	0.51	0.47	0.42	0.39
1993	43.2	44.2	38.0	36.4	0.47	0.48	0.37	0.35
1994	61.6	57.0	35.5	47.6	0.51	0.47	0.31	0.41
1995	71.4	73.7	43.4	58.4	0.48	0.50	0.33	0.44
1996	62.8	84.3	39.4	62.3	0.42	0.56	0.28	0.45
1997	78.1	99.7	39.0	70.2	0.43	0.55	0.27	0.49
1998	74.2	104.4	43.7	68.6	0.40	0.57	0.31	0.49
1999	79.2	110.9	67.0	73.6	0.41	0.57	0.40	0.44
2000	105.2	137.6	100.1	92.6	0.42	0.55	0.44	0.41
2001	111.9	147.4	113.5	94.0	0.42	0.55	0.47	0.39
2002	136.2	179.9	129.1	122.3	0.42	0.55	0.44	0.41
2003	182.0	241.8	187.7	162.9	0.42	0.55	0.45	0.39
2004	243.6	328.0	248.2	221.7	0.41	0.55	0.44	0.39
2005	315.1	416.5	279.7	274.0	0.41	0.55	0.42	0.42
2006	416.3	510.4	333.2	321.5	0.43	0.53	0.42	0.41

Source: China Customs Statistics (1992–2006).

Table I.2   China's exports and imports, by foreign-invested enterprises (FIEs) and all other firms (share of total export or import value in ordinary or processing trade)

| | Export | | | | Import | | | |
| | Ordinary | | Processing | | Ordinary | | Processing | |
Year	FIEs	Other	FIEs	Other	FIEs	Other	FIEs	Other
1992	0.05	0.95	0.39	0.61	0.05	0.95	0.45	0.55
1993	0.09	0.91	0.48	0.52	0.06	0.94	0.53	0.47
1994	0.07	0.93	0.54	0.46	0.05	0.95	0.59	0.41
1995	0.06	0.94	0.57	0.43	0.12	0.88	0.63	0.37
1996	0.12	0.88	0.63	0.37	0.17	0.83	0.67	0.33
1997	0.13	0.87	0.64	0.36	0.22	0.78	0.68	0.32
1998	0.14	0.86	0.66	0.34	0.22	0.78	0.70	0.30
1999	0.16	0.84	0.67	0.33	0.25	0.75	0.72	0.28
2000	0.19	0.81	0.71	0.29	0.26	0.74	0.74	0.26
2001	0.22	0.78	0.72	0.28	0.27	0.73	0.75	0.25
2002	0.23	0.77	0.75	0.25	0.27	0.73	0.77	0.23
2003	0.24	0.76	0.79	0.21	0.29	0.71	0.81	0.19
2004	0.26	0.74	0.81	0.19	0.29	0.71	0.83	0.17
2005	0.27	0.73	0.83	0.17	0.29	0.71	0.84	0.16
2006	0.28	0.72	0.84	0.16	0.32	0.68	0.85	0.15

Source: China Customs Statistics (1992–2006).

A further distinction that can be made in the trade data is between imports or exports made by foreign-invested enterprises (FIEs), or those made by all other firms, including Chinese state-owned enterprises, town and village collectives, and private firms. The FIEs enterprises include both joint ventures between foreign and Chinese firms and, in later years, wholly-owned foreign enterprises. In table I.2, we report the share of ordinary and processing trade accounted for by FIEs and all other firms. For both exports and imports, FIEs accounted for only 5 percent of ordinary trade in 1992 and 39 percent and 45 percent of processing exports and imports, respectively. So joint ventures with foreign firms accounted for very little of ordinary trade flows and less than half of processing trade flows in early years. But the presence of joint ventures and wholly-owned foreign firms increased in both types of trade so that by 2006, FIEs account for 28 percent and 32 percent of ordinary exports and imports, respectively, and 84 percent and 85 percent of processing exports and imports, respectively. That indicates a very dominant presence of foreign firms in processing trade and a substantial presence in ordinary trade, too. The chapters by Wang and Wei and

---

detailed Harmonized System (HS) trade data can be purchased by contacting George Shen, General Manager, China Customs Statistics (CCS) information center, Hong Kong; Tel.+852 9472 6072 / Fax.+852 2891 2963 / georgeshenhkg@yahoo.com.

by Blonigen and Ma document the growth of foreign firms in the Chinese economy and their special presence in processing trade activities. The chapter by Branstetter and Foley compares U.S. firms in China with those from other source countries.

A final way of breaking down the trade data is by type of product. The most commonly used trade classification today is the Harmonized System (HS), used by most countries. The Chinese customs authorities record both exports and imports at HS numbers with up to eight digits, such as "Live pure bred breeding horses," HS 01011100; "Mulberry feeding silk-worm cocoons," HS 50010010; and "Antiques of an age exceeding one hundred years," HS 97060000. A number of chapters in this volume make use of such disaggregate trade categories. To give an initial impression of the importance of each major type of product, in tables I.3 to I.10, we record the values and shares of ordinary and processing exports and imports by major industries. These industries are as follows:

Animals, Food—animals, vegetable products, and foodstuffs (HS 01–24)
Minerals, Wood—mineral and wood products, stone and glass (HS 25–27, 44–49, 68–71)
Chemicals, Plastic—chemicals and allied industries, plastics and rubbers (HS 28–40)
Textiles—textile products, with leather and fur items (HS 41–43, 50–63)
Footwear, Headgear—footwear and headgear articles (HS 64–67)
Metals, Articles—base metals and articles of base metal (HS 72–83)
Machinery, Electrical—machinery and electrical products (HS 84–85)
Transportation—transportation equipment (HS 86–89)
Miscellaneous Manufacturing—miscellaneous manufactured articles, including cameras, clocks, toys, musical instruments, and furniture (HS 90–92, 94–96)
Omitted[3]—arms (HS 93), antiques (HS 97), special categories (HS 98–99)

For ordinary exports in tables I.3 and I.4, the largest dollar increase in exports is in textiles, which increased from about $14 billion to $108 billion over 1992 to 2006, with most of the growth taking place subsequent to China's membership in the World Trade Organization (WTO) at the end of 2001, when the country could begin to enjoy the benefit of the end of the Multifiber Arrangement and the Agreement on Textile and Clothing. This is a subject studied in the chapter by Brambilla, Khandelwal, and Schott. By 2006, the other largest export industries are machinery and electrical ($76 billion), metals and articles of metal ($65 billion), chemicals and plastics

3. The trade omitted from tables I.3 to I.10 is less than 1 percent of the total value in each table. Exports of antiques may be underreported to evade controls on such goods. See Fisman and Wei (2009) for evidence of underreporting on exports by China and other countries to the United States.

Table I.3   Ordinary exports, by major industry (billions of U.S. dollars)

Year	Animals, Food	Minerals, Wood	Chemicals, Plastics	Textiles	Footwear, Headgear	Metals, Articles	Machinery, Electrical	Transport	Miscellaneous Manufacturing
1992	9.1	7.8	3.9	13.9	0.9	2.6	2.8	0.8	1.5
1993	8.0	6.9	4.1	14.9	1.1	2.4	3.0	0.6	1.8
1994	10.5	8.2	5.8	22.8	1.7	3.7	4.4	0.8	3.3
1995	10.1	11.1	8.2	22.1	2.1	6.0	6.3	1.2	4.0
1996	9.6	10.5	7.6	18.1	2.0	5.0	5.1	1.0	3.6
1997	10.4	12.2	8.9	24.9	2.6	6.5	6.0	1.1	5.1
1998	10.1	10.4	8.7	22.9	2.6	6.7	6.1	1.1	5.1
1999	9.7	10.4	9.2	23.9	2.8	7.4	8.4	1.5	5.7
2000	11.5	14.2	11.2	31.1	3.6	10.4	12.0	2.7	8.0
2001	11.8	15.2	12.2	32.5	4.0	10.1	14.1	3.1	8.4
2002	13.3	16.5	14.4	41.3	5.0	11.8	18.9	3.6	11.0
2003	16.2	21.2	18.5	55.2	6.4	15.9	27.8	5.5	14.7
2004	16.8	27.8	24.9	67.8	8.3	30.1	39.4	8.1	19.5
2005	19.9	34.4	33.0	84.1	10.8	40.5	53.6	12.0	25.4
2006	22.8	39.0	40.3	108.2	13.1	65.2	76.4	17.0	32.4

Source: China Customs Statistics (1992–2006).

Table 1.4   Ordinary exports, by major industry (share of total value)

Year	Animals, Food	Minerals, Wood	Chemicals, Plastics	Textiles	Footwear, Headgear	Metals, Articles	Machinery, Electrical	Transport	Miscellaneous Manufacturing
1992	0.21	0.18	0.09	0.32	0.02	0.06	0.06	0.02	0.03
1993	0.18	0.16	0.10	0.35	0.03	0.06	0.07	0.01	0.04
1994	0.17	0.13	0.09	0.37	0.03	0.06	0.07	0.01	0.05
1995	0.14	0.16	0.11	0.31	0.03	0.08	0.09	0.02	0.06
1996	0.15	0.17	0.12	0.29	0.03	0.08	0.08	0.02	0.06
1997	0.13	0.16	0.11	0.32	0.03	0.08	0.08	0.01	0.07
1998	0.14	0.14	0.12	0.31	0.04	0.09	0.08	0.01	0.07
1999	0.12	0.13	0.12	0.30	0.04	0.09	0.08	0.02	0.07
2000	0.11	0.13	0.11	0.30	0.03	0.10	0.11	0.03	0.08
2001	0.11	0.14	0.11	0.29	0.04	0.09	0.11	0.03	0.08
2002	0.10	0.12	0.11	0.30	0.04	0.09	0.13	0.03	0.08
2003	0.09	0.12	0.10	0.30	0.04	0.09	0.14	0.03	0.08
2004	0.07	0.11	0.10	0.28	0.03	0.12	0.15	0.03	0.08
2005	0.06	0.11	0.10	0.27	0.03	0.13	0.16	0.04	0.08
2006	0.05	0.09	0.10	0.26	0.03	0.16	0.18	0.04	0.08

Source: China Customs Statistics (1992–2006).

($40 billion), minerals and wood ($39 billion) and miscellaneous manufacturing ($32 billion), which includes toys. Note that Chinese food and animal products exports continued to grow in absolute value after its membership in the WTO in 2001, in spite of the fear that its agriculture could be decimated by foreign competition once its tariff and quota protection was reduced. The reason behind the agricultural expansion is analyzed in the chapter by Huang, Liu, Martin, and Rozelle.

When measured by the share of ordinary exports, textiles has a declining share, as do the resource-based industries of minerals and woods and animals and foods, despite a rising nominal value of exports in each case. Conversely, the greatest increase in export shares are for the machinery and electrical industry, which triples from 6 percent to 18 percent of exports over 1992 to 2006; and metals and articles of metal, which doubles from 6 percent to 12 percent of exports over 1992 to 2004 and then rises to 16 percent by 2006. Overall, ordinary exports are more diversified across industries than the pattern seen in processing exports, shown in tables I.5 and I.6.

For processing exports, machinery and electrical products experienced phenomenal growth, from $9 to $323 billion over the period, or from 22 percent to 63 percent of the total value. Telecommunications equipment, a subset of machinery and electrical products, is one example of a processing export that has experienced very substantial growth. Besides machinery and electrical, most other categories of processing exports experience a growth in their value of roughly ten times over the fourteen years, so their shares stay roughly constant. The two most significant exceptions are textiles and footwear and headgear, whose combined exports expand from $17 billion to $48 billion, so their combined share falls substantially from 43 percent to 10 percent. (In addition, miscellaneous manufacturing has a declining share.) While these traditional export industries still expand in dollar terms, it is at a rate slower than the total for processing exports and *much* slower than the more technologically advanced products in the machinery and electrical industry. These industry trends in processing exports are studied in the first two chapters in the volume, by Amiti and Freund and by Wang and Wei.

Turning to ordinary imports, in tables I.7 and I.8, these show the highest value and growth in minerals and woods: imports of those products rise from $5 billion to $118 billion, and its import share more than doubles from 16 percent to 35 percent. These imports are likely used for construction in China as well as intermediate inputs needed in other industries. Their rising value and share are indicative of the pressure exerted by China on world markets for such construction and investment materials. Most other categories of imports have roughly constant shares, with import values rising roughly six or seven times over the fourteen years.

Finally, in tables I.9 and I.10, we report the values and shares for processing imports by major industries. Such imports are brought into the country duty-free and must be incorporated into goods that are subsequently

Table 1.5   Processing exports, by major industry (billions of U.S. dollars)

Year	Animals, Food	Minerals, Wood	Chemicals, Plastics	Textiles	Footwear, Headgear	Metals, Articles	Machinery, Electrical	Transport	Miscellaneous Manufacturing
1992	0.8	1.7	2.0	13.1	4.1	1.8	8.6	1.4	6.0
1993	0.9	1.8	2.2	13.5	5.1	2.0	10.6	1.1	6.9
1994	1.9	2.5	3.0	15.7	5.6	2.9	15.2	1.8	8.4
1995	2.3	2.9	4.2	18.8	6.0	5.9	20.8	2.7	10.1
1996	2.9	3.3	4.8	21.9	6.4	5.2	25.2	3.0	11.6
1997	2.9	4.2	5.7	24.0	7.2	6.7	31.4	3.9	13.6
1998	2.5	3.8	6.4	22.9	7.1	5.6	36.4	5.0	14.6
1999	2.5	4.3	6.7	22.7	6.9	5.0	42.8	4.7	15.3
2000	2.7	5.5	8.0	25.0	7.1	6.0	59.5	6.1	17.8
2001	3.1	5.5	8.5	24.9	7.1	5.7	68.7	5.9	17.8
2002	3.5	6.7	9.7	24.7	7.1	6.8	93.9	6.5	20.9
2003	3.7	8.0	11.7	27.3	7.6	8.5	139.7	9.6	25.3
2004	4.9	10.7	15.4	31.3	8.3	12.1	199.9	12.2	32.8
2005	5.8	14.1	20.3	33.9	9.2	14.4	258.3	15.4	44.8
2006	6.6	17.0	24.7	38.4	10.0	16.1	323.4	19.9	53.6

Source: China Customs Statistics (1992–2006).

Table I.6   Processing exports, by major industry (share of total value)

Year	Animals, Food	Minerals, Wood	Chemicals, Plastics	Textiles	Footwear, Headgear	Metals, Articles	Machinery, Electrical	Transport	Miscellaneous Manufacturing
1992	0.02	0.04	0.05	0.33	0.10	0.05	0.22	0.03	0.15
1993	0.02	0.04	0.05	0.30	0.11	0.05	0.24	0.03	0.16
1994	0.03	0.04	0.05	0.28	0.10	0.05	0.27	0.03	0.15
1995	0.03	0.04	0.06	0.26	0.08	0.08	0.28	0.04	0.14
1996	0.03	0.04	0.06	0.26	0.08	0.06	0.30	0.04	0.14
1997	0.03	0.04	0.06	0.24	0.07	0.07	0.31	0.04	0.14
1998	0.02	0.04	0.06	0.22	0.07	0.05	0.35	0.05	0.14
1999	0.02	0.04	0.06	0.20	0.06	0.05	0.39	0.04	0.14
2000	0.02	0.04	0.06	0.18	0.05	0.04	0.43	0.04	0.13
2001	0.02	0.04	0.06	0.17	0.05	0.04	0.47	0.04	0.12
2002	0.02	0.04	0.05	0.14	0.04	0.04	0.52	0.04	0.12
2003	0.02	0.03	0.05	0.11	0.03	0.04	0.58	0.04	0.10
2004	0.01	0.03	0.05	0.10	0.03	0.04	0.61	0.04	0.10
2005	0.01	0.03	0.05	0.08	0.02	0.03	0.62	0.04	0.11
2006	0.01	0.03	0.05	0.08	0.02	0.03	0.63	0.04	0.10

Source: China Customs Statistics (1992–2006).

Table I.7 Ordinary imports, by major industry (billions of U.S. dollars)

Year	Animals, Food	Minerals, Wood	Chemicals, Plastics	Textiles	Footwear, Headgear	Metals, Articles	Machinery, Electrical	Transport	Miscellaneous Manufacturing
1992	3.0	5.3	6.4	1.4	0.0	4.2	9.3	2.8	1.2
1993	1.8	7.2	3.8	0.5	0.0	8.2	11.6	3.5	1.2
1994	2.8	5.1	4.3	1.1	0.0	4.8	13.0	3.1	1.2
1995	5.7	5.8	6.3	1.3	0.0	3.5	15.8	3.3	1.6
1996	5.5	7.5	6.5	1.0	0.0	3.4	10.9	3.3	1.2
1997	4.5	10.8	6.2	0.6	0.0	3.0	10.4	2.2	1.2
1998	4.7	9.2	7.2	0.6	0.0	3.4	14.5	2.6	1.5
1999	5.4	14.3	12.2	0.9	0.0	6.1	22.8	2.9	2.4
2000	7.6	27.9	16.7	1.9	0.0	8.8	29.8	3.8	3.2
2001	7.6	26.2	18.5	2.1	0.0	11.0	36.3	6.4	5.2
2002	7.8	28.4	22.0	2.5	0.1	13.6	42.1	7.2	5.1
2003	12.3	42.5	29.6	3.6	0.1	22.1	58.3	11.8	7.3
2004	17.6	69.7	40.7	5.9	0.2	25.1	67.0	13.0	8.9
2005	17.2	90.1	47.4	6.3	0.2	29.2	65.7	12.8	10.2
2006	17.9	117.7	53.6	7.9	0.3	26.5	77.2	19.6	12.0

Source: China Customs Statistics (1992–2006).

Table I.8   Ordinary imports, by major industry (share of total value)

Year	Animals, Food	Minerals, Wood	Chemicals, Plastics	Textiles	Footwear, Headgear	Metals, Articles	Machinery, Electrical	Transport	Miscellaneous Manufacturing
1992	0.09	0.16	0.19	0.04	0.00	0.12	0.28	0.08	0.04
1993	0.05	0.19	0.10	0.01	0.00	0.22	0.30	0.09	0.03
1994	0.08	0.14	0.12	0.03	0.00	0.14	0.37	0.09	0.03
1995	0.13	0.13	0.15	0.03	0.00	0.08	0.36	0.08	0.04
1996	0.14	0.19	0.16	0.03	0.00	0.09	0.28	0.08	0.03
1997	0.12	0.28	0.16	0.02	0.00	0.08	0.27	0.06	0.03
1998	0.11	0.21	0.16	0.01	0.00	0.08	0.33	0.06	0.04
1999	0.08	0.21	0.18	0.01	0.00	0.09	0.34	0.04	0.04
2000	0.08	0.28	0.17	0.02	0.00	0.09	0.30	0.04	0.03
2001	0.07	0.23	0.16	0.02	0.00	0.10	0.32	0.06	0.05
2002	0.06	0.22	0.17	0.02	0.00	0.11	0.33	0.06	0.04
2003	0.07	0.23	0.16	0.02	0.00	0.12	0.31	0.06	0.04
2004	0.07	0.28	0.16	0.02	0.00	0.10	0.27	0.05	0.04
2005	0.06	0.32	0.17	0.02	0.00	0.10	0.24	0.05	0.04
2006	0.05	0.35	0.16	0.02	0.00	0.08	0.23	0.06	0.04

Source: China Customs Statistics (1992–2006).

Table I.9   Processing imports, by major industry (billions of U.S. dollars)

Year	Animals, Food	Minerals, Wood	Chemicals, Plastics	Textiles	Footwear, Headgear	Metals, Articles	Machinery, Electrical	Transport	Miscellaneous Manufacturing
1992	0.8	3.1	5.4	9.9	0.5	3.0	6.1	0.2	1.9
1993	0.9	3.5	6.3	10.7	0.5	4.2	7.5	0.3	2.1
1994	2.0	4.6	8.8	13.7	0.4	4.9	9.9	0.3	2.3
1995	2.8	5.3	10.6	16.1	0.4	6.0	13.4	0.3	2.8
1996	2.0	6.1	11.3	17.5	0.4	6.1	15.1	0.3	2.9
1997	2.2	7.3	12.4	18.0	0.4	6.9	18.9	0.3	3.0
1998	1.9	6.3	13.0	15.2	0.4	7.0	21.0	0.3	2.8
1999	1.4	6.3	12.8	15.0	0.4	7.5	26.1	0.3	2.9
2000	1.6	7.5	14.8	17.2	0.4	9.3	36.8	0.3	3.8
2001	1.7	6.8	14.6	17.0	0.4	8.8	39.5	0.3	4.0
2002	1.9	7.8	17.8	17.3	0.3	10.3	58.6	0.3	7.1
2003	2.2	9.3	21.2	18.9	0.4	13.2	82.0	0.3	14.5
2004	2.6	13.1	26.2	21.0	0.4	18.0	113.9	0.4	24.7
2005	3.2	16.5	31.5	20.9	0.4	20.8	145.1	0.6	33.6
2006	3.5	19.2	36.5	21.6	0.5	25.9	174.1	0.7	37.9

Source: China Customs Statistics (1992–2006).

Table I.10 Processing imports, by major industry (share of total value)

Year	Animals, Food	Minerals, Wood	Chemicals, Plastics	Textiles	Footwear, Headgear	Metals, Articles	Machinery, Electrical	Transport	Miscellaneous Manufacturing
1992	0.03	0.10	0.17	0.32	0.02	0.10	0.19	0.01	0.06
1993	0.02	0.10	0.17	0.29	0.01	0.11	0.21	0.01	0.06
1994	0.04	0.10	0.19	0.29	0.01	0.10	0.21	0.01	0.05
1995	0.05	0.09	0.18	0.28	0.01	0.10	0.23	0.01	0.05
1996	0.03	0.10	0.18	0.28	0.01	0.10	0.24	0.00	0.05
1997	0.03	0.10	0.18	0.26	0.01	0.10	0.27	0.00	0.04
1998	0.03	0.09	0.19	0.22	0.01	0.10	0.31	0.00	0.04
1999	0.02	0.09	0.17	0.20	0.00	0.10	0.36	0.00	0.04
2000	0.02	0.08	0.16	0.19	0.00	0.10	0.40	0.00	0.04
2001	0.02	0.07	0.16	0.18	0.00	0.09	0.42	0.00	0.04
2002	0.02	0.06	0.15	0.14	0.00	0.08	0.48	0.00	0.06
2003	0.01	0.06	0.13	0.12	0.00	0.08	0.50	0.00	0.09
2004	0.01	0.06	0.12	0.09	0.00	0.08	0.51	0.00	0.11
2005	0.01	0.06	0.11	0.08	0.00	0.08	0.53	0.00	0.12
2006	0.01	0.06	0.11	0.07	0.00	0.08	0.54	0.00	0.12

Source: China Customs Statistics (1992–2006).

exported. Often, the major industries of the import and export products are the same. So it is not surprising to see a rapid growth in the value and share of processing imports within the machinery and electrical industry, which mirrors its very rapid growth in processing exports. Conversely, textiles also has a falling share (though rising value), which again is similar to what we found for processing exports of those products. Besides those two cases, most other industries in table I.10 have constant or slightly declining shares. The exception is miscellaneous manufacturing, whose share of processing imports doubles from 6 percent to 12 percent. Overall, the trends we see in processing imports will be determined by the production of processing exports, and the difference between these two categories of trade indicates the *value added* in processing activities. Because processing exports rely on imports, the value added in this activity is less than for ordinary exports or domestic production. This difference in value added and in the employment created by processing versus ordinary trade is studied in the chapter by Feenstra and Hong.

The Microstructure of Chinese Trade

The volume begins with several chapters that take a detailed look at the microeconomic structure of Chinese trade, by which we mean the details of how China's exports compare with other countries in terms of product quality and variety, firm ownership, contractual trade, and the impact of government policies.

From trade statistics, a striking feature about Chinese exports is its apparent similarity to exports by the United States, Japan, and Europe, where this similarity appears to be increasing over time. For example, during the period from 1996 to 2005, the fraction of HS six-digit product lines exported (by at least US$1 million) by both the high-income countries and China rose from 71.3 percent to 86.3 percent. This is a surprising finding because China's factor endowments, with a vast pool of cheap labor, is not the same as those of the high-income countries. Both Rodrik (2006) and Schott (2008) document this apparent rise in sophistication in China's exports. If China has truly managed to export higher quality products than their endowment would imply, this could represent competitive pressure on firms in the developed world outside traditional labor-intensive sectors.

The first chapter in the volume, by Amiti and Freund, challenges the findings of the existing literature on the product quality and variety of China's exports. They begin by noting that while Broda and Weinstein (2006) find that China was the largest contributor to growth in U.S. varieties, most of that growth was in the early (1972 to 1988) period. Furthermore, while Schott (2008) and Rodrik (2006) both argue that China's exports are in high-quality sectors, more typical of a highly-developed country, that conclusion does not take into account the large amount of processing exports in sectors that may be labeled as high-tech industries.

Since 1992, Amiti and Freund find a substantial reallocation of China's exports away from apparel, textiles, footwear, and miscellaneous manufacturing (including toys) and toward electrical machinery, office machines (which includes computers), and telecommunications. But these are precisely the sectors that rely most heavily on processing trade. The fact that China exports rose in these sectors means that its skill content of exports also rose, making it appear closer to the export structure of a highly developed country. But that effect vanishes when processing trade is omitted. In that case, there was no change in the average skill intensity of China manufacturing exports. Rather, it was a rising skill intensity of *processing imports* that appears to explain the same change for processing exports, but not for the rest of exports. Note that processing trade is disproportionately located in government policy zones. The second chapter, by Wang and Wei, suggests that, once a separate policy zone effect on export sophistication is accounted for, the processing trade effect only shows up in the form of a high unit value within a product category.

Wang and Wei use more detailed micro data than that of the previous chapter to study the factors behind this apparent rise in sophistication. As suggested in the chapter by Amiti and Freund, this phenomenon could be nothing but a statistical mirage due to processing trade. For example, while both the United States and China may export notebook computers, the Chinese producers may have to rely more on importing the most sophisticated components, such as central processing units (CPUs) made by Intel or ADM in the United States. In such a case, the Chinese producers could specialize in the unsophisticated stage of production, even though the final product is classified as sophisticated when it shows up at the customs. If one were able to classify a product further into its components, China and developed countries might be found to produce different components. In this case, they would not compete directly with each other. So under this scenario, there is very little for the developed countries to worry about.[4]

On the other hand, the Chinese authorities at both the regional and central levels have been actively promoting quality upgrades in China's product structure through tax and other policy incentives. A particular manifestation of these incentives is the proliferation of economic and technological development zones, high-tech industrial zones, and export processing zones around the country. Their collective share in China's exports rose from less than 6 percent in 1995 to about 25 percent by 2005. These policy incentives could increase the sophistication of China's exports, though they are

---

4. Koopman, Wang, and Wei (2008) find that the share of domestic value in Chinese exports is only on the order of 50 percent, and the share is lower in sectors that are normally labeled as sophisticated, such as telecommunication equipment, and in exports by foreign-invested firms.

unlikely to be efficient (unless learning by doing confers a significant positive externality). If policy is the primary driver for rising sophistication (rather than the mismeasurement induced by processing trade), then China may indeed represent a more direct competition with producers in developed countries.

Foreign-invested firms in China straddle these two explanations. The share of China's total exports produced by wholly foreign-owned firms and Sino-foreign joint ventures has risen steadily over time, from about 31 percent in 1995 to more than 58 percent by 2005. These foreign-invested firms may choose to produce and export much more sophisticated products than would indigenous Chinese firms. In this scenario, while China-made products may compete with those from developed countries, the profits from such activities go to the gross national products (GNPs) of developed countries. Of course, the presence of foreign firms may help indirectly to raise the sophistication of Chinese exports through various spillovers to domestic firms. These three possible scenarios can reinforce each other. For example, a foreign-invested firm may engage in processing trade while located in a high-tech zone.

Taking into account all these possibilities, Wang and Wei report evidence that neither processing trade nor foreign invested firms play the key role in generating the increased overlap in the structure of exports by China and the high-income countries. Instead, improvements in human capital and government policies in the form of tax-favored, high-tech zones appear to contribute most to the rising sophistication of China's exports. Because most processing trade takes place inside an incentive zone, it is not easy to identify the separate roles of processing trade and government incentives without the kind of detailed microdata used in this chapter. By explicitly analyzing the independent role of government policies in the form of high-tech and other incentive zones, this chapter goes beyond the analysis of Amiti and Freund.

An analysis of unit values in trade by Wang and Wei adds further insights. Processing trade is positively associated with higher unit values. In the absence of data on value added from imported inputs versus domestic inputs, it is difficult to say whether processing trade has generated any skill upgrading for China. However, after controlling for processing trade, exports by foreign-invested firms tend systematically to have higher unit values, suggesting that they produce higher-end product varieties (beyond promoting processing exports). High-tech zones and other policy zones set up by the government are likewise associated with higher unit values (beyond promoting processing trade). Therefore, both foreign-investment and government-policy zones have helped to raise product sophistication, but through somewhat different channels.

For the range of export varieties, or the extensive margin of trade, Amiti and Freund find that its growth over the 1997 to 2005 period has been surprisingly modest. Depending on whether they focus on China's exports to the world or to the United States, and on which country's data are used, they find that the growth in exports due to expanding variety cannot explain more than one-quarter of the overall export growth. That means that the remaining three-quarters or more of the export growth over the decade is explained by the intensive margin, that is, rising exports in product categories that China was exporting all along. We should expect this growth in the intensive margin to bring a drop in prices for imports of China's trading partners, which they confirm for the United States: over 1997 to 2005, they find that average export prices from China to the United States fell by 1.5 percent per year, whereas prices from the rest of the world to the United States rose by 0.4 percent per year.

Falling prices from China is a terms-of-trade gain for the countries importing these goods but poses a challenge to the other countries exporting such goods on international markets. The next two chapters in the volume investigate the impact that China's growing trade has had on its trading partners and other exporters, both in the Asia region and beyond.

Harrigan and Deng adopt a simple version of the Ricardian model with stochastic technologies, due to Eaton and Kortum (2002). In that framework, the market share achieved by each country in their trading partners will depend on that country's size, technical capability, and transport costs to its partners. An improvement in China's technical capability increases the market share in partner countries by an amount that is rising in its initial market share: China gains the most in those markets that it already serves most strongly. Likewise, other exporting countries lose the most in those market already served by China. Harrigan and Deng find some support for this hypothesis for several of China's neighbors—South Korea, Taiwan, and Japan—in their sales to China's top twenty markets.

Harrigan and Deng further investigate how China's exports to nearby versus distant markets vary with weight and transportation mode. They confirm a version of the "Washington apples" hypothesis, whereby China's export prices of goods *net* of transport costs rise to more distant markets: goods shipped farther are higher quality, or of higher value relative to weight. The mode of transport also depends on weight, and, in theory, heavy goods should only be sold in nearby markets and air transport only used for distant markets. Interestingly, they find that air transport from China is used predominantly by private and foreign firms, not the state-owned or collectives, and primarily for their shipments of processing exports. That finding is consistent with a high value of time being placed on processing trade (Harrigan 2006).

Hanson and Robertson also investigate the impact of China's growing trade on other exporters and consider ten developing countries that are similar to China in their share of manufacturing in gross domestic product (GDP) and exports: Hungary, Malaysia, Mexico, Pakistan, The Philippines, Poland, Romania, Sri Lanka, Thailand, and Turkey.[5] They adopt the conventional "gravity" specification of international trade flows, whereby exports in a sector depend on the range of products in that sector, production costs, partner GDP, and the country's distance (and, hence, trade costs) to its partners. As China grows, its export sales will divert demand away from other exporters selling to the same markets. In the gravity equation, this potential diversion is captured by the "supply capacity" of China, which in turn should reflect the range of products it exports and its production costs. Hanson and Robertson consider a counterfactual exercise where the supply capacity for China is held constant at its 1995 estimated value and then project the increase in exports for the ten other developing countries selling to a large set of importers in 2005. That is, they are using the gravity equation to estimate how the exports of the ten developing countries would have evolved had China not grown over 1995 to 2005.

In their results, Hanson and Robertson find a modest impact of China on the competing exporters. For all manufacturing industries, the counterfactual difference in export demand in 2005 does not exceed 2.8 percent, for The Philippines, and could be as low as 0.2 percent, for Mexico.[6] The impacts are somewhat larger when excluding all resource industries or when focusing on particular manufacturing industries. In the combined group of apparel, footwear, electronics, and toys, for example, the increase in exports sales for several countries (Pakistan, Poland, and Romania) is about 5 percent; followed by 4 percent for Mexico; 3 percent for Turkey; and about 2 percent for Hungary, Malaysia, The Philippines, and Thailand.[7] One reason that these estimates are modest in size is that the counterfactual exercise whereby China's supply capacity is held constant is limiting the growth in the *range of products* exported from China and limiting the change in its production costs. From the chapter by Amiti and Freund, we know that the extensive margin of China's exports did not rise that much over 1997 to 2005. The counterfactual exercise used by Hanson and Robertson allows for the intensive margin China's export to grow in response to higher import demand or lower tariffs, but holds constant the extensive margin of exports as well as production costs. But because the extensive margin did not rise that much over 1997 to 2005, this counterfactual still allows for substantial growth in Chinese exports relative to what actually happened. This helps to understand why the counterfactual growth in export sales by other developing countries is not that large.

5. India to also similar to China in its manufacturing share of GDP and exports, but Hanson and Robertson omit that country due to its own strong growth in recent years.

6. See table I.6, column (1). This range of estimates ignores Sri Lanka, which is found to benefit from China's growth and, therefore, exports less in the counterfactual exercise where China's supply capacity is held constant.

7. See table I.6, column (7).

The Macroeconomic Implications of China's Trade

The second set of chapters shifts the focus to the macroeconomic consequences of China's trade. There is no doubt that the boom in China's exports during the past decades is large enough to have significant impacts on its domestic employment and production, as well as on the price levels of its trading partners and pressure for exchange rate adjustment. The big macroeconomic question is the sustainability of the current international equilibrium, whereby China (and other countries) are financing the current account deficits of the United States (and some other countries). In a series of papers, Dooley, Folkerts-Landau, and Garber (2003, 2004a,b,c) argue that China is willing to finance the current account deficits of the United States because it generates urban employment in China. In their view, this system is sustainable so long as expanding exports continue to generate employment gains in China, and they suggest these desired gains are on the order of ten to twelve million persons per year, with about 30 percent of that coming from export growth. Feenstra and Hong investigate whether such employment increases have actually occurred in China due to export growth, relying on input-output analysis to quantify the link between exports and employment.

Like other chapters in the volume, Feenstra and Hong make the distinction between processing and ordinary exports. Processing exports cannot be expected to generate the same employment gains as ordinary exports, particularly when we take into account the direct plus indirect use of labor in each industry: the indirect use comes from labor used to produce the intermediate inputs used in exports. Static estimates of the employment gains generated from $1,000 of exports are about 0.44 person-years for ordinary exports and 0.13 person-years for processing exports, for 2000. But applying these coefficients to the very large increase in exports since 1997 vastly overstates the actual employment gains, by an order of magnitude or more. In other words, the static estimates of employment gains from the input-output tables are unreliable as predictors of future employment growth. Feenstra and Hong argue this finding is due to technological change as well as the shifting composition of industries: exports have shifted toward industries with high labor productivity, implying lower employment gains from any given increase in exports.

Making corrections for the shifting composition of industries, as well as for technological change (proxied by the growth in wages), the predictions from the input-output analysis can match the actual employment growth more closely. Feenstra and Hong find that the predictions of Dooley, Folkerts-Landau, and Garber (2003, 2004a,b,c) are quite close to what occurred in China: employment grew by 7.5 to 8 million per year over 1997 to 2002, with export growth explaining about 30 percent of that increase, and the other employment gains coming from nontraded goods like construction.

Surprisingly, the *domestic* demand for traded goods did not add anything to employment over this period: the increase in demand was offset by productivity growth, leading to negligible job gains from domestic demand for tradable. Exports grew much faster over the 2000 to 2005 period, and so did domestic demand, though the breakdown between nontraded and traded goods is not available. Feenstra concludes that exports have become increasingly important in stimulating employment in China but that the same gains could be obtained from growth in domestic demand, especially for tradable goods, which has been stagnant until at least 2002.

The macroeconomic consequences of China's growth on its second-largest trading partner—Japan—are the focus of the chapter by Broda and Weinstein. They begin with a quotation from the Ministry of Finance in Japan, drawn from a widely read editorial in the *Financial Times,* arguing that China and other East Asian countries bring a "deflationary force" in the global economy due to their high "supply capacity." The words used here mirror the discussion of China's "supply capacity" in the chapter by Hanson and Robertson. But in this case the officials in Japan are not worried about the impact of China's rising export sales on other exports of other developing countries; rather, they are concerned about the impact of low prices from China on Japan itself. China's share of imports in Japan rose starting in 1990, and the U.S. share fell from 1998. At the same time, from 1992 to 2002 the import price index for Japan fell. This coincidence of events has led officials in Japan to believe that the rising imports from China have contributed to deflation.

Broda and Weinstein argue that this belief is misplaced and, in fact, that the fall in import prices is due more to technical issue of the construction of the import price index than to any deflationary pressures from China. When adopting the same formula that is used for the consumer price index, import prices rise instead; the same is true when using superlative formulas (the Törnqvist or Fisher Ideal indexes) constructed over import unit values. Furthermore, statistical analysis shows that the unit values from China did not fall faster than those from countries exporting to Japan (though the Chinese unit values are lower). Broda and Weinstein find, however, that the quality and variety of Chinese exports to Japan rose considerably, but even these effects have only a very small impact on Japanese deflation.

As China's trade surplus exploded in recent years, the role of the Chinese exchange rate in generating this surplus has become an intense subject of debate. In particular, has China's currency been kept artificially low to give its exporters a competitive edge? Would Chinese trade adjust in a responsive way to a renminbi (RMB) appreciation? In chapter 7, Cheung, Chinn, and Fujii provide an analysis of these issues. Their chapter has two parts. First, they assess whether the Chinese real exchange rate is consistent with long-run equilibrium by casting the question in a setting of a cross-country comparison. Second, they estimate the elasticities of China's trade to real exchange rate on both a multilateral and a bilateral (i.e., vis-à-vis the United States) basis.

When assessing the level of real exchange rate, Cheung, Chinn, and Fujii's most important claim is that there is a distinction between *finding* undervaluation and *proving* undervaluation. In terms of point estimates, the Chinese currency is shown to be substantially undervalued from a variety of specifications, sometimes on the order of 50 percent. However, none of the point estimates is obtained with much precision. The estimates are typically within 2 standard deviations from the regression line (conditional mean). In other words, despite the large value of the point estimates, one cannot reject statistically the null hypothesis that there is no undervaluation of the Chinese currency. This does not prove there is no undervaluation because one equally cannot reject statistically the hypothesis that there is a 50 percent undervaluation. What Cheung, Chinn, and Fujii show is that, given the nature of the noise in the relationship between exchange rates and other variables, there is a considerable amount of uncertainty associated with the battery of statistical tools they use. Perhaps future development of statistical tools would allow one to make more precise statements. Frankel, in discussing this chapter, argues that Cheung, Chinn, and Fujii might be overly conservative in acknowledging a lack of precision of the estimates. If several different procedures all point to the same conclusion of an RMB undervaluation, perhaps the uncertainty about this conclusion is smaller than each of the procedures taken alone.

In the second part of the chapter, Cheung, Chinn, and Fujii examine whether and how Chinese trade flows respond to its exchange rate (holding constant other determinants of trade). Economic theory would predict that when the RMB appreciates, Chinese exports are likely to decline, and its imports are likely to increase. While Cheung, Chinn, and Fujii confirm the effect on the exports in the data, they find it difficult to corroborate the predicted effect on imports. In fact, the imports appear to decline also in response to an RMB appreciation. They try a number of fixes, such as separating processing imports from ordinary imports and adding cumulative foreign direct investment (FDI) as a control variable. These modifications do not change the estimated relationship on the import side. A likely remedy in the future is to use much more disaggregated trade data as in some of the other chapters in this volume.

Sectoral Issues and Trade Policies

The third set of chapters in the volume investigates various important sector-level issues. It begins by examining the use of "nontraditional" trade protectionist tools, in particular, antidumping investigations, both against China and by China. This is followed by a chapter that reflects on the country's experience under the Multifiber Arrangement (MFA) and the Agreement on Textiles and Clothing (ATC). China's agricultural trade reform and rural prosperity is the subject of the third chapter, and an investigation into the relationship between China's trade and the environment concludes this section.

On December 1, 2001, China became a full-fledged member of the WTO after an arduous fourteen-year period of negotiations with existing members of the General Agreement on Tariffs and Trade/World Trade Organization (GATT/WTO). Because of China's size and its rising share in world trade, its share in international trade disputes naturally increases over time and, in fact, at a pace that is more than proportional to the growth of its share in world trade. China's WTO membership makes many policymakers and economists anxious about whether the WTO's relatively new dispute settlement mechanism could be stretched beyond its capacity.

Using several newly compiled data sets, Bown provides a rich and systematic look at the incidence and characteristics of trade disputes involving China since its WTO membership. The discussion is placed in a comparative framework: how discriminatory treatment against China by other countries has evolved as compared to the period prior to its membership, and how China's own use of antidumping measures compares to their use by other countries.

Bown reports a number of interesting findings. Antidumping is one of the increasingly popular tools of protectionism used by countries around the world, in part because of the success of the GATT and the WTO in achieving negotiated reductions in tariff rates. Before China acquired its membership in the WTO in December 2001, its exporters faced substantial discriminatory treatment relative to other exporting countries during 1995 to 2001: Chinese exporters were more likely to face antidumping charges than exporters from most other countries, relative to the volume of their exports. For example, while Chinese exports accounted for only 8 percent of the U.S. imports, its share in U.S. antidumping investigations was 13 percent. Similarly, while its share in the European Union's (EU) imports was only 6 percent, its share in the EU antidumping investigations was 14 percent. We do not know from the data whether Chinese exporters were actually dumping more that other producers. But because China was defined as a nonmarket economy, these importing countries used benchmark cost calculations that were biased toward finding dumping by Chinese producers. Partly as a result of this, antidumping cases against Chinese exporters were three to four times more likely to be successful than those against other producers. Some of the "new" countries using antidumping tools were even more aggressive. For example, Argentina and Brazil targeted 21 percent and 16 percent, respectively, of all of their antidumping cases against China, even though China only accounted for 4 percent and 2 percent, respectively, of their import shares.

When China was negotiating its entry into the GATT/WTO during 1991 to 2001, one might hypothesize that China's trading partners may strategically target antidumping cases in sectors in which China had higher tariffs, as a way to pressure China to increase the scope of its own trade liberalization. If this is true, it could give a relatively benign interpretation. Bown formally tests this hypothesis but finds no support in the data. In other words, it is unlikely that China's trading partners employed antidumping investigations systematically as a tool to encourage China to undertake bigger trade liberalizations in the corresponding sectors.

After 2001, the year China joined the WTO, other countries appear to have *increased* their actions against Chinese exports, including the use of China safeguards. For example, both the United States and the EU have increased the share of Chinese exporters in their overall antidumping investigations against foreign producers. Antidumping, tariff barriers, and other trade protection tools are substitutes. Because the Chinese membership in the WTO has placed new limitations on the use of other more traditional protectionist tools, and because antidumping cases against China could still invoke the nonmarket economy clause for the purpose of calculating exporters' costs, it is perhaps not surprising to see the rise of antidumping cases against China. Interestingly, although Chinese textile and garment exports were growing at a phenomenal rate, its trading partners have not raised the frequency of using the antidumping tool against the Chinese in this sector. Part of the reason is that they could use China-specific "special safeguards" to directly impose quantitative restrictions on Chinese exports, as discussed in chapter 9.

Bown then turns to examining China's own use of antidumping investigations against exporters from other countries. Ironically, China had no antidumping and safeguard provisions prior to the mid-1990s. They were imported by China as part of "international best-practices." It launched its first antidumping case in 1997 (one of the editors of this volume was a consultant on behalf of the Canadian and U.S. exporters involved in this case) and its first safeguard investigation in 2002. China has since become one of the top five users of antidumping measures in the world. Just as for its trading partners, the use of antidumping is a substitute for other protectionist instruments for China. While its WTO accession obligations require it to progressively reduce tariff rates across the board, antidumping appears increasingly more attractive to import-competing firms seeking government relief. In the data, Bown finds that industries that had the biggest tariff reductions during the WTO accession are more likely to seek antidumping measures against foreign producers in subsequent years.

Around the time that China's WTO membership took effect, some observers were worried that China will be involved in a huge number of trade disputes both as a complainant (plaintiff) and as a respondent (defendant). This could then pose the risk of overwhelming and even paralyzing the WTO dispute settlement mechanism (as distinct from the antidumping regulations). So far, this has not turned out to be case. China has not been an active participant in WTO litigations against other countries. Similarly, it has been relatively infrequently on the defensive side in WTO litigations. However, the United States has brought several new cases against China in 2008. It will be interesting to see if this signals a change in strategy in general by China's trading partners. Moreover, China has signed up as an "interested third party" in cases involving other complainant and respondent countries. As of 2006, China has been very active in forty different disputes in this indirect capacity. One possible interpretation is that China is actively learning about the dispute settlement mechanism and preparing to become a more active initiator of cases against other countries (as well as a respondent in cases against itself). In this sense, the past may not be a reliable predictor of the future.

The specific trade policies of the textile and apparel industry are discussed in the chapter by Brambilla, Khandelwal, and Schott. Under the GATT, exports of textiles and apparel to developed countries were restricted under the MFA, renamed as the ACT under the WTO. These quotas were eliminated in 2005, at which time exports from China surged. As a result, special "safeguard" quotas were reimposed against Chinese exports in both the United States and Europe. While such safeguard quotas are normally not permitted under the WTO, a special provision agreed to upon China's entry to the WTO in 2001 allowed for their use in textiles and apparel.

Brambilla, Khandelwal, and Schott document the evolution of China's export in textiles and apparel since before its accession to the WTO. They argue that China had faced quotas that were more binding than for many other exporters. For example, they find that the "fill rate" in quota categories, which equals exports divided by the base quota, was 88 percent for China, similar to that in Bangladesh, Cambodia, India, Indonesia, and Pakistan. But all other countries had fill rates that were lower, indicating that the quotas were less binding. In addition, China was not eligible for any growth in its quotas, as most other countries enjoyed.

All that changed when China joined the WTO in 2001. Then it could benefit from the phased reduction in quota levels that other exporters had already experienced. Phase III of the reduction in quotas occurred in 2002, which was the first time that China was eligible for the reductions since joining the WTO. China's overall textile and apparel exports increased by 306 percent that year, which amounted to nearly three-quarters of the total export increase from all countries. By comparison, in 2005, China's exports increased by 271 percent, while global exports fell slightly. In both years, most of the increase in Chinese exports occurred in the intensive margin (selling more within existing categories of goods) rather than the extensive margin. Furthermore, they find some evidence that the increase in exports was accompanied by quality downgrading, as expected when quotas expire.

Thus, the growth in Chinese exports really dates from 2001 and reflects past treatment under the MFA and ACT that put China in a disadvantaged position. From this perspective, the surge in China's textiles and apparel exports after the MFA/ACT expired in 2005 was not surprising. Countries that were impacted most by the growth in Chinese exports in 2005 include those in Central America, Oceania, East Asia, and sub-Sahara Africa. The largest South Asian exporters—Bangladesh, India, and Pakistan—were not impacted to the same degree. The fact that both the United States and Europe reimposed special safeguard quotas on Chinese exports in 2006 will limit its future export growth to those developed countries (while the safeguards are due to expire in 2008, they may be renewed up to 2013). That may allow other countries to reestablish their export position. But for these other developing countries exporting textiles and apparel, the more important trend for the future will be China's shift away from labor-intensive goods and toward more capital and skill-intensive industries. Already, China's former production in textiles and apparel is shifting to lower-wage countries, such as Vietnam, which joined the WTO in 2007. For these reasons, fears that China will permanently displace other exporters of textiles and apparel are probably misplaced.

Under its WTO accession, China had to agree to radical reductions in agricultural tariffs. As the pre-WTO tariff levels were high on many products, most economists and other observers predicted that agriculture was going to be one area in which Chinese producers were not going to be competitive, so that rural income was going to fall and rural poverty was likely to rise after the accession. Fortunately for Chinese rural households, these predictions did not turn out to be true. In fact, agricultural growth continued, which poses a puzzle. Chapter 10 by Huang, Liu, Martin, and Rozelle provides an answer to this puzzle.

China agreed to major reductions in agricultural tariffs as a part of the conditions for gaining the WTO membership, and it followed through on these liberalization promises after the accession, so the phase-in was completed by 2005 as scheduled. The key resolution to the puzzle is to recognize that the high preaccession tariff protection was largely offset by a long list of policy distortions such as a high agricultural tax and a low state mandatory procurement price that generally were unfavorable to rural households and agricultural production. As a result of the domestic policy distortions, the net rate of protection before the WTO membership was in fact negative for many crops. Coinciding with the WTO accession, the Chinese have undertaken numerous domestic reforms that gradually remove these antiagricultural policy distortions. The net effect of trade and domestic policy reforms is a positive boost to many agricultural producers.

The basic tool that Huang, Liu, Martin, and Rozelle use to gauge the net effect of policies is the nominal rate of assistance (NRA), which is based on a comparison between domestic prices of agricultural products and corresponding international prices. The NRA was negative for farmers that produce rice and many other import-competing commodities until around 1995. The NRA continued to improve even after the WTO accession. In addition to removing discriminatory policies against agriculture, the Chinese government also invested in the development and dissemination of agricultural technology, which improved farmer's productivity. Huang, Liu, Martin, and Rozelle give the example of investment in research and development (R&D) for plant biotechnology; the growth of government sponsored R&D was 5.5 percent per year between 1995 and 2000. They report that China now ranks among the global leaders in agricultural biotechnology, with public spending in this area second only to the United States. Therefore, in the period leading up to the WTO accession and in the period since the WTO membership, farmers have gained on net from the whole package of policy reforms and public investment more than they have lost from the reductions in agricultural tariffs.

The final chapter in this section, by Dean and Lovely, deals with China's environment. Here again, conventional wisdom points toward a very negative prognosis: press reports of the pollution in China and the cost to human health are both frequent and disheartening. Without questioning that existing pollution levels (i.e., the stock of pollution) in China are very high, Dean and Lovely argue that a different picture is obtained if one focuses instead on the pollution intensity of industries (i.e., the flow of pollution) over time. In fact, Chinese industrial emissions of water pollution (measured by the chemical oxygen demand, or COD) and air pollution (measured by soot and dust particles) have been declining since 1995, while sulfur dioxide shows only a small increase. What factor can explain the decline in emissions for three out of these four pollutants?

Dean and Lovely use the emissions data to calculate the pollution intensity of thirty-three Chinese sectors, for 1995 and 2004. Using that information, they can compute whether the decline in aggregate industrial emissions reflects the same decline at an industry level (a "technique" effect) or reflects a shift toward cleaner industries (a "composition" effect). They find that the pollution intensity of production has fallen over time for all four pollutants and across nearly all sectors. Thus, there is evidence in favor of a shift toward cleaner production techniques. That may very well reflect the increasing attention given to environmental regulation by government agencies in China, though these agencies are still small and underfunded compared to the scale of the environmental problem.

In addition, Dean and Lovely find that there has been a shift toward cleaner industries in China. From 1995 to 2004, the water pollution intensity of exports fell by 84 percent, and the drop in air pollution intensity is nearly as large. Most of that drop is due to the technique effect rather than a composition effect, however. By reweighting the pollution intensities using processing exports rather than ordinary exports, they find that processing exports are cleaner than ordinary exports for all four pollutants. In addition, ordinary or processing exports are cleaner than the respective imports. They then develop a model to assess the role that production fragmentation through processing trade plays in explaining the pollution intensity of Chinese trade and find empirical support for the hypotheses arising from the model.

Foreign Investment and Trade

Foreign direct investment is another area in which there have been substantial changes in China. The country metamorphosed from being closed to foreign investment in the 1970s to now being the single largest developing country host of FDI. Foreign-invested firms are an important of China's trade story, accounting for more than half of its total exports and imports. Moreover, in recent years, China's modest but increasing outward direct investment has started to attract attention and sometimes anxiety. The last set of chapters examines various issues with regard to FDI.

The chapter by Blonigen and Ma examines the degree to which foreign-invested firms have spurred the growth of domestic Chinese firms. Do Chinese firms catch up with foreign-invested firms in terms of export volume, product composition, and product quality? Blonigen and Ma examine these questions systematically by utilizing the same detailed data at the level of product, region, and firm ownership type (as well as other dimensions).

Over the last twenty years, as the Chinese trade volume rises, the share of exports by state-owned firms has declined steadily, while the share accounted for by foreign-invested firms has been rising steadily. Blonigen and Ma employ two approaches to investigate this topic for the period 1997 to 2005. First, within a typical six-digit product code, they ask whether Chinese firms take up an increasingly big share. Second, for a given product, they ask whether the quality gap between the variety produced by domestic Chinese firms and that by foreign-invested firms narrows over time.

One might guess the answer to the first question from the aggregate data: if the share in total exports by FIEs has been rising, it is also likely to be on an upward trend within a product code, on average. This indeed turns out to be true, but Blonigen and Ma do not stop here. They also ask which factors could either speed up or slow down the expansion of export shares by FIEs across products by exploring cross-product variations in policies that may encourage technological transfers, and variables that may proxy the degree of competition between FIEs and Chinese firms.

The answer to the second question is "not really." That is, there is no evidence of a steady narrowing in export quality (measured by difference in unit values) between FIEs and domestic firms. By this metric, Chinese firms appear to be "falling behind" rather than "catching up" as the unit values of their exports appear to become progressively lower relative to the unit value of the same product produced by FIEs.

The government policies toward FDI are not neutral across sectors. Foreign direct investment in various sectors can be placed in three categories: (a) encouraged, (b) neutral, and (c) restricted. In the "encouraged" sectors, while there is no reduction in the quality gap between domestic and foreign firms, the share by domestic firms in those sectors' total exports actually declined. This suggests that the sector-biased FDI encouragement policies do not systematically help domestic firms to catch up with FIEs, at least not by the criteria that Blonigen and Ma use.

The chapter by Branstetter and Foley sets out to dispel four commonly held perceptions regarding U.S. FDI in China. The first question is, is the U.S. FDI in China large? The answer is no. This can be understood from two levels. First, U.S. multinational firms' investment in China is only a small fraction of their total overseas investment. In 2004, for example, their China operation's shares in their total overseas affiliate sales and assets were a mere 1.9 percent and 0.7 percent, respectively. Second, U.S. FDI in China as a share of China's total inward FDI is also small. In fact, the most important source "country" for FDI in China is Hong Kong. However, this does not mean that FDI is unimportant for China. As we have previously noted, China is among the world's top recipient of FDI.

The second question is, is U.S. FDI in China heavily export-oriented? The answer from Branstetter and Foley is no. They use data on benchmark surveys of U.S. multinational firms and compute sales to local market versus exports. They found no evidence that U.S. affiliates in China are more export-oriented than elsewhere. The notion that U.S. firms invest in China and then sell their products back to the United States en masse does not turn out to be supported by a careful look at the data. Note, however, the authors are not rejecting the possibility that there could be a good deal of indirect exports by U.S. affiliates in China back to the United States. For example, U.S. affiliates could sell machineries and other intermediate inputs to local Chinese firms or other unaffiliated FIEs in China, which in turn may export to the United States and other markets. Checking out this possibility would require data that go beyond what these authors have.

The third question is does investment by U.S. multinational firms in China displace their investment in the United States? The answer is again no. Branstetter and Foley examine whether a U.S. firm's investment in the United States tends to contract whenever it expands its investment in China and find no evidence supporting this notion. In fact, firms that increase employment in China also appear to increase, not decrease, employment in other locations. This suggests that investment in China tends to be a complement to investment in the United States and other locations.

Finally, the fourth question is are U.S. firms aggressively engaging in R&D

in China? At a first glance, the answer may be yes. By the end of 2004, multinational firms had established more than 700 R&D centers in China. Global companies like Microsoft make repeated statements about engaging world-class research in its China-based R&D centers. But after examining data on counts of patents registered in the United States by multinational firms, including those with investors who reside in China, Branstetter and Foley conclude that most multinational firms engage relatively little true cutting-age research in China. Even for Microsoft, China-generated patents accounts for only 4 percent of the stock of all its patents (though the China share in its flow of new patents may be higher and rising). As of now at least, most of the China-based R&D centers probably focus on customizing technologies developed elsewhere to the Chinese market.

China's investment in resource-rich countries in Africa and Latin America, and its attempt to acquire various U.S. companies, have generated attention to its overall outbound FDI. China's newly established sovereign wealth fund—the China Investment Corporation—has further focused the spotlight on its overseas investment activities. The chapter by Cheng and Ma provides a timely and systematic analysis of China's outbound FDI during 2003 to 2006. They reach a number of interesting findings.

First, in spite of the international attention, China's outbound FDI is quite small, accounting for less than 2 percent of global FDI flow in 2006. Second, while the attention has been focused on China's overseas investment in resource sectors, business services turn out to be the biggest area of its investment. It is possible that overseas business services are an important input into the Chinese exports. The importance of business-services investment by Chinese firms simply reflects the importance of exports for the Chinese economy. Cheng and Ma caution, however, that the true sector composition of the Chinese outbound FDI may be different from the official data as a significant fraction of its outbound FDI is reported to go to tax havens. In all likelihood, these investment projects wind up elsewhere, but their true destination and sector composition are not well recorded. Third, the destination country's GDP (but not income), foreign reserve, and currency appreciation are all positively related to China's FDI in that country.

Conclusions

While Chinese GDP doubles once every eight years, its exports and imports have been growing at an even more impressive pace, roughly doubling in value once every three to four years. This poses both opportunities and challenges for China and for the rest of the world. Magazines and airport bookstores are filled with publications with sometimes outlandish claims about the causes and consequences of China's growing trade in the world. This book, by putting together a group of prominent empirical trade economists, aims to clarify a number of misconceptions and enhance our understanding of issues related to China's trade.

In the pages to follow, readers will find detailed analyses of the microstructure of trade, the macroeconomic implications, sector-level issues, and FDI. While the topics are diverse, a common feature is a careful examination of microdata that is conducted under the guidance of economic theories. Some conventional wisdom is overturned; many new data patterns are documented. While this volume is unlikely to be the last word on China's trade, it hopefully will inspire more follow-up research and contribute to well-informed discussion of China's role in world trade.

References

Broda, Christian, and David E. Weinstein. 2006. Globalization and the gains from variety. *Quarterly Journal of Economics* 121 (2): 541–85.
China Customs Statistics. Various years. (Data set). Beijing, China: Customs General Administration, Statistics Department (producer); Hong Kong, China: China Customs Statistics Information Center (distributor).
Dooley, Michael P., David Folkerts-Landau, and Peter Garber. 2003. An essay on the revived Bretton Woods System. NBER Working Paper no. 9971. Cambridge, MA: National Bureau of Economic Research.
———. 2004a. Direct investment, rising real wages and the absorption of excess labor in the periphery. NBER Working Paper no. 10626. Cambridge, MA: National Bureau of Economic Research.
———. 2004b. The revived Bretton Woods System: The effects of periphery intervention and reserve management on interest rates and exchange rates in center countries. NBER Working Paper no. 10331. Cambridge, MA: National Bureau of Economic Research.
———. 2004c. The U.S. current account deficit and economic development: Collateral for a total return swap. NBER Working Paper no. 10727. Cambridge, MA: National Bureau of Economic Research.
Eaton, Jonathan, and Samuel Kortum. 2002. Technology, geography, and trade. *Econometrica* 70 (5): 1741–79.
Fisman, Raymond, and Sahng-Jin Wei. 2009. The smuggling of art, and the art of smuggling: Uncovering illicit trade in cultural property and antiques. *American Economic Journal: Applied Economics.*
Harrigan, James. 2006. Airplanes and comparative advantage. NBER Working Paper no. 11688. Cambridge, MA: National Bureau of Economic Research.
Koopman, Robert, Zhi Wang, and Shang-Jin Wei. 2008. How much of Chinese exports is really made in China? Assessing domestic value added when processing trade is prevalent. NBER working paper no. 14109. Cambridge, MA: National Bureau of Economic Research.
Rodrik, Dani. 2006. What's so special about China's exports? *China & World Economy* 14 (5): 1–19.
Samuelson, Paul. 2002. Where Ricardo and Mill rebut and confirm arguments of mainstream economists supporting globalization. *Journal of Economic Perspectives* 18 (3): 135–146.
Schott, Peter. 2008. The relative sophistication of Chinese exports. *Economic Policy* 53 (January): 5–49.

I

Microstructure of International Trade

The Anatomy of China's Export Growth

Mary Amiti and Caroline Freund

1.1 Introduction

China's real exports increased by more than 500 percent over the last fifteen years. As a result, in 2004, China overtook Japan as the world's third largest exporter, just behind Germany and the United States. This paper decomposes this stunning export growth along various dimensions. In particular, how has China's export structure changed? Has the export sector become more specialized, focusing on particular types of goods, or has it diversified as it has grown? Are China's exports becoming more skill-intensive? How important are new goods in export growth? The answers to these questions have important implications for the global welfare consequences of China's export expansion and for future growth of China's export sectors.

Our analysis shows that China's export structure has transformed dramatically since 1992. There has been a significant decline in the share of agriculture and soft manufactures, such as textiles and apparel, with growing shares in hard manufactures, such as consumer electronics, appliances, and computers. However, a large component of this export growth in machinery has been due to growth in processing trade—the practice of assembling duty-free intermediate inputs. These inputs are generally of high-skill

Mary Amiti is a research officer in international research at the Federal Reserve Bank of New York. Caroline Freund is a lead economist in the Development Economics Research Group at The World Bank.

We would like to thank Jin Hongman of China Customs Statistics for providing us with the data. We are grateful to Robert Feenstra for extended comments and discussions and to Bin Xu, David Weinstein, Shang-Jin Wei, Chong Xiang, and participants at the National Bureau of Economic Research (NBER) preconference and the International Monetary Fund (IMF) for many useful suggestions. The views expressed in this paper are those of the authors and do not necessarily represent those of the World Bank or the Federal Reserve Bank of New York.

content, originating in countries such as the United States and Japan (see Dean, Fung, and Wang 2007). Thus, on the surface, it appears that China is dramatically changing its comparative advantage, yet a closer examination reveals that it is continuing to specialize in labor-intensive goods. We find that the labor intensity of China's exports remains unchanged once we account for processing trade. Further, exports remained highly concentrated in a small fraction of goods—though the particular goods have changed. These patterns are consistent with traditional trade theories, which place specialization and comparative advantage at the center of trade growth.

More recent trade theories emphasize the gains from trade as importing countries access new product varieties. For example, Broda and Weinstein (2006) find that 30 percent of U.S. import growth between 1972 and 2001 was in new varieties (the extensive margin) and that China was the largest contributor to growth in these U.S. varieties; however, most of this growth was in the earlier period from 1972 to 1988. Other papers highlight a strong positive correlation between the number of export varieties a country produces and its living standard (see Funke and Ruhwedel 2001). Hummels and Klenow (2005) find that larger and richer countries export more varieties of goods, using data for 1995. This finding is suggestive that a large portion of China's export growth would be associated with exports of new varieties. However, our analysis of China's export growth patterns between 1997 and 2005 shows that most of its export growth was actually in existing varieties (the intensive margin). This large growth in the intensive margin is also supportive of predictions consistent with traditional theories with an important role for terms-of-trade effects, where the welfare gains for importing countries arise through lower import prices. As China increases its supply of existing varieties on world markets, this is likely to exert downward pressure on world prices of these goods. Indeed, between 1997 and 2005, average prices of goods exported from China to the United States fell by an average of 1.5 percent per year, whereas the average prices of these products from the rest of the world to the United States increased, on average, by 0.4 percent per year.[1]

The rest of the paper is organized as follows. Section 1.2 describes the data. Section 1.3 examines the reallocation of exports across industries. Section 1.4 looks at the skill intensity of exports. Section 1.5 examines whether there has been increased diversification or specialization as exports have grown. Section 1.6 decomposes export growth into the intensive and extensive margins. Section 1.7 compares China's export prices to the United States to those from the rest of the world. Section 1.8 concludes.

---

1. This is a Törnqvist chain-weighted price index using HS ten-digit goods that China exported during this period.

1.2   Data

The most disaggregated export data available for China is at the Harmonized System (HS) eight-digit level, from China Customs Statistics, which includes 8,900 product codes. The trade data are in current U.S. dollars, which we deflate by the U.S. Consumer Price Index (CPI; base year 1992) to generate a constant dollar series. Summary statistics for China's exports are presented in table 1.1, showing that China's real exports to the world increased by 500 percent between 1992 and 2005, from US$84.94 billion to US$525.48 billion. Its share of exports to the United States increased from 10 percent to 21 percent over the sample period. To check for the accuracy of the China export data, we also use data on U.S. imports from China, from the U.S. Bureau of the Census, Foreign Trade Division. This data also has the advantage of being available at an even higher level of disaggregation, at the HS ten-digit, which includes 18,600 product categories.

As there were major reclassifications in the international HS six-digit classifications in 1996 and 2002, in some cases we aggregate the data up to HS six-digit codes and convert them to the same HS six-digit classifications used in 1992 to avoid problems related to reclassification of codes. This reduces the number of product codes for China's world exports to 5,000 products. To examine broader export patterns we divide the data into Standard International Trade Classification (SITC) one-digit codes, which include agriculture (SITC 1 to 4), chemicals (SITC 4), manufactured materials (SITC 5), manufactured materials (SITC 6), machinery (SITC 7) and miscellaneous manufacturers (SITC8).

Table 1.1   **Summary statistics: trade data for China**

	1992	1995	1997	1999	2001	2003	2005
Total exports							
$U.S. billions	84.94	136.50	160.34	163.81	211.19	334.53	525.49
Total processing exports							
$U.S. billions	39.92	67.92	87.59	93.23	117.04	184.56	287.24
Share (%)	0.47	0.50	0.55	0.57	0.55	0.55	0.55
Exports to U.S. (Chinese data)							
$U.S. billions	8.59	22.67	28.70	35.25	43.08	70.59	112.34
Share (%)	0.10	0.17	0.18	0.22	0.20	0.21	0.21
Exports to U.S. (U.S. data)							
$U.S. billions	25.73	41.79	54.87	68.73	81.17	116.32	167.91

Source: China Customs Statistics.
Note: Deflated using 1992 U.S. Consumer Price Index.

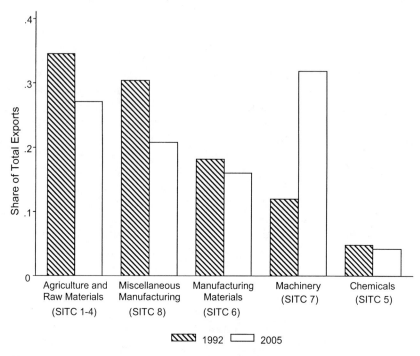

Fig. 1.1 Reallocation of exports across SITC one-digit industries
Note: Column headings include the following industries:
SITC 1–4: Beverages, tobacco, raw materials, mineral fuels, oils, and fats.
SITC 5: Chemicals, dyes, pharmaceuticals, and perfumes.
SITC 6: Leather, rubber, cork and wood products, textiles, metallic and nonmetallic manufactures.
SITC 7: Industrial machinery, office machinery, telecommunications equipment, electrical machinery, transportation equipment.
SITC 8: Prefabricated buildings, furniture, travel goods, clothing, footwear, professional and scientific equipment.

1.3   Reallocation across Industries

China has experienced big changes in its export composition. It has moved from the first stage of agriculture and apparel to more sophisticated manufactured goods. Figure 1.1 shows this by plotting the export share of each one-digit SITC sector in 1992 and 2005. Rapid export growth has been associated with a move out of agriculture and apparel into the machinery and transport sectors. In figure 1.2, we focus on changes within the manufacturing sector. In particular, we look at how trade shares have adjusted in all major two-digit SITC sectors, where major is defined as accounting for at least 3 percent of exports in 1992 or 2005. There is a notable move out of

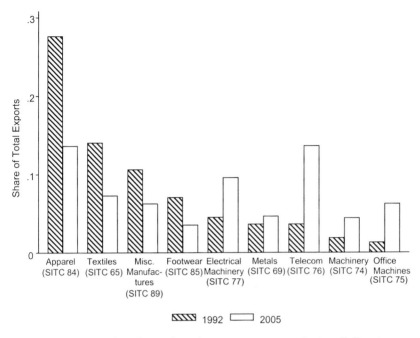

Fig. 1.2 The reallocation of manufacturing exports across major two-digit sectors
Notes: A sector is defined as major if the sector's share of total trade is above 3 percent in 1992 or 2005. These sectors account for about 70 percent of manufacturing exports.

apparel, textiles, footwear, and toys and into electrical machinery, telecom, office machines, and, to a lesser extent, metals.

The strongest overall export growth has been in machinery (SITC 7), and within this broad category, it is telecoms, electrical machinery, and office machines that have experienced the highest growth and make up the largest shares within machinery. The question arises whether China is producing most of the value added of these capital intensive goods or if China is just assembling duty-free imported inputs for export. This practice is known as processing trade and does account for an increasingly large share of China's exports, from 47 percent in 1992 to 55 percent in 2005. According to Dean, Fung, and Wang (2007), imported inputs account for between 52 to 76 percent of the value of processing exports. Figure 1.3 graphs total exports of two-digit machinery categories as a share of total manufacturing exports, in descending order for 2005, and the lighter bars show the portion that is classified as processing trade by China Customs Statistics. This figure reveals that most of the high export growth in machinery is indeed processing trade; thus, only a small share of this growth is likely to be due to high value added production in machinery in China.

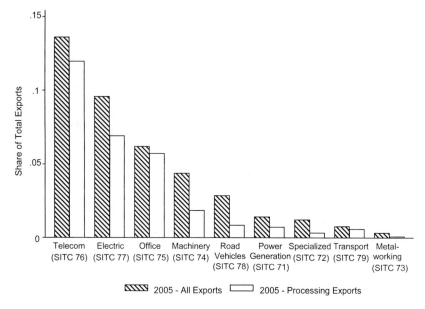

Fig. 1.3 Machinery exports and processing trade

Note: Column headings include the following industries:

SITC 71: Boilers, turbines, internal combustion engines, and power generating machinery.

SITC 72: Agricultural machinery, civil engineering and contractors' equipment, printing and bookbinding machinery, and textile and leather machinery.

SITC 73: Lathes, machines for finishing and polishing metal, soldering equipment, metal forging equipment, and metal foundry equipment.

SITC 74: Heating and cooling equipment, pumps, ball bearings, valves for pipes, and nonelectrical machines.

SITC 75: Typewriters, photocopiers, and data processing machines.

SITC 76: Television receivers, radio receivers, and sound recorders.

SITC 77: Equipment for distributing electricity, electro-diagnostic apparatus, and semiconductors.

SITC 78: Automobiles, trucks, trailers, and motorcycles.

SITC 79: Railroad equipment, aircraft, ships, boats, and floating structures.

1.4   Skill Content of Export Growth

China's export bundle is very different now from what it was in the early 1990s. Rodrik (2006) and Schott (2006) highlight the increasing sophistication of China's exports, as demonstrated by an export pattern that more closely resembles high-income countries than would be expected given its income level. To see whether this increased sophistication has been associated with an increase in the overall skill content of its exports, we rank industries from low- to high-skill intensity on the horizontal axis of figure 1.4 and plot the cumulative export share on the vertical axis. Because indus-

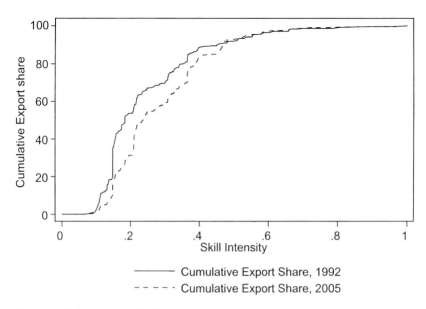

Fig. 1.4   **Skill intensity of China's manufacturing exports**

Notes: Data uses HS six-digit classifications. The skill intensity is measured as the ratio of nonproduction workers to total employment from the Indonesian manufacturing census at the five-digit ISIC level for 1992.

try skill-level data for China were unavailable, we based the skill-intensity ranking on information from Indonesia, another emerging market that is likely to have similar **technologies.**[2] **The** skill intensity is measured as the ratio of nonproduction workers to total employment from the Indonesian manufacturing census at the five-digit International Standard Industrial Classification (ISIC) level for 1992. In figure 1.4, the shift of the curve to the right indicates that the skill content of China's exports has increased over the sample period. For example, in 1992, 20 percent of the least skill-intensive industries produced 55 percent of China's export share. By 2005, the export share that these industries produced fell to 32 percent.[3]

However, given the high share of processing trade in China, an increase in the skill content of China's exports could be due to China importing intermediate inputs with higher skill content that it then assembles for exporting. We assess this possibility by plotting the cumulative of export shares against the skill intensity with nonprocessing manufacturing exports only. That is, we exclude any exports that have been classified as processing trade. From

2. Zhu and Trefler (2005) measure changes in the skill content of exports for all countries using U.S. industry-level skill data to rank the skill intensity of industries, assuming no factor intensity reversals. Our results also hold using U.S. skill data.

3. This approach only gives an indication of shifts between industries; thus, we cannot say if there has been any skill upgrading within an industry.

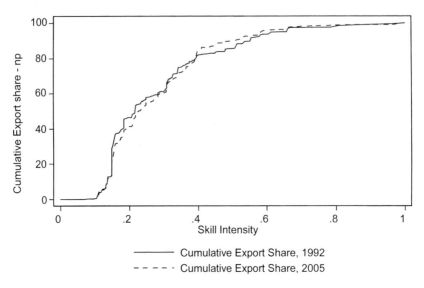

Fig. 1.5   Skill intensity of China's manufacturing exports excluding processing trade

Notes: Data uses HS six-digit classifications. The skill intensity is measured as the ratio of nonproduction workers to total employment from the Indonesian manufacturing census at the five-digit ISIC level for 1992.

figure 1.5, we see that there is hardly any shift in the curve indicating no change in the skill content of China's nonprocessing exports.

Processing exports make up a large share of China's manufacturing exports and by excluding processing exports, we are excluding around 54 percent of China's manufacturing exports (see table 1.1). Although imported inputs account for a large share of the value of processing exports, there still remains a significant amount of value added in China in processing exports, and there could be a shift in the skill content within that portion. To examine this possibility, we compare the change in the skill content of imported manufacturing inputs for processing trade to the skill content of imported inputs for nonprocessing trade in figures 1.6 and 1.7. Using U.S. industry skill data to rank the skill intensity of imports, we find a much larger increase in the skill content of processed imports than of nonprocessing imports. Of course, this rise in the skill content of processing imports does not rule out the possibility that the Chinese value added has become more skill-intensive, too.

Wei and Wang, in chapter 2, also examine how the sophistication of China's goods have changed over time. They use two measures. The first is an index of how different China's export structure is from the export structure of industrial countries (using the Group of Three [G3] to represent industrial countries), which they refer to as a disimilarity index. If China's export

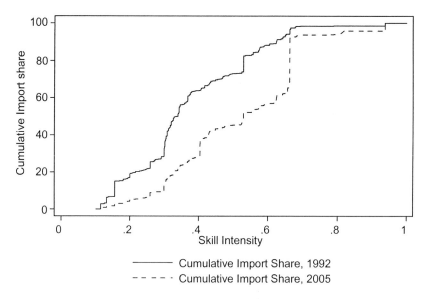

Fig. 1.6   Cumulative import share and skill intensity, processing trade
Notes: Data uses HS six-digit classifications. The skill intensity is measured as the ratio of nonproduction workers to total employment for U.S. four-digit SIC industries in 1992.

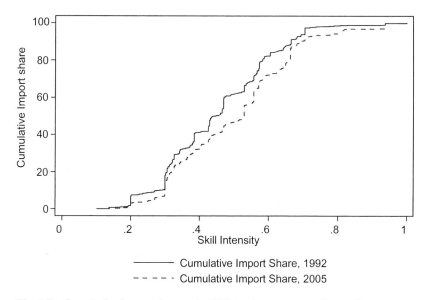

Fig. 1.7   Cumulative import share and skill intensity, nonprocessing trade
Notes: Data uses HS six-digit classifications. The skill intensity is measured as the ratio of nonproduction workers to total employment for U.S. four-digit SIC industries in 1992.

structure becomes more similar to industrial countries', this is interpreted as China's exports becoming more sophisticated. The second is an index of the average value of China's exports, using unit value data. An increase in the average unit value of exports is interpreted as exporting higher-quality or more-sophisticated goods. They examine how the two indexes have changed for seventy-nine cities in China and the determinants of the changes. With respect to the disimilarity index, they find that increased processing trade has not contributed to making regional export patterns more similar to industrial country patterns. However, with respect to unit values, they find strong evidence that processing trade has contributed to higher unit values, especially processing exports in high-tech zones. The unit value results support our conclusions, but the dissimilarity results do not.[4] One possibility is that the unit value index is closer to our measure of skill intensity, as high unit value industries are likely to be more skill-intensive. Together, the results imply that processing trade has contributed to higher unit value and higher skill-intensity goods being exported from China.

1.5   Diversification versus Specialization

We have seen that snapshots of China's export sector taken in 1992 and 2005 look very different, with the increased churning from agriculture and textiles into machinery, electronics, and assembly. As a result of this transformation, China's exports may have become more specialized or more diversified. Traditional trade theory highlights the combination of increased trade and specialization as a key factor in promoting higher living standards. Imbs and Warziarg (2003), however, find that countries tend to diversify production as they grow from low levels of income and that they only begin to specialize once they reach a relatively high level of income. This is consistent with countries moving from exploiting natural resources to developing new industrial sectors as they grow. Hausmann and Rodrik (2003) argue that in the early stage of development, more entrepreneurship and potentially greater diversification may help producers identify the sectors in which it is a competitive producer.

We examine whether China's exports display increased or decreased specialization in figure 1.8 by plotting the inverse cumulative export shares for all products at the HS six-digit level. A shift to the left of the curve would indicate increased specialization. Looking across all products, it appears

---

4. One issue with the dissimilarity index is that regional export shares can divert from industrial country export patterns at the same time as China's total gross exports become more similar to industrial countries. For example, assume processing industries are overall similar to G3 export structure but tend to be geographically specialized, for example, flat screens in one area, computers in another, and so on. Then increasing processing trade in a given region could pull you away from OECD structure, while increasing processing trade overall will pull China as a country toward OECD structure.

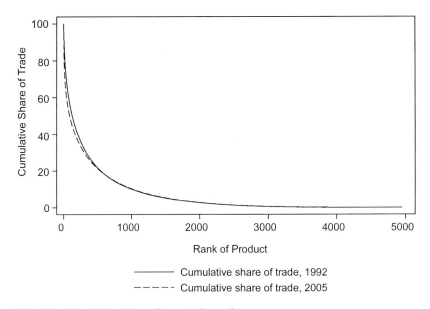

Fig. 1.8   Cumulative share of exports by rank
Notes: Data uses HS six-digit classifications. Rank is largest to smallest by value.

from figure 1.8 that there is hardly any change in the degree of specialization. Yet when we magnify the image of figure 1.8 in figure 1.9, showing the cumulative trade shares when we keep only the largest 500 categories by value, which account for nearly 80 percent of total exports in either of the years, there is a noticeable downward shift in the curve, suggesting there has been an increase in specialization. The pattern is very similar, with a slightly greater increase in specialization, if we only include manufacturing exports.

This finding is confirmed using the Gini coefficient, which is an alternative way to measure changes in specialization, by measuring export equality in each period. It is defined as

$$\text{Gini} \equiv 1 - \frac{1}{n}\sum_i (\text{cshare}_{i-1} + \text{cshare}_i),$$

where there are n products, i is a product's order (1 is smallest, and n is largest), and cshare$_i$ is the cumulative share of exports of the ith product. The Gini coefficient uses the trapezoid approximation to calculate the area between a 45-degree line and the cumulative distribution, weighting each industry as an equal share of the population of industries ($1/n$). A Gini coefficient of zero indicates that export shares are equally distributed across all industry groups; an increase in the Gini coefficient implies an increase in specialization.

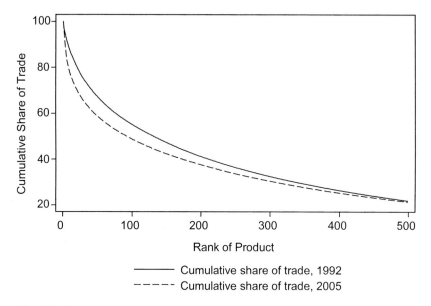

Fig. 1.9   Cumulative share of exports by rank, top 500 products

Notes: Data uses HS six-digit classifications. Rank is largest to smallest by value.

Table 1.2   **Gini coefficient for China's exports**

Period	All	Top 70%	Top 100
1992	0.85	0.46	0.35
2005	0.86	0.55	0.50

Source: China Customs Statistics and authors' calculations.

Table 1.2 reports the Gini coefficient for 1992 and 2005 for the whole sample of products and some subsamples. The Gini coefficient remained unchanged over the sample period at 0.85 when all products are included. However, when a subsample of the largest goods accounting for 70 percent of exports are included, the Gini coefficient increases from 0.46 to 0.55. Similarly, when we only include the top 100 products, which account for 45 percent of exports in the 1992 period and nearly 50 percent in 2005, the Gini coefficient increased from 0.35 to 0.50. Thus, over the period we see enhanced specialization—a smaller number of products account for an increased size of China's exports—though the bundle of goods exported has changed.

1.6   Intensive versus Extensive Margin

Has the large export growth mainly been in new product varieties or existing varieties? A new variety is generally defined as the export of a new product code, that is, a product code for which there are positive exports one period and zero exports in an earlier period. One of the main problems using this definition is that there have been major reclassifications in the trade data in 1996 and 2002 at the HS six-digit level; thus, a product might be classified as a new variety just because there has been a new product code or previous codes were split. For example, in one year, cherry tomatoes were reclassified into a new product code rather than being part of the tomatoes category. In this case, cherry tomatoes would appear to be counted as a new variety even though they were exported in previous periods. In contrast, flat-screen televisions received a new classification, and these are, in fact, new varieties.

1.6.1   Export Shares

There have been various approaches developed to address these reclassification issues. One approach is to use HS six-digit data concorded to the same 1992 product codes, but in general, these categories might be too aggregated to be able to identify new products: by 1992, China was exporting in over 90 percent of these categories. To examine whether export growth is mainly from new goods with this aggregate data, we follow Kehoe and Ruhl (2009) by splitting exports into deciles by value in 1992 and calculate their share of exports in 2005. If export growth is mainly from new goods, we would expect rapid growth in the bottom deciles, where trade was negligible in 1992. Figure 1.10 shows the share of exports in 2005 that is accounted for by the products falling into each decile. The categories that accounted for the bottom 20 percent of trade by value more than doubled between 1992 and 2005, while the categories in the other deciles contracted or remained **constant.**[5] This points to a sizable role for the extensive margin as the least-traded goods grew the fastest.

One problem with this method is that exports tend to be concentrated in a small number of categories. This can be clearly seen in figure 1.11, where we divide exports into deciles according to the number of categories of trade in 1992. For example, the 10th decile is the top 10 percent of product categories when products are ranked by value. The distribution in 1992 is highly skewed, reflecting that only 10 percent of categories accounted for nearly 80 percent of trade. The decline in the share of the top decile shows that there was a sizeable reallocation of trade, but it was not the bottom 50 percent of products that gained. Instead, gains in the trade share were in the four deciles just below the top.

In sum, the results imply that there was a significant reorientation in exports and that the reshuffling of export products during the expansion was mainly in the mid-to-upper rank products. These are products that were in the bottom 20 percent by value but in the mid-to-high range by product

5. Arkolakis (2006) develops a model consistent with this finding.

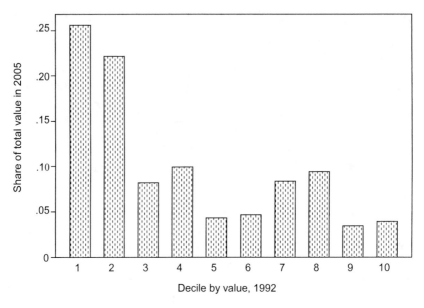

Fig. 1.10   Reallocation of exports by value

Note: Data uses HS six-digit classifications.

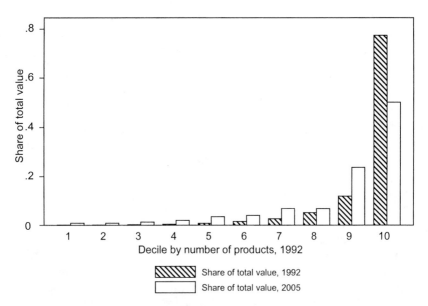

Fig. 1.11   Reallocation of exports by product shares

Note: Data uses HS six-digit classifications.

rank.[6] Taken with the previous results on specialization, this implies that there was a sizable compositional shift over time that led to a more skewed distribution of trade in 2005 as compared with 1992.

1.6.2 Variety Growth

To utilize the more disaggregated trade data at the eight- and ten-digit levels, we examine the contribution of new varieties to export growth using two complementary methods. The first is the Feenstra index of net export variety growth, which provides an indication of the importance of new varieties in trade. The second is a decomposition of export growth into new, disappearing, and existing varieties and offers more information on the magnitude of export creation and destruction. We present the definitions and discuss the strengths and weaknesses of each measure in the following.

Feenstra's (1994) seminal work on measuring import prices incorporating new goods leads to a natural index of variety growth that has been widely used in the literature. Denoting I as the set of varieties available in both periods, $I \subseteq (I_t \cap I_{t-1})$, the Feenstra index of net variety growth is defined as the fraction of expenditure in period $t-1$ on the goods $i \subset I$ relative to the entire set $i \subset I_{t-1}$ as a ratio of the fraction of expenditure in period t on the goods $i \in I$ relative to the entire set $i \in I_t$, minus 1.[7] Let V_{it} be the value of trade at time t in product i ($V_{it} = p_{it} q_{it}$), then

$$(1) \quad \text{Feenstra index of net variety growth} = \frac{\sum_{i \in I} V_{t-1i} / \sum_{i \in I_{t-1}} V_{t-1i}}{\sum_{i \in I} V_{it} / \sum_{i \in I_t} V_{it}} - 1.$$

The index will be equal to zero if there is no growth in varieties relative to the base period and positive if the number of varieties has grown. This measure has the nice feature that if HS trade classifications are split and their share of total trade remains unchanged, the index remains unchanged. However, if growth classifications are split (or reclassified) to a greater extent than shrinking classifications are merged, the index will tend to overstate the extensive margin. A disadvantage of the index for measuring the relative importance of new varieties in export growth is that if there is a lot of churning, with an equal amount of export creation and destruction, it will report net variety growth of nil. To an importer, theory suggests that welfare increases with the number of varieties available, so it is net variety growth that is relevant. To an exporter, however, gross variety changes may be of interest as they provide an indication of how important new goods are to export growth. From the exporter's perspective, the Feenstra index could

---

6. These figures and the estimates of the extensive and intensive margin are very similar if we use only manufacturing trade.
7. From Feenstra (1994), this is the inverse of the lambda ratio minus 1.

understate the importance of new goods in export growth if there is a lot of creation and destruction.

To get an idea of how important churning is, we also calculate the shares of trade growth due to new, disappearing, and existing goods. The decomposition of trade growth is as follows:

$$
(2) \quad \frac{\sum_i V_{it} - \sum_i V_{it-1}}{\sum_i V_{it-1}} = \frac{\sum_{i \in I} V_{it} - \sum_{i \in I} V_{it-1}}{\sum V_{it-1}}
$$

$$
- \frac{\sum_{i \in I^D_{t-1}} V_{it-1}}{\sum V_{it-1}} + \frac{\sum_{i \in I^N_t} V_{it}}{\sum V_{it-1}},
$$

where I^D_{t-1} is the set of products that disappeared between $t-1$ and t, and I^N_t is the set of new products available in year t. This is an identity where total growth in trade relative to the base period is decomposed into three parts: (a) the growth in products that were exported in both periods, the intensive margin; (b) the reduction in export growth due to products no longer exported, disappearing goods; and (c) the increase in export growth due to the export of new products. The share of trade growth due to the extensive margin is defined as the new goods share less the disappearing goods. This decomposition provides an estimate of the extent of churning, but it is less robust to reclassifications than the Feenstra index because growth from products that are reclassified for any reason will be attributed to the extensive margin. We report the share of total export growth of each term on the right-hand side of equation (2); hence, by construction, the intensive and extensive margins sum to 1.[8]

Figure 1.12 plots the Feenstra index of net variety growth and the share of trade growth attributed to the extensive margin on an annual basis for China's exports to the United States at the ten-digit level from 1993 to 2005. What is striking about this figure is the large peak in the growth in the extensive margin around 1996, where there were major reclassifications, and in the following year there is a big fall in variety growth using both measures. This likely reflects that some new classifications were used in the middle of 1996, and old classifications were not retired until the following year. Although the

---

8. Note that there is a direct relationship between the Feenstra index of net variety growth in equation (1) and the decomposition in equation (2). Let the numerator of the first term in the Feenstra index be λ_{t-1} and the denominator λ_t. Then $\lambda_{t-1} = 1 -$ share disappearing • export growth and the denominator is $\lambda_t = 1 -$ share new • export growth/(V_t/V_{t-1}). This highlights how the Feenstra index of net variety growth essentially combines disappearing trade and new trade into one index. For example, consider the U.S. HS ten-digit trade data, line 1 in panel B of table 1.3. Trade growth $(V_t - V_{t-1})/V_{t-1}$ is 168 percent in this period using this data. Because these are shares of trade growth, the value of $(1 - \lambda_{t-1}) =$ share disappearing • export growth $= 0.12 • 1.68 = 0.20$, so $\lambda_{t-1} = 0.80$. To get $(1 - \lambda_t)$, we have share new • export growth/V_t/ $V_{t-1} = 0.29 • 1.68/2.68 = 0.18$ (where 2.68 is V_t/V_{t-1}), so $\lambda_t = 0.82$. Thus, the Feenstra index is $(0.8/.82) - 1 = -0.03$.

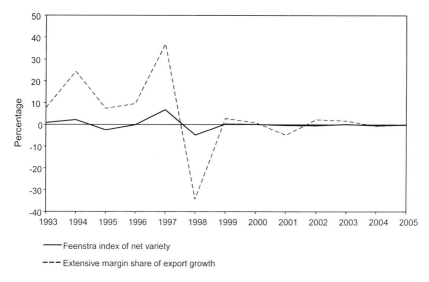

——— Feenstra index of net variety

- - - Extensive margin share of export growth

Fig. 1.12   Growth in extensive margin of U.S. Imports from China, 1992–2005
Note: Data uses HS ten-digit U.S. imports from China.

size of the reclassification effect is smaller using the Feenstra index, reclassifications still clearly play an important role in calculations of the extensive margin using both measures.

To measure growth in the extensive margin, it is more insightful to consider changes over a longer horizon because the value of exports in new product codes are generally small when they are first introduced. But if one just compares year-to-year changes, they would no longer be grouped in the new goods category. In order to minimize the reclassification issues, we report the growth in extensive margin from 1997 to 2005 in table 1.3. Using an earlier period as a base yields wide variations in measures, and comparable U.S. and China data give vastly different results. Panel A of table 1.3 shows calculations using China's eight-digit data. In the first row, where we use data on China's exports to the world from 1997 to 2005 in all eight-digit categories, we see moderate net variety growth of 10 percent, with the extensive margin accounting for 26 percent of total export growth. Recalculating the extensive margin with exports only to the United States, in the second row, we see that the magnitudes of the extensive and intensive margins are roughly the same as with total exports. In order to eliminate the potential problem associated with reclassifications that take place from year to year in China's HS eight-digit data, we also calculate the margins for product codes that existed over the whole period. In this case, we find that the growth in exports to the United States accounted for by new varieties falls markedly, to just 2 percent. This implies that part of the large variety growth found with the full sample is likely a result of reclassifications pushing up the

Table 1.3   Variety growth in China's exports, 1997–2005

			Share of total export growth from:					
No. of Codes	Type	Partner	Feenstra	Intensive	New	Disappearing	Extensive	Total export growth (%)
			A: Extensive margin using eight-digit China data					
1. 7,951	All	World	0.10	0.74 [5,501]	0.33 [1,624]	0.07 [826]	0.26	187
2. 6,357	All	U.S.	0.11	0.76 [3,641]	0.29 [1,980]	0.05 [736]	0.25	243
3. 4,826 (76% of codes)	Exist	U.S.	0.01	0.98 [3,641]	0.02 [935]	0.00 [250]	0.02	212
			B: Extensive margin using ten-digit U.S. data					
1. 14,169	All	U.S.	−0.03	0.83 [7,576]	0.29 [5,122]	0.12 [1,471]	0.17	168
2. 11,444 (81% of codes)	Exist	U.S.	0.02	0.97 [7,576]	0.03 [3,506]	0.00 [362]	0.03	182

Notes: The share of total trade growth from each margin is reported. The extensive margin share is the share of new trade less the share of disappearing trade. The extensive and intensive margin may not sum exactly to 1 because of rounding error. The total number of codes for intensive, new, and disappearing is in brackets.

extensive margin. The existing products codes are likely not to be a random sample because entirely new products—such as a digital camera—will by definition require a new code; thus, this can be taken as a lower bound of the extensive margin.

Panel B of table 1.3 reports the extensive margin using U.S. data at the ten-digit level. The data have more than twice as many codes (over 14,000 for U.S. to China trade), allowing the extensive margin to be larger. Using all of the ten-digit exports from China to the United States, net variety growth is negative and the extensive margin share of trade growth is 17 percent. The smaller value for the extensive margin in the U.S. data, as compared with the China data, is likely a result of there being fewer reclassifications in the United States (81 percent of codes are permanent as compared with 76 percent in the China data). Including only codes that exist between 1997 and 2005, the net variety growth and the extensive margin's share of trade growth are similar, at around 3 percent, and larger than measured using permanent eight-digit codes from the China data. Note that there is still significant growth in the number of new export variety categories, which increased by more than 40 percent, but these new varieties account for a small share of export growth.

Compared to other non-Organization for Economic Cooperation and Development (OECD) countries, China's growth in the extensive margin has been small. Based on the HS ten-digit export data to the United States with all codes included, China ranks 80th out of a total of 133 non-OECD countries using the Feenstra net index of variety measure and 100th using the extensive margin measure.

All of these measures of the extensive margin should be interpreted with caution given that the magnitudes vary considerably depending on whether all product codes are used and whether the base period is before or after the major reclassifications that took place in 1996. The calculations with the more disaggregated U.S. data from 1997 onward indicate that a large portion of China's export growth took place along its intensive margin.

1.7   Export Prices

The large increase in export growth along the intensive margin suggests that China's export growth is likely to put downward pressure on world prices of these goods. Taking the subset of HS ten-digit goods that China exported to the United States between 1997 and 2005, we construct an average export-price index using a chain-weighted Törnqvist index for manufactured goods, defined as follows:

$$\text{Tindex}_t = \prod_i \left(\frac{p_{it}}{p_{it-1}} \right)^{w_{it}}, \text{ where } w_{it} = 0.5 \cdot (\text{share}_{it} + \text{share}_{it-1}),$$

and p_{it} is the unit value, defined as the ratio of the export value from China to the United States of product i at time t to the quantity exported. Note that we only construct export-price indexes to the United States rather than to exports to the world because it is important to have highly disaggregated product-level data to ensure that the units of measurement of quantities are the same within the HS codes. Using more aggregated data, say, at the HS six-digit level runs the risk of having aggregated quantities across different units of measurement. Even at the HS ten-digit level, the quantity data is quite noisy; thus, we clean the data by deleting products with price change of more than 200 percent over this period. After cleaning the data and ensuring that China and the rest of the world export this same subset of products, we are left with 3,800 HS ten-digit product codes within manufacturing. The export-price index for China is weighted by the export value of each of these product codes from China to the United States as a ratio of the total value of these exports, and the export-price index from the rest of the world to the United States is weighted by the export value of each of these same product codes from the rest of the world to the United States as a ratio of total export value of these products.

The Törnqvist export-price index (Tindex) for China between 1997 and 2005 is 0.88, indicating a fall of 12 percent over the period. In contrast, the Tindex for exports of these same HS ten-digit codes from the rest of the world to the United States is 1.03, indicating a 3 percent increase in prices over this period.[9]

The export price decline in China is consistent with a negative terms-of-trade effect, with increased exports pushing down export prices. However, it could also be related to improved productivity in China, declining profit margins, or exchange rate movements.

1.8 Conclusions

This chapter decomposes China's spectacular export growth, of over 500 percent since 1992, along various dimensions. A number of interesting findings emerge. First, churning among different products was significant. China's export structure changed dramatically, with growing export shares in electronics and machinery and a decline in agriculture and apparel. The strongest overall export growth has been in machinery, and within this broad category, telecoms, electrical machinery, and office machines have experienced the highest growth and make up the largest shares within machinery.

Second, despite the shift into these more-sophisticated products, the skill

9. The Fisher price index, which is the square root of the Laspeyres index (that uses base period weights) and the Paasche index (that uses current period weights) gives the same result as the Tindex.

content of China's manufacturing exports remained unchanged once processing trade is excluded. When examining the skill content of China's total manufacturing exports, it looks like there has been an increase over the sample period. However, it turns out that this is mainly due to the increased skill content of imported inputs that are then assembled for export—a practice known as processing trade. This result has implications for other studies that have emphasized the sophistication of China's exports as a potential conduit of China's rapid income growth. We highlight processing trade as the mechanism behind this special feature of China's exports. Of course, there still may be something special about processing trade, perhaps through learning externalities or more growth opportunities in export processing.

Third, export growth was accompanied by increasing specialization. This finding casts some doubt on the notion that export diversification is a key element in export growth. The literature argues that diversification could promote export growth if it makes export discoveries more likely and that it helps alleviate risks associated with shocks to particular sectors. Indeed, traditional thinking highlights trade and specialization, where market forces work to attract resources into the main sectors where relative cost advantages are the greatest.

Fourth, export growth was mainly accounted for by high export growth of existing products (the intensive margin) rather than in new varieties (the extensive margin). Consistent with an increased world supply of existing varieties, we find that China's export prices to the United States fell by an average of 1.6 percent per year between 1997 and 2005, while export prices of these products from the rest of the world to the United States increased by 0.4 percent annually over the same period. Importers have gained from lower prices and from the abundance of products now available in markets around the globe.

References

Arkolakis, C. 2006. Market access costs and the new consumers margin in international trade. University of Minnesota. Mimeograph.

Broda, C., and D. Weinstein. 2006. Globalization and the gains from variety. *Quarterly Journal of Economics* 121 (2): 541–85.

Dean, J., K. C. Fung, and Z. Wang. 2007. Measuring the vertical specialization on Chinese trade. USITC Working Paper no. 2007-01-A. Washington, DC: U.S. International Trade Commission.

Feenstra, R. C. 1994. New product varieties and the measurement of international prices. *American Economic Review* 84: 157–77.

Funke, M., and R. Ruhwedel. 2001. Export variety and economic growth: Empirical evidence from the OECD countries. *IMF Staff Papers* 48 (2): 225–42. Washington, DC: International Monetary Fund.

Hausmann, R., and D. Rodrik. 2003. Economic development as self-discovery. *Journal of Development Economics* 72 (2): 603–33.

Hummels, D., and P. Klenow. 2005. The variety and quality of a nation's exports. *American Economic Review* 95: 704–23.

Imbs, J., and R. Warziarg. 2003. Stages of diversification. *American Economic Review* 93 (1): 63–86.

Kehoe, T., and K. Ruhl. 2009. How important is the new goods margin in international trade? Federal Reserve Bank of Minneapolis Staff Report no. 324. Minneapolis, MN: Federal Reserve Bank of Minneapolis.

Rodrik, D. 2006. What's so special about China's exports? NBER Working Paper no. 11947. Cambridge, MA: National Bureau of Economic Research.

Schott, P. 2006. The relative sophistication of China's exports. NBER Working Paper no. 12173. Cambridge, MA: National Bureau of Economic Research.

Zhu, S. C., and D. Trefler. 2005. Trade and inequality in developing countries: A general equilibrium analysis. *Journal of International Economics* 65:21–48.

Comment   Bin Xu

Amiti and Freund wrote a revealing and stimulating piece on characteristics of China's export dynamics. I summarize their main findings in the following and offer my comments under each of their findings.

Finding 1: The skill content of China's exports increased from 1992 to 2005, but the increase was driven almost entirely by China's processing exports. There was little skill upgrading found in China's nonprocessing exports.

This is a striking result to me. To comment on this result, we need to understand the method used by the authors. The authors first rank China's five-digit International Standard Industrial Classification (ISIC) industries in ascending order of skill intensity. Due to unavailability of relevant Chinese data, the industry skill-intensity ranking is based on Indonesian data. The authors then compute the cumulative export shares of the industries. If a country's cumulative export shares of low-skill industries decrease over time, it is considered as evidence of rising skill content of the country's overall exports. The authors find such a decrease in China's manufacturing exports in the period of 1992 to 2005 but no such a decrease in China's *nonprocessing* manufacturing exports in the same period.

To explain Amiti and Freund's method, let us consider a model of two industries, a low-skill industry 1 and a high-skill industry 2. Denote h_1 and h_2 as skill intensity of exports from 1 and 2, respectively, h_e as skill intensity of total exports, and λ as export share of 1. Then $\lambda h_1 + (1 - \lambda)h_2 = h_e$. By

Bin Xu is a professor of economics and finance at the China Europe International Business School (CEIBS).

definition, an increase in the (relative) skill content of the country's exports refers to an increase in h_e.

The approach of Amiti and Freund is to detect changes in skill content from changes in λ. For China's nonprocessing exports, they find little changes in λ. What does this finding tell us? It tells us that distribution of nonprocessing export shares is quite stable in the period of 1992 to 2005 across Chinese manufacturing industries. In other words, there are little export-share shifts from low-skill industries to high-skill industries with regard to nonprocessing exports. As is clear from the model, a constant λ implies no changes in skill content *only if* h_1 and h_2 are unchanged. In footnote 3 of their paper, Amiti and Freund recognize that their result only gives an indication of shifts between industries (λ) and do not say if there has been any within-industry skill upgrading (h_1 and h_2). Still, I want to caution the reader that one cannot draw a conclusion of no skill upgrading in China's nonprocessing exports without looking at changes in skill intensities of Chinese industries that conduct nonprocessing exports.

I must add that the preceding point does not downgrade the very valuable finding by Amiti and Freund that there exists a sharp difference in across-industry–export-share distribution between processing and nonprocessing exports. This finding calls for future research to explore the underlying reasons for this sharp difference. Given this paper's finding of across-industry skill upgrading in China's processing exports and the likely occurrence of within-industry skill upgrading of Chinese exports, the skill content of China's processing exports should have risen. Amiti and Freund provide some evidence that the skill content of China's processing *imports* increased significantly, which supports an argument that the rising skill content of China's processing exports resulted from rising skill content of China's imports of intermediate goods used in producing processing exports. As the authors recognize, rising skill content of processing imports does not rule out the possibility of skill upgrading of China's value added in the production of processing exports. Future research is needed to estimate the contribution of China's value added to the skill upgrading of its process exports.

Finding 2: China's export growth was accompanied by increasing specialization or decreasing diversification.

To comment on this result, we need to first understand what the authors mean by specialization and diversification. The authors use two measures to gauge the degree of what they call "export specialization." First, they rank products in ascending order of export share, compute the cumulative shares for 1992 and 2005, and compare them. For China's top 500 export products, they find that the cumulative share for 2005 is lower than that for 1992, which they interpret as increased export specialization. Second, they compute a Gini coefficient and find that its value rises for China's exports from 1992 to 2005, which they interpret as indication of increased export specialization.

From the two measures the authors use, it is clear that their definition of export specialization (diversification) is indeed inequality (equality) of export-share distribution. Take an example of three goods. If a country initially exports the three goods evenly, $s_1 = s_2 = s_3 = 1/3$, where s denotes export share, then the Gini coefficient is zero. Suppose later on export shares become $s_1 = 1/6$, $s_2 = 1/3$, and $s_3 = 1/2$, then the Gini coefficient becomes 0.5. This rise in the Gini coefficient indicates that the export-share distribution has become more uneven but does it necessarily mean that the country's export structure has become more specialized? To answer this question, let us rank 1, 2, 3 in ascending order of skill intensity. Suppose initially China's export shares are $s_1 = 1/2$, $s_2 = 1/3$, and $s_3 = 1/6$, where half of China's exports are in the low-skill good 1. Suppose at a later time China's export shares become $s_1 = s_2 = s_3 = 1/3$, which indicates that China's export-share distribution has become more equal. In terms of export specialization, China has become less specialized in the low-skill good 1, but more specialized in the high-skill good 3. This example shows that we really cannot conclude from a more even export-share distribution that export structure has become less (or more) specialized.

The chapter associates increased specialization (accompanying export growth) with traditional trade theory, and more diversified export structure with the cost discovery theory of Hausmann and Rodrik (2003) and the stage-of-diversification theory of Imbs and Wacziarg (2003), and interprets the finding of China's rising export specialization as evidence supporting the traditional trade theory. I don't think this interpretation is proper. In the standard 2×2 Heckscher-Ohlin (HO) model, a country produces both goods (i.e., diversification in production), exports one good, and imports the other good. In this model, export growth cannot be interpreted as rising export specialization. In HO models with more goods than factors, export patterns are indeterminate, and, hence, there is no meaningful definition of export specialization. In multicone HO models, export growth is associated with product specialization, but it is not about increased export shares of a given set of goods. Rather, export growth is usually accompanied by shifting of product mix from one set of goods to another set of goods. In contrast, the associations between diversification and growth in the aforementioned development theories are derived from models of different nature, and it is farfetched to link them to the current context.

Finding 3: China's export growth was driven overwhelmingly by export expansion of existing goods, with only a small contribution from export expansion of new goods.

The authors attempted two approaches. First, they use Harmonized System (HS) six-digit data in concordance to the same 1992 product codes, rank these goods in ascending order of export share, split them into deciles by export value in 1992, and examine the changes of export shares of the deciles from 1992 to 2005. They find that the bottom 20 percent of China's export value more than doubled in this period. In other words, the goods with the lowest export values in 1992 saw the fastest growth in export value in the period. The authors view it as suggesting a sizable role for the extensive margin (i.e., export growth from introduction of new goods).

As the authors point out, HS six-digit categories are too aggregated to be able to identify new products. Low export shares of HS six-digit categories do not necessarily contain new goods, so the observed rapid export expansion in these categories may well be that of the existing goods, that is, the intensive margin. Although this approach based on HS six-digit data does not identify the contributions of the intensive margin and extensive margin, the authors find that the reshuffling of China's HS six-digit categories during the period 1992 to 2005, while occurring mainly in the bottom 20 percent by export value, was mainly in the mid-to-upper range by product category rank (splitting exports into deciles by the number of product categories in 1992), shifting from the top decile to the four deciles below the top. I find this pattern very interesting. If the top decile corresponds to the most labor-intensive goods (large export items of China in 1992), the next four deciles correspond to goods of middle-range skill intensities; then the preceding pattern suggests that there was skill upgrading in China's export structure from 1992 to 2005 in industries of low-to-middle skill intensities (which was exactly what figure 1.4 of the paper shows). Moreover, the fact that it occurred mainly in the bottom 20 percent by export value suggests that this skill upgrading of China's export structure was mainly driven by the expansion of *small* export items whose skill intensities lie in the middle range. I think this is an interesting pattern worthy of further exploration.

To examine the relative contribution of intensive and extensive margins to China's export growth, the authors use the (second) approach of computing the Feenstra (1994) index of variety growth and decomposing export growth into the intensive margin and extensive margin (defined as creation of new export goods less destruction of old goods). They use HS eight-digit data collected by China and HS ten-digit data collected by the United States. To alleviate the distorting effect of a major reclassification of HS codes in 1996, they implement their estimation using the sample period of 1997 to 2005. The results indicate that China's export growth has been small in the extensive margin as compared to other non-Organization for Economic Cooperation and Development (OECD) countries. I think this is a very useful finding as it tells us something important about the mode of China's export growth. Recent studies by Rodrik (2006) and Schott (2008) find that China's exports have more overlaps with that of advanced countries than would be expected from its income level. Given the large overlaps of exports by China and advanced countries, whether China's export growth relies more on the intensive margin or the extensive margin becomes an important factor in assessing the nature of export competition between China and advanced countries.

Finding 4: For the same HS ten-digit goods exported to the United States, the price index for China fell by 13 percent, while the price index of the rest of the world rose by 3 percent, in the period of 1997 to 2005.

Amiti and Freund are not the first to point out that price of China's exports to the U.S. market has been declining relative to that of other countries. Schott (2008) used the same HS ten-digit data, compared Chinese and OECD export unit values, and identified a trend of increasing price discount of Chinese exports that has existed since 1980.

What is behind this trend of falling prices of Chinese exports? One can think of several hypotheses. First, price can be a signal of product quality. Even at the HS ten-digit level, goods are still of great heterogeneity, as one can see from the big variation of unit values of the same good imported from different countries. If one interprets the price difference between Chinese and OECD goods as reflecting product quality difference, as does Schott (2008), one may conclude that falling prices of Chinese goods are of less a concern to advanced countries as they do not directly compete with the high-quality varieties exported by advanced countries. Second, falling prices of Chinese exports may be a result of the increasing volume of Chinese exports. This terms-of-trade hypothesis is proposed by the authors of this chapter, who argue that the large increase in export growth along the intensive margin suggests that China's export growth is likely to put downward pressure on world prices. The authors do not provide, however, any evidence to support this argument. One might be interested to see if there is a positive correlation between growth of China's exports and decline of their prices at the product level. Besides these two hypotheses, falling prices of Chinese exports may be due to some other reasons. For example, Chinese export firms have seen improved productivity and increased domestic competition, both of which may lead to lower export prices. During the 1980s and 1990s, there was depreciation of China's real exchange rate, which may have also played a role in lowering China's export prices during the period.

In sum, I find this chapter by Amiti and Freund very interesting and stimulating. China has emerged as a major force in international trade, yet our understanding of the characteristics of Chinese foreign trade is still quite rudimentary. By identifying several interesting patterns of China's export growth and raising a number of important questions with regard to these patterns, Amiti and Freund's research provides an excellent starting point for further exploration of this topic.

References

Feenstra, Robert C. 1994. New product varieties and the measurement of international prices. *American Economic Review* 84:157–77.

Hausmann, Ricardo, and Dani Rodrik. 2003. Economic development as self-discovery. *Journal of Development Economics* 72 (2): 603–33.

Imbs, Jean, and Romain Wacziarg. 2003. Stages of diversification. *American Economic Review* 93 (1): 63–86.

Rodrik, Dani. 2006. What's so special about China's exports? *China & World Economy* 14 (5): 1–19.

Schott, Peter K. 2008. The relative sophistication of Chinese exports. *Economic Policy* 53:5–49.

2

What Accounts for the Rising Sophistication of China's Exports?

Zhi Wang and Shang-Jin Wei

*Everyone knew that we would lose jobs in labor-intensive indus-
tries like textiles and apparel, but we thought we could hold our
own in the capital-intensive, high-tech arena. The numbers we're
seeing now put the lie to that hope—as China expands its share
even in core industries such as autos and aerospace.*
—Robert Scott, U.S. Economic Policy Institute

2.1 Introduction

China's rise as a trading power has taken the world by storm. Its exports
have risen from 18 billion dollars or less than 4 percent of its gross domestic
product (GDP) in 1980 to more than 760 billion dollars or about 35 percent of its GDP by 2005. Besides the rapid expansion of its trade volume,
researchers have noted another feature: China's level of sophistication has
been rising steadily. This sophistication can be seen in three aspects, two
noted in the literature, and the third presented here, by us. First, as Schott
(2006) noted, China's export structure increasingly resembles the collective
export structure of the high-income countries in a way that seems unusual
given China's endowment and level of development. Second, as Rodrik
(2006) observed, the level of GDP per capita associated with countries
exporting the same basket of goods as China is much higher than China's
actual level of income per capita. Third, as we will show, the fraction of
product lines that the United States, the fifteen-member European Union,
and Japan (referred to hereafter as G3) export and that China does not is
shrinking steadily. Obviously, these three trends are not independent from

Zhi Wang is a senior international economist at Research Division, Office of Economics,
U.S. International Trade Commission. Shang-Jin Wei is the N. T. Wang Professor of Chinese
Business and Economy at Columbia Business School, and a research associate of the National
Bureau of Economic Research.

The views in the chapter are those of the authors and are not the official views of the U.S.
International Trade Commission (ITC), the International Monetary Fund (IMF), or any other
organization that the authors are or have been affiliated with. The authors thank Kyle Caswell
and Chang Hong for efficient research assistance; John Klopfer for able editorial assistance;
and Xuepeng Liu, William Power, participants in the National Bureau of Economic Research
(NBER) conference for the project, and, especially, Galina Hale, for helpful comments.

each other. Taken at their face value, they may suggest that China is competing head to head with producers from developed and developing nations alike. This has generated a tremendous amount of anxiety in many nations. Why would China, a country with an extreme abundance of labor but relative scarcity in capital, skilled labor, and research and development (R&D) investment, produce and export a bundle of goods that resembles those of developed countries? Schott (2006) conjectures that this results from a combination of a large variation in factor endowment and a low factor mobility across regions.

The evolution of China's export sophistication during 1996 to 2005 is traced out in table 2.1. This table shows that the level of dissimilarity between China's export structure and that of the G3 economies declined from 133.7 in 1996 to 121.5 by 2005.[1] During the same period, the number of Harmonized System (HS) six-digit product lines exported by G3 countries but not by China fell from 101 in 1996 to 83 in 2005, out of 4,143 and 4,212 in total, respectively. As a share of the product lines that the G3 export, those not manufactured by China fell from 2.44 percent of the total in 1996 to 1.97 percent in 2005. This count is somewhat misleading as China exports a very small volume (i.e., less than $1 million) in several product lines. Excluding these lines, the share of products exported by the G3 but not by China fell from 28.7 percent (1,189/4,143) in 1996 to 13.7 percent (578/4,212) in 2005.[2]

How much should developed countries be concerned with rising competitive pressure from increasingly sophisticated Chinese exports? The answer depends on the sources of China's rising sophistication. On the one hand, this sophistication, as measured, could be a statistical mirage due to processing trade. For example, both the United States and China may export notebook computers, but Chinese manufacturers may have to import the computer's most sophisticated components, such as central processing units (CPUs) made by Intel or AMD in the United States. In such a case, Chinese producers may specialize in the unsophisticated stage of production although the final product is classified as sophisticated. If one were able to classify a product further into its components, China and developed countries might be found to produce different components. That is, they do not compete directly with each other. In this scenario, there is very little for the developed countries to worry about.

As a variation of this scenario, China and the high-income economies may export the same set of product lines, but they may export very different varieties within each product line, with China exporting varieties of much lower quality.[3] Competition between the high-income economies and China need not be tense.

1. This is computed at national level using equation (2) and excluding the region subscript.
2. There is virtually no product that China exports but G3 does not.
3. Xu (2007) noted that for the same product, the unit value of China's exports tends to be lower than that of rich countries, indicating that China's varieties are of lower quality and pre-

Table 2.1   **Increasing overlaps in the export structure: China relative to the United States, the European Union, and Japan (1996–2005)**

Year	No. of HS six-digit product lines exported by the high-income countries (G3, at least U.S. $1 million) (1)	Also exported by China (at least U.S. $1 million) (2)	Fraction of the product lines exported by the G3 but not by China (3) = 1 − (2)/(1)	Export dissimilarity index (4)
1996	4,126	2,942	28.7	133.7
1997	4,123	3,042	26.2	132.5
1998	4,121	3,041	26.2	130.8
1999	4,120	3,024	26.6	129.2
2000	4,116	3,172	22.9	125.5
2001	4,118	3,184	22.7	124.8
2002	4,184	3,306	21.0	125.4
2003	4,182	3,408	18.5	126.1
2004	4,186	3,515	16.0	123.1
2005	4,179	3,609	13.6	121.5

Source: Authors' computation based on trade statistics from the China Customs Administration and on G3 data downloaded from the UN COMTRADE database.

Note: The export dissimilarity index is computed based on equation (2), explained in the text; smaller values indicate greater overlaps. HS = Harmonized System.

On the other hand, the Chinese authorities, including governments at the regional or local levels, have been actively promoting quality upgrades to China's product structure through tax and other policy incentives. A particular manifestation of these incentives is the proliferation of economic and technological development zones, high-tech industrial zones, and export processing zones around the country. Their collective share in China's exports rose from less than 6 percent in 1995 to about 25 percent by 2005. These policy incentives could increase the similarity of Chinese exports to those of developed countries, though they are unlikely to be efficient (unless learning by doing confers a significant positive externality). If policy is the primary driver for rising sophistication (rather than the mismeasurement induced by processing trade), then China may come into more direct competition with developed countries.

Foreign-invested firms in China straddle these two explanations. The share of China's total exports produced by wholly foreign-owned firms and Sino-

---

sumably of lesser sophistication. Fontagne, Gaulier, and Zignago (2007, tables 1 and 2) show that China's export structure, defined the same way as in Schott (2006) but at the HS six-digit level, is more similar to Japan, the United States, and the European Union than to those of Brazil and Russia. However, judged on unit values, Chinese exports are more likely to be in the low end of the market than are those of the high-income countries.

Table 2.2   Breakdown of China's exports by firm ownership, 1995–2006 (%)

Year	State-owned enterprise	Joint-venture	Wholly foreign-owned	Collective	Private
1995	66.7	19.8	11.7	1.5	0.0
1996	57.0	24.9	15.7	2.0	0.0
1997	56.2	23.9	17.1	2.5	0.0
1998	52.6	24.1	20.0	2.9	0.1
1999	50.5	23.2	22.2	3.5	0.3
2000	46.7	24.2	23.8	4.2	1.0
2001	42.6	24.1	25.9	5.3	2.0
2002	37.7	22.7	29.5	5.8	4.2
2003	31.5	21.5	33.3	5.7	7.9
2004	25.9	21.0	36.1	5.4	11.7
2005	22.2	19.9	38.4	4.8	14.7
2006	19.7	18.7	39.5	4.2	17.8
Average 1996–2004	39.8	22.7	27.8	4.7	4.9

Source: Authors' computation based on official trade statistics from the China Custom Administration.

foreign joint ventures has risen steadily over time, from about 31 percent in 1995 to more than 58 percent by 2005 (table 2.2). These foreign-invested firms may choose to produce and export much more sophisticated products than would indigenous Chinese firms. In this scenario, while China-made products may compete with those from developed countries, the profits from such activities contribute directly to the gross national products (GNPs) of developed countries. Besides the direct effect of foreign-invested firms on China's export upgrading, the presence of foreign firms may help indirectly to raise the sophistication of Chinese exports through various spillovers to domestic firms (Hale and Long 2006). The preceding three possible explanations can reinforce each other rather than be mutually exclusive. For example, a foreign-invested firm may engage in processing trade while located in a high-tech zone.

To the best of our knowledge, direct evidence on the importance of these channels is not yet available in the literature until recently. Using a detailed product-level data set on Chinese exports, the chapter by Amiti and Freund (chapter 1 in this volume) examines the change in the skill content of the Chinese exports. They have found a dramatic transformation of the export structure since 1992. In particular, there has been a significant decline in the share of agriculture and traditional labor-intensive manufacturing products, such as textiles, garments, and shoes, with a growing share in nontraditional manufactures, such as consumer electronics, appliances, computers, and telecommunication equipment. This would seem to suggest a dramatic rise in the skill content of China's exports. They confirm this by measuring the skill content in a sector as the ratio of nonproduction workers to total employment from the Indonesian manufacturing census at the five-digit International Standard Industrial Classification (ISIC) level for 1992 (they don't have access to comparable data for China). However, a prominent feature of the Chinese exports is the role of processing trade—the use of tariff-free imported inputs in the production for exports—accounting for more than half of China's total exports in recent years. It is possible the real skill content in processing exports is low even though they may appear in sectors that otherwise would be classified as having a high-skill content. Outside processing exports, they find very little skill upgrading associated with normal exports. They note, however, that they cannot rule out the possibility that within processing exports, "the Chinese value added has become more skill-intensive."

In this chapter, we measure China's evolving export sophistication, not by the changing share of nonproduction workers in employment, but, following Schott (2006), by an increase in the resemblance of its export bundle to those of high-income countries. Our data set is even more finely disaggregated than what is used in Amiti and Freund (chapter 1 in this volume): our product-level data set on Chinese exports is disaggregated by firm ownership type and incentive status of a production location in about 240 Chinese cities.

Our data set allows us to examine some questions that are not possible to examine in the previous chapter. For example, we can assess respective contributions by processing exports in a high-tech incentive zone, normal exports in a similar zone, and processing exports outside the incentive zones to China's export structure sophistication. This allows us to also reach somewhat different conclusions.

To preview some of our key findings, we will argue that it is important to look both at export structure and at the unit value of exports. We will report evidence that neither processing trade nor foreign-invested firms play an important role in generating the increased overlap between China's export structure and that of the high-income countries. Instead, improvement in human capital and government policies in the form of tax-favored high-tech zones appear to contribute significantly to the rising sophistication of China's exports.

Our finding on the role of processing trade in raising export sophistication appears to be different from the previous chapter in part due to the difference in the data sets (and in part due to the difference in the metric used to assess sophistication). Our more finely disaggregated data shows that the contributions to export structure sophistication from processing and normal exports in a high-tech incentive zone are about the same, and those from processing and normal exports outside any incentive zones are also about the same. This leads us to conclude that it is the incentive zones, not processing trade, that are associated with a more sophisticated export structure. Because processing exports are disproportionately located in various incentive zones, one may not be able to isolate the effect of processing exports without the more disaggregated data.

An analysis of unit values adds important insights. Processing trade is positively associated with higher unit values. In the absence of data on value added from imported inputs versus domestic inputs, it is difficult to say whether processing trade has generated any skill upgrading for China. However, after controlling for processing trade, exports by foreign-invested firms tend to have systematically higher unit values, suggesting that they produce higher-end product varieties (beyond promoting processing exports). High-tech zones and other policy zones set up by the government are likewise associated with higher unit values (beyond promoting processing trade). Therefore, both foreign investment and government policy zones are conducive to greater product sophistication, by increasing the overlap in China's export structure with that of the advanced economies or by producing higher-end varieties within a given product category.

The rest of the chapter is organized as follows: section 2.2 explains the basic specification and the underlying data, section 2.3 reports a series of statistical analyses, and section 2.4 concludes.

2.2   Specification and Data

Our strategy is to make use of variations across Chinese cities in both export sophistication and its potential determinants to study their relationship. We look at two measures of export sophistication: (a) the similarity between local export structure to that of the G3 economies, and (b) the unit value of local exports. We consider several categories of determinants, including the level of human capital, the use of processing trade, and the promotion of sophistication by governments through high-tech and economic development zones.

2.2.1   Data and Basic Facts

Data on China's exports were obtained from the China Customs General Administration at the HS eight-digit level (the most disaggregated level of classification available). The administration's database reports the geographic origin of exports (from more than 400 cities in China), policy zone designation (i.e., whether an exporter is located in any type of policy zone), firm ownership, and transaction type (whether an export is related to processing trade, as determined by customs declarations) for the period from 1995 through 2005.

We link this database with a separate database on Chinese cities, including gross metropolitan product (GMP) per capita, population, college enrollment, and foreign direct investment (FDI) data, downloaded from China Data Online (a site managed by the University of Michigan China Data

Center). Unfortunately, the coverage of this second database is more limited (240 cities from 1996 through 2004), which effectively constrains the ultimate sample for the statistical analyses. Our sample of cities is listed in table 2A.3.

The exports by the G3 economies at the HS six-digit level come from the United Nations' COMTRADE database, downloaded from the World Integrated Trade Solution (WITS). We wish to focus on manufactured goods, not on natural resources, and have, therefore, excluded the goods in HS chapters 1 to 27 (agricultural and mineral products) and raw materials and their simple transformations (mostly at HS four-digit level) in other HS chapters. A list of excluded products is reported in table 2A.4.

Summary statistics are reported in tables 2.1 to 2.6. From table 2.1, we can see that the fraction of HS six-digit product lines that the advanced economies export but China does not declined over time, from 28.7 percent in 1996 to 13.6 percent in 2005. This is consistent with the possibility of a rapid rise in export sophistication by China.

Table 2.2 reports a breakdown of export value by the ownership of exporters. A number of features are worth noting. First, the share of China's exports produced by state-owned firms declined steadily from 66.7 percent in 1995 to 39.8 percent in 2005. This reduction in the role of state-owned firms in exports mirrors the reduced economic role of the state in general. Second, foreign-invested firms (both wholly foreign-owned firms and Sino-foreign joint ventures) play a significant role in China's exports. Their share of China's exports also grew steadily from 31.5 percent in 1995 to 58.3 percent in 2005. The role played by foreign firms in China's export industries is greater than their role in most other countries with a population over ten million. Third, exports by truly private domestic firms are relatively small, though their share in China's exports has similarly increased over time, from basically nothing before 1997 to 17.8 percent by 2005. Some growth in exports by domestic private firms is achieved by a change in firm ownership. For example, the laptop manufacturer Lenovo was established as a partly state-owned firm. By 2003, it was a privately owned firm. By now, Lenovo has attracted foreign investment, acquired the original IBM PC division, and exported products under the IBM brand.

Table 2.3 reports a breakdown of China's exports into processing trade, normal trade, and other categories according to exporters' customs declarations. Processing exports come from three areas: (a) export processing zones, (b) various high-tech zones, and (c) areas outside any policy zones. Collectively, their share of the country's total exports increased from 43 percent (= 0 + 3.2% + 39.8%) in 1995 to 52 percent (= 4.6% + 11.8% + 35.6%) in 2005. As we lack information on the share of processing exports for other countries, we cannot conduct a formal international comparison. Our conjecture is that few developing countries would have a share of processing

Table 2.3   Share of processing trade and policy zones in China's total exports, 1996–2005 (%)

Year	Special economic zones (1)	Exports processing zones (2)	Processing exports in high-tech zones (3)	Normal exports in high-tech zones (4)	Processing exports outside policy zones (5)	Normal exports outside policy zones (6)	All other exports[a] (7)
1995	10.6	0	3.2	2.1	39.8	42.1	2.2
1996	8.7	0	3.9	1.8	45.2	38.3	2.0
1997	8.8	0	4.6	1.7	43.9	39.0	1.9
1998	8.2	0	5.5	1.9	45.5	36.9	1.9
1999	7.0	0	6.4	2.2	45.5	37.0	1.9
2000	7.1	0	7.0	2.6	43.3	38.2	1.8
2001	6.8	0.1	7.4	2.8	43.0	38.0	1.9
2002	6.2	0.7	8.0	3.0	42.2	37.6	2.3
2003	5.3	2.4	9.5	3.4	39.6	37.1	2.7
2004	4.4	3.6	11.0	3.6	37.7	36.4	3.2
2005	4.3	4.6	11.8	3.6	35.6	36.8	3.5
Average 1996–2004	6.3	1.3	8.0	2.8	41.7	37.4	2.4

Source: Authors computed based on official trade statistics from China Custom Administration.

[a]Including international aid, compensation trade, goods on consignment, border trade, goods for foreign contracted projects, goods on lease, outward processing, barter trade, warehouse trade, and entrepôt trade by bonded area.

Table 2.4   Firm structure across trade and policy zones, 1996–2004 (%)

	Special economic zones	Exports processing zones	Processing exports in high-tech zones	Normal exports in high-tech zones	Processing exports outside policy zones	Normal exports outside policy zones	All other exports[a]
1996–2004 average							
State-owned	23.7	0.0	4.8	58.3	28.3	62.5	44.3
Joint-venture	34.3	3.4	33.4	16.9	29.2	13.1	13.0
Wholly foreign	36.3	96.0	61.5	16.3	38.0	6.6	24.0
Collective	1.7	0.6	0.3	1.4	3.1	8.2	4.6
Private	3.8	0.0	0.1	7.1	1.5	9.5	10.4
Total	99.9	100.0	100.0	100.0	100.0	100.0	96.3
1996							
State-owned	29.4		15.6	79.7	40.5	85.7	63.0
Joint-venture	39.5		37.8	13.3	35.2	9.4	10.3
Wholly foreign	30.0		46.2	6.2	22.4	2.2	11.3
Collective	0.9		0.4	0.9	1.9	2.6	3.4
Private	0.0		0.0	0.0	0.0	0.0	0.2
Total	99.8		100.0	100.0	100.0	100.0	88.2
2004							
State-owned	20.5	0.0	2.5	44.0	18.3	41.8	30.3
Joint-venture	30.5	3.0	27.2	16.4	26.3	15.0	15.5
Wholly foreign	37.9	96.5	69.8	23.2	47.9	9.4	29.8
Collective	2.2	0.4	0.2	1.4	3.4	10.3	4.0
Private	9.0	d0.0	0.3	15.1	4.0	23.5	19.7
Total	100.0	100.0	100.0	100.0	100.0	100.0	99.4

Source: Authors computed based on official trade statistics from China Custom Administration.

[a]Including international aid, compensation trade, goods on consignment, border trade, goods for foreign contracted projects, goods on lease, outward processing, barter trade, warehouse trade, and entrepôt trade by bonded area.

Table 2.5   Summary statistics for city-level variables

	N	Mean	Median	Standard deviation	Min.	Max.
GMP per capita (in log)	1981	8.97	8.89	0.63	7.23	11.48
GMP (in log)	1981	14.74	14.71	0.96	11.16	18.13
Student enrollment in colleges and universities as a share of nonagricultural population	1986	0.016	0.009	0.019	0.000	0.155

Note: GMP = gross metropolitan product.

exports as large as China's. On the other hand, we conjecture that China's reported processing trade may be exaggerated due to some firms' desire to evade tariffs on the domestic sale of imported "inputs."[4]

Table 2.4 tabulates the distribution of firm ownership for exports from each type of policy zone. Foreign-invested firms are dominant in processing exports, accounting for 100 percent of exports out of export processing zones, 95 percent of processing exports out of high-tech zones, and 67 percent of processing exports from the rest of China. State-owned firms account for the bulk of the remaining processing trade. Therefore, wholly and partly foreign-owned firms handle most processing exports. The reverse is not true—foreign firms also engage in normal (i.e., nonprocessing) exports, accounting in 2004 for 40 percent of nonprocessing exports out of high-tech zones and for 24 percent of normal trade outside policy zones.

We can compute a breakdown of export type (processing or nonprocessing) by ownership. The result is reported in table 2.6. For both wholly foreign-owned firms and Sino-foreign joint ventures, processing trade accounts for nearly 50 percent of exports. For state-owned firms and collectively owned firms, the share of processing exports in their total exports is 18 percent and 13 percent, respectively. Domestic private firms engage in comparatively little processing trade, making less than 7 percent of their exports in this category.

As part of its development strategy, China established a number of special economic zones and other areas where special incentives were applied following 1979. Five special economic zones (SEZs) were set up and should be distinguished from other special economic areas. These include all of Hainan province, three cities in Guangdong province (Shenzhen, Zhuhai, and Shantou), and a city in Fujian Province (Xiamen). Other special eco-

---

4. Fisman and Wei (2004) provide evidence of massive tariff evasion on China's imports. Fisman, Moustakerski, and Wei (2008) suggest that entrepôt trade via Hong Kong may have been used as a conduit for part of the tariff evasion.

Table 2.6	Summary statistics: other key variables in regression analysis				
	Export dissimilarity index (logged) (1)	Share of processing exports outside policy zones (2)	Share of processing exports in high-tech zones (3)	Share of non-processing exports in high-tech zones (4)	Share of export processing zones (5)
All firms					
N	1,986	1,986	1,986	1,986	1,986
Mean	5.24	0.259	0.0144	0.0068	0.0004
Median	5.26	0.196	0.0000	0.0000	0.0000
SD	0.07	0.233	0.0594	0.0253	0.0057
Min.	4.84	0.000	0.0000	0.0000	0.0000
Max.	5.30	0.996	0.5940	0.4206	0.1534
State-owned firms					
N	1,981	1,981	1,981	1,981	1,981
Mean	5.24	0.168	0.0016	0.0058	0.0000
Median	5.27	0.103	0.0000	0.0000	0.0000
SD	0.06	0.200	0.0105	0.0327	0.0000
Min.	4.92	0.000	0.0000	0.0000	0.0000
Max.	5.30	0.990	0.1822	0.5102	0.0013
Joint-venture firms					
N	1,835	1,835	1,835	1,835	1,835
Mean	5.27	0.430	0.0263	0.0143	0.0004
Median	5.28	0.418	0.0000	0.0000	0.0000
SD	0.04	0.321	0.0875	0.0663	0.0083
Min.	4.95	0.000	0.0000	0.0000	0.0000
Max.	5.30	1.000	0.6985	0.9543	0.3256
Wholly foreign-owned firms					
N	1,552	1,552	1,552	1,552	1,552
Mean	5.27	0.417	0.0448	0.0132	0.0019
Median	5.29	0.378	0.0000	0.0000	0.0000
SD	0.04	0.355	0.1433	0.0481	0.0214
Min.	4.99	0.000	0.0000	0.0000	0.0000
Max.	5.30	1.000	0.9470	0.9898	0.5395
Collectively owned firms					
N	1,640	1,640	1,640	1,640	1,640
Mean	5.28	0.117	0.0021	0.0037	0.0010
Median	5.29	0.001	0.0000	0.0000	0.0000
SD	0.03	0.203	0.0218	0.0228	0.0216
Min.	5.10	0.000	0.0000	0.0000	0.0000
Max.	5.30	1.000	0.5497	0.3115	0.5919
Private firms					
N	1,264	1,264	1,264	1,264	1,264
Mean	5.27	0.055	0.0025	0.0143	0.0000
Median	5.29	0.000	0.0000	0.0000	0.0000
SD	0.04	0.141	0.0378	0.0692	0.0002
Min.	4.96	0.000	0.0000	0.0000	0.0000
Max.	5.30	1.000	1.0000	1.0000	0.0051

Note: SD = standard deviation.

nomic areas are much smaller geographically and are classified as economic and technological development areas (ETDAs), hi-technology industry development areas (HTIDA), and export processing zones (EPZs). Some of these special incentive zones and areas are located within the five SEZs. We will also refer to these incentive zones or areas as "policy zones."

The ETDAs and HTIDAs are tax-favored enclaves established by central or local governments (with approval by the central government) to promote development of sectors designated as "high and new tech," albeit by somewhat poorly defined criteria. In theory, there are differences between the two types of zones. In practice, however, the line between the two is often blurred. The determination of what firms should go into a particular type of zone is somewhat arbitrary; therefore, we group them together in our subsequent discussions. With progressively more ETDAs and HTIDAs being established, their share in China's exports has grown steadily in our sample, from only 4.3 percent in 1995 to 15.4 percent in 2005 (sum of columns [3] and [4] in table 2.3). Because most cities do not yet have such zones, an unweighted average of their share in a city's exports, across all cities and years, comes to only 2 percent (sum of columns [3] and [4] in the top panel of table 2.6).

Dedicated EPZs (which exclusively export processing trade) were first established in 2001 and are present in only twenty-six cities today. By 2005, only 3.5 percent of exports came from all the EPZs together (table 2.3). On simple average (across cities and years), only 0.04 percent of exports come from EPZs. This means that most of China's processing exports are produced outside EPZs. It is useful to bear this in mind when interpreting the regression coefficients in the subsequent tables.

Foreign-invested firms dominate processing exports from EPZs and high-tech zones (in our sample period, 99 percent and 95 percent respectively—see table 2.4) and also took a lion's share of processing trade (67 percent) outside those policy zones. State-owned firms are the major players in normal exports, accounting for 58 percent of normal exports from high-tech zones and 63 percent of normal exports outside policy zones, during our sample period. Though they played a small role in processing trade, collectively owned and private firms produced an important share of China's normal exports, accounting for 8.5 percent of normal exports from high-tech zones and 18 percent of exports outside policy zones (table 2.4).

2.2.2 Basic Specification

We relate the sophistication level of local export structure to its plausible determinants, including the role of processing trade, foreign investment, and local human capital. Formally, the econometric specification is given by the following equation (or by variations to be noted):

(1) $\text{Ln(EDI}_{rft}) = \text{city\_fixed} + \text{year\_fixed} + \beta_1 \text{ EPZ\_share}_{rft}$

$+ \beta_2 \text{ High\_tech\_zone\_processing\_Share}_{rft}$

$+ \beta_3 \text{ Processing\_outside\_anyzone\_share}_{rft}$

$+ \beta_4 \text{ High\_tech\_zone\_nonprocessing\_share}_{rft}$

$+ \beta_5 \text{ Ln(GMP}_{rt}) + \beta_6 \text{ SKILL}_{rt} + \text{other\_controls} + \mu_{rft},$

where Ln(EDI) is the log of a dissimilarity index between a Chinese city's export structure and the combined export structure of the United States, Japan, and the European Union. $\beta_1 \beta_2, \ldots, \beta_6$ are coefficients to be estimated. μ_{rft} is the error term. Other regressors and the sources of our data are explained in table 2A.1. Robust standard errors, clustered by city, are reported.

We define an index for a lack of sophistication by the dissimilarity between the product structure of a region's exports and that of the G3 economies, or the export dissimilarity index (EDI), as:

(2) $$\text{EDI}_{rft} = 100\Big[\sum_i \text{abs}(s_{irft} - s_{i,t}^{ref})\Big],$$

(3) $$\text{where } s_{irft} = \frac{E_{irft}}{\sum_i E_{irft}},$$

where s_{irft} is the share of HS product i at six-digit level in Chinese city r's exports for firm type f in year t, and $s_{i,t}^{ref}$ is the share of HS product i in the six-digit level exports of G3 developed countries. The greater the value of the index, the more dissimilar the compared export structures are. If the two export structures were identical, then the value of the index would be zero; if the two export structures were to have no overlap, then the index would take the value of 200. We regard an export structure as more sophisticated if the index takes a smaller value. Alternatively, one could use the similarity index proposed by Finger and Kreinin (1979) and used by Schott (2006) (except for the scale):

(4) $$\text{ESI}_{rft} = 100\sum_i \text{min}(s_{irft}, s_{i,t}^{ref})$$

This index is bounded by zero and 100. If Chinese city r's export structure had no overlap with that of the G3 developed countries, then the export similarity index (ESI) would be zero; if the two export structures had a perfect overlap, then the index would take the value of 100. It can be verified that there is a one-to-one, linear mapping between ESI and EDI:

(5) $$\text{ESI}_{rft} = \frac{200 - \text{EDI}_{rft}}{2}$$

Table 2A.7 reports regressions that use ESI and EDI in levels, respectively, as the dependent variables. It can be seen that the coefficient on any given regressor always has the opposite sign in each of the two specifications. These linear specifications have the drawback that the error term is far from being normally distributed. A better specification would use logged EDI or logged ESI as the dependent variable. However, log(ESI) is related to log(EDI) only nonlinearly. Economic theory does not give much guidance to the exact functional form. Our experimentation suggests that using log(EDI) as the dependent variable is more likely to produce robustly significant coefficients. Most important, the sign patterns on the coefficient estimates are consistent between regressions using logged EDI and EDI, respectively, as the dependent variables, but they are inconsistent between regressions using logged ESI and ESI as the left-hand-side variables. Therefore, in our analysis, we use log(EDI) as the dependent variable.

2.3   Analysis

2.3.1   Basic Results

Our regression results are reported in table 2.7. In the first four columns, the sophistication of a city's export structure is measured on a year-by-year basis by its similarity with that of the G3 high-income countries. As a robustness check, in the last four columns, export sophistication is measured against the export structure of the high-income countries in a fixed year (2004, the last in our sample period). The change in reference year for export sophistication does not turn out to matter qualitatively.

The coefficient on "export processing zone exports as a share of total city exports" is negative and significant, implying that exports from EPZs tend to be more similar to those of the G3 high-income countries than are typical Chinese exports. However, as a majority of Chinese cities do not have EPZs, this does not contribute much to explaining cross-city differences in export sophistication.

The coefficients on the two variables describing exports from high-tech zones ("processing exports from high-tech zones" and "nonprocessing exports from high-tech zones") are negative and significant, implying that the high-tech zones do contribute to raising the sophistication of the Chinese export structure. Comparing the two point estimates, however, one sees that the nonprocessing exports from the two types of high-tech zones in fact contribute more to raising export sophistication than do processing exports.

The coefficient on processing exports outside any policy zones is positive and significant: the more processing trade outside any policy zones, the less sophisticated a city's exports are. Taking the discussion of the last four coefficients together, we argue that processing trade (outside policy zones) is unlikely to have promoted the resemblance of the Chinese export structure

Table 2.7 What explains cross-city export structure? (export structure dissimilarity between Chinese cities [all firms] and the G3 countries)

Explanatory variables	Yearly benchmark				2004 benchmark			
	(1)	(2)	(3)	(4)	(5)	(6)	(7)	(8)
Export processing zone exports as a share of total city exports	-0.351*** (0.074)	-0.382*** (0.055)	-0.350*** (0.071)	-0.384*** (0.053)	-0.552*** (0.116)	-0.594*** (0.087)	-0.544*** (0.111)	-0.591*** (0.084)
Processing exports in high-tech zones as a share of total city exports	-0.065*** (0.018)	-0.070*** (0.020)	-0.067*** (0.018)	-0.073*** (0.020)	-0.083*** (0.020)	-0.089*** (0.023)	-0.082*** (0.020)	-0.090*** (0.023)
Nonprocessing exports in high-tech zones as a share of total city exports	-0.087* (0.045)	-0.108** (0.053)	-0.093** (0.044)	-0.115** (0.053)	-0.087* (0.049)	-0.116* (0.061)	-0.092* (0.049)	-0.122** (0.061)
Processing exports outside economic zones as a share of total city exports	0.005* (0.003)	0.004 (0.003)	0.004 (0.003)	0.002 (0.003)	0.006* (0.003)	0.004 (0.003)	0.005* (0.003)	0.003 (0.003)
Student enrollment in institutions of higher education as a share of the city nonagricultural population	-0.225*** (0.066)		-0.229*** (0.066)		-0.309*** (0.073)		-0.315*** (0.072)	
Gross metropolitan product (GMP)	-0.003** (0.001)	-0.003** (0.001)	-0.003** (0.001)	-0.003** (0.001)	-0.003* (0.001)	-0.003* (0.002)	-0.003** (0.001)	-0.003*** (0.002)
GMP per capita		-0.006** (0.002)		-0.007*** (0.003)		-0.010*** (0.003)		-0.010*** (0.003)
Foreign-invested firms' share in city exports			0.001 (0.006)	0.004 (0.006)			-0.004 (0.006)	-0.000 (0.007)
Joint-venture firms' share in city exports			0.010*** (0.004)	0.010*** (0.004)			0.009** (0.004)	0.009** (0.004)
City fixed effects	Y	Y	Y	Y	Y	Y	Y	Y
Year fixed effects	Y	Y	Y	Y	Y	Y	Y	Y
Robust (clustered by city)	Y	Y	Y	Y	Y	Y	Y	Y
No. of observations	1,981	1,981	1,981	1,981	1,981	1,981	1,981	1,981
R^2	0.98	0.98	0.98	0.98	0.98	0.97	0.98	0.97

Note: Standard errors in parentheses.
***Significant at the 1 percent level.
**Significant at the 5 percent level.
*Significant at the 10 percent level.

to that of the high-income countries. This argument is consistent with the intuition that processing trade in many areas of China, excepting policy zones, is relatively labor-intensive.

The coefficient on student enrollment in colleges or graduate schools as a share of a given city's nonagricultural population—a proxy for that city's level of human capital—is negative and significant, consistent with the notion that a city with more skilled labor tends to have a more sophisticated export structure. In column (2) of table 2.7, we use GMP per capita as an alternative measure of a city's level of human capital. This variable also produces a negative coefficient, indicating an association between more human capital and more sophisticated export structure.

In columns (3) to (4) of table 2.7, we include measures of the presence of foreign firms in a city. The estimated coefficient for exports by wholly foreign-owned firms as a share of a city's total exports is not significantly different from zero. Interestingly, the share of exports by joint-venture firms has a positive coefficient: the more a city's exports come from joint-venture firms, the less that city's export structure resembles that of the high-income countries. These results suggest that foreign-invested firms in China are not directly responsible for the rising sophistication of China's export structure, or at least not in a simple linear fashion.

As we explained earlier, columns (5) to (8) of table 2.7 replicate the first four columns except that the left-hand-side variables are recalibrated against the export structure of the G3 economies in 2004. The qualitative results remain essentially the same. To summarize the key findings that emerge from the series of regressions in table 2.7, we find the following:

1. Cross-city differences in human capital are linked to cross-city differences in the level of sophistication of export structures. A higher level of human capital, measured either by GMP per capita or by college and graduate school enrollment, is associated with a more sophisticated export structure.

2. High-tech zones are associated with more sophisticated export structures. The higher the share of a city's exports produced in high-tech zones, the more likely that city's export structure is to resemble that of the G3 high-income economies.

3. The EPZs contribute to rising sophistication in export structures. However, because only a small fraction of Chinese cities have EPZs, these play a very small quantitative role in explaining cross-city differences in export-structure sophistication.

4. Processing trade is not generally a major factor in explaining cross-city differences in export-structure sophistication. This can be seen in two ways. First, with regard to exports outside policy zones (which represent the lion's share of all exports), more processing trade is in fact associated with less resemblance to the export structure of the high-income countries.

Second, with regard to exports produced in high-tech zones, nonprocessing trade is more responsible for a resemblance to the export structure of the high-income countries than processing trade.

5. After controlling for exports from major policy zones, foreign invest-ment appears not to play a major role in explaining cross-city differences in the level of sophistication of their export structures. If anything, joint-venture firms may create some divergence between a city's export structure and that of the high-income economies.

These findings reject the view that China's increasingly sophisticated export structure is the product of processing trade or foreign-invested firms. Meanwhile, these findings confirm the importance of human capital and government-sponsored high-tech zones in increasing the sophistication of China's export structure.

The specification used in table 2.7 includes city fixed effects, as is expected in panel regressions such as ours. However, to ensure that the variables we have proposed—processing trade, foreign ownership, high-tech zones, human capital, and so on—collectively have sufficient explanatory power over observed cross-city export-structure dissimilarities, we have run similar regressions without city fixed effects (see table 2A.8). The signs on the coefficient estimates and their statistical significance are generally similar in table 2A.8 and in table 2.7. Equally important, the values of R-square in this second set of regressions lie in the range of 66 to 68 percent. This suggests that much of the cross-city differences in export patterns are explained by the included regressors and not by city fixed effects.

2.3.2   Exports by Firms of Different Ownership

Because China is still transitioning from a centrally planned system to a market-based economy and has become very open to foreign direct invest-ment (as the greatest developing-country recipient of FDI since 1995), its exports are primarily generated by state-owned firms and foreign-invested firms rather than by domestic privately owned firms. State-owned and foreign-invested firms account for 40 percent and 51 percent of China's total exports during our sample period, respectively (table 2.2). It will be beneficial to examine the determinants of export-structure sophistication by firm ownership type.

Table 2.8 reports a series of regressions with the left-hand-side variable being the export-structure dissimilarity index for state-owned firms (but otherwise identically specified as those in table 2.7). The results shown in table 2.8 are qualitatively very similar to those in table 2.7. In particular, differences in the degree of processing trade (outside policy zones) are not shown to be responsible for cross-city differences in export-structure sophis-tication. If anything, processing trade outside policy zones may have reduced the resemblance of Chinese export structures to those of high-income coun-

Table 2.8   State-owned firms' export structure dissimilarity relative to the G3 countries

Explanatory variables	Yearly benchmark				2004 benchmark			
	(1)	(2)	(3)	(4)	(5)	(6)	(7)	(8)
Export processing zone exports as a share of total city exports	−11.88*** (4.040)	−13.21*** (4.427)	−12.16*** (4.016)	−13.49*** (4.411)	−18.84*** (5.449)	−20.83*** (6.099)	−18.97*** (5.431)	−20.96*** (6.089)
Processing exports in high-tech zones as a share of total city exports	−0.010 (0.074)	−0.023 (0.073)	−0.013 (0.074)	−0.027 (0.074)	−0.023 (0.093)	−0.044 (0.091)	−0.025 (0.092)	−0.045 (0.091)
Nonprocessing exports in high-tech zones as a share of total city exports	−0.123** (0.052)	−0.136** (0.053)	−0.124** (0.053)	−0.138** (0.055)	−0.151** (0.066)	−0.171** (0.067)	−0.150** (0.065)	−0.170** (0.067)
Processing exports outside economic zones as a share of total city exports	0.007*** (0.003)	0.006** (0.003)	0.007*** (0.003)	0.007** (0.003)	0.007*** (0.003)	0.007** (0.003)	0.008*** (0.003)	0.007** (0.003)
Student enrollment in institutions of higher education as a share of the city nonagricultural population	−0.166** (0.069)		−0.170** (0.068)		−0.255*** (0.075)		−0.258*** (0.074)	

	(1)	(2)	(3)	(4)	(5)	(6)	(7)	(8)
Gross metropolitan product (GMP)	-0.002*	-0.003*	-0.003*	-0.003*	-0.003*	-0.003*	-0.003*	-0.003*
	(0.001)	(0.001)	(0.001)	(0.001)	(0.001)	(0.001)	(0.001)	(0.001)
GMP per capita		-0.005**		-0.005**		-0.008***		-0.008***
		(0.002)		(0.002)		(0.003)		(0.003)
Foreign-invested firms' share in city exports			0.001	0.002			-0.003	-0.002
			(0.007)	(0.007)			(0.007)	(0.007)
Joint-venture firms' share in city exports			0.006	0.005			0.004	0.003
			(0.005)	(0.005)			(0.005)	(0.005)
	(0.023)	(0.035)	(0.023)	(0.036)	(0.023)	(0.043)	(0.023)	(0.044)
City fixed effects	Y	Y	Y	Y	Y	Y	Y	Y
Year fixed effects	Y	Y	Y	Y	Y	Y	Y	Y
Robust (clustered by city)	Y	Y	Y	Y	Y	Y	Y	Y
No. of observations	1,976	1,976	1,976	1,976	1,976	1,976	1,976	1,976
R^2	0.97	0.97	0.97	0.97	0.97	0.97	0.97	0.97

Note: Standard errors in parentheses.

***Significant at the 1 percent level.

**Significant at the 5 percent level.

*Significant at the 10 percent level.

Table 2.9   **Wholly foreign-owned firms' export structure dissimilarity relative to the G3 countries**

Explanatory variables	Yearly benchmarks		2004 benchmark	
	(1)	(2)	(3)	(4)
Export processing zone exports as a share of total city exports	−0.095 (0.059)	−0.097* (0.057)	−0.112 (0.073)	−0.115 (0.071)
Processing exports in high-tech zones as a share of total city exports	−0.017 (0.012)	−0.016 (0.012)	−0.024* (0.014)	−0.022 (0.014)
Nonprocessing exports in high-tech zones as a share of total city exports	−0.013 (0.011)	−0.013 (0.011)	−0.019 (0.014)	−0.019 (0.014)
Processing exports outside economic zones as a share of total city exports	−0.001 (0.001)	−0.001 (0.001)	−0.007 (0.008)	−0.007 (0.008)
Student enrollment in institutions of higher education as a share of the city nonagricultural population	−0.078 (0.063)		−0.080 (0.074)	
Gross metropolitan product (GMP)	−0.005* (0.003)	−0.003 (0.003)	−0.005 (0.004)	−0.003 (0.003)
GMP per capita		−0.012** (0.005)		−0.012** (0.006)
City fixed effects	Y	Y	Y	Y
Year fixed effects	Y	Y	Y	Y
Robust (clustered by city)	Y	Y	Y	Y
No. of observations	1,548	1,548	1,548	1,548
R^2	0.95	0.95	0.81	0.81

Note: Standard errors in parentheses.
**Significant at the 5 percent level.
*Significant at the 10 percent level.

tries. More human capital, as measured by either GMP per capita or college student enrollment, is associated with an increased resemblance of state-owned-enterprise export structures to that of the high-income countries.

Columns (3) to (4) and (7) to (8) of table 2.8 can be interpreted as a test of possible spillover from foreign-invested firms to local state-owned enterprises in any given city.[5] The coefficients on the shares of wholly foreign-owned firms or joint ventures in a city's total exports are essentially zero, statistically. Therefore, the presence by foreign firms in the same industry and in the same city does not appear to affect whether state-owned-enterprise exports resemble those of the high-income countries.

5. Hale and Long (2006) suggest that foreign firms in China generate technological spillover to local firms in part through the reemployment of skilled labor from foreign-invested firms by local firms.

Table 2.10   **Joint-venture firms' exports structure dissimilarity relative to the G3 countries**

Explanatory variables	Yearly benchmark		2004 benchmark	
	(1)	(2)	(3)	(4)
Export processing zone exports as a share of total city exports	0.013 (0.027)	−0.002 (0.030)	0.000 (0.033)	−0.016 (0.036)
Processing exports in high-tech zones as a share of total city exports	−0.005 (0.010)	−0.006 (0.009)	−0.014 (0.009)	−0.015* (0.009)
Nonprocessing exports in high-tech zones as a share of total city exports	0.001 (0.010)	−0.000 (0.009)	0.001 (0.008)	0.001 (0.008)
Processing exports outside economic zones as a share of total city exports	0.001 (0.001)	0.000 (0.001)	0.003* (0.002)	0.002 (0.001)
Student enrollment in institutions of higher education as a share of the city nonagricultural population	−0.094** (0.039)		−0.104** (0.035)	
Gross metropolitan product (GMP)	−0.001 (0.001)	−0.001 (0.001)	−0.001 (0.001)	−0.001 (0.001)
GMP per capita		−0.004* (0.002)		−0.005** (0.002)
City fixed effects	Y	Y	Y	Y
Year fixed effects	Y	Y	Y	Y
Robust (clustered by city)	Y	Y	Y	Y
No. of observations	1,831	1,831	1,831	1,831
R^2	0.97	0.97	0.96	0.96

Note: Standard errors in parentheses.
**Significant at the 5 percent level.
*Significant at the 10 percent level.

Tables 2.9 and 2.10 report similar regressions for wholly foreign-owned and Sino-foreign joint-venture firms, respectively. In these tables, unlike in tables 2.7 and 2.8, no regressor except the proxies for human capital is statistically significant. This reinforces our earlier conclusion that, during our sample period, foreign-invested firms did not contribute to the rising sophistication of China's export structure. Tables 2.9 and 2.10 suggest that this is true whether foreign firms are located in EPZs, high-tech zones, or elsewhere. Unfortunately, data limitations prevent us from examining whether FDI from different source countries has differentially promoted the sophistication of China's export structure.[6]

6. Xu and Lu (2007) report differences between firms from Hong Kong, Macao, and Taiwan, and those from the United States and other Organization for Economic Cooperation and Development (OECD) countries.

For completeness, we also examine the dissimilarity index of export structures relative to the G3 economies for collectively and privately owned firms, respectively (see tables 2.11 and 2.12). For each type of firm, a higher level of local human capital is associated with the greater resemblance of its exports to those of the high-income countries. For collectively owned firms alone, there is evidence that processing trade both within and without policy zones may have slowed the rise in the sophistication of these firms' export structures. This is consistent with the possibility that most of these collectively owned firms operate in labor-intensive industries.

For domestic private firms (but not for collectively owned firms), EPZs promote a similar export structure to that of the rich countries. However, EPZs do not exist in most cities. In contrast to the state-owned enterprises, wholly foreign-owned firms or joint ventures in the same city have some impact on private firms' export-structure sophistication; both coefficients are negative (the coefficient for wholly foreign-owned firms is statistically significant). This is evidence that the presence of foreign-invested firms may have helped Chinese private firms increase their export sophistication over the sample period.

2.3.3 Unit Value

Recent literature emphasizes the importance of specialization across varieties within a product (Schott 2004); we now look at cross-city differences in the unit value of the same product, where a product is defined both by its HS eight-digit code and by its physical unit code. For example, HS 94053000 refers to "lighting sets used for Christmas trees," but there are two different physical units used to measure the quantities of exports of this product: number of items and mass in kilograms. We take 94053000 (number of items) and 94503000 (kilograms) as two different products in our estimation.

Our assumption is that different unit values for the same product reflect different varieties (and statistical noise). For example, both high-end and low-end digital cameras fit into the same HS eight-digit product classification, but high-end cameras command a higher unit value. We note, however, that differences in unit value within an eight-digit product category may also reflect factors other than quality, such as differences in production costs (see Hallack 2006; Hallack and Schott 2006). We will assume that these factors generate noise in the mapping of unit value against product variety.

We now investigate the roles of processing trade, high-tech zones, and firm ownership in explaining differences in unit value (which proxy for differences in variety) within a product category. To fix intuition, let us look at two examples. As a first example, color video monitors (HS code 852821) were produced and exported in 2005 by local and foreign-invested firms located in EPZs and high-tech zones and also outside policy zones. The average unit value of monitors produced by foreign-invested firms was $241.50.

Table 2.11   Collectively owned firms' export structure dissimilarity relative to the G3 countries

Explanatory variables	Yearly benchmark				2004 benchmark			
	(1)	(2)	(3)	(4)	(5)	(6)	(7)	(8)
Export processing zone exports as a share of total city exports	0.003 (0.005)	-0.005 (0.007)	0.002 (0.005)	-0.006 (0.007)	-0.003 (0.006)	-0.010 (0.007)	-0.004 (0.005)	-0.011 (0.007)
Processing exports in high-tech zones as a share of total city exports	0.028** (0.012)	0.020 (0.013)	0.028** (0.012)	0.019 (0.013)	0.029** (0.011)	0.020* (0.012)	0.028** (0.011)	0.020 (0.012)
Nonprocessing exports in high-tech zones as a share of total city exports	-0.070** (0.029)	-0.089** (0.036)	-0.071** (0.029)	-0.089** (0.036)	-0.066** (0.028)	-0.084** (0.034)	-0.066** (0.029)	-0.084** (0.035)
Processing exports outside economic zones as a share of total city exports	0.009*** (0.003)	0.008** (0.003)	0.009*** (0.003)	0.007** (0.003)	0.010*** (0.003)	0.008*** (0.003)	0.009*** (0.003)	0.008*** (0.003)
Student enrollment in institutions of higher education as a share of the city nonagricultural population	-0.38*** (0.075)		-0.39*** (0.075)		-0.38*** (0.078)		-0.38*** (0.078)	
Chinese gross metropolitan product (GMP)	-0.004 (0.003)	-0.005* (0.003)	-0.004 (0.003)	-0.005* (0.003)	-0.004 (0.003)	-0.006* (0.003)	-0.004 (0.003)	-0.006* (0.003)
Chinese GMP per capita		-0.016** (0.005)		-0.016** (0.005)		-0.016** (0.005)		-0.016** (0.005)
Foreign-invested enterprise firms' share in city exports			-0.010 (0.008)	-0.011 (0.009)			-0.013 (0.008)	-0.013 (0.009)
Joint-venture firms' share in city exports			0.004 (0.005)	0.001 (0.006)			0.003 (0.005)	-0.000 (0.006)
City fixed effects	Y	Y	Y	Y	Y	Y	Y	Y
Year fixed effects	Y	Y	Y	Y	Y	Y	Y	Y
Robust (clustered by city)	Y	Y	Y	Y	Y	Y	Y	Y
No. of observations	1,636	1,636	1,636	1,636	1,636	1,636	1,636	1,636
R^2	0.89	0.87	0.89	0.88	0.87	0.86	0.87	0.86

Note: Standard errors in parentheses.
***Significant at the 1 percent level.
**Significant at the 5 percent level.
*Significant at the 10 percent level.

Table 2.12   Private firms' export structure dissimilarity relative to the G3 countries

Explanatory variables	Yearly benchmark				2004 benchmark			
	(1)	(2)	(3)	(4)	(1)	(2)	(3)	(4)
Export processing zone exports as a share of total city exports	−14.28*** (3.640)	−15.86*** (3.825)	−14.02*** (3.589)	−15.51*** (3.896)	−14.97*** (3.778)	−16.68*** (4.016)	−14.44*** (3.782)	−16.00*** (4.224)
Processing exports in high-tech zones as a share of total city exports	−0.006 (0.014)	−0.012 (0.015)	−0.003 (0.014)	−0.009 (0.014)	−0.005 (0.015)	−0.010 (0.016)	0.002 (0.016)	−0.003 (0.016)
Nonprocessing exports in high-tech zones as a share of total city exports	−0.100 (0.072)	−0.109 (0.070)	−0.094 (0.066)	−0.103 (0.064)	−0.096 (0.072)	−0.105 (0.070)	−0.085 (0.061)	−0.093 (0.059)
Processing exports outside economic zones as a share of total city exports	0.007 (0.008)	0.008 (0.007)	0.008 (0.007)	0.008 (0.007)	0.010 (0.008)	0.010 (0.007)	0.010 (0.007)	0.010* (0.006)
Student enrollment in institutions of higher education as a share of the city nonagricultural population	−0.655*** (0.181)		−0.645*** (0.170)		−0.660*** (0.186)		−0.639*** (0.166)	

	(1)	(2)	(3)	(4)	(5)	(6)	(7)	(8)
Gross metropolitan product (GMP)	-0.019	-0.024**	-0.021	-0.025**	-0.014	-0.020*	-0.017	-0.022**
	(0.015)	(0.010)	(0.015)	(0.010)	(0.014)	(0.011)	(0.013)	(0.010)
GMP per capita		-0.048**		-0.050***		-0.040**		-0.043**
		(0.020)		(0.019)		(0.020)		(0.018)
Foreign-invested enterprise firm export share			-0.086***	-0.091***			-0.179**	-0.184**
			(0.031)	(0.030)			(0.086)	(0.087)
Joint-venture firm export share			-0.003	-0.009			-0.009	-0.015
			(0.015)	(0.015)			(0.018)	(0.018)
City fixed effects	Y	Y	Y	Y	Y	Y	Y	Y
Year fixed effects	Y	Y	Y	Y	Y	Y	Y	Y
Robust (clustered by city)	Y	Y	Y	Y	Y	Y	Y	Y
No. of observations	1,262	1,262	1,262	1,262	1,262	1,262	1,262	1,262
R^2	0.75	0.74	0.76	0.76	0.63	0.62	0.68	0.67

Note: Standard errors in parentheses.

***Significant at the 1 percent level.

**Significant at the 5 percent level.

*Significant at the 10 percent level.

Even monitors produced entirely by foreign-invested firms in China showed variations in unit value dependent on where the producer was located and whether the export was of processing trade or normal trade. The unit value of monitors exported from an EPZ was $347.80; processing-export monitors from a high-tech zone were valued at $456.70, while normal-export monitors from the same zone were sold for $364.80; in distinction, processing-export monitors from outside any policy zone were valued at only $56.80, and normal-trade monitors from outside any policy zone cost $73.60. Ownership also matters. The unit value of a monitor was $207.00 when it was exported by a state-owned firm and only $77.20 when it was exported by a domestic private firm. For comparison, the average unit value of the same product, as exported by producers from the United States, the European Union, and Japan was $467.40.[7] Generally speaking, the unit values of the Chinese exports are lower than those from high-income countries. In this example, of the Chinese varieties, the processing-export monitor produced by a foreign firm located in a high-tech zone had the highest unit value, roughly 98 percent of the value of G3 exports, suggesting that it may substitute closely for the high-income countries' variety.

As a second example, video cameras (HS code 852540) were also produced and exported by firms of various ownership, located in areas with different policy incentives. The average unit value for video cameras exported by foreign-invested firms was $51.50 in 2005, compared to $30.20 for a similar camera made by state-owned firms. Both export type and firm location matter as well. Of processing-exports cameras produced by foreign-invested firms, the unit value was $154.60 for exports from a high-tech zone, $66.30 for those from outside any policy zone, and $51.50 for those assembled in an export processing zone. For normal-export cameras made by a foreign firm, the unit value was $21.60 for those from a high-tech zone, and only $13.20 for those from outside any policy zone. Again, processing exports from a high-tech zone had the highest unit value, and normal exports not from any policy zone had the lowest value. Cameras produced by foreign-invested firms generally had a higher unit value than did local firms. For comparison, the average unit value of a camera manufactured in the G3 countries (the United States, Japan, and the European Union) was $331.50. In this example, even China's priciest variety (a processing export made in a high-tech zone by a foreign firm) had a unit value only 47 percent that of the average G3-exported camera. In this example, the variety of video camera made in China is unlikely to substitute closely for that of a wealthy country.

While these examples are illustrative, we must turn to a regression framework to summarize patterns in the data more efficiently and systematically.

---

7. This figure is taken from information in the UN COMTRADE database; we thank Mark Gehlhar for providing this data.

Additionally, our regression framework explicitly accounts for differences in income across regions, as well as other factors that could account for the differences in unit value. Let $\ln(\text{Unit\_Value}_{rkt})$ denote the natural logarithm of the unit value of city r's export of product k in year t. Our specification relates this variable to city by year fixed effects, product fixed effects, the share of export processing zones in a city's export of a given product, the share of high-tech zones in that city's export of that product (distinguished in regressions between processing and nonprocessing exports), the share of processing trade in that city's export of that product from outside any policy zones, and other control variables.

(6) $\text{Ln}(\text{Unit\_Value}_{rkt}) = \text{city\_year\_fixed} + \text{product\_fixed}$

$$+ \beta_1 \, \text{EPZ\_share}_{rkt}$$

$$+ \beta_2 \, \text{High\_tech\_zone\_Processing\_Share}_{rkt}$$

$$+ \beta_3 \, \text{Processing\_trade\_outside\_anyzone}_{rkt}$$

$$+ \beta_4 \, \text{High\_tech\_zone\_nonprocessing\_share}_{rkt}$$

$$+ \text{other\_controls} + \mu_{rkt}$$

Note that city by year fixed effects are more general than either year fixed effects or city fixed effects. Our regression results are reported in table 2.13. Column (1) shows that both export processing zones and high-tech zones are associated with higher unit values. Of the exports originated from the high-tech zones, those produced by processing trade are linked to higher unit values than those of nonprocessing trade. An increase of 10 percent in processing exports from a high-tech zone as a share of a city's total exports is associated with an increase of 5.9 percent in unit value, whereas an increase of the same magnitude in the share of nonprocessing trade from high-tech zones is associated with a 2.1 percent increase in unit value. An increase of 10 percent in the export share of EPZs in a city's total exports is associated with an increase of 2.1 percent in unit value. With regard to unit value, there is no difference between exports from an export processing zone and nonprocessing exports from a high-tech zone. In comparison, an increase of 10 percent in the share of processing exports originating outside any policy zone is associated with a 1.2 percent increase in unit value. Overall, processing trade appears to be associated with higher-quality varieties than ordinary trade.

To show the role of foreign investment in upgrading the quality of products, column (2) of table 2.13 includes the respective shares of wholly foreign-owned and joint-venture firms in a city's total exports (by HS eight-digit code) as additional regressors. Both new regressors have positive and statistically significant coefficients. An increase of 10 percent in the share of exports made by these two types of firms in a city's total exports of a

Table 2.13   What explains the cross-city difference in the unit values of exports?

Explanatory variables	(1)	(2)	(3)	(4)
Export processing zone exports as a	0.209**	0.068	0.050	0.064
share of total city exports	(0.058)	(0.058)	(0.058)	(0.058)
Processing exports in high-tech zones as	0.589**	0.429**	0.428**	0.434**
a share of total city exports	(0.012)	(0.013)	(0.013)	(0.013)
Nonprocessing exports in high-tech	0.206**	0.171**	0.172**	0.173**
zones as a share of total city exports	(0.008)	(0.008)	(0.008)	(0.008)
Processing exports outside economic	0.119**	0.117**	0.117**	0.119**
zones as a share of total city exports	(0.004)	(0.005)	(0.005)	(0.005)
Foreign-investment enterprise firm		0.198**		0.179**
export share		(0.005)		(0.005)
Joint-venture firm export share		0.222**		0.207**
		(0.004)		(0.004)
Collective and private firm export share			−0.290**	−0.094**
			(0.005)	(0.004)
State-owned enterprise firm export share			−0.196**	
			(0.004)	
Product fixed effects	Y	Y	Y	Y
City year fixed effects	Y	Y	Y	Y
No. of unique cities	238	238	238	238
No. of unique products	6,473	6,473	6,473	6,473
No. of observations	1,256,999	1,256,999	1,256,999	1,256,999
Adjusted R^2	0.794	0.794	0.794	0.794

Notes: The dependent variable is the natural log of the unit value of Harmonized System six-digit products, from 1996 to 2004. The regressions include city by year fixed effects and product fixed effects. Standard errors are given in parentheses.
**Significant at the 5 percent level.

product tends to be associated with an increase in the unit value of the given product by 2.0 percent and 2.2 percent, respectively. This suggests that products from foreign-invested firms—assigned higher values—are generally of higher quality.

Interestingly, this adjustment renders the share of EPZs statistically insignificant. The coefficients on the shares of processing and ordinary trade out of high-tech zones, and on the share of processing trade outside policy zones, while still positive and statistically significant, are now smaller in magnitude (by more than 2 standard deviations, in two out of the three cases). This suggests that part of the higher–unit value effect, previously attributed to processing trade and high-tech zones, is in fact due to the presence of foreign-invested firms in these activities. As noted in the preceding (table 2.4), during the sample period more than 95 percent of exports originating from EPZs and from processing trade in high-tech zones were produced by foreign-invested firms.

Column (3) of table 2.13 includes a regressor of the combined share of collective and private firms in a city's total exports and one of the share of state-owned firms (this column excludes that of shares held by foreign-invested firms). Column (4) of table 2.13 includes the two types of foreign-invested firms plus the combined share of the collective and domestic private firms (leaving out that of state-owned firms). The shares of exports made by collective and domestic private firms, and by state-owned firms, have negative and statistically significant coefficients, indicating that a larger share of Chinese domestic firms in a city's exports is associated with a lower unit value of those exports. This confirms the intuition that, in a given HS eight-digit product line, foreign-invested firms in China produce relatively higher-quality varieties than do Chinese domestic firms.

Taking these unit value results together, we conclude that processing trade (regardless of its origin), high-tech zones, and foreign invested firms are all independently associated with higher unit values, suggesting that they have each individually played a role in leading China to produce and export higher-quality products than it otherwise would have.

2.4   Conclusion

Are China's exports competing head to head with those of high-income countries? This paper addresses this question by examining variations in export sophistication across different cities in China. It looks at both the overlap in product structure between a city's exports and those of the advanced economies and at the unit values of different products.

Estimation shows that China's export structure as a whole has begun increasingly to resemble that of the G3 advanced economies, and the unit values of its exports are also rising over time. If these patterns are generated entirely by the rise of processing trade, then there may not be much genuine increase in the sophistication of Chinese exports. If there has been increase in sophistication, but one brought about solely by foreign investment in China, then the economic profit associated with improved sophistication has accrued to foreign economies rather than to China's. Of course, increased sophistication can also come from a higher level of local human capital or from government policies set up expressly to promote the upgrading of industrial infrastructure, such as government initiatives establishing high-tech policy zones. Regional variations in the use of processing trade and high-tech zones and the availability of skilled labor are assessed in this paper to determine the relative importance of these factors. Econometric analysis conducted in this study helps to clarify this issue.

1. Cross-city differences in human capital are linked to cross-city differences in the sophistication of export structure. A higher level of human

capital is associated with more sophisticated export structures in Chinese cities.

2. High-tech zones are associated both with more sophisticated export structures and with higher unit values. This indicates that the policy zones (especially ETDZs and HTIDZs) set up by central and local governments may have worked to induce firms to upgrade their product ladder to a higher level than they would have otherwise done. In other words, these policy zones not only promoted processing trade, but they also promoted improvements in the sophistication of China's exports.

3. The EPZs contribute both to the rising sophistication of China's export structure and to the rising unit values of its exports. However, because only a tiny fraction of Chinese cities have EPZs and because most of their exports come from foreign-invested firms, EPZs do not contribute greatly to explaining cross-city differences in export sophistication.

4. Processing trade is not generally a major factor in explaining the cross-city differences in export-structure sophistication. This can be seen in two ways. First, with regard to exports originating outside policy zones (which took up the lion's share of China's total exports during our sample period, about 42 percent), more processing trade is in fact associated with a lesser resemblance to the export structure of advanced countries. Second, with regard to exports originating inside of the high-tech zones, products associated with the processing trade do not appear to overlap more with advanced countries' exports than do those associated with nonprocessing trade.

However, processing trade is significantly associated with higher unit values. How can our findings on export structure and unit values be reconciled? If processing-export production outside the policy zones is generally labor-intensive, a higher share in a given city will increase the dissimilarity of that city's export structure to that of the G3 advanced economies. However, processing exports could still be of higher quality (of greater sophistication) than normal trade exports in the same product line if higher-quality materials are used to manufacture the former. In other words, processing trade moves China into the production and export of more sophisticated varieties within a given product category, but not necessarily within those product categories heavily exported by the G3 advanced economies.[8]

5. The export share of foreign-invested firms in a Chinese city does not appear to play a major role in explaining cross-city differences in the sophistication level of export structures. If anything, joint-venture firms may create some divergence between a city's export structure and that of the advanced

---

8. The higher unit values associated with processing exports may simply reflect the higher cost of using imported inputs rather than domestically made inputs. This leaves open the question of whether processing exports generate more value added than do normal exports that use more local or domestic inputs.

economies. However, after controlling for processing trade, both types of foreign-invested firms are found to be strongly associated with higher export unit values. Therefore, foreign investment has been conducive to greater same-product sophistication in China.

Appendix

Table 2A.1   Definition of key variables and their data sources

	Description	Data sources
Dependent variable		
$EDI_{rft} = (iabs[s_{irft} - sref\backslash i,t])$	Absolute export structure dissimilarity index	Calculated by the authors from the Harmonized System six-digit level. Chinese city exports based on official China Customs Statistics. Data on U.S., EU15, and Japanese exports downloaded from World Integrated Trade Solution.
Explanatory variables		
GMP	Gross metropolitan product (10,000 yuan)	China city data, China Data Online
$GMPpc_{rt} = 100\ GMP_r/POP_r$	Chinese GMP per capita (yuan)	China city data, China Data Online
$SKILL_{rt} = 100$(no. of college students)$rt/$ (nonagricultural population)$_{rt}$	Student enrollment in institutions of higher education as a share of the city nonagricultural population	China city data, China Data Online
EPZ_share_{rft}	Export processing zone exports as a share of total city exports	China Customs Statistics
$High\_tech\_zone\_processing\_share_{rft}$	Processing exports in the two high-tech zones as a share of total city exports	China Customs Statistics
$High\_tech\_zone\_nonprocessing\_share_{rft}$	Nonprocessing exports in the two high-tech zones as a share of total city exports	China Customs Statistics
$Processing\_outside\_anyzone\_share_{rft}$	Processing exports outside policy zones as a share of total city exports	China Customs Statistics

(continued)

Table 2A.1   (continued)

	Description	Data sources
Expfiesh$_{rft}$	Foreign-invested enterprise firm exports as share of total city exports	China Customs Statistics
Expjonsh$_{rft}$	Joint-venture firm exports as share of total city exports	China Customs Statistics
expothsh$_{rft}$	Collective and private firm exports as share of total city exports	China Customs Statistics
expsoesh$_{rft}$	State-owned enterprise firm exports as share of total city exports	China Customs Statistics

Table 2A.2   Years of establishment of economic zones, by incentive type

City code	City name	Special economic zone	Economic and technological development area	Hi-technology industry development area	Export processing zone
1100	Beijing CY		1996	1996	2001
1200	Tianjin CY		1996	1996	2001
1301	Shijiazhuang			1996	
1303	Qinhuangdao		1996		2005
1306	Baoding			1996	
1401	Taiyuan		2003	1996	
1502	Baotou			1997	
2101	Shenyang		1996	1996	
2102	Dalian		1996	1996	2001
2103	Anshan			1996	
2201	Changchun		1996	1996	
2202	Jilin			1996	
2301	Harbin		1996	1996	
2306	Daqing			1996	
3100	Shanghai CY		1996	1996	2001
3201	Nanjing			1996	2004
3202	Wuxi			1997	2003
3204	Changzhou			1997	
3205	Suzhou		1996	1997	2001
3206	Nantong		1996		2003
3207	Lianyungang		1996		2004
3211	Zhenjiang				2004
3301	Hangzhou		1996	1996	2001

Table 2A.2   (continued)

City code	City name	Special economic zone	Economic and technological development area	Hi-technology industry development area	Export processing zone
3302	Ningbo		1996		2004
3303	Wenzhou		1996		
3401	Hefei		2005	1996	
3402	Wuhu		1996		2003
3501	Fuzhou		1996	1996	
3502	Xiamen	1995		1996	2002
3601	Nanchang			1996	
3701	Jinan			1996	
3702	Qingdao		1996	1997	2004
3703	Zibo			1999	
3706	Yantai		1996		2001
3707	Weifang			1996	
3710	Weihai			1996	2001
4101	Zhengzhou			1996	2005
4103	Luoyang			1997	
4201	Wuhan		1996	1996	2001
4206	Xiangfan			1997	
4301	Changsha			1996	
4302	Zhuzhou			2000	
4401	Guangzhou		1996	1996	2001
4403	Shenzhen	1995		1996	2002
4404	Zhuhai	1995		1996	
4405	Shantou	1995			
4406	Foshan			1998	
4408	Zhanjiang		1996		
4413	Huizhou			1996	
4420	Zhongshan			1996	
4501	Nanning			1996	
4503	Guilin			1996	
4505	Beihai				2005
4601	Haikou	1995		1996	
4602	Sanya	1995			
5000	Chongqing		2002	2002	2002
5101	Chengdu		2001	1996	2001
5107	Mianyan			1996	
5201	Guiyang			1996	
5301	Kunming			1996	
6101	Xi'an			1996	2004
6103	Baoji			1997	
6104	Xianyang			2002	
6201	Lanzhou			1996	
6301	Xining		2005		
6501	Urumqi		1996	1997	

Note: Cities that did not have any policy zone between 1996 and 2005 are not listed.

Table 2A.3   Chinese cities included in the sample used in regressions (236 in total)

Code	City name	Province	Code	City name	Province	Code	City name	Province
1100	Beijing	Beijing	3404	Huainan	Anhui	4313	Huaihua	Hunan
1200	Tianjin	Tianjin	3405	Maanshang	Anhui	4401	Guangzhou	Guangdong
1301	Shijiazhuang	Hebei	3406	Huaibei	Anhui	4402	Shaoguan	Guangdong
1302	Tangshan	Hebei	3407	Tongling	Anhui	4403	Shenzhen	Guangdong
1303	Qinhuangdao	Hebei	3408	Anqing	Anhui	4404	Zhuhai	Guangdong
1304	Handan	Hebei	3409	Huangshan	Anhui	4405	Shantou	Guangdong
1305	Xingtai	Hebei	3410	Fuyang	Anhui	4406	Foshan	Guangdong
1306	Baoding	Hebei	3411	Suxian	Anhui	4407	Jiangmen	Guangdong
1307	Zhangjiakou	Hebei	3412	Chuxian	Anhui	4408	Zhanjiang	Guangdong
1308	Chengde	Hebei	3413	Liuan	Anhui	4409	Maoming	Guangdong
1309	Changzhou	Hebei	3414	Xuancheng	Anhui	4412	Zhaoqing	Guangdong
1310	Langfang	Hebei	3415	Chaohu	Anhui	4413	Huizhou	Guangdong
1401	Taiyuan	Shanxi	3416	Chizhou	Anhui	4414	Meizhou	Guangdong
1402	Datong	Shanxi	3502	Xiamen	Fujian	4415	Shanwei	Guangdong
1403	Yangquan	Shanxi	3503	Putian	Fujian	4416	Heyuan	Guangdong
1404	Changzhi	Shanxi	3504	Sanming	Fujian	4417	Yangjiang	Guangdong
1405	Jincheng	Shanxi	3505	Quanzhou	Fujian	4418	Qingyuan	Guangdong
1406	Suozhou	Shanxi	3506	Zhangzhou	Fujian	4419	Dongguan	Guangdong
1410	Jinzhong	Shanxi	3507	Nanpin	Fujian	4420	Zhongshan	Guangdong
1501	Hohhot	Inner Mongolia AR	3509	Longyan	Fujian	4421	Chaozhou	Guangdong
1502	Baotou	Inner Mongolia AR	3601	Nanchang	Jiangxi	4424	Jieyang	Guangdong
1503	Wuhai	Inner Mongolia AR	3602	Jingdezhen	Jiangxi	4501	Nanning	Guangxi Zhuan AR
1504	Chifeng	Inner Mongolia AR	3603	Pingxiang	Jiangxi	4502	Liuzhou	Guangxi Zhuan AR
1507	Holunbeir	Inner Mongolia AR	3604	Jiujiang	Jiangxi	4503	Guilin	Guangxi Zhuan AR
2101	Shenyang	Liaoning	3605	Xingyu	Jiangxi	4504	Wuzhou	Guangxi Zhuan AR
2102	Dalian	Liaoning	3606	Yingtan	Jiangxi	4505	Beihai	Guangxi Zhuan AR
2103	Anshan	Liaoning	3607	Ganzhou	Jiangxi	4507	Baise	Guangxi Zhuan AR

Code	City	Province		Code	City	Province		Code	City	Province
2104	Fushen	Liaoning		3611	Fuzhou	Jiangxi		4508	Hechi	Guangxi Zhuan AR
2105	Benxi	Liaoning		3701	Jinan	Shandong		4509	Qinzhou	Guangxi Zhuan AR
2106	Dandong	Liaoning		3702	Qingdao	Shandong		4516	Hezhou Area	Guangxi Zhuan AR
2107	Jinzhou	Liaoning		3703	Zibo	Shandong		4601	Haikou	Hainan
2108	Yingkou	Liaoning		3704	Zaozhuang	Shandong		4602	Sanya	Hainan
2109	Fuxin	Liaoning		3705	Dongying	Shandong		5000	Chongqing	Chongqing
2110	Liaoyang	Liaoning		3706	Yantai	Shandong		5101	Chengdu	Sichuan
2111	Panjin	Liaoning		3707	Weifang	Shandong		5103	Zigong	Sichuan
2112	Tieling	Liaoning		3708	Jining	Shandong		5104	Panzhihua	Sichuan
2113	Chaoyang	Liaoning		3709	Taian	Shandong		5105	Luzhou	Sichuan
2201	Changchun	Jilin		3710	Weihai	Shandong		5106	Deyang	Sichuan
2202	Jilin	Jilin		3711	Rizhao	Shandong		5107	Mianyang	Sichuan
2203	Sipin	Jilin		3713	Dezhou	Shandong		5108	Guangyuan	Sichuan
2204	Liaoyuan	Jilin		3714	Liaochen	Shandong		5109	Suining	Sichuan
2205	Tonghua	Jilin		3715	Linyi	Shandong		5110	Neijiang	Sichuan
2209	Baicheng	Jilin		3720	Laiwu	Shandong		5111	Leshan	Sichuan
2301	Harbin	Heilongjing		4101	Zhengzhou	Henan		5114	Yibin	Sichuan
2302	Qiqihar	Heilongjing		4102	Kaifeng	Henan		5115	Nanchong	Sichuan
2303	Jixi	Heilongjing		4103	Luoyang	Henan		5116	Daxian	Sichuan
2304	Hegang	Heilongjing		4104	Pindinshan	Henan		5201	Guiyang	Guizhou
2305	Shuangyashan	Heilongjing		4105	Anyang	Henan		5202	Liupanshan	Guizhou
2306	Daqing	Heilongjing		4106	Hebi	Henan		5203	Zunyi	Guizhou
2307	Yichun	Heilongjing		4107	Xinxiang	Henan		5301	Kunming	Yunnan
2308	Jiamusi	Heilongjing		4108	Jiaozhuo	Henan		5303	Zhaotong	Yunnan
2309	Qitaiher	Heilongjing		4109	Puyang	Henan		5304	Qujing	Yunnan
2310	Mudanjiang	Heilongjing		4110	Xuchang	Henan		5306	Yuxi	Yunnan
2311	Heihe	Heilongjing		4111	Luohe	Henan		5314	Lijiang	Yunnan
3100	Shanghai CY	Shanghai CY		4112	Sanmenxia	Henan		6101	Xi'an	Shanxi
3201	Nanjing	Jiangsu		4113	Shangqiu	Henan		6102	Tongzhou	Shanxi
3202	Wuxi	Jiangsu		4116	Nanyang	Henan		6103	Baoji	Shanxi
3203	Xuzhou	Jiangsu		4117	Xinyang	Henan		6104	Xianyang	Shanxi

(continued)

Table 2A.3   (continued)

Code	City name	Province	Code	City name	Province	Code	City name	Province
3204	Changzhou	Jiangsu	4201	Wuhan	Hubei	6105	Weinan	Shanxi
3206	Nantong	Jiangsu	4202	Huangshi	Hubei	6106	Hanzhong	Shanxi
3207	Lianyungang	Jiangsu	4203	Shiyan	Hubei	6108	Shangluo	Shanxi
3208	Huaiyin	Jiangsu	4205	Yichang	Hubei	6109	Yanan	Shanxi
3209	Yancheng	Jiangsu	4206	Xiangfan	Hubei	6110	Yulin	Shanxi
3210	Yangzhou	Jiangsu	4207	Ezhou	Hubei	6201	Lanzhou	Gansu
3211	Zhenjiang	Jiangsu	4208	Jingmen	Hubei	6202	Jiayuguan	Gansu
3217	Suqian	Jiangsu	4209	Huanggang	Hubei	6203	Jinchang	Gansu
3301	Hangzhou	Zhejiang	4210	Xiaogan	Hubei	6204	Baiyin	Gansu
3302	Ningbo	Zhejiang	4211	Xianning	Hubei	6205	Tianshiu	Gansu
3303	Wenzhou	Zhejiang	4212	Jingzhou	Hubei	6206	Jiuquan	Gansu
3304	Jiaxing	Zhejiang	4301	Changsha	Hunan	6207	Zhangye	Gansu
3305	Huzhou	Zhejiang	4302	Zhuzhou	Hunan	6208	Wuwei	Gansu
3306	Shaoxing	Zhejiang	4303	Xiangtan	Hunan	6211	Pinliang	Gansu
3307	Jinhua	Zhejiang	4304	Hengyang	Hunan	6212	Qingyang	Gansu
3308	Quzhou	Zhejiang	4305	Shaoyang	Hunan	6301	Xining	Qinghai
3309	Zhoushan	Zhejiang	4306	Yueyang	Hunan	6401	Yinchuan	Ningxia Hui AR
3311	Taizhou	Zhejiang	4307	Changde	Hunan	6402	Shizuishan	Ningxia Hui AR
3401	Hefei	Anhui	4309	Yiyang	Hunan	6501	Urumqi	Xinjiang AR
3402	Wuhu	Anhui	4310	Loudi	Hunan	6502	Kelamayi	Xinjiang AR
3403	Bangbu	Anhui	4311	Chenzhou	Hunan			

Table 2A.4   **Harmonized System (HS) products excluded from export data**

HS code	Description	HS code	Description
01–24	Agricultural products	25–27	Mineral products
4103	Other raw hides and skins (fresh, o	8002	Tin waste and scrap
4104	Tanned or crust hides and skins of	8101	Tungsten (wolfram) and articles the
4105	Tanned or crust skins of sheep or 1	8102	Molybdenum and articles thereof, in
4106	Tanned or crust hides and skins of	8103	Tantalum and articles thereof, incl
4402	Wood charcoal (including shell or n	8104	Magnesium and articles thereof, inc
4403	Wood in the rough, whether or not s	8105	Cobalt mattes and other intermediate
7201	Pig iron and spiegeleisen in pigs,	8106	Bismuth and articles thereof, inclu
7202	Ferro-alloys	8107	Cadmium and articles thereof, inclu
7204	Ferrous waste and scrap; remelting	8108	Titanium and articles thereof, incl
7404	Copper waste and scrap	8109	Zirconium and articles thereof, inc
7501	Nickel mattes, nickel oxide sinters	8110	Antimony and articles thereof, incl
7502	Unwrought nickel	8111	Manganese and articles thereof, inc
7503	Nickel waste and scrap	8112	Beryllium, chromium, germanium, van
7601	Unwrought aluminium	8113	Cermets and articles thereof, inclu
7602	Aluminium waste and scrap	9701	Paintings, drawings and pastels, ex
7801	Unwrought lead	9702	Original engravings, prints and lit
7802	Lead waste and scrap	9703	Original sculptures and statuary, i
7901	Unwrought zinc	9704	Postage or revenue stamps, stamp-po
7902	Zinc waste and scrap	9705	Collections and collectors' pieces
8001	Unwrought tin	9706	Antiques of an age exceeding 100 years
530521	Coconut, abaca (Manila hemp or Musa	811252	Beryllium, chromium, germanium, van

Table 2A.5   **Correlation matrix for key variables (all firms)**

	Export dissimilarity index (logged)	GMP per capita (logged)	GMP (in logged)	Share of joint-venture firm exports	Share of FIE firm exports	Student enrollment in colleges and universities as a share of nonagricultural population	Share of processing exports outside policy zones	Share of processing exports in the two high-tech zones	Share of nonprocessing exports in the two high-tech zones	Share of export processing zone
Export dissimilarity index (in log)	1.00									
GMP per capita (logged)	-0.61	1.00								
GMP (logged)	-0.72	0.62	1.00							
Share of joint-venture firm exports	-0.13	0.09	0.12	1.00						
Share of FIE firm exports	-0.35	0.26	0.23	0.05	1.00					
Student enrollment in colleges and universities as a share of nonagricultural population	-0.47	0.41	0.49	-0.06	0.03	1.00				
Share of processing exports outside policy zones	-0.20	0.08	0.05	0.40	0.33	-0.12	1.00			
Share of processing exports in the two high-tech zones	-0.47	0.32	0.34	0.09	0.43	0.19	0.03	1.00		
Share of nonprocessing exports in the two high-tech zones	-0.40	0.30	0.35	0.05	0.14	0.30	-0.03	0.42	1.00	
Share of export processing zone	-0.27	0.18	0.19	0.02	0.14	0.16	0.00	0.19	0.27	1.00

Notes: GMP = gross metropolitan product; FIE = foreign-invested enterprises.

Table 2A.6 Correlation matrix for key variables, unit value (all firms)

	Unit value of city exports (in log)	Share of joint-venture firm exports	Share of FIE firm exports	Share of processing exports outside policy zones	Share of processing exports in the two high-tech zones	Share of nonprocessing exports in the two high-tech zones	Share of export processing zone	Share of SOE exports	Share of collective and private firm exports
Unit value of city exports (in log)	1.00								
Share of joint-venture firm exports	0.03	1.00							
Share of FIE firm exports	0.01	-0.07	1.00						
Share of processing exports outside policy zones	0.01	0.29	0.30	1.00					
Share of processing exports in the two high-tech zones	0.05	0.10	0.19	-0.01	1.00				
Share of nonprocessing exports in the two high-tech zones	0.05	0.04	0.05	-0.06	0.02	1.00			
Share of export processing zone	0.01	0.00	0.06	0.00	0.00	0.00	1.00		
Share of SOE exports	-0.01	-0.52	-0.43	-0.30	-0.14	-0.05	-0.03	1.00	
Share of collective and private firm exports	-0.03	-0.13	-0.11	-0.10	-0.04	-0.01	0.00	-0.57	1.00

Note: FIE = foreign-invested enterprise; SOE = state-owned enterprise.

Table 2A.7   What explains cross-city export structure?

Explanatory variables	Export dissimilarity index				Export similarity index			
	(1)	(2)	(3)	(4)	(5)	(6)	(7)	(8)
Export processing zone exports as a share of total city exports	-45.89***	-50.98***	-46.02***	-51.63***	22.94***	25.49***	23.01***	25.81***
	(9.01)	(6.62)	(8.58)	(6.54)	(4.50)	(3.31)	(4.29)	(3.27)
Processing exports in high-tech zones as a share of total city exports	-10.73***	-11.49***	-11.22***	-12.16***	5.36***	5.75***	5.61***	6.08***
	(2.88)	(3.34)	(2.82)	(3.27)	(1.44)	(1.67)	(1.41)	(1.64)
Nonprocessing exports in high-tech zones as a share of total city exports	-14.70**	-18.24**	-15.88**	-19.47**	7.35**	9.12**	7.94**	9.73**
	(7.37)	(8.72)	(7.35)	(8.65)	(3.68)	(4.36)	(3.68)	(4.33)
Processing exports outside economic zones as a share of total city exports	0.956*	0.725	0.722	0.445	-0.478*	-0.363	-0.361	-0.222
	(0.533)	(0.533)	(0.523)	(0.524)	(0.266)	(0.267)	(0.261)	(0.262)
Student enrollment in institutions of higher education as a share of the city nonagricultural population	-36.93***		-37.60***		18.46***		18.80***	
	(11.40)		(11.35)		(5.70)		(5.67)	
Gross metropolitan product (GMP)	-0.443*	-0.467**	-0.495**	-0.520**	0.222*	0.234**	0.248**	0.260**
	(0.233)	(0.236)	(0.242)	(0.243)	(0.117)	(0.118)	(0.121)	(0.122)
GMP per capita		-1.04**		-1.15***		0.520**		0.575***
		(0.425)		(0.436)		(0.213)		(0.218)
Foreign-invested firms' share in city exports			0.465	0.839			-0.233	-0.419
			(0.989)	(1.018)			(0.494)	(0.509)
Joint-venture firms' share in city exports			1.91***	1.95***			-0.953***	-0.976***
			(0.68)	(0.69)			(0.34)	(0.345)
City fixed effects	Y	Y	Y	Y	Y	Y	Y	Y
Year fixed effects	Y	Y	Y	Y	Y	Y	Y	Y
Robust (clustered by city)	Y	Y	Y	Y	Y	Y	Y	Y
No. of observations	1,981	1,981	1,981	1,981	1,981	1,981	1,981	1,981
R^2	0.98	0.98	0.98	0.98	0.98	0.98	0.98	0.98

Notes: Standard errors in parentheses. Export dissimilarity index and export similarity index in levels as dependent variables.
***Significant at the 1 percent level.
**Significant at the 5 percent level.
*Significant at the 10 percent level.

Table 2A.8   What explains cross-city export structure, excluding city fixed effects?

Explanatory variables	Yearly benchmark					2004 benchmark		
	(1)	(2)	(3)	(4)	(5)	(6)	(7)	(8)
Export processing zone exports as a share of total city exports	-1.139*** (0.271)	-1.101*** (0.261)	-1.049*** (0.26)	-1.044*** (0.256)	-1.208*** (0.269)	-1.175*** (0.253)	-1.120*** (0.258)	-1.119*** (0.247)
Processing exports in high-tech zones as a share of total city exports	-0.234*** (0.055)	-0.200*** (0.059)	-0.179*** (0.055)	-0.165*** (0.059)	-0.215*** (0.051)	-0.182*** (0.055)	-0.160*** (0.051)	-0.148*** (0.054)
Nonprocessing exports in high-tech zones as a share of total city exports	-0.15 (0.191)	-0.198 (0.185)	-0.169 (0.193)	-0.216 (0.186)	-0.143 (0.17)	-0.192 (0.168)	-0.161 (0.172)	-0.209 (0.169)
Processing exports outside economic zones as a share of total city exports	-0.047*** (0.012)	-0.036*** (0.011)	-0.037*** (0.012)	-0.032*** (0.011)	-0.044*** (0.011)	-0.032*** (0.01)	-0.034*** (0.011)	-0.029*** (0.01)
Student enrollment in institutions of higher education as a share of the city nonagricultural population	-0.741*** (0.149)		-0.787*** (0.151)		-0.733*** (0.138)		-0.779*** (0.14)	
Gross metropolitan product (GMP)	-0.039*** (0.004)	-0.035*** (0.004)	-0.038*** (0.005)	-0.036*** (0.004)	-0.036*** (0.004)	-0.034*** (0.004)	-0.036*** (0.004)	-0.034*** (0.004)
GMP per capita		-0.027*** (0.006)		-0.027*** (0.006)		-0.026*** (0.006)		-0.025*** (0.006)
Foreign-invested firms' share in city exports			-0.066*** (0.019)	-0.043** (0.019)			-0.064*** (0.018)	-0.043** (0.018)
Joint-venture firms' share in city exports			0.007 (0.011)	0.015 (0.01)			0.006 (0.01)	0.013 (0.01)
City fixed effects	N	N	N	N	N	N	N	N
Year fixed effects	Y	Y	Y	Y	Y	Y	Y	Y
Robust (clustered by city)	Y	Y	Y	Y	Y	Y	Y	Y
No. of observations	1,981	1,981	1,981	1,981	1,981	1,981	1,981	1,981
R^2	0.66	0.67	0.67	0.67	0.67	0.67	0.68	0.68

Notes: Standard errors given in parentheses. (log [export dissimilarity index]) as the dependent variable.

***Significant at the 1 percent level.

**Significant at the 5 percent level.

References

Finger, J. Michael, and M. E. Kreinin. 1979. A measure of "export similarity" and its possible uses. *Economic Journal* 89:905–12.

Fisman, Raymond, Peter Moustakerski, and Shang-Jin Wei. 2008. Outsourcing tariff evasion: A new explanation for entrepot trade. *Review of Economics and Statistics,* forthcoming.

Fisman, Raymond, and Shang-Jin Wei. 2004. Tax rates and tax evasion: Evidence from "missing trade" in China. *Journal of Political Economy* 112 (2): 471–96.

Fontagne, Lionel, Guillaume Gaulier, and Soledad Zignago. 2007. Specialisation across varieties within products and North-South competition. CEPII Working Paper no. 2007-06. Paris: Centre d'Etude Prospectives et d'Informations Internationales, May.

Hale, Galina, and Cheryl Long. 2006. What determines technological spillovers of foreign direct investment: Evidence from China. Federal Reserve Bank of San Francisco, Working Paper no. 2006-13. http://ideas.recpec.org/p/fip/fedfwp/2006-13.html.

Hallack, Juan Carlos. 2006. Product quality and the direction of trade. *Journal of International Economics* 68 (1): 238–65.

Hallack, Juan Carlos, and Peter Schott. 2005. Estimating cross-country differences in product quality. Yale University, Working Paper.

Hausmann, Ricardo, Jason Hwang, and Dani Rodrik. 2005. What you export matters. NBER Working Paper no. 11905. Cambridge, MA: National Bureau of Economic Research.

Hummels, David, and Peter Klenow. 2005. The variety and quality of a nation's exports. *American Economic Review* 95:704–23.

Rodrik, Dani. 2006. What's so special about China's exports? NBER Working Paper no. 11947. Cambridge, MA: National Bureau of Economic Research.

Schott, Peter. 2004. Across-product versus within-product specialization in international trade. *Quarterly Journal of Economics* 119 (2): 647–78.

———. 2006. The relative sophistication of Chinese exports. NBER working paper no. 12173. Cambridge, MA: National Bureau of Economic Research.

Xu, Bin. 2007. Measuring China's export sophistication. China Europe International Business School.

Xu, Bin, and Jiangyong Lu. 2007. The impact of foreign firms on the sophistication of Chinese exports. China Europe International Business School and Tsinghua University, Working Paper.

Comment   Galina Hale

Zhi Wang and Shang-Jin Wei present us with a thorough and convincing study of the growing sophistication of Chinese exports in recent years and of the forces behind this trend. We learn that improvements in human capital and tax incentives for high-tech zones are responsible for the expansion

Galina Hale is a senior economist in the research department of the Federal Reserve Bank of San Francisco.

of China's export into more sophisticated categories, while sophistication within categories is driven by a combination of processing trade, foreign direct investment (FDI), and, again, tax incentives for high-tech zones.

These results are important for two reasons. First, rising sophistication of Chinese exports means that even high-income countries will experience competitive pressure from Chinese producers, so understanding its sources will help us evaluate potential shifts in the global division of labor in the future. More specifically, the distributional effects of U.S. imports from China (which in 2008 contributed over 16 percent to U.S. total imports) depend crucially on what types of goods the United States is importing from China. Second, this study contributes to our understanding of China's economic growth. In particular, it suggests that, at least in its export sector, China is following the stages of the East Asian growth miracle—beginning with labor-intensive goods, increasing capital intensity as wealth accumulates and labor becomes more expensive, turning to high-tech goods as technology develops and human capital accumulates, and finally developing into a niche producer of cutting-edge research and development (R&D) intensive goods and services.

The analysis is conducted on two levels. On the first level, the authors study the overlap in Harmonized System (HS) six-digit categories of manufactured goods exported by China and by G3 economies (the United States, Japan, and the European Union)—the larger the overlap, the more sophisticated the structure of Chinese exports. To do so, they construct an export dissimilarity index (EDI) in the spirit of Finger and Kreinin's (1979) export similarity index (ESI) and study the trends and the determinants of these indexes across China's provinces and cities. On the second level, the authors study the unit prices of each of these six-digit categories to investigate the potential increase in sophistication and quality of goods *within* each category.

We learn, as expected, that the similarity of Chinese exports to G3 exports grew at a steady pace between 1996 and 2006. This increase in sophistication is most pronounced among privately owned companies, the share of which has been steadily growing during the period under consideration. The authors are careful to conduct their analysis for firms with different ownerships separately and find that the results do indeed vary by ownership type.

For geographical differences in export sophistication growth, they consider the following possible explanations: processing export, the presence of a high-tech zone, skilled labor, output, and the presence of FDI. Almost all of their results come from differences in the *dynamics* of EDI and explanatory variables across cities because city and year fixed effects are included. The role of cross-city differences may be read from table 2A.8, where city fixed effects are excluded. As expected, the same factors that appear important in the main specification are also responsible for cross-city differences in export sophistication.

The results are summarized well in the paper. I now focus on the difference of the results across different ownership types and on some interpretations I don't necessarily agree with. The reader should keep in mind that city fixed effects absorb all time-invariant differences across cities, while year fixed effects absorb all trends common to all cities. The discussion in the paper occasionally slips into cross-city interpretation (especially in the conclusion), which is not really a problem given that cross-city differences are, in fact, driven by the same factors.

The authors find that in the full sample EDI becomes smaller, that is, exports become more sophisticated, when the share of exports from export processing zones (EPZs) and high-tech zones increases, when the share of population with a university degree increases, and when cities become richer in terms of gross metropolitan product (GMP) per capita.

Although GMP per capita is potentially endogenous (presumably, more sophisticated exports are also more valuable and, thus, increase GMP per capita) and should probably be lagged, I believe it is an important control variable and needs to be included. I disagree, however, with its interpretation as a measure of human capital accumulation in the city—it might be a measure of physical capital accumulation in the city or of changing industrial composition of the city's output, which, again, would be simultaneously determined with more sophisticated exports. I believe the other proxy—share of university students in nonagricultural population—is less likely to be endogenous and is a better proxy for human capital accumulation. In fact, it seems to have an independent effect in the same direction as the per capita GMP: an increase in the share of university students is associated with growing sophistication of the export structure, even controlling for GMP.

Given that processing trade is a large share of Chinese exports, it is very important to include relevant controls. The authors did a great job of controlling for both EPZs and processing trade outside such zones. They find that processing trade is, in fact, in less sophisticated product categories—the larger the share of processing trade, the less sophisticated the exports, ceteris paribus. This effect is driven entirely by state-owned and collective firms, as it is not present for other ownership sectors and is small and not robustly significant for the full sample.

The importance of high-tech zones is also driven by state-owned and collective firms, which is not surprising because it shows a direct effect of the government's policies designed to upgrade the production structure in state-owned enterprises through high-tech zones, R&D subsidies, and links with research centers. Private firms do not enjoy such support.

The authors seem to find consistently that the presence of FDI does not have any effect on the sophistication of Chinese exports. While foreign-invested firms themselves appear to produce more sophisticated product lines (see columns [3] and [4] in table 2.10), there do not seem to be any spillovers, nor do the preceding factors affect the export sophistication of foreign-owned firms. To me, this effect is not surprising: Hale and Long (2008) find that the presence of FDI in a given city and industry increases competition for skilled labor, which may offset any potential positive spillovers from FDI. Hale and Long (2009) also find that spillovers from FDI to total factor or labor productivity do not seem to be present in China, which is consistent with the Wang and Wei results.

Turning to the analysis of unit values, which proxy for the sophistication of exports within each HS six-digit category, I am disappointed that the authors chose a different regression specification. In particular, they chose to include city by year fixed effects, rather than city and year fixed effects separately. While this allows them to focus more squarely on the role of processing trade and high-tech zones, it no longer allows them to test for the effect of human capital accumulation as in previous regressions because the explanatory variable does not vary within city-year. Moreover, it makes results difficult to compare with the preceding analysis. For instance, the authors find that a higher share of processing trade increases the unit values of exports, which is different from the effect of processing trade on EDI. However, we cannot definitively say that the effects differ because the regression specification is not the same.

Overall, the paper presents a very informative and thorough analysis of an issue that is both important and understudied in the literature so far. Any trade economist or macroeconomist who studies Chinese exports needs to keep in mind that massive structural and compositional changes take place in the background and cannot be ignored. Wang and Wei provide an important contribution to our understanding of the sophisticated nature of Chinese economic growth and of geographical differences in Chinese export growth patterns.

My understanding of the results is that the growing sophistication of Chinese exports mostly appears to be driven by government policies targeting the development of high-tech industries and higher education. Going forward, therefore, if one can expect such policies to continue, one should also expect the sophistication of Chinese exports and their competitive pressure on high-income countries to be growing as well.

References

Hale, Galina, and Cheryl Long. 2008. Did foreign direct investment put an upward pressure on wages in China? Federal Reserve Bank of San Francisco, Working Paper no. 2006-25.
———. 2009. Are there productivity spillovers from foreign direct investment in China? *Pacific Economic Review,* forthcoming.
Finger, J. Michael, and M. E. Kreinin. 1979. A measure of "export similarity" and its possible uses. *Economic Journal* 89:905–12.

China's Local Comparative Advantage

James Harrigan and Haiyan Deng

3.1 Introduction

China's trading pattern is often seen as an illustration of the power of the Heckscher-Ohlin approach to explaining world trade: labor abundant China specializes in exporting labor-intensive goods. A broader Heckscher-Ohlin worldview is also perfectly consistent with China's role in performing the labor-intensive tasks in complex international supply chains.

In this paper, we draw attention to a different determinant of China's comparative advantage: her geographical location. We present theoretical models of global bilateral trade that build on the work of Eaton and Kortum (2002) and Harrigan (2006), which show how China's location influences her competitiveness in different markets around the globe, that is, China's "local comparative advantage." The model also shows how the rise of China differentially affects the competitiveness of other low-wage economies.

A key prediction of the theory is that relative transport costs by product and export destination influence China's export success. In particular, the model predicts that China will tend to export "heavy" goods (those with a high transportation cost as a share of value) to nearby export destinations and will export "light" goods to more distant markets. Furthermore, heavy

James Harrigan is a professor of economics at the University of Virginia, and a research associate of the National Bureau of Economic Research. Haiyan Deng is a research fellow at the Conference Board.

We thank conference participants and the organizers, especially Robert Feenstra and our discussant Chong Xiang, for helpful comments. We also thank Jennifer Peck for able research assistance. The views expressed in this document are those of the authors and do not necessarily reflect the position of the Federal Reserve Bank of New York, the Federal Reserve System, the Conference Board, or the National Bureau of Economic Research (NBER).

goods will be sent by ship, while light goods may be shipped by air. Our empirical analysis, which looks at highly detailed Chinese export data in 2006, confirms this prediction of the model: the weight of China's exports is strongly related to distance.

The gravity equation, a relationship between aggregate trade volumes, country size, and distance, is extremely well established empirically and theoretically. Recent research on the trade-distance nexus has started to move beyond the aggregate gravity model and looks at disaggregated trade in theory and in the data. Relevant papers include Baldwin and Harrigan (2007), Deardorff (2004), Evans and Harrigan (2005), Harrigan (2006), Harrigan and Venables (2006), Hummels (2001), Hummels and Klenow (2005), Hummels and Skiba (2004), and Limão and Venables (2002). This line of research has two related purposes: better understanding the effects of distance and transport costs and enriching our models of comparative advantage. The current paper shares these purposes, along with the goal of better understanding China's comparative advantage in particular. In this it is, we hope, complementary to the other papers in this volume.

3.2   Theory

In this section, we present a general equilibrium model of bilateral trade in a multilateral world where relative distance is a key determinant of comparative advantage. Before moving to an exposition of the model, we introduce the interaction between specific trade costs and trade flows in partial equilibrium.

3.2.1   Partial Equilibrium

The simplest explanation for a relation between export prices and distance is the so-called Washington apples effect, which is the basis of the paper by Hummels and Skiba (2004). The theory starts with the observation that per-unit transport costs depend primarily on physical characteristics rather than value; that is, they are specific rather than ad valorem.

Focusing on a single exporting country, the relationship between import and export prices is given by

$$(1) \qquad p_{ic}^{M} = (1 + t_{ic})\, p_{ic}^{X},$$

where p_{ic}^{M} is the cost, insurance, and freight (c.i.f.) import price of good i shipped to country c, p_{ic}^{X} is the free-on-board (f.o.b.) export price, and $t_{ic} \geq 0$ is the cost of transport per dollar of value shipped.[1] The usual "iceberg" assumption is that t_{ic} is a function of distance only. This implies that per-unit

---

1. The constant returns-to-scale assumption that per-unit transport costs are independent of the number of units shipped is inessential.

transport costs are proportional to value and independent of weight, but Hummels and Skiba (2004, table 1) show that the opposite assumption is closer to the truth. Thus, a more realistic assumption about transport costs per dollar of value shipped is that they are given by

$$(2) \qquad t_{ic} = \frac{t(w_i, d_c)}{p_{ic}^X},$$

where w_i is weight per unit, d_c is the distance between the exporter and country c, and the function t is nondecreasing in both arguments. In the remainder of the paper, it is appropriate to interpret w as any physical characteristic of the good (such as volume and perishability, in addition to weight in kilos) that affects shipping costs. The specification in equation (2) has the key implication that shipping costs as a share of f.o.b. price are smaller for higher-priced goods, controlling for weight.

Now consider a high-priced good H and a low-priced good L, and let $\tilde{p} = p_H/p_L$ denote the price of H in terms of L. Equations (1) and (2) imply that the relative import price of the two goods in country c is

$$(3) \qquad \tilde{p}_c^M = \tilde{p}^X \frac{(1 + t_{Hc})}{(1 + t_{Lc})} = \tilde{p}^X \frac{[1 + t(w_H, d_c)/p_H^X]}{[1 + t(w_L, d_c)/p_L^X]}.$$

If the two goods weigh the same, then the high priced good has lower transport costs as a share of f.o.b. price, and the ratio of transport factors in equation (3) will be less than 1, so $\tilde{p}_c^M < \tilde{p}^X$. The law of demand then implies that relative consumption of H will be higher in country c than at home. This is precisely the "shipping the good apples out" effect: good apples and bad apples weigh the same, but it is cheaper as a share of value to ship out the good apples.[2]

The strength of the Washington apples effect is increasing in distance.[3] The intuition is simple: as per-unit transport costs increase with distance, the importance of any difference in f.o.b. prices shrinks.

A similar comparison can be made by reinterpreting the subscripts in equation (3). Now let H and L stand for "heavy" and "light," respectively. Then H will be relatively more expensive in c than at home ($\tilde{p}_c^M > \tilde{p}^X$), with obvious effects on relative consumption. The effect of increasing distance on the strength of this weight effect is, in general, ambiguous and depends

---

2. The antique textbook by Silberberg (1978, chapter 11) has a clear discussion of the Washington apples effect, including some caveats when there are more than two goods.

3. To see this, note that

$$\frac{\partial \tilde{p}^M}{\partial d_c} = \frac{p_L^X - p_H^X}{(p_L^X + t)^2} \frac{\partial t}{\partial d_c} \le 0.$$

In the limit as transport costs go to infinity, f.o.b prices are irrelevant, and the c.i.f. relative price is unity.

on details of the transport cost function $t(w_i, d_c)$.[4] In the case where $t(w_i, d_c)$ has constant elasticities with respect to distance and weight, the effect of greater distance is to amplify the importance of any differences in weight for import prices. Economic intuition suggests that this will be the normal case, unless $t(w_i, d_c)$ increases more rapidly with distance when evaluated at w_L than when evaluated at w_H in some relevant range.

These results about the effect of transport costs on import prices can be restated in terms that will be relevant to our empirical analysis, where we look at variation in export prices from China to different destinations. In our analysis, we will consider narrowly defined product categories that, nonetheless, may comprise many different goods with differing unit values and different weights per unit.

First, the Washington apples effect implies a composition effect: because high-quality goods will be relatively less expensive at greater distances, we should expect higher average unit values across countries as a function of distance.

Second, goods with the same value per unit that differ in weight are subject to the weight-composition effect: distance raises the relative price of heavy goods, which will cause the value-weight ratio to be increasing in distance. Clearly the Washington apples effect and the weight-composition effect are closely related. Indeed, if goods within a category differ only in their value and not their weight, then unit values are proportional to the value-weight ratio, and the two effects are identical.

A final composition effect comes from differences in demand across importers. If higher-income countries demand proportionately more higher-quality goods, or if Chinese exporters price discriminate against high-income importers, then we would also expect a positive association between importer per capita income and average export unit values from China. See Hallak (2006) for evidence on the relation between income per capita and the demand for quality and Feenstra and Hanson (2004) for some evidence on price discrimination in Chinese exports.

3.2.2   General Equilibrium

The Washington apples effect offers a useful starting point for thinking about the effect of specific trade costs on trade patterns, but because it takes f.o.b. prices as given, it cannot be considered a model of trade. Here, we embed the partial equilibrium mechanism in a general equilibrium model

---

4. The relevant cross second derivative is

$$\frac{\partial^2 \tilde{p}^M}{\partial w_H \partial d_c} = \frac{-1}{[p_L^X + t(w_L, d_c)]^2} \left[\frac{\partial t(w_H, d_c)}{\partial w_H} \frac{\partial t(w_L, d_c)}{\partial d_c} \right] + \frac{1}{p_L^X + t(w_L, d_c)} \frac{\partial^2 t(w_H, d_c)}{\partial w_H \partial d_c}.$$

The first term is negative, and the second term is positive, so this derivative cannot be signed.

to address the question: how does China's position on the globe influence its trade pattern?

Our model has N countries, one factor of production (labor), and a continuum of final goods produced under conditions of perfect competition. Goods are symmetric in demand and in expected production cost. Physical geography is unrestricted and summarized by the matrix of bilateral distances with typical element d_{cb} denoting the distance between countries b and c. As in Eaton and Kortum (2002), firms located in each country compete head-to-head in every market in the world, with the low-cost supplier winning the entire market. A firm's cost in a particular market depends on its f.o.b. price and on transport costs between the firm's home and the market (this cost is normalized to zero if the market in question is the home market). By perfect competition, f.o.b. price equals the wage divided by unit labor productivity, which is stochastic. Firms located in c have productivity distributed according to the Fréchet distribution with parameters $T_c > 0$ and $\theta > 1$.

As in Harrigan (2006), consumers value goods that are delivered by air more than goods delivered by ship. Some of the reasons for such a preference are analyzed by Evans and Harrigan (2005) and Harrigan and Venables (2006), but for the purposes of this model, we will simply suppose that utility is higher for goods that arrive by air. Let the set of goods shipped by air be A, with measure also given by A. Utility is

$$(4) \qquad U[x(z)] = \int_{z \in A} a \ln x(z)dz + \int_{z \notin A} \ln x(z)dz,$$

where $a > 1$ is the air-freight preference, x is consumption, and $z \in [0,1]$ indexes goods. An implication of equation (4) is that for a given good, the relative marginal utility if it arrives by air versus ship is a.

We now consider the problem of an exporter in c choosing the optimal shipping mode for selling in b. Let $\tau_{cb}^A[w(z), d_{cb}] \geq 1$ be the iceberg shipping cost for air shipment of good z from c to b, with $\tau_{cb}^S[w(z), d_{cb}]$ defined similarly for surface shipment. Given the premium a that consumers are willing to pay for air shipment, the optimal shipping mode is

$$(5) \qquad \tau_{cb}(z, d_{cb}) = \tau_{cb}^A[w(z), d_{cb}] \text{ if } \frac{\tau_{cb}^A[w(z), d_{cb}]}{a} \leq \tau_{cb}^S[w(z), d_{cb}]$$

$$\tau_{cb}(z, d_{cb}) = \tau_{cb}^S[w(z), d_{cb}] \text{ otherwise.}$$

What are the properties of the transport cost functions? First, order goods by weight, with $z = 0$ being the lightest and $z = 1$ the heaviest. We will make three assumptions about the transport cost functions $\forall b, c, z \in [0,1]$:

Air shipping is expensive

$$(6) \qquad \tau_{cb}^S[w(z), d_{cb}] \leq \tau_{cb}^A[w(z), d_{cb}]$$

Air shipping is proportionately more expensive for heavier goods

(6′)
$$\frac{\partial \ln \tau_{cb}^S}{\partial \ln z} \leq \frac{\partial \ln \tau_{cb}^A}{\partial \ln z}$$

The cost disadvantage of air shipment declines with distance

(6″)
$$\frac{\partial \ln \tau_{cb}^S}{\partial \ln d_{cd}} \geq \frac{\partial \ln \tau_{cb}^A}{\partial \ln d_{cd}}$$

The truth of the first assumption, that air shipment is always more expensive than surface shipment, is obvious to anyone who has ever traveled or shipped a package. The second assumption, that surface shipping costs increase more slowly with weight than air costs, is also reasonable and is consistent with light goods being much more likely to be shipped by air (see Harrigan [2006, table 10] for statistical confirmation of this commonplace observation). The final assumption is consistent with the fact that air shipment is almost never used on short distances. Assumption (6″) is also consistent with a model of a demand for timely delivery: for short distances, timely delivery can be assured by (cheap) surface shipment, while for longer distances only (costly) air shipment can ensure timeliness.

For any pair of countries, the optimal shipping mode will be a function of weight. It is possible that even the lightest goods will be shipped by surface, and it is also possible that even the heaviest goods will be shipped by air. But the normal case in world trade is that some goods are shipped by each mode (e.g., for U.S. trade in 2005, every exporter except Sudan sent some goods by air and some by surface). Let $\bar{z}_{cb}$ denote the dividing line between air-shipped goods ($z \leq \bar{z}_{cb}$) and goods shipped by surface ($\bar{z}_{cb} < z$) in trade between c and b. By assumption (6″), the cutoff will be lower for nearby countries than for faraway countries. These relationships are illustrated in figure 3.1 for exports from China to two countries, one near and one far. In the figure, we illustrate assumption (6′) by having surface transport costs unrelated to weight, while air transport costs are increasing in weight.

As noted in the previous section, the iceberg assumption is not realistic and rules out the important Washington apples effect on relative c.i.f. prices. It was also noted that the Washington apples effect and the weight-composition effect are very closely related. In the specification used in the current section, a Washington apples-like effect appears through the influence of weight on transport costs. Because of symmetry in supply and demand, expected f.o.b. prices from a given exporter are the same for all goods, but c.i.f. prices differ due to differences in weight.

We now turn to a discussion of the trade equilibrium. As discussed in Harrigan (2006), wages in each country c are endogenous and will be determined by the aggregate productivities T_c, labor supplies, and bilateral distances. In this paper, we analyze a single country's exports across its trading partners and, thus, can treat wages as fixed.

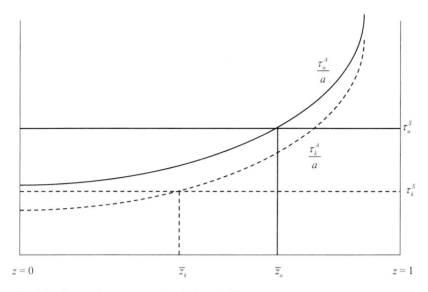

Fig. 3.1   Optimal transport mode choice for Chinese exporters

Notes: The vertical axis is iceberg transport cost factor, and the horizontal axis indexes weight from lightest ($z = 0$) to heaviest ($z = 1$). Country k (Korea) is relatively close to China, while country u (United States) is further away. The horizontal lines are surface transport costs, and the upward sloping lines are air transport costs relative to the air preference parameter a. The vertical lines show the division between optimal mode choices for the two destinations. See text for further discussion.

In keeping with the focus of the paper, we will consider China's probability of successfully competing in different markets and in different goods. In the Eaton-Kortum (2002) model, the probability that China will supply a given market b is the same for all goods (their equation (8), 1748). In the current model, the probability varies and will depend on $\tau_{cb}(z, d_{cb})$ for all countries c. With this modification, the Eaton-Kortum logic goes through otherwise unchanged, so the probability that China will supply good z to country b is

$$(7) \qquad \pi_{Cb}(z) = \frac{T_C[w_C \tau_{Cb}(z, d_{Cb})]^{-\theta}}{\sum_{c=1}^{N} T_c[w_c \tau_{cb}(z, d_{cb})]^{-\theta}} = \frac{T_C[w_C \tau_{Cb}(z, d_{Cb})]^{-\theta}}{\Phi_b(z)}.$$

The summation in the denominator $\Phi_b(z)$ in equation (7) includes country b, which reflects the fact that good z might be produced domestically rather than imported.[5] The economics of equation (7) is fairly simple. The probability that China successfully captures the market for good z in country b depends positively on China's absolute advantage T_C and negatively on

5. Here and in what follows, we let C stand for China, while c is a generic index for any country.

China's wage and transport cost to b, relative to an average of world technology levels and wages weighted by transport costs to the same market.

3.2.3   Implications of Chinese Growth for China's Competitors

A great virtue of the Eaton-Kortum (2002) model is that it is a fully competitive general equilibrium model. Alvarez and Lucas (2007) point out that this implies that all the properties that are known about such models in general can be applied to Eaton and Kortum's model. However, the Eaton-Kortum model has no general analytical solution for equilibrium wages, which makes comparative static analysis problematic. In this section, we show that despite its analytical complexity, the model can be used to answer some important questions about how the rise of China affects the trade performance of China's competitors.

We begin by assuming costless trade. In this case, Alvarez and Lucas (2007) show (1744, equation [6.3]) that equilibrium wages are

$$w_c = \left(\frac{T_c}{L_c} \right)^{1/(1+\theta)},$$

where L_c is country c's labor force. National income is

(8) $\qquad Y_c = w_c L_c = T_c w_c^{-\theta} = \left(\frac{T_c}{L_c} \right)^{1/(1+\theta)} L_c = T_c^{1/(1+\theta)} L_c^{\theta/(1+\theta)}$

Thus, national income is a geometric average of a country's technology level and its labor supply. Setting all transport factors $= 1$, substitution of equation (8) into equation (7) implies

$$\pi_{Cb}(z) = \frac{Y_C}{\sum_{c=1}^{N} Y_c}.$$

Thus, we have that in the frictionless case, the probability that China supplies a given good z to any country is simply China's share in global gross domestic product (GDP).

Now reintroduce transport costs, adopting for the purposes of this section the Eaton-Kortum (2002) assumption that transport costs do not differ across goods. For small transport costs, this will not affect national income much, so we can replace $T_c w_c^{-\theta}$ by Y_c in equation (7). This gives the following approximation to equation (7),

(9) $\qquad \pi_{Cb} \cong \dfrac{Y_C \tau_{Cb}^{-\theta}}{\sum_{c=1}^{N} Y_c \tau_{cb}^{-\theta}} \approx \dfrac{Y_C \tau_{Cb}^{-\theta}}{\Phi}.$

Since equation (9) is independent of z, we can integrate over z and reinterpret equation (9) as giving China's market share in country b. This result is useful because it links China's market share to observables. Because a change of subscripts makes equation (9) applicable to every country's sales in every other country, it also allows us to analyze how international competition is affected by Chinese growth.

By the same reasoning used to derive equation (9), we have the approximation

$$\Phi_b \cong \sum_{c=1}^{N} Y_c \tau_{cb}^{-\theta}.$$

This term is very similar to the country price indexes derived by Anderson and van Wincoop (2003). It is also close to what Harrigan (2003) defines as a country's "centrality" index, which is a GDP-weighted average of a country's inverse bilateral trade costs. It is larger the closer b is to big countries: Belgium will have a large value of Φ_b, while New Zealand will have a small value.

A natural way to consider the impact of China's growth on its neighbors in this model is to ask how an improvement in China's technical capability T_C affects China's export market share. The full general equilibrium effects on global wages and trading patterns of an increase in T_C cannot be found analytically, but we can get an approximate answer by treating China as a small country and by using the preceding approximations. Substituting equation (8) into equation (9), we have

(10)
$$T_C \frac{\partial \pi_{Cb}}{\partial T_C} \cong \frac{1}{1 + \theta} \pi_{Cb} (1 - \pi_{Cb}).$$

This expression says that a 1 percent improvement in T_C raises China's market share in all markets, but the largest gain comes where China's share is already large.[6] The effect on some other country k's market share in b when China grows is given by

(11)
$$T_C \frac{\partial \pi_{kb}}{\partial T_C} \cong -\frac{1}{1 + \theta} \pi_{Cb} \pi_{kb}.$$

Equation (11) states that the biggest market share losses are felt by countries that have large market share where China also has large market share.

Equations (10) and (11) show the impact effect of an increase in T_C before equilibrium adjustments in world wages and trade flows. As noted in the preceding, analytical solutions for these general equilibrium effects are not available, but we can conjecture some effects. Because the impact effect of Chinese growth is largest in markets where China already has a substantial presence, the increased competition from China will be felt most keenly in precisely these markets. By equation (7), these locations will be markets that are close to China and far from the rest of the world, such as East and Southeast Asia. With China's market share rising in these markets, other countries that sell there will suffer loss of market share given by equation (11), with consequent reductions in factor demand. These negative factor demand effects in export markets are, of course, balanced by the consumption gains from cheap Chinese imports at home, plus increased sales of home

---

6. To see this, note that $\pi_{Cb} (1 - \pi_{Cb})$ is increasing in π_{Cb} for $\pi_{Cb} < 0.5$, a condition that holds in the data $\forall b$.

produced products in the Chinese market, with the net effect on real income uncertain. This is an application of an old but sometimes neglected point from trade theory: in a multicountry trade model, technological progress in one country may lower real income in some other countries even as it raises global real income.

3.2.4   Testable Predictions for Chinese Export Data

The theory developed in the previous two sections generates testable predictions about Chinese export data. The simplest are given by equations (10) and (11), which predict how aggregate bilateral trade patterns will change with rapid growth in China. The predictions given by equations (10) and (11) are made holding transport costs and other countries' technology fixed, so even if the model were literally true, the change in trade patterns would be more complex than given by these partial derivatives. However, as we will see in the following, these simple equations turn out to be remarkably useful predictors of changing bilateral trade patterns in markets where China already had a foothold in the mid-1990s.

Turning to product-level data, we can use equation (7) to generate testable predictions about China's export unit values. For a given good z, increases in distance reduce the probability of export success. This is simply the usual gravity effect operating through the extensive margin.

Now consider some set of goods $Z \subseteq [0,1]$. For every good $z \in Z$, the extensive margin effect of distance is operative. However, given our characterization of trade costs in assumptions (6), (6'), and (6''), it is clear that the extensive margin effect is stronger for heavier goods. That is, as distance increases, the probability that a heavy good will be successfully exported decreases faster than the same probability for a lightweight good.

Next consider a heavy good and a light good z^H, $z^L \in Z$. If both goods are exported from China to some group of markets, the weight-composition effect discussed in section 3.2.1 is operative: the more distant the market from China, the greater the relative c.i.f. price of z^H and, thus, the greater the share of z^L in local consumption. If goods weigh the same $\forall z \in Z$, the (very similar) Washington apples logic will apply: high-quality goods will be "light" in the sense of having low shipping costs as a share of f.o.b. value, and, thus, their relative c.i.f. price will be lower, and consumption higher, in more distant markets. These are intensive margin effects because they describe how relative consumption of goods actually exported changes with distance.

With an understanding of how the extensive and intensive margins for goods $z \in Z$ operate as a function of distance, we can now answer the following question: how does the average unit value of exports vary with distance? From what we have just elucidated in the previous two paragraphs, the answer is clear, and we highlight it as the key empirical prediction that we will test when we look at disaggregated export data:

PREDICTION. *For a given set of goods, the average unit value of Chinese exports will be nondecreasing in distance, controlling for other determinants of the demand for quality.*

3.3 Data Analysis

We use two different data sources. Testing the aggregate predictions of equations (10) and (11) requires data on all bilateral trade flows in the world, and our source for this data is the International Monetary Fund (IMF) Direction of Trade Statistics. The IMF does not report data on Taiwan, so we supplement the IMF data from Taiwanese government sources.

To test the predictions about export unit values, we used highly disaggregated Chinese export data from 2006 (China Customs Statistics 1997–2007). Exports are reported by eight-digit Harmonized System (HS) code, importing country, province of origin, type of exporting firm (seven categories that we aggregate as state or collective-owned and private), type of trade (eighteen categories that we aggregate as ordinary, processing, and other), and transport mode (air and sea). Export destinations are classified by the location of the final consumer.

3.3.1 Market Share Changes

Our aggregate data includes bilateral trade among 212 countries, for potentially $212 \times 211 = 44{,}732$ bilateral relationships, many of which are tiny to the point of insignificance. Because our focus is on the rise of China, we restrict most of our attention to the twenty largest markets for Chinese exports, listed in table 3.1.

The model underlying equations (10) and (11) is a static, long-run model, so it is appropriate to test it using long-run changes in trade patterns. We look at changes between 1996 and 2006. The initial date was chosen because it is after the major changes in China's foreign trade regime that were implemented in 1993 to 1994, and before the 1997 Asia crisis that temporarily disrupted trade patterns. This ten-year period covers the era when China continued to liberalize trade, joined the World Trade Organization (WTO), grew at a fantastically rapid rate, and became a major factor in global trade.

The most effective way to evaluate the predictions of equations (10) and (11) is with a series of bivariate scatter plots. Figures 3.2 and 3.3 compare the actual change in China's share of export markets between 1996 and 2006 with the level predicted by China's market share in 1996. We calculate this predicted level neglecting the constant of proportionality $(1 + \theta)^{-1}$ because we have no data on θ. An implication is that the horizontal scale and magnitude of the slope in these charts is not meaningful.

Figure 3.2 shows that the simple model does a startlingly good job of predicting China's export expansion in her top twenty markets, with most of China's big markets lining up on almost a straight line through the origin.

Table 3.1   China's top twenty export markets, 2006

	Distance from Beijing	Exports ($ billions)	% exports sent by air
United States	11,154	203	19
Hong Kong	1,979	155	12
Japan	2,102	92	15
Korea	956	45	14
Germany	7,829	40	33
The Netherlands	7,827	31	22
United Kingdom	8,146	24	15
Singapore	4,485	23	35
Taiwan	1,723	21	26
Italy	8,132	16	9
Russia	5,799	16	7
Canada	10,458	16	12
India	3,781	15	17
France	8,222	14	26
Australia	9,025	14	14
Malaysia	4,351	14	35
Spain	9,229	12	9
United Arab Emirates	5,967	11	7
Belgium	7,969	10	14
Thailand	3,301	10	16

The simple correlation in this chart is 0.48, and the correlation weighted by 2006 export value is 0.77. The two biggest negative outliers are Hong Kong and Russia, where China had small falls in market share. A group of three large East Asian markets (Malaysia, Taiwan, and Thailand) are large positive outliers, probably reflecting their participation in processing trade that boosts gross trade far above the levels predicted by models of trade in final goods such as Eaton-Kortum (2002).

Figure 3.3 includes all of China's export destinations, and the basic message is the same as that of figure 3.2. The unweighted and value-weighted correlations between predicted and actual are 0.35 and 0.46, respectively. The two northeast outliers are Yemen and Mongolia, respectively.

Equation (11) in principle gives predictions for how every bilateral relationship in the world responds to the rise of China. According to the equation, the effect is increasing in China's market share, so we restrict our attention to changes that occur in China's top twenty markets. Figures 3.4, 3.5, and 3.6 show how the other big East Asian exporters (Korea, Taiwan, and Japan) saw their export shares change in China's top twenty markets between 1996 and 2006. In each case, the correlation between predicted and actual is positive, but the relationship is weaker than when looking at China's trade directly.

Figure 3.4 shows that Korea lost market share in Europe, Japan, Austra-

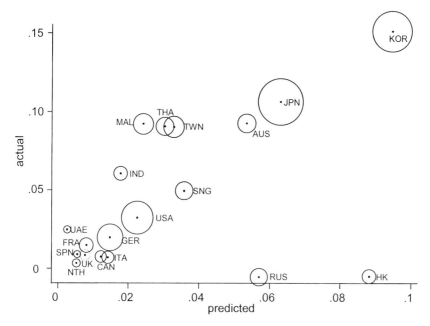

Fig. 3.2   Change in China's export market shares, 1996 to 2006, actual versus predicted, top twenty markets

Notes: Data is total bilateral trade, from International Monetary Fund (IMF) Direction of Trade Statistics (Taiwan data from Taiwan Government sources). Export market share is defined as the exporters share of the importer's aggregate imports. The size of circles is proportional to bilateral trade volume in 2006. Predicted values computed from 1996 trade shares, as given by equations (10)—figures 3.2 and 3.3—and (11)—figures 3.4, 3.5, and 3.6—in the text. Country abbreviations are as follows: USA = United States; UK = United Kingdom; BEL = Belgium; FRA = France; GER = Germany; ITA = Italy; NTH = The Netherlands; CAN = Canada; JPN = Japan; SPN = Spain; AUS = Australia; UAE = United Arab Emirates; TWN = Taiwan; HK = Hong Kong; IND = India; KOR = Korea; MAL = Malaysia; SNG = Singapore; THA = Thailand; RUS = Russia.

lia, and the United States, but had a big increase in trade with Taiwan and the United Arab Emirates. Figure 3.5 shows that Taiwan lost market share everywhere except Italy, but Taiwan's market share losses were much smaller than predicted with respect to Korea and Singapore and, to a lesser extent, Japan. As with figure 3.2, the Korea and Taiwan results are suggestive of the growing importance of processing trade among the middle-income East Asian countries.

Figure 3.6 shows that Japan lost market share in all of China's big export markets, with only trade with Australia holding up substantially better than predicted.

On the whole, the results illustrated in these charts show that the Eaton-Kortum (2002) model is a useful tool for organizing our thinking about

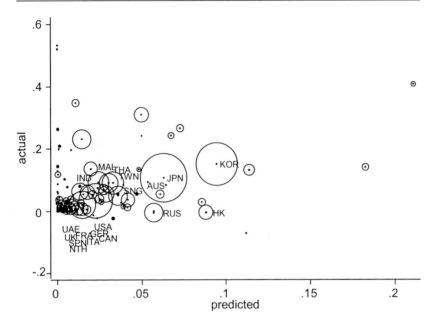

Fig. 3.3   Change in China's export market shares, 1996 to 2006, actual versus predicted, all markets

Note: See notes to figure 3.2.

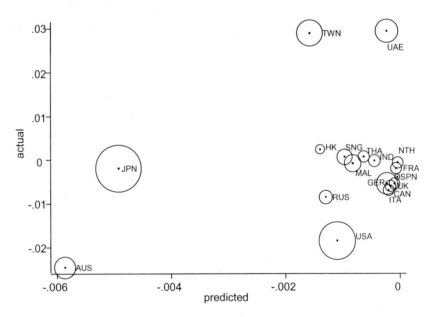

Fig. 3.4   Change in Korea's export market shares, 1996 to 2006, actual versus predicted, China's top twenty export markets

Note: See notes to figure 3.2.

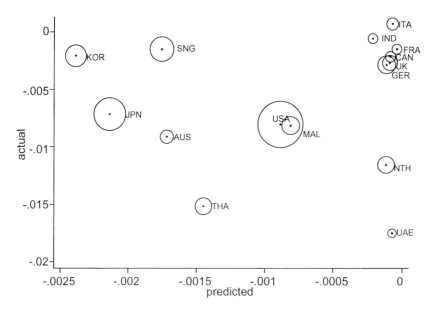

Fig. 3.5   Change in Taiwan's export market shares, 1996 to 2006, actual versus predicted, China's top twenty export markets (excluding Hong Kong)

Note: See notes to figure 3.2.

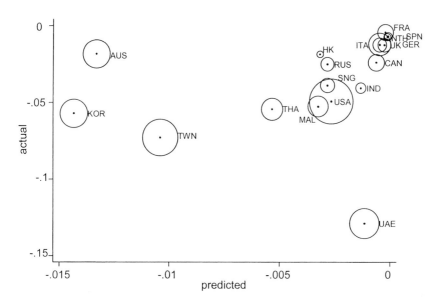

Fig. 3.6   Change in Japan's export market shares, 1996 to 2006, actual versus predicted, China's top twenty export markets

Note: See notes to figure 3.2.

changes in bilateral trade patterns. China's rise has had effects on its own market shares, and the market shares of its principal competitors, that are broadly consistent with the predictions of the model. The notable exceptions to this good fit are countries where China is involved in processing trade, where trade shares rose by more, or fell by less, than the Eaton-Kortum model would predict.

3.3.2   Specification of the Unit Value–Distance Relationship

As discussed in section 3.2.4, we are primarily interested in variation in Chinese export unit values across importing countries. The theory is silent about the appropriate degree of aggregation across products, and we would expect the composition effects to work across broad product categories: China should export heavy products to nearby markets and lighter goods to more distant markets. Nonetheless, there are two compelling reasons to analyze the predictions of the model using the most disaggregated data possible. The first reason is simply that different HS eight-digit categories are measured using different units, and it is literally meaningless to compare unit values measured as (for example) dollars/kilos and dollars/(number of shirts). The second reason is related, which is that there are systematic differences in unit values and per-unit transport costs even among goods measured in common physical units (e.g., dollars/[kilos of diamonds] and dollars/[kilos of coal]). Thus, in all specifications we will include product fixed effects that remove product-specific means and identify remaining parameters using solely cross-country variation.

Province of origin, transport mode, firm type, and trade type are characteristics of exports that are quite likely to be jointly determined with unit value and so cannot be considered exogenous to an equation that explains unit values. Feenstra and Spencer (2005) provide a model and analysis of Chinese export data that support this supposition although they focus on geographical variation within China rather than across China's export markets. These concerns motivate the following specification, where we pool across all characteristics of exports except product and destination:

$$(12) \qquad v_{ic} = \alpha_i + \beta_d d_c + \beta_y y_c + \text{error},$$

where

v_{ic} = log unit value of exports of product i from China to country c.

α_i = fixed effect for eight-digit HS code i.

d_c = distance of c from Beijing.

y_c = log real GDP per capita of c in 2004.

The fixed effect α_i will remove any average differences in unit values across products so that the estimated distance elasticity is meaningful. Note that export values are measured f.o.b, so they do not include transport charges.

The model predicts $\beta_d > 0$: across importers within an eight-digit commodity category, China will sell higher unit value goods to more distant importers. As an additional control motivated by the results of Schott (2004), we include per capita GDP of the importing country.

Notwithstanding the preceding comments about the endogeneity of customs regimes and firm types, preliminary data mining reveals large differences in unit values associated with these categories. This suggests that pooling across all such categories as done in equation (12) may cause aggregation bias. To address this issue, we estimate a model that has separate intercepts and slopes for different customs regimes and firm types. Letting these categories be indexed by j, this model is

$$(13) \qquad v_{ijc} = \alpha_i + \alpha_j + \sum_j (\beta_{jd} d_c) + \beta_y y_c + \text{error}.$$

We do not specify interactions on the GDP per capita variable because this effect is not our primary focus. Because of the endogeneity of the firm and trade type classifications, interpretation of the β_{jd}s in equation (13) will be more reduced form than the interpretation of the β_ds in equation (12).

We measure distance in two ways. The first is simply log kilometers from Beijing to the capital of the importing country, using great-circle distance. The second breaks distance down into two categories:

1–2,500 km	Korea, Taiwan, Hong Kong, Japan
2,500+ km	Rest of world

The motivation for this split can be seen in figure 3.7 which compactly illustrates a number of patterns in China's exports. Because of the Pacific Ocean, there is a natural break in distance at 2,500 kilometers, with four large trading partners (Korea, Taiwan, Japan, and Hong Kong) being less than this distance from Beijing and most other important trading partners, in particular the United States and Western Europe, being at least 5,000 kilometers away. Note that the limitations of our great-circle distance data makes Western Europe seem much closer than it would be for an ocean-going freighter. This caveat is not relevant in regressions where we use the binary distance indicator.

As noted in the preceding, interpretability of regression coefficients is problematic in equations (12) and (13) as we are pooling across such disparate goods. To address this, we split the sample in a number of ways:

1. All observations
2. Observations where unit is a count and where the count is at least two
3. Observations where unit is kilos
4. All of the preceding cuts restricted to manufactured goods

In addition, for each regression, we drop trade flows below \$10,000 to dampen the measurement error that always plagues unit values.

Appropriate estimation of equations (12) and (13) requires careful atten-

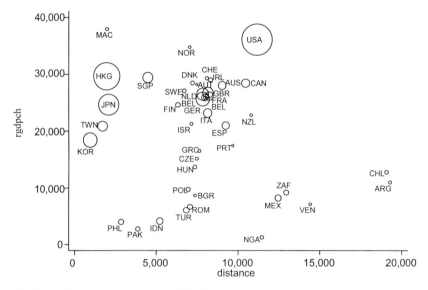

Fig. 3.7   China's export markets, 2006

Notes: The vertical axis is real GDP per capita, and the horizontal axis is distance in kilometers from Beijing. The size of circles is proportional to China's exports to indicated country. All markets where China sold at least $1 billion in 2006 are depicted.

tion to the structure of the data, which is an unbalanced panel with many (at least 1,500) products and relatively few (92) countries. The country-specific data are repeated many times in the sample, but the data does *not* have the structure of a "cluster sample" because each unit i has observations across many countries c. As discussed by Moulton (1990) and Wooldridge (2006), the appropriate estimator in such a model is random effects generalized least squares (GLS), where the random effects are country-specific. A refinement to GLS suggested by Wooldridge is to use a fully robust covariance matrix rather than assume spherical residuals, and we implement this in the following. Because we also have product fixed effects, our equations are estimated in a four-step procedure as follows:

1. Remove product-specific means from all the data using the within transformation.

2. Run pooled ordinary least squares (OLS) on the transformed data.

3. Quasi-difference the transformed data with respect to country-specific means, where the random effects quasi-differencing parameter $\phi \in [0,1)$ is a function of the OLS residuals from step 2.

4. Estimate the model on the quasi-differenced data by OLS, and calculate a robust covariance matrix.

Hansen (2007) shows theoretically that the robust covariance matrix for this mixed fixed effects-random effects model is consistent regardless of the relative size of the two dimensions of the panel. Hansen's Monte Carlo simulations confirm that the asymptotic formula is quite accurate for data dimensions substantially smaller than in our application.

In applying the preceding estimator to equation (13), we found that in every case, the estimated GLS quasi-differencing parameter ϕ was zero. Thus, for equation (13), the estimation technique is simply OLS with product fixed effects and a robust covariance matrix. We also estimated this equation using a different GLS procedure that allows for the error variance to differ by country. The GLS results were very close to the results of OLS with product fixed effects, so we do not report the GLS results to save space.

3.3.3   Estimation Results

Table 3.1 reports China's top twenty export destinations in 2006. While only 16 percent of Chinese exports are sent by air, there is wide variation across markets. The largest share of exports by air, 35 percent, goes to Malaysia and Singapore, a result that is suggestive of China's role in time-sensitive international production networks. A surprisingly (and suspiciously) high share of exports also goes to Hong Kong by air. See Feenstra et al. (1999) for a discussion of the difficulties of separating Chinese exports *to* Hong Kong and exports *through* Hong Kong. As always with aggregate international trade data, the importance of gravity (distance and country size) is clearly visible in table 3.1. We return to an analysis of the share of China's exports that are shipped by air in section 3.4.

Table 3.2 reports results of estimating various versions of equation (12). Focusing first on the full sample, the distance elasticity is 0.074, which is economically significant given the large variation in distance. But this effect is fragile across specifications ranging from 0.044 and statistically insignificant to 0.077. The indicator variable for distance greater than 2,500 kilometers is more consistent: in the full sample, the effect is to raise export unit values by 14.8 percent, and the effect ranges between 9.2 percent and 15.6 percent, depending on the sample. This effect is economically important but somewhat smaller than the distance effect on U.S. import unit values found by Harrigan (2006) and on U.S. export unit values by Baldwin and Harrigan (2007).

While it is not our main focus here, the small size and fragility of the effect of importer GDP per capita on unit values is striking, although consistent with the results of Baldwin and Harrigan (2007) on U.S. data. The overall effect of 0.04 to 0.06 is driven by a fairly large effect of 0.12 on goods measured in kilos and a near-zero effect for goods measured as a count.

Table 3.3 reports results of estimating two versions of equation (13). In the top panel, we show results with firm type interacted with the dummy "far," which is distance > 2,500 kilometers (the excluded dummy is near x state and collective firms). The second panel show results with customs regime interacted with far (the excluded dummy is near x other trade). The effect of importer real GDP per capita on export unit values is consistent with table 3.2.

Table 3.2   China export unit value regressions, 2006

	All products					
	All units		Unit = count, >1		Unit = kilos	
Log importer GDP per	0.059	0.061	−0.038	−0.033	0.122	0.126
capita	(5.82)	(6.08)	(−1.88)	(−1.65)	(12.3)	(12.6)
Log distance	0.074		0.050		0.077	
	(6.09)		(1.39)		(6.54)	
Distance > 2,500 km		0.148		0.144		0.156
		(6.61)		(2.14)		(6.91)
Random effects φ	0.92	0.92	0.88	0.88	0.89	0.88
HS eight-digit fixed						
effects		6,820		1,951		4,334
N		155,419		55,280		87,868

	Manufacturing products only					
	All units		Unit = count, >1		Unit = kilos	
Log importer GDP per	0.040	0.043	−0.045	−0.040	0.117	0.120
capita	(2.81)	(3.03)	(−2.00)	(−1.78)	(7.86)	(8.03)
Log distance	0.058		0.044		0.039	
	(2.94)		(1.02)		(2.08)	
Distance > 2,500 km		0.135		0.143		0.092
		(3.52)		(1.75)		(2.43)
Random effects φ	0.91	0.91	0.89	0.89	0.86	0.86
HS eight-digit fixed						
effects		3,608		1,538		1,644
N		95,534		43,477		41,497

Notes: Independent variable is log Chinese bilateral export unit value by Harmonized System (HS) eight-digit code and importer. The statistical model controls for fixed product effects and random country effects. The median partial differencing parameter for the random effects transformation is φ. Robust *t*-statistics are in parentheses. Observations with export value less than $10,000 excluded from sample. GDP = gross domestic product.

The coefficients on the interactions in table 3.3 are somewhat hard to interpret, so we turn immediately to table 3.4, which reports the linear combinations of interest and associated test statistics from table 3.3. The top panel shows that the distance effect is positive and statistically significant for both types of firms, with the effect a bit larger for state/collective firms than for foreign/private firms. The second panel shows a relatively large and robust effect for ordinary trade of around 0.10. The effect for processing trade is small and positive for goods measured as a count and zero for goods measured in kilos. There is a large negative effect of distance for the trade regime category "other," which accounts for just 4 percent of total exports.

Summarizing the results of this section, we conclude that there is a small but robust positive relationship between distance and export unit values. The

Table 3.3   **China export unit value regressions, 2006, with trade type and firm type controls**

	All observations			Manufacturing observations		
	All	Count	Kilos	All	Count	Kilos
Type of firm (state-collective and private-foreign)						
Log importer GDP	0.067	−0.010	0.117	0.048	−0.023	0.113
per capita	(27.3)	(−1.9)	(49.8)	(14.8)	(−3.9)	(34.0)
Far × state and	0.095	0.087	0.101	0.066	0.082	0.049
collective firms	(12.1)	(4.8)	(12.0)	(6.2)	(4.0)	(3.9)
Far × private and	0.103	0.100	0.118	0.065	0.066	0.083
foreign firms	(13.2)	(5.6)	(14.0)	(6.1)	(3.2)	(6.6)
Near × private and	0.029	0.068	0.024	0.029	0.029	0.059
foreign firms	(3.0)	(3.0)	(2.3)	(2.1)	(1.1)	(3.7)
HS eight-digit fixed						
effects	6,817	1,946	4,332	3,576	1,508	1,643
N	240,473	87,262	134,285	148,637	68,078	64,247
Type of customs regime (ordinary, processing, and other)						
Log importer GDP	0.053	−0.028	0.111	0.033	−0.037	0.103
per capita	(19.3)	(−4.8)	(42.1)	(9.0)	(−5.6)	(27.1)
Far × ordinary	−0.498	−0.480	−0.506	−0.542	−0.392	−0.690
trade	(−30.2)	(−15.7)	(−26.2)	(−25.5)	(−11.9)	(−24.1)
Near × ordinary	−0.615	−0.570	−0.641	−0.627	−0.491	−0.760
trade	(−35.4)	(−17.1)	(−31.8)	(−27.8)	(−13.5)	−25.4
Far × processing	−0.267	−0.195	−0.334	−0.273	−0.158	−0.392
trade	(−15.9)	(−6.4)	(−16.9)	(−12.6)	(−4.7)	−13.3
Near × processing	−0.315	−0.304	−0.321	−0.331	−0.258	−0.402
trade	(−16.8)	(−8.6)	(−14.8)	(−13.5)	(−6.6)	−12.4
Far × other trade	−0.217	−0.226	−0.215	−0.227	−0.149	−0.311
	(−12.2)	(−7.0)	(−10.3)	(−10.0)	(−4.3)	−10.2
HS eight-digit fixed						
effects	6,817	1,949	4,331	3,575	1,511	1,642
N	230,937	88,823	125,089	144,104	68,714	61,013

Notes: This table reports results from twelve regressions. Independent variable is log Chinese bilateral export unit value by Harmonized System (HS) eight-digit code and importing country. All regressions have product fixed effects and importer random effects. Robust *t*-statistics are in parentheses. Observations with export value less than $10,000 are excluded from sample. GDP = gross domestic product.

relationship only disappears for processing trade where the units are kilos. We hesitate to overinterpret the results of tables 3.3 and 3.4 because customs regime, trade type, and export unit value are jointly determined.

3.4   Air Shipment and Chinese Exports

The model developed in sections 3.2.1 and 3.2.2 highlighted the importance of shipping mode choice in determining bilateral trade patterns. The keys to the mechanism are the assumptions on the transport cost functions given by equations (6), (6′), and (6″). Our empirical analysis of export unit

Table 3.4   **Effects of distance on China export unit value, 2006**

	All observations			Manufacturing observations		
	All	Count	Kilos	All	Count	Kilos
Far × state and	0.095	0.087	0.101	0.066	0.082	0.049
collective firms	(12.1)	(4.8)	(12.0)	(6.2)	(4.0)	(3.9)
(Far – Near) ×	0.075	0.033	0.094	0.036	0.037	0.024
private foreign	(4.2)	(2.0)	(12.1)	(3.7)	(2.0)	(2.0)
firms						
(Far – Near) ×	0.116	0.089	0.135	0.085	0.099	0.070
ordinary trade	(16.9)	(5.7)	(18.1)	(9.1)	(5.6)	(6.4)
(Far – Near) ×	0.048	0.109	–0.014	0.058	0.101	0.010
processing trade	(4.4)	(5.3)	(1.1)	(4.0)	(4.3)	(0.5)
Far × other trade	–0.217	–0.226	–0.215	–0.227	–0.149	–0.311
	(–12.2)	(–7.0)	(–10.3)	(–10.0)	(–4.3)	(–10.2)

Notes: This table is based on table 3.3. Each cell represents the point estimate of a linear combination, and the test statistic (square root of a χ^2 test statistic) for the null that the linear combination equals zero. Robust *t*-statistics are in parentheses.

Table 3.5   **Shipment mode for Chinese exports, 2006**

	All firms	State and collective	Private and foreign
	A: Share of exports shipped by air		
All trade types	0.16	0.05	0.20
Ordinary	0.06	0.05	0.07
Processing	0.24	0.03	0.27
Other	0.14	0.11	0.17
	B: Share of total air shipments		
All trade types	1.00	0.07	0.93
Ordinary	0.16	0.05	0.12
Processing	0.80	0.01	0.79
Other	0.04	0.01	0.03

values in the previous section does not control for shipping mode because the core message of the model is that shipping mode and export unit value are jointly determined. Nonetheless, it is instructive to see how the air shipment choice is correlated with firm characteristics, which we do in table 3.5.

Panel A of table 3.5 is a cross-tab of firm type and customs regime and reports the share of exports in each cell that is shipped by air. Panel B of table 3.5 shows the share of total air shipments accounted for by each cell. The overall share of Chinese exports sent by air is fairly small at 16 percent, but this number masks a stark pattern: almost 80 percent of air shipment is processing trade by private and foreign firms. Over a quarter of the value of trade in this cell is sent by air, while the air share in other cells is negligible.

Clearly, timely delivery is very important for this type of trade. We conjecture that the reason for this revealed preference for timely delivery is that with a multistage production process, the cost of delay increases very rapidly in the number of stages and the complexity of production.[7]

3.5 Conclusion

There is little doubt that China has an overall comparative advantage in labor-intensive goods. In this paper, we have argued that understanding Chinese trade also requires accounting for *local* comparative advantage: products where China has a competitive advantage in some locations but not others.

In our formulation of Deardorff's (2004) concept of local comparative advantage, we focus on cost differences due to differences in transport costs and the transport intensity (weight) of goods. In the theory section, we showed that China could be expected to have a comparative advantage in heavy goods in nearby markets and lighter goods in more distant markets. This theory motivates a simple empirical prediction: within a product, China's export unit values should be increasing in distance. We find strong evidence for this effect in our empirical analysis. Splitting up China's export markets into two groups, one nearby (Korea, Taiwan, Hong Kong, and Japan) and one further away, we find that the average unit value of exports sent beyond the nearby group is about 15 percent higher.[8]

We also showed that the Eaton-Kortum (2002) model implies that as China grows, it will gain market share most quickly in markets where it is already competitive, a prediction strongly supported by looking at the growth in China's aggregate bilateral export market shares between 1996 and 2006. A corollary is that China's competitors in export markets will be most squeezed where China starts out with a high market share, a prediction that finds some support in our analysis of how Korea, Taiwan, and Japan export performance has fared in the face of the China's expansion.

Beyond its relevance to Chinese trade, we believe this paper makes the broader point that trade economists should strive to escape the powerful field exerted by the gravity model. Understanding the effect of distance on economic activity is an important intellectual and policy issue, and much can be accomplished outside the simple gravity framework.

7. Harrigan and Venables (2006) model this effect in detail.
8. We refer here to the coefficients in the top panel of table 3.2.

References

Alvarez, Fernando, and Robert E. Lucas Jr. 2007. General equilibrium analysis of the Eaton-Kortum model of international trade. *Journal of Monetary Economics* 54:1726–68.

Anderson, James E., and Eric van Wincoop. 2003. Gravity with gravitas: A solution to the border puzzle. *American Economic Review* 93 (1): 170–92.

Baldwin, Richard E., and James Harrigan. 2007. Zeros, quality, and space: Trade theory and trade evidence. NBER Working Paper no. 13214. Cambridge, MA: National Bureau of Economic Research, July.

China Customs Statistics. 1997–2007. (Data set). Beijing, China: Customs General Administration, Statistics Department (producer); Hong Kong, China: China Customs Statistics Information Center (distributor).

Deardorff, Alan. 2004. Local comparative advantage: Trade costs and the pattern of trade. RSIE Working paper no. 500. Ann Arbor, MI: Research Seminar in Economics.

Eaton, Jonathan, and Samuel Kortum. 2002. Technology, geography, and trade. *Econometrica* 70 (5): 1741–79.

Evans, Carolyn E., and James Harrigan. 2005. Distance, time, and specialization: Lean retailing in general equilibrium. *American Economic Review* 95 (1): 292–313.

Feenstra, Robert C., Wen Hai, Wing T. Woo, and Shunli Yao. 1999. Discrepancies in international data: An application to China-Hong Kong entrepôt trade. *American Economic Review: Papers and Proceedings* 89 (2): 338–43.

Feenstra, Robert C., and Gordon Hanson. 2004. Intermediaries in entrepôt trade: Hong Kong re-exports of Chinese goods. *Journal of Economics & Management Strategy* 13 (1): 3–35.

Feenstra, Robert C., and Barbara J. Spencer. 2005. Contractual versus generic outsourcing: The role of proximity. NBER Working Paper no. 11885. Cambridge, MA: National Bureau of Economic Research, December.

Hallak, Juan Carlos. 2006. Product quality and the direction of trade. *Journal of International Economics* 68 (1): 238–65.

Harrigan, James. 2003. Specialization and the volume of trade: Do the data obey the laws? In *The handbook of international trade,* ed. James Harrigan and Kwan Choi, 85–118. Oxford, UK: Basil Blackwell.

———. 2006. Airplanes and comparative advantage. NBER Working Paper no. 11688. Cambridge, MA: National Bureau of Economic Research.

Harrigan, James, and Anthony J. Venables. 2006. Timeliness and agglomeration. *Journal of Urban Economics* 59:300–316.

Hansen, Christian B. 2007. Asymptotic properties of a robust variance matrix estimator for panel data when T is large. *Journal of Econometrics* 141:597–620.

Hummels, David. 2001. Time as a trade barrier. Purdue University. Unpublished Manuscript. http://www.mgmt.purdue.edu/faculty/hummelsd/.

Hummels, David, and Peter Klenow. 2005. The variety and quality of a nation's exports. *American Economic Review* 95 (3): 704–23.

Hummels, David, and Alexandre Skiba. 2004. Shipping the good apples out? An empirical confirmation of the Alchian-Allen conjecture. *Journal of Political Economy* 112 (6): 1384–1402.

Limão, Nuno, and Anthony J. Venables. 2002. Geographical disadvantage: A Heckscher-Ohlin-Von Thunen model of international specialisation. *Journal of International Economics* 58 (2): 239–63.

Moulton, Brent R. 1990. An illustration of a pitfall in estimating the effects of aggregate variables on micro units. *Review of Economics and Statistics* 72 (1): 334–38.

Schott, Peter K. 2004. Across-product versus within-product specialization in international trade. *Quarterly Journal of Economics* 119 (2): 647–78.

Silberberg, Eugene. 1978. *The structure of economics: A mathematical analysis.* New York: McGraw Hill.

Wooldridge, Jeffrey W. 2006. Cluster sample methods in applied econometrics: An extended analysis. Michigan State University. Unpublished Manuscript. http://www.msu.edu/~ec/faculty/wooldridge/current%20research.htm.

Comment   Chong Xiang

The explosive growth in China's trade with the rest of the world has been one of the hallmark events for globalization over the last decade. Looking ahead, will this growth continue? How will this growth affect China's neighboring countries and trading partners? In addition, which country and which industry will be affected the most? The authors have delivered timely and convincing answers to these questions that have gripped the attention of economists and policymakers alike from a novel angle: the role of geography and trade costs in shaping China's patterns of trade. Geography and trade costs are especially relevant for China's neighboring countries because these countries have different geographical locations relative to China and so are likely to face different degrees of competition from China.

To illustrate the role of geography, the authors consider trade costs that are proportional to weight and independent of value. There are "light," or high-quality goods, and "heavy," or low-quality goods. A super-premium delicious apple and a rotten apple may have very different values, but they cost the same to ship if they weigh the same. This suggests that light goods are more immune to the effects of trade costs over long distances so that China has a comparative advantage in light goods relative to heavy goods in distant markets. The authors deliver this point clearly and concisely in a partial-equilibrium setting.

The authors then consider a general-equilibrium setting à la Eaton and Kortum (2002), where every national market around the world is contended by firms located in each country and the lowest-cost firm wins the entire national market. The authors then rigorously show that as distance increases, the probability that China exports a heavy good decreases relative to the probability of exporting a light good; conditional on being successfully exported, the price of a heavy good increases relative to the price of a light good. Both imply that over long distances, light goods account for larger

Chong Xiang is an associate professor of economics at Purdue University.

shares of China's exports. As light goods have high qualities and high prices, the unit value of China's exports increases in distance. In addition, as air shipping is expensive relative to surface shipping, light goods are more likely to be air-shipped than heavy goods, and so China ships a larger fraction of its exports to distant markets by air.

A bonus of the general equilibrium setting is the predictions concerning China's growth: (a) it is the largest in the markets where China already has a substantial presence; and (b) China's growth leads to the biggest market share losses for the countries that have large market shares where China also has large market shares. These simple, elegant predictions are also parsimonious: they explain the changes in the market shares for China and her trading partners around the globe using nothing more than the allocation of market shares prior to China's growth. These predictions are also broadly consistent with data! The predicted changes in China's market shares and the actual changes have a (weighted) correlation coefficient of 0.46. The predicted changes in the market shares of China's neighboring countries are also positively correlated with the actual changes.

To investigate the relation between unit values for China's exports and distance, the authors employ a rich data set that breaks down China's exports by eight-digit Harmonized System (HS) codes × Chinese customs regions × types of exporting firms × trade regimes. Consistent with the authors' predictions, a 1 percent increase in distance raises the unit value by 6 percent to 12 percent, and the results are strongest for the markets that are more than 2,500 kilometers away from China, for the products whose units are in kilograms (versus those measured in counts), for state and collective firms, and for ordinary trade (versus processing trade).

As one reads the paper, one cannot help being struck by how often processing trade contributes to data "anomalies" at odds with the authors' predictions. (a) Malaysia, Taiwan, and Thailand are "large positive outliers" for the predictions of the growth in China's market shares, "probably reflecting their participation in processing trade . . ." (b) South Korea and Taiwan are also outliers for the predictions of the loss in market shares by China's neighboring countries and these "are suggestive of the growing importance of processing trade among the middle-income East Asian countries." (c) The largest shares of air shipping in China's exports go to Malaysia and Singapore, "a result that is suggestive of China's role in time-sensitive international production networks" (i.e., processing trade). (d) The relation between unit values of China's exports and distance is much weaker for processing trade than for ordinary trade. (e) Processing trade by private and foreign firms accounts for over 80 percent of air shipping in China's exports. These findings point to the significance of processing trade in determining China's comparative advantage and shaping China's trading relationships with her neighboring countries. Although the authors have run out of space in this paper to further investigate the role of processing trade, they have put the issue on the table. The significance of processing trade, and the payoff of understanding it, is likely to grow as China continues her expansion and the world deepens its integration.

Reference

Eaton, Jonathan, and Samuel Kortum. 2002. Technology, geography, and trade. *Econometrica* 70 (5): 1741–79.

4

China and the Manufacturing Exports of Other Developing Countries

Gordon H. Hanson and Raymond Robertson

4.1 Introduction

The explosive growth of China's economy has been extraordinary. Between 1990 and 2005, China's exports increased by twenty-five times in real terms, compared to an increase of about four times in the twelve largest exporting nations (table 4.1). As of 2005, China's exports accounted for 25 percent of the total exports of all countries outside of the top twelve.[1]

What has made China's emergence potentially disruptive is that the country is highly specialized in manufacturing. Over the period 2000 to 2005, manufacturing accounted for 32 percent of China's gross domestic product (GDP) and 89 percent of its merchandise exports, making it more specialized in the sector than any other large developing economy (table 4.2). In consumer goods and other labor-intensive manufactures, China has become a major source of supply, pushing down world product prices. Meanwhile, China has contributed to a boom in demand for commodities, leading to increases in the prices of metals, minerals, and farm goods.

The impact of China's emergence on other developing countries is just beginning to be appreciated (Devlin, Estevadeordal, and Rodriguez-Clare

Gordon H. Hanson is director of the Center on Pacific Economies and a professor of economics at the School of International Relations and Pacific Studies, University of California, San Diego, and a research associate of the National Bureau of Economic Research. Raymond Robertson is an associate professor of economics at Macalester College.

We thank Irene Brambilla, Ernesto Lopez Cordoba, Robert Feenstra, David Hummels, Daniel Lederman, Marcelo Olarreaga, Guillermo Perry, and Christian Volpe for helpful comments.

1. This share excludes Hong Kong and Singapore, which are entrepôt economies and whose exports contain a substantial share of reexports.

Table 4.1   Total exports, by country group (billions of 2000 $U.S.)

Exporter	1990	1991	1992	1993	1994	1995	1996	1997	1998	1999	2000	2001	2002	2003	2004	2005
China	35.9	72.0	89.7	168.2	211.5	250.8	269.4	297.5	296.3	324.8	388.1	389.8	464.1	582.3	749.0	897.7
Sample of ten developing country exporters	79.6	155.0	180.3	208.7	266.1	330.0	360.4	389.6	393.6	422.6	489.5	464.5	491.4	554.3	644.4	696.6
Twelve largest industrialized exporters	1,127.1	1,561.6	1,889.9	2,068.6	2,693.9	3,273.8	3,300.4	3,314.6	3,299.1	3,322.6	3,456.9	3,186.7	3,251.1	3,614.6	4,175.2	4,359.2
Other exporters (developing and developed)	371.6	478.6	563.4	627.7	794.3	937.9	1,006.6	1,034.2	968.4	994.5	1,133.7	1,086.7	1,148.2	1,355.7	1,642.6	1,878.4

Notes: Sample of ten developing country exporters is Hungary, Malaysia, Mexico, Pakistan, The Philippines, Poland, Romania, Sri Lanka, Thailand, and Turkey. The twelve largest industrialized exporters (as of 2005) are Canada, France, Germany, Italy, Japan, Korea, The Netherlands, Spain, Switzerland, Taiwan, the United States, and the United Kingdom; other exporting nations excludes Hong Kong and Singapore.

Table 4.2   Specialization in manufacturing for developing countries

Country	Manufacturing (% merchandise exports)	Manufacturing (% GDP)	GDP per capita (2000 U.S.$)	Population (millions)
China	88.21	32.28	979	1,260.3
The Philippines	85.83	22.56	996	75.8
Pakistan	84.96	15.91	531	138.4
Hungary	83.09	23.48	4,591	10.2
Mexico	82.65	19.96	5,682	97.6
Turkey	80.14	15.48	2,915	67.3
Romania	79.85	24.11	1,805	22.2
Poland	78.32	18.66	4,356	38.4
Malaysia	78.26	30.23	3,894	23.0
India	75.30	15.79	458	1,015.2
Sri Lanka	74.93	16.12	838	18.9
Thailand	74.23	32.60	2,085	61.4
Ukraine	68.89	24.99	691	49.2
Morocco	62.55	17.05	1,240	27.9
South Africa	56.22	19.36	3,072	43.6
Brazil	54.18	—	3,441	173.9
Indonesia	52.15	27.62	842	206.4
Vietnam	46.47	18.47	406	78.4
Senegal	42.64	12.44	424	10.4
Egypt, Arab Republic	35.69	18.54	1,456	67.4
Guatemala	34.53	13.23	1,694	11.2
Colombia	34.25	15.49	2,039	42.1
Argentina	31.36	19.91	7,488	36.9
Zimbabwe	28.34	15.50	586	12.5
Kenya	23.43	11.79	420	30.7
Russian Federation	23.18	17.48	1,811	146.0
Kazakhstan	22.61	15.10	1,329	15.0
Peru	20.44	15.99	2,078	25.9
Cote d'Ivoire	18.17	19.81	621	16.6
Chile	16.15	19.45	4,924	15.4
Venezuela	12.70	18.82	4,749	24.3
Saudi Arabia	10.61	10.20	9,086	20.7
Ecuador	9.93	12.00	1,368	12.3
Iran, Islamic Republic	8.93	12.66	1,634	63.6
Syrian Arab Republic	8.36	10.30	1,128	16.8

Notes: This table shows data for all countries with more than 10 million inhabitants and per capita gross domestic product (GDP) greater than $400 and less than $10,000 (in 2000 prices). Figures are averages over the period 2000–2005. Dash indicates not available.

2005; Eichengreen and Tong 2005; Lopez Cordoba, Micco, and Molina 2005). In the 1980s and 1990s, international trade became the engine of growth for much of the developing world. Trade liberalization and market-oriented reform in Asia and Latin America steered the regions toward greater specialization in exports. There is a popular conception that for non-oil-exporting developing countries, expanding export production has meant specializing in manufacturing. But in actuality, there is considerable heterogeneity in the production structures of these economies, which means there is variation in national exposure to China's industrial expansion.

Even excluding oil exporters and very poor countries, there are many countries that specialize in primary commodities. In Chile, Côte d'Ivoire, Kenya, and Peru, for instance, manufacturing accounts for less than 25 percent of merchandise exports (table 4.2). One might expect this group to have been most helped by China's growth, with the commodity boom lifting their terms of trade. Other countries have diversified export production, spanning agriculture, mining, and manufacturing. In Argentina, Brazil, Colombia, Egypt, Indonesia, and Vietnam, manufacturing accounts for 30 percent to 55 percent of merchandise exports. For this group, China may represent a mixed blessing, increasing the prices of some of the goods they produce and decreasing the prices of others. A third group of countries is highly specialized in manufacturing. In Hungary, Mexico, Pakistan, The Philippines, and Turkey, manufacturing accounts for more than 80 percent of merchandise exports. This last group includes the countries most likely to be adversely affected by China as it has become a rival source of supply in their primary destination markets. Between 1993 and 2005, China's share of total imports rose from 5 percent to 15 percent in the United States and from 4 percent to 12 percent in the European Union.

In this paper, we examine the impact of China's growth on developing countries that specialize in export manufacturing. Using the gravity model of trade, we decompose bilateral trade into components associated with demand conditions in importing countries, supply conditions in exporting countries, and bilateral trade costs. In theory, growth in China's export-supply capabilities would allow it to capture market share in the countries to which it exports its output, possibly reducing demand for imports from other countries that also supply these markets. We calculate the export demand shock that China's growth has meant for other developing countries, as implied by gravity model estimation results.

To isolate economies that are most exposed to China's manufacturing exports, we select developing countries that are also highly specialized in manufacturing. After dropping rich countries, very poor countries, and small countries, we identify ten medium-to-large developing economies for which manufacturing represents more than 75 percent of merchandise exports: Hungary, Malaysia, Mexico, Pakistan, The Philippines, Poland, Romania,

Sri Lanka, Thailand, and Turkey.[2] This group includes a diverse set of countries in terms of geography and stage of development, hopefully making our results broadly applicable. We focus on developing countries specialized in manufacturing as, for this group, the impact of China on their production activities is largely captured by trade in manufactures. Manufacturing is also a sector for which the gravity model is well suited theoretically.

In section 4.2, we use a standard monopolistic-competition model of trade to develop an estimation framework. The specification is a regression of bilateral sectoral imports on importer country dummies, exporter country dummies, and factors that affect trade costs (bilateral distance, sharing a land border, sharing a common language, belonging to a free-trade area, and import tariffs). When these importer and exporter dummies are allowed to vary by sector and by year, they can be interpreted as functions of structural parameters and country-specific variables that determine a country's export supply and import demand. Changes in import-demand conditions can be decomposed into two parts, one that captures changes in income levels in import markets and another that captures changes in sectoral import price indexes for those markets, which are themselves a function of other countries' export supply dummies.

In section 4.3, we report coefficient estimates based on our framework. The data for the analysis come from the United Nations' (UN) COMTRADE database and the Trade Analysis and Information System (TRAINS) data set, which cover the period from 1995 to 2005. We estimate country-sector-year import dummies, country-sector-year export dummies, and sector-year trade cost elasticities using data on a large set of trading economies that account for much of world trade. We begin by reporting estimated sectoral exporter dummy variables for the ten developing-country exporters vis-à-vis China. For nine of the ten countries, export supply dummies are strongly positively correlated with China's, suggesting that their comparative advantage is relatively similar to that of China. The results also describe how each country's export supply capacities have evolved over time. Relative to each of the ten countries, the growth in China's export supply capabilities has been dramatic.

The main results, presented in section 4.4, suggest that had China's export supply capacity been constant over the 1995 to 2005 period, export demand would have been 0.6 percent to 1.8 percent higher in the ten countries studied. The impact is somewhat larger when excluding resource intensive industries or when focusing on industries in which China's revealed comparative advantage appears to be strongest (apparel, footwear, electronics, toys). For

2. In table 4.2, it is apparent India would also satisfy our criteria. We exclude India because its recent growth represents another potentially important global economic shock for other developing countries.

developing countries highly specialized in manufacturing, it appears China's expansion has represented only a modest negative shock.

It is important to note that our results do not represent a general equilibrium analysis of China's impact on other developing economies. China's export growth may have increased the number of product varieties available to these countries, thereby improving consumer welfare (Broda and Weinstein 2005), or had positive effects on the demand for nonmanufacturing output. Our approach does not account for changes in consumer welfare associated with changes in product variety or nonmanufacturing prices. Nevertheless, the results give a sense of the extent to which China is in competition with other large developing country exporters for market share abroad.

By way of conclusion, in section 4.5, we discuss what China's continued growth may mean for manufacturing-oriented developing countries.

4.2   Empirical Specification

Consider a standard monopolistic model of international trade, as in Anderson and van Wincoop (2004) or Feenstra (2004). Let there be J countries and N manufacturing sectors, where each sector consists of a large number of product varieties. All consumers have identical Cobb-Douglas preferences over constant elasticity of substitution (CES) sectoral composites of product varieties, where in each sector n there are I_n varieties of n produced, with country j producing I_{nj} varieties. There are increasing returns to scale in the production of each variety. In equilibrium, each variety is produced by a monopolistically-competitive firm and I_n is large, such that the price for each variety is a constant markup over marginal cost. Free entry drives profits to zero, equating price with average cost.

Consider the variation in product prices across countries. We allow for iceberg transport costs in shipping goods between countries and for import tariffs. The cost, insurance, and freight (c.i.f.) price of variety i in sector n produced by country j and sold in country k is then

$$(1) \qquad P_{injk} = \left(\frac{\sigma_n}{\sigma_n - 1} \right) w_{nj} t_{nk} (d_{jk})^{\gamma_n},$$

where P_{inj} is the free-on-board (f.o.b.) price of product i in sector n manufactured in country j; σ_n is the constant elasticity of substitution between any pair of varieties in sector n; w_{nj} is unit production cost in sector n for exporter j; t_{nk} is 1 plus the ad valorem tariff in importer k on imports of n (assumed constant for all exporters that do not share a free trade area with importer k); d_{jk} is distance between exporter j and importer k; and γ_n is the elasticity of transport costs with respect to distance for goods in sector n.

Given the elements of the model, the total value of exports of goods in sector n by exporter j to importer k can be written as,

(2)
$$X_{njk} = \mu_n Y_k I_{nj} P_{njk}^{1-\sigma_n} G_{nk}^{\sigma_n - 1},$$

where μ_n is the expenditure share on sector n, and G_{nk} is the price index for goods in sector n in importer k. Equation (2) reduces to

(3)
$$X_{njk} = \frac{\mu_n Y_k I_{nj}[w_{nj}\tau_{njk}(d_{jk})^{\gamma_n}]^{1-\sigma_{n=1}}}{\sum_{h=1}^{H} I_{nh}[w_{nh}\tau_{nhk}(d_{hk})^{\gamma_n}]^{1-\sigma_n}},$$

which can be written in log form as

(3′)
$$\ln X_{njk} = \ln \mu_n + \ln \frac{Y_k}{\sum_{h=1}^{H} I_{nh}[w_{nh}\tau_{nhk}(d_{hk})^{\gamma_n}]^{1-\sigma_n}}$$
$$+ \ln(I_{nj}w_{nj}^{1-\sigma_n}) + (1 - \sigma_n)\ln\tau_{njk} + \gamma_n(1 - \sigma_n)\ln d_{jk}.$$

Regrouping terms in (3′), and allowing for measurement error in trade values, we obtain

(4)
$$\ln X_{njk} = \theta_n + m_{nk} + s_{nj} + \beta_{1n}\ln\tau_{jk} + \beta_{2n}\ln d_{jk} + \varepsilon_{njk}.$$

In equation (4), we see that there are five sets of factors that affect country j's exports to country k in sector n. The first term ($\theta_n = \ln\mu_n$) captures preference shifters specific to sector n; the second term ($m_{nk} = \ln\{Y_k/\sum_{h=1}^{H} I_{nh}[w_{nh}\tau_{nhk}(d_{hk})^{\gamma_n}]^{1-\sigma_n}\}$) captures demand shifters in sector n and importer k (which are a function of importer k's income and supply shifters for other countries that also export to k); the third term [$s_{nj} = \ln(I_{nj}w_{nj}^{1-\sigma_n})$] captures supply shifters in sector n for exporter j (which reflect exporter j's production costs and the number of varieties it produces in the sector); the fourth and fifth terms [where $\beta_{1n} = 1 - \sigma_n$ and $\beta_{2n} = \gamma_n(1 - \sigma_n)$] capture trade costs specific to exporter j and importer k (which in the empirical analysis we measure using import tariffs, bilateral distance, whether countries share a common language, whether countries share a land border, and whether countries belong to a free-trade area); and the final term (ε_{njk}) is a residual. Exporter j's shipments to importer k would expand if importer k's income increases, production costs increase or the number of varieties produced decreases in other countries that supply importer k, exporter j's supply capacity expands, or bilateral trade costs decrease.

Our first empirical exercise is to estimate equation (4). Then we use the coefficient estimates to examine the role of China in contributing to changes in import demand in other countries. To motivate this approach, consider import-demand conditions in country k, as embodied in the importer dummy variables in equation (4). In theory,

(5)
$$m_{nk} = \ln Y_k - \ln\left(\sum_{h=1}^{H} I_{nh}w_{nh}^{1-\sigma_n}\tau_{nhk}^{1-\sigma_n}d_{hk}^{\beta_n}\right),$$

which captures average expenditure per imported variety by country k in sector n. Import-demand conditions in k are a function of income in k, export supply conditions in k's trading partners (embodied in the number of varieties they produce and their production costs), and k's bilateral trade costs. Average expenditure per variety in country k would decrease if the number of varieties produced globally increases (because a given sectoral expenditure level would be spread over more varieties) or production costs in other countries increases (which would deflect expenditure away from their varieties). Using equation (4), we can write equation (5) as,

$$(6) \qquad m_{nk} = \ln Y_k - \ln\left(\sum_{h=1}^{H} e^{\hat{s}_{nh}}\tau_{nhk}^{\hat{\beta}_{1n}}d_{hk}^{\hat{\beta}_{2n}}\right),$$

where $\hat{s}_{nh}$, $\hat{\beta}_{1n}$, and $\hat{\beta}_{2n}$ are ordinary least squares (OLS) coefficient estimates from equation (4).[3] Over time, import-demand conditions in k will change as its income changes, its bilateral trade costs change, or export supply conditions in its trading partners change. As China's export-supply capacity in sector n improves (due either to increases in the number of varieties it produces or decreases in its production costs), average expenditure per imported variety in country k would fall, leading to a decrease in the demand for imports from k's trading partners.

Following this logic, we construct the implied change in demand for imports by country k associated with changes in China's export supply capacity. Actual import-demand conditions in sector n for country k at time t are

$$(7) \qquad m_{nkt} = \ln Y_{kt} - \ln\left(\sum_{h\neq c}^{H} e^{\hat{s}_{nht}}\tau_{nhkt}^{\hat{\beta}_{1n}}d_{hk}^{\hat{\beta}_{2n}} + e^{\hat{s}_{nct}}\tau_{nckt}^{\hat{\beta}_{1n}}d_{ck}^{\hat{\beta}_{2n}}\right),$$

where c indexes China. Suppose China had experienced no growth in its export supply capacity between time 0 and time t. The counterfactual import-demand term for country k would then be

$$(8) \qquad \tilde{m}_{nkt} = \ln Y_{kt} - \ln\left(\sum_{h\neq c}^{H} e^{\hat{s}_{nht}}\tau_{nhkt}^{\hat{\beta}_{1n}}d_{hk}^{\hat{\beta}_{2n}} + e^{\hat{s}_{nc0}}\tau_{nckt}^{\hat{\beta}_{1n}}d_{ck}^{\hat{\beta}_{2n}}\right),$$

For each importing country in each sector, we calculate the value,

$$(9) \qquad \tilde{m}_{nkt} - m_{nkt} = -\left[\ln\left(\sum_{h\neq c}^{H} e^{\hat{s}_{nht}}\tau_{nhkt}^{\hat{\beta}_{1n}}d_{hk}^{\hat{\beta}_{2n}} + e^{\hat{s}_{nc0}}\tau_{nckt}^{\hat{\beta}_{1n}}d_{ck}^{\hat{\beta}_{2n}}\right)\right.$$
$$\left. - \ln\left(\sum_{h\neq c}^{H} e^{\hat{s}_{nht}}\tau_{nhkt}^{\hat{\beta}_{1n}}d_{hk}^{\hat{\beta}_{2n}} + e^{\hat{s}_{nct}}\tau_{nckt}^{\hat{\beta}_{1n}}d_{ck}^{\hat{\beta}_{2n}}\right)\right],$$

3. One might imagine estimating equation (4) subject to the constraint in equation (6). In practice, imposing such nonlinear constraints would greatly complicate the regression analysis. As a simple check on whether the constraints on the value of m_{nk} appear to be satisfied in the data, we estimate equation (6) using OLS (after first estimating equation [4]), the results for which are reported in table 4.4. In most specifications, the coefficient on log income ranges between 0.5 and 1.0, and the coefficient on the import price index (constructed from the coefficient estimates) is –0.3 to –0.5. These coefficient signs and magnitudes are roughly consistent with theory.

which shows the amount by which import demand in k would have differed at time t had China's export supply capacity remained unchanged between time 0 and time t.

We refer to the quantity in equation (9) as the counterfactual change in import demand in country k and sector n. For each of the ten developing country exporters, we calculate the weighted average of equation (9) across importers and sectors. The resulting value is the difference in the demand for a country's exports implied by growth in China's export supply capacity. An exporter will be more exposed to China's growth the more its exports are concentrated in goods for which China's export supply capacity has expanded and the more it trades with countries with which China has relatively low trade costs. Obviously, this counterfactual exercise is not general equilibrium in nature and should be interpreted with caution. Still, it may be useful for gauging which export producers have been more exposed to export competition from China.

One problem with estimating equation (4) is that at the sectoral level, there is zero trade between many country pairs.[4] Santos Silva and Tenreyro (2006) propose a Poisson pseudo-maximum likelihood (PML) estimator to deal with zero observations in the gravity model. In our application, this approach is subject to an incidental-parameters problem (Wooldridge 2002). While in a Poisson model it is straightforward to control for the presence of unobserved fixed effects, it is difficult in this and many other nonlinear settings to obtain consistent estimates of these effects. Because, at the sectoral level, most exporters trade with no more than a few dozen countries, PML estimates of exporter and importer country dummies may be inconsistent.

Our approach is to estimate equation (4) using OLS for a set of medium to large exporters (Organization for Economic Cooperation and Development [OECD] countries plus larger developing countries, which together account for approximately 90 percent of world manufacturing exports) and medium-to-large importers (which together account for approximately 90 percent of world manufacturing imports). For bilateral trade between larger countries, there are relatively few zero trade values. Because we do not account explicitly for zero bilateral trade in the data, we are left with unresolved concerns about the consistency of the parameter estimates, which the trade literature has only recently begun to address.[5]

4.3   Gravity Estimation Results

The trade data for the analysis come from the UN COMTRADE database and cover manufacturing imports over the period 1995 to 2005. We examine

---

4. Zero bilateral trade values further complicate estimating equation (4) subject to the constraint in equation (6).
5. See Helpman, Melitz, and Rubinstein (2007).

bilateral trade at the four-digit HS level for the union of the forty largest manufacturing export industries in each of the ten developing-country exporters.[6] The forty industries account for the majority of manufacturing exports in the ten manufacturing exporters, ranging from 71 percent to 90 percent for seven of the ten countries (The Philippines, Mexico, Turkey, Malaysia, Romania, Sri Lanka, Pakistan) and from 48 percent to 62 percent in the three others (Hungary, Poland, Thailand). The tariff data, which are based on Robertson (2007), come from the TRAINS database and are the simple averages of available tariffs at the ten-digit HS level within each four-digit industry. We use the tariffs that are most applicable to each sector-country pair. For some country pairs, these are the importer's most-favored nation (MFN) tariffs; for other pairs (e.g., North American Free Trade Agreement [NAFTA] members), it is tariffs governed by a regional trade agreement; and for others (e.g., United States-Israel), it is tariffs governed by a bilateral trade agreement.[7]

We estimate the gravity equation in equation (4) on a year-by-year basis, allowing coefficients on exporter-country dummies, importer-country dummies, and trade costs to vary by sector and year. The output from the regression exercise is for each sector a panel of exporter- and importer-country dummy variables, trade cost coefficients, intercepts, and residuals. The country-sector dummies are the deviation from U.S. sectoral mean trade by year (as the United States in the excluded country in all regressions). For these coefficients to be comparable across time, the conditioning set for a given sector (i.e., the set of comparison countries) must be constant. For each sector, we limit the sample to bilateral trading partners that have positive trade in every year during the sample period.[8]

4.3.1   Summary of Coefficient Estimates

To provide some background on the industries included in the sample, table 4.3 shows the five largest industries in terms of manufacturing exports for each of the ten developing-country exporters. For nine of the countries (all except Hungary), manufacturing exports are concentrated in a handful of industries, with the top five industries accounting for at least 20 percent of merchandise exports, and for five of the countries, the top five industries account for at least 30 percent of merchandise exports. For seven of the countries, at least one of their top five export industries is also one that accounts for at least 2 percent of China's manufacturing exports.

The regression results for equation (4) involve a large amount of output. In each year, we estimate over 10,000 country-sector exporter coefficients

---

6. Choosing a subset of industries helps keep the dimension of the estimation manageable.
7. We replace missing tariff data with interpolated values based on nonmissing tariff data. See Robertson (2007).
8. This restriction may introduce selection bias into the estimation.

Table 4.3 **Major export industries in ten developing countries**

Country	HS4	Description	Manufacturing rank	Share of country's total exports	Share of China's total exports
Hungary	6204	Female suits	1	0.035	0.026
	6403	Footwear	2	0.026	0.024
	8544	Wire	3	0.023	0.003
	2710	Non-crude oil	4	0.022	0.013
	8708	Motor vehicle parts	5	0.020	0.001
Malaysia	2709	Crude oil	1	0.103	0.048
	8542	Electric circuits	2	0.087	0.001
	4403	Rough wood	3	0.060	0.001
	8527	Receivers	4	0.050	0.023
	4407	Sawn wood	5	0.038	0.001
Mexico	2709	Crude oil	1	0.219	0.048
	8703	Motor vehicles	2	0.066	0.000
	8708	Motor vehicle parts	3	0.054	0.001
	8544	Wire	4	0.041	0.003
	8407	Engines	5	0.036	0.000
Pakistan	5205	Cotton yarn	1	0.186	0.002
	5201	Cotton	2	0.097	0.004
	5208	Cotton fabrics	3	0.063	0.010
	6302	House linens	4	0.061	0.010
	4203	Leather apparel	5	0.056	0.011
The Philippines	8542	Electric circuits	1	0.124	0.001
	1513	Coconut oil	2	0.037	0.000
	8471	Data processing machines	3	0.031	0.005
	2603	Copper	4	0.029	0.000
	7403	Refined copper	5	0.027	0.000
Poland	2701	Coal	1	0.072	0.008
	7403	Refined copper	2	0.047	0.000
	6204	Female suits	3	0.030	0.026
	9403	Furniture n.e.s.	4	0.025	0.003
	6203	Not knit male suits	5	0.022	0.017
Romania	9403	Furniture NES	1	0.079	0.003
	7208	Iron and steel	2	0.076	0.003
	6204	Female suits	3	0.048	0.026
	2710	Non-crude oil	4	0.046	0.013
	9401	Seats	5	0.045	0.002
Sri Lanka	902	Tea	1	0.079	0.003
	6204	Female suits	2	0.068	0.026
	6206	Female blouses	3	0.062	0.015
	7103	Precious stones	4	0.050	0.000
	6203	Male suits	5	0.043	0.017
Thailand	8473	Office machine parts	1	0.049	0.005
	8471	Data processing machines	2	0.048	0.005
	4001	Rubber	3	0.039	0.000
	8542	Electric circuits	4	0.037	0.001
	1701	Sugar (solid)	5	0.028	0.001
Turkey	6110	Sweaters	1	0.049	0.031

(*continued*)

Table 4.3   (continued)

Country	HS4	Description	Manufacturing rank	Share of country's total exports	Share of China's total exports
	6204	Female suits	2	0.048	0.026
	4203	Leather apparel	3	0.045	0.011
	6104	Knit female suits	4	0.042	0.003
	2401	Tobacco	5	0.041	0.001

Notes: This table shows for each country the five largest manufacturing industries in terms of exports, the industry's share in the country's total merchandise exports, and the industry's share in China's merchandise exports (each averaged for the period 1995–2005). HS = Harmonized System; n.e.s. = not elsewhere specified.

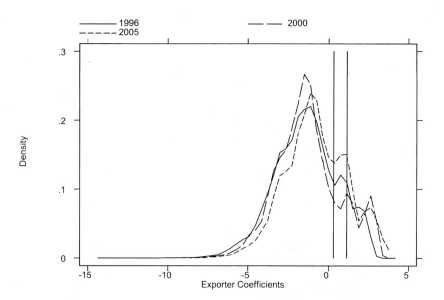

Fig. 4.1   Estimated sector-country exporter coefficients, selected years

and country-sector importer coefficients and over 200 trade cost coefficients. To summarize exporter and import dummies compactly, Figures 4.1 and 4.2 plot kernel densities for the sector-country exporter and importer coefficients (where the densities are weighted by sector-country exports or imports). Figure 4.1 shows that most exporter coefficients are negative, consistent with sectoral exports for most countries being below the United States. Over the sample period, the distribution of exporter coefficients shifts to the right, suggesting other countries are catching up to the United States. Vertical

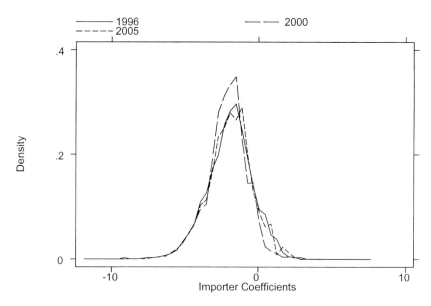

Fig. 4.2   Estimated sector-country importer coefficients, selected years

lines indicate weighted mean values for China's exporter coefficients in 1995 (equal to 0.44) and 2005 (equal to 1.78), which rise in value over time relative to the overall distribution of exporter coefficients, suggesting China's export supply capacity has improved relative to other countries over the sample period. Evidence we report later supports this finding. In figure 4.2, most importer coefficients are also negative, again indicating sectoral trade values for most countries are below those for the United States.

To provide further detail on the coefficient estimates, table 4.4 gives median values of the trade cost elasticities by year, weighted by each sector's share of world trade. The estimates are in line with results in the literature (Anderson and van Wincoop 2004). The coefficient on log distance is negative and slightly larger than 1 in absolute value; adjacency, common language, and joint membership in a free trade agreement are each associated with higher levels of bilateral trade; and the implied elasticity of substitution (given by the tariff coefficient) is close to 3.

4.3.2   Export Supply Capabilities in Developing Countries vis-à-vis China

Of primary interest is how the ten countries' export supply capacities compare to those of China. Figures 4.3, 4.4, and 4.5 plot sectoral export coefficients for each country against exporter coefficients for China over the sample period (using sectoral shares of annual manufacturing exports in each country as weights). For each country, there is a positive correlation

Table 4.4   Median estimated trade cost elasticities

Year	Log distance	Common language	Adjacency	Free trade agreement	Tariff
1995	−1.169	0.732	0.484	0.325	−3.173
1996	−1.174	0.725	0.470	0.313	−3.122
1997	−1.174	0.732	0.468	0.314	−3.109
1998	−1.174	0.761	0.494	0.339	−3.097
1999	−1.171	0.766	0.479	0.337	−3.074
2000	−1.171	0.739	0.432	0.306	−3.051
2001	−1.176	0.744	0.447	0.311	−3.030
2002	−1.176	0.748	0.457	0.323	−3.059
2003	−1.178	0.740	0.448	0.317	−3.031
2004	−1.180	0.733	0.436	0.307	−2.999
2005	−1.181	0.715	0.412	0.289	−2.964

Note: Coefficient estimates are expressed as trade-value-weighted median values for manufacturing industries.

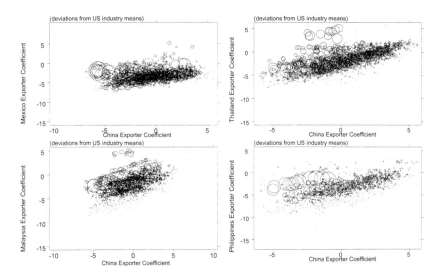

Fig. 4.3   Sectoral export coefficients for selected Pacific Rim developing countries and China

in its sectoral export dummies with China, with the correlation being strongest for Turkey (0.63), Romania (0.59), Hungary (0.48), Thailand (0.48), Malaysia (0.47), Poland (0.45), Sri Lanka (0.45); somewhat smaller for The Philippines (0.33) and Pakistan (0.32); and weakest for Mexico (0.12). The correlation for Mexico appears to be driven by industries related to petroleum, which began the period as major export sectors for the country but have since declined in importance.

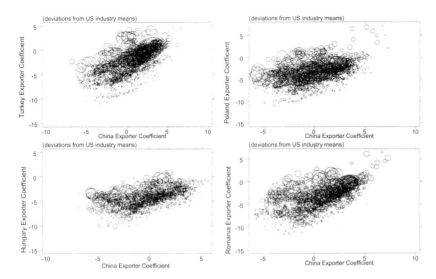

Fig. 4.4   Sectoral export coefficients for selected European developing countries and China

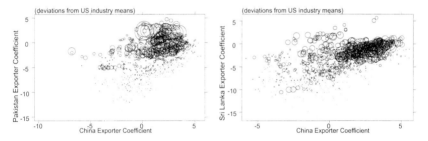

Fig. 4.5   Sectoral export coefficients for selected South Asian developing countries and China

The positive correlation in sectoral export coefficients with China suggests that most of the large developing countries that specialize in manufacturing have strong export supply capabilities in the same sectors in which China is also strong. In other words, the comparative advantage of these countries is closely aligned with that of China. To the extent that the major trading partners of these countries are the same as those of China, they would be exposed to export supply shocks in China, meaning that growth in China would potentially reduce demand for the manufacturing exports that they produce and lower their terms of trade.

To see how export supply capacities have evolved over time, Figures 4.6, 4.7, and 4.8 plot the year-on-year change in country-sector export dummies for each of the ten developing countries against those for China, weighted

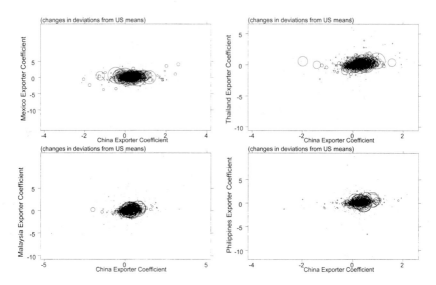

Fig. 4.6   Changes in sectoral export coefficients for selected Pacific Rim countries and China

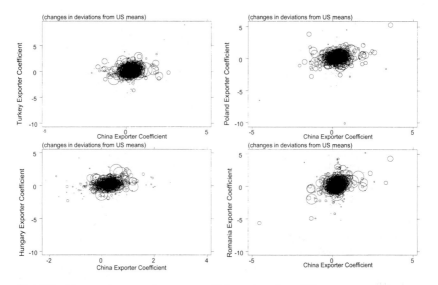

Fig. 4.7   Changes in sectoral export coefficients for selected European countries and China

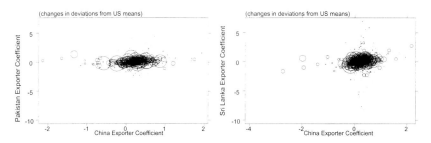

Fig. 4.8   Changes in sectoral export coefficients for selected South Asian countries and China

by each country's sectoral trade shares. Immediately apparent is that the range of growth in China's export supply capacities is large relative to that of any other developing country. Changes in China's export dummies take on a wide range of values, while none of the ten countries shows nearly as much variation. As a consequence, the correlation between changes in sectoral export dummies between each country and China is weaker than the correlation in levels. The strongest correlations in changes are for Romania (0.50) and Malaysia (0.47); followed by Thailand (0.32), Sri Lanka (0.31), Hungary (0.30), The Philippines (0.30), Poland (0.22), and Turkey (0.21); and then by Pakistan (0.16) and Mexico (0.14).

4.4   Counterfactual Exercises

In this section, we compare the change in import-demand conditions facing each of the ten developing-country exporters under two scenarios, one in which import demand evolved as observed in the data (as implied by the coefficient estimates from the gravity model) and a second in which we hold constant the change in China's export supply capabilities. This exercise allows us to examine whether China's growth in export production has represented a negative shock to the demand for exports from other developing countries.

According to the theory presented in section 4.2, sectoral import demand in a country is affected by its GDP and by its sectoral import price index. Its price index, in turn, is affected by export supply conditions in the countries from which it imports goods, weighted by trade costs with these countries. From equation (8), this yields the following relationship:

$$(10) \qquad \tilde{m}_{nkt} = \alpha_0 + \alpha_1 \ln Y_{kt} + \alpha_2 \ln\left(\sum_{h=1}^{H} e^{\hat{s}_{nht}} \tau_{nhkt}^{\hat{\beta}_{1n}} d_{hk}^{\hat{\beta}_{2n}}\right) + \eta_{nkt},$$

where $\hat{m}_{nht}$, $\hat{s}_{nht}$, $\hat{\beta}_{1n}$, and $\hat{\beta}_{2n}$ are OLS coefficient estimates of the sectoral importer dummy, the sectoral exporter dummy, the tariff elasticity, and the distance elasticity from equation (4). In theory, it should be the case that $\alpha_1 = 1$ and $\alpha_2 = -1$.

To verify that the relationships posited by theory are found in the data, table 4.5 shows coefficient estimates for equation (10). Departing from equation (10) slightly, we also include log population as an explanatory variable (to allow demand to be affected by market size and average income), though it is imprecisely estimated in most regressions. We show specifications under alternative weighting schemes and for three sets of industries: all manufacturing industries, excluding core resource-intensive industries,[9] and excluding all resource-intensive industries.[10] Demand conditions in resource-intensive industries may differ from other manufacturing industries due to their reliance on primary commodities as inputs. Coefficients on GDP (α_1 in equation [10]) are all positive and precisely estimated, ranging in value from 0.52 to 1.05. Coefficients on the import price index (α_2 in equation [10]) are all negative and precisely estimated, ranging in value from -0.31 to -0.53. While the coefficient estimates do not exactly match the theoretically predictions, they are broadly consistent with the model.

The next exercise is to use the coefficient estimates to examine the difference in demand for exports faced by the ten developing country exporters that is associated with the growth in China's export supply capacity. The first step is to calculate for each importer in each sector the value in equation (9), which is,

$$
\tilde{m}_{nkt} - m_{nkt} = - \left[\ln\left(\sum_{h \neq c}^{H} e^{\hat{s}_{nht}} \tau_{nhkt}^{\hat{\beta}_{1n}} d_{hk}^{\hat{\beta}_{2n}} + e^{\hat{s}_{nc0}} \tau_{nckt}^{\hat{\beta}_{1n}} d_{ck}^{\hat{\beta}_{2n}} \right) \right.
$$
$$
\left. - \ln\left(\sum_{h \neq c}^{H} e^{\hat{s}_{nht}} \tau_{nhkt}^{\hat{\beta}_{1n}} d_{hk}^{\hat{\beta}_{2n}} + e^{\hat{s}_{nct}} \tau_{nckt}^{\hat{\beta}_{1n}} d_{ck}^{\hat{\beta}_{2n}} \right) \right].
$$

This shows the amount by which average import demand in country k and sector n at time t would have differed had China's export supply capacity (which reflects the number of product varieties it produces and its production costs) had remained constant between time 0 and time t.[11] The second step is to calculate the weighted average value of $\tilde{m}_{nkt} - m_{nkt}$ for each of the ten

---

9. At the two-digit HS level, these industries are beverages, cereals, animal oils and fats, sugar, meat and seafood processing, fruit and vegetable processing, tobacco, nonmetallic minerals, mineral fuels and oils, and inorganic chemicals.

10. In addition to those industries mentioned in note 9, this excludes organic chemicals, pharmaceuticals, fertilizers, plastics, rubber, leather products, and wood products.

11. An alternative to the counterfactual exercise we propose would be to examine the change in China's exports implied by the change in tariffs facing China over the sample period. Were China's economy in steady state, then the change in tariffs would be the primary shock affecting the country's exports. However, over the sample period, China very much appears to be an economy in transition to a new steady state, associated with a sectoral and regional reallocation of resources brought about by the end of central planning. Thus, focusing on tariffs alone would miss the primary shock to China's export growth.

Table 4.5   **Correlates of country sector import dummies**

	Without trade weights			With trade weights		
Sample	All manufacturing	Exclude core resource intensive	Exclude all resource intensive	All manufacturing	Exclude core resource intensive	Exclude all resource intensive
Log GDP	0.939	0.983	1.045	0.529	0.520	0.664
	(0.03)	(0.01)	(0.02)	(0.07)	(0.05)	(0.03)
Log population	−0.127	−0.125	−0.228	0.041	0.062	−0.032
	(0.05)	(0.05)	(0.02)	(0.08)	(0.03)	(0.03)
Log import price index	−0.358	−0.386	−0.307	−0.531	−0.477	−0.303
	(0.05)	(0.08)	(0.01)	(0.09)	(0.12)	(0.03)
R^2	0.376	0.378	0.499	0.278	0.184	0.520
N	128942	108097	84724	128942	108097	84724

Notes: This table shows regression of country-sector import dummies on log GDP, log population, and the log import price index. Standard errors (clustered by industry and year) are in parentheses. The sample spans 1995–2005 for one of three groups of industries (all manufacturing, excluding core resource intensive industries, excluding all resource intensive industries). All regressions include sector-year dummy variables. Weighted regressions use the share of a sector in a country's manufacturing exports as weights.

developing country exporters, using as weights the share of each importer and sector in a country's total manufacturing exports (where these shares are averages over the sample period).[12]

Table 4.6 shows the results from the counterfactual calculation where year 0 corresponds to 1995 and year t corresponds to 2005.[13] The first column shows results in which we set α_2 from equation (10) equal to –1, as implied by theory. In 2005, the difference in export demand ranges from 3.3 percent in Romania to –1.1 percent in Sri Lanka, with The Philippines and Mexico among the most affected countries and Pakistan and Turkey also among the least affected. The mean difference across countries is 1.6 percent. Thus, in the developing countries we consider, demand for exports, on average, would have been 1.6 percent higher had China's export supply capacity remained constant from 1995 to 2005. The negative difference for Sri Lanka indicates that China's export supply capacities declined in the country's primary export industries (which include tea). The second column shows results in which we set α_2 equal to –0.5, which is at the upper end of the coefficient estimates for table 4.5. The mean difference in export demand across countries drops to 0.8 percent. For no country does China represent a negative export demand shock of greater than 1.7 percent.

Columns (3) to (6) repeat the results, excluding resource-intensive industries from the sample. China's comparative advantage appears to lie in labor-intensive activities rather than industries that use oil, minerals, timber, or foodstuffs intensively. In column (3), the mean difference across countries is 2.7 percent (compared to 1.6 percent in column [1]), indicating that China's impact is indeed larger for industries that do not use resources intensively. The most affected countries are Pakistan, Romania, Mexico, Malaysia, and The Philippines. In column (4), in which the value of α_2 is set to –0.5, the mean difference across countries is 1.3 percent.

Finally, columns (7) and (8) show results when we limit the industries to apparel, footwear, electronics, and toys. These include labor-intensive industries (or, in electronics, industries with labor-intensive stages of production), in which one might imagine that China's comparative advantage is strongest. For these industries, China's impact is indeed larger, at least for some countries. The counterfactual increase in export demand would be 3.0 percent across all countries, with values over 4.0 percent occurring in Romania, Poland, Pakistan, and Mexico.

12. In taking this weighted average across industries, we are approximating for the percentage change in imports with the log change. This approximation becomes less precise as the growth in imports becomes larger. In unreported results, we experimented with using the percentage change. The findings are similar to what we report in table 4.6.

13. Because we do not estimate equation (4) subject to the constraint in equation (6), one needs to be careful in interpreting our results. The counterfactual exercises we report apply to changes in demand conditions rather than changes in trade. Absent imposing the equilibrium conditions implied by the model, we cannot interpret the counterfactual exercises as implying how trade would change.

Table 4.6   Counterfactual difference in export demand

	All manufacturing industries		Excluding core resource industries		Excluding all resource industries		Apparel, footwear, electronics, toys	
	(1)	(2)	(3)	(4)	(5)	(6)	(7)	(8)
Hungary	0.025	0.013	0.028	0.014	0.029	0.015	0.018	0.009
Malaysia	0.019	0.010	0.032	0.016	0.034	0.017	0.020	0.010
Mexico	0.002	0.001	0.032	0.016	0.034	0.017	0.042	0.021
Pakistan	0.014	0.007	0.015	0.007	0.041	0.021	0.049	0.025
The Philippines	0.028	0.014	0.028	0.014	0.032	0.016	0.015	0.008
Poland	0.018	0.009	0.018	0.009	0.022	0.011	0.052	0.026
Romania	0.033	0.017	0.034	0.017	0.040	0.020	0.055	0.028
Sri Lanka	-0.011	-0.006	-0.016	-0.008	-0.007	-0.004	-0.006	-0.003
Thailand	0.017	0.009	0.019	0.010	0.023	0.012	0.023	0.012
Turkey	0.018	0.009	0.021	0.011	0.021	0.011	0.033	0.017
Mean	0.016	0.008	0.021	0.011	0.027	0.013	0.030	0.015

Notes: This table shows how manufacturing export demand would have differed in 2005 for a given country had China's export supply capacities remained unchanged between 1995 and 2005, based on the methodology outlined in the text. For columns (1), (3), (5), and (7), α equals -1. For columns (2), (4), (6), and (8), α equals -0.5.

The counterfactual exercises indicate that had China's export supply capacities remained unchanged, demand for exports would have been modestly larger for other developing countries that specialize in manufacturing exports. To repeat, across all manufacturing industries, the average difference in export demand is 0.8 percent to 1.6 percent; for non-resource-intensive industries, the average difference is 1.3 percent to 2.7 percent. These are hardly large values, suggesting that even for the countries that would appear to be most adversely affected by China's growth, it is difficult to find evidence that the demand for their exports has been significantly reduced by China's expansion.

4.5   Discussion

In this paper, we use the gravity model of trade to examine the impact of China's growth on the demand for exports in developing countries that specialize in manufacturing. China's high degree of specialization in manufacturing makes its expansion a potentially significant shock for other countries that are also manufacturing oriented. Of the ten developing countries we examine, nine have a pattern of comparative advantage that strongly overlaps with China, as indicated by countries' estimated export supply capacities. Yet, despite the observed similarities in export patterns, we find that China's growth represents only a small negative shock in demand for the other developing countries' exports. While there is anxiety in many national capitals over China's continued export surge, our results suggest China's impact on the export market share of other manufacturing exporters has been relatively small.

There are several important caveats to our results. Our framework and analysis are confined to manufacturing industries. There may be important consequences of China for developing-country commodity trade, which we do not capture. The counterfactual exercises we report do not account for general-equilibrium effects. There could be feedback effects from China's growth on prices, wages, and the number of product varieties produced that cause us to misstate the consequences of such shocks for other developing countries. There are also concerns about the consistency of the coefficient estimates, due to the fact that we do not account for why there is zero trade between some countries.

References

Anderson, James E., and van Wincoop, Eric. 2004. Trade costs. *Journal of Economic Literature* 42 (3): 691–751.

Broda, Christian, and David Weinstein. 2006. Globalization and the gains from variety. *Quarterly Journal of Economics* 121 (2): 541–85.

Devlin, Robert, Antoni Estevadeordal, and Andrés Rodriguez-Clare. 2005. *The emergence of China: Opportunities and challenges for Latin America and the Caribbean.* Washington, DC: Inter-American Development Bank.

Eichengreen, Barry, and Hui Tong. 2005. Is China's FDI coming at the expense of other countries? NBER Working Paper no. 11335. Cambridge, MA: National Bureau of Economic Research.

Feenstra, Robert C. 2004. *Advanced international trade: Theory and evidence.* Princeton, NJ: Princeton University Press.

Helpman, Elhanan, Marc J. Melitz, and Yona Rubinstein. 2007. Trading partners and trading volumes. Harvard University. Mimeograph.

Lopez Cordoba, Ernesto, Alejandro Micco, and Danielken Molina. 2005. How sensitive are Latin American exports to Chinese competition in the U.S. market? Inter-American Development Bank. Mimeograph.

Robertson, Raymond. 2007. World trade and tariff data. Macalester College. Mimeograph.

Santos Silva, J. M. C., and Silvana Tenreyro. 2006. The log of gravity. *The Review of Economics and Statistics* 88 (4): 641–58.

Wooldridge, Jeffrey M. 2002. *Econometric analysis of cross section and panel data.* Cambridge, MA: MIT Press.

Comment   Irene Brambilla

Much has been speculated and argued in light of China's exceptional growth and progressive integration into world markets. The discussion has ranged from competition effects, whereby China may be crowding other countries out both as recipients of foreign direct investment (FDI) and as suppliers in international markets, to positive effects such as the increase in business opportunities and the potentially huge expansion in demand for commodities.

Within this broad topic, Hanson and Robertson look into a very specific question: the effect of China's expansion in the manufacturing exports of a selected group of ten developing countries. They perform a neat and simple empirical exercise where they first estimate a gravity equation model and then run a counterfactual exercise to simulate what demand for exports of these ten countries would have been in the absence of China's relative expansion during the last decade.

Results are sobering. They show that, on average, manufacturing exports of the ten selected industrialized economies would have been only 1.6 percent higher (0.8 percent on a different specification) had China not expanded

Irene Brambilla is an assistant professor of economics at Yale University, and a faculty research fellow of the National Bureau of Economic Research.

between 1995 and 2005. Results vary by country, with the effect being largest for Romania: the impact of China on Romanian manufacturing exports is 3.3 percent. The most unusual case is Sri Lanka, where the impact on exports is positive.

In December 2001, China signed its much anticipated accession to the World Trade Organization (WTO). How are Hanson and Robertson's results compatible with this event? How does it happen that the most-populated, fastest-growing country in the world has such seemingly small impact on international markets?

Supply-Side Factors versus Market Access

One answer is that Hanson and Robertson's counterfactual exercise is *not* designed to simulate China's accession to the WTO, or, more generally, to simulate China's newly granted market access. It is a supply-side exercise. They look at export supply capacity.

It is worth taking a look at how export supply capacity enters into the gravity equation. Let us consider a pair of countries, Mexico and the United States, for example. Exports from Mexico to the United States in a particular industry depend on three factors: (a) demand conditions in the United States, given by the share of the industry in total consumption, by income in the United States, and by what is being offered by Mexico's competitors; (b) Mexico's supply capacity, that is, the cost of production and availability of varieties in Mexico; (c) finally, gravity-type variables such as bilateral distance, cultural barriers, and trade policy variables (i.e., tariffs) also play a role. Demand conditions conceptually refer to *residual* demand conditions, that is, U.S. demand for Mexican products given the "state" of Mexico's competitors, including China. Thus, residual demand for Mexican products depends on among other things, the varieties and prices offered by China, where prices are determined by production costs, tariffs, distance, and other gravity-type variables.

Here is where the counterfactual exercise comes into place. The exercise compares 1995 and 2005. In actuality, between 1995 and 2005, conditions in China and in other countries change. In the counterfactual exercise, Mexico's exports to the United States are simulated for the year 2005 using some of China's conditions in 1995. This is later aggregated across industries and countries of destination, to compute the total impact on Mexico's exports by comparing actual exports in 2005 with simulated exports in that same year.

The distinction between supply capacity and market access refers to which conditions are kept constant at their 1995 level and which conditions are allowed to vary. Hanson and Robertson choose to keep the number of varieties and costs of production constant at their 1995 level, thus focusing on a supply-side mechanism. In doing so, they abstract from the changes in tariffs that occurred between 1995 and 2005. The supply-side factors can be broadly understood as improvements in infrastructure, information technology, regulation, human capital, and other variables that affect production costs. An alternative question could look at the impacts of change in market access. In this exercise, the counterfactual exports of 2005 would be generated using the tariffs of 1995, and, as expected, would yield higher impacts on the exports of the selected ten countries, Mexico included among them.

There is a small caveat to the export supply capacity counterfactual exercise. Supply-side conditions are not exogenous of market access and gravity-type variables. In the model, the number of varieties is an equilibrium result, determined jointly with prices and quantities and affected by market access variables such as tariffs. If we consider that tariffs faced by China fell between 1995 and 2005, the measured increase in export supply capacity is partially an endogenous response to the tariff change, and the counterfactual estimates provide an upper bound. Additionally, demand-side conditions are estimated as an exporter dummy, which in the model is well determined but in practice can capture unobserved market access variables such as nontariff barriers that might have also changed between 1995 and 2005. The textile and apparel sectors are examples where nontariff barriers dropped between 1995 and 2005.

Looking into Specific Industries

Differences across industries are another point to consider. China's expansion has been far from homogeneous. Between 1995 and 2005, changes in China's market share in world exports have ranged from a decrease of 68 to an increase of 73 percentage points across Harmonized System (HS) six-digit products in the COMTRADE data set. Of nearly 5,000 HS six-digit products with positive exports from China in both years, the increase in market share has been below 2 percentage points for over half of them, while for forty-eight product lines, the increase in China's market share has been above 40 percentage points. Naturally, these forty-eight industries are at greater risk of suffering a large negative impact from China's expansion in supply. The extent of the impact on aggregate countrywide results in the ten countries subject to study depends on the importance of the industries where China's expansion has been largest in these countries' composition of exports.

Table 4.3 in the paper reports the five most important industries in each of the ten selected countries, defined as the five industries with largest share in total exports. By showing that these industries are not as important within China's exports, Hanson and Robertson support their claim that there is not much overlap between China's and the ten countries' composition of exports.

Table 4C.1

| | Correlation | | Highly endangered products |
	Values (1)	Rank (2)	(3)
Hungary	−0.023	−0.0201	195
Sri Lanka	−0.035	0.0223	119
Mexico	0.002	0.1048	31
Malaysia	0.0262	0.111	19
The Philippines	0.0169	0.1137	155
Poland	−0.0006	0.0569	76
Romania	−0.0066	0.0116	223
Thailand	0.0497	0.1987	31
Turkey	0.0294	0.1048	43

Source: UN COMTRADE.

It is potentially more informative to look at this from the angle of changes in China's market shares in world exports. Column (1) in table 4C.1 shows the correlation between two variables: (a) changes in China's market share in world exports between 1995 and 2005; and (b) the participation of each product in total country exports for each of the ten countries.[1] Observations are defined at the HS six-digit level. The coefficients are very close to zero, indicating that industries in which China has expanded are of low relative importance within the exporting structure of each country. Column (2) shows analogous correlations using ranks of products instead of shares. This result is consistent with finding a low *aggregate* impact of China on total country exports.

Column (3) looks at the forty-eight product lines in which the market share of China has increased by more than 40 percentage points. These are the products that are more at risk of suffering the impact of China's expansion. For each of the ten countries, HS six-digit product lines are sorted in order of importance according to their share in total country exports. Column (3) displays the position in the ranking of the *first* product that overlaps with the products in which China's expansion has been largest. In the case of Hungary, for example, the result is 195. This means that *none* of Hungary's 194 most important product lines are among the "highly endangered products" for which the share of China has increased by more than 40 percentage points.

The bottom line is that there is not much overlap between products of

---

1. Let m, l, and h denote value of imports, industries and HS six-digit products. The first variable is defined as $(m_{h,China,2005}/\Sigma_l m_{h,l,2005}) - (m_{h,China,1995}/\Sigma_l m_{h,l,1995})$. The second variable is $(m_{h,l,1995}/\Sigma_k m_{k,l,1995})$.

large expansion of Chinese exports and products in which the ten countries specialize, which largely explains the low aggregate numbers. These empirical facts are consistent with the econometric findings in the paper obtained using structural methods. Additionally, they suggest that, albeit low in aggregate, the impact of China's expansion is potentially large in specific industries and in countries in which the composition of exports is more similar to China's.

II

Macroeconomic Issues

5

China's Exports and Employment

Robert C. Feenstra and Chang Hong

5.1 Introduction

In a series of papers, Dooley, Folkerts-Landau, and Garber (2003, 2004a,b,c, 2005) lay out a vision of a "revived Bretton Woods system" to explain international trade and monetary arrangements today. According to their vision, this system has the following elements:

1. Under the old Bretton Woods system, European countries adopted undervalued exchange rates and capital controls, allowing them to pursue export-led growth. They eventually graduated to flexible exchange rate and capital mobility, thereby jointly forming a "capital account" region (along with Canada and Latin America).

2. Another group of countries, including Asia and especially China, make up the new periphery and again adopted undervalued exchange rates and capital controls to pursue export-led growth. These countries form a "trade account" region. China, in particular, needs to employ some 200 million persons from the rural area, or 10 to 12 million persons per year in the urban areas, which is facilitated by the inflow of foreign direct investment (FDI).

3. The United States is at the center, and its budget and current account deficits have their counterpart in the trade surpluses in Asia. The U.S. current account deficit is financed through official inflows from the trade account region and private inflows from the capital account region.

Robert C. Feenstra is a professor of economics at the University of California, Davis, and a research associate of the National Bureau of Economic Research. Chang Hong is a professor of economics at Clark University.

The authors thank Caroline Freund and Michael Dooley for comments and Zhi Wang for providing the 2000 input-output table used in our calculations as well as other data.

4. The system is sustainable so long as the trade account region continues to finance the U.S. trade deficit and protectionism does not occur. Threats of protectionism are offset by the profits earned by foreign investors in the "trade account" region, especially China. Conversely, the trade deficits run by the United States (or, equivalently, the Treasury bills held by China) are a form of collateral that prevents the Chinese from seizing the assets of foreign firms, which would lead the United States to default on its financial obligations.

Some of these various hypotheses are more controversial than others. For example, Wei (2007) objects to the idea that U.S. Treasury bills held by China act as collateral against the Chinese seizing foreign plants, arguing that (a) most FDI in China does not come from the United States but rather from Hong Kong; (b) there is no recent history of China seizing control of foreign firms; (c) there is even less history of the United States defaulting on its Treasury bill obligations. But this final idea of U.S. Treasury bills acting as collateral is not really essential for the rest of the theory, and controversy over it need not detract from the other hypotheses.[1] The focus of this paper is on the least controversial of their hypotheses, and that is the idea that expanding exports from China serve to create employment in the urban areas.

Our goal is to quantitatively evaluate this employment hypothesis, that is, to answer the question of how much employment is created by rising Chinese exports. Even this hypothesis is not as straightforward as it might seem. A recent article in the *Economist* entitled "The Jobless Boom" notes that employment growth has been lower than overall economic growth across various countries of Asia, especially in China, and that this ratio has been falling over time.[2] Citing a study by the Asian Development Bank (Felipe and Hasan 2006a,b), the article suggests that the reasons for this weak employment growth has been the shift toward more productive, capital-intensive industries. Dooley, Folkerts-Landau, and Garber (2004a, 4) themselves do not expect the employment growth to come entirely from exports and, in fact, suggest that employment growth of 3 million workers per year in China will come from rising exports.

A logical starting point to determine the employment effect of exports is to look at the calculations from input-output (IO) tables for China, with both the direct and indirect demand for labor from ordinary and processing exports. As reviewed in section 5.2, an increase in ordinary exports of $1,000 (the annual wage in manufacturing in 2000) leads to employment of 0.44 person-years in 2000 and 0.34 person-years in 2002, with much smaller effects from processing exports. But surprisingly, applying these static employment

---

1. In fact, Dooley et al. (2004c) motivate the collateral idea by noting that the rest of their theory does not necessarily imply a *trade deficit* in the United States as center country; by adding the trade deficits as collateral, that limitation of the theory is overcome.

2. See *The Economist*, January 14, 2006, 46–47.

coefficients to compute the implied employment gains due to the growth in domestic demand and exports, over 1997 to 2002 and 2000 to 2005, leads to employment gains that *vastly exceed the actual employment increase in China.* In other words, the static employment coefficients are an unreliable guide to computing the actual employment effects of export growth.

One reason why the static employment effects are unreliable has already been suggested: changes in the industry composition of exports toward more productive industries. This source of aggregate productivity growth is sometimes called the "Denison effect" in the U.S. literature (Nordhaus 1992, 215), as discussed in section 5.3. Shifting toward more productive industries means that the labor needed to produce any given output is reduced. We show in section 5.4 that accounting for the Denison effect reduces the employment impact of exports by about 25 percent from the initial calculations, but we still predict employment gains due to rising exports that are much too high.

Besides the shifting composition of industries, aggregate productivity can rise due to technological progress and capital accumulation. We do not attempt to fully account for this second source of productivity growth, but make a limited attempt by using the growth in wages over time: in our calculations with the IO tables, rising wages means reduced employment growth. We show in section 5.5 that this factor further reduces the employment gains that we can expect from exports to 45 percent of the initial calculation for ordinary exports and 75 percent of the initial calculation for processing exports. These are rules of thumb that can be used to reduce the static employment coefficients for exports.

In section 5.6, we investigate the growth in domestic demand in China over 1997 to 2002, when our data is most complete. Looking first at traded goods (agriculture, mining, and manufacturing) and accounting for the Denison effect, we find that the net employment growth in those sectors due to rising domestic demand is *actually negative.* That is, the shift toward more productive industries has outstripped the increase in final demand, leading to no net job creation. The only source of employment gains during 1997 to 2002 was in the nontraded sectors, such as construction, and final consumer services like restaurants, health services, education, and so on. Taking into account the same factors as for exports, that is, shifting demand across industries and rising wages, we find that the impact of domestic demand on employment is 75 percent smaller than the initial calculation from the IO table, which gives us another rule of thumb.

Using these rules of thumb we *revise* the static employment coefficients, and in section 5.7, recalculate the impact of rising exports and domestic demand on labor demand in China. We find the implied employment growth from exports is modest over the 1997 to 2002 period: not more than 2.5 million jobs added per year. During the 2000 to 2005 period, exports grew much faster, so the employment impact is also higher: exports added as much as

7.5 million jobs per year. However, domestic demand led to three times more employment gains than did exports, while productivity growth subtracted the same amount again from employment. This calculation confirms the suggestion in Dooley, Folkerts-Landau, and Garber (2004a, note 5) that about 30 percent of the employment growth in China will come from rising exports. We conclude in section 5.8 that exports have become increasingly important in stimulating employment in China but that the same gains could be obtained from growth in domestic demand, especially for tradable goods, which has been stagnant until at least 2002 and possibly beyond (Aziz and Cui 2007).

5.2   Employment Gains in China

We begin by reviewing the recent growth in employment, gross domestic product (GDP), and exports in China. Throughout the paper, we focus on the period 1997 to 2005, which gives us two overlapping five-year intervals to work with: 1997 to 2002 and 2000 to 2005. Despite the relatively short span of years and closeness of these two intervals, we will find substantial changes in the Chinese economy over this time.

In table 5.1, we list total employment, broken down by urban and rural, as well as GDP and its components during these years. Total employment has grown by 7.5 to 8 million workers per year over this period, while urban employment has grown slightly faster: 8 to 8.5 million workers, as there was some migration out of the countryside. Real GDP and its components, as well as all trade data, is measured in constant 2000 US$.[3] Real GDP growth doubled from 5.7 percent per year over 1997 to 2002 to 11.0 percent in 2000 to 2005.[4] Notice that the growth of $C + G$ is much less in the 2000 to 2005 period than is the growth in investment, indicating that an increasing share of domestic demand is for construction projects and other investments.

In table 5.2, we provide the data on Chinese ordinary and processing trade, again in constant 2000 US$. Both exports and imports grew by more than 20 percent per year over the 2000 to 2005 period, which greatly outstripped their prior growth: the boom in Chinese trade is really a feature of the twenty-first century. Note that the trade balance listed in the final column of table 5.2 does not match the values for $(X - M)$ given in the final column of table 5.1 because $(X - M)$ includes both goods and services as used in GDP accounts, whereas the trade balance in table 5.2 is just for merchandise trade.

3. We lack specific deflators for components of GDP and trade, and the overall Chinese inflation rate is erratic over this period, including some years of deflation. Because our trade data is reported in US$, we decide to use constant 2000 US$ to measure all other values, converted with the nominal yuan/dollar rate and using the U.S. Consumer Price Index (CPI).

4. The real GDP figures we are using are deflated by the U.S. CPI, as explained in note 3, and are based on expenditure GDP rather than production GDP. For these reasons, the growth rates differ from those sometimes reported in the press.

Table 5.1   **China's employment and gross domestic product (GDP)**

Year	Millions of persons			U.S.$ billions, 2000			
	Employment	Urban	Rural	GDP	$C + G$	Investment	$X - M$
1997	698	208	490	1,057	623	388	46
2000	721	232	489	1,193	743	421	29
2002	737	248	490	1,392	829	527	36
2005	758	273	485	2,009	1,043	856	110
	Growth (million per year)			Growth rate (% per year, compound)			
	Employment	Urban	Rural	GDP	$C + G$	Investment	$X - M$
1997–2002	7.8	8.0	−0.2	5.7	5.9	6.3	−4.9
2000–2005	7.5	8.4	−0.9	11.0	7.0	15.3	30.7

Source: China Statistical Yearbook, various years.

Table 5.2   **China's ordinary and processing trade**

Year	Ordinary exports	Processing exports	Total exports	Ordinary imports	Processing imports	Total imports	Trade balance
1997	89	107	196	77	75	152	44
2000	112	138	249	133	93	225	24
2002	139	172	312	166	117	283	29
2005	305	367	672	340	242	582	90
			Growth rate (% per year, compound)				
1997–2002	9.3	10.0	9.7	16.5	9.2	13.1	−7.9
2000–2005	22.2	21.7	21.9	20.8	21.2	20.9	30.1

Source: China customs trade data.

A logical starting point to determine the impacts of export growth on employment are the studies by Chen et al. (2004), using a 1995 IO table for China, and Lau et al. (2006b,c), using a 2002 IO table; both of these estimates are summarized in Chen et al. (2008). From the 1995 table, Chen et al. (2004) estimate that $1,000 of ordinary exports from China leads to 0.70 person-years of employment, and $1,000 of processing exports leads to 0.06 person-years, or roughly one-tenth as much as for ordinary exports. Those estimates are shown in table 5.3 and have been falling over time. Using the 2002 IO table, Lau et al. (2006b,c) estimate that $1,000 of ordinary exports from China leads to 0.36 person-years of employment (which is one-half as much as they found for 1995), and $1,000 of processing exports leads to 0.11 person-years (which is twice the estimate for 1995), so processing exports lead to about three-tenths the employment of ordinary exports.

We will refer to these employment estimates computed from the IO tables

Table 5.3   Static employment coefficients (implied employment increase per $1,000 of exports or domestic demand in person-years)

Source	Ordinary exports	Processing exports	Domestic demand
Chen et al. from 1995 IO[a]	0.703	0.057	n.a.
Our estimates 2000 IO[b]	0.444	0.130	0.562
Lau et al. from 2002 IO[c]	0.363	0.111	0.492

Note: IO = input-output; n.a. = not available.
[a]Chen et al. (2004, tables 7, 8) and also Chen et al. (2008, table 1).
[b]Author estimates for 2000 IO table, as described in the appendix.
[c]Lau et al. (2006c, table 4) for ordinary and processing exports and also Chen et al. (2008, table 1), with domestic demand coefficient computed as explained in the text.

as "static employment coefficients" because they each refer to a single year. The change in these static employment coefficients can be due to either of the factors we identified in the introduction: shifting composition of exports across industries and technological progress. We will attempt to measure the importance of each of these but first need to replicate the results of Lau and his coauthors for one year. Using the IO table for 2000, we find that $1,000 of ordinary exports from China leads to 0.44 person-years of employment, and $1,000 of processing exports leads to 0.13 person-years. So again, processing exports leads to about three-tenths the employment of ordinary exports. Our estimates for 2000 are also shown in table 5.3 and fall neatly in between the estimates of Chen et al. (2004) and Lau et al. (2006b,c), giving us some confidence that our employment estimates are consistent with theirs.

The methodology we have used to obtain the static employment coefficients from the 2000 IO table is discussed in the appendix and is briefly summarized as follows. Denote the sources of demand by $j = D, O, P$ for domestic demand, ordinary exports, and processing exports, respectively. Then the portion of value added going to labor from $1 demand of type j in sector i is B_{Lit}^j, which is computed from the IO table as the sum of direct plus indirect payments to labor. Our calculations are only for 2000, which we denote $t = 0$, but the same calculations are made by Chen et al. (2004) and Lau et al. (2006b,c) for 1995 and 2002. Having obtained these coefficients B_{Lit}^j for each sector, these are averaged across sectors:

$$(1) \qquad \overline{B}_{Lt}^D \equiv \frac{\sum_i D_{it} B_{Lit}^D}{\sum_i D_{it}}, \text{ and } \overline{B}_{Lt}^j \equiv \frac{\sum_i X_{it}^j B_{Lit}^j}{\sum_i X_{it}^j}, \text{ for } j = O, P,$$

where D_{it} denotes domestic demand in sector j, while X_{it}^O denotes ordinary exports, and X_{it}^P denotes processing exports.

Notice the averaged terms $\overline{B}_{Lt}^j$ refer to the portion of value added going to labor. To convert this into employment, we need to divide by a wage. For the 2000 IO table, we have used the average 2000 wage, which was $842 per year. So the static employment coefficients shown in table 5.3 for 2000 are obtained as:

(2) $$\overline{C}_{L0}^{j} \equiv \overline{B}_{L0}^{j}/\$842, \quad \text{for } j = D, O, P,$$

We are unsure what wages were used by Chen et al. (2004) and Lau et al. (2006b,c) for 1995 and 2002, but the calculation is presumably analogous to that in equation (2), which we will write in other years as:

(2') $$\overline{C}_{Lt}^{j} \equiv \overline{B}_{Lt}^{j}/W_{t}.$$

In table 5.3 we also show the static employment coefficient for *domestic demand,* which equals $C + I + G$. For 2000, we have computed the domestic coefficients as in equations (1) and (2), for $j = D$. For 2002, we choose $\overline{C}_{Lt}^{j}$ so that the implied employment from domestic demand plus exports just equals the *actual* employment in each year. That is, we have chosen $\overline{C}_{Lt}^{D}$ so that:

(3) $$\overline{C}_{Lt}^{D} D_{t} + \overline{C}_{Lt}^{O} X_{t}^{O} + \overline{C}_{Lt}^{P} X_{t}^{P} = L_{t},$$

where L_{t} is employment in year t. Notice that this full-employment condition also holds in 2000 by construction of the static employment coefficients from the IO table.

Despite the fact that the static employment coefficients are obtained for a single year, there is a strong temptation to apply them over time, that is, to use these coefficients to predict the future course of employment due to export growth. There are potentially large errors associated with that procedure, however. To see this point theoretically, take the difference of equation (3) over a five-year period. After some simplification, we obtain the equation:

(4) $$\Delta L_{t} = \Delta D_{t} \frac{1}{2}(\overline{C}_{Lt}^{D} + \overline{C}_{Lt-5}^{D}) + \Delta X_{t}^{O} \frac{1}{2}(\overline{C}_{Lt}^{O} + \overline{C}_{Lt-5}^{O})$$

$$+ \Delta X_{t}^{P} \frac{1}{2}(\overline{C}_{Lt}^{P} + \overline{C}_{Lt-5}^{P}) + \Delta \overline{C}_{Lt}^{D} \frac{1}{2}(D_{t} + D_{t-5})$$

$$+ \Delta \overline{C}_{Lt}^{O} \frac{1}{2}(X_{t}^{O} + X_{t-5}^{O}) + \Delta \overline{C}_{Lt}^{P} \frac{1}{2}(X_{t}^{P} + X_{t-5}^{P}),$$

where $\Delta D_{t} = D_{t} - D_{t-5}$ is the change over a five-year interval and likewise for every other variable. On the first line of equation (4), we have the change in domestic demand and exports times the average employment coefficients, and on the second line we have the change in the employment coefficients times the average demand. Generally, the employment coefficients are *falling* over time, as can be seen by comparing the rows of table 5.3. It follows that the last three terms of equation (4) is negative and potentially quite large: the fall in each employment coefficient is multiplied by the average level of demand and not just its growth. Because these terms are negative and potentially large, it follows that the first three terms on the right are potentially much larger than the actual increase in employment.

This theoretical result is confirmed in table 5.4, where we take the static employment coefficients and apply them to the change in exports over the two five-years periods, 1997 to 2002 and 2000 to 2005. In the first row of table 5.4, for example, we use our estimates of the C_{l0}^j employment coefficient from the 2000 IO table, as shown in table 5.3, and multiply each of the employment coefficients by the real change in domestic demand, ordinary exports, and processing exports over 1997 to 2002. That is, we compute:

$$(5) \qquad \text{Prediction 1} = \Delta D_t \overline{C}_{L0}^D + \Delta X_t^O \overline{C}_{L0}^O + \Delta X_t^P \overline{C}_{L0}^P,$$

which is similar to the first three terms of equation (4). From domestic demand, we predict an employment increase of 216 million persons, and for ordinary processing exports, we predict an employment increase of 31 million persons.[5] Summing over these, we obtain nearly 250 million workers, as compared to an *actual* employment increase of only 39 million! We see that simply multiplying the real changes in demand and exports by the employment coefficients, as in equation (5), massively overstates the true change in employment.

The situation is even worse over the 2000 to 2005 period, where now we use the static employment coefficients of Lau et al. (2006c) from the 2002 IO table. Again, we multiply the employment coefficients by the real change in domestic demand and exports, as in equation (5), and predict an increase in employment in China of 550 million workers, as compared to the actual increase of only 37 million! Thus, the predicted employment impact *vastly exceeds* the actual employment increase. The difference between the predicted and actual employment increases is due to fall in the employment coefficients, as shown by the final terms of equation (4).

We conclude from these calculations that the static employment coefficients, times the changes in demand, do not provide reliable estimates of the actual employment gains in China. Reasons for this have already been suggested: the static employment coefficients do not take into account the changing industry composition of domestic demand and exports, and the coefficients can also fall due to technological progress and capital accumulation. We now examine each of these explanations in turn.

---

5. The rise in domestic demand of $411.5 billion in table 5.4 is taken from the IO tables for 1997 and 2002 and exceeds the rise in domestic demand of $345.4, taken from $C + I + G$ in the national accounts, table 5.1. We use domestic demand from the IO tables for consistency with later calculations. If instead we use the national accounts figure to predict employment gains in table 5.4, then we obtain 225 million workers over 1997 to 2002, which is somewhat less than what we report in table 5.4.

Table 5.4   **Implied Chinese employment from domestic demand and exports (using static employment coefficients)**

| Source | Period | Growth in demand (U.S.$ billions, 2000) | | Implied employment increase[a] (millions of persons) | | | Actual employment increase[b] (millions of persons) |
		Domestic demand	Exports	Domestic demand	Exports	Total	
Author estimates from 2000 IO	1997–2002	411.5	115.5	231.1	30.8	261.8	39.2
Lau et al. (2006c) from 2002 IO	2000–2005	735.0	422.7	361.6	95.6	457.2	37.4

Note: IO = input-output.

[a]Uses the static employment coefficients from table 5.3 and multiplies these by the real growth in domestic demand, ordinary exports, and processing exports.

[b]Actual employment increase comes from the China Statistical Yearbook of each year (see table 5.1).

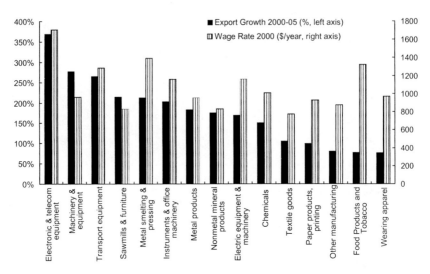

Fig. 5.1   Growth in total exports, 2000–2005, and industry wages, 2000

5.3   Shifting Composition of Exports and Domestic Demand

The static employment coefficients computed from the IO table refer to the employment impact of an additional $1,000 in *average* exports or domestic demand, that is, using the same composition of output that occurred in the year of the IO table, as shown by taking the averages in equation (1). But that is not a good guide for the effects of an actual change in demand because with shifting comparative advantage, export growth may be in industries different from in the past. In addition, for domestic demand, the growth in China in recent years has been especially strong in investment (as shown in table 5.1), especially construction, which differs in its labor requirements from other industries.

The growth in exports is shown in figures 5.1 and 5.2, where we graph the percentage increase over 2000 to 2005 in total and ordinary exports, respectively, and industry wages in 2000. Regardless of whether we use total or ordinary exports, the industry with the greatest percentage increase in exports was electronic and telecommunications equipment, and that industry also had the highest wage in 2000.[6] Overall, there is a positive correlation between the percentage growth in exports, and the real wage in 2000, with food products and tobacco appearing as an outlier (and a relatively small export industry). The fact that the percentage increase in exports differs substantially across industries, meaning that the use of "average" exports as

---

6. This industry also had by far the greatest increase in real exports over 2000 to 2005, exceeding $160 billion, though the majority of those sales were for processing exports.

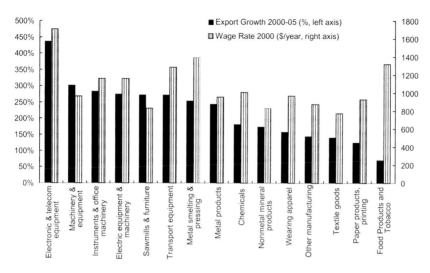

Fig. 5.2   Growth in ordinary exports, 2000–2005, and industry wages, 2000

in Chen et al. (2004) and Lau et al. (2006b,c) will lead to inaccurate results. Instead, we want to use the "marginal" exports, that is, the *actual increase* in exports that occurred in each industry over the five-year period.

In theoretical terms, we want to compare the results of using *aggregate* employment coefficients, as shown in table 5.3, with using *disaggregate* sector-level coefficients. To obtain the disaggregate results, write the full-employment condition equation (1) alternatively as:

$$(6) \qquad \sum_i C^D_{Lit} D_{it} + C^O_{Lit} X^O_{it} + C^P_{Lit} X^P_{it} = \sum_i L_{it},$$

where C^D_{Lit}, C^O_{Lit}, and C^P_{Lit} are the disaggregate employment coefficients by IO sectors and likewise for domestic demand D_{it}, ordinary exports X^O_{it}, and processing exports X^P_{it}. Taking the difference of equation (6) over a five-year interval, we obtain:

$$(7) \qquad \Delta L_t = \sum_i \left[\Delta D_{it} \frac{1}{2}(C^D_{Lit} + C^D_{Lit-5}) + \Delta X^O_{it} \frac{1}{2}(C^O_{Lit} + C^O_{Lit-5}) \right.$$

$$+ \Delta^{XP}_{it} \frac{1}{2}(C^P_{Lit} + C^P_{Lit-5}) \right]$$

$$+ \sum_i \left[\Delta C^D_{Lit} \frac{1}{2}(D_{it} + D_{it-5}) + \Delta C^O_{Lit} \frac{1}{2}(X^O_{it} + X^O_{it-5}) \right.$$

$$+ \Delta C^P_{Lit} \frac{1}{2}(X^P_{it} + X^P_{it-5}) \right].$$

By using the sectoral data in the 2000 IO table, we can make an alternative prediction of the employment gains from the first two lines of equation (7):

$$(8) \qquad \text{Prediction 2} = \sum_i (\Delta D_{it} C_{Li0}^D + \Delta X_{it}^O C_{Li0}^O + \Delta X_{it}^P C_{Li0}^P),$$

where we are using employment coefficients from the year 2000 table in place of the average employment coefficients that appear in equation (5). Note that these are obtained from the 2000 IO table by dividing B_{Li0}^j by the wage in each sector:

$$(9) \qquad \text{Prediction 2 uses: } C_{Li0}^j \equiv \frac{B_{Li0}^j}{W_{i0}}, \text{ for } j = D, O, P.$$

Comparing the new prediction obtained from the disaggregate coefficients in equation (8) with that from the aggregate coefficients in equation (5), because $\Delta D_t = \Sigma_i \Delta D_{it}$ and $\Delta X_{t=}^j \Sigma_i \Delta X_{it}^j$, we obtain:

(10)   Prediction 2 − Prediction 1

$$= \sum_i [\Delta D_{it} (C_{Li0}^D - \overline{C}_{L0}^D) + \Delta X_{it}^O (C_{Li0}^O - \overline{C}_{L0}^O) + \Delta X_{it}^P (C_{Li0}^P - \overline{C}_{L0}^P)].$$

If there is a negative correlation between the growth in demand and the employment coefficients in each sector, as we would expect if growth in output occurs in the more efficient sectors, then equation (10) is negative, and our second prediction of employment growth is less than the first. This reduction in employment gains comes from shifts toward more productive industries and is an example of what Nordhaus (1992, 215) calls the "Denison effect." Nordhaus refers to the work of Edward Denison (1967, 1980), who demonstrated that if resources shift from low-productivity to high-productivity industries, like from agriculture to manufacturing, then the economy would show aggregate productivity growth even if sectoral productivity growth was zero in both sectors. The aggregate productivity growth is due to a "reallocation effect" across industries. The flip side of this aggregate productivity growth is that the labor needed to produce any given output is reduced, as we are showing in equation (10).

Another interpretation of the calculation in equation (8) can be obtained by taking the averages:

$$(11) \qquad \tilde{C}_{L0}^D \equiv \frac{\sum_i \Delta D_{it} C_{Li0}^D}{\sum_i \Delta D_{it}}, \text{ and } \tilde{C}_{L0}^j \equiv \frac{\sum_i \Delta X_{it}^j C_{Li0}^j}{\sum_i \Delta X_{it}^j}, \text{ for } j = O, P.$$

Notice that equation (11) is an average of the sectoral employment coefficients C_{Li0}^j in 2000, but using the change in domestic demand and exports as weights, rather than their average levels as in equations (1) and (2). Again, because $\Delta D_t = \Sigma_i \Delta D_{it}$ and $\Delta X_{t=}^j \Sigma_i \Delta X_{it}^j$, it is immediate that prediction 2 in equation (8) can be alternatively written as:

(12)   Prediction $2 = \Delta D_t \tilde{C}_{L0}^D + \Delta X_t^O \tilde{C}_{L0}^O + \Delta X_t^P \tilde{C}_{L0}^P$,

which is the change in demand times the revised employment coefficients. From equations (11) and (12), we can see our second prediction of the rise in employment uses *actual* or "marginal" increase in exports and domestic demand, rather than the "averages" used in equations (1) and (2) and equation (5).

In the following sections, we implement this second prediction, as well as a third variant, using the 2000 IO table. In sections 5.4 and 5.5, we focus on the growth of exports, over 1997 to 2002 and 2000 to 2005, and in section 5.6 discuss the growth in domestic demand, in which case we do not have disaggregate data for 2005, so we are restricted to investigating 1997 to 2002.

5.4   Growth of Exports, 1997 to 2002 and 2000 to 2005

In table 5.5, we report the employment gains over 1997 to 2002 and 2000 to 2005 using the disaggregate increase in exports over these two periods (prediction 2a). In the former period, 1997 to 2002, the employment growth is 22.7 million persons, rather than 30.8 million from table 5.1. So the shift toward more productive industries reduces the employment growth by 25 percent (or 17 percent for ordinary exports and 52 percent for processing exports). A similar decline is seen over 2000 to 2005, when using the actual rather than the average increase in exports reduces employment growth from 115.4 million (prediction 1) to 86.1 million (prediction 2a), again a decline of 25 percent.[7] We conclude that the employment gain from increased exports is reduced once we account for the industry composition of exports, as suggested by Felipe and Hasan (2006a,b).

The adjustments we have made for prediction 2a can be extended in two directions: we have the data to take into account the provincial compositions of exports, along with provincial wages by industry; or to account for the differing wages paid by types of firm ownership (state-owned, collective, or private) and the exports by firm ownership and industry as well as wages by firm ownership and industry. To the extent that exports are shifting to more productive provinces (e.g., coastal) or firms (e.g., private), the estimated employment gains are reduced.

It should be noted that the maintained assumption in these calculations is that the national IO table for 2000 applies equally well across provinces and across types of firm ownership. We have only very limited data that could be

---

7. If instead of using the industry wages in prediction 2, as in equation (9), we instead continued to use the overall average wage of \$842 in 2000, then the predicted employment impact of exports is reduced by 15 percent as compared with the first prediction. That reduction comes from using the disaggregate calculation as in equation (8), but with the average wage of \$842 in equation (9). The additional 10 percent reduction for prediction 2 is obtained by using the industry wages, as in equation (9).

Table 5.5   Implied increase in Chinese employment from exports (using input-output table in 2000, and industry wages in 2000)

Author estimates using 2000 input-output table	Period	Implied employment increase (millions of persons)			Percentage reduction from Prediction 1	
		Ordinary export	Processing export	Total export	Ordinary export	Processing export
Prediction 1, from table 5.4: using average exports, and average wages in 2000	1997–2002	22.3	8.5	30.8		
	2000–2005	85.7	29.7	115.4		
Prediction 2a: using industry exports, and industry wages in 2000	1997–2002	18.6	4.1	22.7	17	52
	2000–2005	69.4	16.7	86.1	19	44
Prediction 2b: using industry-province exports, and industry-province wages in 2000	1997–2002	17.0	3.5	20.6	24	59
	2000–2005	63.2	14.4	77.5	26	52
Prediction 2c: using firm-ownership exports, and firm-ownership wages in 2000	1997–2002	17.2	3.9	21.0	23	54
	2000–2005	59.1	15.1	74.1	31	49

Source: Authors' calculations as explained in the text.

used to test this assumption. To the extent possible, we applied the methods of Bernstein and Weinstein (2002) and found that the 2000 IO table appears to hold reasonably well across provinces except for Guangdong (where labor compensation was higher than predicted from the national IO table). Because Guangdong was the only outlier, and because our ability to construct an alternative IO table for Guangdong is extremely limited, we continued to apply the national table across all provinces and types of firm ownership.

Focusing first on the provincial effects (prediction 2b), accounting for the shift in exports by industry and province further reduces the employment impact of increased exports, to 20.6 million persons over 1997 to 2002, or one-third less than the initial calculation. For 2000 to 2005, the implied increase in employment is 77.5 million persons, which is also one-third less than the initial calculation. The employment effects that are obtained when we instead take into account the shift in exports by industry and firm ownership (prediction 2c) are similar to those that take into account provincial effects: the predicted employment gains are reduced by about one-third from the initial calculations. The data we have available do not allow us to take into account both of these effects at the same time. In any case, for 2000 to 2005, the implied increase in employment is still much larger than the actual increase of 37 million, which calls for an explanation.

5.5   Increase in Wages due to Productivity Gains

A final limitation of the static employment coefficients computed from the IO table, and also a limitation of our results reported in table 5.5, is that we have assumed that wages are constant over time. That is, we are using wages in 2000: either at the overall wage in equation (2) or the industry wage in equation (9). But, of course, real wages will rise over time due to both productivity gains and capital accumulation. With rising wages, any implied increase in value added and payments to labor will correspond to a smaller increase in employment.

For our next calculation, we divide the direct plus indirect payments to labor from the 2000 IO table by the real 1997 and 2002 wages, respectively, when estimate labor demand in each year. That is, we obtain the employment coefficients in each year as:

$$(13) \qquad \hat{C}^j_{Lit} \equiv \frac{B^j_{Li0}}{W_{it}} \text{ and } \hat{C}^j_{Lit-5} \equiv \frac{B^j_{Li0}}{W_{it-5}}, \text{ for } j = D, O, P.$$

Then our third prediction of the employment gains for rising demand is:

$$(14) \quad \text{Prediction 3} = \sum_i (D_{it}\hat{C}^D_{Lit} - D_{it-5}\hat{C}^D_{Lit-5} + X^O_{it}\hat{C}^O_{Lit} - X^O_{it-5}\hat{C}^O_{Lit-5}$$

$$+ \Delta X^P_{it}\hat{C}^P_{Lit} - \Delta X^P_{it-5}\hat{C}^P_{Lit-5}).$$

Note that if instead of the estimates in equation (13), we had used the true employment coefficients C^j_{Lit} obtained from the IO table in each year, then equation (14) would be an exact prediction of the change in employment: there would be no error involved. So the difference between the third prediction, which uses the industry wages in each year, and the actual changes in employment occurs because (a) we are using wages in equation (13) that do not differ between domestic and export production, and (b) we are still using coefficients B_{Li0}^{j} from 2000 rather than allowing these coefficients to change over time. In brief, we still do not accurately predict employment changes with equation (14) because we are not allowing the IO table to change over time, and our wage data is not detailed enough. Still, we find that this third prediction is a further improvement over our earlier calculations.

In table 5.6, we show how the implied employment effects are further reduced when we allow for the actual increase in wages over 1997 to 2002 or 2000 to 2005. For 1997 to 2002, we find that the employment gains due to ordinary exports range from 5 to 10 million (predictions 3a, 3b, and 3c), which are reduced by 55 percent or more as compared to the initial calculation. For processing exports, the implied employment effects range from −1.4 to 1.7 million, a reduction of at least 80 percent from the initial calculation. Over this period, most of the increase in exports over these years can be explained by the shift in workers toward more efficient industries, firms, and provinces, so the employment gain is very modest. Over 2000 to 2005, we also find that the employment gains due to increased ordinary exports are reduced by 55 percent from our initial calculation, while the employment gains due to processing exports are reduced by about 75 percent.

To sum up, our calculations have reduced the employment impact of increased exports by *more than one-half* of the initial calculation for ordinary exports, and at least *three-quarters* for processing exports. Are these results in table 5.6 believable? The smaller employment gains indicate an efficient reallocation of resources, which is plausible. We note that these efficiency gains come from reallocations across many industries (as well as province and firm ownership) and do not simply reflect a rural-urban migration. Indeed, agriculture and manufacturing industries tend to rise or fall together in our calculations: allowing for rising wages over time, we find that the increase in exports is associated with rising employment in both agriculture and the sum of all manufacturing industries. So the net changes in implied employment reported in tables 5.5 and 5.6 would be similar if we omitted agriculture and reported instead the changes in manufacturing employment due to exports.

5.6   Shifting Composition of Domestic Demand, 1997 to 2002

To measure domestic demand, we rely on the sum of $C + I + G$ by industry from the IO tables, which we have for the years 1997, 2000, and 2002, but not for 2005.[8] So to evaluate the change in employment due to domestic

---

8. Imports are treated entirely as intermediate inputs in the IO table, so need not be deducted from $C + I + G$.

Table 5.6   Implied Chinese employment from exports (using input-output table in 2000, and industry wages by year)

Estimates using 2000 input-output table	Period	Implied employment increase (millions of persons)			Percentage reduction from Prediction 1	
		Ordinary export	Processing export	Total export	Ordinary export	Processing export
Prediction 2a, table 5.5: using firm-ownership exports, and firm-ownership wages in 2000	1997–2002	17.2	3.9	21.0	23	54
	2000–2005	59.1	15.1	74.1	31	49
Prediction 3a: using industry exports, and industry wages by year	1997–2002	4.7	-1.4	3.3	79	117
	2000–2005	37.9	7.8	45.7	56	74
Prediction 3b: using industry-province exports, and industry-province wages by year	1997–2002	5.7	0.1	5.8	74	99
	2000–2005	36.5	7.8	44.4	57	74
Prediction 3c: using firm-ownership exports, and firm-ownership wages by year	1997–2002	10.3	1.7	12.0	54	80
	2000–2005	38.3	8.1	46.4	55	73

Source: Authors calculations as explained in the text.

demand, we are restricted to the five-year period 1997 to 2002 and will not be able to report any results for 2000 to 2005. Furthermore, domestic demand is not broken down by province nor by the type of firm ownership. So the calculations for domestic demand will *only* be broken down by industry over 1997 to 2002.

The implied employment increase due to the growth in domestic demand are reported in table 5.7, where we distinguish domestic demand for tradable goods (all manufacturing plus mining and agriculture) and nontraded goods (all utilities and services, including construction).[9] That is, we have recomputed the employment coefficients shown in equations (1) and (2) and equations (10) and (11) for domestic demand by separating traded from nontraded goods. Traded goods are shown in panel A of table 7. We find that domestic demand for tradable goods has risen by a very modest amount in real terms over 1997 to 2002, $24 billion, shown in the first column. Multiplying that increase in demand by the static employment coefficient of 0.525, we obtain a modest rise in employment of 12.7 million persons, as shown in the third column (prediction 1).

However, if instead we use the actual change in demand rather than its "average" change, then fall in demand would actually lead to *reduced* employment of 9.9 million workers when holding wages fixed at their 2000 levels (prediction 2). Allowing for the growth of wages between 1997 and 2002, the implied fall in employment is even higher, 49.8 million workers, due to the fall in domestic demand (prediction 3). Only a very small amount, 3.3 million workers, is made up by the increase in demand due to rising exports, so the net change in employment due to domestic demand plus exports is a fall of some 47 million jobs.

Because employment actually increased by 39 million jobs over 1997 to 2002, the gap must be made up by the nontraded sector, which is confirmed in the next row of table 5.7. An initial calculation using a static employment coefficient gives a rise in employment of 203 million (prediction 1, panel B). Use the actual change in demand rather than its "average" change, then the employment increase becomes 166 million workers when holding wages fixed at their 2000 levels (prediction 2). Allowing wages to rise over 1997 to 2002, the employment gain in nontradable goods is 111 million workers (prediction 3). That is an enormous rise in employment due to domestic demand, which far exceeds any of our calculations for exports. The sector with the largest increase in domestic demand is construction, which accounts for at least half of the overall rise in employment. Employment gains are also shown in final consumer services like real estate, restaurants, health services, education, and so on.

The changes in domestic demand for tradable and nontradable goods

---

9. Tradable goods are defined as sectors 1–22 of the 2000 IO table, and nontradable goods as sectors 23–40.

Table 5.7 Implied Chinese employment from domestic demand and exports, 1997–2002 (using input-output table in 2000 and industry wages, 2000 or by year)

Author estimates using 2000 input-output table	Growth in demand (U.S.$ billions, 2000)		Implied employment increase (millions of persons)		Percentage reduction from Prediction 1	
	Domestic demand	Total export	Domestic demand	Total export	Domestic demand	Total export
A. Traded goods						
Prediction 1: using average demand, average wages in 2000	24.1	115.5	12.7	30.8		
Prediction 2: using industry demand, industry wages in 2000	24.1	115.5	−9.9	22.7	−178	26.3
Prediction 3: using industry demand, industry wages by year	24.1	115.5	−49.8	3.3	−492	89.3
B. Nontraded goods						
Prediction 1: using average demand, average wages in 2000	387.4	0	203.3	0		
Prediction 2: using industry demand, industry wages in 2000	387.4	0	165.7	0	18.5	n.a.
Prediction 3: using industry demand, industry wages by year	387.4	0	110.8	0	45.5	n.a.
C. All goods						
Prediction 1: using average demand, average wages in 2000	411.5	115.5	216.0	30.8		
Prediction 2: using industry demand, industry wages in 2000	411.5	115.5	155.8	22.7	27.9	26.3
Prediction 3: using industry demand, industry wages by year	411.5	115.5	61.0	3.3	72	89.3

Source: Authors calculations as explained in the text.

Note: n.a. = not available.

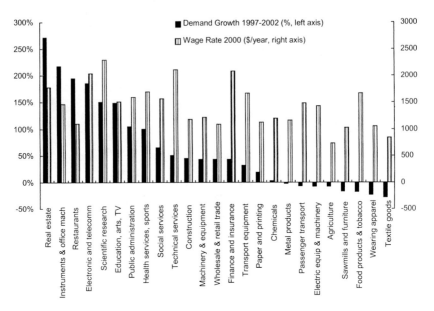

Fig. 5.3   Growth in domestic demand, 1997–2002, and industry wages, 2000

are graphed in figure 5.3, along with the industry wages in 2000.[10] Sectors with the greatest increase in demand include a few tradable industries, like instruments and office machinery and electronic and telecommunication equipment, but many more nontraded goods: real estate, restaurants, scientific research, education, public administration, health and social services, and so on. At the far right of the figure, sectors like textile, wearing apparel, food products, furniture, and agriculture all have *negative* growth in real demand over 1997 to 2002. We find it quite remarkable that the rapidly growing Chinese economy did not generate more domestic demand for its own tradable goods over this period! Domestic demand should be treated as a viable alternative to exports as a source of employment growth but did not function in that way, presumably because the income gains in China did not lead to a commensurate rise in consumption. Aziz and Cui (2007) argue that one reason for this outcome is that household income did not rise by as much as GDP.

That estimate for rising employment due to nontraded goods can be combined with the fall in employment in tradable goods to obtain a total implied change in employment of 61 million workers (prediction 3, panel C). That is our final estimate for 1997 to 2002. In principle, this estimate of 61 + 3.3 = 64.3 million jobs added over 1997 to 2002, from both domestic demand and exports, should equal the actual gain in employment of 39 million jobs. The

10. For convenience, we omit the petroleum and mining sectors in figure 5.3 as well as several other smaller sectors.

discrepancy between these numbers (25 million) can be due to multiple causes: we have not been able to distinguish domestic demand by firm ownership or province; we have used a fixed 2000 IO table; and the wage data we use is not as detailed as we would like. But we feel that even if these improvement were made to our calculations, the overall message of table 5.7 would not change: the vast majority of job growth over 1997 to 2002 is due to the increase in demand for nontraded goods, especially the construction sector. The main reason that employment has grown as much as it has in China over 1997 to 2002 is due to the increase in domestic demand for nontradable goods!

Furthermore, it is important to recognize that our final estimate of 61 million jobs gained over 1997 to 2002, from prediction 3, is vastly better than our initial calculation of 216 million jobs (prediction 1, panel C). Comparing these two numbers, we see that the initial calculation is reduced by 72 percent due to the adjustments we have made. That is nearly the same adjustment (75 percent) that we found in the previous section for processing trade but larger than the adjustment (45 percent) that we found for ordinary exports. It is noteworthy that a downward adjustment of 45 percent is shown in table 5.7 for the nontradable sector, where the employment gains were reduced from 203 million in our initial calculation to 61 million (prediction 3). The fact that *total* employment generated from domestic demand is revised downward by nearly 75 percent reflects the very weak growth in demand for tradable goods, leading to negative employment gains once we account for the industry composition of demand and wage increases over time. In other words, the Denison effect operates very strongly in the pattern of domestic demand for tradable goods, as we have already seen for exports.[11]

5.7   Implied Growth in Employment Once Again

Let us now summarize what we have learned from the last three sections and return to the calculations of employment growth. In table 5.8, we show again the static employment coefficients for 2000 (our calculations) and 2002 (from Lau et al. 2006b,c). We found in section 5.2 that those coefficients vastly overstate the actual change in employment over 1997 to 2002 or 2000 to 2005. But by using improved calculations, we were able to reduce the predicted employment growth. Our final calculations showed that the employment growth for ordinary exports was 55 percent lower than obtained from the static employment coefficients, while that employment growth from processing exports and domestic demand were 75 percent lower (and possibly more). We apply those rules of thumb to the initial static employment coefficients to obtain *revised* employment coefficients, as shown in table 5.8.

11. Note that in figure 5.3, the industry with tradable-good industry with the highest percentage increase in domestic demand is instruments and office machinery, followed by electronic and telecommunication equipment. The latter industry has among the highest wage of any tradable industry and also shows the highest percentage increase in exports (both for ordinary and processing exports).

Table 5.8   Revised employment coefficients (implied employment increase per $1,000 of exports or domestic demand in person-years)

Source	Ordinary exports	Processing exports	Domestic demand
Author estimates from 2000 IO[a]	0.444	0.130	0.562
Revised estimates for 2000 IO[b]	0.444 × 0.45 = 0.20	0.130 × 0.25 = 0.03	0.562 × 0.25 = 0.14
Lau et al. from 2002 IO[c]	0.363	0.111	0.492
Revised estimates for 2000 IO[b]	0.363 × 0.45 = 0.16	0.111 × 0.25 = 0.03	0.492 × 0.25 = 0.12

Note: IO = input-output.
[a]From table 5.3.
[b]Revised as explained in the text and shown in the table.
[c]Lau et al. (2006c, table 4), Chen et al. (2008, table 1), and from table 5.3.

For example, instead of the initial calculations for the 2000 IO table, we now predict that $1,000 in ordinary exports generates 0.44 × 0.45 = 0.20 person-years of employment, while $1,000 in processing exports or domestic demand generates 0.13 × 0.25 = 0.03 and 0.53 × 0.25 = 0.13 person-years, respectively. For 2002, we now predict that $1,000 in ordinary exports generates 0.36 × 0.45 = 0.16 person-years of employment, while $1,000 processing exports of domestic demand generates 0.11 × 0.25 = 0.03 and 0.44 × 0.25 = 0.11 person-years, respectively. These estimates are upper bounds because we obtained lower employment impacts in some calculations, but we shall use these adjustments as conservative.

We use the revised employment coefficients in table 5.8 to recalculate the employment gains for both periods, as shown in table 5.9. For 1997 to 2002, we find that the growth in domestic demand (for nontradable goods, in particular), leads to an increase in employment of 57.8 million workers. In addition, the growth in exports (for ordinary exports, especially), leads to an increase in employment of 12.2 million workers, or about 2.5 million workers per year. Summing over domestic demand and exports, we predict employment gains of 70 million from 1997 to 2002, as compared to the *actual* employment increase of 39 million.[12] So our prediction is nearly twice as big as the actual gain, but that is a great improvement over our initial calculation (table 5.4), where the predicted employment gain was 216 million—more than five times greater than the actual increase! The gap between our revised

12. Note that the predicted employment gains in table 5.9 are not exactly the same as the final row of table 5.7 because in table 5.9, we are using the rules of thumb shown in table 5.8 to reduce the static employment coefficients, that is, the coefficient for ordinary exports is reduced by 55 percent, and the coefficients for processing exports and domestic demand are reduced by 75 percent. Those rules of thumb are broadly consistent but not identical to the calculations in the final row of table 5.7.

Table 5.9   Implied Chinese employment from domestic demand and exports (using revised employment coefficients)

Source	Period	Growth in demand (U.S.$ billions, 2000)		Implied employment increase[a] (millions of persons)			Actual employment increase[b] (millions of persons)
		Domestic demand	Exports	Domestic demand	Exports	Total	
Author estimates from 2000 IO	1997–2002	411.5	115.5	57.8	12.2	70.0	39.2
Lau et al. (2006c) from 2002 IO	2000–2005	735.0	422.7	90.4	37.9	128.3	37.4

Note: IO = input-output.

[a]Uses the revised employment coefficients from table 5.8 and multiplies these by the real growth in domestic demand, ordinary exports, and processing exports.

[b]Actual employment increase comes from the China Statistical Yearbook of each year (see table 5.1).

employment gain over 1997 to 2002 and the actual is due to the fall in the labor coefficients B_{Lit}^j from the IO table, reflecting technological progress and capital accumulation.

In later period, 2000 to 2005, the growth in domestic demand and exports are both stronger. We again use the revised employment coefficient from table 5.8 for 2002 and multiply those by the real changes in domestic demand and exports. We find that the growth in domestic demand (especially investment) leads to an increase in employment of 90.4 million workers. In addition, the growth in exports adds employment of another 38 million workers. By coincidence, the predicted employment impact of exports is nearly exactly equal to the *actual* rise in employment of 37 million workers, or 7.5 million per year.

However, the role of domestic demand over 2000 to 2005, which added 90.4 million to employment is more than twice as large as the role of exports. Based on that evidence, we could not refute the claim that *domestic demand* is responsible for the employment increase. Whether we want to claim that it is domestic demand or exports that are responsible is really just an exercise in semantics, however: the fact is that both have played an important role in stimulating employment growth, and the sum of them (128.3 million) is still considerably larger than the actual employment gains (37.4 million) over this period. Again, we would attribute the gap between the predicted and actual employment gains as due to technological progress and capital accumulation, as well as illustrating the limits of how far we can push our calculations from the IO table. We have made a substantial improvement over the initial calculations, whose predictions were off by an order of magnitude, but still have not obtained a precise accounting of the causes of employment growth.

5.8   Conclusions

Dooley et al. (2003, 2004a,b,c) argue that the current systems of current account imbalances is sustainable so long as China is willing to absorb the Treasury bills used to finance the U.S. deficits. And that willingness is tied to its desire to move workers from unproductive rural employment into urban, manufacturing jobs. These authors suggest that China needs to reemploy some 200 million persons from the countryside, or 10 to 12 million persons per year in the urban areas, and that growth in exports will explain about 30 percent if these employment gains.

We have evaluated this hypothesis by using calculations on the employment impact of exports and domestic demand from Chinese IO tables. We have started with the calculations of Chen et al. (2004) and Lau et al. (2006b,c) for 1995 and 2002 and added our own calculation for the 2000 IO table. The static employment coefficients obtained from these tables summarize the amount of employment generated by $1,000 in exports or domestic demand for one year. By construction, these static employment coefficients are consistent with the full-employment condition for the economy. But the static employment coefficients do a very poor job at predicting the *future* growth in employment from the future growth in exports or domestic demand. We have shown that the errors involved in this forward-looking forecast are enormous, which means that the static employment coefficients are highly unreliable for that purpose.

To improve on that situation, we have proposed adjustments to the static employment coefficients. These adjustments take into account the future growth in export and domestic industries, which may be quite different from their former growth, as well as rising wages over time. The adjustments partially close the gap between predicted and actual employment growth, even when using an IO table for a single year. Using the *revised* employment coefficients, we find that export growth over 1997 to 2002 explains at most one-third of the total employment growth in the economy (2.5 out of 7.5 to 8 million workers per year). For 2000 to 2005, however, export growth was faster and, in principle, can explain the entire employment growth of 7.5 million workers per year. However, the rise in domestic demand—especially for investment—generated employment gains that are more than two times larger than those for exports, which confirms the relative importance of exports as compared to domestic demand suggested by Dooley et al. (2004a). The same amount of employment is reduced by productivity growth in the economy, so the net gain is back to 7.5 million workers per year, somewhat less than the goal put forth by Dooley et al. (2003, 2004a,b,c).

The other key finding is that over 1997 to 2002, the rise in domestic demand was *nearly entirely* in the nontradable sector: predicted employment for tradable goods actually fell. This is very surprising but reflects the shift in expenditure in China toward construction projects as well as nontradable consumer goods. We do not have the detailed data to evaluate whether the same shift occurred during 2000 to 2005, but from the aggregate GDP data, there has been substantially faster growth in investment instead of in private and public consumption $C + G$. So we speculate that domestic demand for tradable goods continues to lag, despite the newspaper reports of rising consumer expenditures; this view is also put forth by Aziz and Cui (2007), who point to the slow growth in household income as an explanation.

The importance of this finding is that China could certainly turn toward domestic demand instead of export (and consumer expenditures, in particular) as an engine to stimulate employment. The transition from export-led growth to domestic demand would undoubtedly rely on many economic and policy actions that are now only beginning: a real appreciation as the prices of nontradable goods begin to rise, shifting domestic demand toward both imports and exportable goods; accompanied by some nominal appreciation of the yuan; fiscal policies that allow for greater security of income in old age, allowing higher expenditures today; reform of the banking sector;

and so on. We believe that it is these features—and not the reliance on export-led growth—that should determine the future path of the government and trade accounts in China and ultimately restore greater balance to these accounts.

Appendix

Chinese Input-Output Table

The structure of China's extended IO table separates domestic input from ordinary and processing imported inputs. The direct input requirement coefficient matrix is presented in table 5A.1:

- A^{DD}, A^{DO}, A^{DP} are ($n \times n$) matrixes of direct input requirement of domestic products for one unit of domestic product, ordinary export, and processing export, respectively.
- A^{MD} and A^{OO} are the ($n \times n$) matrixes of direct input requirement coefficients of ordinary import for one unit domestic production and ordinary exports.
- A^{PP} is the ($n \times n$) matrix of direct processing import requirement coefficient of producing one unit processing export.
- A_V^D, A_V^O, and A_V^P are each an $1 \times n$ vector of direct value added caused by one dollar of sector j's production in domestic products, ordinary export, or processing exports.
- A_L^D, A_L^O, A_L^P are each an ($1 \times n$) vector of direct labor demand generated by one dollar production of domestic products, ordinary export, or processing exports.
- E^O and E^P are each an $n \times 1$ vector of ordinary export and processing export, respectively.

Total Value Added (VA) Coefficient Matrix

To calculate the total economy value added, we must consider the linkages between sectors. When one unit domestic product is produced, it generates a first round of value added, which is the direct value added A_V^D. However, in order to produce this unit of domestic product, intermediate inputs must be used. The production of these intermediate inputs hence creates the second round of value added, which is named indirect value added ($A_V^D \cdot A^{DD}$). This process of creating indirect value added can continue on and on, as intermediate inputs are needed to produce other intermediate inputs. Therefore, the total domestic VA induced by a unit domestic production is the sum of first round direct domestic VA and all the indirect domestic VA. Hence, we derive the total domestic VA coefficient (B_V^D) aroused by domestic production as:

Table 5A.1   **Input-output table: direct input requirement coefficient matrix**

	Domestic product	Ordinary export	Process export	Subtotal	$C + I + G$	Export	Total output
Domestic intermediate input	A^{DD}	A^{DO}	A^{DP}				X^D
Ordinary import input	A^{MD}	A^{OO}	0				
Process import input	0	0	A^{PP}				
Value added	A_V^D	A_V^O	A_V^P				
Labor	A_L^D	A_L^O	A_L^P				
Total input	X^D	E^O	E^P				

(A1) $$B_V^D = A_V^D + A_V^D \bullet A^{DD} + A_V^D \bullet A^{DD} \bullet A^{DD} + A_V^D \bullet (A^{DD})^3$$
$$+ \ldots = A_V^D \bullet (I - A^{DD})^{-1}$$

Similarly, producing one unit of ordinary or processing export products also requires domestic made intermediate goods, which in turn generates many rounds of VA from these domestic intermediate inputs. We thus have:

(A2) $$B_V^P = A_V^P + B_V^D \bullet A^{DP}.$$

(A3) $$B_V^O = A_V^O + B_V^D \bullet A^{DO},$$

where B_V^i represents the total VA coefficient vector for production i, for $i = D$ (domestic), O (ordinary), and P (processing) respectively.

For the same reason, total import content caused by Domestic Production and exports are defined using i as a $(1 \times n)$ vector of one's:

(A4) $$B_M^D = i \bullet A^{MD} \bullet (I - A^{DD})^{-1}.$$

(A5) $$B_M^O = i \bullet A^{OO} + i \bullet A^{MD} \bullet (I - A^{DD})^{-1} \bullet A^{DO}.$$

(A6) $$B_M^P = i \bullet A^{PP} + i \bullet A^{MD} \bullet (I - A^{DD})^{-1}.$$

This is conceptually similar to the vertical specialization (VS) as in Hummels, Ishii, and Yi (2001) and Dean, Fung, and Wang (2007).

We estimate the total value added B using equations (A1) to (A6). The results are reported in table 5A.2.

Other Data

In table 5A.3, we show the allocation of value added to labor and capital, along with the share of value added within the sum of value added plus

Table 5A.2   Total value added and import content, 2000

Input-output industries	BVD	BVO	BVP	BMD	BMO	BMP
1. Agriculture	0.969	0.896	0.625	0.031	0.104	0.375
2. Coal mining and processing	0.945	0.811	0	0.055	0.189	0
3. Crude petroleum and natural gas products	0.957	0.814	0.762	0.043	0.186	0.238
4. Metal ore mining	0.908	0.623	0.370	0.092	0.377	0.630
5. Non-ferrous mineral mining	0.944	0.772	0.443	0.056	0.228	0.557
6. Manufacture of food products and tobacco processing	0.965	0.909	0.474	0.035	0.091	0.526
7. Textile goods	0.956	0.899	0.256	0.044	0.101	0.744
8. Wearing apparel, leather, furs, down, and related products	0.958	0.909	0.171	0.042	0.091	0.829
9. Sawmills and furniture	0.915	0.674	0.225	0.085	0.326	0.775
10. Paper and products, printing, and record medium reproduction	0.928	0.760	0.335	0.072	0.240	0.665
11. Petroleum processing and coking	0.865	0.268	0.343	0.135	0.732	0.657
12. Chemicals	0.923	0.664	0.345	0.077	0.336	0.655
13. Nonmetal mineral products	0.926	0.737	0.352	0.074	0.263	0.648
14. Metals smelting and pressing	0.901	0.635	0.404	0.099	0.365	0.596
15. Metal products	0.901	0.655	0.404	0.099	0.345	0.596
16. Machinery and equipment	0.890	0.591	0.347	0.110	0.409	0.653
17. Transport equipment	0.895	0.647	0.311	0.105	0.353	0.689
18. Electric equipment and machinery	0.899	0.680	0.174	0.101	0.320	0.826
19. Electronic and telecommunication equipment	0.855	0.702	0.184	0.145	0.298	0.816

20. Instruments, meters, cultural and office machinery	0.857	0.550	0.191	0.143	0.450	0.809
21. Maintenance and repair of machinery and equipment	0.907	0	0	0.093	0	0
22. Other manufacturing products	0.929	0.767	0.385	0.071	0.233	0.615
23. Scrap and waste	1	0	0	0	0	0
24. Electricity, steam, and hot water production and supply	0.930	0	0	0.070	0	0
25. Gas production and supply	0.921	0	0	0.079	0	0
26. Water production and supply	0.954	0	0	0.046	0	0
27. Construction	0.916	0.723	0	0.084	0.277	0
28. Transport and warehousing	0.944	0.806	0.717	0.056	0.194	0.283
29. Post and telecommunication	0.941	0.850	0.388	0.059	0.150	0.612
30. Wholesale and retail trade	0.949	0.835	0.672	0.051	0.165	0.328
31. Eating and drinking places	0.967	0.921	0.274	0.033	0.079	0.726
32. Passenger transport	0.928	0.766	0.633	0.072	0.234	0.367
33. Finance and insurance	0.974	0.907	0.875	0.026	0.093	0.125
34. Real estate	0.968	0	0	0.032	0	0
35. Social services	0.929	0.769	0.579	0.071	0.231	0.421
36. Health services, sports, and social welfare	0.927	0.741	0	0.073	0.259	0
37. Education, culture and arts, radio, film, and television	0.957	0.871	0.755	0.043	0.129	0.245
38. Scientific research	0.893	0	0	0.107	0	0
39. General technical services	0.951	0.824	0.622	0.049	0.176	0.378
40. Public administration and other sectors	0.944	0.807	0	0.056	0.193	0

Table 5A.3   Division of value added, 2000 and 2002

	From 2000 input-output table				2002
	Domestic production	Ordinary exports	Processing exports	Combined production	Combined production
Value added/(Value added + imports)	0.94	0.62	0.20	0.36	n.a.
Compensation of employees/Value added	0.54	0.50	0.45	0.54	0.48
Net taxes on production/ Value added	0.14	0.16	0.18	0.15	0.14
Gross capital income/ Value added	0.31	0.34	0.37	0.31	0.37

Notes: n.a. = not available. Figures reported here are only for the direct use of labor and imports in each type of production and do not take into account the indirect usage through domestic intermediate inputs.

imports used for each type of production: domestic production, ordinary exports, and processing exports. For each type of production, about one-half of value added goes toward compensating labor, with the remainder divided between capital income (one-third) and taxes on production (one-sixth). The amount of value added differs a great deal across type of production, however: it is 94 percent of the sum of value added plus imports used in domestic production, 62 percent for ordinary exports, and 20 percent for processing exports.

We have also confirmed that the employment levels in table 5.1 are consistent with the IO table itself, as described in table 5A.4. In the first column, we list the economywide compensation to labor from the various years of the IO tables and, in the next columns, the real agricultural and manufacturing wages (in US$, 2000). China employs one-half of its workers in agriculture and one-half in manufacturing, so we take the simple average of these two wages to obtain the average wage, which is $842 in 2000, for example. Dividing the labor compensation from the IO table by the average wage, we obtain employment of 716.5 million persons in 2000, which is very close to the 720.5 million persons reported in table 5.1.

For years before and after 2000, however, there is an inconsistency between the actual employment figures reported by the China Statistical Yearbook, in the last column of table 5.4, and the implied employment obtained by dividing total compensation from the IO tables by average wages from the China Statistical Yearbook, in the second-to-last column. Implied employment even falls over 1997 to 2002, which does not seem believable. The problem appears to be an inconsistency between the wage series we use (from the China Statistical Yearbook) and the wages that are implicit in the IO

Table 5A.4   Wages and employment

Year	Compensation from IO table (U.S.$ millions, 2000)	Agriculture sector wage (U.S.$, 2000)	Manufacturing sector wage (U.S.$, 2000)	Real wage[a] (average; U.S.$, 2000)	Implied employment[b] (millions of persons)	Actual employment[c] (millions of persons)
1995	334,000	476.6	699.4	520	641.9	680.7
1997	501,101	557.9	767.8	618	811.0	698.2
2000	603,003	626.2	1057.0	842	716.5	720.9
2002	712,224	740.0	1272.4	1,006	708.0	737.4
2005	n.a.	894.1	1695.5	1,468		758.3
			Using revised wage data[d]			
1997	501,101	602.5	829.2	715.9	700.0	698.2
2002	712,224	710.4	1221.5	966.0	737.3	737.4

Note: IO = input-output; n.a. = not available.

[a] Average wage is the simple average of manufacturing and agriculture sectors. Source for wage data is the China Statistical Yearbook, 2006.

[b] Implied employment = real compensation from IO table/real average wage.

[c] Actual employment data come from China Statistical Yearbook of each year.

[d] The revised wage data multiplies 1997 wages by 1.08, and multiplies 2002 wages by 0.96 so that the implied employment is roughly equal to actual employment.

tables, at least in 1997 and 2002.[13] It is essential that the implied employment from the IO table in each year equal actual employment in the economy. To achieve this, we inflate the 1997 wages from the China Statistical Yearbook by 8 percent and deflate the 2002 wages by 4 percent, obtaining the revised wages reported in the bottom of table 5.4. Those adjusted wages lead to implied employment from the IO tables that is roughly equal to that reported by the China Statistical Yearbook. We will continue to use this simple adjustment to 1997 and 2002 wages in all our calculations.

References

Aziz, Jahangir, and Li Cui. 2007. Explaining China's low consumption: The neglected role of household income. IMF Working Paper no. 07/181. Washington, DC: International Monetary Fund.

Bernstein, Jeffrey R., and David E. Weinstein. 2002. Do endowments predict the location of production? Evidence from national and international data. *Journal of International Economics* 56 (1): 55–76.

Chen, Xikang, Leonard K. Cheng, K. C. Fung, and Lawrence J. Lau. 2004. The estimation of domestic value added and employment induced by exports: An application to Chinese exports to the United States. Paper presented at the AEA conference, Boston.

Chen, Xikang, Leonard K. Cheng, K. C. Fung, Lawrence J. Lau, Yung Wing Sung, C. Yang, K. Zhu, J. Pei, and Z. Tan. 2008. Domestic value added and employment generated by Chinese exports: A quantitative estimation. FREIT Working Paper no. 7. http://eitt.org/WorkingPapers/Papers/TradePolicyGeneral/FREIT007.pdf.

Dean, Judith M., K. C. Fung, and Zhi Wang. 2007. Measuring the vertical specialization in Chinese trade. U.S. International Trade Commission, Working Paper.

Denison, Edward. 1967. *Why growth rates differ.* Washington, DC: Brookings Institution.

———. 1980. *Accounting for slower growth: The United States in the 1970s.* Washington, DC: Brookings Institution.

Dooley, Michael P., David Folkerts-Landau, and Peter Garber. 2003. An essay on the revived Bretton Woods system, NBER Working Paper no. 9971. Cambridge, MA: National Bureau of Economic Research.

———. 2004a. Direct investment, rising real wages and the absorption of excess labor in the periphery. NBER Working Paper no. 10626. Cambridge, MA: National Bureau of Economic Research. Also published in *G7 Current Account Imbalances: Sustainability and Adjustment*, Richard H. Clarida, ed., 103–27. Chicago: The National Bureau of Economic Research, 2007.

———. 2004b. The revived Bretton Woods system: The effects of periphery intervention and reserve management on interest rates and exchange rates in center coun-

13. For 2000, when we have the most complete IO table available, it lists both labor compensation and employment at the end of the year. So the wages being used in the IO table can be computed, and they are highly consistent with both the wages and actual employment figures used in table 5.4 for 2000. For 1997 and 2002, however, the IO table is less complete and, in particular, does not list employment so that implied wages cannot be computed.

tries. NBER Working Paper no. 10331. Cambridge, MA: National Bureau of Economic Research.

———. 2004c. The U.S. current account deficit and economic development: Collateral for a total return swap. NBER Working Paper no. 10727. Cambridge, MA: National Bureau of Economic Research.

———. 2005. *International Financial Stability: Asia, Interest Rates, and the Dollar.* Deutsche Bank. http://people.ucsc.edu/~mpd/InternationalFinancialStability _update.pdf.

Felipe, Jesus, and Rana Hasan. 2006a. The challenge of job creation in Asia. ERD Policy Brief no. 44. Manila, The Philippines: Asian Development Bank. http:// www.asiandevbank.org/Documents/EDRC/Policy_Briefs/PB044.pdf.

———. 2006b. Labor markets in a globalizing world. In *Labor markets in Asia: Issues and perspectives,* ed. Jesus Felipe and Rana Hasan, 63–142. London: Palgrave Macmillan.

Hummels, David, Jun Ishii, and Kei-Mu Yi. 2001. The nature and growth of vertical specialization in world trade. *Journal of International Economics* 54:75–96.

Lau, Lawrence J., Xikang Chen, Leonard K. Cheng, K. C. Fung, Yun-Wing Sung, Cuihong Yang, Kunfu Zhu, Zhipeng Tang, and Jiansuo Pei. 2006a. Estimates of U.S.-China trade balances in terms of domestic value added. Stanford Center for International Development Working Paper no. 295. Stanford, CA: Stanford University.

———. 2006b. The estimation of domestic value added and employment generated by U.S.-China trade. Institute of Economics Working Paper no. 2. Hong Kong: Chinese University of Hong Kong.

———. 2006c. Estimation of domestic value added and employment induced by China's exports. Unpublished Manuscript.

Nordhaus, William. 2002. Productivity growth and the new economy. *Brookings Papers on Economic Activity,* Issue no. 2:211–65. Washington, DC: Brookings Institution.

Wei, Shang-Jin. 2007. Comment on Direct Investment, rising real wages, and the absorption of excess labor in the periphery. In *G7 Current Account Imbalances: Sustainability and Adjustment,* ed. Richard Clarida, 128–32. chicago: National Bureau of Economic Research

Comment   Michael Dooley

This chapter provides a careful evaluation of the contribution of export growth to growth in manufacturing employment in China in recent years. Feenstra and Hong are generous in citing my work with Folkerts-Landau and Garber as providing an incentive to evaluate the role of export industries in absorbing some 250 million underemployed workers over the next decade or so. They find that our back-of-the-envelope calculation that exports have generated one-third of the growth in employment is roughly consistent with their estimates generated from input-output data adjusted for productivity

Michael Dooley is a professor of economics at the University of California, Santa Cruz, and a research associate of the National Bureau for Economic Research.

growth. These adjustments reflect the fact that in traded goods industries, output has grown much faster than labor inputs.

Their interpretation of this evidence, however, is quite different from ours. They observe that shifting toward domestic demand might stimulate more employment for a given growth rate. We have argued that an effective development strategy provides workers capital and technology that generates an improvement in labor productivity. It follows that relatively slow growth in employment is a necessary condition for a successful development strategy.

Productivity growth could, in principle, come from growth in traded (including agriculture) or nontraded goods output. Moreover, this growth in output could be supported by domestic or foreign demand. In any case, employment must grow more slowly than output for real wages to rise. If productivity did not increase, there would be little point in switching labor from one sector to another.

Feenstra and Hong provide important evidence that domestic demand for traded goods has actually declined in China in recent years and suggest that policies that encourage the domestic demand would be just as effective as export demand in supporting traded-goods industrialization and growth. True, but if the mechanism for accomplishing this is real appreciation of the exchange rate China would lose the incentive for foreign firms to risk their capital in China and the associated transfers of technology.

We do not offer, nor have we found, a theoretical reason for favoring one development strategy over another. For example, the strategy of import substitution industrialization popular in Latin America until recently might have succeeded. The idea here was to switch domestic demand from imports to domestic manufactured goods. It was assumed that productivity growth in the industrial sector would generate economic growth and rising real wages. But the clear evidence is that it did not.

There is the possibility, of course, that this need not have been a problem for the international system at all. If there is unemployed labor and inefficient capital formation in emerging markets, why not reform their domestic institutions and rely on domestic markets to create employment and economic growth? A recurrent criticism of our approach is that we focus on growth in export industries and participation in international financial markets and neglect the contribution of development of domestic goods and financial markets. Clearly, domestic demand that supports the expansion of high-productivity jobs and capital accumulation is as good as international demand.

We do not know why inward looking development polices such as the import substitute industrialization popular in Latin America have been such dismal failures or why it has proven so difficult to reform domestic financial markets. We only point out that if we were responsible for the development strategy of a poor country, we would not find many historical examples of successful inward looking strategies. The only thing we are sure of is that we reject categorically assertions that "economic theory" tells us much about what will and will not be a successful development strategy.

It would be wonderful to reform the domestic financial systems in emerging markets because this would liberate domestic savings for efficient capital formation. But we observe that it is more effective to bypass the domestic financial system by allowing capital flight from the country to return in the form of direct or equity investment. This replaces the distorted domestic allocation incentives. It also threatens the rents captured by domestic financial institutions as their business is lost to international markets. The domestic reaction, of course, is to tighten controls on capital flows. But at some point the threat of replacement will generate reform.

From a macroeconomic perspective, China's large savings have been more than sufficient to finance its own development. However, its poor domestic financial system, its need for foreign technology and management skills, and its need to pry open foreign markets were insurmountable barriers to a purely domestic approach based on domestic demand. The solution to the problem came about perhaps by chance—implement the macroeconomic policies outlined in the preceding, let foreign financial markets partially intermediate Chinese savings, let foreign capital profit from the strategy, and thereby split the interests of foreign labor and capital to keep open the export markets.

6

Exporting Deflation?
Chinese Exports and
Japanese Prices

Christian Broda and David E. Weinstein

The spectacular growth of China in the last two decades has caused China to replace Japan as the major new source of U.S. imports and destination for our exports. This perception has not gone unnoticed by Japanese who often bemoan the relative decline of the perceived importance of Japan with the phrase, "Japan Passing." Much less well known in the United States is how the rapid growth of trade with China is affecting the world's second largest economy. The explosion of trade between Japan and China has had profound impacts on the Japanese economy and is frequently seen as a source of Japan's persistent deflation. For example, in a now famous article in the *Financial Times,* the Vice Minister and Deputy Vice Minister for International Affairs at the Japanese Ministry of Finance wrote:

> The entry of emerging market economies—such as China and other east Asian nations—into the global trading system is a powerful additional deflationary force. Their combined supply capacity has been exerting downward pressure on the prices of goods in industrialised economies. . . . China is exporting deflation and its effects are not limited to neighboring Hong Kong and Taiwan.[1]

Christian Broda is a professor of economics at the Graduate School of Business, University of Chicago, and a faculty research fellow of the National Bureau of Economic Research. David E. Weinstein is the Carl Sumner Shoup Professor of the Japanese Economy at Columbia University, and a research associate of the National Bureau of Economic Research.

The authors want to thank the National Science Foundation (NSF; grant SES-0452460) for funding for this project. David Weinstein would like to also thank the Center for Japanese Economy and Business. This work was supported by the James S. Kemper Foundation Faculty Research Fund at the Graduate School of Business, University of Chicago. Alexis Antonaides and Jessie Handbury provided excellent research assistance for this project. We also want to thank Joshua Aizenman, Mary Amiti, and Robert Feenstra for excellent comments.

1. See Masahiro Kawai and Haruhiko Kuroda, "Time for a switch to global reflation," *Financial Times,* December 2, 2002, 23.

This notion that China was exporting deflation by exporting goods at low prices was repeated by market analysts and policymakers both inside and outside of Japan.[2]

In this chapter, we assess the impact that Chinese exports have had on Japanese consumer prices in the years between 1992 and 2005. We start by showing that although the official Japanese import price index (IPI) is based on a Laspeyres index formula, it differs importantly to a standard Laspeyres index in terms of how goods are sampled and weighted. As a result, we show an IPI computed using a pure Laspeyres formula would have resulted in substantial *inflation* over this period. This suggests that one cannot separate one's interpretation of the direction in which aggregate Japanese prices were moving from the methodologies used. The fact that index number problems are sufficiently large in Japanese import price data to bias the numbers downward by 1 percentage point per year could easily have confused policymakers and economists alike about how trade was affecting price movements in Japan.

Despite this aggregate pattern, the notion that China might be exporting deflation may be warranted given the importance of China in Japan's trade and the perception that Chinese products are falling in price. The rise in importance of China in Japan's import and export structure over this period has been dramatic and has happened simultaneously with a sharp decline in the importance of the United States. In 1992, the United States exported three times as much to Japan as China; by 2005, China was exporting twice as much as the United States. Moreover, between 1992 and 2005, the number of new imported varieties entering Japan rose by 32 percent, and China played an enormous role in this expansion—accounting for 11 percent of the total. This is more than twice the level we observed in the United States over a similar period. The fact that the United States and China have traded places, or at least traded trade shares, is not a fact that is well known in the United States and is likely to dramatically alter Japanese-United States relations in the future.

Understanding the price impact of the expansion of Chinese exports is more complex. Although China plays a large role in Japanese imports, we find no evidence that import prices from China fell faster than those from other countries. In those categories where China already had a presence in 1992, we do not find that Chinese prices fell more rapidly than those of other exporters to Japan. Moreover, the impact of Chinese competition to other exporters is also small. There is no evidence that the entry of Chinese firms into new markets has any significant impact on the pricing behavior of other

2. The idea that the presence of China might be reducing prices is also popular in the United States. Broda and Romalis (2008) estimate the impact that China has had on the prices of goods paid by different income groups in America. Bergin and Feenstra (2007) argue that the rise in China's share of U.S. imports may explain the lower pass-through of exchange rates to U.S. import prices.

exporting countries.[3] Clearly, what is driving the rapid expansion of Chinese exports into Japan is not lower prices for existing goods.

Given the large growth of varieties coming from China, it is possible that the popular belief that China is exporting deflation is being driven by the constant introduction of cheap Chinese products in Japanese markets. It is important to notice that the introduction of new products would not be captured in existing price indexes, which usually ignore product entry and exit.[4] In order to identify the impact that a new product has on prices, we need to understand its welfare implications. Intuitively, the introduction of a new product reduces the cost of living for consumers (i.e., the true price index) if the *price-per-unit quality* of the new product is *lower* than that of existing products (i.e., higher quality or lower price than existing products) or if the new product is sufficiently different from existing products that consumers value the additional choice. Lower price-per-unit quality and higher variety of Chinese products could also explain the large increase in Chinese shares in the recent period.

We use a constant-elasticity-of-substitution (CES) aggregator to back out the implied impact of new products on the Japanese cost of living. We find that there has been a remarkable decrease in the price-per-unit quality of Chinese exports. Price-per-unit quality of Chinese exports halved during this period, due largely to quality upgrading. This is one of the most dramatic increases in quality that we observe in the data. In other words, while prices of Chinese products as computed in official statistics are not falling by more than those of other exports to China, the quality of Chinese products is rising relative to those of other countries. However, we find the quantitative significance of this quality growth to be small. If the Japanese were to correct for the increase in quality in Chinese products in the IPI, then the quality-adjusted import price inflation would only be 1 percentage point smaller than the actual import inflation over the 1992 to 2004 period.

While the specific price impact of new products from China is small, the impact of all new and higher quality imports can account for a fall in Japanese import prices of as much as 10 percentage points over the 1992 to 2004 period. This is smaller than the impact that new products had in the United States and several other developed countries (see Broda and Weinstein 2006) but still important given that the official IPI has been relatively flat over this entire period. However, given that imports are such a small share of Japan's

---

3. The impact of Chinese imports on the pricing of *domestic* competitors is beyond the scope of this paper. This might be an important channel through which Chinese imports affect Japanese prices, but a clean match between trade data and data on domestic prices is hard to obtain.

4. This is a problem in the computation of most price indexes around the world, not only the Japanese IPI. To confirm that this is true in the Japanese case, we show that one can replicate the official IPI very closely using unit value data for the set of imports that are common throughout the period. This is strong evidence that the impact of new and better products is not captured in official statistics.

overall consumption, the deflationary impact of new imported goods in Japan's is still small, at around 1 percentage point throughout the entire period.[5]

In sum, China is not placing a strong deflationary impact on the actual Japanese IPI either directly through lower inflation of existing Chinese products or through competition to other Japanese exporters. Moreover, the magnitude of the effect of new goods from China in Japanese import prices is clearly deflationary, but the effect is small. Taking into account all of Japan's new imported products, this effect can explain part of the perception that globalization is reducing import prices in Japan. Despite the large impact of new and better products in the quality-adjusted IPI, the low level of imports in consumption suggest that the impact of globalization on consumer prices is still small in Japan.[6]

6.1   Japan's Trade with China

6.1.1   Overview

We first provide an overview of Japanese exports and imports. For our initial overview of Japanese import and export data, we rely on the aggregates provided by the Japanese Ministry of Finance.[7] Between 1988 and 2006, Japanese imports rose by 181 percent, and Japanese exports rose by 122 percent in nominal terms. Interestingly, imports from and exports to the United States rose at rates that were only a third as fast (46 and 47 percent, respectively). By contrast, exports to China rose by 454 percent, and imports from China rose by a whopping 810 percent. These numbers do not simply reflect rapid growth from a low base. Of the 84 trillion yen worth of total new trade that arose during this period, over one-third was due to trade with China.

Figure 6.1 documents movements in the import structure of Japan. The figure makes clear the very rapid change in position of the United States and China. Although one cannot see it in the figure, in 1975 Japan not only imported more from the United States than China, but it also imported more from the United States than all of East Asia. East Asia gradually overtook China as a source of Japanese imports in the late seventies, but the rise of imports from China did not really take off until 1990. Until 1998, the rise of imports from China did not entail any deterioration in the share of imports emanating from the United States. Thereafter, the importance of the United

---

5. This number is roughly coming from the fact that the import share of Japan is around 10 percent.

6. An important channel that we do not explore in this paper is the exact quantitative role that globalization has on Japan's prices through the competitive pressure that imported goods put on *domestic* producers.

7. See http://www.customs.go.jp/toukei/info/index_e.htm.

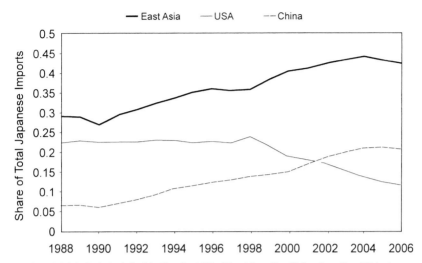

Notes: East Asia is defined to be Cambodia, China (Hong Kong), China (Taiwan), Korea, Dem. PP. Rep., Korea, Rep. of, Malaysia, Myanmar, Philippines, Singapore, Sri Lanka, Thailand, Viet Nam, Indonesia; China is defined to be China and China (Hong Kong).

Fig. 6.1   Share of Japanese imports by source country or region

Notes: East Asia is defined to be Cambodia; China; China (Hong Kong); China (Taiwan); Korea, Dem. PP. Rep.; the Republic of Korea; Malaysia; Myanmar; The Philippines; Singapore; Sri Lanka; Thailand; Vietnam; Indonesia; China is defined to be China and China (Hong Kong).

States as a Japanese trading partner entered a steep decline. Interestingly, all of the increase in imports from East Asia reflects the growth in imports from China. In fact, the share of imports from East Asia excluding China (and Hong Kong) actually fell from 23 percent in 1988 to 22 percent by 2006. Thus, the growth in imports from China was not matched by a more general growth in imports from East Asia more broadly.

One can observe a similar pattern in the export flows emanating from Japan as shown in figure 6.2. Although Japanese exports to China have not overtaken those to the United States, there is clear evidence of a dramatic change in the relative positions of the two countries. Between 1988 and 2006, the share of Japanese exports going to either China or the United States stood at a remarkably stable 42 percent. However, in 1988, 34 percent of Japanese exports were destined for the US as compared to only 23 percent by 2006. Thus, on both the import and export side one can observe a dramatic increase in the interdependency of the Japanese and Chinese economies.

Tables 6.1 and 6.2 report changes in the importance of the top twenty-five exporters to Japan by aggregating up nine-digit bilateral data supplied by the Japan Tariff Association. We shift to these data because it allows us to examine Japanese trade in far more detail than the Ministry of Finance (MOF) data. The top twenty-five exporters accounted for 88 percent of all Japanese imports in both 1992 and 2005. The rise in oil prices over this

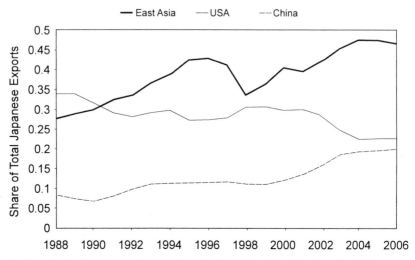

Notes: East Asia is defined to be Cambodia, China (Hong Kong), China (Taiwan), Korea, Dem. PP. Rep., Korea, Rep. of, Malaysia, Myanmar, Philippines, Singapore, Sri Lanka, Thailand, Viet Nam, Indonesia; China is defined to be China and China (Hong Kong).

Fig. 6.2   Share of Japanese exports by source country or region
Note: See figure 6.1 notes.

time period has dramatically increased the importance of countries like Saudi Arabia, United Arab Emirates, Iran, and Qatar as a source of imports. Other than shifts due to the rise in oil prices, there do not appear to be any substantial shifts in the relative rankings of East Asian sources of supply, with the major exception of Hong Kong. Hong Kong appears to have fallen dramatically as a source of supply as goods are shipped from other locations in China. Interestingly, imports from the other growing giant, India, actually fell as a share of total Japanese imports by 30 percent, indicating that the remarkable recent growth in that country has not produced a comparable increase in exports to Japan.

6.1.2   Growth in Varieties

There are many ways in which one can define a "variety." In this paper, we define varieties as in Broda and Weinstein (2006), that is, the imports of a Harmonized System (HS) nine-digit good from a particular country. This definition is close to the concept first suggested by Armington (1969) and is consistent with a wide class of monopolistic competition models.

Table 6.3 documents that the number of varieties entering Japan rose by 32 percent between 1992 and 2005, that is, from 71,666 varieties in 1992 to just under 95,000 varieties in 2005. There is always a question when using this definition of variety growth about how much of the growth can be attributed to an increase in the number of categories and how much is due to an increase in new varieties per se. As one can see from the table, the count

Table 6.1   **Ranking in terms of goods imported by Japan**

Country	1992	1995	2000	2005	Change 1992–2005
United States	1	1	1	2	–1
China	2	2	2	1	1
Australia	3	4	7	5	–2
Indonesia	4	6	5	7	–3
Republic of Korea	5	3	3	6	–1
Germany	6	7	10	9	–3
SU ARAB	7	12	9	3	4
United Arab Emirates	8	10	6	4	4
Taiwan	9	5	4	8	1
Canada	10	8	12	14	–4
Malaysia	11	9	8	11	0
Thailand	12	11	11	10	2
France	13	15	16	15	–2
United Kingdom	14	13	14	19	–5
Italy	15	16	19	18	–3
Switzerland	16	18	23	24	–8
Singapore	17	14	15	20	–3
Brazil	18	19	25	26	–8
Iran	19	23	18	13	6
Russia	20	17	21	21	–1
The Philippines	21	20	13	16	5
Qatar	22	31	17	12	10
Hong Kong	23	25	36	39	–16
India	24	22	29	28	–4
Oman	25	34	33	29	–4

of new varieties entering Japan rose 32 percent over this time period, whereas the average number countries exporting a particular variety grew by 31 percent. Thus, virtually all of the increase in new varieties imported by Japan can be ascribed to new sources of imports of particular nine-digit goods.

In table 6.4, we report the relative contributions of different exporters to Japanese import variety growth. China's contribution is roughly double that of the next highest contributor over this time period, Vietnam. Although non-Chinese, East-Asian exporters did not expand their total exports to Japan dramatically over this time period, they did play a central role in the expansion of new varieties entering Japan. Just over a quarter of new varieties entering Japan came from these countries, and East Asia as a whole accounted for 37 percent of Japanese variety growth. By contrast, the number of varieties coming from the largest exporter to Japan over this time period, the United States, actually fell slightly. Thus, the picture of what is happening with the number of varieties complements that of what happened with imports as a whole—there was a substantial expansion of varieties

Table 6.2   Share of total Japanese imports of the top 25 exporters in 1992

Country	1992	1995	2000	2005	Change 1992–2005
United States	0.224	0.224	0.190	0.124	–0.100
China	0.073	0.107	0.145	0.210	0.138
Australia	0.053	0.043	0.039	0.048	–0.006
Indonesia	0.052	0.042	0.043	0.040	–0.012
Republic of Korea	0.050	0.051	0.054	0.047	–0.002
Germany	0.046	0.041	0.034	0.035	–0.012
SU ARAB	0.044	0.029	0.037	0.056	0.012
United Arab Emirates	0.042	0.030	0.039	0.049	0.007
Taiwan	0.041	0.043	0.047	0.035	–0.006
Canada	0.033	0.032	0.023	0.017	–0.016
Malaysia	0.028	0.031	0.038	0.028	0.000
Thailand	0.026	0.030	0.028	0.030	0.005
France	0.023	0.020	0.017	0.017	–0.007
United Kingdom	0.021	0.021	0.017	0.013	–0.008
Italy	0.018	0.019	0.014	0.013	–0.005
Switzerland	0.014	0.012	0.009	0.010	–0.004
Singapore	0.013	0.020	0.017	0.013	0.000
Brazil	0.012	0.012	0.008	0.009	–0.004
Iran	0.011	0.008	0.014	0.020	0.009
Russia	0.010	0.014	0.012	0.012	0.002
The Philippines	0.010	0.010	0.019	0.015	0.005
Qatar	0.009	0.006	0.015	0.021	0.011
Hong Kong	0.009	0.008	0.004	0.003	–0.006
India	0.009	0.009	0.007	0.006	–0.003
Oman	0.008	0.006	0.005	0.005	–0.003

from East Asia, and especially from China, and a relative decline of the importance of the United States.

6.2   Implications for Japanese Prices

The preceding data preview suggests a number of important possibilities of the impact of globalization and Chinese exports in particular on Japan. In order to examine this, it is important to keep track of impacts arising from the price movements of existing goods and those of new goods entering Japan. To the extent that exports from China have driven down the price of existing imports relative to exports, this would be reflected as a terms-of-trade gain in Japan statistics. By contrast, the availability of new imported products would tend to drive down Japanese prices, but this effect would be mostly missed by official statistics. This happens as new varieties effectively constitute a fall in price from the reservation level to the observed level, but this fall in prices is ignored by most statistical offices around the world.

A goal of this paper is to examine the importance of these forces in the

Table 6.3	Variety in Japan's imports (1992–2005)			
	Total no. of varieties (country-good pairs)	Median no. of exporting countries	Average no. of exporting countries	Share of total U.S. imports in year
All 1992 goods	71,666	15.0	17.0	1.00
All 2005 goods	94,707	19.0	22.2	1.00
Common 1992–2005				
1992	58,641	15.0	17.4	0.67
2005	75,519	21.0	23.2	0.69
1992 not in 2005	13,025	12.0	15.1	0.33
2005 not in 1992	19,188	15.0	18.2	0.31

case of Japan. However, before we do so, we need to delve a little deeper into the data. One possible source of Japanese import data are the official IPIs provided by the Bank of Japan. These indexes are based on a sample of 896 prices in the 1995 base index and 1601 prices in the 2000 index (Bank of Japan 2002). This is between 1–2 percent of the total number of unit values reported in the Japan Tariff Association data. Thus, the sample of prices used in the official index is much smaller than that universe of import prices. We will compare the Bank of Japan data with indexes derived using the data from the Tariff Association.

6.2.1   The Official Import Price Index (IPI)

The Japanese IPI is not constructed as a simple Laspeyres index. The Japanese IPI is computed using a nonrandom sample of import prices. In particular, the index samples commodities with a minimum transaction value (18.8 billion yen in 2000).[8] These prices are then averaged together using weights that are set every five years. The fact that weights are not updated annually but at longer frequencies (most recently 1995 and 2000) will give rise to differences between what are considered best-practice indexes formulas and official Japanese indexes.

Finally, it is worth noting that the IPI, like most official indexes, cannot be used to assess the importance of new varieties entering Japan. The importance of this can be seen by examining the last four rows of table 6.3. Only about two-thirds of the varieties that were imported in 1992 were also imported in 2005, and, similarly, one-third of the goods imported in 2005 were not imported in 1992. This underscores the importance played of new and disappearing varieties in import flows and suggests that an index based on a common set of goods is going to miss a lot of the implied price changes.

8. See http://www.boj.or.jp/en/type/exp/stat/pi/data/ecgpi00.pdf.

Table 6.4 Country contribution to growth in Japanese varieties (%)

Country	1992–1998 Contribution	1992–1998 Average share of Japanese imports	1999–2005 Contribution	1999–2005 Average share of Japanese imports	1992–2005 Contribution	1992–2005 Average share of Japanese imports
China	9.3	10.5	11.8	17.8	11.2	14.2
Vietnam	5.3	0.5	6.6	0.8	6.2	0.6
Thailand	4.0	2.8	4.9	3.0	4.6	2.9
India	3.2	0.9	5.1	0.6	4.4	0.7
Indonesia	4.8	4.6	2.6	4.2	4.3	4.4
Korea, Republic of	4.2	4.7	2.7	4.9	4.2	4.8
The Philippines	3.6	1.2	1.5	1.8	3.0	1.5
Malaysia	3.5	3.1	1.4	3.4	2.9	3.3
Mexico	2.9	0.5	2.4	0.5	2.7	0.5
Italy	2.3	1.8	3.3	1.5	2.6	1.7
Spain	2.4	0.4	2.7	0.4	2.5	0.4
Belgium	2.4	0.6	2.3	0.5	2.2	0.5
Israel	2.3	0.3	1.5	0.2	1.9	0.3
Brazil	0.7	1.1	4.0	0.8	1.9	1.0
Canada	3.4	3.1	-0.3	2.1	1.8	2.6
Australia	2.4	4.7	-0.1	4.2	1.4	4.4
Austria	1.3	0.3	1.7	0.3	1.3	0.3
Finland	1.8	0.3	1.0	0.3	1.3	0.3
Taiwan	1.8	4.0	0.8	4.0	1.2	4.0
The Netherlands	1.8	0.6	-0.2	0.5	0.9	0.6
France	2.2	2.0	-0.5	1.8	0.9	1.9
Russia	0.1	1.2	2.2	1.2	0.8	1.2
Denmark	0.9	0.6	1.4	0.6	0.8	0.6
South Africa	0.7	0.8	1.4	0.9	0.7	0.8

United Arab Emirates	0.7	3.5	0.7	3.8	0.7	3.6
Singapore	1.1	1.7	-0.5	1.5	0.7	1.6
New Zealand	0.6	0.7	0.7	0.6	0.7	0.6
Peru	0.5	0.1	0.6	0.1	0.6	0.1
Argentina	0.1	0.2	1.1	0.1	0.5	0.1
Sweden	0.8	0.7	-0.2	0.6	0.5	0.6
Iran	0.5	1.0	0.2	1.6	0.5	1.3
Norway	1.2	0.3	-0.8	0.3	0.4	0.3
Chile	0.3	0.8	0.5	0.8	0.4	0.8
Ireland	1.4	0.6	-0.5	0.9	0.3	0.8
Colombia	0.3	0.1	0.2	0.1	0.2	0.1
Pakistan	0.3	0.2	0.4	0.1	0.2	0.1
Puerto Rico	0.2	0.1	0.0	0.2	0.2	0.2
Germany	0.9	4.0	0.1	3.6	0.1	3.8
United Kingdom	2.0	2.1	-1.5	1.6	0.1	1.9
Oman	0.2	0.6	0.0	0.6	0.1	0.6
Brunei	0.1	0.5	0.0	0.4	0.1	0.4
Qatar	0.0	0.8	0.1	1.6	0.1	1.2
Kuwait	0.2	0.8	-0.2	1.2	0.1	1.0
Papua New Guinea	-0.1	0.2	0.2	0.1	0.1	0.1
Nigeria	0.1	0.0	0.0	0.2	0.0	0.1
Su Arab	0.4	3.3	-0.4	3.8	0.0	3.6
Venezuela	0.0	0.1	-0.1	0.1	0.0	0.1
United States	2.1	22.8	-2.9	16.8	-0.1	19.8
Switzerland	-0.3	1.1	1.1	1.0	-0.2	1.1
Hong Kong	-0.5	0.8	-0.7	0.4	-0.8	0.6

Note: Countries are ranked by average share of Japanese imports from 1992 to 2005.

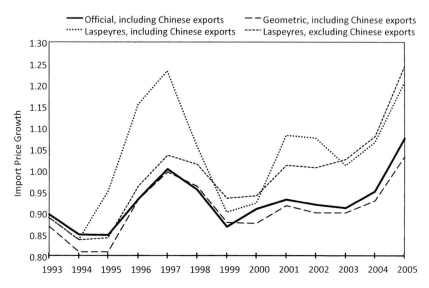

Fig. 6.3   Laspeyres index versus official import price index

Notes: Geometric and Laspeyres indexes are computed using unit value data. Unit values are trimmed to remove unit values whose ratios increase by more 3 or fall by more than 0.3. We also drop all imports of less than 1 million yen. Base years for the official index are 1990, 1995, and 2000. Base years for the other indexes are 1992 and 2000.

However, a major advantage of using the official data is that by defining products precisely, the official index avoids the problem that movements in unit values may reflect changes in the composition of underlying goods rather than changes in the prices themselves. Certainly, it is easy to find in the data examples of wild unit value movements that almost surely reflect measurement issues, but these data problems have to be set against the fact that by working with unit value data, one can have access to a vastly broader set of price data. Moreover, by working with unit values, one can also use comparable quantity data.

To further assess the relative costs and benefits of unit value versus official import price data, we can compare the actual import inflation that would be implied from unit value data in the recent years. In order to deal with data problems in the unit value data, we dropped observations where the ratio of the future price to the past price exceeds 3 or is less than 0.33 or if the units reported for the quantity data changed. We built all of our indexes with base years of 1992 and 2000 so that the rebasing closely matches that of the official index. Figure 6.3 presents a comparison between our Laspeyres index and the official one. Interestingly the geometric price index computed using unit value data using the basic index formulas tracks the official index very closely, but our pure Laspeyres index exhibits much more import price inflation. Although the documentation for the Japanese IPI is not sufficiently

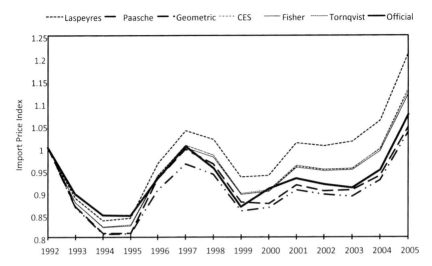

Fig. 6.4   Formula biases in Japanese import price indexes

Notes: Geometric and Laspeyres indexes are computed using unit value data. Unit values are trimmed to remove unit values whose ratios increase by more 3 or fall by more than 0.3. We also drop all imports of less than 1 million yen. Base years for the official index are 1990, 1995, and 2000. Base years for the other indexes are 1992 and 2000. The Paasche, CES, Fisher, and Törnqvist indexes are all computed using the current and base year weights (i.e., not chained weights).

detailed to let us know how the sampling affects the index, it appears to dramatically reduce IPIs. Nevertheless, the correlation between the annual inflation rates between the unit value index that uses a Laspeyres formula and the official index is 0.952, and 0.948 with the unit value index that uses a geometric formula. This high correlation suggests that despite the noise in the unit values, the index based on unit values traces the official inflation rates very closely. In the rest of the paper, we will use this remarkable relationship as an important building block for understanding the impact that formula and variety changes can have on the Japanese IPI.

Given that a unit value price index traces the official index so closely, we can assess the sensitivity of inflation rates to various formula biases. Figure 6.4 shows the IPI using a Laspeyres formula and a number of other indexes—Fisher, Törnqvist, CES, geometric, and Paasche—together with the official IPI. If the index were closer to a pure Laspeyres, it would have significant upward bias. All of these indexes are constructed with base years of 1992 and 2000. Between 1992 and 2005, the Laspeyres index rose 1.1 percent per year faster than the geometric index (which closely matches the official index) and 0.6 percent per year faster than the Törnqvist and Fisher indexes. The Törnqvist and geometric indexes differ in that the former uses weights from both the base and final year, while the latter only uses weights from the earlier year. Interestingly, the geometric price index seems to understate inflation relative to the superlative indexes. These large differences underscore the importance of using the same methodology when making inferences between price indexes in a country (or across countries as in Broda and Weinstein 2007).

According to the Bank of Japan Web site, between 1992 and 2002, import prices fell by 9 percent or almost 1 percent per year. Given that Consumer Price Index (CPI) inflation over this time period averaged 0.2 percent, it is argued that dropping import prices tended to pull down average prices in Japan. The surprising conclusion is that a Japanese IPI based on a pure Laspeyres methodology registered an average inflation rate of 0.0 percent over the same time period.[9] This suggests that the perception that import prices were falling as Japan entered into a period of deflation was driven by the fact that the IPI is not constructed like a pure Laspeyres index. Had the IPI been constructed as a pure Laspeyres index like the CPI, the inflation rates of import prices would have been higher.[10]

The dispersion in the formula biases is also remarkable. One of the striking features of the plot is the behavior of prices between 1992 and 2002. Much of the inflation in Japanese import prices is driven by a very rapid increase in import prices at the end of the sample. If we focus on the period between 1992 and 2002, the time when MOF officials were making their statements, the drop in import prices is a bit more pronounced. Almost this entire drop occurred between 1997 and 2002. Thus, there is some evidence that import prices were falling in Japan around the time that Japan entered deflation. We also can rerun this analysis using annual base updating. Interestingly, updating the base years each year tends to cause measured inflation to rise in these data. Annual base updating causes the Fisher and Törnqvist indexes to rise by 0.7 and 0.6 percent faster, respectively, over the whole time period. The Laspeyres inflation rate rises by a whopping 1.5 percent per year with annual base updating.

This suggests that the recent move to increase the rate of base updating in CPI could cause Japanese inflation to appear to be higher. Our data suggests that had the (BOJ) been using a superlative index like the Fisher or Törnqvist and updating the base annually, they would have found that prices had actually been rising slightly between 1992 and 2002 and even between 1997 and 2002. This type of index would have shown that between 1997 and 2002, prices didn't actually fall by 9 percent; they actually rose by 2 percent! Similarly, using superlative indexes with base years of 1992 and 2000, half

---

9. The reason for this difference can be traced to what is referred to in the literature as the upper-level substitution bias that is not corrected using a Laspeyres index, but is accounted for using a geometric index.

10. Similarly, the fact that the Bureau of Labor Statistics's import and export price indexes are essentially pure Laspeyres indexes indicates that the different formulas used by international statistical agencies can produce substantially different pictures of what is happening to import prices.

Table 6.5	Formula biases of import price indexes (1992–2005)					
	Laspeyres	Paasche	Geometric	CES	Fisher	Official
Median bias of index relative to Törnqvist	0.4	–0.6	–0.7	0.0	–0.1	–0.4
Standard deviation of measurement error	0.6	0.6	0.8	0.2	0.1	2.0

of the price drop disappears. As one can see in figure 6.4, superlative indexes computed with these base years suggest a fall in prices of only 5 percent. Thus, formula bias may be the reason why it appeared that Japanese deflation occurred at the same time as import price deflation.

Figure 6.4 also provides other interesting facts. Not surprisingly, the two superlative indexes, the Fisher and Törnqvist, yield almost identical rates of inflation. Perhaps more surprising is that the CES price index is also almost indistinguishable from the superlative indexes. This will be a useful fact that we will use later to argue that the variety bias using a CES aggregator is probably a reasonable approximation of the true bias.

These biases are summarized in table 6.5. For each index, we express the bias in terms of the implied average annual inflation rate using that formula relative to the Törnqvist formula. Clearly, the choice of formula matters enormously. In nine out of the thirteen years between 1992 and 2005, the Törnqvist index differed from the official index in sign; this, in conjunction with the fact that the official index differs from the conventional Laspeyres index, suggests that the precise methodology used to sample prices can qualitatively affect our understanding of what is happening to Japanese import prices. Nevertheless, no matter how we compute Japanese IPIs using common goods, it appears that there is no clear declining trend in import prices.

6.2.2   Chinese Export Prices

It is possible that China is having an impact on Japanese import prices that is more subtle than what we can detect using aggregate IPIs. China is often seen as a low-cost competitor in many markets, and this is something that we can see clearly in our data. In table 6.6, we report regressions in which we regress the log unit values on a dummy that equals 1 if the source is China. We include HS nine-digit fixed effects in the first set of regressions and HS four-digit fixed effects in the second set to control for cross-product variation in prices. The coefficient on the China dummy corresponds to how much cheaper Chinese imports are than other imports in the same nine- or four-digit category.

The results using the nine-digit dummies indicate that in 1992, Chinese

Table 6.6 Regressions of prices and price variation against a dummy variable indicating China's presence in the market

	Unweighted regressions				Weighted by share in year or average share in both years			
	$LN(P_{92})$	$LN(P_{05})$	$LN(P_{05}/P_{92})$	P_{05}/P_{92}	$LN(P_{92})$	$LN(P_{05})$	$LN(P_{05}/P_{92})$	P_{05}/P_{92}
China dummy	−0.92	−1.04	0.013	0.014	−0.413	−0.948	0.056	0.048
	(0.021)	(0.018)	(0.012)	(0.014)	(0.012)	(0.008)	(0.008)	(0.009)
No. of observations	63,690	86,766	25,423	25,423	63,690	86,766	25,423	25,423
9-digit HS fixed effects	Yes	Yes	Yes	Yes	Yes	Yes	Yes	Yes
R^2	0.8	0.77	0.22	0.22	0.97	0.95	0.60	0.61

Notes: Standard errors in parentheses. HS = Harmonized System.

exports to Japan were 0.0.92 log units cheaper than other exports in the same nine-digit category. This means that Chinese exports were 60 percent cheaper than other imports in the same narrowly defined category in 1992 and 65 percent cheaper in 2005. If we weight the observations by the share, there appears to be a bit steeper decline: weighted Chinese prices were 34 percent cheaper in 1992 and 61 percent cheaper in 2005. However, it is difficult to tell from these two cross-sectional regressions whether the drop in relative prices was due to the entry of new, cheaper Chinese imports or declines in the price of existing imports.

In order to examine the source of this price decline, we focus on the set of common Chinese imports. Here again, we drop unit values whose relative price movements are not in the interval [0.3, 3] or if the units change and include HS nine-digit dummies. The data does not suggest that the prices of goods exported by China in 1992 fell at a faster rate than those exported by other countries over this time period. Essentially, the relative prices of Chinese prices show no relative decline compared to those of other countries in the same product categories. This suggests that whatever is driving the rapid expansion of Chinese exports to Japan, it is not a general decline in prices charged by Chinese producers for existing goods.

These results differ from those of Schott (2006), who found that unit values of Chinese exports to the United States declined substantially. This result seems to be due to the treatment of Hong Kong. In our data, if we treat Hong Kong and China as two different countries, we obtain an analogous result with Chinese prices falling significantly, but prices from Hong Kong rising significantly. These two forces cancel each other out and may reflect that the composition of goods passing through Hong Kong is changing but that there is no significant change in Chinese exports broadly defined.

We have already seen that China has been playing a major role in the expansion of new varieties into Japan. One possible implication of this is that the entry of new Chinese products is driving down the prices of other competing exporters. In order to examine this, we regressed the change in the log of the average price of the other exporters in a HS nine-digit category on whether a Chinese firm entered that sector or exited. We also include year-HS four-digit interaction dummies to control for industry level variation that might be correlated with Chinese entry or exit.

In the first three columns of table 6.7, we report the results from this exercise. When we do not include HS four-digit year effects, we find that the entry of a Chinese exporter into a new market is associated with an 0.8 percent decline in the prices charged by other firms. However, when we include HS four-digit year effects, this relationship loses statistical significance. Moreover, the exit of China from a Japanese import market is not associated with any increase in the relative prices of the other goods. In order to see whether the effect of Chinese entry or exit might take some time to have an impact on the prices of other producers, we also ran specifications in which we

Table 6.7   **Fixed effects regressions of year-on-year log price change of non-Chinese exports to Japan against dummy variables indicating China's entry or exit from the market (1992–2005)**

China Entry$_t$	−0.008	−0.004	−0.002	−0.006	−0.002	0.000
	(0.003)	(0.003)	(0.004)	(0.004)	(0.004)	(0.004)
China Exit$_t$	−0.004	−0.004	−0.004	−0.002	−0.004	−0.004
	(0.003)	(0.004)	(0.004)	(0.004)	(0.004)	(0.005)
China Entry$_{t-1}$		0.000	0.001		0.006	0.006
		(0.004)	(0.004)		(0.004)	(0.004)
China Exit$_{t-1}$		0.000	0.003		0.002	0.003
		(0.004)	(0.004)		(0.004)	(0.005)
China Entry$_{t-2}$			0.002			0.004
			(0.004)			(0.004)
China Exit$_{t-2}$			−0.004			−0.001
			(0.004)			(0.004)
Constant	−0.006	0.001	0.009			
	(0.001)	(0.001)	(0.001)			
No. of observations	89,717	79,317	70,200	89,717	79,317	70,200
No. of years	13	12	11	13	12	11
No. of year-HS code combinations	0	0	0	15,500	14,123	12,798
R^2	0.00	0.00	0.00	0.00	0.00	0.00

Notes: Standard errors in parentheses. HS = Harmonized System.

included one- and two-year lags of the entry and exit variables. Neither of these variables was significantly associated with a price change of imports of the other goods changed.

Our results from these exercises indicate that Chinese exports do not appear to have a differential impact on Japanese import prices when examined through conventional approaches. Chinese export prices into Japan are not falling faster than prices of other comparable nine-digit goods. Moreover, the entry or exit of a Chinese firm in a nine-digit sector does not tend to cause any significant movement in the prices of other firms.

6.3   The Variety Effect

The results from the previous section suggest that China has been a major contributor to the expansion in new varieties that have been entering the Japanese market over the last fifteen years. In particular, China and other exporters that have entered the Japanese market could have an impact on inflation in Japan through the expansion of exported varieties. Common goods price indexes cannot measure the impact of new varieties on prices by definition. However, if we think about the entry of new goods as unmeasured price drops, and consumption goods are produced using these inputs, it is possible that consumer prices might be falling as a result of the entry of new producers into the market.

We now turn to understanding this effect more clearly. Our estimation framework is identical to that of Broda and Weinstein (2006), and we repeat some of their underlying theory here in an abbreviated format.

We begin by assuming that consumers purchase and derive utility from a final good U_t that is produced using domestic and foreign varieties.

$$(1) \qquad U_t = (D_t^{(\kappa-1)/\kappa} + M_t^{(\kappa-1)/\kappa})^{\kappa/(\kappa-1)}; \kappa > 1,$$

where M_t is the composite imported good to be defined in the following, D_t is the domestic good, and κ is the elasticity of substitution between both goods. Moving to the second tier, we define the composite imported good as:

$$(2) \qquad M_t = \left(\sum_{g \in G} M_{gt}^{(\gamma-1)/\gamma} \right)^{\gamma/(\gamma-1)}; \gamma > 1,$$

where M_{gt} is the subutility derived from the consumption of imported good g in time t, γ denotes the elasticity of substitution among imported goods, and G is the set of all imported goods. This subutility function can be represented by:

$$(3) \qquad M_{gt} = \left[\sum_{c \in C} d_{gct}^{1/\sigma_g} (m_{gct})^{(\sigma_g-1)/\sigma_g} \right]^{\sigma_g/(\sigma_g-1)}; \sigma_g > 1 \; \forall g \in G,$$

where σ_g is the elasticity of substitution among varieties of good g, which is assumed to exceed unity; for each good, imports are treated as differentiated across countries of supply, c (as in Armington 1969); m_{gct} corresponds to the imports of good g from country c in time t, that is, we identify varieties of import good g with their countries of origin; C is the set of *all* countries; and d_{gct} denotes a taste or quality parameter for good g from country c.

We will work with the main proposition of Broda and Weinstein (2006), which is an extension of one found in Feenstra (1994). Let I be the set of goods available at some time, I_t be set of goods available in time t, and I_g be the set of varieties in good g that are available in two time periods. We denote the price and quantity vectors by $\mathbf{p}_t$, and $\mathbf{x}_t$ and individual prices of varieties by p_{gct}.

PROPOSITION (*Broda and Weinstein 2006*): *If $I_g \neq \emptyset \; \forall g \in G$ and $d_{gct} = d_{gct-1}$ for $c \in I_g \; \forall g \in G$, then the exact aggregate IPI with variety change is given by:*

$$(4) \qquad \Pi^M(\mathbf{p}_t, \mathbf{p}_{t-1}, \mathbf{x}_t, \mathbf{x}_{t-1}, I) = \text{CIPI}(I) \prod_{g \in G} \left(\frac{\lambda_{gt}}{\lambda_{gt-1}} \right)^{w_{gt}/(\sigma_g - 1)},$$

where CIPI refers to the conventional CES IPI:

$$(5) \quad \text{CIPI}(I) = \prod_{g \in G} P_g(I_g)^{w_{gt}} \text{ and } P_g(\mathbf{p}_{gt}, \mathbf{p}_{gt-1}, \mathbf{x}_{gt}, \mathbf{x}_{gt-1}, I_g) = \prod_{c \in I_g} \left(\frac{P_{gct}}{P_{gct-1}} \right)^{w_{gct}},$$

where w_{gt} are log-change ideal weights, and:

(6) $$\lambda_{gt} \equiv \frac{\sum_{c \in I_g} p_{gct} x_{gct}}{\sum_{c \in I_{gt}} p_{gct} x_{gct}} \text{ and } \lambda_{gt-1} \equiv \frac{\sum_{c \in I_g} p_{gct-1} x_{gct-1}}{\sum_{c \in I_{gt-1}} p_{gct-1} x_{gct-1}}.$$

In order to compute the impact of new varieties on the Japanese economy given by equation (4). Our identification strategy is identical to that in Feenstra (1994) and Broda and Weinstein (2006).

6.4   Results

6.4.1   The Quality of Chinese Exports

Before we turn to estimating the bias in the Japanese IPI due to new varieties entering Japan, it is useful to examine what has been happening to the quality of imports by country. The first point to realize is that with the CES approach we have adopted, we can measure both the relative quality of new varieties as well as quality upgrading of existing varieties.

A maintained assumption in our proposition is that the set of common goods does not experience quality upgrading. If we suspected the goods of a country, say, China to be increasing over time, we could drop those goods from the set of common goods and consider them as goods that disappeared in the first period and were replaced in the second. In this case, the contribution to quality of these goods would appear as a drop in the λ ratio. An alternative method of identifying implied quality changes is to examine how the shares of the common goods after controlling for price changes. This is the approach we follow in this section.

To see how to measure quality upgrading of existing goods in the CES framework, consider the CES demand function:

(7) $$s_{igvt} = \left(\frac{p_{igvt}/d_{igvt}}{P_{gt}} \right)^{1-\sigma_g},$$

where s_{igvt} is the share of expenditures on variety v in time t, and E_{gt} is aggregate expenditure on good g in time t. If we take logs of equation (7), we obtain:

(8) $$\ln s_{igvt} = (1 - \sigma_g)\ln\left(\frac{p_{igvt}}{d_{igvt}} \right) - (1 - \sigma_g)\ln P_{gt}.$$

We can rewrite this as:

(4′) $$\ln s_{igvt} = \phi_{gt} + \left\{ (1 - \sigma_g)\ln\left(\frac{p_{igvt}}{d_{igvt}} \right) - \left[\overline{(1 - \sigma_g)\ln\left(\frac{p_{igvt}}{d_{igvt}} \right)} \right] \right\},$$

where the terms with bars over them indicate the average for a good in time t.

In this case, the term in curly brackets can be thought of as how move-

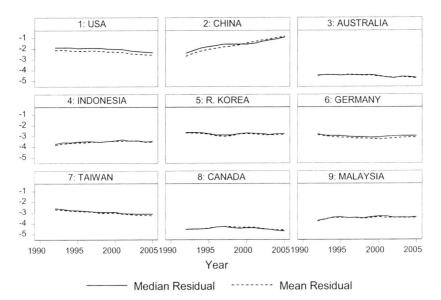

Fig. 6.5   Mean residuals for goods exported to Japan in all years from 1992 to 2005, top nine exporters to Japan in 1992 (excluding Organization of the Petroleum Exporting Countries [OPEC] countries)

Note: Graphs by exporter rank in 1992.

ments in price-per-unit quality have been affecting market shares. In particular, if the price-per-unit quality is high for a given variety in a moment in time, this term will be positive. This suggests that if we regress the shares of products on HS nine-digit year fixed effects, the residuals can be interpreted as how price-per-unit quality has been affecting the market share of that country.[11] If we think that price-per-unit quality of the common exports have remained relatively constant over time, we should expect that this residual should not demonstrate any trend. However, if price-per-unit quality is falling, then we should expect to see this residual rise.

In order to see what was happening to these residuals, we estimated equation (6) and included country dummies so that each country's residuals would be normalized around zero.[12] We then plotted the mean and median residuals for the nine largest non-oil exporters to Japan (see figure 6.5). The results are quite striking. For most countries, there is little movement in the mean or median residuals; however, Chinese residuals exhibit a dramatic rise

11. An alternative interpretation is that the residual captures the number of subvarieties of the product. However, to the extent that one can think of expansions of subvarieties of a good (e.g., increasing the number of car models) as a rise in quality, this interpretation is isomorphic to a quality story.

12. Because of the size of the data set, we limited our analysis to the 100 largest exporters to Japan in 1992.

over time. Of the 100 largest exporters to Japan, China exhibits the highest increase in market share due to quality-adjusted price movements. Chinese market share rose by a factor of 3.3 (1.2 log units) due to quality upgrading. By contrast of the fifty largest exporters to Japan, most experienced market share shifts due to quality-adjusted price movements of less than plus or minus 26 percent. This suggests that a major reason for the increase in the intensive margin of Chinese exports is lower price-per-unit quality.

We can do a back-of-the-envelope calculation to get some sense of how much price-per-unit quality needed to fall in order to produce this rise in market share. If the quality of the remains unchanged, then we can rewrite equation (4) as:

$$\Delta \ln\left(\frac{p_{igvt}}{d_{igvt}}\right) = \frac{\Delta \ln s_{igvt}}{(1 - \sigma_g)}.$$

The median change in the log share of a Chinese variety during this period was 1.45, and the median elasticity estimate was 2.9. Substituting these values into the preceding equation suggests that the price-per-unit quality of the typical Chinese good fell by 54 percent over this time period. This suggests substantial quality upgrading by Chinese manufacturers.

6.4.2   Globalization and Japanese Prices

In order to estimate the impact of new varieties on Japanese prices as indicated by equation (4), we need to compute the lambda ratios and estimate the elasticities. To simplify the analysis, we define "goods" as HS four-digit categories, which divides Japanese imports into just over 1,000 categories.

Table 6.8 documents the summary statistics for the lambda ratios. In the typical sector, the lambda ratio is 0.96. This implies that if all varieties entered utility symmetrically, then the number of varieties would have increased by about 4 percent over this time period. Most of the ratios are distributed relatively narrowly around this value; however, the distribution reveals that there are more sectors with substantial drops in the lambda ratio than sectors with substantial increases. This is consistent with the evidence we presented earlier indicating that, on net, there has been an increase in new varieties entering Japan.

The median lambda ratio for Japan is extremely close to Broda and Weinstein's (2006) computation of the lambda ratio for the United States between 1990 and 2001 (0.95). Moreover, the distribution of lambda ratios is also quite similar. The 5th percentile in Japan is 0.35 compared to 0.34 in the United States, and the 95th percentiles are 1.7 and 1.8, respectively. This suggests that the importance of new sources of supply have been approximately the same for the two economies. In particular, it suggests that even though China only accounted for one-half the amount of net new variety growth

Table 6.8   **Distribution of lambda ratios and sigmas**

Percentile	Lambda ratio	Sigma
1	0.07	1.25
5	0.35	1.48
10	0.57	1.64
25	0.84	2.07
50	0.96	2.93
75	1.03	4.76
90	1.27	11.43
95	1.68	25.03
99	5.18	108.19
No. of observations	1,074	1,074

in the United States as in Japan, this did not change overall growth in new varieties in the two countries.

The distribution of elasticities of substitution is also quite similar to that obtained on U.S. data. The median elasticity for Japanese imports is 2.9, which is the same value found in Broda and Weinstein (2006). However, the distribution of sigmas is somewhat more spread out for Japan, with more elasticities taking on both large and small values. If we apply this elasticity estimate to the results of the previous section, then this implies that the price-per-unit quality fell by 0.63 ($= 1.2/1.9$) log units, or 47 percent over this time period. This suggests that the reason for the dramatic rise in Chinese exports is not price drops but rapid quality upgrading.

When we compute the magnitude of the new good bias as indicated by equation (12), we find it to be 6.1 percent between 1992 and 2005, or about 0.48 percent per year. This is actually somewhat smaller than Broda and Weinstein's (2006) estimate for the United States between 1990 and 2001 (0.8 percent per year). This suggests that the impact of variety growth in Japan was, if anything, less than that in the United States. In addition, the relatively small impact of variety growth on Japanese import prices indicates that the entry of low-cost Chinese exporters cannot be having a substantial impact on Japanese prices. Given that Japan's imports of goods and services to gross domestic product (GDP) ratio averaged only 9 percent over this time period, the impact of a 0.5 percent per year bias in import prices on Japanese deflation is only 0.04 percent per year. To the extent that new imported varieties simply replaced domestic ones, this may be an overestimate. Moreover, if we were to assume that the growth in varieties in services imports did not match that of goods, the impact would be smaller still. This indicates that there cannot be a large effect of new imported varieties in general, and China's entry into Japanese markets in particular, on aggregate Japanese prices.

6.5   Conclusion

The paper highlights the importance of using the same methodology across price indexes when making economic comparisons between them. Between 1992 and 2002, the Japanese IPI registered a decline of almost 9 percent, and Japan entered a period of deflation. However, we show that this may be due to formula biases. Had the IPI been computed using a pure Laspeyres index, the IPI would have hardly moved at all over the same time period, indicating that formula bias may be important for interpreting the behavior of prices. A Laspeyres version of the IPI would have risen 1 percentage point per year faster than the official index.

Second, we show that Chinese prices did not behave differently from the prices of other importers. Although Chinese prices tended to be substantially lower than the prices of other exporters, they do not exhibit a differential trend. However, we estimate that the typical price-per-unit quality of a Chinese exporter fell by half between 1992 and 2005. Thus, the explosive growth in Chinese exports is attributable to growth in the quality of Chinese exports and the increase in new products being exported by China.

Finally, the increase in new imported products entering Japan is only associated with relatively small price movements. The IPI adjusted for new imports rose only 0.5 percentage points per year slower than the unadjusted index. This suggests that the very substantial changes in quality and expansion of China in new markets do not appear to have produced much of an impact on aggregate Japanese prices. In short, China does not seem to be exporting deflation to Japan.

References

Armington, Paul. 1969. A theory of demand for products distinguished by place of production. *IMF Staff Papers* 16:159–78.
Bank of Japan. 2002. Revision of the wholesale price index (switchover to the 2000 base Corporate Goods Price Index [CGPI]). Bank of Japan. Mimeograph.
Bergin, Paul, and Robert C. Feenstra. 2007. Pass-through of exchange rates and competition from Mexico and China. University of California, Davis. Mimeograph.
Broda, Christian, and David E. Weinstein. 2006. Globalization and the gains from variety. *Quarterly Journal of Economics* 121 (2): 541–85.
———. 2007. Defining price stability in Japan: A view from America. NBER Working Paper no. 13255. Cambridge, MA: National Bureau of Economic Research, July.
———. 2008. *Prices, poverty and inequality.* Washington, DC: AEI Press.
Feenstra, Robert C. 1994. New product varieties and the measurement of international prices. *American Economic Review* 84 (1): 157–77.
Schott, Peter K. 2006. The relative sophistication of Chinese exports. NBER Work-

ing Paper no. 12173. Cambridge, MA: National Bureau of Economic Research, April.

Comment   Joshua Aizenman

The remarkable growth experience of Japan from the 1950s has led observers in the 1980s to credit Japan with finding a superior system to the U.S. capitalism, viewing Japan as the "rising sun" that will overtake the United States. Yet the stagflation of the 1990s abruptly put the end to these claims, inducing some policymakers in Japan to look for external scapegoats stopping Japan's aspirations to regain its prominence. This interesting paper investigates the degree to which the deflation-stagflation decade of the 1990s in Japan was due to globalization and Chinese imports. After a careful investigation of these allegations, the authors unambiguously conclude that this was not the case.

Chapter's Investigation Strategy

The authors evaluate carefully the impact that Chinese exports have had on Japanese prices during 1992 to 2005, applying a methodology inspired by Feenstra (1994) and Broda and Weinstein (2006). They use a constant elasticity of substitution (CES) aggregator to infer the implied impact of new products and quality upgrade on the Japanese cost of living. Regressing the shares of products on the Harmonized System (HS) nine-digit year fixed effects, the residuals are interpreted as the impact of price-per-unit quality on the market share of that country. The outcome is remarkable: out of the 100 largest exporters to Japan, China exhibits the highest increase in market share due to quality-adjusted price movements.

The main results show that, while the official Japanese import price index has fallen over this period, an import price index computed, using the same methodology as the consumer price index, would have resulted in substantial *inflation* over this period. Given the large growth of varieties coming from China, the popular belief that China is exporting deflation may be driven by the constant introduction of cheap Chinese products in Japanese markets. Such new products would reduce the cost of living for consumers if the *price-per-unit quality* of the new product is *lower* than that of existing products, or if the new product is actually adding new valuable choices to the consumers. To clarify these issues, the authors use a CES aggregator to back out the

Joshua Aizenman is presidential chair and professor of economics at the University of California at Santa Cruz, and a research associate of the National Bureau of Economic Research.

implied impact of new products on the Japanese cost of living. The findings are remarkable—the price-per-unit quality of Chinese exports halved during this period due to quality upgrading. Yet the quantitative significance of quality growth was small—only 1 percent smaller than the actual import inflation over the 1992 to 2004 period. While the specific price impact of new products from China is small, the impact of all new and higher-quality imports can account for a fall in Japanese import prices of about 10 percent over the 1992 to 2004 period. Yet imports are only 10 percent of Japan's consumption; hence, the deflationary impact of new imported goods in Japan is small, about 1 percent.

Comments

While the small gross domestic product (GDP) share of imports to Japan suggests that the impact of foreign prices on domestic inflation or deflation is small, the paper's methodology may also be useful in reviewing the experience of countries with greater import penetration, like Korea, whose imports are about 40 percent of its GDP, and its inflation is about is about 2 percent.

1. In reading the results, one should keep in mind that the CES aggregator applied in the paper may overstate the ultimate impact of variety or quality on Japan's prices and welfare, as some of the new varieties are not new: they were produced in Japan, but growing fragmentation may shift production to China and other countries. To illustrate this concern, the purchase of the personal computer (PC) unit of IBM by China's leading computer maker, Lenovo, in 2004, transformed a U.S. PC into a Chinese variety in a CES Armington aggregation. Yet a more plausible interpretation may view it as a reincarnation of an IBM PC, with limited impact on the spectrum of varieties consumed.[1] A similar concern arises in circumstances when, due to cost considerations, a Japanese producer (say Sony) licenses the production of a product (say TV) from Japan to China (or any other destination), and the licensed TV would be sold as a Chinese product. The new imported variety should be balanced by the "drop" in "Japanese" varieties.[2] In this situation, we may end up with no "new variety" or "better quality" effect. Yet welfare gain would arise from cheaper TV prices or Sony's higher profits.

2. Due to data limitations, the study relies on the available unit values instead of on the specification prices. Some argued that multinationals' activities may increase the gap between the two, due to transfer pricing and

---

1. If one views the Lenovo PC as a perfect substitute for the IBM, one would record it as a drop in U.S. verities, and a rise in Chinese verities, with no significant impact on the consumer. If the two are viewed as imperfect substitutes, then there would be secondary effects determined by the substitutability of the disappearing IBM PC with the appearing Lenovo PC.

2. If the overall quality of the Chinese- and the Japanese-produced TV is similar, there would be no new varieties gains even if Sony were to keep some production of the TV in Japan.

other concerns.[3] This concern is relevant due to the sizable increase in Japanese foreign direct investment (FDI) in China from 2001, a sizeable portion of which may be of the vertical nature.

3. While the CES aggregator is a convenient structure, Hummels and Lugovskyy (2005) argue that a generalized version of Lancaster's "ideal variety" model can better match facts, where entry causes crowding in variety space, so that the marginal utility of new varieties falls as the market size grows. This crowding effect may be mitigated by income effects, as richer consumers will pay more for varieties closer matched to their ideal types.

Conclusion

The authors convincingly showed that Japan's deflation is "domestically produced"—the impact of imported deflation is close to zero. Hence, the alleged "Chinese exported deflation" as the interpretation for the deflationary patterns in Japan over 1992 to 2004 is invalid. This result is reassuring, as we may expect that the impact of import prices on the Japanese Consumer Price Index (CPI) should be small as Japan is relatively closed to the import of goods. Furthermore, a country with an independent and competent central bank should be able to deal with challenges associated with import penetrations (see Jeanne and Svensson [2004] and Auerbach and Obstfeld [2003]). More important, the paper's methodology is very useful in understanding the experience of any country with greater import penetration.

References

Auerbach, Alan J., and Maurice Obstfeld. 2003. The case for open-market purchases in a liquidity trap. NBER Working Paper no. 9814. Cambridge, MA: National Bureau of Economic Research.

Broda, Christian, and David E. Weinstein. 2006. Globalization and the gains from variety. *Quarterly Journal of Economics* 121 (2): 541–85.

Eden, Lorraine, and Peter Rodriguez. 2004. How weak are the signals? International price indices and multinational enterprises. *Journal of International Business Studies* 35:61–74.

Feenstra, Robert C. 1994. New product varieties and the measurement of international prices. *American Economic Review* 84 (1): 157–77.

Feenstra, Robert C., and Clinton R. Shiells. 1997. Bias in US import prices and demand. In *The economics of new goods,* ed. T. F. Bresnahan and R. J. Gordon, 249–76. Chicago: University of Chicago Press.

Hummels, David, and Volodymyr Lugovskyy. 2005. Trade in ideal varieties: Theory and evidence. Purdue University. Unpublished Manuscript.

3. Eden and Rodriguez (2004) review the earlier debate over methods for calculating import price indexes, concluding that unit values were inferior to specification prices (Lipsey 1994; Feenstra and Shiells 1997). They argue that multinational enterprise activities strengthen the case for specification prices. A 10 percent increase in the intrafirm trade share of U.S. imports widens the gap between the specification price and unit value by 1.3 percent, with transfer price manipulation further increasing the gap.

Jeanne, Olivier, and Lars E. O. Svensson. 2004. Credible commitment to optimal escape from a liquidity trap: The role of the balance sheet of an independent central bank. NBER Working Paper no. 10679. Cambridge, MA: National Bureau of Economic Research.

Lipsey, Robert. 1994. Quality change and other influences on measures of export prices of manufactured goods and the terms of trade between primary products and manufacturers. NBER Working Paper no. 4671. Cambridge, MA: National Bureau of Economic Research.

China's Current Account and Exchange Rate

Yin-Wong Cheung, Menzie D. Chinn, and Eiji Fujii

7.1 Introduction

China—and Chinese economic policy—has loomed large on the global economic stage in recent years. Yet, even as arguments over the normalcy of the Chinese trade balance and the value of the Chinese currency continue, there is substantial debate in both academic and policy circles surrounding what the determinants of these variables are.

Interestingly, there are very few studies that simultaneously assess the Chinese exchange rate and trade/current account balance. This is partly an outcome of the peculiar characteristics of the Chinese economy. In this study, we attempt to inform the debate over the interactions between the exchange rate and the current account by recourse to two key methodologies. First, we identify the equilibrium real exchange rate from the standpoint of cross-country studies. Second, we attempt to obtain more precise estimates of Chinese trade elasticities, both on a multilateral and bilateral (with the United States) basis. In doing so, we hope to transcend the current limited debate based upon rules of thumb.

Yin-Wong Cheung is a professor of economics at the University of California, Santa Cruz, and a guest professor of economics at the Shandong University. Menzie D. Chinn is professor of public affairs and economics at the Robert M. La Follette School of Public Affairs and the Department of Economics, University of Wisconsin, and a research associate of the National Bureau of Economic Research. Eiji Fujii is a professor of economics at the Graduate School of Systems and Information Engineering, University of Tsukuba.

We thank the discussant Jeffrey Frankel, Shang-Jin Wei, Arthur Kroeber, Xiangming Li, Jaime Marquez, and conference participants for comments and discussion; and Kenneth Chow, Guillaume Gaulier, Chang-Tai Hsieh and Hiro Ito for providing data. Cheung acknowledges the hospitality of the Hong Kong Institute for Monetary Research, where part of this research was conducted. Faculty research funds of the University of California, Santa Cruz, the University of Wisconsin, and Grants-in-Aid for Scientific Research are gratefully acknowledged.

To anticipate our results, we obtain several interesting findings. First, the renminbi (RMB) was substantially below the value predicted by our cross-country estimates (although that conclusion does not survive the advent of revised data). The economic magnitude of the misalignment is substantial—on the order of 50 percent in log terms. However, we also find that the misalignment is typically not statistically significant, in the sense of being more than 1 standard error away from the conditional mean. Moreover, substantial revisions to the underlying data provide even more reason to be circumspect about estimates of currency misalignment.

Second, we find that Chinese multilateral trade flows do respond to relative prices—as represented by a trade-weighted exchange rate—but that that relationship is not always precisely estimated. In addition, the direction of effects is different than expected a priori. For instance, we find that Chinese ordinary imports rise in response to a RMB depreciation. However, Chinese exports do appear to respond to RMB depreciation in the expected manner, as long as a supply variable is included. So, in this sense, Chinese trade is not exceptional.

Furthermore, Chinese trade with the United States appears to behave in a standard manner—especially after the expansion in the Chinese manufacturing capital stock is accounted for. Thus, the China-U.S. trade balance should respond to real exchange rate and relative income movements in the anticipated manner. However, in neither the case of multilateral nor bilateral trade flows should one expect quantitatively large effects arising from exchange rate changes. And, of course, our results are not informative with regard to the question of how a change in the RMB U.S. dollar (USD) exchange rate would affect the overall U.S. trade deficit.

Finally, we highlight the fact that considerable uncertainty surrounds both our estimates of RMB misalignment and the responsiveness of trade flows to movements in exchange rates and output levels. In particular, our results for trade elasticities are sensitive to econometric specification, accounting for supply effects, and the inclusion of time trends.

7.2 Placing Matters in Perspective

A discussion of the Chinese economy, and its interaction with the global economy, is necessarily complicated, in large part because of its recent—and incomplete—transition from a central command economy to a market economy.[1]

Take, for instance, the proper measure of the exchange rate in both nominal and real terms, the central relative prices in any open macroeconomy.

---

1. See Cheung, Chinn, and Fujii (2007a) for discussion of various issues related to the transformation of the Chinese economy.

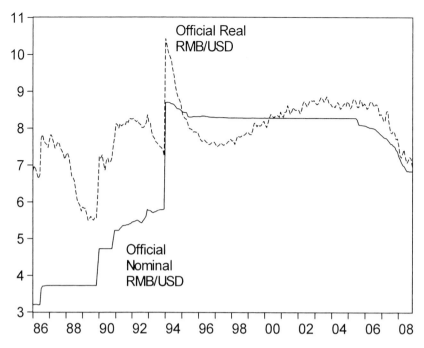

Fig. 7.1   Official nominal and real RMB/USD, 1986M01–2008M11

Sources: IMF, *International Financial Statistics,* and authors' calculations.

Figure 7.1 depicts the official bilateral value of the Chinese currency over the last twenty years. Taking the standard approach in the crisis early warning system literature, one can calculate the extent of exchange rate overvaluation as a deviation from a trend. Adopting this approach in the case of China would not lead to a very satisfactory result. Consider first what a simple examination of the bilateral real exchange rate between the United States and the RMB implies. In figure 7.1, the rate is expressed so higher values constitute a weaker Chinese currency. Over the entire sample period, the RMB has experienced a downward trend in value.

However, as with the case with economies experience transitions from controlled to partially decontrolled capital accounts and from dual to unified exchange rate regimes, there is some dispute over what exchange rate measure to use. In the Chinese case, an argument can be made that, with a portion of transactions taking place at swap rates, the 1994 "mega-devaluation" was actually better described as a unification of different rates of exchange. Figure 7.2 shows the official rate (the solid line) at which some transactions took place, and a floating rate—often called the "swap-market rate"—shown with the thick dashed line. Using a transactions-weighted average of these two rates (called the "adjusted rate") yields a substantially

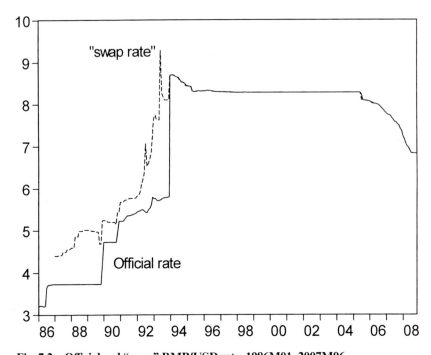

Fig. 7.2   Official and "swap" RMB/USD rate, 1986M01–2007M06

Sources: IMF, *International Financial Statistics* and Fernald, Edison, and Loungani (1999).

different profile for the RMB's path, with a substantially different (essentially flat) trend, as depicted in figure 7.3.[2]

The trade-weighted exchange rate is arguably more relevant. Figure 7.4 depicts the International Monetary Fund's (IMF)s effective exchange rate index (logged) and a linear trend estimated over the available sample of 1986-2008M09. Following the methodology outlined in Chinn (2000a), Cheung, Chinn, and Fujii (2009a) test for cointegration of the nominal (trade weighted) exchange rate and the relative price level. We find that there is evidence for cointegration of these two variables, with the posited coefficients. This means that we can use this trend line as a statistically valid indication of the mean value, which the real exchange rate series reverts to. Interestingly, repeating this procedure for the more recent period yields a 14.2 percent *over*valuation in 2008M09.

It is obviously an understatement to say that the Chinese current and trade accounts have elicited substantial interest in policy and academic circles over the past few years, in part because of the apparent break in the behavior of these flows. Figure 7.5 shows the current account balance expressed in dollar

2. See Fernald, Edison, and Loungani (1999) for a discussion in the context of whether the 1994 "devaluation" caused the 1997 to 1998 currency crises.

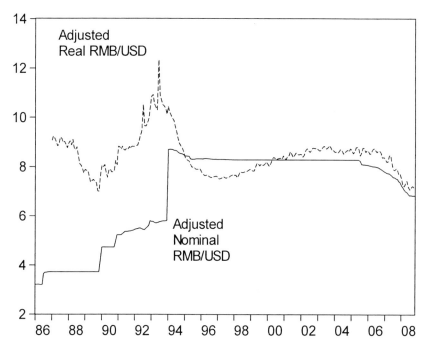

Fig. 7.3   Adjusted nominal and real RMB/USD, 1986M01–2008M11

Sources: IMF, *International Financial Statistics,* Fernald, Edison, and Loungani (1999), and authors' calculations.

terms and as a share of gross domestic product (GDP). Clearly, the Chinese current account balance has ballooned in recent years, sparking the debate over the "normalcy" and propriety of a large emerging market running such a large surplus. Of course, normalcy is in the eye of the beholder. Chinn and Ito (2007) argue that China's current account surplus over the 2000 to 2004 period—while exceeding the predicted value—was within the statistical margin of error, according to a model of the current account based upon the determinants of saving and investment.[3]

The current account balance is driven largely by the trade balance.[4] Figure 7.6 shows the trade balance in dollar terms. Until about 2004, the Chinese trade account was in rough balance, with deficits against other countries offsetting a trade surplus with the United States.

This brings us to one interesting aspect of the Chinese experience—the

---

3. Chinn and Ito's analysis is based upon the Chinn and Prasad (2003) approach to estimating the "normal" level of a current account balance, using as fundamentals the budget balance, per capita income, demographic variables, and various other control variables.

4. Although the gap has increased in recent years, with the current account exceeding the trade balance as income on China's increasing foreign exchange reserves offsets income payments to a greater and greater extent.

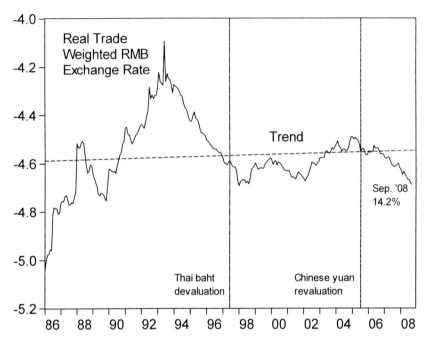

Fig. 7.4   Log trade-weighted real RMB exchange rate, 1986M01–2008M11, and linear time trend

Sources: IMF, *International Financial Statistics* and authors' calculations. Pre-1994 data from March 2007 *International Financial Statistics.*

fact that such a large portion of the Chinese surplus is accounted for by the United States. Figure 7.6 also shows the bilateral surplus with the United States, highlighting the fact that the behavior of overall Chinese trade balances differs substantially from that of the China-U.S. trade balance.[5] This divergence reflects in part China's role in the global supply chain.

It is because of this disjuncture between some of the measures of equilibrium exchange rates and the behavior of the external accounts that we adopt the procedure of examining first a model of the equilibrium exchange rate, and then—taking the exchange rate as largely exogenous—estimating the responsiveness of trade flows to the various macroeconomic variables in a partial equilibrium framework.

5. Note that in this figure, we have used the Chinese measure of the China-U.S. trade balance, which differs from the U.S. measure, due to both differences in valuation measures and treatment of reexports via Hong Kong.

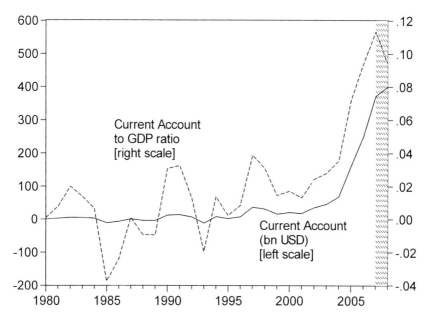

Fig. 7.5   Current account balance (in billions of U.S. dollars, left scale) and current account-GDP ratio (right scale)

Source: IMF, *World Economic Outlook* (October 2008).

Note: Statistics for 2008 are IMF projections.

7.3   The Chinese Equilibrium Exchange Rate

7.3.1   An Overview of Approaches

Several surveys have compared the estimates of the degree to which the RMB is misaligned. The Government Accountability Office (2005) provides a comparison of the academic and policy literature, while Cairns (2005b) briefly surveys recent point estimates obtained by different analysts. Here, we review the literature to focus primarily on the economic and econometric distinctions associated with the various analyses. We also restrict our attention to those studies conducted in recent years.

Many of these papers fall into familiar categories, either relying upon some form of relative purchasing power parity (PPP) or cost competitiveness calculation, the modeling of deviations from absolute PPP, a composite model incorporating several channels of effects (sometimes called "behavioral equilibrium exchange rate models"), or flow equilibrium models. Table 7.1 provides a typology of these approaches, further disaggregated by the data dimension (cross-section, time series, or both).

The relative PPP comparisons are the easiest to make, in terms of calculations. However, relative PPP in levels requires the cointegration of the

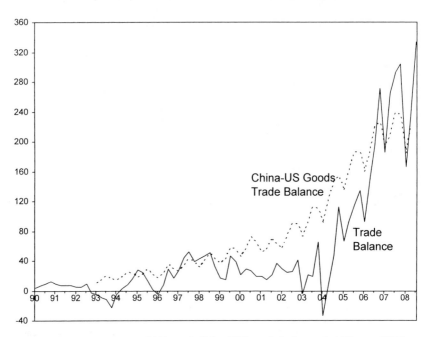

Fig. 7.6   Trade balance and bilateral China-U.S. trade balance, in billions of U.S. dollars at annual rates

Sources: CEIC, BEA/Census via Haver, and authors' calculations.

Note: China-U.S. balance is simple average of Chinese and U.S. data.

relevant price indexes with the nominal exchange rate (or, equivalently, the stationarity of the real exchange rate), but these conditions do not necessarily hold and are seldom tested for. Wang (2004) reports some IMF estimates of unit labor cost-deflated RMB. This series has appreciated in real terms since 1997; of course, this comparison, like all other comparisons based upon indexes, depends upon selecting a year that is deemed to represent equilibrium. Selecting a year before 1992 would imply that the RMB has depreciated over time.

Bosworth (2004), Frankel (2006), Coudert and Couharde (2005), and Cairns (2005b) estimate the relationship between the deviation from absolute PPP and relative per capita income. All obtain similar results regarding the relationship between the two variables, although Coudert and Couharde fail to detect this link for the RMB.

Wang (2004) and Funke and Rahn (2007) implement what could broadly be described as behavioral equilibrium exchange rate (BEER) specifications. These models incorporate a variety of channels through which the real exchange rate is affected. Because each author selects different variables to include, the implied misalignments will necessarily vary, as discussed in Dunaway et al. (2009) as well as McCown, Pollard, and Weeks (2007).

Table 7.1   Studies of the equilibrium exchange rate of the renminbi

	Relative PPP, competitiveness	Absolute PPP-income relationship	Balassa-Samuelson (with productivity)	BEER	Macroeconomic balance/ External balance
Time series	CCF (2009a); Wang (2004)	Bosworth (2004)	CCF (2009a)	Zhang (2001); Wang (2004); Funke and Rahn (2005)	Bosworth (2004); Goldstein (2004); Wang (2004)
Cross section		Frankel (2006); Coudert and Couharde (2005)			
Panel		Cairns (2005b); CCF (2007b)		CCF (2009a)	Coudert and Couharde (2005)

Notes: Relative purchasing power parity (PPP) indicates the real exchange rate is calculated using price or cost indexes and no determinants are accounted for. Absolute **PPP** indicates the use of comparable price deflators to calculate the real exchange rate. Balassa-Samuelson (with productivity) indicates that the real exchange rate (calculated using price indexes) is modeled as a function of sectoral productivity levels. Behavioral equilibrium exchange rate (BEER) indicates composite models using net foreign assets, relative tradable to nontradable price ratios, trade openness, or other variables. Macroeconomic balance indicates cases where the equilibrium real exchange rate is implicit in a "normal" current account (or combination of current account and persistent capital inflows, for the external balance approach). CCF denotes Cheung, Chinn, and Fujii.

A different set of approaches eschews the price-based approaches and views the current account as the residual of savings and investment behavior. The equilibrium exchange rate is derived from the implied medium-term current account using import and export elasticities. In the IMF's macroeconomic approach, the norms are estimated. Coudert and Couharde (2005) implement a closely related approach for China.

A final set of approaches, popular in the policy arena, focuses on the persistent components of the balance of payments (Goldstein 2004; Bosworth 2004). This last set of approaches—what we will term the "external accounts approach"—is perhaps most useful for conducting short-term analyses. But the wide dispersion in implied misalignments reflects the difficulties in making judgments about what constitutes *persistent* capital flows. For instance, Prasad and Wei (2005), examining the composition of capital inflows into and out of China, argue that much of the reserve accumulation that has occurred in the period before the current account surge was due to speculative inflow; hence, the degree of misalignment was small. That assessment has been viewed as less applicable as the current account balance has surged in the past two years.[6]

Two observations regarding these various estimates are of interest. First, as noted by Cairns (2005a), there is an interesting relationship between the particular approach adopted by a study and the degree of misalignment found. Analyses implementing relative PPP and related approaches indicate the least misalignment. Those adopting approaches focusing on the external accounts yield estimates that are in the intermediate range. Finally, studies implementing an absolute PPP methodology result in the greatest degree of estimated undervaluation.

Given that the last approach is the most straightforward in terms of implementation, we adopt it, cognizant of the tendency of this approach to maximize the estimated extent of misalignment.

7.3.2   A Framework

The key problem with explaining the Chinese exchange rate and current account imbalance is that China deviates substantially from cross-country norms for at least its currency value.

Following Cheung, Chinn, and Fujii (2007b), we exploit a well-known relationship between deviations from absolute PPP and real per capita income using panel regression methods. By placing the RMB in the context of this well-known empirical relationship exhibited by a large number of developing and developed countries, over a long time horizon, this approach addresses the question of where China's real exchange rate stands relative to

---

6. In addition, such flow-based measures must be conditioned on the existence of capital controls, the durability and effectiveness of which must necessarily be a matter of judgment.

the equilibrium level. In addition to calculating the numerical magnitude of the degree of misalignment, we assess the estimates in the context of statistical uncertainty. In this respect, we extend the standard practice of considering both economic and statistical significance in coefficient estimates to the prediction aspect.

The price-level variable in the Penn World Tables (Summers and Heston 1991) and other PPP exchange rates attempt to circumvent measurement problems arising from heterogeneity in goods baskets across countries by using *prices* (not price indexes) of goods and calculating the aggregate price level using the same weights. Assume for the moment that this can be accomplished, but that some share of the basket (α) is nontradable (denoted by N subscript), and the remainder is tradable (denoted by T subscript). Then:

(1) $$p_t = \alpha p_{N,t} + (1 - \alpha)p_{T,t}.$$

By simple manipulation, one finds that the real exchange rate is given by:

(2) $$q_t \equiv s_t - p_t + p_t^* = (s_t - p_{T,t} + p_{T,t}^*) - \alpha(p_{N,t} - p_{T,t}) + \alpha(p_{N,t}^* - p_{T,t}^*).$$

Rewriting, and indicating the first term in parentheses, the intercountry price of tradables, as $q_{T,t}$ and the intercountry relative price of nontradables as ω_t $\equiv (p_{N,t} - p_{T,t}) - (p_{N,t}^* - p_{T,t}^*)$, leads to the following rewriting of equation (2):

(2′) $$q_t = q_{T,t} - \alpha\omega_t$$

This expression indicates that the real exchange rate can appreciate as changes occur in the relative price of traded goods between countries or as the relative price of nontradables rises in one country, *relative to another.* In principle, economic factors can affect one or both.

Models that center on the relative price of nontradables include the well-known approaches of Balassa (1964) and Samuelson (1964). In those instances, the relative price of nontradables depends upon sectoral productivity differentials, as in Hsieh (1982), Canzoneri, Cumby and Diba (1999), and Chinn (2000b). They also include those approaches that include demand-side determinants of the relative price, such as that of De Gregorio and Wolf (1994), who observe that if consumption preferences are not homothetic and factors are not perfectly free to move intersectorally, changes in per capita income may result in shifts in the relative price of nontradables.

This perspective provides the key rationale for the well-known positive cross-sectional relationship between relative price (the inverse of q, i.e., $-q$) and relative per capita income levels. We exploit this relationship to determine whether the Chinese currency is undervalued. Obviously, this approach is not novel; it has been implemented recently by Frankel (2006) and Coudert and Couharde (2005). However, we will expand this approach along several dimensions. First, we augment the approach by incorporating the time series dimension.[7] Second, we explicitly characterize the uncertainty surrounding our determinations of currency misalignment. Third, we examine the stability of the relative price and relative per capita income relationship using (a) subsamples of certain country groups and time periods, and (b) control variables.

7.3.3   The Basic Bivariate Results: Using the 2007 Vintage Data

We compile a large data set encompassing up to 160 countries over the 1975 to 2005 period. Most of the data are drawn from the World Bank's *World Development Indicators (WDI)*. Because some data are missing, the panel is unbalanced. The data appendix provides greater detail on the data used.

Extending Frankel's (2006) cross-section approach, we estimate the real exchange rate-income relationship using a pooled time series cross-section ordinary least squares (OLS) regression, where all variables are expressed in terms relative to the United States;

$$(3) \qquad r_{it} = \beta_0 + \beta_1 y_{it} + u_{it},$$

where $r = -q$ is expressed in real terms relative to the U.S. price level, y is per capita income also relative to the United States.[8] The results are reported in the first two columns of table 7.2, for cases in which we measure relative per capita income in either USD exchange rates or PPP-based exchange rates.

One characteristic of estimating a pooled OLS regression is that it forces the intercept term to be the same across countries and assumes that the error term is distributed identically over the entire sample. Because this is something that should be tested, rather than assumed, we also estimated random effects and fixed effects regressions. The former assumes that the individual specific error is uncorrelated with the right-hand-side variables, while the latter is efficient when this correlation is nonzero.[9]

Random effects regressions do not yield substantially different results from those obtained using pooled OLS. Interestingly, when allowing the within and between coefficients to differ, we do find differing effects. In particular, with USD-based per capita GDP, the within effect is much stronger than the between. This divergence is likely picking up short-term effects,

---

7. Coudert and Couharde (2005) implement the absolute PPP regression on a cross-section, while their panel estimation relies upon estimating the relationship between the relative price level to relative tradables to nontradables price indexes.

8. β_0 can take on currency specific values if a fixed effects specification is implemented. Similarly, the error term is composed of a currency specific and aggregate error if the pooled OLS specification is dropped. Note that this analysis differs from that in Cheung, Chinn, and Fujii (2007b), in that we use an updated and revised data set and exclude China from the regression.

9. Because the price levels being used are comparable across countries, in principle there is no need to incorporate country-specific constants as in fixed effects or random effects regressions. In addition, fixed effects estimates are biased in the presence of serial correlation, which is documented in the subsequent analysis.

Table 7.2   The panel estimation results of the real exchange rate-income relationship: 2006 vintage data

	U.S.$-based GDP				PPP-based GDP			
	Pooled OLS (1)	Between (2)	Fixed effects (within) (3)	Random effects (4)	Pooled OLS (5)	Between (6)	Fixed effects (within) (7)	Random effects (8)
GDP per capita	0.259***	0.259***	0.387***	0.309***	0.317***	0.309***	0.386***	0.361***
	(0.003)	(0.013)	(0.020)	(0.012)	(0.005)	(0.025)	(0.020)	(0.013)
Constant	−.023***	−.040	—	.099***	−.147***	−.184***	—	−.084**
	(0.008)	(0.044)		(0.036)	(0.010)	(0.055)		(0.037)
Adjusted R^2	0.564	0.677	0.800	0.564	0.413	0.467	0.800	0.413
F-test statistic			33.557***				54.362***	
Hausman test statistic				19.013*				0.167
No. of observations	4,600				4,600			

Notes: GDP = gross domestic product; PPP = purchasing power parity; OLS = ordinary least squares. The data covers 168 countries over the maximum of a thirty-one-year period from 1975 to 2005. The panel is unbalanced due to some missing observations. Heteroskedasticity-robust standard errors are given in parentheses underneath coefficient estimates. For the fixed effects models, the F-test statistics are reported for the null hypothesis of the equality of the constants across all countries in the sample. For the random effects models, the Hausman test statistics test for the independence between the time-invariant country-specific effects and the regressor.

***Significant at the 1 percent level.

**Significant at the 5 percent level.

Relative price level

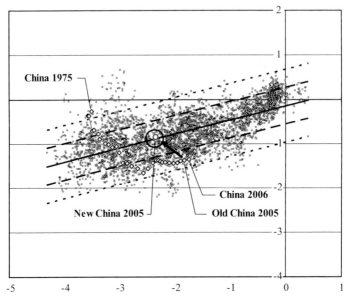

Relative per capita income in PPP terms

Fig. 7.7   The rate of RMB misalignment based on the pooled OLS estimates with the PPP-based per capita income, 1975–2005

Sources: Chinese 2006 data are from *World Economic Outlook.* "New China 2005" observation is based upon 2007 International Comparison Program data.

where output growth is correlated with other variables pushing up currency values. This pattern, however, is not present in results derived from the PPP-based output data.

Interestingly, the estimated elasticity of the price level with respect to per capita income does not appear to be particularly sensitive to measurements of per capita income. In all cases, the elasticity estimate is always around 0.26 to 0.39, which compares favorably with Frankel's (2006) 1990 and 2000 year cross-section estimates of 0.38 and 0.32, respectively.[10]

One of the key emphases of our analysis is the central role accorded the quantification of the uncertainty surrounding the estimates. That is, in addition to estimating the economic magnitude of the implied misalignments, we also assess whether the implied misalignments are statistically different from zero. In figure 7.7, we plot the actual and resulting predicted (inverse) rates and standard error bands derived from the PPP-based data. The results

---

10. Note that, in addition to differences in the sample, our estimates differ from Frankel's in that we measure each country's (logged) real GDP per capita in terms relative to the United States rather than in absolute terms.

pertaining to USD-based per capita GDP data are qualitatively similar and, thus, are not reported for brevity.

It is interesting to consider the path that the RMB has traced out figure 7.7. It begins the sample as overvalued, and over the next three decades, it moves toward the predicted equilibrium value and then overshoots, so that by 2005 to 2006, it is substantially undervalued by about 60 percent in log terms (50 percent in absolute terms).[11] It is indeed a puzzle that the RMB path is different from the one predicted by the Balassa-Samuelson hypothesis. In comparing the observations at 1975 and 2004, we found that countries including Indonesia, Malaysia, and Singapore also experienced an increase in their income but a decrease in their relative price level. On the other hand, Japan—a country typically used to illustrate the Balassa-Samuelson effect, has a positive relative price level—income relationship. We reserve further analysis for future study.

In this context, we make two observations about these estimated misalignments. First, the RMB has been persistently undervalued by this criterion since the mid-1980s, even in 1997 and 1998, when China was lauded for its refusal to devalue its currency despite the threat to its competitive position.

Second, and perhaps most important, in 2005, the RMB was more than 1 standard error—but less than 2 standard errors—away from the predicted value, which in the present context is interpreted as the "equilibrium" value. In other words, by the standard statistical criterion that applied economists commonly appeal to, the RMB is not undervalued (as of 2005) in a statistically significant sense. Similarly, we could not assert that the estimated degree of undervaluation is statistically significant in 2006. The wide dispersion of observations in the scatter plots should give pause to those who would make strong statements regarding the exact degree of misalignment.

In Cheung, Chinn, and Fujii (2007b), we extended this analysis to allow for heterogeneity across country groupings (industrial versus less-developed, high versus low, and regional) and time periods. After conducting various robustness checks, we conclude that although the point estimates indicate the RMB is undervalued in almost all samples, in almost no case is the deviation statistically significant, and indeed, when serial correlation is accounted for, the extent of misalignment is not even statistically significant at the 50 percent level. These findings highlight the great degree of uncertainty surrounding empirical estimates of equilibrium real exchange rates, thereby underscoring the difficulty in accurately assessing the degree of RMB undervaluation.

Notice that the deviations from the conditional mean are persistent; that is, deviations from the real exchange rate-income relationship identified by

---

11. The deviations when using per capita income in USD, rather than PPP, terms are somewhat smaller—55 percent in log terms (42 percent in absolute terms).

the regression are persistent or exhibit serial correlation. This has an important implication for interpreting the degree of uncertainty surrounding these measures of misalignment. Frankel (2006) makes a similar observation, noting that half of the deviation of the RMB from the 1990 conditional mean exists in 2000. We estimate the autoregressive coefficient in our sample at approximately 0.95 (derived from PPP-based per capita income figures) on an annual basis. A simple, ad hoc adjustment based upon the latter estimate suggests that the standard error of the regression should be adjusted upward by a factor equal to $[1/(1 - \hat{\rho}^2)]^{0.5} \approx 3$. After controlling for serial correlation, the actual value of the RMB is always within 1 standard error prediction interval surrounding the (predicted) equilibrium value in the last twenty plus years! Combining this result and the large data dispersion observed in figure 7.7, it is clear that the data are not sufficiently informative for making a sharp inferences regarding misalignment—not just for the recent period but for the entire sample period.[12]

7.3.4   The Basic Specification Updated: The 2008 Vintage Data

Recently, the World Bank reported new estimates of China's GDP and price level in 2005, measured in PPP terms. These estimates, based on the International Comparison Project's work, incorporated new benchmark data on prices. The end result was to reduce China's estimated GDP per capita by about 40 percent and increase the estimated price level by the same amount.[13] Using the updated data, one finds that China's 2005 observation lying essentially on the regression line, highlighted as "New China 2005" in figure 7.7. In other words, the new estimates erase our estimated undervaluation.

However, taking proper account of this issue involves a slightly more involved approach. This is because data for *many* other countries were substantially revised as well. This means that we need to reestimate the regressions. We report these results in table 7.3.

Focusing on the PPP-based data, one finds that the pooled OLS results indicate a smaller impact of income on relative price levels than obtained using the earlier data. The coefficient drops from 0.3 to 0.2. In fixed effects regressions, the between coefficient drops, while the within rises. Given the change in the sample period and the change in the estimated coefficients, one would not be too surprised to find the estimated misalignments change. However, the *magnitude* of the change in the implied misalignment for the RMB is surprising. Essentially, as of 2006, there is no significant misalignment, in

---

12. The discussant, Jeffrey Frankel, has observed that the 5 percent significance level might be too high a hurdle to jump for policy purposes. Even when reducing the significance levels to 40 percent, we would not reject the no-undervaluation null hypothesis, after accounting for serial correlation.

13. Statistics are from Asian Development Bank (2007). See also Elekdag and Lall (2008) and International Comparison Program (2007) for discussion.

Table 7.3   The panel estimation results of the real exchange rate-income relationship: 2008 vintage data

	U.S.\$-based GDP				PPP-based GDP			
	Pooled OLS	Between	Fixed effects	Random effects	Pooled OLS	Between	Fixed effects	Random effects
GDP per capita	.211***	.196***	.552***	.482***	.194***	.188***	.415***	.302***
	(.002)	(.012)	(.008)	(.006)	(.004)	(.019)	(.023)	(.013)
Constant	-.099***	-.157***	—	0.623***	-.276***	-.310***	—	-.078**
	(.008)	(.040)		(.026)	(.010)	(.045)		(.035)
Adjusted R^2	.541	.585	.894	.541	.300	.365	.740	.300
F-test statistic			82.484***				42.765***	
Hausman test statistic				112.50***				35.122***
No. of observations	3,946				4,031			

Notes: GDP = gross domestic product; PPP = purchasing power parity; OLS = ordinary least squares. The data covers 168 countries over the maximum of a twenty-seven-year period from 1980 to 2006. The panel is unbalanced due to some missing observations. For the fixed effects models, the *F*-test statistics are reported for the null hypothesis of the equality of the constants across all countries in the sample. For the random effects models, the Hausman test statistics test for the independence between the time-invariant country-specific effects and the regressor.

***Significant at the 1 percent level.

**Significant at the 5 percent level.

Relative price level

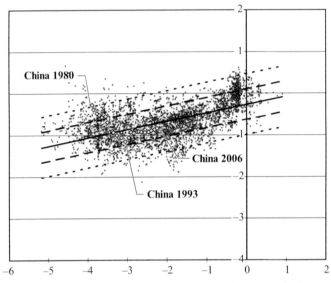

Relative per capita income in PPP terms

Fig. 7.8   The rate of RMB misalignment based on the pooled OLS estimates with the PPP-based per capita income, 2008 vintage data

either the economic or statistical sense. The undervaluation is on the order of 10 percent in log terms, and the maximal undervaluation is in 1993.[14]

This outcome is clearly illustrated in figure 7.8, where we present the scatterplot of the price level against per capita income but utilizing the most recent data. These figures summarize our basic finding: namely that the substantial misalignment—on the order of 40 percent—detected in our previous analysis disappears in this analysis.[15]

14. We also estimated equation (3) using the year-by-year cross-section regression method. The implied pattern of RMB misalignment is comparable with the one discussed in the preceding. For instance, RMB is found to be overvalued before the 1980s, display a large amount of undervaluation from the late 1980s to 2004, and be slightly overvalued in 2005. All these year-by-year cross-section estimates of the degree of undervaluation are not statistically significant. The average of these year-by-year undervaluation estimates from 1975 to 2005 is 15.5 percent. The value is similar to the undervaluation estimate of 16 percent reported in Arvind Subramanian (2008), who obtains his estimate based upon the methodology outlined in Johnson, Ostry, and Subramanian (2007). We believe utilizing panel regression—as we do—and focusing specifically on the most recent period provides a more accurate assessment of the current degree of currency misalignment.

15. We have not controlled for additional effects in these regressions. However, our basic results do not change with the inclusion of other variables including demographics and institutional factors. See Cheung, Chinn, and Fujii (2009b).

One might take this development as justification for our earlier conclusions that the statistical evidence for undervaluation was misplaced. However, our confidence bands were drawn based upon sampling uncertainty. The revision in China's position reflects measurement error, which we did not take into account in our previous analysis.

The seemingly ephemeral nature of our undervaluation estimate reinforces the point that we have only investigated one approach of the several laid out in table 7.1. Our discussant has observed that other indicators also inform the debate over whether the RMB is misaligned. The burgeoning trade surplus and reserves accumulation, as well as the rapid growth rate (exceeding what is widely perceived as the sustainable rate), point to an undervalued currency, at least conditional upon the level of other policy variables.

We would not disagree with the view that multiple approaches should be used to assess currency misalignment. In that respect, we have somewhat more evidence for RMB undervaluation than one would gain from merely looking at the Penn effect, especially as the revised PPP data have cast into doubt our estimates of misalignment.

Nonetheless, to the extent that almost all such estimates indicate quantitatively substantial undervaluation, and sustained deviation from the price line, we are willing to consider the possibility that the real rate can be controlled for sustained periods of time. Taking the real exchange rate as somewhat exogenous, we can then plausibly consider the effects of changes in the RMB's value on Chinese trade flows.

7.4   A Closer Look at Trade Elasticities

7.4.1   Survey of Trade Elasticity Estimates

The extant literature documenting the price and income responsiveness of Chinese trade flows is relatively small, and given the rapid pace of structural transformation, some of the earlier studies spanning the transition period is of limited relevance.

With respect to Chinese multilateral trade elasticities, there are few academic studies. One widely cited estimate from Goldman Sachs is for a Chinese export price elasticity of 0.2 and an import price elasticity of 0.5.[16] Presumably, similar estimates underlie Goldstein's (2004) calculations although they are not reported.

Kwack et al. (2007) uses a gravity model augmented with a Consumer Price Index (CPI)-deflated real exchange rate to estimate elasticities over the 1984 to 2003 period. Using a panel of twenty-nine developed and developing

16. O'Neill and Wilson (2003) as cited in Morrison and Labonte (2006).

countries, they obtain a Chinese multilateral import price elasticity of 0.50 and an income elasticity of 1.57.[17]

Thorbecke and Smith (forthcoming) do not directly examine the implications for both imports and exports, but do focus on the impact of RMB appreciation on exports, taking into account the integration of the production chain in the region. Using a sample of thirty-three countries over the 1994 to 2005 period and a trade-weighted exchange rate that measures the impact of how bilateral exchange rates affect imported input prices, they find that a 10 percent RMB appreciation in the absence of changes in other East Asian currencies would result in a 3 percent decline in processed exports and an 11 percent decline in ordinary exports. If other East Asian currencies appreciated in line with the RMB, then the resulting change in the processed exports would be 9 percent.

Marquez and Schindler (2007) argue that the absence of useful price indexes for Chinese imports and exports requires the adoption of an alternative model specification. They treat the variable of interest as world (import or export) trade shares, broken down into "ordinary" and "parts and components." Using monthly Chinese imports data from 1997 to July 2006, they find ordinary trade-share income elasticities ranging from –0.021 to –0.001 (i.e., the coefficients are *in the wrong direction*), and price elasticities from 0.013 to 0.021.[18] The parts and components price elasticities are in the wrong direction and statistically significantly so. Interestingly, the stock of foreign direct investment (FDI) matters in almost all cases. Because the FDI stock is a smooth trend, it is not clear whether to attribute the effect explicitly to the effect of FDI or to other variables that may be trending upward over time, including productive capacity.

For export shares (ordinary goods), they find income elasticities ranging from 0.08 to 0.09 and price elasticities ranging from 0.08 to 0.068. For parts and components export share, the income coefficient ranges from a 0.042 to 0.049. Their preferred specification implies that a 10 percent real appreciation of the Chinese RMB reduces the Chinese trade balance between $75 billion and $92 billion.

Garcia-Herrero and Koivu (2007) come closest to our approach. They examine data over the 1995 to 2005 period, breaking the data into ordinary and processing/parts imports and exports. They relate Chinese exports to the world imports and the real effective exchange rate, augmented by a proxy measure for the value added tax rebate on exports and a capacity utilization variable. In both import and export equations, the stock of FDI is included.

17. Wang and Ji (2006) adopt a related approach and find essentially zero effect of nominal exchange rates on Chinese imports and exports.
18. Marquez and Schindler (2007) conjecture that this counterintuitive result arises from the role of state-owned enterprises. They also observe that this result can occur under certain configurations of substitutability between imported and domestic goods.

One notable result they obtain is that for Chinese imports, the real exchange rate coefficient has a sign opposite of anticipated in the full sample.

Another particularly interesting result they obtain is that post-World Trade Organization (WTO) entry, Chinese income and price elasticities for exports rise considerably. On the import side, no such change is obvious with respect to the pre- and post-WTO period.

In the bilateral vein, Mann and Plück (2007) investigate China-U.S. trade. Using an error correction model specification applied to disaggregate bilateral data over the 1980 to 2004 period, they find extremely high income elasticities for U.S. imports from China: for capital and consumer goods, the estimated long-run income elasticities are 10 and 4, respectively. The consumer good price elasticity is not statistically significant, while the capital good elasticity is implausibly high, around 10.[19] On the other hand, U.S. exports to China have a relatively low income elasticity of 0.74 and 2.25 for capital and consumer goods, respectively. The price elasticity estimates are not statistically significant. In general, they have difficulty obtaining sensible coefficient estimates.

Thorbecke (2006) examines aggregate bilateral U.S.-China data over the 1988 to 2005 period. Using both the Johansen maximum likelihood method as well as Stock and Watson's (1993) dynamic OLS methodology, he finds statistically significant evidence of cointegration between incomes, real exchange rates, and CPI-deflated trade flows.

U.S. imports from China have a real exchange rate elasticity ranging from 0.4 to 1.28 (depending upon the number of leads and lags in the dynamic ordinary least squares [DOLS] specification). The income elasticity ranges between 0.26 to 4.98. In all instances, substitution with Association of Southeast Asian Nations (ASEAN) trade flows is accounted for by the inclusion of an ASEAN/dollar real exchange rate. Interestingly, the income elasticities are not statistically significant, even when quantitatively large. For U.S. exports to China, he obtains exchange rate elasticities ranging from 0.42 to 2.04, and income elasticities ranging from 1.05 to 1.21.

7.4.2   Multilateral Trade Elasticities

First, let us consider Chinese trade flows with respect to the rest of the world. We estimate the following equations, where the designations import and export are from the Chinese perspective,

(4) $$\mathrm{ex}_t = \beta_0 + \beta_1 y_t^* + \beta_2 q_t + \beta_3 z_t + u_{1,t},$$

and

---

19. Mann and Plück (2007) use disaggregate U.S. trade flow and price index data from the Bureau of Economic Analysis (BEA). The reported income elasticities are for matched expenditure series, for example, investment activity as the income variable in a regression involving capital goods.

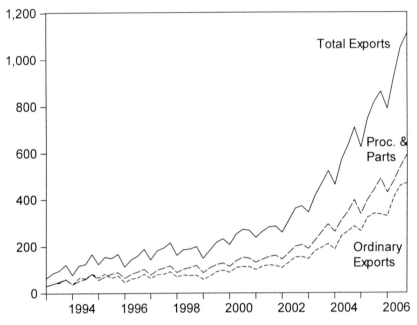

Fig. 7.9   Chinese total, ordinary, and processing and parts exports, in billions of U.S. dollars, at annual rates

(5) $$im_t = \gamma_0 + \gamma_1 y_t + \gamma_2 q_t + \gamma_3 w_t + u_{2,t},$$

where y is an activity variable, q is a real exchange rate (defined conventionally, so that a rise is a depreciation), and z is a supply-side variable. The variable w is a shift variable accounting for other factors that might increase import demand. The equations are estimated using the Stock-Watson (1993) dynamic OLS regression method with two leads and lags of first differences of the right-hand-side variables.

For the dependent variables, we have collected data on Chinese exports and imports from as early as 1980, to 2006, on a monthly basis. These data are in turn broken into ordinary and processing and parts trade flows. The multilateral data is sourced from Chinese Customs via CEIC. Import data are on a cost, insurance, and freight (c.i.f.) basis, while export data are free on board (f.o.b.). We convert the monthly data into quarterly by simple averaging. These series are depicted in figures 7.9 and 7.10.

One particularly difficult issue involves price deflators. Until 2005, the Chinese did not report price indexes for imports and exports. This limitation explains Marquez and Schindler's (2007) reliance on a trade share variable. We attempt to circumvent this difficulty in a different manner, by relying on several proxy measures. Because the trade flows are reported in U.S. dollars,

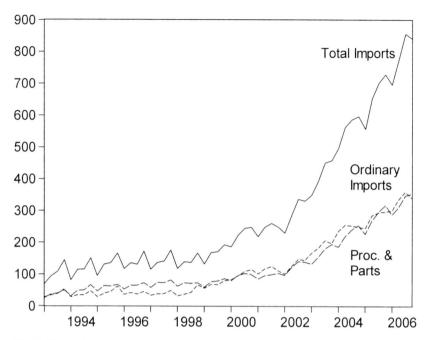

Fig. 7.10   Chinese total, ordinary, and processing and parts imports, in billions of U.S. dollars, at annual rates

the price measures we consider include the U.S. CPI-all, the PPI for finished goods, the price indexes reported by Gaulier, Lemoine, and Ünal-Kesenci (2006, hereafter GLÜ-K), both at the aggregate level, and by stage of production, and, finally, using the Hong Kong reexport indexes.

In the following, we report only the results based upon the PPI, the category-specific GLÜ-K indexes, and the Hong Kong unit value indexes; the remaining results are available upon request. We select these indexes (shown in figures 7.11 and 7.12) mostly on the grounds of pragmatism. The PPI appears to be a good proxy for tradable goods prices, while the GLÜ-K indexes are carefully constructed and documented.

The Hong Kong unit value indexes have typically been used in empirical analyses as proxy measures for Chinese trade (see Cheung 2005). We use the Hong Kong to China reexport unit value indexes to deflate Chinese imports and the Hong Kong to U.S. reexport unit value indexes to deflate Chinese exports.

The GLÜ-K indexes have the drawback of being available only at the annual frequency, and then only up to 2004. We have used quadratic interpolation to translate the annual data into quarterly.

Our measure of the real exchange rate, q, is the IMF's CPI-deflated trade-

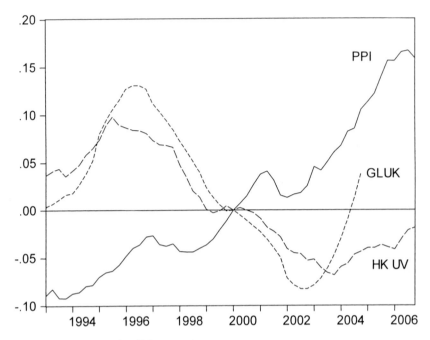

Fig. 7.11   Deflators for Chinese exports
Sources: U.S. PPI, consumption good-based price index from Gaulier, Lemoine, and Ünal-Kesenci (2006) and Hong Kong reexport to world unit value index.
Note: All series in logs, rescaled to 2000Q1 = 0.

weighted index. For y^*, we use rest-of-the-world GDP evaluated in current U.S. dollars, deflated into real terms using the U.S. GDP deflator, while y is measured using real GDP (production based) expressed in real 1990 RMB. For z, we assume that supply shifts out with the capital stock in manufacturing (Chinn 2005). This capital stock measure was calculated by Bai, Hsieh, and Qian (2006). This series is extended by assuming a 12 percent growth rate in 2005 and 2006, and interpolated to quarterly frequency using quadratic match averaging.

In table 7.4, we present the results for Chinese exports, with panel A for aggregate flows, panel B for ordinary exports, and panel C for parts and processing. For each flow, we present coefficient estimates pertaining to real trade flows calculated using alternative deflators. The results in column (1) pertain to PPI-deflated series, while those in column (2) pertain to that obtained when deflating with the GLÜ-K price series, and column (3) pertains to Hong Kong reexport unit value index-deflated series. For now, the z term is suppressed.

There are two uniformly consistent results in all the regression results reported in table 7.4. First, the income variable enters in with a very high (perhaps implausibly high) and statistically significant coefficient. Second,

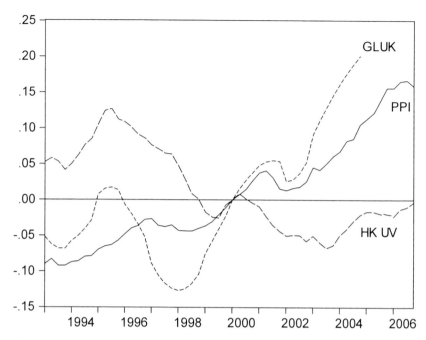

Fig. 7.12   Deflators for Chinese imports

Sources: U.S. PPI, capital good-based price index from Gaulier, Lemoine, and Ünal-Kesenci (2006) and Hong Kong reexport to China unit value index.

Note: All series in logs, rescaled to 2000Q1 = 0.

the real exchange rate enters in with a strongly negative sign—that is, greater RMB depreciation induces less exports.[20]

Because these results seem so counterintuitive, we appeal to a supply shift variable. The standard imperfect goods model of imports and exports typically relies upon the real exchange rate index measuring the relative price of traded goods well. However, our exchange rate measure is the CPI-deflated exchange rate, which may or may not be a good measure of relative traded goods prices.[21] Hence, we add in a measure of the supply side. In line with the approach adopted in Helkie and Hooper (1988), we use a measure of the Chinese capital stock in manufacturing.

The results using this supply variable are quite interesting. As reported in table 7.5, the supply variable coefficient is now the only one that is consistently significant. In addition, the income and price coefficients now take

20. In these, and subsequent, estimates, the inclusion of a time trend often results in substantially different point estimates for the income elasticity. This outcome occurs because Chinese GDP and rest-of-the-world GDP look similar to a deterministic time trend.

21. Here we have adjusted the official rate to reflect the fact that many transactions took place through swap centers during the period leading up to 1994. See Fernald, Edison, and Loungani (1999).

Table 7.4   **Chinese export elasticities**

	PPI (1)	GLÜ-K (2)	HK UV (3)
	A. Aggregate exports		
y^*	5.23***	5.30***	6.01***
	(0.29)	(1.42)	(0.35)
q	−1.63***	−2.14***	−1.69***
	(0.39)	(0.68)	(0.47)
z			
Adjusted R^2	0.89	0.76	0.88
Standard error	0.186	0.272	0.223
Sample	93Q3–06Q2	93Q3–04Q2	93Q3–06Q2
	B. Ordinary exports		
y^*	4.98***	4.82***	5.76***
	(0.32)	(1.52)	(0.38)
q	−1.46***	−2.00***	−1.51***
	(0.42)	(0.73)	(0.50)
z			
Adjusted R^2	0.85	0.68	0.84
Standard error	0.209	0.293	0.244
Sample	93Q3–06Q2	93Q3–04Q2	93Q3–06Q2
	C. Processing and parts exports		
y^*	5.35***	5.14***	6.13***
	(0.27)	(1.15)	(0.33)
q	−1.86***	−2.68***	−1.92***
	(0.37)	(0.56)	(0.45)
z			
Adjusted R^2	0.92	0.84	0.90
Standard error	0.171	0.220	0.208
Sample	93Q3–06Q2	93Q3–04Q2	93Q3–06Q2

Notes: Point estimates are obtained from dynamic ordinary least squares (2,2). Robust standard errors are given in parentheses. The price elasticity estimate should be positive for Chinese exports. PPI indicates U.S. producer price index-finished goods is used as the deflator; GLÜ-K indicates the Gaulier, Lemoine, and Ünal-Kesenci (2006) consumer good index is used as the deflator; HK UV indicates the Hong Kong unit value index for reexports to the world is used as the deflator.

***Significant at the 1 percent level.

on more plausible coefficients, even though they are often not statistically significant.

In panel A, overall exports are examined. The only statistically significant coefficients are on the supply variable. Of course, as suggested by Marquez and Schindler (2007), the differing behavior of ordinary and processing exports suggests that aggregation is inappropriate. Panel B reports the results for ordinary exports. Here, one finds that the rest-of-the-world activity is not a good predictor of exports, while the price variable is an important determinant. Using either GLÜ-K or Hong Kong indexes, one

Table 7.5   **Chinese export elasticities in the presence of Chinese capital stock**

	PPI (1)	GLÜ-K (2)	HK UV (3)
	A. Aggregate exports		
y^*	0.57	−0.56	0.31
	(0.40)	(0.53)	(0.40)
q	−0.06	0.26	0.27
	(0.23)	(0.22)	(0.22)
z	1.68***	2.35***	2.06***
	(0.16)	(0.16)	(0.15)
Adjusted R^2	0.98	0.98	0.99
Standard error	0.077	0.080	0.076
Sample	93Q3–06Q2	93Q3–04Q2	93Q3–06Q2
	B. Ordinary exports		
y^*	0.04	−1.26	−0.22
	(0.55)	(0.75)	(0.55)
q	0.31	0.61*	0.64*
	(0.32)	(0.31)	(0.32)
z	1.83***	2.51***	2.22***
	(0.22)	(0.22)	(0.22)
Adjusted R^2	0.96	0.96	0.97
Standard error	0.106	0.108	0.105
Sample	93Q3–06Q2	93Q3–04Q2	93Q3–06Q2
	C. Processing and parts exports		
y^*	0.98***	0.26	0.72**
	(0.30)	(0.32)	(0.31)
q	−0.47**	−0.62***	−0.14
	(0.19)	(0.16)	(0.18)
z	1.52***	1.99***	1.91***
	(0.11)	(0.10)	(0.11)
Adjusted R^2	0.92	0.99	0.99
Standard error	0.065	0.060	0.062
Sample	93Q3–06Q2	93Q3–04Q2	93Q3–06Q2

Notes: Point estimates are obtained from dynamic ordinary least squares (2,2). Robust standard errors are given in parentheses. The price elasticity estimate should be positive for Chinese exports. PPI indicates U.S. producer price index-finished goods is used as the deflator; GLÜ-K indicates the Gaulier, Lemoine, and Ünal-Kesenci (2006) consumer good index is used as the deflator; HK UV indicates the Hong Kong unit value index for reexports to the world is used as the deflator. Supply is the Bai, Hsieh, and Qian (2006) measure of the Chinese capital stock in manufacturing.

***Significant at the 1 percent level.

**Significant at the 5 percent level.

*Significant at the 10 percent level.

finds an export elasticity of approximately 0.6. At the same time, a 1 percent increase in the Chinese manufacturing capital stock induces between a 2.2 and 2.5 percent increase in real exports.

Strangely, the rest-of-the-world GDP does affect positively processing output. Thorbecke and Smith (forthcoming) argue that Chinese processing output is fairly sophisticated in nature; if so, that might explain the greater income sensitivity of such exports.

In table 7.6, we turn to examining Chinese imports. We rely upon the same breakdown, with panel A pertaining to aggregate imports, panel B to ordinary imports, and panel C to processing and parts imports.

Aggregate imports appear to respond strongly to income, and in the expected direction. On the other hand, we replicate Marquez and Schindler's (2007) results with regard to the price elasticity. A weaker RMB induces greater imports, rather than less. This is true also for ordinary imports. Only when moving to parts and processing imports does one obtain some mixed evidence, and there the results are still toward finding a wrong-signed coefficient.

The Marquez and Schindler (2007) results suggest including a role for FDI as our w variable. However, inclusion of a cumulative FDI variable is insufficient to overturn this result on a consistent basis.

In panel D of table 7.6, we interpret w as real total exports, in the specification involving parts and processing imports. Then we obtain a negative estimated elasticity for the real exchange rate although the results can hardly be considered robust.

Given these mixed results, we have to be very careful in interpreting the estimated elasticities until such time as we have a long time series on Chinese trade prices.

7.4.3   China-U.S. Trade Elasticities

In order to examine the behavior of the bilateral China-U.S. trade balance, it is necessary to modify equations (4) and (5) to take into account the substitutability between Chinese goods and goods from competing countries. The resulting specifications are given by:

$$(6) \qquad ex_t = \beta_0 + \beta_1 y_t^* + \beta_2 q_t + \beta_3 z_t + \beta_4 \tilde{q}_t + u_{3,t},$$

and

$$(7) \qquad im_t = \gamma_0 + \gamma_1 y_t + \gamma_2 q_t + \gamma_3 w_t + \gamma_4 \tilde{q}_t + u_{4,t},$$

where q_t is the bilateral real exchange rate, and $\tilde{q}_t$ is an effective real exchange rate relative to China's other trading partners.

Two sets of bilateral data are obtained; the first is sourced from the People's Republic of China Customs agency, and the second from U.S. Customs. The valuation conventions differ between the Chinese and U.S. data as does the

Table 7.6   **Chinese import elasticities**

	PPI (1)	GLÜ-K (2)	HK UV (3)
	A. Aggregate imports		
y	1.78***	1.41***	2.16***
	(0.06)	(0.04)	(0.06)
q	1.48***	0.39**	1.54***
	(0.38)	(0.19)	(0.32)
Adjusted R^2	0.99	0.98	0.99
Standard error	0.056	0.050	0.055
Sample	94Q4–06Q2	94Q4–04Q2	94Q4–06Q2
	B. Ordinary imports		
y	2.16***	2.40***	2.54***
	(0.26)	(0.32)	(0.27)
q	2.75**	2.25**	2.80**
	(1.18)	(1.06)	(1.19)
Adjusted R^2	0.85	0.94	0.94
Standard error	0.209	0.152	0.196
Sample	94Q4–06Q2	94Q4–04Q2	94Q4–06Q2
	C. Processing and parts imports		
y	1.68***	0.85***	2.06***
	(0.08)	(0.13)	(0.06)
q	1.15***	–0.25	1.20***
	(0.35)	(0.34)	(0.28)
R^2	0.98	0.88	0.99
Standard error	0.072	0.080	0.060
Sample	94Q4–06Q2	94Q4–04Q2	94Q4–06Q2
	D. Processing and parts imports		
y	–0.40*	–1.86*	–0.04
	(0.20)	(0.93)	(0.25)
q	–0.13	–1.64***	–0.16
	(0.23)	(0.58)	(0.22)
w	1.10***	1.20***	0.96***
	(0.13)	(0.40)	(0.12)
Adjusted R^2	0.99	0.89	0.99
Standard error	0.037	0.074	0.035
Sample	94Q4–06Q2	94Q4–04Q2	94Q4–06Q2

Notes: Point estimates are obtained from dynamic ordinary least squares (2,2). Robust standard errors are given in parentheses. The price elasticity estimate should be negative for Chinese imports. PPI indicates U.S. producer price index-finished goods is used as the deflator; GLÜ-K indicates the Gaulier, Lemoine, and Ünal-Kesenci (2006) capital goods and parts index is used as the deflator for aggregate, capital goods for ordinary and parts for processing and parts; HK UV indicates the Hong Kong unit value index for reexports is used as the deflator. The demand shift variable w is total real exports.

***Significant at the 1 percent level.
**Significant at the 5 percent level.
*Significant at the 10 percent level.

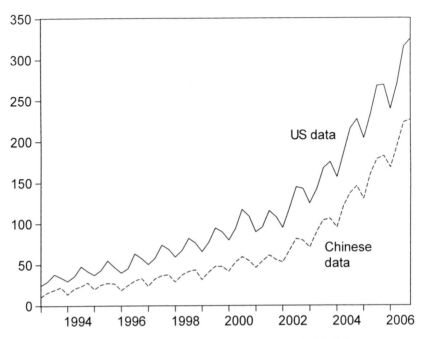

Fig. 7.13   Chinese exports to the United States, in billions of U.S. dollars, at annual rates

coverage. These differences are discussed in detail by Schindler and Beckett (2005). The relevant bilateral series are presented in figures 7.13 and 7.14.

Now y^* is measured using U.S. real GDP (in chained 2000 dollars). q_t is calculated by deflating the Chinese RMB (taking into account the transactions taking place at swap rates pre-1994) by the Chinese and U.S. CPI. $\tilde{q}_t$ is calculated using time-varying trade weights based on Chinese trade flows and bilateral real exchange rates calculated using CPIs. In the calculation of trade weights, we omitted Hong Kong, due to the difficulties in interpreting the trade with that economy.

Once again, our chief difficulty arises from the absence of an appropriate deflator. The Bureau of Labor Statistics (BLS) reports a price index for Chinese imports into the United States starting from 2004 onward, which affords a much too short time series for purposes of estimation. While the Chinese import price series has tracked the import price index for East Asian newly industrializing countries (NICs) over the period that we have Chinese statistics, it is clearly inappropriate to use the NICs series going back before June 1997 as China did not move its exchange rate with the other East Asian countries. Hence, for Chinese exports to the United States, we use a variety of proxy measures. The first is the U.S. PPI for all finished goods. The second is a composite measure, that is, the reported U.S. import series for Chinese

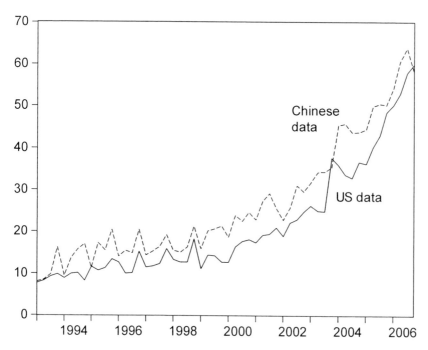

Fig. 7.14   Chinese imports from the United States, in billions of U.S. dollars, at annual rates

goods from January 2004 onward, the NICs series from January 2000 to end-2003, and the GLÜ-K consumer goods index from 1992 to end-1999. The third is the Hong Kong unit value index for reexports to the United States.

The BLS does not report a price index for U.S. exports to China. Because according to Chinese statistics, over half of Chinese imports from the United States are categorized as machinery and electrical equipment in 2006, we chose to use as one of our proxies for Chinese import prices, the U.S. capital goods export price index, in addition to the U.S. PPI. A final proxy measure is the Hong Kong unit value index for imports from the United States. This means there are three deflators for each trade flow measure.

The results for Chinese exports are reported in table 7.7. The three left-hand-side columns pertain to results obtained using U.S. data, while the three right-hand-side columns pertain to results obtained using Chinese data. We do not report results omitting the supply shift variable as this leads to implausibly high income elasticities.

The estimated income elasticities based on U.S. data are positive but not statistically significant. On the other hand, there is a strong, statistically significant coefficient on the bilateral real exchange rate. In other words, as the Chinese currency depreciates against the dollar, Chinese exports to the United States increase. In addition, as the Chinese currency depreci-

Table 7.7   Chinese bilateral export elasticities (China–United States)

| | US data | | | Chinese data | | |
	PPI (1)	P (2)	HK UV (3)	PPI (4)	P (5)	HK UV (6)
y^*	0.03	0.59	0.56	−1.75*	−1.19	−0.62
	(0.80)	(0.73)	(0.75)	(0.99)	(0.92)	(0.99)
q	0.80***	1.27***	1.05***	1.55***	2.03***	1.65***
	(0.22)	(0.22)	(0.20)	(0.30)	(0.29)	(0.31)
$\tilde{q}$	0.47	0.68	1.04	1.31	1.52	1.08
	(0.72)	(0.67)	(0.71)	(0.88)	(0.89)	(0.80)
z	.82***	2.14***	2.04***	3.12***	3.45***	2.98***
	(0.32)	(0.31)	(0.33)	(0.47)	(0.45)	(0.46)
Adjusted R^2	0.99	0.99	0.99	0.99	0.99	0.99
Standard error	0.040	0.039	0.042	0.049	0.048	0.048
Sample	93Q4–06Q2	93Q4–06Q2	93Q4–06Q2	93Q4–06Q2	93Q4–06Q2	93Q4–06Q2

Notes: Point estimates are obtained from dynamic ordinary least squares (2.2). Robust standard errors are given in parentheses. PPI indicates that U.S. producer price index-finished goods is used as the deflator; P indicates that the composite import price deflator is used (see text); HK UV indicates that the Hong Kong unit value index for reexports to the United States is used. Supply is the Bai, Hsieh, and Qian (2006) measure of the Chinese capital stock in manufacturing.

***Significant at the 1 percent level.

**Significant at the 5 percent level.

*Significant at the 10 percent level.

ates against its trade partners, it gains a larger share of exports—vis-à-vis ASEAN and other economies—to the United States.[22] However, this estimated effect is not particularly large and is nowhere near statistical significance. Finally, the supply shift variable comes in with a large positive and statistically significant coefficient.

Interestingly, when we use Chinese data, we obtain a negative coefficient on U.S. income (significant in one instance). The other results remain intact, however. Hence, we can be reasonably confident that the bilateral real exchange rate does have an effect on bilateral trade flows.

Which set of estimates should we place more weight on? Because Schindler and Beckett (2005) argue that most of the error in calculating trade balances is attributable to China's inability to identify correctly the destination of Chinese exports transshipped through Hong Kong, we believe the results based on U.S. data are of greater reliability, at least insofar as Chinese exports are concerned. For Chinese imports of U.S. goods, Chinese data may be more reliable.[23]

In contrast to the results obtained for Chinese exports to the United States, Chinese imports from the United States are relatively well explained by Chinese income and—at least for U.S. data—the real exchange rate. Both elasticities are statistically significant and in the anticipated direction when using U.S. data. However, the Chinese exchange rate relative to other trading partners once again do not enter in with any sort of recognizable pattern. Despite the similarity in the time series behavior of the U.S. and Chinese data, when the latter are used, the coefficient on the bilateral real exchange rate is no longer statistically significant, nor is the sign negative.

7.4.4   Policy Implications of the Estimates

There are some complications in drawing out the policy implications of these regression estimates. First, it is clear that the estimates are not robust to specification. Second, some of the key point estimates are not statistically significant. Third, some of the point estimates—when statistically significant—are counterintuitive. In particular, the results pertaining to import elasticities are problematic.

For instance, consider a 10 percent appreciation. Using the point estimates from table 7.5, column three of panels B and C for exports, one finds that Chinese real exports (in 2000$) decline from 952.3 billion (recorded in 2006) to 927.4 in the long run. On the other hand, using column three estimates from panels B and D from table 7.6, one finds that Chinese imports also *decline,* from 581.6 billion to 510.5 billion. This means that the trade balance *increases* from 400.9 billion to 416.9 billion, in response to a 10

---

22. For a discussion of the complementary/substituting aspect of Chinese and ASEAN trade, see Ahearne et al. (2003).
23. See also the discussion in Fung and Lau (2001).

percent real appreciation. (Note that parts and processing imports fall as total exports rise.)

The ordinary goods import price elasticity estimate of +2.8 drives this result. Alternative econometric specifications lead to different estimates. For instance, using a single equation error correction model, allowing for coefficient shifts with Chinese accession to WTO, leads to a statistically insignificant estimate of the price elasticity. In the 2000 to 2006 period, the implied price elasticity is zero. Using this point estimate, then a 10 percent appreciation would actually lead to a shrinkage of the trade balance from 400.9 billion to 355.2 billion. This estimate of 45.7 billion (2000$) is somewhat less than the $88.6 billion current dollars reported in Marquez and Schindler (2007).

Although the China-U.S. trade balance is not, macroeconomically speaking, very interesting, for political reasons it has taken on heightened visibility.[24] We can apply our estimates to answering the question of what would happen in response to a 10 percent appreciation of the RMB against the USD. Because both export and import and price elasticities are approximately unity (see column three in tables 7.7 and 7.8), this implies the China-U.S. trade balance would respond fairly strongly to RMB appreciation. Assuming unitary elasticities, the 2006 trade balance of 229.3 billion (2000$) would fall to 195.9 billion, or by 33.4 billion. Of course, this does not mean that the overall U.S. trade deficit would shrink. In fact, the deficit could be reallocated to other countries, even as the Chinese surplus with the United States fell.

Interestingly, our estimate is not that far away from Thorbecke's (2006) estimate of a long-run decrease of 29 billion dollars in response to a 10 percent appreciation in 2005.

The ex-U.S. trade-weighted exchange rate ($\tilde{q}$) should capture the effect of the changes in the value of the RMB relative to the currencies of other countries that also export to the United States. Unfortunately, the point estimate is not statistically significant at conventional levels. Hence, one can take the foregoing calculation in either of two ways. First, it assumes that the RMB moves against the U.S. dollar, while holding its position relative to its trading partners constant—that is, other countries aside from the United States move their currencies in line with China's. Second, the other country effect is absent.

7.5   Concluding Thoughts

This study has aimed to illuminate some of the determinants of the Chinese exchange rate and China's external balance. In documenting the em-

---

24. See, for instance, Frankel and Wei's (2007) analysis of determinants of the Treasury's decisions regarding currency manipulators.

Table 7.8   Chinese bilateral import elasticities (China–United States)

	U.S. data			Chinese data		
	PPI (1)	P (2)	HK UV (3)	PPI (4)	P (5)	HK UV (6)
y	1.45***	2.02***	1.85***	1.24**	1.81***	1.65***
	(0.33)	(0.35)	(0.32)	(0.46)	(0.48)	(0.45)
q	−1.31***	−1.13***	−0.99***	0.25	0.43	0.57
	(0.33)	(0.32)	(0.32)	(0.39)	(0.42)	(0.45)
$\tilde{q}$	−0.26	0.69	−0.21	0.36	1.32	0.42
	(1.06)	(1.10)	(1.04)	(1.51)	(1.56)	(1.51)
Adjusted R^2	0.95	0.96	0.97	0.95	0.96	0.97
Standard error	0.101	0.101	0.100	0.087	0.091	0.087
Sample	94Q4–06Q2	94Q4–06Q2	94Q4–06Q2	94Q4–06Q2	94Q4–06Q2	94Q4–06Q2

Notes: Point estimates are obtained from dynamic ordinary least squares (2.2). Robust standard errors are given in parentheses. PPI indicates that U.S. producer price index-finished goods is used as the deflator; P indicates that the U.S. capital goods export price deflator is used (see text); HK UV indicates that the Hong Kong unit value index for imports from the United States is used.

***Significant at the 1 percent level.

**Significant at the 5 percent level.

pirical record, we have highlighted one particularly important fact: many of the empirical relationships that can be identified are of a tenuous nature.

Turning first to the real value of the RMB, we reiterate the findings of Cheung, Chinn, and Fujii (2007b)—namely that the relationship between real per capita income and the real value of a currency in PPP terms is quite diffuse. We can be quite certain that a relationship exists, but the exact magnitude of the slope coefficient is subject to substantial uncertainty. And this is even before one adds in model uncertainty and measurement error, the latter of which has been spectacularly demonstrated as being of consequence. Hence, we cannot reject the null hypothesis of no undervaluation at conventional levels of statistical significance. Of course, it is critical to remember that the failure to reject a null is *not* the same as acceptance of the null hypothesis.[25] Even now, with the benefit of updated Chinese price and income data, we could also not reject the null that the RMB was 40 percent undervalued.

The same characterization applies to our findings regarding trade elasticities, perhaps even more so than in the case of the exchange rate. That outcome occurs for a number of reasons, in our view. First, in the approach adopted, we rely solely upon a single country's data, rather than appealing to cross-country data. Second, the data pertain to an economy experiencing rapid structural changes. These structural changes include a rapid build up in the capital stock, motivating our use of a proxy measure of China's supply capacity.[26]

We also freely acknowledge that our approach, while fully in the spirit of conventional approach, may miss some important aspects of China's recent macroeconomic behavior. In particular, some observers have noted that the decline in import growth during the 2005 to 2006 period was associated with a decline in consumption, which, in turn, has been driven by a declining disposable income-GDP ratio and a rising saving-disposable income ratio (International Monetary Fund 2006). Because consumption behavior clear affects imports and exports, omission of this factor is something to be examined in subsequent work.

With these caveats in mind, we conclude that there is some evidence that Chinese trade flows respond to changes in real exchange rates—as well as income levels. However, the price elasticities do not appear reliably estimated, and some estimates are counterintuitive.

Our bottom line conclusion regarding the estimated elasticities is that the real exchange rate effect on overall trade flows—using typical point

25. This is cogently discussed in Frankel (1990).

26. Marquez observes that assuming a constant income elasticity of imports while the import-GDP ratio increases over time presupposes a very specific behavior for the marginal propensity to import. An alternative is to impose a constant marginal propensity to import and retrieve the implied time varying income elasticities.

estimates—is relatively small and sometimes goes in the direction opposite of anticipated. Using some plausible estimates and zeroing out perverse estimates, we obtain for a 10 percent RMB real appreciation a 46 billion (2000$) reduction in the Chinese trade balance, which, while not inconsequential, is still not tremendously large when measured against a 2006 balance of 401 billion (2000$).

These findings suggest that exchange rate policy alone will not be sufficient to reduce the Chinese trade surplus, especially when taken in the context of a trend increase in China's manufacturing capacity. Depending upon which specification is selected, slower growth in the rest of the world could have substantial impact on Chinese exports. With less circumspection, one can assert that slower growth in the United States would have a substantial impact on the U.S. trade deficit with China.

Appendix
Data Appendix

The data used for the real exchange rate portion of the paper (section 7.3) were drawn from a number of different sources. For most countries, data were available from 1971 through 2006 and drawn from the World Bank's *World Development Indicators* (2007 and 2008 editions). Taiwanese data are drawn from the Central Bank of China; International Center for the Study of East Asian Development (ICSEAD); and Asian Development Bank, *Key Indicators of Developing Asian and Pacific Countries* (through 2005).

The data used for the trade elasticities portion of the paper (section 7.4) are drawn from a variety of sources.

- Official exchange rates from IMF *International Financial Statistics* and "swap rates" from personal communication with John Fernald.
- Total Chinese exports and imports, from Chinese Customs, via CEIC.
- China-U.S. trade flows, from China Customs, via CEIC, and from U.S. BEA/Census via Haver.
- Price deflators from various sources.
  - U.S. CPI-all and PPI (finished goods), from U.S. Bureau of Labor Statistics, via Federal Reserve Economic Data (FRED) II.
  - Overall price indexes for Chinese exports and imports, and category-specific price indexes, in USD terms, as described in Gaulier, Lemoine, and Ünal-Kesenci (2006); personal communication from Guillaume Gaulier.
  - Price indexes for U.S. imports from China, East Asian Newly Industrializing Countries (NICs), from Bureau of Labor Statistics.

- Chinese real GDP seasonally adjusted (from CEIC). U.S. real GDP drawn from Bureau of Economic Analysis (June 28, 2007 release).
- The Chinese nominal and real trade-weighted exchange rates from IMF *International Financial Statistics.*
- The bilateral USD/RMB exchange rate adjusted for swap transactions was provided by John Fernald.
- Chinese CPI drawn from CEIC, updated using IMF *International Financial Statistics* year-on-year growth rates.
- The Chinese capital stock in manufacturing, as described in Bai, Hsieh, and Qian (2006), was provided by Chang-Tai Hsieh. This series is assumed to grow by 12 percent in 2005 and 2006, and is interpolated to a quarterly frequency using quadratic match averaging.

References

Ahearne, Alan, John Fernald, Prakash Lougani, and John Schindler. 2003. China and emerging Asia: Comrades or competitors? *International Finance Discussion Paper* no. 789. Washington, DC: Federal Reserve Board.

Asian Development Bank. 2007. *Purchasing power parities and real expenditures.* Manila, The Philippines: Asian Development Bank.

Bai, Chong-En, Chang-Tai Hsieh, and Qingyi Qian. 2006. Returns to capital in China. *Brookings Papers on Economic Activity* Issue no. 2:61–101. Washington, DC: Brookings Institution.

Balassa, Bela. 1964. The purchasing power parity doctrine: A reappraisal. *Journal of Political Economy* 72 (6): 584–96.

Bosworth, Barry. 2004. Valuing the renminbi. Paper presented at the Tokyo Club Foundation for Global Studies meeting, Tokyo, Japan.

Cairns, John. 2005a. China: How undervalued is the CNY? IDEAglobal Economic Research, Research Report, June 27.

———. 2005b. Fair value on global currencies: An assessment of valuation based on GDP and absolute price levels. IDEAglobal Economic Research, Research Report, May 10.

Canzoneri, Matthew, Robert Cumby, and Behzad Diba. 1999. Relative labor productivity and the real exchange rate in the long run: Evidence for a panel of OECD countries. *Journal of International Economics* 47 (2): 245–66.

Cheung, Yin-Wong. 2005. An analysis of Hong Kong export performance. *Pacific Economic Review* 10 (3): 323–40.

Cheung, Yin-Wong, Menzie Chinn, and Eiji Fujii. 2007a. *The economic integration of greater China: Real and financial linkages and the prospects for currency union.* Hong Kong: Hong Kong University Press.

———. 2007b. The overvaluation of renminbi undervaluation. *Journal of International Money and Finance* 26 (5): 762–85.

———. 2009a. The illusion of precision and the role of the renminbi in regional integration. In *Prospects for monetary and financial integration in East Asia: Dreams and dilemmas,* ed. K. Hamada, B. Reszat, and U. Volz, 325–56. Northampton, MA: Edward Elgar.

————. 2009b. Pitfalls in measuring exchange rate misalignment: The yuan and other currencies. *Open Economies Review* 20 (2): 183–206.

Chinn, Menzie. 2000a. Before the fall: Were East Asian currencies overvalued? *Emerging Markets Review* 1 (2): 101–26.

————. 2000b. The usual suspects? Productivity and demand shocks and Asia-Pacific real exchange rates. *Review of International Economics* 8 (1): 20–43.

————. 2005. Supply capacity, vertical specialization and tariff rates: The implications for aggregate U.S. trade flow equations. NBER Working Paper no. 11719. Cambridge, MA: National Bureau of Economic Research, October.

Chinn, Menzie, and Hiro Ito. 2007. Current account balances, financial development and institutions: Assaying the world "saving glut," *Journal of International Money and Finance* 26 (4): 546–69.

Chinn, Menzie, and Eswar Prasad. 2003. Medium-term determinants of current accounts in industrial and developing countries: An empirical exploration. *Journal of International Economics* 59 (1): 47–76.

Coudert, Virginie, and Cécile Couharde. 2005. Real equilibrium exchange rate in China. CEPII Working Paper no. 2005-01. Paris: Centre d'Etude Prospectives et d'Informations Internationales, January.

De Gregorio, Jose, and Holger Wolf. 1994. Terms of trade, productivity, and the real exchange rate. NBER Working Paper no. 4807. Cambridge, MA: National Bureau of Economic Research.

Dunaway, Steven Vincent, Lamin Leigh, and Xiangming Li. 2009. How robust are estimates of equilibrium real exchange rates: The case of China. *Pacific Economic Review* 14 (3): 361–75.

Elekdag, Selim, and Subir Lall. 2008. International statistical comparison: Global growth estimates trimmed after PPP revisions. *IMF Survey Magazine,* January 8. Washington, DC: International Monetary Fund.

Fernald, John, Hali Edison, and Prakash Loungani. 1999. Was China the first domino? Assessing links between China and other Asian economies. *Journal of International Money and Finance* 18 (4): 515–35.

Frankel, Jeffrey A. 1990. Zen and the art of modern macroeconomics: A commentary. In *Monetary policy for a volatile global economy,* ed. W. S. Haraf and T. D. Willett, 117–23. Washington, DC: AEI Press.

————. 2006. On the Yuan: The choice between adjustment under a fixed exchange rate and adjustment under a flexible rate. In *Understanding the Chinese economy,* ed. Gerhard Illing, 246–75. CESifo Economic Studies, vol. 52. Oxford, UK: Oxford University Press.

Frankel, Jeffrey A., and Shang-Jin Wei. 2007. Assessing China's exchange rate regime. *Economic Policy* 22:575–627.

Fung, K. C., and Lawrence J. Lau. 2001. New estimates of the United States–China bilateral trade balances. *Journal of the Japanese and International Economies* 15:102–30.

Funke, Michael, and Jörg Rahn. 2005. Just how undervalued is the Chinese renminbi? *World Economy* 28:465–89.

Garcia-Herrero, Alicia, and Tuuli Koivu. 2007. Can the Chinese trade surplus be reduced through exchange rate policy? BOFIT Discussion Paper no. 2007-6. Helsinki, Finland: Bank of Finland, March.

Gaulier, Guillaume, Françoise Lemoine, and Deniz Ünal-Kesenci. 2006. China's emergence and the reorganization of trade flows in Asia. CEPII Working Paper no. 2006-05. Paris: Centre d'Etude Prospectives et d'Informations Internationales, March.

Goldstein, Morris. 2004. China and the renminbi exchange rate. In *Dollar adjust-*

ment: How far? Against what? ed. C. Fred Bergsten and John Williamson, 197–230. Washington, DC: Institute for International Economics.

Government Accountability Office. 2005. International trade: Treasury assessments have not found currency manipulation, but concerns about exchange rates continue. Report to Congressional Committees GAO-05-351. Washington, DC: Government Accountability Office, April.

Helkie, William L., and Peter Hooper. 1988. An empirical analysis of the external deficit, 1980–86. In *External deficits and the dollar, the pit, and the pendulum,* ed. Ralph C. Bryant, Gerald Holtham, and Peter Hooper, 10–56. Washington, DC: Brookings Institution.

Hsieh, David. 1982. The determination of the real exchange rate: The productivity approach. *Journal of International Economics* 12 (2): 355–62.

International Comparison Program. 2007. Preliminary results: Frequently asked questions. http://siteresources.worldbank.org/ICPINT/Resources/background er-FAQ.pdf.

International Monetary Fund (IMF). 2006. People's Republic of China: 2006 Article IV consultation—Staff report. IMF Country Report no. 06/394. Washington, DC: International Monetary Fund, October.

Johnson, Simon, Jonathan Ostry, and Arvind Subramanian. 2007. The prospects for sustained growth in Africa: Benchmarking the constraints. IMF Working Paper no. 07/52. Washington, DC: International Monetary Fund.

Kwack, Sung Yeung, Choong Y. Ahn, Young S. Lee, and Doo Y. Yang. 2007. Consistent estimates of world trade elasticities and an application to the effects of Chinese yuan (RMB) appreciation. *Journal of Asian Economics* 18:314–30.

Mann, Catherine, and Katerina, Plück. 2007. The U.S. trade deficit: A disaggregated perspective. In *G7 current account imbalances: Sustainability and adjustment,* ed. R. Clarida, 247–82. Chicago: University of Chicago Press.

Marquez, Jaime, and John W. Schindler. 2007. Exchange-rate effects on China's trade. *Review of International Economics* 15 (5): 837–53.

McCown, T. Ashby, Patricia Pollard, and John Weeks. 2007. Equilibrium exchange rate models and misalignments. Office of International Affairs Occasional Paper no. 7. Washington, DC: U.S. Department of the Treasury, March.

Morrison, Wayne, and Marc Labonte. 2006. China's currency: Economic issues and options for U.S. trade policy. CRS Report for Congress no. RL32165. Washington, DC: GPO.

O'Neill, Jim, and Dominic Wilson. 2003. How China can help the world. Goldman Sachs Global Economic Outlook Paper no. 97.

Prasad, Eswar, and Shang-Jin Wei. 2005. The Chinese approach to capital inflows: Patterns and possible explanations. NBER Working Paper no. 11306. Cambridge, MA: National Bureau of Economic Research, April.

Samuelson, Paul. 1964. Theoretical notes on trade problems. *Review of Economics and Statistics* 46 (2): 145–54.

Schindler, John W., and Dustin H. Beckett. 2005. Adjusting Chinese bilateral trade data: How big is China's trade surplus? International Finance Discussion Paper no. 2005-831. Washington, DC: Federal Reserve Board, April.

Stock, James, and Mark, Watson. 1993. A simple estimator of cointegrated vectors in higher order integrated systems. *Econometrica* 61:783–820.

Subramanian, Arvind. 2008. Fact check, reality check? New GDP data. *Business Standard,* January 11.

Summers, Robert, and Alan Heston. 1991. The Penn World Tables (Mark 5). An expanded set of international comparisons. *Quarterly Journal of Economics* 106:327–68.

Thorbecke, Willem. 2006. How would an appreciation of the renminbi affect the U.S. trade deficit with China? *BE Press Macro Journal* 6 (3): Article 3.

Thorbecke, Willem, and Gordon Smith. Forthcoming. How would an appreciation of the RMB and other East Asian currencies affect China's exports? *Review of International Economics.*

Wang, Jiao, and Andy G. Ji. 2006. Exchange rate sensitivity of China's bilateral trade flows. BOFIT Discussion Paper no. 2006-19. Helsinki, Finland: Bank of Finland, December.

Wang, Tao. 2004. Exchange rate dynamics. In *China's growth and integration into the world economy,* ed. Eswar Prasad, 21–28. Washington, DC: International Monetary Fund.

Zhang, Zhichao. 2001. Real exchange rate misalignment in China: An empirical investigation. *Journal of Comparative Economics* 29:80–94.

Comment   Jeffrey Frankel

When one reads in the second paragraph of this nice chapter, "there are very few studies that simultaneously assess the Chinese exchange rate and trade/current account balance," one's first reaction is: "That is true; I wonder why analysts haven't addressed them together. This will be a useful contribution." And the chapter does turn out to be a useful contribution; the authors do their usual careful job with the econometrics, while linking directly to some of the most important questions in international macroeconomic policy today.

One doesn't have to read much further, however, before being reminded why quantitative research on the Chinese exchange rate and trade balance has been stunted. There are reasons to be pessimistic about getting good results econometrically. First, as the authors say, "the data pertain to an economy experiencing rapid structural changes." Second, the exchange rate has usually been de facto fixed, in the past under a dual exchange rate system and even today supported by capital controls. Neither the domestic financial market, nor international capital flows, nor the exchange rate itself are determined by market forces. Flexibility in the nominal exchange rate has been so low and the current "misalignment" probably so high, that there is little hope in estimating an econometric equation to determine the exchange rate. According to some theories, one gets the same real exchange rate regardless of the regime: if nominal flexibility is suppressed, then fundamentals show up in the price level instead. But we know that, in practice, if a country like China holds the nominal exchange rate fixed at a time, it will prevent or at

Jeffrey Frankel is the James W. Harpel Professor of Capital Formation and Growth at the Kennedy School of Government, Harvard University, and a research associate of the National Bureau of Economic Research.

least delay real adjustment from occurring.[1] This is especially true if the authorities sterilize their reserve inflows, as the People's Bank of China was remarkably successful at doing, at least through 2007. One need not pass judgment on the wisdom of Chinese policy, let alone call it "manipulation," to realize that the renminbi (RMB) has been sufficiently insulated from market forces that models designed for other countries are unlikely to work well in this context.

Cheung, Chinn, and Fujii (CCF) estimate the RMB to be undervalued on the order of 50 percent in log terms. This is close to some other estimates of purchasing power parity (PPP)-based relationships, such as my own 45 percent (in log terms), relative to the line representing the Balassa-Samuelson (B-S) relationship. In other words, it is not just that China's absolute prices are at current exchange rates only an estimated 23 percent of prices in the United States, but they are low by 45 percent even after taking into account what is normal for countries at China's stage of development, as measured by income per capita. Admittedly, the extant range of estimates of undervaluation is far larger once one ventures beyond the B-S/PPP approach.

Large as the CCF point estimate is, probably their most important message is that the standard error on their calculation is so large that this undervaluation is not statistically significant. I hadn't done this particular test myself, but one probably shouldn't be surprised. It continues in the train of negative findings regarding models of exchange rate determination that has been the dominant tradition ever since Meese-Rogoff. And one can eyeball from the graphs that the R^2 of the relationship is sufficiently low that most countries will find themselves within the "normal range of variation" around the B-S line.[2]

Note that this is very different from saying that the B-S relationship itself is not statistically significant. It is significant, in the results of CCF, as in my results[3] and those of many others before us. What then should one make of the undervaluation estimate for the RMB? I will come back to this later.

Sticking to the chapter itself for now, there are two directions to go, from the finding of statistical insignificance. The first is to note that the absence of statistically significant predictive power, or even stable explanatory power contemporaneously, undermines the argument of those who would say that the RMB is clearly undervalued based on economic fundamentals. The authors write, "These findings highlight the great degree of uncertainty

---

1. The evidence does not suggest that nominal exchange rate regimes strongly affect the speed of adjustment of the real exchange rate (Chinn and Wei 2008). But this may just reflect that prolonged misalignments are as possible under floating exchange rates as under fixed rates, even though arising from different causes.

2. I am here using the term "Balassa-Samuelson relationship" to refer to the correlation between real exchange rates and real income or labor productivity. As CCF point out, there are other theories that could explain the correlation besides the one that Balassa and Samuelson had in mind, which was faster productivity growth in tradables than nontradeables.

3. See Frankel (2006).

surrounding empirical estimates of equilibrium real exchange rates, thereby underscoring the difficulty in accurately assessing the degree of RMB undervaluation." One could point out that the disagreement among economists, using different economic models, particularly the tendency of some prominent international economists (though a minority)[4] to say that the RMB is very fine where it is, thank you, undermines the claim that any objective mode of inquiry would find the RMB clearly undervalued.

This is a very important point, as the "misalignment" or even "manipulation" is the position of U.S. politicians of both parties and could well result in Congress passing the aggressive sort of legislation that it has been threatening for years. It is also in some sense now the position of the International Monetary Fund (IMF), explicitly in its recent Article IV consultations and implicitly in the research agenda associated with the Multilateral Consultative Group on exchange rate surveillance. And if one cannot come up with a clear unambiguous answer to the question for the RMB, what hope is there for other exchange rates, where it is typically far more difficult still to pronounce the currency unambiguously undervalued or overvalued. Often, as for the U.S. dollar, one criterion like PPP can point in one direction, while other criteria, like the current account balance or overall balance of payments, point just as clearly in the opposite direction. This is not the case with China.

The econometric approach taken by the chapter itself goes in the direction of concluding, "We can never reliably say what determines exchange rates; so let's just take them as given, and go on to the other half of the topic, the effect of exchange rates, however they are determined, on trade flows." Here statistical significance is more easily obtained, but some of the point estimates are less than what one would normally expect, as the authors note. Exports are found to respond to depreciation in the usual positive way. But imports are also found to respond positively to depreciation. This is not what is normally expected (though it apparently is what Marquez and Schindler also found).

I have one thought here. It has probably already occurred to CCF (and Marquez as well), so let me phrase it as a question. We know that Chinese trade is heavily dominated by gross exports that have high import content.[5] Most obviously, many of the imports are raw materials or intermediate inputs that go into production generally, and especially production of exports. The econometricians have separate statistics on "parts and processing imports"; the perverse sign applies at least as strongly to "ordinary imports" as to these. But I suspect that even among "ordinary imports," a lot is reexported after the contribution of some domestic value added. So the question is this: could the perverse sign of the effect of the exchange rate on imports reflect

---

4. See Mundell, McKinnon, Cooper, and Dooley and Garber.
5. See Koopman, Wang, and Wei (2008).

that component of imports which is closely tied to exports, where the sign is clear?[6] Perhaps the authors should consider adding an additional term to equation (7), so it reads:

$$im_t = \gamma_0 + \gamma_1 y_t + \gamma_2 q_t + \gamma_3 w_t + X_4 ex_t + u_t.$$

The additional terms is exports, ex_t, and the coefficient X_4 represents their import content. Because exports are endogenous, the equation would have to be identified by means of foreign income y_t^*, which enters the export equation. Perhaps controlling for exports would restore γ_2, the coefficient on the real exchange rate, to its conventional sign.

I want to return now to the question how to think about residuals from the B-S relationship. Cheung, Chinn, and Fujii say, "It is indeed a puzzle that the CNY path is different from the one predicted by the Balassa-Samuelson hypothesis." This refers not just to the magnitude of the residuals, but to the movement over time: the failure of the Chinese currency to appreciate in real terms as the economy has experienced rapid growth in income per capita.

Let me begin by suggesting a distinction between the B-S relationship and the B-S effect.[7] Most discussion of B-S talks as if countries are always on the B-S line, except perhaps for minor regression errors. Specifically, the B-S effect is the proposition that for every 1 percent increase in labor productivity or income per capita, there is a .3 percent real appreciation (or whatever the estimate is); in other words, all movements are implicitly assumed to be movements along the line. But we know the residuals are large *and we have lots of well-articulated theories to explain this,* theories of real effects following from monetary disturbances, or other demand-side disturbances. These theories encompass a large share of open-economy macroeconomics outside B-S. There is no reason why we have to choose between B-S and theories of devaluation or monetary policy. Both are important. The theories of devaluation and monetary policy are the obvious candidates to explain the residuals from the B-S relationship (or some share of those residuals; nothing fits perfectly).

Real exchange rates are influenced not solely by the long-term trend of the B-S effect nor solely by the short-term fluctuations of monetary policy and nominal exchange rate changes, but rather are influenced by both.[8] A reasonable characterization is that in the long run, B-S factors dominate, but in the short run, monetary factors can pull the real exchange rate away from the B-S equation. This framework contains the powerful prediction that if

6. We also know that exports are much larger than imports for China; so either way, we are left with the conclusion that a real appreciation would reduce the trade surplus, as desired.

7. This is in addition to the distinction vis-à-vis "the Balassa-Samuelson theory," flagged in my second footnote.

8. One does not necessarily need prices of nontraded goods to be sticky—let alone prices of traded goods—to get the result that devaluations or changes in monetary policy can have transitory effects on the real exchange rate in the short run. See Dornbusch (1973).

a country lies substantially off the B-S regression line in one year, it can be expected to return part way—not necessarily all the way—to the regression line over the subsequent decade. This claim has important implications for our ability to make predictions and, furthermore, is borne out by data from the last two decades.

Here are examples of what I have in mind as possible explanations, anytime one observes a country lying well below the B-S line:
Macro influences such as:

- Devaluation in the presence of either sticky goods prices or nontraded goods.
- "Exogenous" depreciation under floating, with either sticky prices or nontraded goods.
- Monetary contraction/deflation, with a fixed exchange rate.
- Increased demand for currency, for example, arising from rapid supply-led growth, with a fixed exchange rate.

In the case of China, it is the last of these cases that is the relevant one. The RMB was de facto fixed to the dollar for the last ten years or so.[9] If one goes back further, the exchange rate regime was different, but the currency has never floated or been determined in a flexible way. Yet China has experienced tremendous growth in productivity and real income over the last quarter-century, perhaps the greatest the world has ever known. So even if the RMB had been on the B-S line thirty years ago, it would not be on it today. According to some theories, the exchange rate regime makes no difference: if the exchange rate is held fixed, then the economic fundamentals that would show up as a nominal appreciation under floating will instead show up in the form of inflation. You will get the same real exchange rate either way. But this is not how the world works. In addition to heavy foreign exchange intervention, the authorities made heavy use of capital controls and sterilization, with the result that the trend rate of increase in the money supply did not noticeably exceed the trend rate of growth of the real economy during the years 2005 and 2006 despite the large balance-of-payments surplus. The large reserve inflows finally in 2007 to 2008 showed up in accelerating money growth, an overheating economy, and inflation, as some of us predicted they would. But the dollar peg had already greatly delayed and diminished the effect on the real exchange rate.

This puts the CCF finding regarding the estimated undervaluation of the RMB in a very different light. Ideally, we would add to the B-S equation additional terms to capture monetary influences that in the short or medium run pull the real exchange rate away from its equilibrium value.

---

9. The Chinese authorities in 2005 announced a more flexible regime. But Frankel (2009), Frankel and Wei (2007), and others statistically infer the true regime and find that it is still rather close to a dollar peg.

Possible variables include real interest rates, acceleration in the real money supply, sudden nominal devaluations or revaluations. I tried some of these recently and got nowhere. But that may reflect a failure of my specification. For example, none of these terms would capture the presumed source of the large Chinese residual: an essentially fixed exchange rate during a period of rapid supply-side growth. So we need a better specification to capture the intermediate-term macro influences. In the meantime, my point still holds. Whether the distance between China's real exchange rate and the B-S line is statistically significant is not necessarily the point.

I am not suggesting that one should pronounce the RMB substantially undervalued based solely on a point estimate. For one thing, aside from statistical significance, I don't think any of us has really known or felt entirely comfortable with what goes into the estimated Chinese price level in the Penn World Table. Cline and Williamson (2008), for example, argued that the data were biased in the direction of exaggerating the true undervaluation.[10]

I can tell you how I think of the RMB problem, when we turn from the mores of scholarly papers to the world of policy. I can think of four or five independent criteria for addressing the question whether China should, in its own interest, allow the RMB to float upward. For most countries, some of these criteria would point in opposing directions. Correspondingly, for most countries, I am not willing to proclaim publicly that I view their currencies as either overvalued or undervalued. For China, it seems to me that the criteria tend all to point in the same direction:

1. PPP/B-S.
2. Trade balance/balance of payments/level of reserves.
3. Overheating economy.
4. Desirability of an economy as large as China's having its own monetary policy, without relying on capital controls to continue to insulate against disturbances in the future.
5. Desirability of choosing a time of strength to make the move away from a peg, rather than waiting for a time of weakness or even crisis.

It is on this basis that I do take the stand that China should let the currency appreciate. (This has nothing to do with pressure from U.S. politi-

10. Soon after the NBER conference, such doubts were proven spectacularly right when the International Bank for Reconstruction and Development (2007) released the preliminary results of a new study of absolute PPP, under the International Comparison Project, using much more extensive data, in particular for China, than had previously been available. According to the new numbers, which pertain to 2005, China's price level was 42 percent of the U.S. price level. This is far less of an undervaluation against the dollar. The new numbers show China's real income per capita to be 9.8 percent of the U.S. level. Because the new International Comparison Project numbers on prices and real incomes are both more up to date and more reliable than those previously available, it makes sense to reestimate the B-S estimation. Subramanian (2008) has done this; he computes that the RMB is 15 percent below where it ought to be. Certainly the new International Comparison Project numbers imply that the RMB is far less undervalued under the B-S criterion than had previously been estimated.

cians, which I regard as ill-advised for a whole other set of reasons). What the CCF paper has to offer—the estimate of undervaluation relative to B-S and estimates of what effect an appreciation would have on exports and imports—are useful inputs to these considerations.

References

Chinn, Menzie, and Shag-Jin Wei. 2008. A faith-based initiative: Does a flexible exchange rate regime really facilitate current account adjustment? NBER Working Paper no. 14420. Cambridge, MA: National Bureau of Economic Research, October.

Cline, William, and John Williamson. 2008. Estimates of the equilibrium exchange rate of the renminbi. In *Debating China's exchange rate policy,* ed. Morris Goldstein and Nicholas Lardy. Washington, DC: Petersen Institute for International Economics.

Dornbusch, Rudiger. 1973. Devaluation, money and nontraded goods. *American Economic Review* 63 (December): 871–80.

Frankel, Jeffrey. 2006. On the yuan: The choice between adjustment under a fixed exchange rate and adjustment under a flexible rate. In *Understanding the Chinese economy,* ed. Gerhard Illing, 246–75. CESifo Economic Studies, vol. 52. Oxford, UK: Oxford University Press.

———. 2009. New estimation of China's exchange rate regime. *Pacific Economic Review* 14, no. 3 (August): 346–60.

Frankel, Jeffrey, and Shang-Jin Wei. 2007. Assessing China's exchange rate regime. *Economic Policy* 51:575–614.

International Bank for Reconstruction and Development. 2007. *2005 International Comparison Program: Preliminary results.* Washington, DC: International Bank for Reconstruction and Development.

Koopman, Robert, Zhi Wang, and Shang-Jin Wei. 2008. How much of Chinese exports is really made in China? Assessing domestic value added when processing trade is pervasive. NBER Working Paper no. 14109. Cambridge, MA: National Bureau of Economic Research, June.

Subramanian, Arvind. 2008. Fact check, reality check? New GDP data. *Business Standard,* January 11.

III

Sectoral Issues and Trade Policies

8

China's WTO Entry
Antidumping, Safeguards, and
Dispute Settlement

Chad P. Bown

8.1 Introduction

Policymakers choose to enter into trade agreements like the World Trade Organization (WTO) for many political and economic reasons. However, economic theorists have posited two reasons central to this decision: first, that "large" countries seek reciprocal market access commitments to neutralize the terms-of-trade effects of trade liberalization; and second, that many countries seek an externally enforced contract in order to credibly commit domestic sectors to policy reform.[1] From the broad perspective of economic theory, China's 2001 WTO accession might be motivated along the following lines: China agreed to undertake substantial import liberalization in exchange for greater certainty with respect to market access for its exports, and China's program of reform would gain domestic credibility from trading partners' threat and actual use of WTO dispute settlement procedures to ensure that China was living up to its liberalization commitments.

This chapter examines China's political-economic experience in the face

Chad P. Bown is an associate professor of economics at Brandeis University.

Thanks to Rachel McCulloch; Shang-Jin Wei, Thomas J. Prusa; Martin Feldstein; Richard Cooper; Lee Branstetter; Bruce Blonigen; Will Martin; Henrik Horn; Hylke Vandenbussche; Patrick Messerlin; conference participants at the National Bureau of Economic Research (NBER); and seminar participants at Brandeis University, Kiel, Sciences-Po in Paris, Louvain, and the Research Institute of Industrial Economics (IFN) in Stockholm for useful comments. Matthew Niedzwiecki and Paul Deng provided outstanding research assistance. The World Bank provided financial support for the collection of data used in this project. All remaining errors are my own.

1. For economic theory formalizing the first argument, see Bagwell and Staiger (1999); for the second, see Maggi and Rodriguez-Clare (1998, 2007). For recent empirical evidence supporting the first theory, including estimates using data from China, see Broda, Limão, and Weinstein (2008) and Bagwell and Staiger (2006).

of "frictions" in the international trading system as it transitions to full WTO membership. We use a number of newly compiled data sources that track areas of international political-economic tensions associated with China's increased trade. We focus on both its own exports and the potential changes in policy treatment they face across foreign markets as well as China's imports and its own changes in trade policy associated with the market access commitments it undertook as part of its 2001 accession. While certainly only a part of the landscape, the data characterizing the changing nature of trade policies by China and its trading partners helps us characterize China's actual WTO accession experience thus far.

With respect to policies facing China's exports, we examine data on WTO members' use of antidumping import restrictions against Chinese firms prior to and following its 2001 accession. While most economists view antidumping as economically baseless and little more than an easy-to-access tool of protectionism, there are many insights to be gained from examining its use, especially when it comes to China's exporters' experience. An additional benefit to studying antidumping is that it is a measurable and relatively transparent policy whose use has spread to many developed and developing countries. While it is certainly not the only tool of protectionism, antidumping is increasingly one of the few WTO-consistent instruments of protection that remains available to policymakers as more and more countries bind their import tariffs under the WTO and take on other liberalization commitments.[2]

Therefore, in section 8.2 of this chapter, we present data revealing the historic foreign use of antidumping against China's exporters. These measures reveal one contributing explanation for China's desire to seek WTO entry. By using a number of measures across virtually all of the major antidumping users in the WTO system, we find that China's exporters faced substantial discriminatory treatment relative to other exporting country targets during the 1995 to 2001 period. We also introduce a regression approach that exploits variation across China's exported products to examine a previously unexplored potential explanation for this feature of the data—that is, that foreign users were more likely to target China's products that were benefiting from high Chinese import tariffs. The theory is that high-tariff products may have been targeted to assist negotiators extract market access commitments from China. Nevertheless, we find no robust evidence of this relationship in the data.

---

2. As further motivation on welfare-economic grounds, Gallaway, Blonigen, and Flynn (1999) present evidence from a study of the cumulative effects of U.S.-imposed antidumping that it was the second most costly trade policy program in terms of lost U.S. economic welfare in 1993 at $3 billion, trailing only the Multi-Fiber Arrangement. Thus, despite any given antidumping measure only covering a handful of imported products, the fact that antidumping-using countries do not stop using the policy once they have started and that imposed measures are infrequently revoked once implemented, the cumulative impact of the policy can be substantial for lost economic welfare.

We also examine WTO member use of antidumping against China since its WTO accession to assess whether there is any associated *change* to the pattern of discrimination it has faced. As we also explore in section 8.3, any change in the use of antidumping against China by WTO members must be viewed in light of the potential for members to substitute alternative policy instruments—such as transitional "China safeguards," other safeguards, countervailing and antisubsidy measures, as well as other import restrictions. Nevertheless, as a preview to our results, while there are certainly new pressures put on foreign policymakers since 2002 that we are unable to formally control for—generated by the combination of China's expanding exports and the fact that policymakers can no longer funnel discrimination against China into their "normal" application of tariffs—there is evidence from antidumping and other new China-specific forms of contingent protection that policymakers are *increasing* discrimination against China's exporters under these particular provisions.

The next set of questions we explore concerns China's own import market access liberalization commitments associated with its WTO accession. An important question facing all countries that have undertaken substantive, new market access commitments is whether they are subsequently able to live up to them, despite the political-economic pressure imposed by domestic, import-competing firms that call for the imposition of new trade restrictions. To examine this issue, we examine data on China's own new and growing use of antidumping as well as other import-restricting measures. In the period since its accession, China has become one of the five most frequent users of antidumping in the WTO system. We describe the composition of sectors and foreign countries that are the targets of China's increasingly important antidumping use, as well as potential explanations for these targets. Finally, in a formal regression analysis, we focus on a subsample of China's antidumping activity and search for evidence of a relationship between the size and timing of China's own import-market liberalization and its subsequent use of antidumping to reimpose trade restrictions. For products within the chemicals sector—the dominant industrial user of antidumping within China—we find economically significant evidence that the larger was the accession year (2001–2002) tariff reduction, the greater is the probability that the product subsequently sought new protection from imports via antidumping during the immediate post-accession period.

Finally, in section 8.5 of this chapter, we examine data on how China has been learning to manage trade frictions through the formal, multilateral auspices of WTO dispute settlement proceedings. The data indicates that, despite predictions based on its share of global trade and diversity of trading partners that might have led to expectations that China would be a frequent litigant in WTO disputes, such activity did not materialize in the first five years after its accession. Instead, China has stood on the sideline of other countries' disputes learning about the process in anticipation. Nevertheless, a flurry of disputes initiated between 2006 and 2008 as well as other related policy changes and external shocks indicates that China's role in future WTO dispute settlement may be substantially altered going forward.

8.2   Foreign Use of Antidumping against China's Exports

Prior to China's accession to the WTO in 2001, existing members were unconstrained by WTO rules for how to treat imports from China. That is, while WTO members are expected to afford one another most-favored-nation (MFN) treatment for the application of tariffs, members were nevertheless not required to offer such treatment to nonmembers like China. Nevertheless, some countries did offer Chinese exports reasonable access to their markets—either through voluntary MFN treatment or sometimes even preferential treatment through programs such as the Generalized System of Preferences.[3]

Despite not being bound by WTO rules with how to treat imports from China—meaning that a country could simply unilaterally raise tariff rates applied against imports from China prior to its 2001 accession without being in violation of any multilateral rules—a number of countries nevertheless chose to limit China's exports by resorting to policies of administered protection. In this section, we examine how a number of WTO members treated imports from China under the most common form of administered import protection—antidumping.

We begin this section by documenting the growing use of antidumping across the WTO membership over time. We then examine antidumping use from the perspective of China's exporters—focusing on which trading partners have been using it and against which Chinese export industries it has been used. We then compare the use of antidumping against China to the use of antidumping against other frequently targeted exporting countries to illustrate the discriminatory nature of the policy, and we examine whether there is evidence that how Chinese exporters were treated under the policy prior to its WTO accession has subsequently changed. Finally, we provide a more formal regression analysis into the question of whether antidumping use against China's exports prior to its 2001 accession might be understood as the WTO membership strategically targeting Chinese industries with high import tariffs, perhaps to increase the depth of China's own import market access liberalization commitments.

8.2.1   Antidumping Proliferation across the WTO Membership

Antidumping use has proliferated across the WTO membership over the last twenty years. According to WTO (2007a,c), forty-two different WTO

---

3. For example, the United States Congress voted on a year-to-year basis during the 1990s, after floor debates over a number of issues including its humanitarian record, on whether to continue to grant China MFN status.

Table 8.1   Use of antidumping by World Trade Organization (WTO) members, 1995–2001 and 2002–2006

Country	New antidumping investigations		New antidumping measures imposed	
	1995–2001	2002–2006	1995–2001	2002–2006
"Historical" developed economy users				
Australia	139	34	41	30
Canada	102	35	67	17
European Union	246	96	161	70
United States	256	82	165	74
Share of total	0.39	0.29	0.40	0.22
"New" developing country users				
Argentina	165	40	95	57
Brazil	96	30	51	15
India	252	124	152	179
Mexico	49	33	51	31
South Africa	156	40	93	27
Turkey	35	56	22	85
Share of total	0.40	0.39	0.43	0.46
China	20	83	0	92
Share of total	0.01	0.10	0.00	0.11
Other WTO members	377	186	187	179
Share of total	0.20	0.22	0.17	0.21
Total	1,893	839	1,085	856

Source: Data for the initiations and measures used in this table compiled by the author from WTO (2007a,c).

Note: "New antidumping measures imposed" implies measures imposed that year (i.e., not necessarily measures from investigations that started in that year). This explains why there were more measures imposed over the 2002–2006 period (856) than there were new investigations initiated during that period (839).

members initiated antidumping investigations during the 1995 to 2006 period, while thirty-eight of those countries imposed at least one import restriction under their domestic antidumping laws. The import-restricting policy has gone from one used primarily by four "historical users" (United States, European Union [EU], Canada, and Australia) in the 1980s, to a trade policy instrument used by an increasing share of the WTO membership, including a number of developing countries (Prusa 2001; Zanardi 2004).

Table 8.1 breaks down country-level antidumping using two rough measures (new investigations and new measures imposed) during two subperiods of the WTO era (1995–2001 and 2002–2006) around the date of China's WTO accession. As the table reveals, roughly 80 percent of all new antidumping investigations and measures imposed during the 1995 to 2001 period was the work of only ten countries—the previously mentioned four "historical" developed-economy users, and six "new" developing-country users (Argentina, Brazil, India, Mexico, South Africa, and Turkey).[4] It is worth noting the continued importance of these particular ten countries because they serve as the focus of our empirical analysis of antidumping use vis-à-vis China described below. We focus on these countries' use of the import-restricting policy because we have detailed data on it from an independent source that allows us to pursue questions that could not be addressed by assessing what countries report to the WTO alone.[5]

While table 8.1 suggests that the *developed* economies have reduced their relative use of antidumping over the period since China's accession, the combined efforts of these ten countries continue to dominate global use of the policy. Together, they contributed 83 percent of the new investigations and 68 percent of the new measures imposed even as the total antidumping use by WTO members continues to grow, especially with the emergence of China itself as a major new user (10 percent of investigations, 11 percent of new measures imposed by all WTO members) between 2002 and 2006.

8.2.2 Which Countries Use Antidumping to Restrict Imports from China?

Next we switch perspectives from the users of antidumping to its primary target—exporting firms from China.[6] Figure 8.1 illustrates that the most frequent users of antidumping overall (the ten countries from table 8.1) are also the countries most frequently targeting China with antidumping. By 2001, these ten countries were initiating roughly sixty new investigations of dumping by Chinese exporters per year. Since 1999, the number of new investigations against Chinese exports from the four historical developed-economy users of antidumping (United States, EU, Canada, and Austra-

---

4. For a survey of the research literature on antidumping, see Blonigen and Prusa (2003). As Zanardi (2004) reports, each of the "new user" countries had implemented antidumping legislation prior to the WTO's inception: South Africa (1914), Argentina (1972), India (1985), Mexico (1986), Brazil (1987), and Turkey (1989). Nevertheless, the "historical" users (United States, EU, Canada, and Australia) were the dominant users of antidumping throughout the 1980s; the new users did not begin intensively using antidumping to restrict imports until they undertook their substantial trade liberalization programs of the late 1980s or early 1990s. As we discuss in substantial detail below, China began its use of antidumping in 1997.

5. While data reported in WTO (2007a,c) are the most up-to-date information available regarding notification of investigations and notification that countries are imposing measures, the data suffer from a number of flaws that prevent them from being useful for detailed analysis. For example, the two columns of data for the 2002 to 2006 period of table 8.1 should not be misinterpreted as yielding information on the share of investigations during that period that resulted in measures being imposed. Countries are also not required to report to the WTO the Harmonized System (HS) product codes of the imports facing antidumping activity as well as a number of other pieces of important information for empirical analysis. The data appendix describes the features of the *Global Antidumping Database* (Bown 2007), which contains the detailed data that we rely on for most of the empirical analysis.

6. For prior studies of China as target on different samples of data, see Messerlin (2004) and Liu and Vandenbussche (2002).

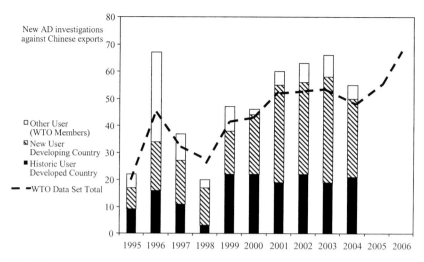

Fig. 8.1   WTO member new antidumping investigations against Chinese exports, 1995–2006

Sources: Data in the bars are compiled from Bown (2007) and are only available through 2004. Aggregate data on total investigations against China's exporters by year from an alternative data source (WTO 2007b) are represented by the dotted line.

Notes: "Historic User" includes the four developed economies of United States, EU, Canada, and Australia; "New User" includes the six developing economies of Argentina, Brazil, India, Mexico, South Africa, and Turkey. "Other User" is all other WTO members, including Taiwan (even prior to its WTO accession). The 1996 "Other User" surge is due to twenty-nine initiations by Peru against China's textile and footwear products.

lia) has leveled off at roughly twenty per year. On the other hand, with the exception of a slight drop in 2004, there has been an upward trend in the number of new investigations per year by the new-user developing-country group—starting from a low of eight new cases in 1995 to thirty or more new cases against China per year in the 2001 to 2004 period.

A comparison of this aggregated data of antidumping use against China during its pre-accession (1995–2001) versus post-accession (2002–2006) period provides our first indicator that there is no prima facie evidence that WTO membership has thus far limited the incidence of China exporter's facing new investigations of dumping behavior. In section 8.2.4, we examine other features of the data underlying country-specific use of antidumping to focus on this question in more depth.

8.2.3   Which Chinese Export Sectors Are Targeted by Antidumping?

Figures 8.2 and 8.3 examine foreign antidumping use against China's exports over the 1995 to 2004 period via examination of the sectors that are most frequently targeted.

Consider first figure 8.2, which examines the combined data for the historical, developed-economy users of antidumping—the United States, EU,

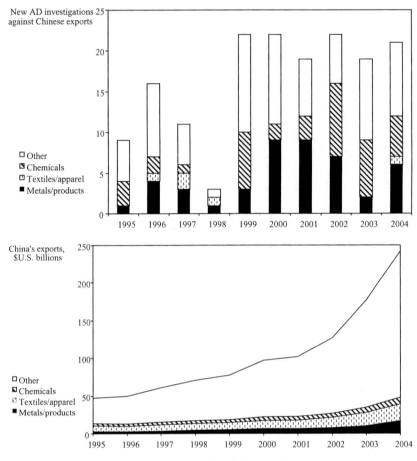

Fig. 8.2   Antidumping by four "Historic User" developed countries by export sector, 1995–2004: *A,* New antidumping investigations against Chinese exports; *B,* Chinese exports to Historical User countries by sector

Sources: Antidumping data compiled from Bown (2007); HS system export data are from Comtrade.

Notes: "Historic User" includes the United States, EU, Canada, and Australia; "New User" is Argentina, Brazil, India, Mexico, South Africa, and Turkey. "Metals/products" are HS chapters 72–83, "Textiles/apparel" are 50–63, "Chemicals" are 28–38.

Canada and Australia. Panel A of figure 8.2 presents the data for the use of antidumping by sector, while panel B of figure 8.2 presents the information on these sectors' shares of Chinese exports to these four markets during the time period. A substantial share of the investigations targeting Chinese products have been in the steel and industrial chemicals categories, which are the traditional sectoral users of antidumping across using countries. Prior to 2004, Chinese textile and apparel exports were not yet a substan-

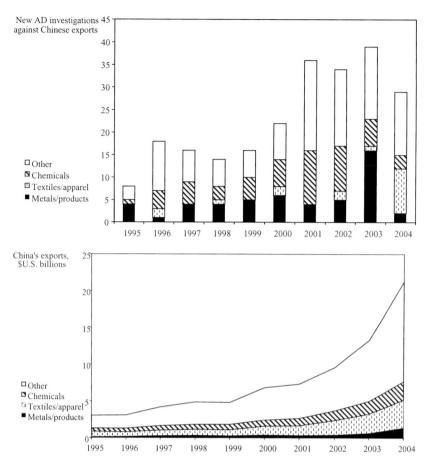

Fig. 8.3   Antidumping by six "New User" developing countries by export sector, 1995–2004: *A*, New antidumping investigations against Chinese exports; *B*, Chinese exports to New User countries by sector

Sources: Antidumping data compiled from Bown (2007); HS system export data are from Comtrade.

Notes: "New User" is Argentina, Brazil, India, Mexico, South Africa, and Turkey. "Metals/products" are HS chapters 72–83, "Textiles/apparel" are 50–63, "Chemicals" are 28–38.

tial target of developed-economy antidumping—for the most part because these user countries were able to limit imports through other trade policy instruments such as the WTO Agreement on Textiles and Clothing, which contained its own transitional safeguard provision during the phase-out of the Multi-Fiber Arrangement. Furthermore, as we discuss in more detail in section 8.3, WTO members need not resort to antidumping to limit imports of Chinese textile and apparel products given that the terms of China's 2001 WTO accession provide a transitional textile and apparel product safeguard policy instrument that can be used until 2008. Furthermore, while imports of textile and apparel products from China have risen in these countries during this time period, their share of China's total exports to these economies is in decline as China diversifies its export basket.

Figure 8.3 illustrates the developing country "new user" targeting of Chinese products by sector. How developing countries have targeted China with antidumping appears quite similar to the developed economies' use of antidumping during this time period. Antidumping use against China is also dominated by the steel and industrial chemicals industries in these developing countries, and Chinese exports in these industries are relatively stagnant (as a share of total Chinese exports to these markets) over this time period. Nevertheless, there has been a recent increase in the share of antidumping cases in textile and apparel products—as some countries have shifted toward the antidumping policy instrument to protect these sectors—as well as other industries, of which other manufacturing products are also frequently targeted. As panel B of figure 8.3 indicates, antidumping is increasing at the same time that these developing countries' imports from China in these categories have also been increasing dramatically.

8.2.4   How Do Antidumping-User Countries Treat China Relative to *Other* Exporters?

Examining China as an antidumping target in isolation is a limiting exercise for a number of reasons. The first is because as a discretionary trade policy, antidumping has the distinguishing feature that user countries can vary the extent to which their particular application *discriminates* among targeted trading partners. In this section, we examine how China as an antidumping target compares to *other* countries targeted by antidumping. Tables 8.2 and 8.3 provide summary data on how major users of antidumping treat China in terms of various discretionary elements that affect the scope of each user's discrimination.

Consider table 8.2, where we examine first the United States' use of antidumping over the 1995 to 2001 period vis-à-vis its most targeted trading partners. By cutting the data in a variety of ways, the evidence clearly indicates that while the policy could be applied in a relatively nondiscriminatory manner, the United States exhibited considerable discrimination vis-à-vis China during this time period. China is the most frequently investigated foreign target of U.S. antidumping, facing 13 percent of all investigations. It was the largest target despite being only the fifth largest exporter overall to the U.S. market during the 1995 to 2001 period with 8 percent of the U.S. import market (final column), trailing Canada, the EU, Japan, and Mexico. Second, 68 percent of the U.S. investigations that Chinese exporters faced resulted in the imposition of a final antidumping measure—a rate that is much higher than the average of 53 percent across all investigated countries. Third, despite an incentive for antidumping authorities to seek to name

Table 8.2 Historical user antidumping (AD) against China, 1995–2001 and 2002–2004, by AD-imposing country

Exporting country target	Antidumping investigations[a]	Investigations resulting in measures[b]	Only country named in investigation[b]	Mean margin conditional on measures imposed (%)	Share of AD-imposing country import market[c]
United States					
1 China	31 (0.13)	21 (0.68)	13 (0.42)	131.77	0.08 (5)
2 Japan	24 (0.10)	16 (0.67)	7 (0.29)	65.23	0.13 (3)
3 EU	24 (0.10)	12 (0.50)	5 (0.21)	18.07	0.19 (2)
4 Korea	19 (0.08)	9 (0.47)	2 (0.11)	17.73	0.03 (7)
5 Taiwan	16 (0.07)	10 (0.63)	2 (0.13)	12.55	0.03 (6)
All other	124 (0.52)	57 (0.46)	18 (0.15)	68.62	0.54
Total	238 (1.00)	125 (0.53)	47 (0.20)	66.16	1.00
2002–2004					
1 China	25 (0.26)	19 (0.76)	13 (0.52)	148.38	0.13 (3)
2 India	9 (0.09)	3 (0.33)	2 (0.22)	40.43	0.01 (14)
3 EU	8 (0.08)	2 (0.25)	0 (0.00)	15.09	0.19 (1)
4 Japan	6 (0.06)	2 (0.33)	3 (0.50)	91.29	0.09 (5)
5 South	5 (0.05)	0 (0.00)	3 (0.60)	.	0.00 (27)
All other	43 (0.45)	16 (0.37)	8 (0.19)	36.10	0.58
Total	96 (1.00)	42 (0.44)	29 (0.30)	88.83	1.00
European Union					
1995–2001					
1 China	36 (0.14)	19 (0.53)	16 (0.44)	59.52	0.06 (4)
2 India	24 (0.10)	15 (0.63)	6 (0.25)	52.88	0.01 (20)
3 Korea	21 (0.08)	9 (0.43)	6 (0.29)	27.51	0.02 (9)
4 Thailand	14 (0.06)	10 (0.71)	1 (0.07)	33.83	0.01 (21)
5 Taiwan	13 (0.05)	8 (0.62)	6 (0.46)	26.15	0.03 (7)
All other	142 (0.57)	91 (0.64)	13 (0.09)	40.80	0.87
Total	250 (1.00)	152 (0.61)	48 (0.19)	42.40	1.00

(*continued*)

Table 8.2 (continued)

Exporting country target	Antidumping investigations[a]	Investigations resulting in measures[b]	Only country named in investigation[b]	Mean margin conditional on measures imposed (%)	Share of AD-imposing country import market[c]
2002–2004					
1 China	16 (0.28)	15 (0.94)	10 (0.63)	61.99	0.10 (2)
2 Russia	6 (0.11)	3 (0.50)	1 (0.17)	30.70	0.05 (5)
3 Vietnam	4 (0.07)	2 (0.50)	1 (0.25)	7.70	0.00 (40)
4 U.S.	3 (0.05)	2 (0.67)	2 (0.67)	98.50	0.16 (1)
5 Norway	3 (0.05)	2 (0.67)	2 (0.67)	31.25	0.04 (6)
All other	25 (0.44)	11 (0.44)	4 (0.16)	23.59	0.64
Total	57 (1.00)	35 (0.61)	20 (0.35)	43.18	1.00
Australia					
1995–2001					
1 EU	23 (0.18)	4 (0.17)	11 (0.48)		0.23 (1)
2 Indonesia	14 (0.11)	2 (0.14)	5 (0.36)		0.03 (10)
3 China	13 (0.10)	2 (0.15)	7 (0.54)		0.07 (4)
4 Korea	11 (0.09)	5 (0.45)	2 (0.18)		0.04 (6)
5 Thailand	9 (0.07)	5 (0.56)	3 (0.33)		0.02 (11)
All other	55 (0.44)	18 (0.33)	11 (0.20)		0.62
Total	125 (1.00)	36 (0.29)	39 (0.31)		1.00
2002–2004					
1 EU	6 (0.24)	2 (0.33)	3 (0.50)		0.23 (1)
2 Korea	5 (0.20)	4 (0.80)	2 (0.40)		0.04 (7)
3 China	4 (0.16)	3 (0.75)	2 (0.50)		0.11 (4)
4 Canada	2 (0.08)	1 (0.50)	2 (1.00)		0.01 (13)
5 Thailand	2 (0.08)	1 (0.50)	0 (0.00)		0.03 (10)
All other	6 (0.24)	4 (0.67)	0 (0.00)		0.57
Total	25 (1.00)	15 (0.60)	9 (0.36)		1.00

				Canada		
1995–2001	1 EU	11 (0.12)	5 (0.45)	3 (0.27)	45.90	0.10 (2)
	2 U.S.	10 (0.11)	7 (0.70)	8 (0.80)	42.80	0.67 (1)
	3 China	10 (0.11)	6 (0.60)	5 (0.50)	45.17	0.03 (5)
	4 Brazil	5 (0.06)	3 (0.60)	1 (0.20)	28.00	0.00 (11)
	5 Taiwan	5 (0.06)	3 (0.60)	0 (0.00)	49.90	0.01 (6)
	All other	49 (0.54)	31 (0.63)	3 (0.06)	35.76	0.17
	Total	90 (1.00)	55 (0.61)	20 (0.22)	39.12	1.00
2002–2004	1 China	7 (0.26)	5 (0.71)	3 (0.43)	49.96	0.06 (3)
	2 Taiwan	3 (0.11)	1 (0.33)	0 (0.00)	68.94	0.01 (8)
	3 Korea	2 (0.07)	2 (1.00)	0 (0.00)	135.00	0.02 (6)
	4 U.S.	2 (0.07)	1 (0.50)	1 (0.50)	165.00	0.61 (1)
	5 Mexico	1 (0.04)	1 (1.00)	0 (0.00)	98.00	0.04 (5)
	All other	12 (0.44)	6 (0.50)	0 (0.00)	76.18	0.26
	Total	27 (1.00)	16 (0.59)	4 (0.15)	81.80	1.00

Sources: Antidumping data compiled from Bown (2007). Harmonized System import data from Comtrade.

Notes: European Union (EU) import data is extra-EU imports only. For consistency, this table only allows for one "EU" entry for each product-specific investigation, hence total number of investigations and imposed measures may differ from table 8.1 due to aggregation of EU member cases per investigation.

[a]Numbers in parentheses are share of total.

[b]Numbers in parentheses are share of target country's investigations.

[c]Numbers in parentheses are rankings.

Table 8.3 New user antidumping (AD) against China, 1995–2001 and 2002–2004, by AD-imposing country

	Exporting country target	Antidumping investigations[a]	Investigations resulting in measures[b]	Only country named in investigation[b]	Share of AD-imposing country import market[c]
			Argentina		
1995–2001	1 China	32 (0.21)	28 (0.88)	22 (0.69)	0.04 (5)
	2 Brazil	30 (0.20)	20 (0.67)	17 (0.57)	0.23 (2)
	3 EU	19 (0.13)	9 (0.47)	10 (0.53)	0.27 (1)
	4 Taiwan	9 (0.06)	9 (1.00)	0 (0.00)	0.01 (11)
	5 South Africa	9 (0.06)	5 (0.56)	1 (0.11)	0.00 (23)
	All other	50 (0.34)	35 (0.70)	18 (0.36)	0.44
	Total	149 (1.00)	106 (0.71)	68 (0.46)	1.00
2002–2004	1 China	6 (0.22)	5 (0.83)	6 (1.00)	0.05 (4)
	2 Brazil	3 (0.11)	2 (0.67)	2 (0.67)	0.33 (1)
	3 U.S.	2 (0.07)	2 (1.00)	0 (0.00)	0.17 (3)
	4 Korea	2 (0.07)	2 (1.00)	0 (0.00)	0.01 (10)
	5 Mexico	2 (0.07)	2 (1.00)	0 (0.00)	0.03 (7)
	All other	12 (0.44)	9 (0.75)	3 (0.25)	0.42
	Total	27 (1.00)	22 (0.81)	11 (0.41)	1.00
			Brazil		
1995–2001	1 China	15 (0.16)	12 (0.80)	14 (0.93)	0.02 (7)
	2 EU	13 (0.14)	8 (0.62)	3 (0.23)	0.27 (1)
	3 U.S.	13 (0.14)	6 (0.46)	5 (0.38)	0.23 (2)
	4 South Africa	4 (0.04)	3 (0.75)	1 (0.25)	0.00 (25)
	5 Mexico	3 (0.03)	3 (1.00)	0 (0.00)	0.02 (12)
	All other	45 (0.48)	22 (0.49)	10 (0.22)	0.45
	Total	93 (1.00)	54 (0.58)	33 (0.35)	1.00

2002–2003	1 China	9 (0.28)	6 (0.67)	8 (0.89)	0.05 (4)
	2 India	5 (0.16)	4 (0.80)	2 (0.40)	0.01 (17)
	3 EU	5 (0.16)	3 (0.60)	2 (0.40)	0.25 (1)
	4 U.S.	5 (0.16)	1 (0.20)	2 (0.40)	0.20 (2)
	5 Romania	1 (0.03)	1 (1.00)	1 (1.00)	0.00 (73)
	All other	7 (0.22)	4 (0.57)	0 (0.00)	0.49
	Total	32 (1.00)	19 (0.59)	15 (0.47)	1.00
India					
1995–2001	1 China	41 (0.18)	38 (0.93)	24 (0.59)	0.03 (9)
	2 EU	33 (0.15)	26 (0.79)	6 (0.18)	0.23 (1)
	3 Taiwan	17 (0.08)	14 (0.82)	2 (0.12)	0.01 (20)
	4 Korea	16 (0.07)	14 (0.88)	2 (0.13)	0.02 (14)
	5 Japan	16 (0.07)	13 (0.81)	2 (0.13)	0.05 (5)
	All other	102 (0.45)	87 (0.85)	8 (0.08)	0.66
	Total	225 (1.00)	192 (0.85)	44 (0.20)	1.00
2002–2004	1 China	25 (0.20)	22 (0.88)	12 (0.48)	0.05 (4)
	2 EU	13 (0.11)	9 (0.69)	2 (0.15)	0.18 (2)
	3 Taiwan	11 (0.09)	8 (0.73)	1 (0.09)	0.01 (17)
	4 Korea	9 (0.07)	7 (0.78)	1 (0.11)	0.03 (6)
	5 Singapore	8 (0.07)	5 (0.63)	0 (0.00)	0.02 (11)
	All other	56 (0.46)	34 (0.61)	5 (0.09)	0.70
	Total	122 (1.00)	85 (0.70)	21 (0.17)	1.00
Mexico					
1995–2001	1 U.S.	14 (0.30)	11 (0.79)	13 (0.93)	0.73 (1)
	2 China	6 (0.13)	5 (0.83)	5 (0.83)	0.02 (6)
	3 EU	5 (0.11)	2 (0.40)	4 (0.80)	0.09 (2)
	4 Russia	4 (0.09)	3 (0.75)	0 (0.00)	0.00 (31)
	5 Taiwan	3 (0.07)	3 (1.00)	2 (0.67)	0.01 (7)
	All other	14 (0.30)	10 (0.71)	8 (0.57)	0.15
	Total	46 (1.00)	34 (0.74)	32 (0.70)	1.00

(continued)

Table 8.3 (continued)

Exporting country target	Antidumping investigations[a]	Investigations resulting in measures[b]	Only country named in investigation[b]	Share of AD-imposing country import market[c]
2002–2003				
1 China	6 (0.25)	6 (1.00)	6 (1.00)	0.06 (3)
2 U.S.	6 (0.25)	5 (0.83)	6 (1.00)	0.60 (1)
3 Russia	2 (0.08)	2 (1.00)	1 (0.50)	0.00 (27)
4 Ukraine	2 (0.08)	2 (1.00)	1 (0.50)	0.00 (33)
5 Romania	2 (0.08)	2 (1.00)	0 (0.00)	0.00 (54)
All other	6 (0.25)	3 (0.50)	3 (0.50)	0.34
Total	24 (1.00)	20 (0.83)	17 (0.71)	1.00
South Africa				
1995–2001				
1 EU	24 (0.18)	14 (0.58)	12 (0.50)	0.43 (1)
2 India	18 (0.13)	13 (0.72)	10 (0.56)	0.01 (15)
3 China	15 (0.11)	13 (0.87)	2 (0.13)	0.04 (5)
4 Korea	11 (0.08)	11 (1.00)	3 (0.27)	0.02 (10)
5 Hong Kong	7 (0.05)	6 (0.86)	0 (0.00)	0.01 (12)
All other	61 (0.45)	36 (0.59)	5 (0.08)	0.50
Total	136 (1.00)	93 (0.68)	32 (0.24)	1.00
2002–2004				
1 China	5 (0.28)	1 (0.20)	1 (0.20)	0.07 (4)
2 Taiwan	3 (0.17)	0 (0.00)	0 (0.00)	0.02 (10)
3 Indonesia	2 (0.11)	1 (0.50)	2 (1.00)	0.01 (21)
4 EU	2 (0.11)	0 (0.00)	2 (1.00)	0.41 (1)
5 India	2 (0.11)	0 (0.00)	2 (1.00)	0.01 (12)
All other	4 (0.22)	3 (0.75)	2 (0.50)	0.49
Total	18 (1.00)	5 (0.28)	9 (0.50)	1.00

Turkey

1995–2001	1 China	9 (0.29)	8 (0.89)	6 (0.67)	0.02 (8)
	2 Korea	4 (0.13)	4 (1.00)	1 (0.25)	0.02 (6)
	3 Taiwan	3 (0.10)	3 (1.00)	1 (0.33)	0.01 (15)
	4 EU	2 (0.06)	1 (0.50)	0 (0.00)	0.50 (1)
	5 Thailand	2 (0.06)	1 (0.50)	0 (0.00)	0.00 (29)
	All other	11 (0.35)	8 (0.73)	0 (0.00)	0.44
	Total	31 (1.00)	25 (0.81)	8 (0.26)	1.00
2002–2004	1 China	35 (0.52)	32 (0.91)	27 (0.77)	0.04 (5)
	2 Taiwan	8 (0.12)	7 (0.88)	0 (0.00)	0.01 (15)
	3 Thailand	6 (0.09)	5 (0.83)	0 (0.00)	0.00 (28)
	4 India	5 (0.07)	4 (0.80)	0 (0.00)	0.01 (16)
	5 Vietnam	4 (0.06)	4 (1.00)	0 (0.00)	0.00 (56)
	All other	9 (0.13)	6 (0.67)	2 (0.22)	0.93
	Total	67 (1.00)	58 (0.87)	29 (0.43)	1.00

Sources: Antidumping data compiled from Bown (2007). Harmonized System import data from Comtrade.

Notes: For consistency, this table only allows for one European Union ("EU") entry for each product-specific investigation, hence total number of investigations and imposed measures may differ from table 8.1 due to aggregation of European Union (EU) member cases per investigation. Brazil and Mexico only contain detailed information on antidumping investigations completed through 2003.

[a]Numbers in parentheses are share of total.

[b]Numbers in parentheses are share of target country's investigations.

[c]Numbers in parentheses are rankings.

exporters from additional countries in investigations, China was the *only* country named in 42 percent of the investigations that its exporters faced, while the average across all cases was 20 percent.[7] Finally, in the investigations that resulted in final antidumping measures being imposed, the average antidumping duty facing exporters from China was 131.77 percent—almost twice as high as the average facing all exporters.[8] These combined features of the data for the U.S. use of antidumping indicate that, in practice, antidumping in the United States has resulted in discriminatory treatment of imports from China relative to other source countries during the 1995 to 2001 period.[9]

While these results are neither the only, nor perhaps a fundamental motivating force behind China's seeking WTO accession, the data does suggest a potential expected benefit associated with China's full membership in the organization—less discriminatory treatment in export markets relative to other foreign competitors. One potential benefit of China's accession could be to reign in foreign use of antidumping against China's exporters so that they received tariff treatment that was closer to that provided by a strict application of the WTO's MFN principle.

As we explore with greater rigor in a regression analysis described in section 8.2.5, there are a number of potential contributing factors behind the decision to target China during its pre-accession period. For example, one potential explanation is that WTO members used antidumping as a policy

7. The option to "cumulate" imports from multiple countries in the injury investigation potentially increases the probability of an affirmative injury decision (Hansen and Prusa 1996) as well as heading off a potential increase in imports from exporting countries not named in the investigation.

8. Note that this chapter does not pursue an empirical investigation into the interesting follow-up question of *how*—legally and administratively—countries "get away with" discriminating against China via application of higher antidumping duties than those that face other foreign suppliers. First, WTO members differ in when they have agreed to reclassify China as a market economy as opposed to a non-market economy (NME). For example, under the terms of the 1999 U.S.-China bilateral agreement, the U.S. is authorized to continue using the unfavorable NME designation to evaluate Chinese dumping until 2014. Non-market economy status grants antidumping investigators the discretion to designate surrogate countries to be used to estimate measures of Chinese firms' costs. Second, Chinese firms may be less likely to represent themselves in the U.S. antidumping process, which can result in investigators using the best information available (BIA) practices. Both NME and BIA affect the construction of the normal value measure from which to compare the export price in the U.S. market. For an analysis of administrative procedures in the U.S. antidumping process that influence the differential between China and other antidumping-targeted countries, as well as how these dumping margins may be changing over time, see Blonigen (2006). See also the discussion in Moore (2006) and Moore and Fox (forthcoming).

9. There are additional potentially discriminatory elements of the antidumping policy that we do not capture in the tables. First, because antidumping is also a foreign-*firm*-specific trade policy, the instrument can be used to discriminate across firms within a country. The data reported in tables 8.2 and 8.3 are the average margin imposed against all firms within that country. Second, firms across countries may differ in their likelihood of receiving offers of the preferable outcome of "price undertakings," relative to facing the imposition of duties. Third, foreign targets may also be treated systematically different in sunset or administrative reviews of antidumping, affecting when a measure that has been imposed is *removed*.

to complement their negotiations strategy in order to extract more import market accession concessions from China as part of the accession. Under the assumption that this was a determinant of antidumping use prior to its accession, an important follow-up question is whether there is evidence that the United States has *changed* its treatment of China under antidumping after 2001 and there is nothing more to extract from China in terms of commitments associated with its WTO accession.

The second panel of rows in table 8.2 illustrates characteristics of U.S. antidumping use between 2002 to 2004, which is the most recent time period since China's 2001 accession for which comprehensive data is available across countries. Note that there is no evidence from this table that the United States has lessened its discriminatory treatment of China via the antidumping policy relative to the pre-accession period. Over 26 percent of all U.S. investigations during 2002 to 2004 targeted China, up from 13 percent in 1995 to 2001. The U.S. imposed import restrictions in 76 percent of the cases in which China was investigated, up from 68 percent in 1995 to 2001. Furthermore, China was the only country named in 52 percent of the cases in which it was investigated (up from 42 percent in 1995 to 2001), and it faced a conditional mean duty of 148.38 percent (up from 131.77 percent in 1995 to 2001). There is thus no evidence from this data that China's WTO membership beginning at the end of 2001 has had a disciplining effect on the U.S. use of antidumping vis-à-vis its exports.[10]

The other three sets of panels in table 8.2 extend the analysis of cross-country use of antidumping by breaking down the data in a similar fashion for the three other developed-economy users (EU, Canada, Australia) and examining the discriminatory application of their antidumping vis-à-vis China. While these users do not appear to discriminate between China and other targeted exporters along each of the same indicators and to quite the same degree as the United States did between 1995 and 2001, there is nevertheless substantial evidence of significant differential treatment facing China's exporters and other major targets of antidumping. Next, with respect to whether WTO accession has curtailed these countries from targeting China with antidumping cases, we conclude that there is also no evidence of this effect. There is some evidence of a general downward trend in the collective use of antidumping by the EU, Australia, and Canada during the 2002 to 2004 time period. Nevertheless, while the overall use of antidumping by these countries may have declined, an increasing share of these countries' total caseload continues to target China with new investigations: in the EU, 28 percent of all cases targeted China (up from 14 percent in 1995 to 2001),

---

10. This is not necessarily surprising for reasons we discuss in section 8.5. Because of the self-enforcing nature of WTO dispute settlement and the fact that until 2008 China did not begin the attempt to formally enforce its market access rights—by challenging U.S. use of antidumping, for example.

in Australia it was 16 percent (up from 10 percent in 1995 to 2001), and in Canada it was 26 percent (up from 11 percent in 1995 to 2001).

Table 8.3 presents a similar breakdown of the data for the six major *developing* country "new users" of antidumping (Argentina, Brazil, India, Mexico, South Africa, Turkey). Evidence from these users also indicates a distinct pattern of a discriminatory application of the policy vis-à-vis China.[11] Furthermore, the discriminatory application appears to be intensifying in the period since China's WTO accession—China is the most targeted foreign country in all six of these new users over the 2002 to 2004 period, despite being no larger than the third largest foreign supplier to any of these markets. One interpretation of this change is that it appears that many of these developing countries are more than simply concerned with the implications of preference erosion associated with China's WTO accession (and receipt of MFN treatment) and having to compete on equal terms with Chinese exporters in foreign markets. Many industries in these developing countries are also concerned for their domestic markets and have increasingly sought new import restrictions to prevent Chinese exports entering their markets as well.

While we have found no evidence that the severity of discrimination facing China's exporters under foreign use of antidumping has improved relative to China's pre-WTO accession period, we cannot make the bolder claim that the WTO accession has not had any impact on its use. As the last column in each country panel in tables 8.2 and 8.3 indicates, China's export share in each of these economies' import markets has also increased during this time period. Ceteris paribus, an export increase means more products to potentially target with antidumping. Furthermore, there are real reasons to expect countries to undertake more discrimination vis-à-vis China within the antidumping trade policy instrument for the post-accession (when compared to the 1995–2001) period. Prior to 2001, if a foreign government felt domestic political pressure to discriminate vis-à-vis imports from China, it may have been able to do so by raising tariffs directly. Now that China is a member of the WTO, in the face of China's booming exports, a WTO member that seeks to legally discriminate against Chinese exports must now funnel that discrimination into a WTO-consistent policy instrument or face risk of a trade dispute. Raising trade barriers against China alone via antidumping protection is one such mechanism—we explore other substitute import-restricting instruments (safeguards, countervailing measures) in the next section. An alternative way to implicitly discriminate against China relative to other foreign producers in a WTO consistent manner is to find a legal way to grant the non-Chinese producers preferential access—examples

11. We do not provide summary data on the average size of the measure imposed by the developing countries as it would be nontrivial to construct. Unlike the developed-economy users, developing countries are less likely to impose antidumping in the form of simple ad valorem duties and are more likely to impose them as specific duties (denominated in import or export currencies), price undertakings, or other combinations thereof.

would include offering unilateral preferences if the exporters are in developing countries under the Generalized System of Preferences (GSP) or by forming a preferential trade agreement on a reciprocal basis.[12]

8.2.5   Did Pre-Accession Antidumping against China Target Its High Tariffs?

Unlike many other exporting countries that were also subject to antidumping trade restrictions imposed during the 1995 to 2001 period, China stands out for one other reason: it was simultaneously negotiating the terms of its own accession into the WTO. Thus, one question to explore is whether a contributing explanation for the discriminatory application of antidumping during the 1995 to 2001 period (illustrated in tables 8.2 and 8.3) is that existing WTO members were using the policy to complement pressure being placed on China to liberalize import markets under accession negotiations. We investigate this question by asking whether Chinese goods that benefited from higher import tariff protection were more likely to be targeted with foreign antidumping investigations, once we control for other product-level differences. Evidence of such a relationship would be consistent with a more charitable interpretation of the discriminatory application of antidumping—that is, that that foreign trading partners were strategically using antidumping to attempt to increase the tariff liberalization commitments that China was willing to undertake under the terms of its 2001 WTO accession.[13]

We formalize this inquiry by estimating a model of the determinants of a foreign antidumping investigation over a Chinese export product i each year during the 1995 to 2001 period.[14] We construct an unbalanced panel for $t = 1995, \ldots, 2001$ of yearly Chinese exports of 4,589 different six-digit Harmonized System (HS) products i to an aggregated, rest-of-the-world trading partner called "Foreign."[15] For our baseline estimates, Foreign will

12. For a discussion of examples of U.S. preferential trade agreements negotiated between 2002 and 2005 with exporting countries that compete with Chinese exporters in important product categories like textiles and apparel, see Bown and McCulloch (2007).

13. The argument is that, in the presence of a foreign antidumping law, China implicitly assists its exporters by liberalizing its imports of the same product. Foreign countries are more likely to use antidumping against China's exports if China's imports are protected by high tariffs because it is easier for foreign competitors to show evidence that Chinese firms "dumped" their exports if those firms are protected by high tariffs at home. A protected home market faces less competition (from imports), resulting in higher domestic prices and, thus, higher dumping margins when less than fair value determinations are constructed from price-to-price comparisons. For a discussion in the case of China, see Messerlin (2004).

14. Using indicators or counts of measures imposed instead of investigations is likely to give similar results, given the results of tables 8.2 and 8.3. Furthermore, evidence dating back to Staiger and Wolak (1994) indicates that even a mere antidumping investigation can have a destructive effect on a country's exports, even if no trade-restricting measures are ultimately imposed, suggesting that investigations are an important indicator with which to begin.

15. The panel is unbalanced because we condition on there being nonzero exports of the product in that year for there to be an observation.

be the combination of fifteen antidumping-using countries—the ten major users listed in table 8.1 in addition to less frequent users such as Colombia, Indonesia, Korea, New Zealand, and Taiwan.[16]

We formally estimate this relationship after controlling for a number of other factors and by using two types of models. The first model is a binomial probit in which the dependent variable is an indicator for whether *any* one of the fifteen countries initiated an antidumping investigation against Chinese exports of the product in year *t*. The second model is a negative binomial regression model in which the dependent variable is the *count* of the number of antidumping investigations that the fifteen countries cumulatively undertook against Chinese exports of the product in year *t*.[17] Our explanatory variable of interest is China's pre-accession MFN applied tariff for product *i*—evidence of a positive relationship between the size of the Chinese import tariff and the event of foreign antidumping investigations against Chinese exports would support the theory that China's high tariffs were a contributing determinant to which of its products were being targeted with antidumping.

There are, of course, a number of other determinants of foreign-country antidumping activity against China's exports that we seek to control for in the estimation. For example, we expect a *positive* relationship between antidumping use in year *t* and two explanatory variables: the size of China's exports of the product (given by the aggregated value of China's exports of the product to "Foreign" in $t-1$) as well as the level of recent growth of those exports (given by the growth of the aggregated value of China's exports of the product between $t-2$ and $t-1$). We also control for whether there has been recent prior antidumping activity in the same product against China's exports with an indicator that takes on a value of 1 if the same product was subject to an investigation in either $t-2$ or $t-1$. Next, we use year dummies to control for year-to-year macroeconomic shocks in indicators such as exchange rates and exchange rates, which Knetter and Prusa (2003) have shown affect aggregate filings across countries via the business cycle. Finally, as there are certain industries that are simply more frequent users of antidumping across countries, we include industry dummies in the estimation as well.[18] The industry dummies should also help control for the influence of

16. In the aggregate, these fifteen countries received slightly less than 50 percent of China's exports during this time period. This percentage is not larger primarily because the list of fifteen countries omits two of China's top four export destination markets in Hong Kong (24.0 percent of exports in 1997) and Japan (17.4 percent of exports in 1997), neither of which used antidumping against any exporter with any frequency during this time period.

17. A closely related framework is Knetter and Prusa (2003), which examines determinants of antidumping-using countries' aggregate yearly filings over time. In contrast, we examine determinants of filing against different products within a single country over time.

18. The industry definitions that we use can be found in the data appendix. There are a number of potential reasons why certain industries—such as steel and chemicals—are frequent targets of antidumping across all using countries. For example, the nature of evidence required

political-economic elements that we do not control for separately because we are using a "Foreign" aggregate.

Table 8.4 presents our estimates of the binomial probit and negative binomial regression models. The models relate potential determinants of an aggregated "Foreign" that potentially initiates new antidumping investigations against a Chinese exported product i over $t = 1995, \ldots, 2001$. Consider first the estimates of the marginal effects of the binomial probit model reported in column (1). The signs of the estimated effects are broadly consistent with the underlying theory. As for the control variables, China's larger export product categories are more likely to be investigated than export products with lesser value. The greater is the recent export growth of the product, the more likely it is to be targeted as well, though this effect is not statistically significant. Products that were targets in the recent past ($t - 2$ or $t - 1$) are also more likely to be targeted in t. This relationship holds even after we control for industry-level effects that indicate it is more likely that products in industries such as chemicals, textiles and apparel, footwear, metals, and transportation equipment are all more likely than the omitted industry category (other miscellaneous products) to be investigated.

Nevertheless, the key variable of interest is the effect of China's pre-accession import tariff rate on the probability that that export product is subject to a foreign antidumping investigation. In column (1), the estimate of 0.015 is positive and statistically significant, which provides preliminary evidence in support of the underlying theory that export products with higher import tariffs face a higher probability of being targeted with a foreign antidumping investigation. The economic effect implied by the estimate is also sizable. The model's predicted probability that an average Chinese export product is investigated with an antidumping case in a given year is 0.0084. The mean applied tariff in the underlying data was 0.241 (i.e., 24.1 percent), so a 10 percentage point increase in this variable above the average (to 0.341) increases the predicted probability of an investigation to 0.01.

Despite preliminary evidence of higher tariff products being more likely to be targeted with foreign antidumping, as a simple robustness check, we reestimate the binomial probit model on the same sample of 1995 to 2001 data except we redefine the "Foreign" aggregate of Chinese trading partners to only include the four developed economy historical users of antidumping—the United States, EU, Canada, and Australia. A number of reasons motivate construction of such a sensitivity analysis. First, these four economies are relatively large destination markets for China's exports, thus also provide much of the variation of the key control variables. Second, the four developed economies were among the major *demandeurs* during China's

---

in antidumping laws may make it biased toward use by cyclical, capital-intensive industries with high fixed costs. On the other hand, the highly concentrated nature of these industries may make it easier for antidumping to be used in a cross-industry retaliatory manner to facilitate internationally collusive outcomes.

Table 8.4   Determinants of Foreign antidumping (AD) investigations across China's exported products

Explanatory variables [expected sign]	Binomial probit model[a]		Negative binomial regression model[b]	
	Foreign is aggregate of 15 AD-using countries (1)	*Foreign* is aggregate of U.S., EU, Canada, or Australia only (2)	*Foreign* is aggregate of 15 AD-using countries (3)	*Foreign* is aggregate of U.S., EU, Canada, or Australia only (4)
Size [+] (value of Chinese exports of *i* to *Foreign* in $t-1$ [\$U.S.][c])	0.021*** (0.004)	0.008*** (0.002)	5.036*** (4.92)	3.462*** (2.85)
China's pre-accession tariff rate [+] (1996 MFN applied tariff rate[d] over *i*)	0.015*** (0.004)	−0.001 (0.002)	1.012*** (3.35)	0.991 (1.32)
Prior AD target [+] (indicator for Chinese exports of *i* facing prior *Foreign* AD investigation in $t-1$ or $t-2$)	0.053*** (0.007)	0.089*** (0.016)	6.432*** (15.06)	18.537*** (17.07)
Recent export growth [+] (% difference between $t-1$ and $t-2$ value of Chinese exports of *i* to *Foreign*)	0.001 (0.000)	0.000* (0.000)	1.063 (1.49)	1.094** (2.29)
Chemicals	0.007* (0.004)	0.001 (0.002)	1.827** (2.20)	1.266 (0.52)
Textiles and apparel	0.007** (0.003)	0.000 (0.001)	2.089*** (3.04)	1.082 (0.17)
Footwear	0.010* (0.007)	0.019* (0.010)	2.162** (2.04)	6.339*** (3.51)
Metals	0.040*** (0.009)	0.015*** (0.006)	6.144* (1.85)	6.485*** (4.54)

Transportation equipment	0.010*	0.003	2.074**	1.865
	(0.007)	(0.004)	(1.97)	(0.99)
Other industries[e]	Yes	Yes	Yes	Yes
Year dummies	Yes	Yes	Yes	Yes
No. of observations	28,265	28,264	28,265	28,264
Pseudo R^2	0.14	0.23	0.13	0.23
Predicted probability (at means)	0.0084	0.0024		

Notes: Sample is an unbalanced panel of 4,589 6-digit Harmonized System products i China exported to the aggregated "Foreign" between $t = 1995, \ldots, 2001$. The fifteen AD-using countries of "Foreign" in columns (1) and (3) are Argentina, Australia, Brazil, Canada, Colombia, the European Union (EU), India, Indonesia, Korea, Mexico, New Zealand, South Africa, Taiwan, Turkey, and the United States. Estimates for the probit model are transformed into marginal effects, with robust standard errors in parentheses. Estimates for the negative binomial model are transformed into incidence rate ratios, with t-statistics in parentheses. MFN = most-favored nation.

[a] Dependent variable is indicator for whether Foreign initiated any new antidumping investigations over i in t.

[b] Dependent variable is count of new Foreign antidumping investigations over i in t.

[c] Rescaled by \$1 billion.

[d] Rescaled by 100 (i.e., so 25% = 0.25) in the probit regression.

[e] Other industry category estimates available upon request. The omitted industry category is "Miscellaneous products" (Harmonized System Chapters 90–97).

***Significant at the 1 percent level.

**Significant at the 5 percent level.

*Significant at the 10 percent level.

WTO accession negotiations. Finally, these are the countries with historical "experience" in using antidumping. Thus, these four countries were the most likely (of any of the antidumping users) to have the ability to manipulate use of antidumping away from capture of domestic industry and toward its use for strategic purposes during China's pre-accession negotiations. Nevertheless, as the estimates in specification (2) indicate, when we estimate the model on these four countries' use of antidumping against China, the positive and significant impact of the China pre-accession tariff disappears.

Columns (3) and (4) of table 8.4 present additional robustness checks on these two sets of results. These specifications use the same explanatory variables and underlying samples of data as columns (1) and (2); in them, we simply redefine the dependent variable as the *counts* of antidumping investigations (as opposed to a 0/1 indicator) facing product i in year t, and we estimate this relationship via a negative binomial regression model.[19] The estimates presented are the model coefficients transformed into incidence rate ratios (IRRs), which are more straightforward to interpret. In specification (3), which is estimated on the sample of cumulated exports to and antidumping investigations by 15 antidumping-using countries, the estimated IRR for the pre-accession applied tariff is greater than 1 and statistically significant at 1.012. The IRR estimate implies that a one unit increase in the applied tariff (from 24.1 percent to 25.1 percent, as we have rescaled this variable for the negative binomial specifications) increases the count of yearly investigations in that product by 1.2 percent. Nevertheless, in specification (4), when we redefine the "Foreign" aggregate in the sample to only include cumulated exports to and antidumping use by the United States, EU, Canada, and Australia, the positive impact of the pre-accession tariff disappears. In fact, because the estimated IRR of 0.991 is less than 1, the estimated impact of a higher pre-accession tariff is to *reduce* the number of antidumping investigations in the developed economy users, though this effect is not statistically significant.

Therefore, we conclude that there is no robust evidence that pre-accession use of antidumping against China was driven by strategic considerations. To the extent that there was, on average, a propensity for Chinese exports of products with higher (Chinese) pre-accession import tariffs to be the target of foreign antidumping, the antidumping over such products was initiated by the *developing* country users. It was unlikely that these countries were targeting such products with the strategic purpose of influencing China's

---

19. For a discussion of the negative binomial regression model, see Greene (2000, 880–91). Of the 28,265 product-year observations in the 1995 to 2001 sample, there were 455 nonzero entries. While the count variable could range between zero and fifteen in principal (the number of antidumping-imposing countries in the sample), the maximum was three, and only twenty-three products faced investigations in two different countries in the same year. Thus, there is little additional variation to be gained in using the negative binomial regression model relative to the binomial probit.

tariff liberalization commitments under its WTO accession negotiations. An alternative explanation is that the positive correlation simply reflects a common political economy pressure facing makers of the same product in China and these other developing countries. It is simply that the political pressure was manifest in different policy instruments—the political pressure from import-competing firms within the other developing countries led them to pursue import protection via new antidumping against China's exports, while the political pressure from import-competing firms within China led them to pursue import protection via higher applied tariffs. This would also make sense because China did not have an active antidumping policy in place during most of this time period.

8.3 Trade Policy Substitution? Other WTO-Consistent Policies to Restrict Imports from China

One expected benefit to China from WTO accession was that access to a rules-based system with potential enforcement through effective dispute-settlement provisions would lead to nondiscriminatory treatment for its exporters as trading partners would be required to abide by the agreement's MFN principle of equal tariff treatment. An additional potential benefit to accession might be to help reign in foreign use of antidumping against China's exports, as well as perhaps reducing the discriminatory nature of its application. The data presented in the last section indicates little evidence through 2004 that this has been the case. Nevertheless, it is important to recognize that *even if* WTO members had applied a less discriminatory antidumping policy against China's exports since 2001, an important question is whether there were simply other potentially substitutable import-restricting policies that members had been using to manage China's export growth instead.

This section examines WTO member use of a number of other trade policy instruments to assess the likelihood of such trade policy substitution: the transitional product-specific China safeguard; the WTO's "regular" safeguard policy; other negotiated safeguard-like trade restrictions such as the reemergence of "grey-area" measures and "voluntary" export restraints (VERs) that were banned by the WTO in prior contexts; and, finally, countervailing measures under "antisubsidy" policies. The resort to such policies in addition to antidumping has arisen as WTO members are now otherwise required to offer Chinese exporters MFN treatment through their tariff schedules.

8.3.1   The Transitional Product-Specific China Safeguard

A unique feature of China's 2001 WTO accession is establishment of a "Transitional Product-Specific Safeguard Mechanism" (section 16, WTO 2001), which any WTO importing country can use against China's exports until 2014.[20] As described in Bown and Crowley (2007a), many character-istics of this new "China safeguard" are at odds with core WTO principles and established instruments of administered import protection available to members.[21] The most radical change introduced by the new China safeguard is the weakened evidentiary criterion—even relative to antidumping—that members must satisfy in order to meet WTO legal requirements to impose a new barrier to Chinese trade. Not only is the threshold domestic injury requirement lower than that required under the "regular" WTO safeguard, but a clause in this new safeguard allows a second country to justify its own imposition of a new import restriction after a first country has implemented a China-safeguard on the basis of a "trade deflection" threat alone, without having to carry out its own injury investigation.[22]

What countries are using the China safeguard to restrict imports from China, and what sectors are being targeted? Table 8.5 provides information on twenty-one China-safeguard investigations that WTO members have ini-tiated since China's 2001 accession. As of data reported to the WTO by June 2007, seven recent cases had been resolved with the imposition of new trade restrictions, eight of the investigations concluded with no new measures imposed, and a number of others are still either unresolved or have been resolved without notification to the WTO.[23] The products under investiga-tion have some overlap with the sectors that typically dominate antidump-ing investigations (steel and chemicals), though there is also use to restrict

20. The question of how to accommodate the accession of a substantial new member such as China into the General Agreement on Tariffs and Trade (GATT)/WTO system is not new, as Japan's 1955 entry into the GATT raised similar concerns. A 1987 GATT working party pointed out that, despite the desire at the time for some existing members to introduce a new Japan-specific safeguard:

> Japan became a contracting party in September 1955 without any new general safeguard clause being added to the General Agreement. Some [13 out of 34] contracting parties invoked Article XXXV ["Non-Application of the Agreement between Specific Contracting Parties"] on Japan's accession. In a number of cases, Japan negotiated bilateral trade agree-ments containing special safeguard clauses which were followed by the countries concerned disinvoking Article XXXV. (GATT 1987, 2).

21. First, the allowance of a China-specific trade restriction on imports of fairly traded goods is otherwise inconsistent with MFN treatment. Second, the use of the new China safe-guard also does not require the policy-imposing country to immediately compensate China for withdrawing trade concessions which weakens the commitment to the WTO's reciprocity principle as well.

22. See Bown and Crowley (2007a) and the discussion of Article 16.8 of China's accession terms (WTO 2001). See also the discussion in Messerlin (2004) and Andersen and Lau (2002). Bown and Crowley (2007b) provide evidence of trade deflection in the context of Japanese exports being targeted with discriminatory import restrictions. See also Durling and Prusa (2006) for evidence of trade deflection in the hot-rolled steel market.

23. Interestingly, in at least five of the cases in the table that did not result in new measures (four for the United States, one for Canada) the domestic administering authority in charge of the domestic injury/market disruption investigation found evidence in favor of new measures and recommended that a new China safeguard import restriction be applied. Despite this rec-ommendation, the final policy decision in each case was not to apply measures.

Table 8.5 World Trade Organization (WTO) members' transitional product China safeguard investigations, 2002–2006

Investigating country	Product	Year of investigation	Outcome of investigation
1. United States	Pedestal actuators	2002	No measure imposed[a]
2. United States	Steel wire garment hangers	2002	No measure imposed[a]
3. India	Industrial sewing machine needles	2002	Unresolved[b]
4. Peru	Textile products and clothing	2003	Definitive safeguard as specific duty
5. United States	Brake drums and rotors	2003	No measure imposed
6. United States	Ductile iron waterworks fittings	2003	No measure imposed[a]
7. Poland	Footwear	2004	No measure imposed
8. United States	Uncovered innerspring units	2004	No measure imposed
9. Canada	Barbeques	2005	No measure imposed[a]
10. Colombia	Certain textile products	2005	Definitive safeguard as ad valorem duty
11. Colombia	Stockings and hosiery	2005	Definitive safeguard as ad valorem duty
12. Colombia	Made-up textile products	2005	Preliminary safeguard as ad valorem duty (definitive safeguard decision unresolved)
13. United States	Circular welded non-alloy steel pipe	2005	No measure imposed[a]
14. India	Industrial sewing machine needles	2005	Unresolved[b]
15. Colombia	Made-up textile products	2006	Unresolved
16. Ecuador	Textile products	2006	Unresolved
17. Ecuador	Taps, cocks, and valves for domestic use	2006	Unresolved
18. Turkey	Float glass	2006	Definitive safeguard as quantitative restriction
19. Turkey	Polyvinyl chloride (PVC)	2006	Definitive safeguard as specific duty
20. Turkey	Porcelain tiles	2006	Definitive safeguard as specific duty
21. Taiwan	Towelling products	2006	Unresolved

Source: Data compiled by the author from reports to the WTO Committee on Safeguards, available at www.wto.org, as well as national government sources.

Notes: Data not inclusive of all textile and apparel safeguard investigations, as China's 2001 WTO accession terms allowed for a separate transitional safeguard that countries can use for such products until 2008 (e.g., see table 8.6).

[a]Indicate cases in which the domestic investigating agency found evidence of injury/market disruption but the country nevertheless decided against imposing measures.

[b]India renotified the WTO Committee on Safeguards of the request for consultations with China in 2005.

footwear and other manufactures. Since the January 2005 expiration of the Multi-Fiber Arrangement (MFA) and transitional Agreement on Textiles and Clothing (ATC), resort to the China safeguard has not surprisingly been dominated by textiles and apparel cases. While most of the countries resorting to the China safeguard are developing countries, some of these countries (e.g., India, Turkey) are also some of the biggest new users of antidumping. At a basic level, there is thus some evidence of substitutability between a country's use of antidumping to target imports from China and use of a China-specific safeguard since 2002, suggesting the data presented in tables 8.2 and 8.3 is understating the true level of trade policy discrimination that China's exports continue to face despite its accession to the WTO.

8.3.2   The Transitional Textiles and Apparel China Safeguard and Related Voluntary Export Restraints

Table 8.5 does not include all transitional China-safeguard measures; certain WTO members have either imposed or threatened to impose additional safeguard restrictions on Chinese exports of textile and apparel products that are not reported there. Such trade restrictions can be justified under a separate transitional product safeguard mechanism and are available for WTO members to restrict imports of such products from China through 2008.[24] One distinguishing feature between the textiles and apparel China safeguard cases that are treated separately from China-safeguard cases involving other products is that there is much less transparency—regarding information over investigations or outcomes—in the former. Moreover, the initiation of safeguard investigation for textile and apparel products and the imposition of trade-restricting measures are frequently not reported to the WTO Committee on Safeguards.[25]

In particular, noticeably absent from table 8.5 are a number of high-profile textile and apparel China-safeguard cases initiated by the United States and the European Union. In the United States, one important way in which this safeguard is distinct is that its injury investigations take place outside of the

---

24. According to WTO's Trade Policy Review of China (2006, 60, emphasis added):

Article 242 of China's Working Party Report permits WTO Members to request consultations with China if the Member believes that imports of textiles and apparel products of Chinese origin covered by the ATC [i.e., the 1995–2005 Agreement on Textiles and Clothing] are causing market disruption; during the consultation, China will hold exports of the products in question at a level no greater than 7.5% (6% for wool) above the amount entered during the first 12 months or the most recent 14 months preceding the month in which consultations were requested. The restraints established as a result of these consultations will be effective for a year from the date on which consultations were requested unless otherwise agreed. Members *can not use simultaneously* measures under this provision, and the *transitional product-specific* safeguard measures under Article 16 of China's Protocol of Accession. Article 242 covers a period up to 2008.

25. It is for this reason that table 8.5 does not include all countries' use of the transitional product-specific China safeguard investigations or impositions.

U.S. International Trade Commission's quasi-judicial investigative process that otherwise handles the injury investigations for antidumping, global safeguards, other China safeguards, as well as countervailing duty cases. Instead, the textile and apparel China-safeguard injury investigations are handled internally by the U.S. Department of Commerce's Office of Textile and Apparel (OTEXA). Table 8.6 reports data from OTEXA's Web site on the textile and apparel products for which U.S. producers initiated safeguard investigations and requested import restrictions for 2003 to 2005.

A common resolution to these U.S. and EU textile and apparel investigations is China frequently agreeing to *voluntarily* restrain exports and undertake other grey-area measures—a practice that has been explicitly *discouraged* in other WTO Agreements.[26] For example, shortly after the expiration of the MFA/ATC in January 2005, a surge in textile and apparel imports from China triggered U.S. and EU investigations and led each trading partner to negotiate a settlement with China. In the face of the threat of discriminatory import restrictions in each case, China instead agreed to establish an explicit mechanism to voluntarily restrain export growth in a number of politically sensitive product categories.[27]

8.3.3 The Use of New Trade Restrictions under the WTO Agreement on Safeguards

A third alternative to antidumping that is another WTO-sanctioned trade policy that a member can use to restrict imports from China is a "global safeguard" applied under the rules set out by the WTO Agreement on Safeguards. Admittedly, a fundamental distinction between a global safeguard measure and antidumping (or either of the new "China safeguards," for

---

26. The VERs were a trade-restricting policy outcome that was frequently used in the 1970s and 1980s, but one which was banned under the WTO's Agreement on Safeguards' Article 11:1(b).

27. The WTO's Trade Policy Review of China (WTO 2006, 60–61) explicitly describes the VER settlements between the EU and China and the United States and China in these investigations as follows:

> On 10 June 2005, China and the European Communities signed a Memorandum of Understanding (MOU), placing export restraints on ten categories of Chinese textiles and clothing exports to the EC until 31 December 2007. The growth rates of these exports would be limited to between 8% and 12.5% per year. As a quid pro quo, the EC agreed to end its ongoing safeguard investigation on these products and to refrain from adopting measures as permitted under Article 242 of China's WTO Working Party Report, in categories not covered by the MOU. . . . .Under the Interim Measures, MOFCOM compiles a "Catalogue of Textiles Products Subject to Interim Export Administration", including exports of textiles and clothing subject to restrictions imposed by countries or regions unilaterally, and textile exports subject to temporary quantitative control under bilateral agreements. For each product listed in the Catalogue, the quota is partly assigned through a bidding system, and partly allocated based on the exporter's share in China's total export value for the previous year in the respective categories. . . . A similar agreement was signed with the United States on 8 November 2005. The restraints on certain categories of textiles and clothing exports from China are effective from 1 January 2006 to 31 December 2008; exports of these products are expected to increase by 8% to 10% in 2006, by 13% in 2007, and 17% in 2008.

Table 8.6   **U.S. textile and apparel safeguard investigations of Chinese exports, 2003–2005**

OTEXA category	Product
	2003 investigations
222	Knit fabric
349/649	Cotton and man-made fiber brassieres
350/650	Cotton and man-made fiber dressing gowns
	2004 investigations
222	Knit fabric
301	Combed cotton yarn
447	Wool trousers
620	Other synthetic filament fabric
338/339	Cotton knit shirts and blouses
340/640	Men's and boys' cotton and man-made fiber shirts not knit
347/348	Cotton trousers
349/649	Brassieres and other body supporting garments
350/650	Dressing gowns and robes
352/652	Cotton and man-made fiber underwear
638/639	Man-made fiber knit shirts and blouses
647/648	Man-made fiber trousers
	2005 investigations
226	Cheeseclothes, batistes, lawns/voiles
301	Combed cotton yarn
332/432/632	Cotton wool and man-made fiber socks
338/339	Cotton knit shirts and blouses
340/640	Men's and boy's cotton and man-made fiber woven shirts
341/641	Women's and girls' cotton and man-made fiber woven shirts and blouses
342/642	Cotton and man-made fiber skirts
345/645/646	Cotton and man-made fiber sweaters
347/348	Cotton trousers
349/649	Cotton and man-made fiber brassieres and other body supporting garments
350/650	Dressing gowns and robes
351/651	Cotton and man-made fiber nightwear
352/652	Cotton and man-made fiber underwear
359/659	Cotton and man-made fiber swimwear
363	Cotton terry and other pile towels
369/666	Curtains and drapery
443	Men's and boy's wool suits
619	Polyester filament fabric, light weight
620	Other synthetic filament fabric
634/635	Other men's and boy's man-made fiber coats and women's and girls' man-made fiber coats
638/639	Knit man-made fiber shirts and blouses
647/648	Man-made fiber trousers

Sources: Requests for China Textile Safeguard Action, downloaded from the Office of Textile and Apparel's Web site, http://otexa.ita.doc.gov/safeguard_all.htm, last accessed 29 September 2006.

Note: OTEXA = Office of Textile and Apparel.

that matter) is that the basic WTO conditions require a global safeguard be applied on a nondiscriminatory basis. Nevertheless, there are a number of exceptions to this rule. The result is that countries frequently structure the imposition of new safeguard measures to allow for a discriminatory impact against exporters with certain characteristics, many of which have important potential implications for a country like China.

Discretionary elements of the Agreement on Safeguards allow a safeguard-imposing country to potentially discriminate implicitly against exporters with certain characteristics.[28] First, import-restricting measures are frequently imposed as quantitative restrictions or tariff rate quotas, policies that require government officials to make the secondary choice of a decision rule for how to allocate import licences (and, thus, market share) across many potential exporters. When imposing such policies, the WTO rules suggest that imposing countries allocate licences based on historical market share in a recent three-year period, a decision rule that implicitly discriminates against new entrants. Second, countries that impose a global safeguard are encouraged by an explicit provision to exempt developing countries from the measure, provided those exporters are de minimus suppliers (less than 3 percent of the import market individually, less than 9 percent collectively). Such exemptions obviously discriminate against even developing countries that are non-de minimus suppliers, as they will face trade barriers under the measure that other foreign competitors do not. Finally, many safeguard-imposing countries frequently exempt from the safeguard's application the imports coming in from preferential trade agreement (PTA) partners. This also serves to implicitly discriminate against non-PTA partner foreign suppliers who face an import restriction under the global safeguard that key foreign competitors in other trading partners do not.[29]

Since the WTO's 1995 inception, member countries have imposed over seventy-five new global safeguard trade restrictions, after more than 145 safeguard investigations. Not surprisingly, many of the major users of global safeguards are the major users of antidumping and the China safeguard,

28. Bown and McCulloch (2004) provide a discussion and empirical analysis of the following discriminatory elements in global safeguard cases initiated between 1995 and 2000.

29. This does not even consider examples of global safeguards applied in clear violation of WTO MFN rules, such as the steel safeguard imposed by the United States in 2002. This policy not only exempted entire countries from the trade restriction (e.g., North American Free Trade Agreement [NAFTA] partners Canada and Mexico), it also introduced discriminatory "product exclusions" that the United States Trade Representative (USTR) granted to exporters at the level of a foreign firm-specific product. For a discussion and empirical analysis, see Bown (2004). A typical exclusion might be as narrowly defined as a trademarked product that only one foreign firm could produce legally. For example, see product exclusion N454.01 granted to the United Kingdom firm Somers Forge, Ltd. on 11 June 2002, "Forged alloy steel die blocks of round or rectangular cross section. U.S. Trademark No. 1213781, commonly known as 'VMC' or 'HYTUF'," or exclusion N408.10 granted to the Japanese firm Daido Steel on 22 August 2002, "A specialized, high grade tool steel, known as Daido's proprietary grade NAK 55, that is used for the construction of plastic molds." See the USTR's Web site, "President Bush Takes Action on Steel," http://www.ustr.gov/sectors/industry/steel.shtml, last access date of 29 February 2004.

after it has agreed to upper limits on its import tariffs (i.e., tariff bindings) through a trade agreement, as China did when it acceded to the WTO in 2001. Hoekman and Kostecki (2001) refer to these as the "escape valve" and "insurance" motives. Bagwell and Staiger (1990), for example, use a repeated-game setting to show that allowing such trade restrictions to be imposed at times of increased trade volumes (when there is a strong terms-of-trade gain motive for a country to impose a new tariff) allows trading partners to sustain lower cooperative tariffs. Once a safeguard or antidumping provision is in place, there is then a substantial body of research examining political-economic explanations for which industries seek and receive protection under its provisions.[33] Until recently, for reasons related to both data availability and the frequency with which the policy was used, research into determinants of use of antidumping and safeguards has focused almost exclusively on historical users such as the United States and EU.

In presenting a first empirically oriented examination of China's own use of antidumping, this section proceeds in two steps. First, much like the approach we took for the other major users of antidumping presented in section 8.2, we characterize the data by focusing first on how China has been using antidumping over time, which exporting sectors and trading partners it has targeted, as well as the discriminatory nature of its use. Then we focus on one particular Chinese import-competing sector's use of antidumping and present a more formal regression approach in which to examine whether there is a relationship between China's post-accession use of antidumping and the pattern and timing of tariff liberalization it took on as part of its WTO accession commitments.

8.4.1   China's Adoption and Use of Import-Restricting Antidumping and Safeguards

Figure 8.4 illustrates China's growing use of antidumping between 1997 and 2005 over time and across sectors. As shown in panel A of figure 8.4, Chinese industries initiated only three investigations in 1997, the year China implemented its antidumping law. However, since 2002, the number of new requests for antidumping import restrictions has grown to between twenty and thirty per year.[34] In a more formal regression framework in the next section, we examine whether there is evidence of a relationship between the post-accession use of antidumping and the level and timing of market

---

33. Blonigen and Prusa (2003) provide a detailed survey of the political-economic literature on antidumping, while Bown and Crowley (2005) survey the literature on safeguards. Examples of important determinants include (a) the standard political-economy explanations (e.g., Grossman and Helpman 1994; Mayer 1984) for differential provision of import protection across industries, (b) use by industries with imperfectly competitive market structures so as to segment markets internationally, and (c) the potential retaliation threat explanation (e.g., Blonigen and Bown 2003).

34. According to Kennedy (2005), China reformed its 1997 antidumping law in November 2001 to bring it into conformity with WTO obligations.

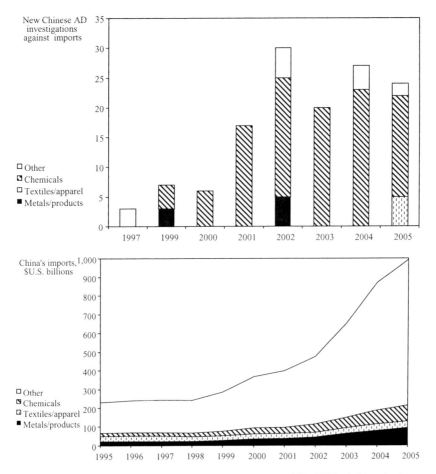

Fig. 8.4   Antidumping by China and imports by sector, 1995–2005: *A*, New Anti-dumping Investigations against Chinese Imports; *B*, Chinese imports by sector

Sources: Antidumping data compiled from Bown (2007); HS system import data are from Comtrade.

Notes: "Metals/products" are HS chapters 72–83, "Textiles/apparel" are 50–63, "Chemicals" are 28–38.

access commitments that China undertook as part of its 2001 accession to the WTO.

Figure 8.4 also documents the sectoral distribution of China's antidumping investigations, revealing that they have been dominated by the industrial chemicals sector, with only a small fraction of use by the steel, textile and apparel, and other import-competing industries. Panel B of figure 8.4 illustrates the share of these particular industries' imports in China's total imports received over the 1995 to 2005 period. Not surprisingly, there is nothing apparent in the raw trade data that would appear to justify why these particular Chinese industries have become the predominant users of antidumping within China.

Table 8.7 provides more detail as to the outcomes of the Chinese antidumping investigations across exporting country targets with data broken down by its pre-accession (1997–2001) versus post-accession (2002–2004) use. When we compare this data to similarly broken out data for the other major users of antidumping illustrated in tables 8.2 and 8.3, these data indicate that China may be using antidumping quite differently. Not only are Chinese cases dominated by a particular sector (chemicals, see figure 8.4), but data on the overall caseload of Chinese investigations and outcomes (table 8.7) also indicate that there is much less differentiation or discrimination across targeted exporting countries. Each of the targeted countries is a major source of Chinese imports, and they each lose a similar proportion of investigations so that the result is that their exporters each face new trade restrictions with similar frequency. China also rarely names only one country in an antidumping investigation over an imported product, which is another potential means of discriminating across exporters that other antidumping-using countries have used. Furthermore, unlike many other new users of antidumping, China almost exclusively applies import restrictions as ad valorem duties, and the duties imposed do not appear be radically different across countries either. To summarize the implications of this table—unlike the evidence for other country users in tables 8.2 and 8.3—China applied antidumping in a relatively nondiscriminatory manner during this time period, that is, for China, there is no country that it treats like others treat China.

Next, because so much of the antidumping caseload within China is focused on industrial chemicals, we illustrate in figure 8.5 additional information on the exporting targets involved in these cases. Consistent with the features of its overall nondiscriminatory application of the policy documented in table 8.5, it appears from panels A and B of figure 8.5 that the vast majority of the chemicals industry requests for new antidumping protection target China's major sources for its chemical imports over the 1997 to 2005 period—the United States, EU, Korea, Japan, Russia, and Taiwan.

Finally, we point out that Chinese industries have only pursued one safeguard investigation since the 2001 WTO accession. This occurred during the global steel crisis of 2002 and is associated with a cross-country surge in steel safeguard investigations—led by the United States and followed by at least eight other WTO members. The result of this particular Chinese safeguard investigation was that it followed the U.S. lead and imposed definitive safeguard restrictions on steel imports that lasted between May 2002 and December 2003.[35]

35. According to WTO (2006, 87), China imposed a preliminary safeguard in the form of tariff quotas in May 2002 for 180 days. It then imposed definitive safeguard "on five of the eleven products investigated on 20 November 2002. Although the measures were expected to remain for three years, they were terminated on 26 December 2003."

Table 8.7   China's use of antidumping (AD), 1997–2001 and 2002–2004

Years	Exporting country target	Antidumping investigations[a]	Investigations resulting in measures[b]	Only country named in investigation[b]	Mean margin conditional on measures imposed (%)	Share of China's import market[c]
1997–2001	1 Korea	8 (0.30)	7 (0.88)	3 (0.38)	28.43	0.10 (5)
	2 Japan	4 (0.15)	3 (0.75)	0 (0.00)	31.50	0.20 (1)
	3 U.S.	4 (0.15)	3 (0.75)	0 (0.00)	60.17	0.11 (4)
	4 EU	3 (0.11)	3 (1.00)	0 (0.00)	44.47	0.15 (2)
	5 Russia	2 (0.07)	2 (1.00)	1 (0.50)	22.75	0.03 (7)
	All other	6 (0.22)	4 (0.67)	0 (0.00)	36.38	0.41
	Total	27 (1.00)	22 (0.81)	4 (0.15)	36.29	1.00
2002–2004	1 Japan	16 (0.21)	14 (0.88)	0 (0.00)	70.72	0.19 (1)
	2 Korea	16 (0.21)	13 (0.81)	0 (0.00)	35.92	0.11 (4)
	3 U.S.	14 (0.18)	12 (0.86)	0 (0.00)	67.57	0.09 (5)
	4 EU	8 (0.11)	6 (0.75)	1 (0.13)	75.58	0.13 (2)
	5 Taiwan	7 (0.09)	5 (0.71)	1 (0.14)	28.42	0.13 (3)
	All other	15 (0.20)	13 (0.87)	0 (0.00)	42.94	0.35
	Total	76 (1.00)	63 (0.83)	2 (0.03)	54.34	1.00

Sources: Antidumping data compiled from Bown (2007) and is based on investigations initiated by 2004 for which complete information on the case's resolution is available. Harmonized System import data from Comtrade.

Notes: In some cases, China investigates firms from the European Union (EU), while in other cases it investigates firms from subsets of one or more EU member countries only. For consistency, this table only allows for one "EU" entry for each product-specific investigation. "All other" countries investigated twice include India, Indonesia, Malaysia, Singapore, and Thailand, and "all other" countries investigated once include Canada, Iran, Kazakhstan, Mexico, and Ukraine.

[a]Numbers in parentheses are share of total.

[b]Numbers in parentheses are share of target country's investigations.

[c]Numbers in parentheses are rankings.

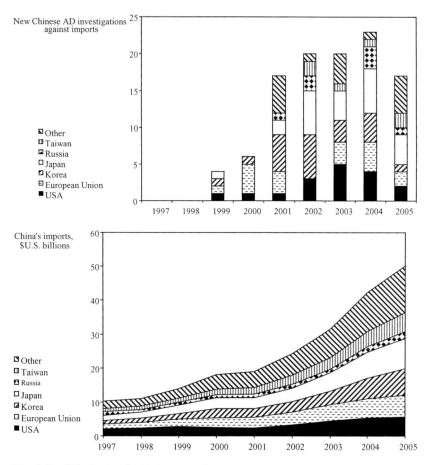

Fig. 8.5   China's chemical industry antidumping use and imports by target country, 1997–2005: *A,* **China's chemical industry new antidumping investigations;** *B,* **China's chemical industry imports**

Sources: Antidumping data compiled from Bown (2007); HS system import data are from Comtrade.

Note: "Chemicals" are HS chapters 28–38.

8.4.2   What Explains China's Use of Antidumping?

Given that China's use of antidumping is concentrated almost exclusively in the industrial chemicals sector, there is little to be gained by an attempt to exploit across-industry variation to explain this newly imposed protection. Kennedy (2005, 423) conjectures that chemicals (and steel) are the primary industrial users of antidumping within China for a number of reasons: they are large, concentrated, and state-owned, and they are less involved than other industries in international production sharing or joint ventures, and they primarily produce for the domestic market. Thus, in this section, we provide a more formal empirical investigation into the potential within-sector determinants of which chemical products sought post-WTO accession protection under China's antidumping law. While such an approach obviously limits our insights to one industry, focusing on the chemicals sector alone does simplify our data collection work in that we will not need to construct measures to control for between-sector differences in political-economic determinants of demands for import protection.

The time series features of figures 8.4 and panel A of figure 8.5 provide anecdotal evidence that there is a surge in industrial-chemical products that sought antidumping protection immediately after China's WTO accession in 2001. In the following, we provide a regression approach in which we examine more formally whether there is a link between the size and timing of the trade liberalization undertaken and the subsequent resort to anti-dumping protection in this industry.[36] Our approach is to focus on roughly 450 different six-digit industrial chemical products in chapters 28 (Inorganic Chemicals) and 29 (Organic Chemicals) of the Harmonized System (HS) classification system, nineteen of which were produced by Chinese industries that sought protection under antidumping at least once between 2001 and 2005. These chemical products alone formed the basis of nearly 60 percent of all new antidumping investigations initiated by China during the 2001 and 2005 period.[37]

Before turning to the formal regression analysis, consider first figure 8.6, which motivates our approach by plotting over the 1996 to 2005 period the product-level average of two different data series—MFN applied tariff and import values—associated with two different categories of chemical products—those products that sought post-accession antidumping protection versus those that did not. First, both product categories indicate a similar time trend—applied MFN tariff rates are falling over the period, and Chinese imports are increasing dramatically over the period. One apparent difference from the raw data, however, is that products facing antidumping during the 2001 to 2005 period were also those that experienced a sharper

36. Feinberg and Reynolds (2007) present evidence of this relationship on a different sample of data. They examine the 1995 to 2003 period and the link between trade liberalization and the subsequent use of antidumping on a cross-country sample of data at a much higher level of disaggregation—that is, twenty-one different HS section-level heading industries based on WTO-provided antidumping filings data. Our approach exploits more disaggregated data and also focuses only the within-sector, product-level variation within one sector within one country.

37. According to the data collected in Bown (2007), 70 of the 123 Chinese antidumping investigations initiated between 2001 and 2005 (aggregating investigations of firms from different EU-member countries consistently into one EU observation) contained products in chapters 28 or 29 of the HS system.

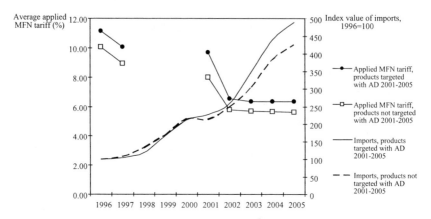

Fig. 8.6   China's tariff liberalization, imports, and antidumping use over chemical products, 1996–2005

Source: Data compiled by the author based on averages from nineteen (432) different six-digit HS products in HS chapters 28 and 29 that China targeted (did not target) with new antidumping investigations over the 2001–2005 period.

reduction in China's applied MFN tariff rate in the accession year of 2001 to 2002. One explanation consistent with this figure is that products that delayed tariff liberalization until 2001 were the products that subsequently felt the pressure to *reimplement* protection in the form of new antidumping import restrictions quickly thereafter.[38]

Table 8.8 provides a more formal econometric analysis of the link between tariff liberalization and subsequent antidumping use. There we report marginal effects estimates of the binomial probit model of determinants of whether each of roughly 450 particular six-digit HS products in the chemical industry sought antidumping protection (= 1) in China during the 2001 to 2005 period.[39] After controlling for the size of imports of the product (0.117), evidence from column (1) indicates that a larger reduction in applied tariffs in 2001 to 2002 is associated with a higher probability of seeking antidumping protection from imports at some point over the subsequent period. The size (–0.017) of the marginal effect is also *economically* significant—

38. A second interesting feature of the data series in figure 8.6 is that imports in products targeted with antidumping appear to be growing more rapidly since 2001. And this is despite the combination of two factors—they face, on average, higher levels of applied MFN tariff rates than products not subsequently targeted with antidumping, *and* many of the products also subsequently faced additional Chinese antidumping import restrictions.

39. By choosing the product as the unit of observation, as opposed to a product-foreign exporter pair, we abstract from potential partner-specific (e.g., retaliatory) considerations that have been shown to affect antidumping use for other countries (e.g., Blonigen and Bown 2003). While this a potential limitation of the current approach, given the evidence from table 8.6 that China appears to apply antidumping is a relatively nondiscriminatory manner, eliminating this potential source of variation may not come at as great a cost as might be the case for other antidumping-user countries.

Table 8.8   **Marginal effects estimates of probit model of China's chemical industry choice to initiate antidumping over an imported product**

| Explanatory variables [expected sign] | Dependent variable: Indicator that the 6-digit chemical product faced at least one Chinese antidumping investigation between 2001 and 2005 | | | |
	(1)	(2)	(3)	(4)
Size [+]				
(value of Chinese pre-accession	0.117**	0.136**	0.163***	0.162**
imports of the product [$U.S.,	(0.059)	(0.061)	(0.063)	(0.063)
in 2000][a])				
Accession year tariff reduction [–]				
(difference between 2001 MFN	–0.017***	–0.023***	–0.022***	–0.023***
applied tariff rate and 2002	(0.006)	(0.006)	(0.006)	(0.006)
MFN applied tariff rate)				
Tariff liberalization commitment [–]				
(difference in 1996 MFN applied		0.008	0.008	0.008
tariff rate and 2005 MFN		(0.006)	(0.006)	(0.006)
bound tariff rate commitment)				
Post-accession tariff overhang [–]				
(difference between 2005 MFN			–0.047*	–0.047*
applied tariff rate and 2005			(0.027)	(0.027)
MFN bound tariff rate				
commitment)				
Pre-accession import growth [+]				
(% difference between 2000 value				0.000
of imports and 1996 value of				(0.003)
imports)				
No. of observations	457	457	457	454
Pseudo R^2	0.09	0.11	0.12	0.12
Predicted probability (at means)	0.032	0.030	0.029	0.029

Notes: The unit of observation is 6-digit product in chapter 28 (Inorganic Chemicals) or 29 (Organic Chemicals) of the Harmonized System. *Notes:* Robust standard errors are in parentheses.
[a]Rescaled by $1 billion.
***Significant at the 1 percent level.
**Significant at the 5 percent level.
*Significant at the 10 percent level.

the implication is that an additional 1 percentage point reduction in the applied MFN tariff leads to an additional 1.7 percentage point increase in the predicted probability of an antidumping investigation when the model is evaluated at the means of the data.[40]

In the remaining columns, we add additional controls as a robustness

40. When evaluated at the means of the data, the model's predicted probability of an investigation is 0.032. Thus, an additional 1 percentage point reduction in the applied MFN tariff (e.g., from the mean reduction of –2.24 percentage points to –3.24 percentage

check on the sensitivity of this result. In column (2), we add a control for the size of the *overall* tariff liberalization commitment the product has to undergo between 1996 (the first year for which we have disaggregated tariff data) and 2005. Perhaps surprisingly, the size of the *overall* tariff reduction commitment undertaken between 1996 and 2005 is negatively related to the decision to seek antidumping protection, though the estimate is not statistically significant.[41] Furthermore, the size of the impact of the accession-year tariff liberalization commitment impact increases to –0.023. Next, in column (3), we also control for the product's post-accession "tariff overhang" defined as the difference between the 2005 applied MFN tariff rate and the 2005 MFN bound tariff rate commitment. The smaller this difference (i.e., the closer is the applied rate to the binding), the higher is the probability that the product seeks additional protection via antidumping, perhaps because it has no other WTO-consistent form to implement additional protection.[42] Finally, in column (5), we control for whether the product experienced a pre-accession surge in imports. While we expect this to be positively related to requests for antidumping protection between 2001 to 2005, there is no evidence of this relationship from this specification. Nevertheless, the sign and estimated size of the coefficients on the other variables of interest remain unchanged.

In summary, there is some evidence from examination of Chinese chemical products—by far the dominant user of antidumping within China during its immediate post-accession period—that there is a relationship between the size of the tariff liberalization undertaken between 2001 and 2002 (the year of its WTO accession) and China's subsequent use of antidumping between 2001 and 2005. In particular, an additional 1 percentage point reduction in the MFN applied tariff rate during 2001 to 2002 is associated with a 1.7 to 2.3 percentage point increase in the probability that a given chemical product seeks an antidumping investigation over the subsequent five year period. This is a large effect given that the predicted probability of the average product seeking antidumping protection during the period is

---

points) leads to an increase in the predicted probability of an investigation by 1.7 percentage points to 0.049. Note that this tariff reduction is well within 1 standard deviation of the applied tariff reduction in the sample, which is 1.23 percentage points.

41. One explanation for a potential positive estimated effect is that it could instead be picking up the effect of the underlying ability of producers of certain products to organize politically—that is, domestic producers of products unable to maintain (applied MFN) tariff protection over the 1996 to 2005 period (in the face of WTO accession) are also unable to organize politically and convince Chinese government authorities that they should receive special import protection under antidumping. Note finally that, in unreported results, we have ruled out the possibility that this result is driven by collinearity between the 2001 to 2002 tariff change and the broader 1996 to 2005 tariff change.

42. Though statistically significant and consistent with what theory would predict, economically, this effect is quite small as there is actually quite little difference in the underlying data between the applied rates and bound rates (–0.2 percentage points) and that could be a statistical anomaly associated with averaging the actual tariff bindings (made at the eight-digit level) to the six-digit level required for the empirical analysis.

only 2.9 to 3.2 percent. It is also apparent that it may be the timing of the effect that matters, as there is no statistically significant relationship between the probability of a post-accession antidumping investigation and the size of the *overall* trade liberalization commitment made for the 1996 to 2005 time period.

8.5   China in WTO Dispute Settlement

Negotiating a successful accession into the WTO is itself an important achievement. Nevertheless, it does not automatically follow that, upon becoming a member of the organization, an acceding country necessarily receives equal treatment under WTO rules. Furthermore, becoming a member does not by itself imply that the country's own policymakers continue to live up to the trade liberalizing commitments that they or their predecessor agreed for the country to take on. An implication of this for the WTO is that, as a self-enforcing agreement, it is sometimes through resort to formal dispute settlement litigation and threats (and follow through) of retaliation that the bargain of countries exchanging a balance of market accession concessions "works" and the benefits of WTO membership are conferred.

Therefore, an important source from which to track China's transition to full WTO membership is its experience in formal WTO dispute settlement. Upon receiving entry into the organization in 2001, it would not have been surprising to observe an almost immediate onslaught of formal China-centered disputes, simply because the country is involved in a substantial share of global trade in many sensitive product categories with dozens of different trading partners.[43] This includes disputes both in which China would be a respondent (defendant), with its policies being challenged by other WTO members who may have been biding their time until 2002 when China would finally also face the discipline of international rules, and also in which China would be a complainant (plaintiff) going on the offensive to enforce the market access commitments that the existing WTO members had promised.

Instead, as we illustrate in the next two sections, China has been largely and conspicuously absent from major WTO litigation in the initial period

---

43. Horn, Mavroidis, and Nordström (2005) provide evidence from a 1995 to 1998 sample of data that the pattern of actual disputes compares favorably to that predicted from a simple probabilistic model that links the frequency of disputes simply to the amount of trade a country undertakes as well as the diversity of its trading partners. The implication from such a model for a country like China is that, simply because it is a country that is involved in a substantial amount of international trade with many countries, it would likely see itself involved in many formal WTO trade disputes, even when abstracting from the likelihood that certain traded products may be more likely to face disputes than others. This idea is also supported by the evidence provided in Bown (2005a, b) which examines trade dispute data from the period prior to China's WTO accession and finds that the decision of a WTO member to actively participate in a potential trade dispute is positively related to the country's market access interest at stake.

following its 2001 accession. Nevertheless, there are increasing signs that this grace period may be coming to an end, which may foreshadow a major shift in China's role in formal WTO dispute settlement going forward.

8.5.1   China as Complainant

The top half of table 8.9 presents an up-to-date breakdown of China's formal participation in WTO trade dispute proceedings as a *complainant* (plaintiff). Perhaps surprisingly, China has filed thus far only three formal disputes of its own as a complainant.[44] In its first dispute, it participated as a co-complainant (along with eight other countries) in the formal challenge to the U.S. use of a safeguard to restrict steel imports in 2002. While China ultimately benefited from the successful resolution to this case—the United States complied with WTO legal rulings and removed the steel safeguard measure in December 2003—this outcome was arguably a by-product of the legal efforts undertaken by more active WTO members in the case such as the EU, which successfully identified politically sensitive U.S. export products to target for retaliation threats.[45] The second case over Coated Paper in 2007 turned out to be a nondispute when the U.S. temporary trade restriction that China was intending to challenge was removed. China's third dispute initiation in September 2008 has challenged newly imposed U.S. antidumping and CVD import restrictions on Chinese-produced steel pipes and tubes, tires, and laminated woven sacks.

There are a number of complementary reasons to indicate some surprise that China has not yet played a more active offensive role as a complainant in WTO trade disputes. First, the most common measure to challenge under formal WTO dispute settlement is increasingly another country's antidumping import restrictions.[46] When combining the feature of frequent WTO

---

44. This is perhaps surprising because some countries immediately take part in formal trade disputes upon entry into the WTO. For example, almost immediately after acceding in 1996 and 1997, respectively, Ecuador and Panama joined (as co-complainants) the ongoing, U.S.-led trade dispute against the EU's import-restricting banana regime, as bananas are an important export sector for both of these economies.

45. Despite its lack of prior experience in such cases, there is, nevertheless, some evidence from the case that China put itself in the position to take appropriate retaliatory action if the EU's efforts were not successful at getting the United States to comply. According to WTO (2006, 87–88, emphasis added):

In response to a safeguard measure imposed by the United States, China notified the Committee on Safeguards in May 2002, its proposed suspension of concessions and other obligations, in accordance with Article 12.5 of the Agreement on Safeguards. The proposed suspension, which would have taken effect from March 2005 *or from the fifth day following a DSB decision that the measures adopted by the United States were inconsistent with the WTO Agreement,* would have taken the form of an increase in duty of 24% on selected products originating in the United States.

46. Bown and Hoekman (2008) report that over 25 percent of all formal WTO disputes between 1999 and 2006 related to antidumping. This is likely because of a number of factors, including (a) the increasing resort to antidumping globally, (b) its relative transparency, and (c) the fact that an antidumping measure is foreign-country specific, so successful removal (via

Table 8.9   China as complainant and respondent in formal World Trade Organization (WTO) dispute settlement, 2002–December 5, 2008

WTO dispute	Respondent	Complainant	Issue under dispute	Year initiated; resolution
China as complainant				
1. DS252	U.S.	China[a]	Safeguard on imports of certain steel products	2002; U.S. removed safeguard in 2003 after adverse Panel and Appellate Body ruling
2. DS368	U.S.	China	Preliminary antidumping and countervailing duty determinations on coated free sheet paper	2007; terminated when U.S. did not implement trade restriction after negative final injury determination
3. DS379	U.S.	China	Definitive antidumping and countervailing duties on certain products from China	2008; ongoing[b]
China as respondent				
1. DS309	China	U.S.	Value-added tax on integrated circuits	2004; settled with China agreeing to amend or revoke the measures at issue
2. DS339, DS340, DS342	China	EU, U.S., Canada	Imports of automobile parts	2006; ongoing[b]
3. DS358, DS359	China	U.S., Mexico	Refunds, reductions, or exemptions from taxes and other payments	2007; settled with China agreeing to remove subsidies at issue
4. DS362	China	U.S.	Protection and enforcement of intellectual property rights	2007; ongoing[b]
5. DS363	China	U.S.	Trading rights and distribution services for certain publications and audiovisual entertainment products	2007; ongoing[b]
6. DS372, DS373, DS378	China	EU, U.S., Canada	Measures affecting financial information services and foreign financial information suppliers	2008; settled with China agreeing to eliminate discriminatory restrictions on foreign firms

Source: Data compiled by the author from the WTO Web site, www.wto.org.

[a]Eight other countries (European Union [EU], Japan, New Zealand, Norway, Switzerland, Korea, Taiwan, and Brazil) also filed formal WTO disputes over the 2002 U.S. steel safeguard.

[b]Through December 5, 2008.

filings over antidumping measures with evidence from the data presented in section 8.2 regarding the discriminatory treatment of China under foreign antidumping (even after its 2001 accession), it would not have been surprising to see China begin to start filing earlier as well as more disputes over this issue. This also suggests the potential scope for a substantial number of Chinese disputes over this issue in the future.

There are a number of potential contributing explanations worthy of discussion, even though they are not empirically testable at this stage, given the lack of data on Chinese disputes. One contributing explanation is certainly China's continued NME designation, which allows policymakers in certain trading partners substantial discretion with how they can construct estimates that China's exporters have dumped.[47] Nevertheless, in the case of the United States, the 2007 U.S. decision to now impose countervailing duties against China—that is, implicitly treating China as a market economy under one law—while continuing to treat China as an NME under another trade law (antidumping), does raise the possibility of China pursuing a dispute in this area. While it is too early to tell with any certainty, this may be one of the arguments behind the WTO dispute that China initiated against the United States in 2008.

A second potential explanation for China's failure to challenge other countries' use of antidumping through formal WTO disputes is if it had decided instead to take matters into its own hands by using its own antidumping trade policy to retaliate in order to lessen the likelihood of future discriminatory. However, this appears to be an unlikely explanation for China's failure to challenge other countries' use of antidumping. The data presented in section 8.4 indicate that China's use of antidumping has been fairly limited—that is, dominated by the chemicals industry—and its own application of antidumping has been relatively nondiscriminatory across foreign export targets in rough proportion to the size of their chemical exports to China.

8.5.2   China as Respondent

The lower half of table 8.9 presents information on the formal WTO trade disputes that China has been involved in as a *respondent* (defendant) country. Just as China has been infrequently on the offensive in WTO litigation, it has also infrequently had to defend itself from foreign challenges thus far.[48]

---

formal WTO litigation) will not necessarily generate positive spillovers to other trading partners, which limits the free-rider problem associated with organizing to pursue a WTO dispute in the first place. See also Bown (2005b).

47. The argument is, even if China filed a WTO dispute and won a case against an antidumping-imposing country, because of China's continued NME status, the using country would still have substantial discretion to identify an alternative means of imposing a WTO-consistent trade restriction that would leave China's exporters no better off than if it had not pursued the case at all.

48. It is somewhat surprising, for example, to not have seen the United States actively pursuing WTO disputes against China sooner than it ended up doing so, given the political pressure

Prior to a flurry of formal disputes filed in 2006 to 2008, China has only been challenged in one dispute (in 2004)—a value added tax on integrated circuits in a case the United States brought that China quickly settled.

Between 2006 and 2008, the United States and other WTO members filed a number of new disputes against China, perhaps signaling an end to the no-litigation standoff in the initial period following China's 2001 accession. In 2006, the United States, EU, and Canada initiated a challenge over China's alleged discriminatory treatment of imports of auto parts. The United States initiated a second dispute in 2007 along with Mexico, accusing China of offering tax refunds and industrial subsidies in violation of its WTO commitments. In 2007, the United States filed two complementary disputes that challenged China's treatment of intellectual property (IP)-intensive industries such as movies, music, and books. The first alleges that China has failed to sufficiently legislate and enforce laws protecting the IP of U.S. firms (thus failing to live up to its commitments under the Trade-Related Aspects of Intellectual Property Rights [TRIPS] Agreement), the second alleges that U.S. firms face discriminatory barriers when attempting to distribute their IP-intensive products and services within China (a violation of the General Agreement on Trade in Services [GATS]). In 2008, the United States, EU, and Canada initiated a challenge to the way in which China regulated foreign firms like Bloomberg, Dow Jones, and Thomson-Reuters that sought to provide financial information services to Chinese consumers.

As the issues at stake under these disputes are fundamental to China's continued efforts at reform, it will be important to watch how both sides choose to proceed in these—as well as other impending WTO challenges to China's policies—going forward.

8.5.3   China as an Interested Third Party

While until recently China has not been a frequent primary litigant—as either a complainant or respondent—in WTO trade disputes, table 8.10 indicates that China has substantial experience following WTO disputes as an *interested third party* in cases involving another complainant and respondent country. In more than forty different disputes, China has been extremely active in observing the WTO dispute settlement process through this manner.

World Trade Organization members have many reasons to observe and weigh in on such disputes in this third party role. One economically motivated reason to closely follow a dispute is the country's own market access interests over a disputed product—for example, China may want to make sure that any settlement or resolution to the case between the two disputing parties does not involve a negotiated outcome in which market access

---

imposed by many domestic constituencies. That is, protectionist sentiment in the U.S. Congress vis-à-vis China that focused on the growth of China's bilateral trade surplus with the United States and calls for the yuan to be revalued long preceded the eventual flurry of new U.S. disputes against China in 2006 to 2008.

Table 8.10 China as an interested third third party in formal World Trade Organization (WTO) dispute settlement, 2002–December 5, 2008

WTO dispute	Respondent	Complainant	Issue under dispute
1. DS108	U.S.	EU	Tax treatment for "Foreign sales corporations"
2. DS174, DS290	EU	U.S., Australia	Trademarks and geographical indications
3. DS207	Chile	Argentina	Price band system and safeguard measures for agriculture
4. DS212	U.S.	EU	Countervailing measures concerning certain products
5. DS243	U.S.	India	Rules of origin for textiles and apparel products
6. DS245	Japan	U.S.	Measures affecting the importation of apples
7. DS248, DS249, DS251, DS253, DS254, DS258	U.S.	EU, Japan, Korea, Switzerland, Norway, New Zealand	Safeguard on imports of certain steel products
8. DS257	U.S.	Canada	CVD determination on softwood lumber
9. DS264	U.S.	Canada	Dumping determination on softwood lumber
10. DS265, DS266, DS283	EU	Australia, Brazil, Thailand	Export subsidies on sugar
11. DS267	U.S.	Brazil	Subsidies on upland cotton
12. DS269, DS286	EU	Brazil, Thailand	Customs classification of frozen boneless chicken cuts
13. DS270	Australia	Philippines	Imports of fresh fruit and vegetables
14. DS273	Korea	EU	Measures affecting trade in commercial vessels
15. DS276	Canada	U.S.	Exports of wheat and treatment of imported grain
16. DS277	U.S.	Canada	USITC investigation on softwood lumber
17. DS280	U.S.	Mexico	Countervailing duties on steel plate
18. DS281	U.S.	Mexico	AD measures on cement
19. DS282	U.S.	Mexico	AD measures on oil country tubular goods
20. DS287	Australia	EU	Quarantine regime for imports
21. DS291, DS292, DS293	EU	U.S., Canada, Argentina	Approval and marketing of biotech products
22. DS294	U.S.	EU	Calculating dumping margins (zeroing)
23. DS295	Mexico	U.S.	Definitive AD measures on beef and rice

24. DS296	U.S.	Korea	CVD investigation on DRAMS
25. DS299	EU	Korea	Countervailing measures on DRAMs
26. DS301	EU	Korea	Trade in commercial vessels
27. DS302	Dominican Republic	Honduras	Importation and internal scale of cigarettes
28. DS308	Mexico	U.S.	Tax measures on soft drinks and other beverages
29. DS312	Korea	Indonesia	AD duties on imports of certain paper
30. DS315	EU	U.S.	Selected customs matters
31. DS316	EU	U.S.	Trade in large civil aircraft
32. DS317	U.S.	EU	Trade in large civil aircraft
33. DS320	U.S.	EU	Continued suspension of obligations in the EC—hormones
34. DS321	Canada	EU	Continued suspension of obligations in the EC—hormones
35. DS322	U.S.	Japan	Zeroing and sunset reviews
36. DS323	Japan	Korea	Import quotas on dried laver and seasoned laver
37. DS331	Mexico	Guatemala	AD duties on steel pipes and tubes
38. DS332	Brazil	EU	Imports of retreaded tires
39. DS347	EU	U.S.	Trade in large civil aircraft (second complaint)
40. DS353	U.S.	EU	Trade in large civil aircraft (second complaint)
41. DS366	Colombia	Panama	Indicative prices and restrictions on ports of entry

Source: Data compiled by the author from the WTO Web site, www.wto.org.

Notes: CVD = countervailing duty; USITC = U.S. International Trade Commission; AD = antidumping; DRAMS = dynamic random access memory semiconductors; EC = European Community.

between the two disputants is restructured in a way that discriminates against its exporters. Second, a country without a market access interest at stake in a particular case may still have a systemic interest if it affects an interpretation of a WTO rule or procedure affecting its economic interests somewhere else. Third, countries may also choose to participate via this route as it provides them with a lower (resource and political) cost of learning about the WTO litigation experience in a way that will likely pay off in future disputes that they are involved in as complainants or respondents.

What is clear from the table is that China has chosen to participate in many different types of disputes over a range of traded products—import restrictions and export promotion, contingent protection, intellectual property, and so on. China is likely using this strategy in part to keep abreast of how the rules are slowly adjusting as the WTO case law and judicial interpretations begin to fill out some of the missing areas not explicitly covered by WTO rules.[49] Furthermore, China is also likely using this opportunity to learn about how the interplay between law, political posturing, and economics in WTO litigation plays out. China must certainly recognize the inevitability as a larger trader that it will be a frequent target of formal dispute settlement activity, and likely sooner rather than later.

8.5.4   China in Future WTO Dispute Settlement

Our discussion of China's future in WTO litigation is mere speculation, of course. It is also likely that China may find itself involved in future WTO trade litigation over issues that have not yet arisen. One feature of China's trade is that a new controversy over Chinese export products appears to surface in media headlines almost every day—whether it be recent allegations of melamine in pet food and dairy products, diethylene glycol in toothpaste, lead paint in children's toys, banned antibiotics in farmed seafood, and so on. In each of the instances thus far, importing countries have imposed trade restrictions that appear, if the prima facie evidence in news reports is accurate, to be justifiable under WTO provisions. Thus, it is not likely that any of these product bans would be subject of future trade dispute challenges.[50]

Nevertheless, the increasing frequency of such incidents suggests that sooner or later a policymaker will face domestic political pressure to impose an import restriction over some new concern that ultimately will be determined to not be based on sound scientific evidence, and in such a case, China

---

49. While no strict stare decisis rule applies in WTO case law, nevertheless, decisions made in panel reports and by the Appellate Body are frequently based on prior decisions, suggesting that precedent matters at least implicitly.

50. While under the GATT, imposing import restrictions to protect human, animal, or plant health was justified under Article XX, much of this has been expanded under the WTO to be covered under the Agreement on Sanitary and Phytosanitary (SPS) measures as well as the Agreement on Technical Barriers to Trade (TBT).

may seek to file a dispute to protect its market access rights.[51] Perhaps more important, the changing nature of trade and many of these controversies over the impact of imported products is likely to affect future institutional arrangements over consumer protection, health, and safety.

8.6 Conclusion

This chapter examines a number of different newly compiled data sets to assess issues surrounding China's 2001 accession to the WTO. I use data from the foreign use of antidumping during the 1995 to 2001 period to document the discrimination that China faced under this one particular trade policy, identifying one of the potential benefits its exporters may have expected to receive with WTO membership. Nevertheless, while a number of other factors were also changing during the time period—including WTO members being required to otherwise offer China MFN treatment and China's own rising exports—since 2001, there is no evidence that foreign discrimination vis-à-vis China via antidumping has improved. Furthermore, there are a number of additional trade policy instruments (e.g., China safeguards) that have also developed since 2001 that countries are also resorting to so as to continue to discriminate against Chinese exports in certain products. Finally, we also are able to find no robust evidence that there is a strategic relationship between China's own high import-tariff products and which export products foreign users were targeting with antidumping.

Regarding its own introduction of new import-restricting measures, we find that while China is now in the top five, in terms of the countries that most frequently implement new antidumping trade restrictions, the post-2001 surge in Chinese use is dominated by its industrial chemicals industry. Unlike the other major users of antidumping that are each increasingly applying their measures in a discriminatory fashion, we also provide evidence that China applies such new trade restrictions in a much less discriminatory (i.e., non-MFN) fashion. Finally, we also provide some evidence from a sample of Chinese chemical industry data that the cross-product variation in demands for new antidumping measures during the post-accession is related to the severity of the accession year tariff liberalization undertaken in 2001–2002.

Last, while it is somewhat surprising that China was not a frequent litigant in formal WTO dispute settlement activity in the early years after its acces-

---

51. There are a number of examples in WTO cases in which one country imposes an import ban on a product that it claimed was based on health (or environmental protection) purposes but which another trading partner challenged. These include U.S. challenges to EU bans on hormone-treated beef and genetically modified foods, as well as foreign challenges to U.S. measures to restrict tuna and shrimp imports that it alleged were necessary to protect the lives of dolphins and sea turtles, respectively.

sion, since 2006 it has increasingly been confronted by other WTO members in formal dispute settlement. Furthermore, given its share in world trade and the political sensitivity of the sectors involved in many of its traded products, it is likely to be involved in many more disputes going forward.

Appendix

Data Appendix

Antidumping Data

What governments report to the WTO regarding their use of antidumping is limited and frequently inconsistent with what is reported in official national government publications. We rely on data reported to the WTO (e.g., WTO 2007a, b, c) only infrequently in this chapter, and we use it primarily to supplement information from our other sources of data that may not be available in the most recent years (e.g., table 8.1 and figure 8.1).

The source of the data on antidumping use for the empirical analysis is the *Global Antidumping Database,* a cross-country data collection project funded by the World Bank and Brandeis University, which contains more detailed data, including dates associated with the investigation, countries targeted, measures imposed, HS products affected, and so on. The database derives from data hand-collected from official national government publications, and it covers nineteen policy-using countries which account for roughly 90 percent of the antidumping activity undertaken by all WTO members over the 1995 to 2004 period. Bown (2007) provides a users manual describing the source of the underlying country of the major users described in the text.

Data collected on China's use of antidumping, as reported in the *Global Antidumping Database* and Bown (2007), is translated to English from official Chinese government Web sites. China's dumping determination data is taken from the Bureau of Fair Trade for Imports and Exports (MOFCOM, http://dcj.mofcom.gov.cn/), its injury investigations are handled by the Bureau of Industry Injury Investigation (MOFCOM, http://gpj.mofcom.gov.cn/). Additional information was collected from the China Trade Remedy Information Web site (http://www.cacs.gov.cn/DefaultWebApp/index.htm).

Import and Export Data

Product-level import and export data at the six-digit HS level is from Comtrade, taken from World Integrated Trade Solution (WITS) database.

Tariff Data

China's applied MFN tariff rates (available for years 1996, 1997, 2001–2005) and its final WTO tariff binding schedule (submitted in 2001) are

Table 8A.1

Harmonized System chapters	Description
01–05	Animal and animal products
06–15	Vegetable products
16–24	Foodstuffs
25–27	Mineral products
28–38	Chemicals and allied industries
39–40	Plastics/rubber
41–43	Leather
44–49	Wood and wood products
50–63	Textiles and apparel
64–67	Footwear/headgear
68–71	Stone/glass
72–83	Metals
84–85	Machinery/electrical
86–89	Transportation
90–97	Miscellaneous

available at the eight-digit product level from the WTO Integrated Database, taken from WITS. I use simple averaging to aggregate the tariff rates from the eight-digit to the six-digit level to match them with the six-digit Chinese import and export data.

Industry Categories

I allocate products from HS chapters into broad industry categories according to table 8A.1.

References

Andersen, Scott, and Christian Lau. 2002. Hedging hopes with fears in China's accession to the World Trade Organization: The transitional special-product safeguard for Chinese exports. *Journal of World Intellectual Property* 5 (3): 405–76.

Bagwell, Kyle, and Robert W. Staiger. 1990. A theory of managed trade. *American Economic Review* 80 (4): 779–95.

———. 1999. An economic theory of GATT. *American Economic Review* 89 (1): 215–48.

———. 2006. What do trade negotiators negotiate about? Empirical evidence from the World Trade Organization. NBER Working Paper no. 12727. Cambridge, MA: National Bureau of Economic Research, December.

Blonigen, Bruce A. 2006. Evolving discretionary practices of U.S. antidumping activity. *Canadian Journal of Economics* 37 (3): 874–900.

Blonigen, Bruce A., and Chad P. Bown. 2003. Antidumping and retaliation threats. *Journal of International Economics* 60 (2): 249–73.

Blonigen, Bruce A., and Thomas J. Prusa. 2003. Antidumping. In *Handbook of international trade*, ed. E. Kwan Choi and James Harrigan, 251–84. Oxford, UK: Blackwell.

Bown, Chad P. 2004. How different are safeguards from antidumping? Evidence from U.S. trade policies toward steel. Brandeis University. Mimeograph.

———. 2005a. Participation in WTO dispute settlement: Complainants, interested parties and free riders. *World Bank Economic Review* 19 (2): 287–310.

———. 2005b. Trade remedies and World Trade Organization dispute settlement: Why are so few challenged? *Journal of Legal Studies* 34 (2): 515–55.

———. 2007. Global antidumping database. [Version 1.0 published as World Bank Policy Research Paper no. 3737, October 2005. Current version 3.0, June, updated data available at http://www.brandeis.edu/~cbown/global_ad/].

Bown, Chad P. and Meredith A. Crowley. 2005. Safeguards. In *The World Trade Organization: Legal, economic and political analysis,* ed. Patrick F. J. Macrory, Arthur E. Appleton, and Michael G. Plummer, 43–66. New York: Springer.

———. 2007a. China's export growth and the China safeguard: Threats to the world trading system? Federal Reserve Bank of Chicago Working Paper no. 2004-28. Chicago: Federal Reserve Bank of Chicago, June.

———. 2007b. Trade deflection and trade depression. *Journal of International Economics* 72 (1): 176–201.

Bown, Chad P., and Bernard M. Hoekman. 2008. Making trade agreements relevant for poor countries: Why dispute settlement is not enough. *Journal of World Trade* 42 (1): 177–203.

Bown, Chad P., and Rachel McCulloch. 2004. The WTO agreement on safeguards: An empirical analysis of discriminatory impact. In *Empirical methods in international trade,* ed. Michael G. Plummer, 145–68. Cheltenham, UK: Edward Elgar.

———. 2007. U.S. Trade Policy toward China: Discrimination and Its Implications. In *Challenges to the Global Trading System: Adjustment to Globalization in the Asia Pacific Region,* ed. Sumner La Croix and Peter A. Petri, 58–82. Oxford, UK: Routledge.

Broda, Christian, Nuno Limão, and David E. Weinstein. 2008. Optimal tariffs and market power: The evidence. *American Economic Review,* 98 (5): 2032–65.

Department of Commerce. 2007. Commerce applies anti-subsidy law to China. Press release, March 30, http://www.commerce.gov/opa/press/Secretary_Gutierrez/2007 _Releases/March/30_Gutierrez_China_Anti-subsidy_law_application_rls.html.

Durling, James P., and Thomas J. Prusa. 2006. The trade effects associated with an antidumping epidemic: The hot-rolled steel market, 1996–2001. *European Journal of Political Economy* 22 (3): 675–95.

Feinberg, Robert M., and Kara M. Reynolds. 2007. Tariff liberalization and increased administered protection: Is there a quid pro quo? *The World Economy* 30 (6): 948–61.

Gallaway, Michael P., Bruce A. Blonigen, and Joseph E. Flynn. 1999. Welfare costs of the U.S. antidumping and countervailing duty laws. *Journal of International Economics* 49 (2): 211–44.

GATT. 1987. Negotiating group on safeguards: Work already undertaken in the GATT on safeguards. GATT Document no. MTN.GNG/NG9/W/1. Geneva: GATT. http://www.worldtradelaw.net/history/ursafeguards/W1.pdf.

Greene, William H. 2000. *Econometric analysis.* 4th ed. Upper Saddle River, NJ: Prentice Hall.

Grossman, Gene M., and Elhanan Helpman. 1994. Protection for sale. *American Economic Review* 84 (4): 833–50.

Hansen, Wendy L., and Thomas J. Prusa. 1996. Cumulation and ITC decision-making: The sum of the parts is greater than the whole. *Economic Inquiry* 34 (4): 746–69.

Hoekman, Bernard M., and Michael M. Kostecki. 2001. *The political economy of the world trading system: The WTO and beyond.* 2nd ed. New York: Oxford University Press.

Horn, Henrik, Petros C. Mavroidis, and Håkan Nordström. 2005. Is the use of the WTO dispute settlement system biased? In *The WTO and international trade law/ dispute settlement,* ed. Petros C. Mavroidis and Alan Sykes. Cheltenham, UK: Edward Elgar.

Jung, Youngjin. 2002. China's aggressive legalism: China's first safeguard measure. *Journal of World Trade* 36 (6): 1037–60.

Kennedy, Scott. 2005. China's porous protectionism: The changing political economy of trade policy. *Political Science Quarterly* 120 (3): 407–32.

Knetter, Michael M., and Thomas J. Prusa. 2003. Macroeconomic factors and antidumping filings: Evidence from four countries. *Journal of International Economics* 61 (1): 1–17.

Liu, Xiang, and Hylke Vandenbussche. 2002. European union anti-dumping cases against China: An overview and future prospects with respect to China's World Trade Organization membership. *Journal of World Trade* 36 (6): 1125–44.

Maggi, Giovanni, and Andres Rodriguez-Clare. 1998. The value of trade agreements in the presence of political pressures. *Journal of Political Economy* 106 (3): 574–601.

———. 2007. A political-economy theory of trade agreements. *American Economic Review* 97 (4): 1374–1406.

Mayer, Wolfgang. 1984. Endogenous tariff formation. *American Economic Review* 74 (5): 970–85.

Messerlin, Patrick A. 2004. China in the World Trade Organization: Antidumping and safeguards. *World Bank Economic Review* 18 (1): 105–30.

Moore, Michael O. 2006. U.S. facts-available antidumping decisions: An empirical analysis. *European Journal of Political Economy* 22 (3): 639–52.

Moore, Michael O., and Alan Fox. Forthcoming. Why don't foreign firms cooperate in U.S. antidumping investigations? An empirical analysis. *Weltwirtschaftliches Archiv.*

Prusa, Thomas J. 2001. On the spread and impact of antidumping. *Canadian Journal of Economics* 34 (3): 591–611.

Staiger, Robert W., and Frank A. Wolak. 1994. Measuring industry-specific protection: Antidumping in the United States. *Brookings Papers on Economic Activity, Microeconomics:* 51–118.

World Trade Organization (WTO). 2001. Accession of the People's Republic of China." http://www.wto.org/, document number WT/L/432.

———. 2006. Trade policy review: Report by the secretariat: People's Republic of China—Revision. WTO report no. WT/TPR/S/161/Rev.1, 26 June. http://www.wto.org/.

———. 2007a. AD measures: By reporting member. http://www.wto.org/english/tratop_e/adp_e/adp_stattab7_e.xls.

———. 2007b. AD initiations: By exporting country. http://www.wto.org/english/tratop_e/adp_e/adp_stattab1_e.xls.

———. 2007c. AD initiations: By reporting member. http://www.wto.org/english/tratop_e/adp_e/adp_stattab2_e.xls.

———. 2007d. Statistics on safeguard measures. http://www.wto.org/english/tratop_e/safeg_e/safeg_e.htm.

———. 2007e. Statistics on subsidies and countervailing measures. http://www.wto.org/english/tratop_e/scm_e/scm_e.htm.

Zanaradi, Maurizio. 2004. Antidumping: What are the numbers to discuss at Doha? *The World Economy* 27 (3): 403–33.

Comment   Thomas J. Prusa

Any comprehensive discussion of China's impact on the trading environment should include a discussion of rising protection against Chinese exports and the looming threat of China retaliating with its own intensive use of contingent protection. Chad Bown does a first-rate job of addressing the major trends. I have no reservations recommending this chapter to anyone interested in getting a quick picture of protectionist trends involving China.

Before making some specific comments on Bown's chapter, I would like to take a moment to draw attention to the significant time and effort Bown invested in compiling the trade dispute data set used to write this chapter. Data collection is among the least glamorous aspects of the research process. Moreover, in the case of Bown's database, the fact that most of the benefits of his time and sweat will ultimately accrue to others makes his endeavor even more noteworthy. While the World Trade Organization's (WTO) Web site provides information on trade disputes between member states, the WTO's official listing includes only the most basic case information (e.g., products and countries involved, dates, outcomes, etc.). Bown spearheaded a World Bank effort to compile detailed information on a wide variety of trade disputes—antidumping, countervailing duty, safeguards, and formal WTO disputes—initiated by WTO members.[1] Prior to Bown's efforts, detailed antidumping case information was only available for the European Union (EU) and the United States; there were no public databases for any of the other types of trade disputes or for antidumping actions by other countries. Bown's database gives researchers an opportunity to better understand the incidence and pattern of trade disputes across all WTO members. The current chapter is an example of the type of research that is now possible thanks to Bown's efforts. The database is a tremendous public good, and many of us owe him a debt of gratitude for his efforts.

Turning now to the current chapter, Bown documents a number of important trends in the use of trade remedies against and by China. First, Bown documents the widespread use of antidumping measures against China. Bown shows that China is the leading target on a worldwide basis, accounting for about 20 percent of all the cases reported by the ten most active users of antidumping. China is the leading target for six of the ten most active users in the early period (1995–2001) and for nine of the ten in the later period (2002–2004). Although he does not report China's share of all cases filed worldwide, it is reasonable to believe that the trends reported for these ten countries are representative of the overall worldwide trend because

Thomas J. Prusa is an associate professor of economics at Rutgers University, and a research associate of the National Bureau of Economic Research.

1. See http://people.brandeis.edu/~cbown/global_ad/.

they account for over 80 percent of the new antidumping cases worldwide. Simply put, the data presented confirm what many of us thought: China is in the bulls-eye of trade protection around the world.

Second, it appears that contingent protection against Chinese exports has increased since China joined the WTO. This finding must be carefully interpreted—the important comparison Bown is making is the number of trade cases against China in the post-WTO era versus those in the pre-WTO period. The issue is complicated because China's exports have increased and trade disputes are clearly related the volume of trade. Hence, it is not surprising that there are more antidumping cases filed against China in recent years. Bown's analysis does not tell us whether China has faced more antidumping actions than it would have without WTO membership. That is, we do not know whether WTO membership has failed to discipline the actions of China's trading partners. At first blush, however, Bown's data suggest that WTO membership has done little to reduce the contingent protection applied on Chinese exporters. This is only a modest complaint as an empirical study controlling for the various incentives for industries/countries to name China would be a full paper by itself.

Third, Bown documents the potentially alarming rise in China's own use of contingent protection. In the last five years, China's use of antidumping has tripled; recent trends indicate that China (along with India) will soon be the two largest users of antidumping, displacing the two longtime leaders, the EU and the United States. Bown highlights one interesting difference in China's use of antidumping as compared the United States and the EU: nondiscrimination. That is, Bown shows that China does not often target single suppliers in their antidumping investigations; Chinese cases tend to target multiple suppliers. As I will discuss in the following, this differs from the pattern of protection that China often experiences where Chinese firms are the only exporters targeted. While filing against multiple countries does make protection more MFN-like, it isn't clear that this pattern is preferable. Is it better to have all foreign suppliers facing high duties or only a single supplier? Antidumping proponents will argue that the discriminatory aspect of antidumping duties is desirable—only sanction the "unfair" trader(s). The fact that China is so often targeted does seem problematic, but we need to have a better idea of the motivation for the protection before concluding that discrimination is bad.

One reason why I like Bown's article is that it touches on many issues that can be examined in greater detail in future work. Here are some questions that Bown's chapter stimulated; I hope they are pursued in the near future.

Is China Unfairly Targeted?

Bown's compilations reveal that about 20 percent of all antidumping cases target China. Bown argues China's 20 percent share is unusually large. For instance, in the case of the United States and the EU, China's share of antidumping cases is about twice as large as its share of the respective import market. Similarly large, often significantly larger, differences exist for other major antidumping users. This is true for both the early (1995–2001) and later (2002–2004) periods. For instance, China's share of antidumping cases is about six times larger than its import market share in Argentina, Brazil, India, and Mexico. In the case of Canada and Turkey, China's share of antidumping cases is more than ten times larger than its import market share. Overall and on a country-by-country basis, China is named far more frequently than its import market share might predict.

Moreover, Bown's statistics might be understating the extent to which China has been targeted. The reason is that a given antidumping *investigation* may involve multiple foreign suppliers. In a manner consistent with WTO reporting requirements, countries tally antidumping cases on a country-by-country basis. Thus, one investigation involving seven countries will result in seven cases. Unless one carefully controls for the fact that there is usually a single investigation, it is easy to understate how important China is to current trade disputes. From my perusal of Bown's database, it appears that the vast majority of investigations involve China—to a far greater extent than his tabulations indicate.

Let me give an example of my point. As of early 2008, there were thirty-eight active antidumping cases in the United States, with China accounting for seventeen of the cases.[2] Thus, at first blush, it appears that China is involved in slightly less than half the disputes. However, when one looks at the products involved it becomes clear that these thirty-eight cases actually involve twenty distinct *investigations*. Of these twenty investigations, eight involve just a single foreign supplier, and in all but one instance, the single country investigated is China. Twelve investigations involve multiple suppliers. Of the twelve multiple supplier investigations, China is named ten times. Thus, China is involved in seventeen of twenty active investigations. No other country is named more than three times. Japan—the country that dominated U.S. contingent protection in the 1980s and 1990s, is currently only subject to one investigation. It appears that China really is the country driving the current contingent protection. It would be useful to construct similar tallies for other antidumping users. The issue of an inordinate focus on China might be more severe than Bown suggests.

On the other hand, import market share may not be the right basis to judge whether China is subject to unusual scrutiny. The WTO antidumping code's de minimis standard for import market share is quite small. Technically, all that the WTO requires is China's exporters have at least 3 percent of a country's import market when it is the only country investigated and potentially as little as 0.5 percent when multiple countries are investigated. One would think that this is an easy threshold to meet. Perhaps another

---

2. See www.usitc.gov for U.S. antidumping statistics.

pertinent measure would be China's increase in import market share. In a follow-up study, it would be interesting to see if China has gained significant market share in the years prior to the filing of antidumping actions. My own sense is the answer will be yes.

Does Contingent Protection Discriminate against China?

Bown documents that China is often the only country named in a given antidumping investigation and that the propensity for this to happen has increased since its 2001 accession. He then makes a compelling argument that application of antidumping against China has become *more* discriminatory in recent years. I think this is an excellent insight and one that bears more consideration.

I have several specific follow-up questions. First, while the number of Harmonized System (HS) line items involved in these cases might be quite small, it would be interesting to know how much larger the tariff differentials are for the affected products. How steep is the discrimination? Did China face less discrimination in the pre-WTO era? Second, even in light of what will likely be large differences in tariffs, what is the impact of antidumping actions on Chinese exports? Is the elasticity of Chinese exports to antidumping duties similar to that for other suppliers? Third, are Chinese exports prone to more diversion to third markets? Fourth, if diversion is indeed found, to what extent does one country's use of antidumping trigger others?

How Much Do Current Rules Discriminate against China?

As discussed in the preceding, Bown documents that Chinese firms are often the target of contingent protection. He also shows that (a) a greater fraction of Chinese cases result in measures taken and (b) Chinese cases result in higher duties than others.

On the first point, Bown may understate the difference between China and other countries. Given that China accounts for so many cases, it would have been useful for Bown to report statistics for "all targets but China" rather than "all targets" in table 8.2. To get a sense of why, I took the data reports in table 8.2 and recalculated the percentage of cases resulting in measures. In my tabulation (see table 8C.1), the "others" category means all countries except China. As is clearly seen, China fares far worse than other targets for most major antidumping users. In the United States, for example, for the most recent period, 76 percent of Chinese cases result in duties, which compares with only 33 percent of non-Chinese cases. In the EU, 94 percent of Chinese cases result in measures taken; by contrast, only 48 percent on non-Chinese cases result in measures taken. In India, currently the world's most active antidumping user, 88 percent of Chinese cases and 65 percent on the non-Chinese cases result in duties. Only in the case of South Africa does China fare better than other targets.

The next question is how much do these differences matter? Using these

Table 8C.1   **Fraction of cases resulting in measures taken**

	Early period (1995–2001)		Late period (2002–2004)	
Importer	China	All but China	China	All but China
United States	0.68	0.51	0.76	0.33
European Union	0.53	0.62	0.94	0.48
Australia	0.15	0.31	0.75	0.57
Canada	0.60	0.61	0.71	0.55
Argentina	0.88	0.66	0.83	0.80
Brazil	0.80	0.54	0.67	0.56
India	0.93	0.83	0.88	0.65
Mexico	0.79	0.72	1.00	0.77
South Africa	0.87	0.66	0.20	0.31
Turkey	0.89	0.78	0.91	0.83

statistics, along with the number of cases filed by each country, I estimate that Chinese exporters would be subject to about 25 percent fewer measures if they had the same success rate as non-Chinese firms. Let me stress that this is a back-of-the-envelope calculation and really should be carefully redone control for other mitigating factors. The next step would be to also do an adjustment for the size of the duties imposed and the Chinese export elasticity so as to get a sense of how much trade is affected by the discriminatory application of the rules.

Certainly Bown's chapter makes me wonder why China fares so poorly. One possibility is that current antidumping rules are designed particularly to restrict exporters like China. If so, what rules and do those rules make economic sense? Perhaps, the rules are particularly effective for sanctioning nonmarket economies. If so, how does China compare with, say, Vietnam? Another possibility is that the evolution of discretionary practices emphasized by work by Bruce Blonigen has particularly made matters difficult for the Chinese. Of course, this means Blonigen's insight about U.S. practice has spread to other antidumping users. It would be interesting to see the answers to these questions in future work.

Is China Motivated by Retaliation?

Many antidumping provisions are broadly defined. Depending on your perspective, this is one of its failures or its virtues. What really constitutes injury? How much impact is necessary to satisfy "causation"?

One consequence is that it is often hard to know the true motivation for not just a particular dispute but also for a change in policy application. For many users, there appears to be some evidence that countries are filing cases with strategic incentives in mind. Bown has a fine paper exploring this idea, and I have also written on this idea. In this case of China, public statements by government officials have explicitly mentioned that they view their own use of antidumping as partly motivated by retaliation for what they perceive as unjust application by other countries. It would be an interesting to see whether there is any statistical evidence for this or whether Chinese officials are simply making vague threats.

Overall, my comments point to future work rather than any particular shortcomings with the analysis in this chapter. I think Bown provides an excellent summary and overview of trade protection against and by China since the inception of the WTO in 1995. The data and analysis contained in the Bown article will serve as an excellent reference for many graduate students, researchers, and policymakers in the future.

China's Experience under the Multi-Fiber Arrangement (MFA) and the Agreement on Textiles and Clothing (ATC)

Irene Brambilla, Amit K. Khandelwal, and Peter K. Schott

9.1 Introduction

On January 1, 2005, restrictions on the fourth and final set of textile and clothing products regulated by the Agreement on Textile and Clothing (ATC), the successor of the Multi-Fiber Arrangement (MFA), were removed. The gradual expiration of these quotas starting in 1995 ended decades of bilateral nontariff-barrier protection in this industry and set the stage for a substantial reallocation of production and exports across countries. Though many analysts expected China's share of the United States' textile and clothing (T&C) imports to rise when the ATC expired in 2005, predictions varied widely.[1] In fact, China's overall T&C export quantities to the United States increased 39 percent in 2005, with exports of goods whose quotas were relaxed in the beginning of that year jumping 270 percent.

Irene Brambilla is an assistant professor of economics at Yale University, and a faculty research fellow of the National Bureau of Economic Research. Amit K. Khandelwal is an assistant professor of economics and finance at the Columbia Graduate School of Business. Peter K. Schott is a professor of economics at Yale School of Management, and a research associate of the National Bureau of Economic Research

Special thanks to Ronald Foote of the U.S. Census Bureau and Ross Arnold and Keith Daly of the U.S. Office of Textiles and Apparel (OTEXA). Schott thanks the National Science Foundation (SES-0241474 and SES-0550190) for research support. We thank Judy Dean, Joseph Francois, James Harrigan and especially Rob Feenstra for helpful comments and suggestions. Excellent research assistance was provided by Matthew Flagge and Rocky Huarng. Any opinions, findings, and conclusions or recommendations expressed in this material are those of the author and do not necessarily reflect the views of the National Science Foundation.

1. For example, the computational general equilibrium (CGE) study by Rivera, Agama, and Dean (2003) predicted that China's textile and apparel exports would increase between 8 and 104 percent, respectively, following the elimination of quotas in developed countries. Nordas (2004) predicted that China's post-MFA/ATC textile and clothing market share in the United States would increase by 7 and 34 percentage points, respectively. Diao and Somwaru (2001) estimated a more moderate growth of 6 percent in Chinese T&C exports to the world.

This paper uses a new data set of U.S. import quotas to examine China's relative performance in the U.S. market under the ATC. Our analysis reveals that China's T&C exports to the United States were relatively restrained along three dimensions. First, China's quotas were more likely to be binding than the quotas imposed on other countries. Second, China's quotas grew at a slower rate than the quotas of most other countries. Finally, the United States appears to have placed relatively greater restrictions on China's ability to shift quota allocations across different categories of goods or across years.

China's rapid increase in U.S. market share as quotas were relaxed came at the expense of both domestic manufacturers and the United States' other trading partners. We show that T&C exports from virtually all countries decreased in 2005, and that for some regions, for example, sub-Saharan Africa, these declines represented an abrupt reversal of several years of previously robust T&C export growth. These reversals suggest that, over time, the MFA and ATC had evolved from a regime intended to protect domestic U.S. manufacturers into one that also guaranteed smaller developing countries access to the U.S. market. Among developing countries, only those from South Asia managed to defend market share in the face of substantial Chinese growth, but even South Asia's response was not uniform across products.

The T&C quotas under the ATC were relaxed in four phases. Though China's response to the final phase of reductions was dramatic, it was predictable given China's reaction to earlier quota relaxations, particularly when one focuses on goods for which China's quotas were binding. China, being outside the WTO, was ineligible for the first two phases of quota reductions in 1995 and 1998. After joining the WTO in December 2001, its quotas on these goods, as well as its quotas on Phase III goods, were lifted simultaneously in January 2002.

The four panels of figure 9.1 trace out China's U.S. exports of T&C goods according to the phase in which quotas were relaxed. *Solid* lines track the evolution of total exports, while *dashed* lines report China's exports in goods whose quotas were binding the year before removal. The years along the x-axis in each panel notes the year in which China's quotas in each set of goods were relaxed. As indicated in the figure, China's exports of Phase I and II goods increased relatively modestly after quota removal (42 and 32 percent, respectively) compared with Phase III and Phase IV goods (305 and 271 percent, respectively). China's response in previously bound goods, by contrast, was substantially larger across the three Phases—II, III, and IV—in which goods faced binding quotas, increasing 825, 322, and 330 percent, respectively. As we document in the following, China's Phase IV growth in 2005 appears to have had an especially large and negative impact on nearly all regions' exports that year.

Examination of export price changes under the ATC suggests a realloca-

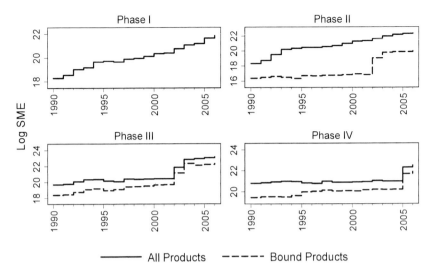

Fig. 9.1   China's T&C exports, by phase

Notes: Bound products are those with > 90 percent fill rates one year prior to integration. Log scale approximates actual percentage changes. Years along the x-axis display the year in which quotas on the noted goods are phased out.

tion of exports within as well as across countries as quotas were relaxed. We find the removal of quotas to be accompanied by large declines in export unit values across all U.S. trading partners. In the final phase, China's unit values in unbound versus bound products fell 31 and 41 percent, respectively. These declines, as well, were anticipated by previous phases of liberalization. Consistent with models of quality upgrading in response to quantitative restrictions, we also document evidence of relative quality downgrading within China's Phase IV products as their quotas were lifted.

The remainder of this paper is organized as follows. In section 9.2 we briefly summarize the MFA and ATC regimes. Section 9.3 provides a detailed description of the contents of the U.S. MFA/ATC database constructed for this paper. Sections 9.4, 9.5, and 9.6 examine countries' quantity and unit value responses to quota relaxation. Section 9.7 concludes.

9.2   The MFA and the ATC

The MFA grew out of a series of voluntary export restraints imposed, initially, by the United States on Japanese textile exports in 1955. By the end of the 1950s, the United Kingdom also began to limit imports from Hong Kong, India, and Pakistan (Spinanger 1999). Quotas on cotton textiles and apparel products were first institutionalized with the Short-Term Arrangement in 1961, which was extended to two subsequent Long-Term Arrangements throughout the 1960s and early 1970s. As the Asian economies' textile and apparel production continued to grow, developed countries sought a more systematic mechanism to deal with "market disruptions" in other fiber markets. This search lead to the signing of the MFA, in 1974, which, although "temporary" at first, ultimately lead to an additional thirty years of protection. As a result of the MFA, T&C products were kept out of multilateral trade negotiations under the General Agreement on Tariffs and Trade (GATT) and its successor, the World Trade Organization (WTO).[2]

A major development of the Uruguay Round was the signing of the Agreement on Textile and Clothing (ATC) in 1994. The ATC ended the MFA and began the process of integrating textile and clothing products into GATT/WTO rules by removing their quotas. Integration occurred over the four phases outlined in table 9.1. During each phase, importing countries were to integrate a portion of all T&C products covered by the ATC. The particular products integrated in each phase were importing-country specific but subject to two rules. First, the products retired in each phase had to include goods from all four major textile and clothing segments, that is, Yarn, Fabrics, Made-Up textile products (e.g., table linen, carpets, and curtains), and Clothing. Second, the chosen products had to represent a set portion of each country's 1990 T&C imports, by volume. In Phase I, which began on January 1, 1995, countries had to integrate products representing 16 percent of their 1990 import volumes. An additional 17 and 18 percent of 1990 export volumes were integrated at the beginning of Phases II and III on January 1, 1998, and January 1, 2002, respectively. Finally, on January 1, 2005, Phase IV of the ATC culminated in the integration of the remaining 49 percent of export volumes, and all quotas were abolished.

Perhaps unsurprisingly given countries' ability to choose which quotas to retire in each phase, quotas removed during the first two phases of the ATC were, in general, not very painful for producers in developed countries. In the United States, ATC products accounted for 17.1 billion square meter equivalents (SME) worth of imports in 1990.[3] However, U.S. imports of products actually subject to quotas in that year totaled just 12.2 billion SMEs (United States International Trade Commission [USITC] 2004). As a result, the United States found it relatively easy to defer removal of quotas on "sensitive" products until the third phase. Products such as tents and life jackets, for example, were included in the ATC but had not been subject to U.S. import quotas. The United States integrated these products in the first phase. As indicated in the final column of table 9.1, the United States retired a total of 4,875 ten-digit Harmonized System (HS) product codes across the four phases, of which 62 percent were retired in 2005. In this paper, these

2. For a more extensive discussions of the road to the ATC, see Spinanger (1999) and Francois and Woerz (2006).

3. Product quotas under the MFA and ATC were set in terms of SME, with each product having an explicit "conversion factor" to determine the SME of their native units (e.g., pairs of socks). Examples of SME are provided in table 9.4.

Table 9.1   **Agreement on Textiles and Clothing (ATC) integration schedule**

Phase	Starting date	Share of export volume integrated	Increase in quota growth rate	No. of HS products integrated
I	January 1, 1995	16	16	318
II	January 1, 1998	17	25	744
III	January 1, 2002	18	27	745
IV	January 1, 2005	49	n.a.	2,978

Source: OTEXA.

Notes: Table describes the four phases of the ATC and quotas. The first three columns describe aspects of the ATC that were common to all signatories. The final column reports the integration of products as implemented by the United States. Quota growth acceleration was advanced one phase for countries with less than 1.2 percent of the importing country's total quotas in 1991. HS = Harmonized System. n.a. = not applicable.

4,875 HS codes are our definition of the set of T&C products imported by the United States and governed by the ATC.[4]

In addition to gradually removing quotas, the ATC improved developing countries' access to developed-country markets by accelerating quota growth over the four phases of quota removal. These changes were governed by what is referred to as the ATC's "growth-on-growth" provision and are summarized in the third column of table 9.1. At the beginning of Phase I, existing quota growth rates were accelerated 16 percent per year, while they were accelerated by 25 and 27 percent in Phases II and III, respectively. A group with a base quota growth rate of 6 percent in 1994, for example, would grow at 6.96 percent (0.06×1.16) per year during Phase I, 8.7 percent (0.0696×1.25) per year over Phase II, and 11.05 (0.087×1.27) percent per year during Phase III.[5]

China's exclusion from the WTO prior to 2001 rendered it ineligible for ATC integration benefits during its first two phases. After China was admitted formally into the WTO on December 11, 2001, the United States removed its quotas on China's Phase I and II imports simultaneously with the quotas on its Phase III goods on the scheduled Phase III removal date, that is, January 1, 2002. After WTO accession, China also received growth rate increases consistent with the ATC.[6]

As part of its entry into the WTO, China agreed to special safeguard provisions, subject to "consultations," that would limit its exports to countries experiencing market disruptions after the ATC was phased out. Under the guidelines governing China's accession into the WTO, WTO members

4. We are grateful to Keith Daly at OTEXA for providing us with this list.
5. Quota growth acceleration was advanced one phase for countries with less than 1.2 percent of the importing country's total quotas in 1991.
6. China's growth rates were increased by 27 percent plus an additional prorated increase to account for its three weeks of WTO membership in 2001 (USITC 2004).

could enter negotiations for new safeguards on Chinese products provided those countries could show evidence of the existence or threat of a market disruption and a role for Chinese goods in that disruption (WTO 2001). The safeguard provision was applicable until December 31, 2008.[7]

When quotas on the final set of products expired on January 1, 2005, domestic textile and apparel industry groups successfully lobbied for new safeguards against China on twenty-two MFA groups of products, and they remained effective until the end of 2008. However, the United States and China reached a memorandum of understanding that the United States would "exercise restraint" on additional safeguards. Table 9.2 lists the quota levels that were operative until 2008.

9.3   The U.S. MFA/ATC Database

This section describes our construction of the U.S. MFA/ATC database and summarizes its contents. The database is assembled from U.S. trading partners' Expired Performance Reports, which were used by the U.S. Office of Textile and Apparel (OTEXA) to monitor trading partners' compliance with the MFA and ATC quotas. Generously provided by Ron Foote of the U.S. Census Bureau, they document imports, base quotas, and quota adjustments (defined in the following) by groups of products (referred to as "MFA groups") and years for all countries with which the United States negotiated bilateral quota arrangements. The database covers 1984 to 2004.[8]

Between 1984 and 2004, the United States signed bilateral MFA/ATC agreements with the seventy-one countries listed in table 9.3. Seven of these countries—Barbados, Canada, Lebanon, Pacific Islands, Portugal, Spain, and Trinidad and Tobago—were not subject to what is known as "specific limits," the most restrictive quota classification and the focus of our analysis (see the following discussion). The details of an agreement were negotiated over an "agreement term," which typically lasted several "agreement periods." For most countries, an agreement period corresponded to a full calendar year.[9] The United States negotiated quotas on 149 three-digit MFA specific-limit groups; on average, each group contains seventeen HS products. The MFA groups span four T&C "segments": Yarn, Fabric, Made-Ups, and Clothing. Examples of MFA groups in each segment are provided in table 9.4.

Quotas were negotiated on individual MFA groups as well as on both

---

7. For additional details regarding the post-ATC Chinese safeguards, see Dayaratna-Banda and Whalley (2007).

8. Data for 1986 are missing. Refinement of the raw data is discussed in a technical appendix available from the authors on request.

9. For some countries, including Brazil, Indonesia, and Sri Lanka, the agreement period in early years covered overlapping calendar years. All periods were standardized to match the calendar year under the ATC.

Table 9.2   Chinese quotas under safeguards, 2006–2008, by Mult-Fiber Arrangement (MFA) category

	Unit	2004 quota	2005 exports	2006 quota	2007 quota	2008 quota
200 Yarns and sewing thread[a]	kg	939,116	n.a.	n.a.	n.a.	n.a.
300/301 Carded and combed cotton yarn[a]	kg	2,671,428	n.a.	n.a.	n.a.	n.a.
200/301[a]	kg		6,949,753	7,529,582	8,832,199	10,131,052
222 Knit fabric	kg	10,619,328	18,145,812	15,966,487	18,728,689	21,482,908
229 Special purpose fabric[b]	kg		29,001,226	33,162,019	39,237,301	45,007,492
332/432/632 Hosiery[c]	dpr	42,433,990	58,230,777	n.a.	n.a.	n.a.
332/432/632-B Baby socks[c]	dpr			61,146,461	71,724,800	80,866,195
332/432/632-T Baby socks[c]	dpr			64,386,841	75,443,136	85,058,437
338/339 Cotton knitted shirts and blouses	doz	2,523,532	20,624,490	20,822,111	23,893,373	26,938,606
340/640 Men's and boys' woven shirts	doz	2,345,946	6,173,242	6,743,644	7,738,332	8,724,590
345/645/646 Sweaters	doz	1,030,348	7,850,557	8,179,211	9,477,660	10,581,854
347/348 Cotton trousers	doz	2,421,922	18,379,851	19,666,049	22,566,791	25,442,951
349/649 Brassieres	doz	17,729,479	20,717,107	22,785,906	26,146,827	29,479,266
352/652 Underwear	doz	5,276,745	18,175,964	18,948,937	21,957,081	24,302,011
359-S/659-S Swimwear	kg	750,959	5,951,219	4,590,626	5,267,743	5,990,767
363 Cotton terry towels	no	24,773,109	87,842,008	103,300,000	118,600,000	134,828,519
443 Men's and boys' wool suits	no	140,015	1,613,356	1,346,082	1,544,629	1,756,637
447 Men's and boys' wool trousers	doz	76,352	203,332	215,004	246,718	280,581
619 Polyester filament fabric[b]	m2		60,348,016	55,308,506	63,466,510	72,177,600
620 Other synthetic filament fabric[b]	m2		83,531,558	80,197,248	92,026,342	103,755,190
622 Glass fabric[b]	m2		30,274,778	32,265,013	37,846,860	43,412,575

(continued)

Table 9.2 (continued)

	Unit	2004 quota	2005 exports	2006 quota	2007 quota	2008 quota
638/639 MMF knitted shirts and blouses	doz	2,712,680	3,762,225	8,060,063	9,248,922	10,427,707
647/648 MMF trousers	doz	2,974,238	6,490,061	7,960,355	9,134,507	10,298,709
666 Window blinds/window shades	kg	573,372	0	964,014	1,106,206	1,268,884
847 Silk blend and other vegetable fiber trousers[b]	doz		15,714,461	17,647,255	20,250,225	23,029,668

Source: Authors' calculations from the trade data and OTEXA.

Notes: Table reports the safeguards imposed on Chinese products in 2005.

[a]In 2004, quotas were placed on MFA 200 and the group MFA 300/301. In 2006, quotas were reimposed on MFA 200 and MFA 301 to reflect a new group category, MFA 200/301. Using the footnotes in the Office of Textile and Apparel (OTEXA) expired performance reports, we aggregated 2005 exports to reflect this new group and denote 2005–2008 exports and quotas within 200 and 300/301 with "n.a."

[b]No specific limit quotas in 2004.

[c]In 2004, quotas were applied on MFA group 332/432/632, and in 2006, quotas were imposed on two new group categories, 332/432/632-B and 332/432/632-T. We were unable determine if the quota levels for these two new MFA groups reflect an aggregate quota or not, so we report the 2006–2008 figures for 332/432/632-B and 332/432/632-T as reported in the official OTEXA documents, and denote 2006–2008 quotas for 332/432/632 with "n.a." For 2005 exports, we aggregate the exports from MFA 332, 432, and 632 using the trade data and the Harmonized System-MFA concordance described in the text.

Table 9.3   **List of countries in U.S. Multi-Fiber Arrangement/Agreement on Textiles and Clothing database**

Argentina	Dominican Republic	Kenya	Oman	Sri Lanka
Bahrain	Egypt	Korea, South	Pacific Islands[a]	Taiwan
Bangladesh	El Salvador	Kuwait	Pakistan	Thailand
Barbados[a]	Fiji	Laos	Panama	Trinidad and Tobago[a]
Belarus	Germany, East	Lebanon[a]	Peru	Turkey
Brazil	Guam	Lesotho	Philippines, The	Ukraine
Bulgaria	Guatemala	Macau	Poland	United Arab Emirates
Burma	Haiti	Macedonia	Portugal[a]	Uruguay
Cambodia	Honduras	Malaysia	Qatar	USSR
Canada[a]	Hong Kong	Maldive Islands	Romania	Vietnam
China	Hungary	Mauritius	Russia	Yugoslavia
Colombia	India	Mexico	Singapore	
Costa Rica	Indonesia	Nepal	Slovak Republic	
Czech Republic	Jamaica	Nigeria	South Africa	
Czechoslovakia	Japan	Northern Mariana	Spain[a]	

Note: Table displays the set of countries with which the United States negotiated quantitative restrictions on apparel and textile imports between 1984 and 2004.
[a]Countries not subject to specific limits (see text).

aggregations and subsets of groups, which are known as "merged" and "part" groups, respectively. As a result, country-year-group observations in the database actually encompass a mixture of groups, merged groups, and part groups. For simplicity, we refer to all of these observations as being at the "group" level for the remainder of the paper.

The negotiated quota for any particular group is stated in terms of SME of fabric. To pool potentially diverse groups with different native units—for example, pairs of gloves and dozens of shirts—the ATC established "conversion factors" to concord native units into SME. These conversion factors are used to aggregate base quotas and import levels and to provide a means of shifting quotas across groups with different units (e.g., shirts to socks).

The Expired Performance Reports refer to nine possible classifications of negotiated quantities. In this paper, we focus exclusively on "specific limit" quotas, which, according to OTEXA, were the most restrictive quotas used under the MFA/ATC. The other classifications are designated consultation levels, minimum consultation levels, other groups, restraint limits, guaranteed access levels, designated consultation provisions, agreed limits, and tariff preference levels. Several of these designations are not actually quotas, but rather served as watch lists. Their application is noted in the MFA/ATC database.[10]

10. For some countries, there was another layer of quotas known as "aggregate group limits." A specific limit was a group-specific quota, while the group limit imposed an aggregate quota over several MFA groups. A group could, therefore, be bound by a specific limit (individual, merged, or part), subject to an aggregate specific limit, or both. One potential explanation for aggregate limits is that it limited the use of flexibilities across MFA groups (see the following). We ignore these aggregate limits in this paper, but they are available in the MFA/ATC database.

Table 9.4   **Sample Office of Textile and Apparel category descriptions**

MFA group description	Segment	Unit	Square meter conversion
218 Yarns of different colors (cotton and/or man-made fiber)	Yarn	sqm	1
219 Duck fabric (cotton and/or man-made fiber)	Yarn	sqm	1
606 Non-textured filament yarn (man-made fiber)	Yarn	kg	20.1
621 Impression fabric (man-made fiber)	Fabric	kg	14.4
628 Twills/sateens staple/filament fiber (man-made fiber)	Fabric	sqm	1
629 Other fabrics of staple/filament fiber (man-made fiber)	Fabric	sqm	1
348 Women's and girls' trousers, breeches, and shorts (cotton)	Apparel	doz	14.9
350 Robes, dressing gowns, etc. (cotton)	Apparel	doz	42.6
431 Gloves and mittens (wool)	Apparel	dpr	1.8
433 Men's and boys' suit-type coats (wool)	Apparel	doz	30.1
836 Dresses (silk or non-cotton vegetable fibers)	Apparel	doz	37.9
362 Bedspreads and quilts (cotton)	Made-ups	no	5.8
464 Blankets (wool)	Made-ups	kg	2.4
465 Floor coverings (wool)	Made-ups	sqm	1
665 Floor coverings (man-made fiber)	Made-ups	sqm	1

Source: U.S. Multi-Fiber Arrangement/Agreement on Textiles and Clothing database.

Note: Examples of Multi-Fiber Arrangement (MFA) groups, native units, and the conversion factors to square meters.

Specific quotas grew at fixed, known rates over an agreement term. Overall, they grew an average of 6 percent per year, but growth varied across countries and groups. China, for example, faced annual specific quota growth rates of 1 to 2 percent, and wool products experienced slower growth than cotton goods.[11]

The U.S. MFA/ATC database records the "base" quota, the "adjusted base" quota, and the total exports for each specific limit by country and year. The base quota is the originally negotiated quota level determined at the start of an agreement term. Adjusted base quotas reflect the use of what are known as "flexibilities," which allowed countries to exceed their base quota in a given period by borrowing unused base quota, up to a specified percentage of the receiving group, across groups within a year and across years within a group. Countries could apply multiple flexibilities on a group, and the adjustments had to be met by corresponding offsets in the lending groups.

There were three major flexibilities:

1. *Carryforward and carryforward-used:* A carryforward allowed countries to borrow base quota from the subsequent period within a group. A carryforward-used offset a carryforward. For example, in 1997 Macau car-

11. We include only specific-limit groups in our examination of fill rates in the following. In our regression analysis, nonspecific limit groups are treated as unbound; the regressions include all T&C HS codes from all T&C exporters.

ried forward 20,419 SME in group 338 ("Men/boys knit shirts"). The flexibility was then offset in 1998, under a carryforward-used, by –20,419 SME. Borrowing was subject to a country-product-specific upper bound.

2. *Carryover and shortfall-used:* A carryover utilized unused quota from the previous period within a group, subject to a country-product-specific maximum. A shortfall-used offset a carryover.

3. *Shift-add, shift-subtract, swing:* Shift-add, shift-subtract, and swings allowed across-group base movements within a year, subject to limits.

After accounting for all flexibilities, the adjusted base quota for a given year reflects the country-group deviation in that year from the original base quota. For example, China's 2002 base quota for group 219 ("duck fabric") was 2.6 million SME. China made two adjustments on this group that year. First, it borrowed 2 percent from the previous year's unused quota (carryover). Second, it added 5 percent of its original base quota from another group (swing). These adjustments resulted in an adjusted base quota of 2.8 million SME for group 219 in 2002. If a country made no adjustment on a group, the adjusted base quota simply remained at the base quota.

Table 9.5 compares countries' aggregate adjusted base quotas and exports across all groups from 1984 to 2004. Results are reported for the thirty countries with the largest aggregate adjusted base quotas. As indicated in the first two columns of the table, China, Taiwan, and Hong Kong exhibit the highest levels of both adjusted base quota and exports between 1984 and 2004. The final column of table 9.5 reports countries' aggregate "fill rates," which equal exports as a percentage of adjusted base quota. Although adjusted base quotas can exceed base quotas, fill rates cannot exceed 100 because they are defined as exports over adjusted base. As indicated in table 9.5, Bangladesh, China, Indonesia, Pakistan, India, and Sri Lanka all exhibit aggregate fill rates in excess of 80 percent over the sample period. Countries with relatively low fill rates include Jamaica, Guatemala, Colombia, and Honduras.

Fill rates provide a useful indication of quota restrictiveness. We follow the USITC (and Evans and Harrigan 2005) in defining a binding quota as one in which the fill rate exceeds 90 percent. Here, too, results are reported for the thirty countries with the largest base quota. As indicated in table 9.6, Bangladesh, India, and China exhibited the largest share of binding quotas over the sample period, in each case above 60 percent. We note that using a more liberal or conservative definition for binding quotas, that is, fill rates of 80 and 95 percent, respectively, does not result in any substantial reranking of counties in terms of which are most constrained over the sample period.

Interestingly, we find that less than 30 percent of the quotas were binding for other major developing East Asian economies such as South Korea, Taiwan, and Malaysia. Thus, even though these countries were subject to a relatively large fraction of specific limits (see table 9.7), these limits appear

Table 9.5   **Total specific limit fill rates, top 30 countries**

Country	Adjusted base quota (SME)	Export (SME)	Fill rate (%)
China	28.4	24.9	88
Taiwan	26.3	16.6	63
Hong Kong	22.8	17.1	75
Korea, South	21.3	13.3	63
Turkey	13.0	5.7	44
Pakistan	12.4	10.3	84
Malaysia	11.0	3.8	35
Thailand	11.0	6.9	63
Indonesia	10.3	8.8	85
Philippines, The	9.6	6.9	72
India	8.4	7.3	87
Bangladesh	8.0	7.0	88
Egypt	7.1	1.9	27
Brazil	6.9	2.4	35
Sri Lanka	5.4	4.4	81
Singapore	3.8	1.6	43
Mexico	3.0	1.2	39
Macau	2.8	1.9	69
Dominican Republic	2.6	1.7	66
Romania	1.9	0.4	21
United Arab Emirates	1.8	1.1	60
Japan	1.6	1.0	61
Jamaica	1.5	0.3	20
Colombia	1.5	0.2	10
Honduras	1.3	0.3	25
Mauritius	1.1	0.5	44
Costa Rica	1.1	0.6	51
Guatemala	0.9	0.7	73
Poland	0.9	0.1	13
Cambodia	0.9	0.8	85

Source: Authors' calculations from U.S. Multi-Fiber Arrangement/Agreement on Textiles and Clothing database.

Notes: Quantities are in billions of square meters. SME = square meter equivalents. Data for specific limits only. Percentage fill rate is exports divided by base quota. Countries sorted by aggregate base quota under the Multi-Fiber Arrangement/Agreement on Textiles and Clothing.

to have been relatively weak. This outcome may be driven in part by these countries' relatively fast movement into more sophisticated manufactures over the sample period. Indeed, we show in the next section that the share of East Asian observations with binding quotas diminishes over time.

Heterogeneity in fill rates is also apparent across MFA groups. Table 9.8 reports aggregate fill rates for the ten largest MFA groups. Trousers and knit shirts are the most constrained groups, with exporters filling more than 80 percent of the allocated quota. Textile groups such as cotton sheeting fab-

Table 9.6   **Top 30 countries in terms of binding quotas, 1984–2004 (%)**

| | Binding Quotas | | |
Country	Liberal definition	Default definition	Conservative definition
Bangladesh	89	81	75
India	76	65	57
China	72	64	55
Indonesia	73	59	50
Pakistan	67	57	47
Guatemala	67	45	32
Hong Kong	52	42	34
Macau	52	41	32
United Arab Emirates	48	39	28
Philippines, The	53	37	30
Sri Lanka	50	36	27
Thailand	51	36	25
Cambodia	42	32	28
Korea, South	42	30	19
Taiwan	43	30	21
Dominican Republic	50	29	17
Malaysia	32	23	16
Singapore	29	22	15
Costa Rica	36	21	12
Turkey	22	18	15
Colombia	26	18	11
Mauritius	18	14	11
Brazil	16	12	8
Romania	16	11	8
Mexico	16	9	7
Egypt	12	9	6
Poland	14	8	5
Japan	10	7	3
Jamaica	5	2	1
Honduras	0	0	0

Source: Authors' calculations from U.S. Multi-fiber Arrangement/Agreement on Textiles and Clothing database.

Note: Table reports the fraction of specific limits with fill rates that exceed 80, 90, and 95 percent, respectively.

ric and cotton poplin exhibited fill rates around 50 percent. The database reveals that the (weighted) average fill rate across all years and exporters for textile groups was only 48 percent compared to 72 percent for apparel groups. These fill rates are consistent with research showing that developed countries apply greater protection to industries where escaping competition from developing countries is harder. Khandelwal (2007), for example, argues that it is harder for developed economies to differentiate their products in terms of quality in apparel versus textiles.

Table 9.7   Fraction of specific limits, top 30 countries (%)

Country	Fraction of specific limits
China	61
Korea, South	53
Taiwan	51
Hong Kong	46
Indonesia	42
Thailand	41
Malaysia	39
Mexico	38
Sri Lanka	38
Romania	33
Philippines, The	31
Japan	31
Pakistan	25
Turkey	25
India	22
Macau	22
Brazil	22
Poland	22
Singapore	21
United Arab Emirates	20
Bangladesh	20
Mauritius	18
Cambodia	17
Dominican Republic	16
Jamaica	15
Egypt	9
Colombia	6
Guatemala	4
Costa Rica	4
Honduras	4

Source: Authors' calculations from U.S. Multi-fiber Arrangement/Agreement on Textiles and Clothing database.

Notes: The table reports the fraction of Multi-Fiber Arrangement groups exported by the country that were subject to specific limits from 1990–2004. The table lists the thirty countries with the largest aggregate base quotas.

Table 9.8 also shows that while there is heterogeneity in aggregate fill rates across products, China's fill rates exhibited substantially less variation: in all but two of the ten groups, China's fill rates exceeded 90 percent. The third and fourth columns of table 9.8 report Bangladesh's and India's fill rates in the major groups. Although Bangladesh was bound in the apparel groups, the United States did not impose specific limits on Bangladesh in the major textile groups, even though Bangladesh exported these products (with the exception of cotton yarns [300/301]). India's fill rates varied widely in the ten groups and was not subject to quotas for underwear, man-made fiber knit shirts, and man-made fiber sweaters.

Table 9.8   **Fill rates by Office of Textile and Apparel category, top 10 categories**

MFA group/Description	Fill rate (%)	China's fill rate (%)	Bangladesh's fill rate (%)	India's fill rate (%)	Base quota (SME)
300/301 Cotton yarns	54	52		12	7.2
313 Cotton sheeting fabric	50	93		70	8.6
314 Cotton poplin/ broadcloth fabric	51	95		54	4.8
315 Cotton printcloth fabric	67	97		75	8.0
340/640[a] Non-knit shirts	69	99	64	99	12.8
347/348 Cotton trousers	83	99	99	98	10.3
352/652[a] Underwear	77	85	97		8.6
638/639 Man-made fiber knit shirts	83	98	96		9.5
645/646 Man-made fiber sweaters	55	95	92		7.9
647/648[a] Man-made fiber trousers	80	99	100	93	8.5

Source: Authors' calculations from U.S. Multi-Fiber Arrangement/Agreement on Textiles and Clothing database.

Notes: Table reports the average fill rates for the twenty largest Multi-Fiber Arrangement (MFA) groups. Quantities are in billions of square meters. SME = square meter equivalents.

[a]China's quotas were negotiated on the subgroups.

9.4   The Relative Restrictiveness of U.S. T&C Quotas

In this section, we demonstrate the relative restrictiveness of China's quotas in terms of the number of goods subject to quotas, how quickly quotas were allowed to grow, and the extent to which China was allowed to shift quota allocations across products and time.

9.4.1   Quota Coverage, Fill Rates, and ETEs

The share of a country's MFA groups that are covered by specific limits provides one measure of cross-country variation in quota restrictiveness. Table 9.7 reports these shares for the major T&C exporters in the pooled 1990 to 2004 data set.[12] As indicated in the table, China, at 61 percent, exhibits the highest share of exports covered by specific limits between 1990 and 2004. Shares for other large Asian exporters are 53 percent for Korea, 51 percent for Taiwan, and 46 percent for Hong Kong. By comparison, just 20 percent of India's MFA groups were subject to specific limits.

---

12. We match the quota data to U.S. import data using a concordance HS-MFA group concordance provided by OTEXA. We have not yet processed the concordance mapping MFA groups to the Tariff Schedule of the United States (TSUSA), which would allow an analysis of U.S. T&C imports for earlier years.

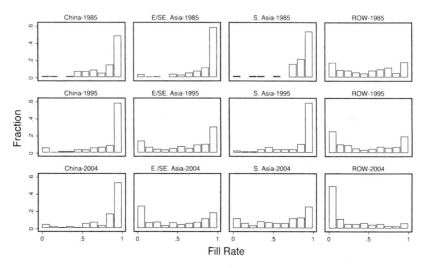

Fig. 9.2   Fill rates by region, 1984–2004

Fill rates, discussed in the preceding, are a second measure of quota restrictiveness. As reported in table 9.5, many countries, particularly those in South Asia, exhibited aggregate fill rates over the pooled sample period that are similar to those experienced by China. Fill rates, however, varied substantially over time, as can be seen in figure 9.2, which reports the distribution of fill rates for China and three regions—East/Southeast (E/SE) Asia, South Asia, and the rest of world (ROW)—which, together, comprise all other countries in the sample.[13] Distributions are reported for three cross-sections, 1985, 1995, and 2004. Each row and column of the figure contains histograms for a different year and region, respectively. In each histogram, the last bin reports the share of binding quotas (i.e., those with fill rates exceeding 90 percent). As indicated in the last three columns of the figure, countries in East/Southeast Asia, South Asia, and ROW experienced more-or-less steady declines in binding quotas over the two decades. East/Southeast Asia's binding quotas, for example, drop from 60 percent in 1985 to less than 20 percent in 2004, while the fraction for South Asia decline from 60 and 70 percent in 1985 and 1995, respectively, to 30 percent in 2004.[14] China's distribution of fill rates, on the other hand, remained essentially constant over the sample period. This evidence suggests that China's T&C

13. The East/Southeast Asian countries are Cambodia, Hong Kong, Indonesia, South Korea, Laos, Macau, Malaysia, The Philippines, Singapore, Taiwan, Thailand, and Vietnam. The South Asian countries are Bangladesh, India, Maldive Islands, Nepal, Pakistan, and Sri Lanka.
14. The distributions reported in figure 9.2 exclude phased-out MFA groups, that is, the figure displays the distributions of fill rates among quotas still applied to the countries.

exports to the United States remained relatively constrained throughout the MFA and ATC. China's fraction of binding quotas, coupled with the relatively high extensive-margin constraint described in the preceding, provide the first two pieces of evidence that China faced a tighter quota regime compared to other countries.

Andriamananjara, Dean, and Spinanger (2004) argue that the price wedge created by the quota rents is a better measure of how tightly a quota binds than its fill rate.[15] The origin of these price wedges and the degree to which they can be observed varies by country. While some countries, such as Hong Kong, created secondary markets to freely trade license permits, others allocated licenses based on various criteria. China's quotas, for example, were managed by its Ministry of Foreign Trade and Economic Cooperation (MOFTEC). The Ministry of Foreign Trade and Economic Cooperation auctioned off only a small share of the quotas available under the MFA. The rest were distributed to firms according to measures of past performance including: their ability to fill at least 90 percent of their previous quotas, their ability to export other products not subject to constraints, and their ability to improve the quality of their exports (Yang 1995).

One way to measure the price wedge created by quota rents is to compute quotas' export tax equivalents (ETEs). Under a perfectly competitive T&C market, the ETE of a quota depends on the prices of quota licenses:

$$(1) \qquad \text{ETE}_{cmt} = \frac{l_{cmt}}{uv_{cmt} - l_{cmt}},$$

where l_{cmt} is the license price paid by the firms in country c in order to export products in MFA group m at time t (measured in dollars per SME), and uv_{cmt} is the free-on-board unit value.

We find that fill rates and estimated ETEs are roughly consistent in indicating the extent to which China's exports face a binding quota. Using data on Chinese export license prices available for a subset of MFA groups from 1999 to 2004, we compute the ETEs of U.S. import quotas on Chinese products for these groups.[16] As indicated in table 9.9, which summarizes the results of regressing the log of ETE on MFA group fill rates as well as year fixed effects, fill rates and ETEs are positively correlated. The estimated coefficient is 2.1 and highly significant; it implies that a 10 percentage point increase in the fill rate is associated with a 21 percent rise in the ETE. Column (2) reports an analogous regression but includes MFA group fixed effects and, therefore, relies solely on variation within groups to identify the

---

15. In countries where export licenses are used to ensure quota adherence, for example, quotas could be binding even if fill rates are low due to insufficient or misallocation of licenses. According to Andriamananjara, Dean, and Spinanger (2004), the internal license allocation regime was inefficient and expensive in many countries.

16. Data on Chinese export license prices are available at www.chinaquota.com. Unfortunately, similar data are not available for all countries in our sample.

Table 9.9   Export tax equivalents (ETE) and fill rates

	Fill rate	
	2.1***	1.4***
	0.2	0.2
Year fixed effects	Yes	Yes
Category fixed effects	No	Yes
R^2	0.21	0.80
No. of observations	417	417

Source: Chinese export license prices obtained from www.chinaquota.com.

Notes: The dependent variable is the log export tax equivalent (see text). The second column includes Office of Textile and Apparel category fixed effects.

***Significant at the 1 percent level.

correlation coefficient. As indicated in table 9.9, the estimated coefficient is 1.4. These relationships are intuitive: one would expect that firms pay higher license prices for products in which capacity to export is tighter. While license price data is only available for China in select years and MFA groups, we interpret these results as providing support for our and others' use of fill rates as a gauge of quota restrictiveness.

Our results regarding the relative restrictiveness of U.S. import quotas on China compared to its other trading partners are consistent with the more detailed inquiry of Francois and Woerz (2006), who estimate ETEs in a gravity-based econometric model that does not require observation of license prices. They find that China's ETEs increased nonlinearly under the ATC and estimate China's ETEs in 2002 at 8 percent and 67 percent for Chinese textiles and apparel, respectively. By comparison, they estimate India's ETEs at only 2 percent for textiles and 5 percent for apparel.

9.4.2 Quota Growth Rates

The evolution of countries' fill rates over time implies that quota growth exceeded export growth for all regions except China. Figure 9.3 traces out the median year-over-year growth in base quota for the four regions over the sample period. For East/Southeast Asia, South Asia, and ROW, the step increases in base quota growth rates match the ATC growth-on-growth provision described in table 9.1. Annual growth for ROW, for example, increased by 16 percent (from 6.00 to 6.96 percent) at the beginning of Phase 1, by 25 percent (to 8.7 percent) at the beginning of Phase II, and by an additional 27 percent (to 11.05 percent) at the beginning of Phase III. The step functions for East and South Asia exhibit identical increases.

China's trajectory of base quota growth, in contrast, is essentially flat. Prior to the ATC, China's growth was roughly equal to that for East/Southeast Asian countries, but in 1994, China's base quota growth was frozen (set to zero). China became eligible for the growth-on-growth provision in 2002,

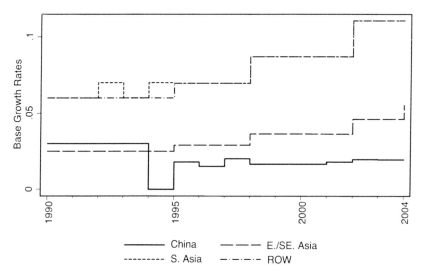

Fig. 9.3   Median base growth rate by region, 1990–2004

after entry into the WTO, and its median growth rate ticked up slightly, but the magnitude of the increase was small given China's low growth rate. China's overall base growth rate was much lower than ROW for the remainder of the ATC. This restrictiveness also varied across MFA groups. For example, the United States imposed slower quota growth for wool products (1 percent for all region in 1995) but even lower growth in these products for China (0.5 percent) overall growth.

9.4.3   Flexibilities

The restrictiveness of the U.S. quota regime can also be measured in terms of countries' ability to adjust their base quotas over time. As discussed in the preceding, the MFA/ATC agreements granted trading partners limited flexibility to borrow and lend quotas across groups and years in response to demand and supply shocks. To our knowledge, use of flexibilities has received little attention in the literature. In this section, we examine both the use of flexibilities as well as their intensity, conditional on use. We find that China's adjustments to its base quotas were more frequent and smaller than those of other countries.

Table 9.10 demonstrates that China made relatively greater use of flexibilities in terms of frequency than many countries between 1984 and 2004. During this period, China made an adjustment to 92 percent of its quotas. Indeed, a striking feature of the data is that China made at least one adjustment to every quota group between 2000 and 2004.

One potential explanation for China's relatively frequent adjustments is that it faced more restrictive caps on its ability to reallocate quotas across

Table 9.10   Flexibility use, 1984–2004

Country	Fraction of groups with adjustments	Flexibility adjustment margin
Cambodia	99	15
Guatemala	97	7
Bangladesh	97	11
Dominican Republic	95	8
India	93	8
Philippines, The	92	11
China	92	5
Indonesia	89	10
Pakistan	88	8
Sri Lanka	88	11
United Arab Emirates	84	6
Macau	81	6
Thailand	80	6
Honduras	78	4
Hong Kong	75	5
Taiwan	71	5
Korea, South	65	4
Turkey	60	2
Costa Rica	60	1
Singapore	52	0
Malaysia	50	0
Colombia	45	0
Romania	30	0
Brazil	27	0
Mauritius	25	0
Mexico	25	0
Egypt	16	0
Poland	15	0
Japan	7	0
Jamaica	6	0

Source: Authors' calculations from U.S. Multi-Fiber Arrangement/Agreement on Textiles and Clothing database.

Notes: The first column reports the median flexibility adjustment margin between 1984–2004. The second column displays the fraction of Multi-Fiber Arrangement groups that were subject to at least one flexibility adjustment. The table lists the thirty countries with the largest aggregate base quotas.

groups and time. If flexibility caps were small, a desired increase in one group might involve more transfers across groups or years than if the caps were large. Unfortunately, the Expired Performance Reports do not provide comprehensive information on countries' flexibility limits over the entire sample period.[17] Details available for 1997, however, indicate that China was allowed

17. Flexibilities were capped at an amount determined by the country's bilateral agreement. Unfortunately, we do not have these details for all agreements in the database.

across-group shifts up to a maximum of 5 percent of the receiving group's base quota and across-time movements of up to 3 percent. Bangladesh and Jamaica, by contrast, were permitted shifts of up to 7 percent across groups and 11 percent across time.

While some countries, notably India and Bangladesh, also made frequent use of the flexibility provisions, among these countries, China faced relatively tighter "flexibility margins" across groups. We define these margins to be the absolute percentage deviation of the adjusted base from the original base for a particular country, group, and year. They are computed across all groups in which adjustments are observed. China's median margin, at 5 percent, is the lowest among countries that made adjustments on at least 80 percent of its quota groups. China's margin was also about half the level exhibited by India and Bangladesh.

Another potential explanation for China's greater use of flexibilities was the relative restrictiveness of its quotas. Given the relatively high number of products bound by quotas, their relatively high fill rates, and their relatively low annual growth rates, frequent adjustments to its base levels may have been necessary to respond to given demand or supply shocks.[18] Countries relatively less constrained by their quota levels and growth rates, by contrast, would have more room to respond without making as many adjustments. Moreover, China was limited in its ability to shift quotas to respond to these shocks. Though we do not pursue this topic here, it is likely that data on countries' flexibility limits and usage under the MFA/ATC could be used to help construct and calibrate a model of optimal quota borrowing and lending.

9.5 Quantity Responses to ATC Phaseouts

In this section, we examine China and other countries' export quantity responses to the ATC phaseouts. We show that countries' export growth occurred primarily in incumbent products, that it varied according to the relative restrictiveness of China's quotas, and that China's export surge in 2005 had ample precedent in prior phases of quota liberalization.

9.5.1 Overview

Figure 9.4 provides an overview of U.S. T&C consumption from 1990 to 2006 according to whether goods were sourced from domestic manufacturers, China, or other U.S. trading partners (ROW).[19] As indicated in the figure, the contribution of domestic producers and other trading partners

18. Indeed, Francois and Woerz (2006) find that China's ETEs spiked to 25 and 112 percent for textiles and apparel, respectively, in 2004, when China no longer had the ability to carry forward additional quota levels because of imminent end of the MFA/ATC regime.

19. U.S. production figures are taken from a report of U.S. T&C production published quarterly by OTEXA (OTEXA 2007). This publication states that exports at the MFA group level are unreliable, so we set exports to zero to calculate the domestic market size.

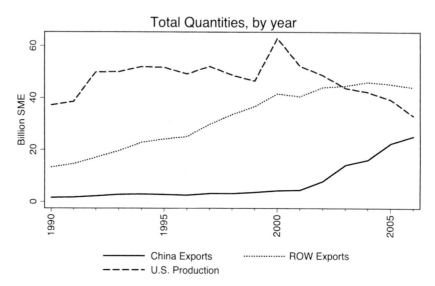

Fig. 9.4   T&C quantities, by region

rose more or less steadily through the 1990s. China's exports, on the other hand, remained relatively flat for the reasons outlined above until 2001. After 2001, China's exports surge, other trading partners' exports begin to level off, and U.S. production starts a long-run decline. Between 2000 and 2006, China's total T&C exports increased almost sixfold from 4.3 billion to 25 billion SME.

To gain a better sense of the potential impact of China's reaction to quota relaxation on other regions' exports, figure 9.5 plots the evolution of export quantities by region between 2000 and 2006. Several regions' exports—for example, North America, the Caribbean, and Oceania—end this period lower than they started, with losses for some (e.g., Oceania) being deeper than others. Other regions experienced reversals of robust export growth during the period. Central America's long-running increase in T&C exports between 2000 and 2005, for example, declined precipitously in 2006. The importance of this reversal is underscored by the fact that T&C goods accounted for roughly three-quarters of Central America's total manufacturing exports to the United States in 2004. Similar reversals were experienced by South America, the former Soviet Union, East Asia, the Middle East, and sub-Saharan Africa. For each of these regions, T&C exports in 2006 were lower than their maximum between 2000 and 2005. South and Southeast Asia, and, although a bit more erratic, the European Union (EU) and North Africa, were the only regions to experience steady export growth between 2000 and 2006.

In the remainder of this section, we provide a more formal assessment of China's impact on other U.S. trading partners' T&C exports to the United States.

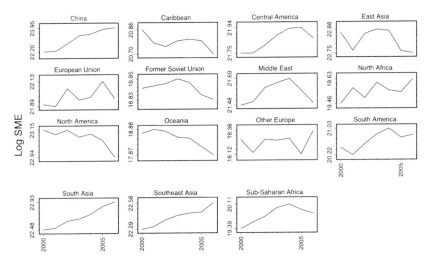

Fig. 9.5   Exports to the United States, 2000–2006, by region

9.5.2   Intensive versus Extensive Margin Export Growth as Quotas Are Removed

Export growth in response to quota relaxation has two potential sources. The first is net growth within countries' continuing products, that is, along their "intensive" margin. The second is net growth due to adding new products or dropping previously exported products, that is, along their "extensive" margin.[20] A priori, it is not obvious which margin will dominate; depending upon assumptions, shifting resources into additional product lines may be more profitable than increasing the capacity of existing product lines.

Table 9.11 decomposes countries' aggregate export quantity growth in percentage terms in the year following each phase of ATC integration. We document export patterns by ATC integration to emphasize the similarities in exporting behavior across each integration stage. Except for China, responses are reported by region. The first column for each phase notes regions' aggregate growth, while the subsequent two columns decompose this aggregate growth into the parts due to countries' intensive and extensive margins. Each panel reports the change in quantities in the year of integration for each phase. That is, the first panel reports growth in 1995, the second panel in 1998, and so on. Since China became eligible for Phase I and II integration in 2002, the bottom row reports China's response in this year for those phases. As indicated in table 9.11, export growth coinciding with Chinese quota relaxation primarily occurs through the intensive margin. For China, the intensive margin represents more than 90 percent of growth in

---

20. As noted earlier, the United States imposed quotas at the level of three-digit MFA groups. These groups contain a median of nineteen HS products.

Table 9.11   Aggregate growth decomposition, by phase and region

Region	Phase I			Phase II			Phase III			Phase IV		
	Aggregate growth	Intensive margin	Extensive margin	Aggregate growth	Intensive margin	Extensive margin	Aggregate growth	Intensive margin	Extensive margin	Aggregate growth	Intensive margin	Extensive margin
China	9	16	−6	9	10	−1	306	288	17	271	269	2
Caribbean	47	23	24	0	0	−1	−12	−12	0	−1	1	−2
Central America	33	6	27	−10	−3	−7	6	10	−4	1	3	−2
East Asia	−10	−10	0	24	24	0	57	22	36	−24	−25	0
European Union	2	3	−1	−3	−3	0	13	12	2	64	64	0
Former Soviet Union	−50	−45	−5	−21	−22	1	−18	−18	0	−61	−51	−10
Middle East	−34	−43	9	−1	−2	2	15	13	2	−12	−12	0
North Africa	−46	−31	−15	23	23	0	−8	−27	19	−4	−4	0
North America	13	10	3	5	5	0	4	5	−1	−14	−13	−1
Oceania	−42	12	−54	48	45	3	−15	−15	1	−52	−49	−3
Other Europe	102	−36	138	12	−6	18	21	−9	30	−30	−30	−1
South America	−65	−58	−7	−51	−51	0	44	44	−1	−13	−12	−1
South Asia	33	33	0	18	18	0	5	3	2	20	19	0
Southeast Asia	−47	8	−54	18	18	0	−13	−13	0	0	0	0
Sub-Saharan Africa	−53	−42	−11	10	−25	34	69	60	9	−16	−15	−1
All regions	3	2	1	3	3	0	31	27	4	14	14	0
All regions (ex. China)	3	1	2	2	2	0	9	6	4	−2	−1	0
China (2002)	42	41	1	32	21	11						
All regions (2002)	8	19	−12	14	11	3						

Notes: Decomposition table reports aggregate growth, decomposed into the extensive and intensive margins, by phase and region, in year of integration. In this table, the integration years for Phase I–IV are for 1995, 1998, 2002, and 2005, respectively. Extensive margin is defined as the net square meter equivalents (SME) quantity growth in varieties that enter and exit in the year of integration. Intensive margin is defined as the net SME quantity growth in continuing varieties in the year of integration. Note that the aggregate growth values for Phase I and II differ from the previous table because this table reports values for 1995 and 1998, respectively. The bottom rows in each panel report Phase I and II export growth for China and all regions in 2002, the year that China was eligible for Agreement on Textiles and Clothing liberalization. The sum of the intensive and extensive margin may not sum to aggregate growth due to rounding.

Phases I, III, and IV, and two-thirds of growth in Phase II. Across all other U.S. trading partners, the intensive margin represented the more important margin of adjustment in Phases II to IV.

Table 9.11 also provides an initial view of the contemporaneous response of China's export growth following each integration phase. China's overall response in the year of each phaseout was 42, 32, 306, and 271 percent for Phases I to IV, respectively. We note that China's Phase III increase accounted for 71 percent of the total increase in Phase III exports in 2002 (i.e., 22 of 31 percentage points). In 2005, aggregate exports from all countries excluding China actually *fell* 2 percent, a signal that China's impact on other U.S. trading partners was potentially large in this final phase.

9.5.3   Reactions to Relaxation of China's Quotas

Other U.S. trading partners' reaction to the relaxation of China's quotas varied according to their relative restrictiveness. As noted in the preceding, we classify China's quotas in the year prior to each phase as being binding if they exhibit a fill rate in excess of 90 percent.[21] To estimate the differential growth associated with relaxation of bound and unbound quotas, we regress the change in country-products' export quantity on region-year dummies interacted with a dummy variable indicating whether China's quota was previously binding.[22]

$$(2) \quad \Delta \ln q_{crht} = \beta_{1rt} \text{ChinaBound}_{h,t-1} + \beta_{2rt} \text{ChinaUnbound}_{h,t-1} + v_{crht},$$

where $\Delta \ln q_{crht}$ is the change in export quantity of country c in region r in HS product h between years t and $t + 1$, and β_{1rt} and β_{2rt} are region-year dummies. These region-year dummies are interacted with $\text{ChinaBound}_{h,t-1}$, a dummy variable that equals unity if China's quota in product h in year $t-1$ had a fill rate exceeding 90 percent, and $\text{ChinaUnbound}_{h,t-1}$ is a dummy variable that equals 1 if China was not subject to a binding quota. Vis-à-vis the aggregate growth pattern displayed in table 9.11, this regression differences out the country-product fixed effects. β_{1rt} and β_{2rt}, therefore, identify the average quantity change across countries in region r within country-products in which China faced binding and nonbinding quotas, respectively.[23] We focus here on other countries' responses in goods in which China faced nonbinding and binding quotas to gain insight into how these regions were influenced by China. Toward that end, the coefficients we report for Phases I to III are for 2002; for Phase IV, we report coefficients for 2005. In line with the results of table 9.11, equation (2) concentrates on countries' reactions along the intensive margin.

Table 9.12 reports ordinary least squares (OLS) estimates for four separate

21. Results do not change when we perturb this cutoff.
22. Because fill rates are available at the MFA group level, we attribute group-level fill rates to all HS products in the group.
23. We exclude the constant in this regression, and standard errors are clustered by exporting country.

Table 9.12 Agreement on Textiles and Clothing phase-outs: export quantities and binding quotas (Δ Ln [SME])

	Phase I		Phase II		Phase III		Phase IV	
	Unbound	Bound	Unbound	Bound	Unbound	Bound	Unbound	Bound
x China	0.41***	0.00	0.93***	2.26***	1.36***	1.81***	1.28***	1.73***
	0.11	0.00	0.11	0.24	0.14	0.18	0.07	0.08
x Caribbean	0.21	0.00	-0.16	-0.17	-0.38	-0.25*	-0.36***	-0.30***
	0.33	0.00	0.27	0.17	0.58	0.14	0.05	0.06
x Central America	-0.26*	0.00	-0.13	-0.05	0.30*	0.10	-0.19	-0.26***
	0.15	0.00	0.11	0.07	0.17	0.10	0.11	0.04
x East Asia	0.16	0.00	0.17**	-0.68***	0.09	0.00	-0.22***	-0.58***
	0.13	0.00	0.07	0.19	0.10	0.16	0.08	0.10
x European Union	0.01	0.00	-0.02	-0.12	-0.01	0.05	-0.15***	-0.20***
	0.05	0.00	0.04	0.16	0.04	0.08	0.02	0.04
x Former Soviet Union	0.09	0.00	0.28	-0.07	-0.49***	-0.22	-0.92***	-1.14**
	0.43	0.00	0.24	0.22	0.11	0.45	0.30	0.56
x Middle East	-0.07	0.00	0.08	0.11	0.11	-0.22	-0.32***	-0.42***
	0.25	0.00	0.15	0.24	0.20	0.14	0.09	0.16
x North Africa	0.35	0.00	0.33***	0.31	-0.17***	-0.25	0.01	-0.09
	0.28	0.00	0.01	0.26	0.04	0.50	0.03	0.08
x North America	0.01	0.00	0.05	-0.19	-0.11***	-0.07***	-0.29**	-0.20**
	0.04	0.00	0.07	0.16	0.02	0.00	0.12	0.09
x Oceania	-0.26**	0.00	-0.17***	-0.55***	-0.13	0.03	-0.19***	-0.26***
	0.10	0.00	0.06	0.06	0.25	0.29	0.05	0.09
x Other Europe	0.06	0.00	-0.12***	1.72**	-0.11	0.14	-0.02	-0.04
	0.06	0.00	0.03	0.71	0.10	0.12	0.10	0.15
x South America	-0.15	0.00	0.03	0.33*	0.21	0.29	-0.14	-0.11
	0.15	0.00	0.17	0.18	0.14	0.25	0.10	0.08

x South Asia	0.31***	0.00	0.36***	-0.07	0.22*	0.34	0.09	-0.08
	0.10	0.00	0.12	0.21	0.12	0.37	0.11	0.09
x Southeast Asia	0.34	0.00	0.23	0.20	0.26	0.06	-0.04	-0.11
	0.26	0.00	0.14	0.28	0.22	0.28	0.07	0.09
x Sub-Saharan Africa	-0.10	0.00	0.02	0.16**	0.38*	-0.26	-0.31**	-0.50***
	0.14	0.00	0.18	0.08	0.20	0.40	0.14	0.12
R^2	0.00		0.00		0.00		0.00	
No. of observations	41,100		88,818		97,482		431,069	

Notes: Table regresses change in the (log of) country-product quantity on year-region-Unbound versus Bound interactions. Each column reports the result of a regression encompassing all the products whose quotas were relaxed in the noted phase. Phases I–III report year-region fixed effects for year 2002, the year China entered the World Trade Organization, and Phase IV reports fixed effects for 2005. Bound refer to the Harmonized System codes in which China had greater than a 90 percent fill rate in the previous year. Standard errors clustered by exporting country.

***Significant at the 1 percent level.

**Significant at the 5 percent level.

*Significant at the 10 percent level.

estimations of equation (2), one for each phase of ATC integration. There are two columns for each phase: the first reports countries' average growth in products where China previously faced nonbinding quotas (β_{2rt}), while the second column reports countries' average growth in products where China previously faced binding quotas (β_{1rt}).

Results for Phase I in the first panel of table 9.12 contain all zeros in the binding column because none of China's quotas on Phase I products were binding in 2001.[24] The second panel reports the 2002 region-year fixed effects for Phase II products. Results in this column indicate that China averaged 153 percent ($e^{0.93} - 1$) export growth in nonbinding products and an incredible 855 percent ($e^{2.26} - 1$) average increase in bound products. Note that the growth rates for Phase II are higher than the aggregate growth rate reported at the bottom of table 9.11; this discrepancy is likely due to the fact that small products grew faster than the large products.[25] Results for East Asia and South Asia suggest that exports from these regions increased in products where China's quotas were not binding but declined in the products where China faced binding quotas. Estimates for Phase III show a similar result with respect to China's response, but more muted responses by other countries. China's exports in products subject to binding quotas increased 511 percent compared to 291 percent in unbound products.

The point estimates for Phase IV are perhaps the most dramatic. Here, too, China's export quantity growth is significantly higher in its bound versus unbound products, 463 percent versus 261 percent. Response to Chinese growth are equally dramatic, with nine of fourteen regions experiencing negative and significant declines in China's bound products. These response contrast starkly with those associated with Phase III.

Variation in countries' reactions to the removal of Chinese quotas likely reflects differences in comparative advantage across T&C products. Though formal assessment of countries' elasticities of substitution with Chinese exports requires structural estimation beyond the scope of this chapter, the results in table 9.12 can be used to provide a rough guide as to which countries were the biggest "losers" with respect to China. Toward that end, table 9.13 reports the results of a Phase IV regression like that in equation (2) but at the country level. Countries are ordered according to their average response in China's previously bound products, with an asterisk denoting statistically significant responses. Of the 143 countries in table 9.13, average exports fell in 102 countries, and these drops were statistically significant for

24. Phase I products were placed in the 9xx MFA groups that were a collection of products with which the United States was relatively unconcerned and, therefore, integrated early. The U.S. MFA/ATC database does not have quota information for these MFA groups. We interpret the fact that this information is missing as evidence that goods in these groups were unconstrained by quotas, and this fact was confirmed through correspondences with OTEXA.

25. See Arkolakis (2007) for a model of market penetration implying that low-volume products grow faster than high-volume products as trade costs fall.

Table 9.13 "Winners and Losers"

Kuwait (−2.89)*	Taiwan (−0.55)*	United Arab Emirates (−0.26)*	Mozambique (0.05)
Russia (−2.81)*	Swaziland (−0.54)*	Ukraine (−0.25)	Malawi (0.05)
Maldives (−2.35)*	Sweden (−0.52)*	El Salvador (−0.23)*	Slovakia (0.06)
Micronesia (−2.14)*	Ghana (−0.51)*	Guatemala (−0.23)*	Trinidad and Tobago (0.09)
Georgia (−1.99)	Mali (−0.48)	Gambia (−0.23)*	Iceland (0.09)
Guinea (−1.85)*	Bahrain (−0.48)	Turkey (−0.23)*	Vietnam (0.09)
Oman (−1.82)*	Mauritius (−0.47)	Czech Republic (−0.21)	Chile (0.11)
Suriname (−1.38)	Slovenia (−0.46)*	Lebanon (−0.21)	Germany (0.12)
Cyprus (−1.35)*	Poland (−0.45)*	Nicaragua (−0.21)	Cambodia (0.12)
Albania (−1.25)*	Venezuela (−0.45)*	Colombia (−0.20)	Indonesia (0.13)
Kyrgyzstan (−1.24)*	Argentina (−0.45)*	Ecuador (−0.18)	Bangladesh (0.15)
Kazakhstan (−1.21)	Hungary (−0.44)*	Brunei (−0.17)	Switzerland (0.16)
Azerbaijan (−1.13)	Barbados (−0.40)*	Australia (−0.15)	Armenia (0.16)
Tajikistan (−1.09)	Belarus (−0.39)*	Brazil (−0.15)	Uzbekistan (0.18)
Macedonia (Skopje) (−1.00)*	Malaysia (−0.39)*	Belgium (−0.15)	Cook Islands (0.18)
South Africa (−0.98)*	Honduras (−0.37)*	Ireland (−0.14)	Bolivia (0.22)
Ivory Coast (−0.91)*	Costa Rica (−0.36)	United Kingdom (−0.14)	Jordan (0.24)
Ethiopia (−0.91)	Romania (−0.35)*	Italy (−0.13)*	Peru (0.24)*
Syria (−0.90)*	Finland (−0.35)*	Spain (−0.13)	Panama (0.25)
Moldova (−0.87)*	Greece (−0.35)	Japan (−0.12)	Botswana (0.26)
Korea, South (−0.85)*	Guyana (−0.34)	Namibia (−0.11)	Uganda (0.30)*
Mongolia (−0.84)*	Dominican Republic (−0.34)*	Uruguay (−0.10)	Saudi Arabia (0.32)
Nepal (−0.77)*	Haiti (−0.34)	Portugal (−0.10)	Nigeria (0.48)*
Israel (−0.72)*	Fiji (−0.33)	Croatia (−0.10)	Qatar (0.51)
Singapore (−0.69)*	Latvia (−0.32)	Estonia (−0.07)	Bosnia-Hercegovina (0.63)
Zambia (−0.69)	Sri Lanka (−0.31)*	Mexico (−0.07)	Senegal (0.67)*
Bermuda (−0.69)	Canada (−0.31)*	Paraguay (−0.04)	British Virgin Islands (0.69)

(continued)

Table 9.13 (continued)

Sierra Leone (−0.68)	Austria (−0.31)*	Turkmenistan (−0.04)	San Marino (0.75)*
Jamaica (−0.65)	New Zealand (−0.31)	Kenya (−0.02)	Malta (0.90)*
Cape Verde (−0.62)*	Zimbabwe (−0.30)*	Morocco (−0.02)	Bahamas (1.35)*
Hong Kong (−0.62)*	France (−0.30)*	Tanzania (0.01)	Netherlands Antilles (1.60)
Belize (−0.61)	Egypt (−0.29)	Lithuania (0.02)	Laos (1.88)*
Denmark (−0.59)*	Norway (−0.28)	Tunisia (0.02)	Somalia (1.94)
Madagascar (−0.57)*	Philippines, The (−0.28)*	Pakistan (0.02)	Tokelau (2.05)
Lesotho (−0.57)*	Bulgaria (−0.27)	India (0.03)	Mauritania (3.43)
Macao (−0.55)*	Thailand (−0.26)*	Netherlands, The (0.05)	

Notes: Table regresses change in the (log of) country-product quantity on country-year fixed effects on the set of China's Phase IV products that were subject to binding quotas in 2004. The 2005 coefficients for each country are reported in parentheses.

*Export response is statistically significant at the 10 percent confidence level (robust standard errors).

54 countries. Statistically significant declines range from a low of 13 percent ($e^{0.14} - 1$) for Italy to a high of more than 80 percent for Kuwait, Russia, the Maldives, Micronesia, Guinea, and Oman. Remarkably, only *eight* countries exhibit a statistically significant increase in exports. Three of the largest South Asian exporters—Bangladesh, India, and Pakistan—report positive but statistically insignificant changes in exports. Though these countries fare much better than others, it is possible their export growth might have been much higher in the absence of robust Chinese growth.

Declines among sub-Saharan African exporters may have been particularly economically significant. These countries experienced increasing T&C exports to the United States from 2000 to 2004 because of modifications made to the rules-of-origin requirements under AGOA; as shown in figure 9.5, the region's T&C exports doubled between 2000 and 2004. These modifications—collectively referred to as the "Special Rule"—allowed countries to satisfy rules-of-origin requirements using fabric of any origin provided that the clothing assembly took place within the countries' borders. As discussed in Dayaratna-Banda and Whalley (2007), firms responded to the Special Rule by importing fabrics from Asian countries for assembly in Africa.[26] The Special Rule also lead to substantial inward foreign direct investment as multinational firms located the final stages of production in Africa to "hop" over quotas (Frazer and Van Biesebroeck 2007). These responses contributed to a boom in sub-Saharan T&C production, particularly in Madagascar, Lesotho, and Swaziland. Between 2000 and 2004, for example, Lesotho's T&C exports to the United States nearly quadrupled, to $455 million, as the number of T&C factories located in the country doubled from 21 to 47 (IMF 2007). In the year following the end of the ATC in 2005, however, Lesotho's T&C production shrank considerably.[27] Both the value and quantity of its T&C exports to the United States fell 14 percent; in China's bound products, the average Lesotho export fell 43 percent. These declines were accompanied by a 30 percent fall in employment, to 35,000 workers, and one quarter of its production facilities being shuttered (IMF 2007).

The most plausible explanation for the sharp decline in sub-Saharan T&C production following the end of the ATC (and, therefore, the end of the Special Rule's value) is that African production costs are prohibitive, either because relatively low wages are in fact relatively high in quality- or productivity-adjusted terms or because transport costs make multinational production absent an extra inducement infeasible. Further research into the reasons behind this decline would be useful both for evaluating appropriate policy responses and for understanding the dynamics of sub-Saharan African economies.

---

26. The following African Growth and Opportunities Act (AGOA) countries were not eligible for the Special Rule provision: Botswana, Gabon, Mauritius, Namibia, Seychelles, and South Africa (www.agao.gov).

27. As noted by Dayaratna-Banda and Whalley (2007), sub-Saharan T&C exports in 2005 were also hurt by an appreciation of the South African Rand.

9.6   Price Responses to ATC Phaseouts

A second margin along which countries might react to the removal of import quotas is price. In this section, we examine the evolution of the United States' T&C import free-on-board unit values (i.e., import value per SME) subsequent to each Phase of ATC integration. In contrast to the results reported above, we here focus on countries' unit value changes in response to their own, not China's, quota relaxations.

Table 9.14 reports the results of a regression similar to equation (2) but where the dependent variable is the log difference in unit value rather than export quantity, and where the binding dummy takes a value of one if the country-product was constrained in its country of origin the prior year. As a result, coefficient estimates are with respect to 1995, 1998, 2002, and 2005 for Phases I through IV, respectively, in the upper portion of table 9.14. China's response to its Phase I and II good quota relaxations in the year in which those quotas were actually removed (i.e., 2002) are reported at the bottom of table 9.14.

As indicated in table 9.14, China's average unit values fell in the years that its products were integrated. Here, as in the preceding, responses varied according to whether China faced binding quotas. Unit value declines for exports previously restrained by China's binding quotas were larger in all integration phases. In 2002, Chinese unit values for bound Phase II products fell 55 percent ($e^{-0.81} - 1$) versus 32 percent for unbound products. For Phase III and IV products, the declines for China were 48 versus 42 percent, and 41 versus 31 percent, respectively. More broadly, though unit value responses vary across phases, they are generally negative and significant for East Asia, Southeast Asia, and South Asia and generally larger in bound products than unbound products.

One explanation for China's and other countries' unit value declines is simply that as quotas are relaxed, goods prices decline, and firms slide down their demand curves as prices and quantities adjust to the previously unrealizable competitive outcome. Indeed, Francois and Worz (2006) estimate the export tax equivalent of Chinese quotas to be 25 percent for textiles and 110 percent for apparel in 2004. With the quotas removed, ETEs, by definition, fall to zero.

Declining prices might also accompany quota relaxation as a result of quality downgrading. It is well known in the international trade literature that firms facing quotas have an incentive to export higher-margin goods; see, for example, the theoretical research of Krishna (1987) and Das and Donnenfeld (1987) and the empirical studies of Aw and Roberts (1986) and Feenstra (1988). Evans and Harrigan (2005), for example, find that U.S. imports of products facing binding quotas exhibit a 6.3 percent price premium relative to unbound imports. Under the assumption that prices reflect only vertical product differentiation, the results reported in table 9.14

Table 9.14   ATC phase-outs: unit values and binding quotas (Δ Ln [Price])

	Phase I		Phase II		Phase III		Phase IV	
	Unbound	Bound	Unbound	Bound	Unbound	Bound	Unbound	Bound
			Integration year					
× China	-0.17		-0.07	0.11	-0.54***	-0.66***	-0.37***	-0.53***
	0.10		0.05	0.14	0.06	0.09	0.02	0.03
× Caribbean	-0.08		-0.10		-0.17*		-0.02	
	0.24		0.08		0.10		0.03	
× Central America	-0.13		-0.01		-0.03		-0.03	-0.03
	0.18		0.06		0.06		0.02	0.49
× East Asia	0.07		-0.08**		-0.17***	-0.14	-0.01	-0.15**
	0.06		0.03		0.03	0.14	0.01	0.06
× European Union	0.00		-0.01		-0.01		0.01*	0.05
	0.04		0.02		0.02		0.01	0.13
× Former Soviet Union	0.03		-0.11		0.13	-0.09	0.16***	0.03
	0.47		0.12		0.09	0.39	0.03	0.18
× Middle East	0.00		0.05		-0.04	-0.15	0.02	0.02
	0.21		0.06		0.05	0.33	0.02	0.16
× North Africa	0.31		0.06		0.10		0.03	
	0.30		0.09		0.08		0.03	
× North America	0.01		0.05		0.00		0.03*	
	0.08		0.04		0.04		0.02	
× Oceania	0.10		-0.08		0.01		0.03	
	0.18		0.08		0.08		0.03	
× Other Europe	0.04		-0.01		-0.13**		0.01	0.16
	0.12		0.07		0.06		0.02	0.70
× South America	0.39**		-0.07		-0.06		0.04**	-0.17
	0.15		0.06		0.05		0.02	0.35

(continued)

Table 9.14   (continued)

	Phase I		Phase II		Phase III		Phase IV	
	Unbound	Bound	Unbound	Bound	Unbound	Bound	Unbound	Bound
× South Asia	0.12		-0.02	-0.10	-0.15***	-0.49*	-0.07***	-0.20**
	0.09		0.04	0.86	0.04	0.27	0.01	0.08
× Southeast Asia	0.26**		-0.13***		-0.13***	0.12	-0.04***	-0.14*
	0.10		0.04		0.03	0.39	0.01	0.07
× Sub-Saharan Africa	0.18		-0.16		-0.19**		0.07***	
	0.21		0.10		0.08		0.02	
Year 2002 × China	-0.14*		-0.38***	-0.81***				
	0.08		0.05	0.13				
No. of observations	41,100		88,818		97,482		431,069	

Notes: Table regresses change in the (log of) country-product unit value on year-region-Unbound versus Bound interactions. Each column reports the result of a regression encompassing all the products whose quotas were relaxed in the noted phase. Phase I, II, and III report year-region fixed effects for year 1995, 1998, and 2002, respectively. The bottom panel reports 2002 fixed effects for Phases I and II for China. Phase IV reports fixed effects for 2005. Bound refers to the Harmonized System codes in which countries had greater than a 90 percent fill rate in the previous year. Robust standard errors are reported.

***Significant at the 1 percent level.

**Significant at the 5 percent level.

*Significant at the 10 percent level.

provide prima facie evidence that China's T&C quality fell following the removal of quotas.

Quality upgrading in response to quantitative restrictions is possible through changes in demand or changes in supply-side characteristics. In the former, imposition of quota rents leads to identical markups across products that induce consumers to substitute toward higher-priced varieties. This effect is similar to Alchian and Allen's (1964) Washington apples story where higher-priced goods are shipped over greater distances to lower the per dollar transport costs (see also Hummels and Skiba 2004). Boorstein and Feenstra (1991) infer quality in this context by comparing a unit value index, which uses quantity weights, to an exact price index, which uses value weights: if the unit value index increases by more than the exact price index, consumption has shifted toward more expensive goods and average quality of goods from the restricted country increases. Using this method to study the effects of quota removal, Harrigan and Barrows (2006) find that the quality of China's bound products fell 7 percent more than its unbound products when quotas were removed in 2005.

Here, we complement Harrigan and Barrows (2006) by using an approach developed in Khandelwal (2007) to measure quality changes within countries' products. As discussed in detail in the appendix, this approach uses a discrete choice demand system to infer country-product (i.e., variety) quality, relative to the average U.S. domestic quality, by estimating differences in relative market shares after controlling for prices. We then examine how these measures of country-product quality react to quota removal using a specification analogous to the ones employed in the preceding:

$$(3) \qquad \Delta\theta_{cht} = \beta_{1rt}\text{China Bound}_{h,t-1} + \beta_{2rt}\text{China Unbound}_{h,t-1} + v_{crht},$$

where θ_{cht} is the estimated quality of country c in product h at time t obtained from a implementing the approach discussed in the appendix. In this specification, we regress the change in country-product quality on region-year fixed effects that are interacted with ChinaBound$_{h,t-1}$, a dummy variable which equals unity if China's quota in product h in year $t-1$ had a fill rate exceeding 90 percent, and ChinaUnbound$_{h,t-1}$, a dummy variable that equals 1 if China was not subject to a binding quota. To focus attention on China, we estimate a single ROW fixed effect for each year for all other countries and, as before, run the regressions separately by phase. For Phases I and II, we report coefficients for 2002 when China became eligible for integration, rather than the phaseout defined under the ATC. Coefficients and standard errors are reported in table 9.15.

The coefficients generally report a positive change in quality in the year of integration for both bound and unbound varieties and for both China and the ROW. On first inspection, these results appear inconsistent with the idea that dismantling quotas results in quality downgrading. Recall, however, that our measure of country-product quality reflects consumers' valuation of

Table 9.15   Agreement on Textiles and Clothing phase-outs: export qualities and binding quotas

	Phase I		Phase II		Phase III		Phase IV	
	Unbound	Bound	Unbound	Bound	Unbound	Bound	Unbound	Bound
China	0.10*		0.49***	0.81***	0.99***	1.03***	1.01***	0.72***
	0.05		0.08	0.19	0.14	0.21	0.06	0.08
Rest of world	−0.01		0.03	−0.12***	0.07**	0.40***	−0.03*	0.15***
	0.01		0.02	0.03	0.03	0.05	0.01	0.02
Difference-in-difference	0.11**		0.47**		−0.29		−0.47***	
	0.05		0.21		0.26		0.11	
Within R^2			0.01		0.01		0.01	
No. of observations	40,186		88,415		97,106		429,488	

Notes: Table regresses change in the country-product quality on year-region-Unbound versus Bound interactions. The procedure to estimate quality is discussed in the appendix. Bound refer to the Harmonized System codes in which China had greater than a 90 percent fill rate in the previous year. Phase I–III coefficients are for 2002, the year China entered the World Trade Organization, and Phase IV reports 2005 coefficients. The difference-in-differences are computed as the change in China's bound and unbound coefficients minus the analogous difference in Rest of world coefficients.

***Significant at the 1 percent level.

**Significant at the 5 percent level.

*Significant at the 10 percent level.

Chinese goods relative to "outside goods," which, in this case, are domestic varieties. These relative valuations complicate the evaluation of the results in table 9.15 because, for example, a deterioration in the quality of the outside good would lead to increase in the quality of the imported varieties. That is, our measure of quality does not separately identify shifts in preferences across HS products versus shifts in preferences toward the outside good.[28]

We use the coefficients reported in table 9.15 to compute a difference-in-differences estimate of China quality upgrading in bound products that uses quality change in unbound products and the ROW as baselines.[29] First, we take the difference between China's change in quality for bound and unbounded varieties; for Phase IV this is $0.72 - 1.01$, or -0.29. This first difference controls for country-specific changes in technology or shifts in demand that are common to all varieties within the country. Second, we compare this difference to the analogous difference in the ROW's coefficients for China's bound and unbound products; for Phase IV this is $-0.29 - 0.18$, or -0.47. This second difference nets out changes in consumers' valuation across varieties. For example, suppose there is a positive technology shock to the Chinese T&C industry. The first difference would control for the technology shock because the shock would be common to China's bound and unbound exports. Now suppose an extreme winter increases the demand for winter clothing; this shock, common to both China and ROW assuming away compositional differences, is controlled by differencing Chinese quality with the ROW within products. In this way, the difference-in-differences estimate provides an uncontaminated estimate of the relative Chinese bound-versus-unbound quality change following each phaseout.

Difference-in-difference estimates for each Phase are reported in the bottom panel of table 9.15. As mentioned earlier, China's Phase I products were not subject to binding quotas, so we merely report the difference between China's and the ROW's unbound quality changes, which is positive and significant at the 10 percent level. For Phase II, we find that China's bound products actually increase in quality, an outcome that is inconsistent with theory. One possible explanation for this result is that Phase II products were only marginally binding in a way that our assessment of bindingness does not pick up.

We do find relative declines in China's bound products' quality in response to Phases III and IV, though only the latter estimate is statistically significant at conventional levels. In both Phases, China registered improvements

---

28. See Nevo (2003) for a detailed discussion on this point. We note that the quality levels could be biased upward if measurement error in the prices leads to attenuation bias in α. Assuming that the attenuation bias is the same in bound and unbound products, this possibility provides further motivation for computing difference-in-differences estimates. Problems associated with measurement error are also mitigated by our use of trade costs as an instrument for price.

29. Actually, this is a triple difference specification, but because we focus on *changes* in quality, the time difference is already assumed.

in quality within bound and unbound varieties, but ROW quality increases by more. These results appear consistent with theory and complement the across-good shifts in demand identified by Harrigan and Barrows (2006) for Phase IV products. They also support the idea that restrictions on China were relatively more stringent.

9.7   China's T&C Future

China's share of U.S. T&C imports jumped threefold, from 10 to 33 percent, between the time it joined the WTO in December 2001 and the end of the ATC regime in 2005. This growth, and in particular China's surging exports in the early months of 2005, spurred domestic firms and other developing countries to lobby the United States, successfully, for the reimposition of T&C quotas on China. By the middle of 2005, the United States and China had agreed to new limits on China's exports in a subset of T&C categories previously covered by Phase IV of the ATC. These categories are listed in table 9.2; they are to remain in effect until 2008.

Some analysts believe that China's large increase in Phase IV exports in early 2005 occurred primarily as a hedge against future protectionist measures. By dramatically increasing their exports early in the year, this line of thinking goes, Chinese firms would be able to establish higher base levels for an inevitable new round of quotas. Table 9.2 provides some evidence in favor of this hypothesis, as the new, post-ATC quota levels agreed to in 2005 were substantially larger than the levels previously imposed by the ATC. Going forward, it is not clear that China will be free of quotas after 2008. According to its WTO accession documents, WTO member countries are allowed to impose product-specific safeguards on China to prevent market disruptions until 2013. As a result, the United States might continue to apply quotas or resort to other forms of protection, such as antidumping remedies, once the current safeguards are removed (Bown 2007). Dayaratna-Banda and Whalley (2007) argue that the new safeguards are merely a means of reimposing an MFA/ATC regime on China, with the major exception that quotas now just apply to China as opposed to all developing economies.

China's exports to the EU also surged after the ATC expired. This increase induced a similar response in the EU, with the result that China and the EU also signed a new bilateral agreement in 2005 restricting China's imports in ten groups of T&C products through 2007.[30] As was well reported at the time, China satisfied its quotas in these goods by September 2005, with the result that $501 million worth of Chinese goods backed up on European ports.[31] Only after high-level negotiations led to an amended quota

30. Dayaratna-Banda and Whalley (2007) report that China has either signed, or is in negotiations to sign, similar quota agreements with Brazil, Turkey, Canada, Mexico, and Peru.

31. See "Europe and China in Accord Over End to a Textile Dispute," *New York Times,* September 6, 2005.

Table 9.16   EU safeguards on China's textile and clothing, 2006–2007, by Multi-fiber Arrangement groups

	Unit	2006 quota	2007 quota	2007 quota growth
Cotton fabrics	kg	61,948,000	69,692,000	12.5
T-shirts	no	540,204,000	594,000,000	10.0
Children's sublimit	no	45,017,000	49,518,000	10.0
Pullovers	no	189,719,000	220,000,000	16.0
Men's trousers	no	338,923,000	383,000,000	13.0
Blouses	no	80,493,000	88,543,000	10.0
Bed linen	kg	15,795,000	17,770,000	12.5
Dresses	no	27,001,000	29,701,000	10.0
Brassieres	no	219,882,000	248,000,000	12.8
Table and kitchen linen	kg	12,349,000	13,892,000	12.5
Flax or ramie yarn	kg	4,740,000	5,214,000	10.0

agreement for 2005 were these goods allowed into the EU. The EU's new safeguards remain in effect until December 31, 2007; they are summarized in table 9.16.

Many observers have reacted to China's T&C export growth with the claim that all of the world's T&C production will relocate to China once its quotas are abolished permanently. Interestingly, Chinese officials appear to be looking beyond their dominance of apparel and textiles and have voiced concern that rising wages will erode their comparative advantage in this sector vis-à-vis even lower-wage countries like Vietnam, Cambodia, and Bangladesh.[32] Though such an outcome appears unlikely, at least in the near term, these countries have become more important sources of T&C exports in recent years. In the year after its trade relations with the United States were normalized in 2001, for example, Vietnam's T&C exports to the United States increased 240 percent, though its market share in terms of quantity in 2005 remained under 2 percent. Until 2007, when it, too, joined the WTO, Vietnam's exports were hampered by U.S. quotas on twenty-five groups of T&C products until 2007, when Vietnam was admitted into the WTO.

Given the large T&C export capacity of China, China's dominance of the T&C market should continue into the near future, especially as the new safeguards expire. As China continues its transition toward more capital- and skill-intensive industries, however, it is likely that the relative importance of apparel and textiles in the Chinese economy will fall. Already, T&C exports have declined to 11 percent of the country's total exports to the United States, down from 26 percent in 1990. As this transition continues, it is likely that countries at earlier stages of development, such as Cambodia and Vietnam, will become bigger players.

32. See the discussions of the 2007 China Development Forum, "Towards New Models of Economic Growth," available at http://www.cdrf.org.cn/en/.

Appendix

Quality Estimation

This appendix explains how to identify quality from the T&C import data. The framework is based on the approach taken by Khandelwal (2007), and the reader is referred to that paper for additional details.

We assume that consumers have discrete choice preferences and select the one country-product variety that provides them with the highest utility. The (indirect) utility that consumer obtains from purchasing variety ch is:

(A1) $$V_{chnt} = \theta_{1ch} + \theta_{2t} + \xi_{cht} - \alpha p_{cht} + \varepsilon_{chnt},$$

where $\theta_{ch} + \theta_t + \xi_{cht}$ denotes the quality of variety ch at time t, P_{cht} denotes its price, and ε_{chnt} is a random consumer-variety specific term. The random term ε introduces horizontal differentiation; its inclusion precludes prices from being sufficient statistics for quality.[33] The random term ε can be decomposed into two randomly distributed components:

(A2) $$\varepsilon_{chnt} = \psi_{hnt} + (1 - \sigma) v_{chnt},$$

with $0 \leq \sigma < 1$. The ψ term is a consumer-HS product random effect that provides consumer n with an idiosyncratic utility from choosing a variety that resides in product h. This term generates a nested logit system which is a more flexible demand model because it alleviates the independence of irrelevant alternatives (IIA) problem found in simple logit models. The product-level random effect creates correlation across varieties within the same HS code, which means that consumers are more likely to substitute toward varieties within the same product.[34]

Under the assumption that v is an independently and identically distributed (i.i.d) extreme value idiosyncratic shock, we can aggregate over all individual purchases in the economy to obtain aggregate market shares for each variety (e.g., see Berry 1994). In order to complete the demand system, the consumer is allowed to choose an "outside" good if none of the inside varieties provides him or her with a high enough utility. In this context, the outside good market share is the U.S. market share.

The aggregation leads to the following demand system equation:

(A3) $$\ln s_{cht} - \ln s_{0t} = \theta_{1ch} + \theta_{2t} - \alpha p_{cht} + \sigma \ln s_{c|ht} + \xi_{cht}$$

The left-hand side of the demand system measures the variety's market share s_{cht} relative to the outside good market share (s_{0t}). We run regression

---

33. In a vertical market, prices are sufficient statistics for quality. Here, a variety that happens to possess a low quality, θ_{ch}, and a high price, p_{cht}, may still be purchased if the consumer draws a high ε_{chnt}.

34. As σ goes to zero, the within-product correlation also goes to zero, and the model converges to a standard logit model.

(A3) separately for aggregates of the MFA groups.[35] This allows price sensitivities and year fixed effects to vary by aggregate leading to more flexible parameter estimates. The portion of observed quality are captured by country-product (θ_{1ch}) and year (θ_{2t}) fixed effects. The price is denoted by p_{cht}, where α captures price sensitivity (a semielasticity). The $s_{c|ht}$ term results from the demand structure that nests varieties within products. This term captures the variety's market share *within* product h at time t. Finally, ξ_{cht} is the unobserved component of quality that becomes the residual of the estimating equation. Because this term is potentially correlated with prices, we have the classic simultaneity problem associated with estimating demand curves. We identify the equation by instrumenting price with trade costs.[36] The estimated qualities are defined by $\theta_{cht} = \theta_{1ch} + \theta_{2t} + \xi_{cht}$. The interpretation of these quality measures is that conditional on price, the variety with higher market shares have higher quality.[37]

References

Alchian, A., and W. Allen. 1964. *University economics.* Belmont, CA: Wadsworth.

Andriamananjara, S., J. Dean, and D. Spinanger. 2004. Trade apparel: Developing countries in 2005. Kiel Institute of World Economics, Working Paper.

Arkolakis, C. 2007. Market access costs and the new consumers margin in international trade. Yale University. Mimeograph.

Aw, B. Y., and M. Roberts. 1986. Measuring quality change in quota-constrained import markets. *Journal of International Economics* 21:45–60.

Berry, S. 1994. Estimating discrete-choice models of product differentiation. *RAND Journal of Economics* 25:242–62.

Berry, S., J. Levinsohn, and A. Pakes. 1995. Automobile prices in market equilibrium. *Econometrica* 63:841–90.

Boorstein, R., and R. Feenstra. 1991. Quality upgrading and its welfare costs in U.S. steel imports, 1969–1974. In *International trade and trade policy,* ed. E. Helpman and A. Razin, 157–86. Cambridge, MA: MIT Press.

Bown, C. 2007. China's WTO entry: Antidumping, safeguards and dispute settlement. NBER Working Paper no. 13349. Cambridge, MA: National Bureau of Economic Research.

35. Market share within an MFA group sum to 1, but we pool observations over aggregates of the MFA groups. For example, one aggregate includes dresses that differ according to fabric (e.g., MFA groups 336, 436, 636, 736, and 836). The MFA groups are classified into forty-three aggregates.

36. Hummels and Skiba (2004) find evidence supporting the Alchian-Allen conjecture that export quality increases with trade costs. This potentially raises concerns that trade costs may be correlated with variety quality. However, the exclusion restriction remains valid as long as transport costs affect *average* quality and not the time-specific deviation, ξ_{cht}. Because the nest-share term is also endogenous, we use the number of varieties within HS product to instrument this term (Berry, Levinsohn, and Pakes 1995)

37. Note that this intuition for quality is similar to that found in Hallak and Schott (2007). The results of these regressions are available upon request.

Das, S., and S. Donnenfeld. 1987. Trade policy and its impact on quality of imports: A welfare analysis. *Journal of International Economics* 23:77–95.

Dayaratna-Banda, O., and J. Whalley. 2007. After the MFA, the CCAs (China containment arrangements). CIGI Working Paper no. 24. Waterloo, Canada: Centre for International Governance Innovation.

Diao, X., and A. Somwaru. 2001. Impact of the MFA phase-out on the world economy an intertemporal, global general equilibrium analysis. TMD Discussion Paper no. 79. Washington, DC: International Food Policy Institute, Trade and Macroeconomics Division.

Evans, C., and J. Harrigan. 2005. Tight clothing: How the MFA affects apparel exports. In *International trade in East Asia,* ed. T. Ito and A. Rose, 367–90. Chicago: University of Chicago Press.

Feenstra, R. 1988. Quality change under trade restraints in Japanese autos. *Quarterly Journal of Economics* 103:131–46.

Francois, J., and J. Woerz. 2006. Rags in the high rent district: The evolution of quota rents in textiles and clothing. CEPR Working Paper no. 5477. London: Centre for Economic Policy Research.

Frazer, G., and J. Van Biesebroeck. 2007. Trade growth under the African Growth and Opportunity Act. NBER Working Paper no. 13222. Cambridge, MA: National Bureau of Economic Research.

Hallak, J., and P. Schott. 2007. Estimating cross-country differences in product quality. Yale University. Mimeograph.

Harrigan, J., and G. Barrows. 2006. Testing the theory of trade policy: Evidence from the abrupt end of the Multifibre Arrangement. NBER Working Paper no. 12579. Cambridge, MA: National Bureau of Economic Research.

Hummels, D., and A. Skiba. 2004. Shipping the good apples out? An empirical confirmation of the Alchian-Allen conjecture. *Journal of Political Economy* 12 (6): 1384–1402.

International Monetary Fund (IMF). 2007. End of quotas hits African textiles. *IMF Survey Magazine: In the News,* July 5.

Khandelwal, A. K. 2007. The long and short (of) quality ladders. Columbia Business School. Mimeograph.

Krishna, K. 1987. Tariffs versus quotas with endogenous quality. *Journal of International Economics* 23:97–112.

Nevo, A. 2003. New products, quality changes and welfare measures computed from estimated demand systems. *The Review of Economics and Statistics* 85 (2): 266–75.

Nordas, H. 2004. The global textile and clothing industry post the agreement on textiles and clothing. WTO Discussion Paper no. 5. Geneva, Switzerland: World Trade Organization.

Office of Textiles and Apparel (OTEXA), U.S. Department of Commerce. 2007. *U.S. imports, production, markets, import production ratios, and domestic market shares for textile and apparel product categories.* Washington, DC: OTEXA.

Rivera, S., L. Agama, and J. Dean. 2003. Africa beyond 2005: Understanding the impact of eliminating NTBs and tariffs on textiles and clothing. International Trade Commission. Mimeograph.

Spinanger, D. 1999. Textiles beyond the MFA phase-out. *World Economy* 22: 455–76.

United States International Trade Commission (USITC). 2004. Textile and apparel: Assessment of the competitiveness of certain foreign suppliers to the U.S. market. Investigation no. 332–448. Washington, DC: USITC.

World Trade Organization. 2001. Report of the working party on the accession of china. WT/ACC/CHN/49. Geneva, Switzerland: World Trade Organization.

Yang, Y. 1995. China's textile and clothing exports: Challenges in the post-MFA period. *Pacific Economic Papers* 250:6.7–6.12.

Comment   Joseph Francois

Introduction

Since its origins in 1947, the multilateral trading system has seen quotas imposed on products ranging from cheese and butter to high definition televisions, steel, and motor vehicles. Quantitative restrictions on international trade flows, and, more broadly speaking, the entire class of nontariff barriers (NTBs), have proven an important feature of the policy landscape. For this reason, estimates of the trade cost-equivalents of NTBs are critical inputs to the assessment of the welfare impact of trade policy, as well as to actual trade negotiations. They also influence the trade patterns at the core of the raft of recent econometric work based on the gravity model (Anderson and van Wincoop 2003 2004).

The launching of the World Trade Organization (WTO) brought with it the dismantling of the single biggest system of quota restrictions to emerge as part of the General Agreement on Tariffs and Trade (GATT)-based trading system—an elaborate system of bilateral quotas on textiles and clothing trade. The process of dismantling these quotas under the Agreement on Textiles and Clothing (ATC) was staged over a ten-year period ending in 2005. In their paper, Brambilla, Klandelwal, and Schott examine the impact of the Multi-Fiber Arrangement (MFA) and ATC on China. They provide a valuable and detailed examination of the utilization of quotas, the impact of quotas, and their expansion on exports during the MFA and ATC, and their role in the surge of exports from China after quotas ended. Their findings fit with other recent estimates (Francois and Woerz 2009; Martin 2004; Andriamananjara, Dean, and Spinanger 2004). While by construction the quotas were increased over time, the technical liberalization of a quota does not guarantee de facto relaxation of implicit trade barriers when the external environment is also changing. In the case of China, quotas on Chinese exports to both the United States and European Union (EU) clearly grew at a rate unable to keep up with the rapid expansion of potential trade due to a mix of both underlying supply and demand growth. As a result, China was more constrained than other countries under the ATC, and, consequently, there was a surge in China's market share when quotas were lifted.

Joseph Francois is a professor of economics with a chair in economic theory at Johannes Kepler Universität Linz.

In my comments, I will focus on two issues. One is the broader context of the ATC phaseout, in terms of its origins and related concerns about quota liberalization on smaller, less-competitive suppliers. The second is the pattern of restrictions on China relative to other major suppliers under the ATC regime.

The ATC and MFA in Context

Like agriculture, the textile and clothing sectors emerged in the early years of the GATT system as politically sensitive sectors. As such, they were treated as special cases within the world trading system, with their own regulatory framework. While technically in violation of the GATT, the quotas were first institutionalized in the beginning of the 1960s with the Short-Term Arrangement (STA) for international trade in cotton textiles. The STA aimed at an orderly opening of restricted markets to avoid (for importing countries) "detrimental market disruptions." The definition of "market disruption" adopted by the Contracting Parties in 1960 entailed the possibility of singling out imports of particular products from particular countries as the disrupting source. This opened the door for a series of bilaterally negotiated quota restrictions that became the rule in the following Long-Term Arrangement (LTA) in 1962. Details on the subsequent evolution of acronyms are provided in table 9C.1.

By the start of the 1970s, it had become apparent that the multiplicity of makeshift arrangements protecting the textile and clothing industries had to be replaced. Resulting negotiations led to the MFA, which went into effect in 1974. Over time, its product coverage was extended from cotton to noncotton textiles and clothing. The final MFA (known as MFA IV) was extended several times, leading in the end to the ATC in 1995. Like the preceding arrangements, the MFA provided rules for the imposition of quotas, either through bilateral agreements or unilateral actions, whenever actual or perceived surges of imports caused market disruption. (Baughman et al. 1997; Krishna and Tan 1997). This included the threat of a surge. In the years leading up to the Uruguay Round Agreements, six developed participants actively applied quotas under the MFA—the EU, the United States, Canada, Norway, Finland, and Austria. These were applied almost exclusively on imports from developing countries. Sweden liberalized its textile and clothing regime in 1991 and actually managed to withdraw from the MFA. Sadly, Sweden was forced to rejoin this regime when it joined the EU. Two other developed-country participants, Japan and Switzerland, did not impose MFA quotas, but instead restricted themselves to "signaling" a readiness to apply quotas by the act of being signatories to the MFA agreement, combined with (active) import surveillance. As shown by Winters (1994), import surveillance can, at least in concentrated industries, induce a fall in import levels as producers are trying to forestall explicit quotas. The restrictiveness of the applied MFA quotas, and subsequent ATC quotas, var-

Table 9C.1   **A parade of acronyms: the evolution of quotas**

Year	Overview of events
1955–57	U.S.–Japan dispute leads to a 5-year agreement limiting textile exports
1958	United Kingdom imposes "voluntary" limitation on cotton textile and clothing products with Hong Kong by threatening to otherwise impose quotas at levels lower than prevailing volumes.
1959	United Kingdom signs restraint agreements with India and Pakistan.
1960	General Agreement on Tariffs and Trade Contracting Parties recognize the problem of "market disruption" to serve as an "excuse" for establishing future nontariff barriers.
1961	**STA:** The Short-Term Arrangement (STA) is agreed.
1962	**LTA1:** The Long-Term Arrangement (LTA) is agreed, to commence October 1, 1962, and last for five years.
1963–65	United States tries and fails to establish agreement on trade in wool products
1966	The United Kingdom implements a global quota scheme in violation of the LTA. The LTA provides only for product-specific restraints.
1967	**LTA2:** Agreement is reached to extend the LTA for three years.
1969–71	United States negotiates voluntary export restraints with Asian suppliers on wool and man-made fibers.
1970	**LTA3:** Agreement is reached to extend the LTA for three years. It was later extended three months more, to fill the gap until the Multi-Fiber Arrangement (MFA) came into effect.
1973	**MFA I:** The MFA is agreed, to commence January 1, 1974, and to last for four years.
1977	The European Economic Community and the United States negotiates bilateral agreements with developing countries prior to agreeing to extension of the MFA.
1977	**MFA II:** The MFA is extended for four years.
1981	**MFA III:** The MFA is renewed for five years. The United States, under pressure from increased imports resulting from dollar appreciation, negotiates tough quotas.
1986	**MFA IV:** The MFA is extended for 5 years, to conclude with the expected end of the Uruguay Round (UR).
1991	**MFA IV+:** The MFA is extended pending outcome of the UR negotiations.
1993	The UR draft final act provides for a 10-year phase-out of all MFA and other quotas on textiles in the Agreement on Textiles and Clothing (ATC). MFA extends until UR comes into force. ATC allows credit for liberalization in products that are not actually restricted.
1995	**ATC1:** 1st ATC tranche liberalized 16% of 1990 imports.
1998	**ATC2:** 2nd ATC tranche liberalized 17% of 1990 imports.
2001	**ATC3:** 3rd ATC tranche liberalized 18% of 1990 imports.
2005	**ATC4:** 4th ATC tranche liberalized 49% of 1990 imports.
	Déjà vu all over again: United States and European Union reimpose quotas on China.

Source: Based on an update of Francois, Glismann, and Spinanger (2000), from Francois and Woerz (2009).

ied from product to product and from supplier to supplier. Norway dropped the use of binding quotas with the shift from MFA to ATC.

The Ministerial Declaration at Punta Del Este in 1986 that launched the Uruguay Round stated that the "Negotiations in the area of textiles and clothing shall aim to formulate modalities that would permit the eventual integration of this sector into GATT on the basis of strengthened GATT rules and disciplines." In plain English, this was a promise to developing countries that MFA quotas were finally going to be eliminated. Indeed, this promise was critical to convincing developing countries to sign on at the creation of the then new WTO. The Uruguay Round of GATT negotiations launched at Punta Del Este led to the ATC in 1995. The ATC was the institutional embodiment of the promise to end quotas in an orderly process. Indeed, it was flagged as a major showpiece in the Uruguay Round Agreements and an important source of trade-based income gains linked to the introduction of the WTO (Harrison, Rutherford, and Tarr 1995; Francois, McDonald, and Nordström 1995; Hertel et al. 1995). By design, the agreement mapped a gradual phaseout of the quota restrictions carried over from the MFA regime on a ten-year timetable leading to full elimination.

Though the ATC was a response to developing-country demands, a number of developing countries expressed concern from the outset, and some even mounted a rearguard action in the end of the ATC phaseout to try and block final quota elimination. In combination with regional agreements, the quotas had led to a distorted pattern of exports, with high import shares for Eastern European and Mediterranean suppliers in the EU market and likewise for Mexico in the U.S. market. For instance, Spinanger (1999) reports evidence that the EU quotas in textile and clothing prevented diversification of the market across exporting countries based on relative costs. In the case of the EU, these distortions were also intentionally used for a discriminatory trade policy with the aim to spur development in certain countries at the expense of other developing countries. With China more restricted than other suppliers (a fact confirmed by the Brambilla, Khandelwal, and Schott estimates), there was genuine concern that smaller, less-competitive suppliers would be hurt in the competitive shuffle following liberalization.

Related to concerns about smaller exporters, there was also concern that the MFA and ATC had induced too much specialization in unconstrained exporters (for example, Bangladesh). Through the quota system, some small, unconstrained exporters were largely protected from the competition of other, bigger suppliers for a long time. Thus, the quota system might have induced strong and persistent specialization in textiles and clothing in these countries, while in the absence of the quotas the need to diversify into other industries may have been stronger. The worry was that removal of the quotas against all suppliers would suddenly make such a failure all too obvious (Spinanger 1999).

What actually happened? As Brambilla, Khandelwal, and Schott note, we did indeed see a surge in exports from China after the ATC quotas were eliminated. From their detailed analysis, they also report that unit values fell in products where quotas were lifted. China moved to lower prices and higher volumes in liberalized products (consistent with loss of quota rents in export pricing). This is only part of the story, however. Because China's quota growth rates did not keep up with growth in supply conditions in China (where growth was around ten percent a year), let alone the combined impact of income growth (i.e., rising demand) in North America and Europe, the quotas on China were still largely binding when they expired. The outcome was political theater, new quotas on China, and revitalization of managed trade in the sector. I will focus on the pattern of protection against China in the next section.

The Impact of the Quotas

The impact of quantitative restrictions on trade is reflected in per-unit economic rent generated by a binding quota. This is because a binding quota effectively limits the supply of the good in the importing market, resulting in a price markup and giving economic rents to those suppliers who have access to the market (i.e., those who are able to export inside the quota). Because the quotas on textiles and clothing were administered as "voluntary" export restraints by the suppliers, often with the quotas distributed by auction, these rents can alternatively be seen as an implicit tax on exports. For these reasons, the effect of the quotas in the literature is generally expressed as an export tax equivalent (ETE). In their paper, Brambilla, Khandelwal, and Schott use ETEs to focus in detail on how quotas impacted China. I will focus here on how, at the same time, these quotas had a broadly more restrictive impact on China than on other suppliers, again in terms of ETEs. To do this, I will make some comparisons based on ETEs for a wider set of countries, though at a more aggregate level.

Table 9C.2 reports information on the top five suppliers in textiles and clothing for the quota using importers: Canada, the United States, and the EU. Because China ranged among the top suppliers for all quota users in 2001, the evolution of the Chinese ETEs as implied by the quotas can be read from table 9C.2. The tariff and ETE estimates in table 9C.2 come from Francois and Woerz (2009). Other data come from Martin (2004) and the World Bank's *World Development Indicators* database. Canada was the quota user most compliant with the ATC among all three. The reduction in price wedges for China was especially impressive. During the life of the ATC, the ETE was reduced to zero from an estimated 30.4 percent of export price for clothing. Indeed, with most suppliers, liberalization was substantial in Canada, if not complete, even if some high barriers remained, mostly against minor suppliers (for instance, Jamaica, Qatar, and Morocco).

While there was a clear pattern toward liberalization for imports to the EU, the degree of liberalization was more limited than in the Canadian

Table 9C.2 **Top 5 import suppliers**

	2001 import share	2001 tariff	ETEs as % of export price 1996	ETEs as % of export price 2004
EU15: textiles				
Turkey	14.0	0.0		
China	9.1	8.2	18.6***	14.0***
India	8.1	7.5	6.6***	2.0***
United States	4.7	6.4		
Pakistan	4.6	0.0	13.1***	3.2***
All	100.0	1.8	1.8	0.7
EU15: clothing				
China	17.1	10.6	48.5**	19.4***
Turkey	8.5	0.0		
Romania	6.6	0.0		
Tunisia	6.2	0.0		
India	5.8	8.5	19.3***	
All	100.0	3.2	13.1	3.6
United States: textiles				
Mexico	12.7	0.1		
European Union	10.9	8.5		
China	10.2	7.4	6.5***	7.2***
Canada	7.7	0.0		
Pakistan	5.4	9.0	5.2***	
All	100.0	7.9	3.8	3.5
United States: clothing				
China	13.3	9.8	43.3***	48.1***
Mexico	12.1	0.1		
Hong Kong	6.9	11.5		
European Union	4.5	10.1		
Indonesia	4.3	12.7		
All	100.0	9.9	10.2	14.5
Canada: textiles				
United States	54.2	0.0		
European Union	8.7	9.4		
China	7.4	13.5	5.9***	
Korea, Republic of	4.4	10.3		
India	3.6	10.9	0.1	
All	100.0	5.2	0.5	0.0
Canada: clothing				
China	27.4	15.6	30.4***	
United States	12.0	0.0		
European Union	8.0	16.3		
India	7.8	17.7		
Hong Kong	6.4	17.9		
All	100.0	14.5	11.6	0.1

Source: Francois and Woerz (2009).

Note: ETEs = export tax equivalents

***Estimated bilateral ETEs significant at the 1 percent level.

**Estimated bilateral ETEs significant at the 5 percent level.

case. Although trade with China became more liberalized, the degree of protection remained high at the end of the ATC. Table 9C.2 shows the fall in protection against China. However, the tariff equivalents at the end of the ATC remained substantial. The removal of the quota system by 2005 thus implied a substantial surge in imports from China. Indeed, as Brambilla, Khandelwal, and Schott note, in 2004 and 2005, we saw a tremendous increases in China's market share in the EU market, leading to a reimposition of quotas by the middle of 2005.

Most interesting is the experience with the United States. The ETEs for China actually went up. The observed backloading of trade liberalization vis-à-vis China should not be surprising and cannot be ascribed purely to noncompliance with the ATC. Nor is it the case that China was alone. China's experience was instead a consequence, in part, of the design of the system. From table 9C.2, U.S. protection against restricted suppliers went up for fifteen WTO exporters of textiles. Only four WTO suppliers—Cambodia, Macedonia, Brazil, and Pakistan—faced falling export tax equivalents during the ATC in the U.S. market. For clothing, three suppliers—Uruguay, Cambodia, and India—saw a fall in their ETEs, while nine suppliers faced increasing price distortions—Turkey, Bulgaria, China, Poland, Hungary, Slovakia, Romania, and the Czech Republic.

In the case of China, the spike in U.S. quotas follows from the interaction of several factors. The first factor is the failure of quota growth to keep up with growth in potential trade. This is illustrated in table 9C.3, which highlights the strong expansion of the Chinese economy and, thus, the huge increase in export potential over the life of the ATC. This growth well surpassed quota growth rates. While the Chinese quotas on the U.S. market increased by 33 percent in textiles and 41 percent in clothing between 1994 and 2004, Chinese gross domestic product (GDP) rose by 170 percent over the same period. With a cumulative growth of 61 percent, U.S. GDP growth—as a proxy for the growth of import demand—itself outstripped the rate of quota expansion. Another factor in spiking ETEs was the ability to "borrow forward" on quotas. This meant that, for example, in late 2000, importers could borrow against 2001 quota limits. Obviously, by late 2004, there were no more quotas to borrow against, contributing to the late surge in U.S. ETEs as the system, by construction, became increasingly restrictive.

Closing Comments

Careful empirical analysis of quota regimes, like those provided by Brambilla, Khandelwal, and Schott, offer valuable insight regarding the political difficulties that followed the ATC's end days. The ATC embodied commitments to a ten-year, staged reduction in quotas. The process was advertised as orderly, systematic, and transparent. Yet the end of the ATC brought with it sudden surges in imports from China, panicked trade ministers, rushed

Table 9C.3   Cumulative growth: 1994–2004 (%)

| | Quota growth | | | | GDP growth | |
| | textiles | | clothing | | | |
	U.S.	EU	U.S.	EU	Per capita	In total
Importer						
United States					49	66
European Union					55	61
Exporter						
Bangladesh	168		168		26	53
China	33	50	41	38	151	171
Hong Kong	37	16	17	22	1	16
India	141	50	116	79	57	84
Indonesia	134	83	133	117	19	35
Korea, Republic of	37	70	12	38	34	44
Pakistan	139	79	150	119	30	63
Sri Lanka	134	204	132	204	43	56
Philippines, The	134	112	119	112	1	21
Thailand	127	116	123	116	−10	−1

Sources: Martin (2004), Eurostat, IFS, and Francois and Woerz (2009).

meetings, and the reimposition of quotas on China by late 2005 in both the United States and EU. This episode is fully consistent with recent estimates of the price impact of quotas. A key implication from the results of this research is that the problem of China's textile and clothing sector integration was basically deferred rather than managed in stages. This was not solely a result of the ATC itself, but was certainly reinforced by insufficient predefined quota expansion rates during a period of outstandingly strong expansion of China's supply potential and demand growth in North America and Europe.

An important underlying question is the extent to which managed trade in textiles and clothing is really a thing of the past. There was a de facto peace clause during the MFA and ATC. Exporters agreed to managed trade, and importers agreed not to support antidumping and countervailing duty investigations. Obviously, this cease fire is over. We may yet see a return to managed trade. In addition, there are now countries outside the original MFA importer club—Korea, Brazil, South Africa, and Mexico, for example—who may themselves succumb to similar pressure to manage trade in these sector as they move up the value added ladder and their own producers fall under rising competitive pressure from importers. The MFA (and ATC) may be dead. However, we cannot assume the political economy fundamentals that drove the creation of the system in the first place really have been put to rest.

References

Anderson, J., and E. van Wincoop. 2003. Gravity with gravitas: A solution to the border puzzle. *American Economic Review* 93 (1):170–92.
———. 2004. Trade costs. *Journal of Economic Literature* 42 (3): 691–751.
Andriamananjara, S., J. Dean, and D. Spinanger. 2004. Trading apparel: Developing countries in 2005. USITC and Kiel Insitut for World Economics. Mimeograph
Baughman, L., R. Mirus, M. Morkre, and D. Spinanger. 1997. Of tyre cords, ties, and tents. *The World Economy* 4:407–34.
Francois, J., H. H. Glismann, and D. Spinanger. 2000. The cost of EU trade protection in textiles and clothing. Kiel Working Paper no. 997. Kiel, Germany: Kiel Institute for the World Economy, August.
Francois, J., B. McDonald, and H. Nordström. 1995. Assessing the Uruguay Round. In *The Uruguay Round and the developing economies,* ed. W. Martin and L. Alan Winters, 117–214. Cambridge, UK: Cambridge University Press.
Francois, J., and J. Woerz. 2009. Non-linear panel estimation of import quotas: The evolution of quota premiums under the ATC. *Journal of International Economics* 78 (2): 181–91.
Harrison, G. W., T. F. Rutherford, and D. G. Tarr. 1995. Quantifying the Uruguay Round. In *The Uruguay Round and the developing economies,* ed. W. Martin and L. A. Winters, 215–84. World Bank Discussion Paper no. 307. Washington, DC: World Bank.
Hertel, T. W., W. Martin, K. Yanagishima, and B. Dimaranan. 1995. Liberalizing manufactures in a changing world economy. In *The Uruguay Round and the developing economies,* ed. W. Martin and L. A. Winters, 73–96. World Bank Discussion Paper no. 307. Washington, DC: World Bank.
Krishna, K., and L. H. Tan. 1997. The multifibre arrangement in practice: Challenging the competitive framework. In *East Asian trade after the Uruguay Round,* ed. D. Robertson, 59–77. Cambridge, UK: Cambridge University Press.
Martin, W. 2004. Implications for Pakistan of abolishing the textile and clothing quotas. Report by the World Bank, April 30. Washington, DC: World Bank.
Spinanger, D. 1999. Textiles beyond the MFA Phase-out. *The World Economy* 22 (June): 455–76.
Winters, L. A. 1994. The EC and protection: The political economy. *European Economic Review* 38 (3–4): 596–603.

10

Agricultural Trade Reform and Rural Prosperity
Lessons from China

Jikun Huang, Yu Liu, Will Martin, and Scott Rozelle

China's agriculture has grown rapidly in recent years, despite radical reductions in agricultural tariffs (Huang and Chen 1999; Huang, Rozelle, and Chang 2004). China's agriculture has moved from a focus on self-sufficiency and industry-first growth, through the Open Door Policy of the 1980s, to a much more market-oriented regime. Accession to the World Trade Organization (WTO) was allowed only after China promised major institutional reforms and a virtually unprecedented degree of tariff reduction, the abolition of export subsidies, and introduction of constraints on domestic support (Lardy 2001; Bhattasali, Li, and Martin 2004).

In response to the commitment to reform trade as well as domestic markets, there were fears that such sharp liberalization would have dire consequences for the rural population. In poor countries, government officials know that agricultural price shifts can have important effects on domestic food production, farm household incomes, national poverty rates, and overall rural stability. Many voices focused on the cuts in agricultural tariffs and warned that poverty in China would be exacerbated and rural incomes would fall if the nation were to follow through with their ambitious domestic market and trade liberalization policies (Carter and Estrin 2001; Li, Zhai, and Wang 1999; Schmidhuber 2001; Ni 2007). Even in light of these concerns, policymakers have pushed ahead.

Jikun Huang is director of the Center for Chinese Agricultural Policy. Yu Liu is a doctor and assistant research fellow in the Economic Forecasting Department of the State Information Center, Beijing. Will Martin is research manager of rural development in the Develoment Research Group at the World Bank. Scott Rozelle is the Helen F. Farnsworth Senior Fellow in the Freeman Spogli Institute for International Studies, Stanford University.

The views expressed in this paper are those of the authors alone and not those of the World Bank or any other individual or institution.

By the mid-2000s, the concerns about rural incomes of critics of trade policies had not been realized. Even scholars who have long worried about poor income growth in the rural areas are admitting the incomes and rural welfare are rising as never before. Although the gap in incomes between urban and rural people remains large, conventional measures of this gap are overstated by neglecting the lower costs of living in rural areas and by the exclusion of rural migrants living in urban areas when calculating average urban incomes (Sicular et al. 2006; Chen and Ravallion 2007; National Bureau of Statistics of China [NBSC] 2007).

Although there has long been an interest in the agricultural economy (e.g., Lardy 1983; Sicular 1988a; Lin 1992; Rosen, Huang, and Rozelle 2004), it is quite surprising to many that the agricultural sector of China actually has a very impressive record. Growth rates of gross domestic product (GDP), agricultural value added, and food per capita increased dramatically between the early 1980s and the mid-2000s. Indeed, China's performance in agriculture over the past two decades was more impressive than any other country in Asia. Markets have boomed. The structure of agriculture has fundamentally shifted. Despite having the largest population in the world and high income growth (which has radically changed consumption patterns), China has remained a net exporter of agricultural products until very recently, with a recent switch to net import status due largely to increased cotton imports needed for burgeoning exports of textiles and clothing. A report by the National Bureau of Statistics of China (NBSC 2006) demonstrates that rural incomes grew robustly between 2002 and 2005 and did so in all income deciles and all provinces (see table 10.2).

The overall goal of this paper is to address these questions using two specific approaches. The first is to present estimates of indicators of direct and indirect interventions of China's government in agriculture from 1981, when it first became possible to assess the stance of trade policies, to 2005, when almost all of China's WTO commitments had been phased in. To achieve this objective, we examine the differences in prices between international prices and domestic prices at the border (Nominal Rates of Assistance [NRA] at the market level and NRA_f at the farm level). Because input-related policies were relatively small over most of our sample period, we focus on the transfers associated with changes in commodity prices, although we include the effects of input measures in our estimates of support to farmers. In the most general terms, we find that China shifted from an economy that was highly distorted with a generally taxed agricultural sector, to one that was highly integrated with the world economy.

In the second part of the paper, we seek to understand what allowed the rural economy to do as well as it has in the face of falling prices for some products. To do so, we examine four factors: investments in agricultural technology; the policy responses aimed at deregulating agricultural markets and promoting structural adjustment; the new set of programs that has redirected resources toward rural infrastructure and services as well as relatively nondistorting transfer programs and tax cuts; and policies aimed at facilitating the movement of labor from agriculture to industry and from rural to urban.

The wide scope of our goals and objectives necessitate certain limitations. First, the absence of data precludes our examining the entire agricultural sector. Instead, we examine commodities that account for two-thirds or more of gross output value over our study period. Second, although we are able to judge from the price trends and our understanding of domestic marketing and trade policy reforms the broad sources of the shifts in the distortions of the agricultural economy, we cannot identify the exact source of changes and must rely on earlier work by the authors and others examining these causal linkages in more detail (Huang and Rozelle 1996; de Brauw, Huang, and Rozelle 2004). Third, because of the complexity of agricultural trade instruments during the period—including state trading, quotas, licenses, tariffs, and exchange rate distortions—we were forced to use price comparison approaches even though exchange rates were distorted by a two-tier exchange rate system up to 1994. During this period, we used an exchange rate adjusted for the two-tier exchange rate system to compare international prices with prices in China's domestic economy, an approach used in (Huang, Liu, et al. 2009).

Before showing these results in the following section, we discuss our quantitative approach and sources of data. The results of the distortion analysis are presented and discussed in the next section. The following section discusses three policy responses that are likely part of the reason for the robust performance of China's rural sector. The final section concludes.

10.1   Methodology and Data Sources

In this paper, we have utilized the approach specified in Anderson et al. (2008). The approach is primarily based on comparisons between domestic and international prices. During the reform era, these price comparisons provide indicators of the incentives for production, consumption and trade, and of the income transfers associated with interventions.

Our approach essentially creates two main measures of distortions for each commodity. The basic measure in our analysis is the NRA, used to compare the prices of commodities in the domestic economy (at the port) with the international prices of commodities at the border (that is, cost, insurance, and freight [c.i.f.] in the port for importables; free on board [f.o.b.] in the port for exportables).

Because of barriers within the domestic economy, the extent of protection (or disprotection) provided by trade policies may not be the same as the protection to farmers. Because we have independent observations on the prices obtained by farmers in local markets we are able to estimate the *nominal rate of assistance at the farm level* taking into account *both* border distortions and domestic distortions affecting farmer returns (NRA$_f$s). NRA$_f$s are calculated after allowing for quality adjustment; taxes or subsidies; and transport, storage, and handling costs in moving commodities from the farm to the wholesale level. Differences between NRAs and NRA$_f$s can arise from subsidy or transfer payments that cause the prices received by farmers to differ from what they would receive under competitive internal market conditions.[1]

10.1.1   The Data

In compiling our data, we necessarily had to make choices on commodity coverage. We included eleven commodities: rice, wheat, maize, soybeans, cotton, pork, milk, poultry, fruit (using apples as a representative product), vegetables (using tomatoes as a representative product), and sugar (both sugarbeet and sugarcane). Over the study period, these commodities accounted for roughly 75 percent (in the late 1980s) and 60 percent (during the early 2000s) of the value of agricultural output in China. Because production and consumption decisions were only gradually being allowed to respond to domestic prices, and because we do not have access to reliable data on secondary market exchange rates prior to 1981, we focus on the period from 1981.

Much of the data on margins, transportation costs, and other transaction costs are from an extensive set of surveys by Huang and Rozelle during the 1990s and the early 2000s, surveys which also served to establish which commodity price series provided appropriate bases for price comparisons. Some of this was previously reported in Rozelle et al. (2000) and Huang, Rozelle, and Chang (2004), which provided information on substantial quality differences between some imported and domestic commodities and resulting methodologies for ensuring valid price comparisons. For more recent years, survey teams from the Center for Chinese Agricultural Policy interviewed traders in ten cities around China in 2006. The complete data series are in the appendixes of Huang et al. (2007).

When calculating the rate of support to farmers, we took into account direct support measures using data from the Price Department of the National Development and Reform Commission. These measures included three applying since 2002—direct grain supports, the seed subsidy program, and agricultural machinery subsidies. We also took into account the negative assistance imposed by agricultural taxes on production of specific commodities. We did not take into account the input subsidy program that pays subsidies to state-owned enterprises (SOEs) producing fertilizers and mulching film on the grounds that all or part of this may be a subsidy to the

---

1. While NRAs only measure differences in output prices, there may also be distortions on the input side; our NRA$_f$ measures include a number of budget support and tax measures. The assumption and methods that were used to generate our exchange rate series are in Martin, Huang, and Rozelle (2006).

SOEs, rather than to the farmers. Nor did we include the "grain for green" payments made to convert fragile agricultural land to forest or pasture (see OECD [2008] for details of both of these measures).

10.2   Results

10.2.1   The Role of Domestic Price and Marketing Policy

Before examining the role of distortions at the border, it is useful (and necessary) to examine the relationship between the available domestic price series for farm and retail prices for two major grain crops (figure 10.1, panels A and B). The importance (and role) of China's domestic price and marketing policy for rice and wheat (the two largest crops in China—one an exportable and the other an importable) can be seen by comparing the state-set urban retail price and the state-set farm-gate procurement price with the rural retail price, a free market price. Until 1992, the urban retail price for rice was generally well below the free market price in rural areas, despite the costs associated with transferring rice to urban areas. Only urban residents could buy rice at these low prices and only with ration coupons that were available in limited quantities.

The relatively low selling price of grain at the farm gate by farmers shows that China's food system in the 1980s was set up to transfer income from rural to urban people (figure 10.1, panels A and B). The amount that farmers received for their mandatory deliveries was far below the free market price although, in the case of rice, it was above the urban retail price, suggesting urban prices were held down by a subsidy as well as by taxation of farmers. However, there is some question about the effects of the depressed rural prices on farmers' incentives given the inframarginal nature of many of these transfers (Sicular 1988b). This is because from the mid-1980s, farmers were able to sell additional amounts at higher market prices once they had met their obligation to deliver a quota at the low purchasing price. As shown by Sicular (1988b), the higher out-of-quota price is the relevant incentive for production at the margin. However, as shown by Wang, Rozelle, and Huang (1999), even such policies may not be fully decoupled from incentives, with seemingly inframarginal transfers giving rural household members an incentive to move out of agriculture.

After 1992, however, changes to China's domestic marketing and procurement system appear to have eliminated this additional layer of taxation and regulation for producers of rice and wheat (figure 10.1, panels A and B). In the early 1990s, the urban price began to rise above the farm gate price; urban and rural retail prices also came much closer together. The gap between urban and rural retail prices essentially disappeared. And the gap between the rural retail price and the farm price declined, possibly suggesting an improvement in marketing efficiency (Park et al. 2002).

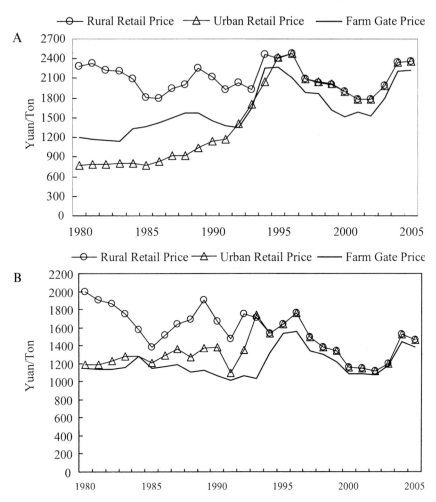

Fig. 10.1   Rural retail price (free market price), urban retail price, and farm-gate sales price in China, 1980–2005 (real 2005 yuan): *A*, Rice; *B*, Wheat
Source: NDRC (2005).

10.2.2   Nominal Rates of Assistance for China's
Main Agricultural Commodities

In this section, we focus on the distortions faced by farmers in China between 1981 and 2005. To do so, we examine plots of NRAs and NRA_fs over time for an illustrative subsample of our eleven commodities. A more comprehensive analysis is contained in Huang, Rozelle, et al. (2009).

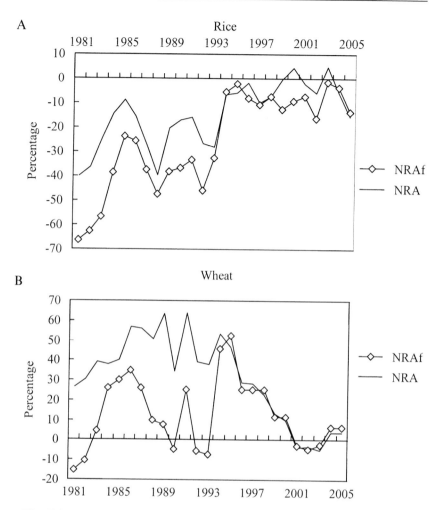

Fig. 10.2   Nominal rates of assistance (NRAs) and nominal rates of assistance for farmers (NRA_f s) for rice and wheat in China, 1981–2005: *A*, Rice; *B*, Wheat
Source: Huang et al. (2007).

Distortions to the Grain Economy before 1995

The distortions to the rice economy of China in the 1980s and early 1990s are characterized by two important features (figure 10.2, panel A). First, the NRA of rice, an exportable commodity, is negative in every year between 1980 and 1995. Ranging between –40 and –10, the negative NRAs show that China was highly competitive in international rice markets during these years. Trade policy, and particularly the state trading monopoly, kept exporters from shipping large quantities of rice onto world markets and kept market prices of rice in China's port cities below world prices.

The second feature demonstrates how domestic marketing and procurement placed a greater tax on farmers and insulated the domestic price of rice from the world market price even if trade policy had been liberalized (figure 10.2, panel A). The state's artificially low procurement price kept the price received by farmers systematically below the free market price of rice as seen by the NRA_fs. Because of this, the total tax on rice ranged from −70 in the early 1980s to −30 in the early 1990s. Rice producers were among the most heavily taxed farmers in China—given the large share of the crop's sown area and large negative rates of disprotection.

Unlike rice, the NRA measures show that trade policy offered high rates of protection for wheat in China between 1981 and the mid-1990s (figure 10.2, panel B). In most years after 1980, the free market price of wheat in China's port cities was about 60 percent above international prices (cost, insurance, and freight [cif], China's port cities). Unlike rice farmers, wheat producers—who have been shown to produce at a higher cost than producers in many other countries (Huang and Ma 2000)—benefited from high market prices for their marginal output. By keeping out imports and keeping domestic prices high, trade policy appears to have been focused on food self-sufficiency, rather than on providing inexpensive food to urban consumers.

The differences between rice and wheat illustrate that trade liberalization in China should not have been expected to hurt everyone and emphasize the importance of looking at distortions on a commodity by commodity basis. Trade liberalization clearly had the potential to help rice producers, in particular. By contrast, the removal of the high protection rates for wheat observed in the 1980s and early 1990s would have had the potential to hurt wheat producers. Our analysis of why trade policy reform has been accompanied by rural income rises seems most relevant for the case of crops, such as wheat, that were receiving positive protection in the 1980s and 1990s.

Domestic marketing policies, however, were working in the opposite direction. The trends in NRA_fs show how the forced deliveries under wheat quotas largely insulated farmers from much of the benefit of protection (figure 10.2, panel B). Although there was still positive protection for wheat in most years between 1980 and 1995, the average rates were lower (all below 50 percent except for in 1994 and 1995) and were zero and even slightly negative in five of the sixteen years (1981, 1982, 1990, 1992, and 1993). These figures suggest that policy for wheat was trying to increase production through the higher market prices, but to transfer income from producers to consumers through the inframarginal transfers captured in the NRA_f. Huang et al. (2007) show that the story for maize is similar to that of wheat.

Distortions to the Grain Economy after 1995

After 1995, our distortions analysis shows that China's international trade and domestic marketing policies have changed strikingly (figure 10.2, right-hand sides of panels A and B). That China's reformers were able to eliminate the procurement policies that had been taxing rice and wheat (and maize) farmers is apparent from the way the differences between NRAs and NRA_fs narrow and disappear. In other work, Huang, Rozelle, and Chang (2004) show that elimination of the procurement quota system contributed significantly to a reduction in the tax burden on farmers. In part, then, procurement policy reform itself was important in increasing rural incomes to farmers during the 1990s.

The liberalization of domestic policies in the mid-1990s was accompanied by liberalization of trade policy, at least in the case of China's major food grains. After 1995, the taxation and subsidization of rice and wheat were being phased out as the NRAs for rice steadily rose (became less negative), and the NRAs for wheat fell. Likely in part in preparation for its accession to the WTO, China's leaders liberalized trade for its main food grains to such an extent that between 1995 and 2001, most of the protection for these crops was eliminated. Since 2001, the NRAs for both rice and wheat have been almost zero.

Edible Oils, Milk and Sugar

Outside the grain economy, marketing and trade reform, as in the case of wheat, removed positive protection from a number of key commodities. The biggest difference between the analysis of distortions for grain crops and cash crops (in our case, for soybeans) is that domestic marketing policy has historically played less of a role for cash crops. Although some counties had procurement delivery quotas for soybean producers, this was not as widespread as for grain, and the implicit taxes on soybeans in counties with quotas were generally lower than for staple grains. There was, as a consequence, little difference between the graphs for NRAs and NRA_fs. The same applies for the remaining commodities (livestock, horticulture, and milk and sugar) because there was no state-mandated procurement for these commodities. As a result, the discussion in the rest of this section focuses on trade policy.

Before 1995, our analysis shows that soybeans fluctuated between being taxed and protected (figure 10.3). Although the average level of protection was roughly zero, it varied from –20 percent up to 30 percent. A paper by Rozelle and Huang (2004) shows that much of this fluctuation was due to domestic policy cycles that switched between encouraging and discouraging production while allowing little trade.

The trends in NRAs after 1995 show the strong commitment to trade liberalization for soybeans (figure 10.3, right-hand side of the graph). Begin-

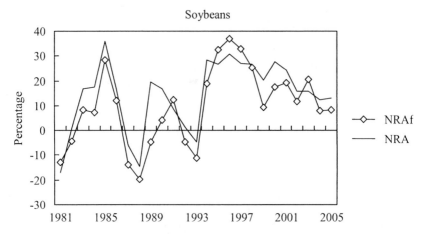

Fig. 10.3   Nominal rates of assistance (NRAs) and nominal rates of assistance for farmers (NRA$_f$s) for soybean in China, 1981–2005
Source: Huang et al. (2007).

ning in the late 1990s and continuing through 2005, protection for soybeans fell from around 30 percent to almost zero. This falling protection, in fact, should not be a surprise given the integration of China into world soybean markets and the monotonic rise in imports (which exceeded 25 million tons in 2005). The story of soybeans after 1995 parallels that of wheat. In fact, because of the high level of imports, the case of soybean producers often raised in discussions about the adverse effects of trade policies on farmers (see Rozelle and Huang [2004] for a complete description). In fact, Rozelle and Huang (2004) empirically show using CAPSiM (an agricultural simulation model developed by the authors) that soybean prices and the incomes of soybean producers would have been higher in the absence of trade reform. Therefore, in the case of soybeans, the government carried through with its commitment to trade reform.

Protection of milk and sugar began earlier and remained higher than for soybeans. During the 1980s, the NRAs for milk and sugar were large and positive (figure 10.4, panels A and B), with milk ranging between 50 and over 200 percent between 1980 and 1987, and sugar above 40 percent through the late 1990s. The NRAs for milk fell dramatically in the late 1980s and subsequently fluctuated between zero and 50 percent. Protection for sugar also fell in the late 1980s, but subsequently rose, with the average NRA fluctuating around 40 percent.

Livestock and Horticultural Commodities

The case of livestock (figure 10.5 for pork) and horticulture (not shown here—see Huang et al. 2007) show that trade liberalization directly helped

A
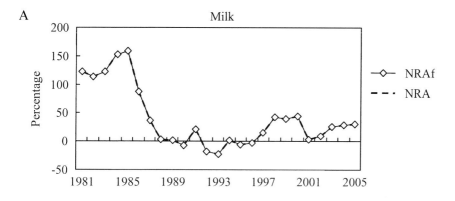

B
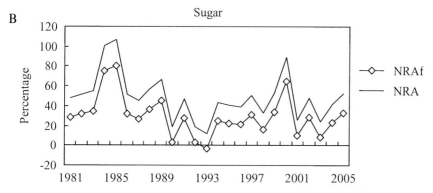

Fig. 10.4   Nominal rates of assistance (NRAs) and nominal rates of assistance for farmers (NRA_fs) for industrial processed goods (milk and sugar production) in China, 1981–2005: *A*, Protection measures for milk; *B*, Protection measures for sugar

Source: Huang et al. (2007).

raise farm incomes in certain regions and sectors. During the early reform era there was heavy implicit taxation of livestock and horticultural commodities. Although China can competitively produce labor-intensive livestock and horticultural products, producers were not encouraged to produce or export these commodities on a large scale. Part of the resistance to exports was from China's own barriers, such as quotas on exports to Hong Kong. Another part of the price gap shown in these figures reflects trade barriers facing China in export markets. While there quite possibly were grounds for some of these barriers (for example, foot and mouth disease is widespread in China), even blatantly false claims could not be contested because China was not a WTO member. As a consequence, China's livestock and horticultural producers produced commodities far below the world market price yet were unable to increase exports into global markets.

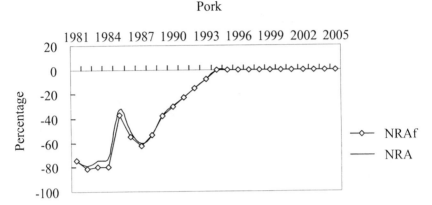

Fig. 10.5   Nominal rates of assistance (NRAs) and nominal rates of assistance for farmers (NRA$_f$s) for pork in China, 1981–2005

Source: Huang et al. (2007).

Notes: These measures are calculated in the same way as NRAs and NRA$_f$s reported for other commodities. However, the true NRAs for these commodities become zero after 1994 because China has no policies holding their prices below world levels.

Aggregate Impacts

We separated the commodities in our study into importable and exportable groups and used production weights at undistorted prices to aggregate them. Assuming that our study commodities largely reflect the distortions to all commodities, there is a striking pattern (figure 10.6, left-hand side of figure) that reinforces the positive relationship between trade liberalization and rural incomes. In the 1980s and through the mid-1990s, importables (such as wheat, soybeans, milk and sugar) were protected. On average, their protection rates were between 15 and 35 percent. The same was true for exportables, except the distortions show that commodities such as rice, livestock commodities, and horticultural commodities were taxed at rates ranged from 40 to 50 percent. With exportable agricultural products accounting for a larger share of output than importables, China's average agricultural distortions were negative. In other words, China was taxing its agriculture—with both its international trade and domestic marketing policies.

One of the main findings of this study is evident from the right-hand side of figure 10.6. After 1995, the NRAs of importables fell from around 20 percent to less than 10 percent. During this period, the NRAs of exportables rose, or the implicit taxes on them fell, from about 40 percent to around 15 percent. When taken together, the distortions in China's agriculture fell to less than 10 percent. In many years, overall protection was between 0 and –5 percent. The combination of domestic marketing reforms and international

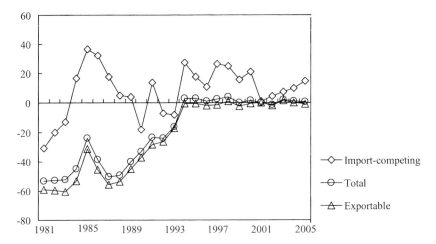

Fig. 10.6   Rates of assistance (including subsidy/taxes on inputs) for farmers that produce importable commodities, exportable commodities and for all of agriculture (11 commodities) in China, 1981–2005

Source: Authors' spreadsheet using methodology from Anderson et al. (2008) and Huang et al. (2007).

trade liberalization has created an economy that is one of the least distorted in the world. It also helped China enjoy rising incomes (in the aggregate) at the same time that it was reforming trade policies. One key to this was the removal of agricultural taxation. Another was allowing farmers to produce the goods that would generate the greatest benefit at international prices.

When considering the impact of trade reform on the agricultural sector, it is not sufficient to consider only the instruments directly affecting the sector. The pathbreaking study of distortions to agricultural incentives in developing countries (Krueger, Schiff, and Valdés 1991) showed that the indirect taxation of agriculture resulting from protection to other sectors was generally more important than direct agricultural distortions.

In the case of China, this question requires particular attention because there have been enormous reductions in nonagricultural barriers, including tariffs, exchange rate overvaluation, quotas, and licensing. We have combined estimates of these distortions into a composite measure of nonagricultural distortions depicted as an NRA for nonagricultural tradeables in figure 10.7. In a simplified two-sector model, what matters is the relative rate of assistance (RRA) also shown in this figure. This figure shows that the agricultural sector benefited from a rapid reduction in both direct and indirect taxation between the early 1980s and 1995. In the period since 1995, the RRA has become positive and continued to rise, albeit at a much slower rate than in the 1981 to 1995 period. The reduction in taxation of the agri-

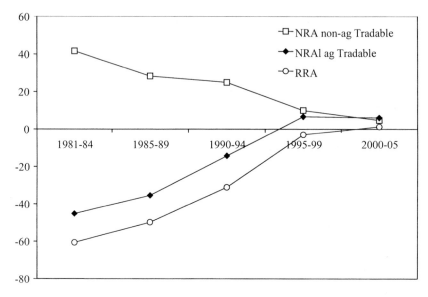

Fig. 10.7   Agricultural and nonagricultural protection and the relative rate of assistance to agriculture
Source: Huang et al. (2007).

cultural sector evident in this diagram is consistent with the improvement in the terms of trade for agriculture relative to nonagriculture within China observed by Zhu and Hong (2007) using data on relative prices for agricultural and nonagricultural goods.

Distinguishing the Impacts of WTO Accession

One final issue that needs to be recognized when considering the impacts of reforms associated with WTO accession is the nature of commitments in the WTO. China's main WTO accession commitments on agriculture were commitments that tariffs would not rise above the bound levels agreed in China's WTO accession schedule. These commitments were negotiated through an intensive process that took into account the market access interests of existing members and the previously prevailing applied tariff rates. Given the nature of China's trade regime, however, the relationship between these tariff rates and China's actual protection was weak. For many products, the relationship between domestic and world prices was determined more by state trading, quotas and licenses than by tariffs.

Table 10.1 shows the relationship estimated by Ianchovichina and Martin (2004) between applied protection prior to accession, the applied tariff, and the bound tariff associated with WTO accession. From table 10.1, it is clear that the applied tariffs for many commodities were strikingly above

Table 10.1	Actual protection, applied tariffs, and out-of-quota tariff bindings (%)		
	Actual protection 1995	Applied tariff	Out-of-quota tariff bindings
Rice	–5	114	65
Wheat	25	114	65
Corn	20	114	65
Soybean	30	22	3
Sugar	44	114	50
Cotton	20	30	40

the protection actually provided. For rice, the applied tariff of 114 percent was quite irrelevant, with the actual protection applied being negative. Similarly, the applied rates of protection on wheat and maize were far below the applied rates of 114 percent. For only a few commodities, such as soybeans, did the bound rate agreed at the WTO require reductions in the protection previously applied. This distinction between reductions in applied rates and reductions in actual agricultural protection is extremely important. Much of the concern about potential adverse impacts of WTO commitments expressed either in prospect by authors such as Schmidhuber (2001) or Carter and Estrin (2001) or retrospectively by authors such as Ni (2007) is based on the reductions in tariff rates required by WTO accession.

10.3 Policies to Support Market and Trade Liberalization

Our analysis that documents reductions in the distortions to China's agriculture helps us meet our first objective. China's policymakers have successfully carried out their promises to liberalize markets and trade. In some sense, the analysis also helps explain the second puzzle. Because of the rising share of livestock and horticulture in China's agricultural economy, and because trade liberalization actually eliminated negative protection in these sectors, the average level of protection (combining the net effects of commodities that were having their positive protection removed and the commodities that were being less taxed) moved toward zero. In this way, trade policy was helping to increase farm incomes. In the period since 1995, liberalization elsewhere in the economy reduced the taxation of the agricultural sector leading to the rise in the relative rate of assistance noted in figure 10.7. In this way, trade policy changes can contribute, in part, to the explanation of how rural China avoided declining during trade liberalizations.

However, the story needs more explanation. In part, the additional explanation is needed because rural incomes not only rose on average, but rose *in all provinces* (table 10.2). The rise in income occurred in all provinces, including those in northern, northeastern, and northwestern China. In

Table 10.2   Real per capita net income of rural households, by province in China, 2000–2005 (in real 2005 yuan)

	2000	2005	Growth in 2005 over 2000 (%)	Annual growth rate (%)
Beijing	4,790	7,346	53.36	8.93
Tianjin	3,830	5,580	45.68	7.82
Hebei	2,711	3,482	28.41	5.13
Shanxi	2,127	2,891	35.90	6.33
Inner Mongolia	2,318	2,989	28.97	5.22
Liaoning	2,671	3,690	38.18	6.68
Jilin	2,215	3,264	47.37	8.06
Heilongjiang	2,339	3,221	37.75	6.61
Shanghai	5,809	8,248	41.97	7.26
Jiangsu	3,960	5,276	33.25	5.91
Zhejiang	4,603	6,660	44.70	7.67
Anhui	2,095	2,641	26.08	4.74
Fujian	3,467	4,450	28.36	5.12
Jiangxi	2,255	3,129	38.77	6.77
Shangdong	2,960	3,931	32.80	5.84
Henan	2,195	2,871	30.80	5.52
Hubei	2,526	3,099	22.68	4.17
Hunan	2,452	3,118	27.17	4.92
Guangdong	3,838	4,690	22.22	4.10
Guangxi	1,991	2,495	25.32	4.62
Hainan	2,346	3,004	28.06	5.07
Chongqing	2,015	2,809	39.39	6.87
Sichuan	2,109	2,803	32.90	5.85
Guizhou	1,513	1,877	24.02	4.40
Yunnan	1,615	2,042	26.40	4.80
Tibet	1,414	2,078	46.99	8.01
Shanxi	1,620	2,053	26.68	4.84
Gansu	1,656	1,980	19.53	3.63
Qinghai	1,729	2,151	24.40	4.46
Ningxia	1,891	2,509	32.64	5.81
Xinjiang	1,796	2,482	38.24	6.69
National average	2,462	3,255	32.21	5.74

Source: NBSC, Statistical Yearbook of China, 2001–2006.

Note: Values are in real 2005 yuan using rural consumer price index by province.

these regions of China, farmers produce many crops (wheat, maize, soybeans, and cotton) that were still receiving positive protection during the late 1990s and early 2000s. With this set of crops accounting for a large share of the crop area in northern, northeastern, and northwestern China, there remains a puzzle to explain. Why did incomes rise in those areas even though we know that incomes of some producers would have suffered from trade liberalization-induced cuts in protection. Part of the explanation is presumably the reduction in the cost structure resulting from rapid liberalization in the rest of the economy. In the rest of this section, we discuss several key policy reforms that we believe contributed to rural incomes rising even while agricultural protection fell.

10.3.1   Development and Dissemination of Agricultural Technology

The importance of agricultural research and extension in increasing agricultural productivity in developing countries is now widely recognized. Successful development has been shown to be tied closely to productivity growth in the agricultural sector (World Bank 2008). In a country like China, where agriculture is dominated by small, poor farms, it is even more important.

During the reform era, it was not always clear whether China would be able to maintain the pace of technological advance needed to maintain farm incomes in a dynamic economy. While decollectivization played the key role in boosting productivity (Lin 1992) in the early stages of reform, this provided only a one-off boost to productivity. After 1985, the evidence suggests that technological advance has been the main engine of productivity growth (Huang and Rozelle 1996). China was one of the first countries to develop and extend Green Revolution technology in the 1960s, 1970s, and 1980s. Hybrid rice was developed by China's scientists in the late 1970s and, until the mid-1990s, it was the only country in the world to have commercialized this new technology.

Despite these and other successes, China's system of agricultural research faced great challenges by the late 1980s (Pray, Rozelle, and Huang 1997). Research investment, almost totally publicly funded, was declining. Incentives were poor, and funding was being allocated in ways that did not always reward excellence. The system was not responding to many demands for new technologies and the extension system was in shambles.

A nationwide reform in research was launched in the mid-1980s (Pray, Rozelle, and Huang 1997). The reforms attempted to increase research productivity by shifting funding from institutional support to competitive grants, supporting research useful for economic development, and encouraging applied research institutes to support themselves by selling the technology they produced. In addition, in the late 1980s and early 1990s, new horticultural seeds, improved breeding livestock (Rae et al. 2006), and new technologies for dairy were all imported (Ma et al. 2006).

After declining between the early 1980s and the mid-1990s (Pray, Rozelle, and Huang 1997), investment in research and development (R&D) also began to rise. Funding was greatly increased for plant biotechnology, although only Bt cotton has been commercialized in a major way to date (Huang et al. 2002). China now ranks among the global leaders in agricultural biotechnology. In the late 1990s, China invested more in agricultural biotechnology research than all other developing countries combined. Its public spending on agricultural biotechnology was second only to the United States and, according to some projections, it will soon outspend the U.S. government on plant biotechnology research. Investment in government-sponsored R&D

Table 10.3   Annual growth rate of yield and total cost of main grain crop in China, 1985–2004 (%)

	1985–1994		1995–2004	
Crop	Output (1)	Input (2)	Output (3)	Input (4)
Early indica	0.05	1.72	0.08	−2.31
Late indica	1.37	2.12	0.80	−1.16
Japonica	1.79	3.99	0.17	−1.99
Wheat	2.84	2.58	1.38	−0.22
Maize	3.66	1.87	1.04	−0.63
Soybean	0.71	2.24	1.06	−1.36

Source: Jin et al. 2007.

increased by 5.5 percent annually between 1995 and 2000 and by over 15 percent per year after 2000 (Hu et al. 2007). During the past decade, the increase in investment in rural research and development has been the most rapid of any large nation.

The investment in R&D has been paying off. During China's early reform period, the yields of major food crops rose steadily (table 10.3, column [1]). Although some of that yield increase came from greater efficiency in input use, technological improvements appear to have accounted for some of this growth because indexes of aggregated inputs (that is, measures of land, labor, and material inputs) for rice, wheat, and maize actually fell for all the crops during the early 1980s (column [2]).

Although there was concern about the effect of the slowdown in R&D spending during the 1980s and early 1990s, the analysis shows that the growth of output continued to outpace that for inputs (table 10.2, columns [3] and [4]). And, productivity trends continued to rise (table 10.4, column [2]). During this time—and during the early reform period—China's total factor productivity (TFP) has been rising at the healthy rate of about 2 percent per year. Such rises, which occurred in all provinces and with all crops, could not have helped but increase incomes—of all farmers—regardless of whether the crop was being protected or taxed.

10.3.2   Policies to Encourage Market Integration and Efficiency

Price and marketing reforms have been key components of China's transition strategy from a centrally planned to a market-oriented economy. These policies were implemented in a gradual way (Sicular 1995). In the initial years, there was little effort to move the economy to one in which most all resources and factors were allocated according market price signals. Over time, the government's position on market reform has gradually evolved. As officials in charge of the overall economic reforms began to be committed to use markets as the primary means to allocate resources for the economy,

Table 10.4   **Annual growth rate of main grain crop's total factor productivity (TFP) and decomposition into technical efficiency (TE) and technical change (TC) in China, 1985–2004 (%)**

	1985–1994			1995–2004		
Crop	TFP (1)	TE (2)	TC (3)	TFP (4)	TE (5)	TC (6)
Early indica	1.84	−0.03	1.88	2.82	0	2.82
Late indica	1.85	0.26	1.59	2.92	0.21	2.71
Japonica	−0.12	−0.37	0.26	2.52	0.15	2.37
Wheat	0.25	1.08	−0.83	2.16	1.06	1.10
Maize	1.03	0.61	0.42	1.70	−0.23	1.94
Soybean	0.11	0.19	−0.09	2.27	−0.08	2.35

Source: Jin et al. 2007.

the commitment to allowing markets in agriculture also deepened (Sicular 1995).

As markets began to emerge, China's leaders took steps to encourage the efficiency of markets and, perhaps more important, stepped aside and allowed them to expand in an environment with minimal distortions. Above all, national and regional governments invested in the hardware—roads, landline telephones, and cellular technology—that reduced transaction costs and accelerated the flow of information and goods (Park et al. 2002). Many regional and local governments invested in marketing sites and tried to attract commercial interests to set up businesses. Finally, except for a short period in the late 1990s, government officials have stepped back and allowed the entry of private traders and private transport and have done little to interfere with markets. Licensing fees and taxes are low or nonexistent. Markets were encouraged for both agricultural outputs and inputs.

In assessing the health of the rural economy, it is important to understand how China's markets are functioning. Markets—whether classic competitive ones or some workable substitute—increase efficiency by facilitating transactions among agents to allow specialization and trade and by providing information through a pricing mechanism to producers and consumers about the relative scarcity of resources. With better markets, producers can begin to specialize, become more efficient, and increase their incomes.

According to price data from private reporting stations and information firms, it appears that China's markets function relatively well. For example, maize prices in for different cities in Northeast China track each other closely (Rozelle and Huang 2003). Soybean prices in markets in different regions of the country move almost in perfect concert with one another (Rozelle and Huang 2004). Rice markets also have been shown to function as well as or better than those in the United States in terms of the efficiency of moving commodities around and between China's producing and consuming regions (Huang, Rozelle, and Chang 2004). Horticultural, dairy, and livestock markets are all dominated by millions of small traders who are operating in extremely competitive environments (Wang et al. 2007; Wu, Huang, and Rozelle 2007; Bi, Huang, and Rozelle 2007).

The improvement in markets has allowed individual producers to specialize as never before. According to one national survey, the number of villages that have become specialized producers of a single commodity rose from less than 20 percent in 1995 to nearly 40 percent in 2004 (Rosen, Huang, and Rozelle 2004). Such integration has allowed relatively small and poor farmers to participate in emerging markets and to accrue the substantial income gains associated with moving from subsistence to a market orientation (Wang et al. 2007; Bi, Huang, and Rozelle 2007; Balat and Porto 2006). In fact, in a recent survey of the greater metropolitan Beijing area, it was found that poor farmers living in poor villages were the main beneficiaries of new demands for horticultural commodities.

Most important, according to de Brauw, Huang, and Rozelle (2004), when markets in China have begun to become more competitive and efficient, they have led to rising productivity and efficiency. The link between improved markets and rising incomes is important because it is consistent with our puzzle. Even where market and trade liberalization has reduced protection and necessarily adversely affected income, the rising productivity and efficiency effects have at least partly offset these negative impacts. This interpretation is supported by the modeling work in Huang et al. (2005), which finds when trade policy positively affects some prices (e.g., horticultural crops) but negatively affects others (e.g., wheat), farmers mitigate the downside effects by transferring production into the commodities with rising prices.

10.3.3   Public Investment, Services, and Subsidies

Any visitor to most parts of rural China is struck by one thing: agriculture is still being carried out in many environments that can only be described as backward. Except in a few suburban and coastal regions, the infrastructure in rural China is extremely poor. Roads and bridges, irrigation and drainage, drinking water, schools, and health facilities are far from modern and decades behind the infrastructure in China's cities. Yet development economists know that for a country to modernize, its infrastructure has to be able to support the production and marketing activities of a complex economy.

Although the stock of infrastructure is poor, there have been improvements in recent years. Research has shown that, on average, each village in China had about one infrastructure project during the late 1990s (Luo et al. 2007). This is far higher than in most other developing nations in Asia. In recent years, the level of investment activity has risen sharply (to almost one project per year). Most of these projects are public goods (and not activities, such as orchards, in which governments frequently invested during the 1980s). In addition, research suggests that this investment is being targeted fairly well, with increasing amounts going to poor, minority, and remote parts of China.

Although the level of public goods investment per capita has risen from about 40 to 100 U.S. dollars (in purchasing power parity [PPP] terms), it is still far below the levels that were enjoyed by rural residents in Japan during the 1950s and South Korea during the 1970s (Luo et al. 2007). Quality, while rising, is still low in many villages (Liu et al. 2009). China is just beginning the process of narrowing the gap between rural and urban infrastructure, and it will take an enormous and sustained effort to transform the rural economy.

10.3.4   Education and Health Programs

Rural services—in particular education and health—are perhaps the weakest part of the rural economy, despite the recognition by development economists of their importance. Rural education by any metric is abysmal. Fees—until recently—were high, even for elementary school. Buildings and equipment are outdated and poor. Teaching quality is poor. Because of poor education, there is evidence that even as the nation accelerates its drive toward industrialization and urbanization—and agriculture is becoming more complex and demanding—retention rates for farm children remain very low beyond the compulsory nine years of schooling. Partly because tuition and associated fees are so high—an estimated one-quarter of total expenditure for many poor households—participation rates in high school (grades 10–12) are less than 15 percent for the rural population. A national survey found that nearly half of rural residents believe education has not improved in recent years (Liu et al. 2007).

There has been a new surge of interest by the government in improving rural education and reducing the cost of education—especially in poor, rural areas. In 2005, fees for elementary schools were eliminated in poor areas. In 2006, this was expanded to the entire rural economy. By 2007, all compulsory education (grades 1–9) was supposed to be free. The income effects of such policies are potentially enormous. Huang, Rozelle, and Chang (2004) show that the elimination of government tuition fees provided a benefit more than twice as large as the losses resulting from tariff reductions for China's protected crops.

The national and regional governments have also begun to build a rural health care program. In its initial years, while funding was scarce, it is in high demand. By 2007, the government was investing up to thirty yuan per capita into the program.

10.3.5   Farm Subsidies and Taxes

The government launched a massive program of direct subsidies in 2004, and this program is projected to expand further in the coming years. Designed in part to boost production of grain (for national food self-sufficiency) and in part as a rural income transfer, the national Grain Subsidy and the national new technology program have in a very short time become fixtures in the rural economy. Nearly 80 percent of farm households receive subsidies. Participation in the program is as high in poor areas as is it is in higher-income areas (Tan et al. 2006). Although they were relatively small in the first year of the program, by the second year, between the two programs, many farmers were receiving about ten to fifteen yuan per mu, which is more than seventy yuan per acre.

While farmers were obviously predisposed to favoring the program (who does not like direct subsidies?), there are several issues that China must weigh in considering the long-term benefit and sustainability of the program. First is whether payments under the Grain Subsidies should be counted toward the nation's aggregate measure of support (AMS) at the WTO. In its accession to WTO, China agreed to keep its distorting payments in agriculture below 8.5 percent of agricultural GDP. Obviously, if these payments were counted against the AMS, China could rapidly approach its maximum level of payments. But there is a question about whether these payments are "distorting or not." In 2004, a survey by the Research Center for the Rural Economy (RCRE) found that more than 70 percent of the payments were decoupled, with farmers receiving the payment whether they planted grain or any other crop. If this were the case, then such payments arguably could be counted as pure, unlinked transfers and not be counted. However, during the second year of the program, there was more of an effort to target households that produced grain. If the payment is linked to the type of crop planted, it is likely to be classified as a distorting subsidy with careful accounting needed to ensure it does not violate the restriction on distorting subsidies under China's WTO commitments.

In addition to subsidies, the national government has eliminated almost all taxes and fees in rural villages. In 2001 and 2002, all fees were converted to a single agricultural tax that was not to exceed 8.5 percent of a household's (village's) gross value of agricultural output. However, no sooner had this been implemented than the tax was eliminated altogether. By 2007, surveys showed that farmers were paying almost no taxes.

When added together, the recent policy innovations in rural infrastructure, free rural school tuition, grain and other agricultural subsidies, tax reductions, and health insurance subsidies are substantial. These government programs have likely injected enough funds to contribute importantly to the observed improvements in household incomes in rural areas.

10.3.6 Improving Mobility of Labor out of Agriculture

China began the period under study with around half of its workforce in agriculture and will reduce this fraction to just a few percent by the time she reaches high income status. The rate of migration out of agriculture consistent with China's growth path is one of the most rapid ever observed. In almost all rapidly growing economies, the resistance to this adjustment, particularly due to sector-and region-specific investments in human capital, is frequently seen as the source of a "farm problem" in which farm incomes fall below incomes in the rest of the economy.

The usual resistances to labor out-migration are compounded by a number of China-specific factors. One is the *hukou* residence permit system, which has restricted mobility of labor into urban areas (see Sicular and Zhao 2004). Another is the land tenure system, where households leaving the agricultural sector completely must relinquish their land without compensation (Zhao 1999). Other China-specific resistances have come from factors such as the low quality of educational opportunities in rural areas discussed in the preceding. Unless these structural rigidities to mobility of labor out of agriculture are reduced, the effectiveness of other reforms, such as tax cuts or price supports, is likely to be diminished greatly, as excess labor remains bottled up in agriculture, earning low returns. Where out-migration is feasible, de Brauw and Giles (2008) show that it increases the living standards of the family members remaining, and tends to increase their land holdings, although not necessarily their investment in other assets.

During the period we consider, the *hukou* system has been relaxed considerably, to the point where it is regarded by some, but not all, labor economists as a relatively minor source of resistance to overall labor mobility out of agriculture. Relatively little appears, so far, to have been done to change the land tenure system to reduce this barrier to mobility. The improvements in rural education discussed in the preceding seem likely to play a key role in enhancing mobility, both by increasing returns from work outside agriculture and by lowering the costs of adjusting (Fan, Hertel, and Wang 2004).

10.4   Conclusions and Implications

The main finding of this paper is that the nature of policy intervention in China's agriculture has changed dramatically over the past twenty-five years, transforming the agricultural sector from one characterized by high and variable distortions to one that is relatively liberal. In the 1980s and early 1990s (or the *early reform period*), there were distortions in both external and domestic policies that isolated domestic producers and consumers from international markets.

During the early reform period, domestic marketing and pricing policies actually served to make the prices that domestic producers and consumers faced almost independent from the effects of trade policy. In the case of rice and other exportable commodities, heavy border distortions that reduced domestic prices were compounded by a domestic procurement system that depressed farm prices and the prices paid by urban consumers.

Similar dynamics characterized importable commodities such as wheat and soybeans where, despite fairly high rates of protection from trade policies, producer prices were relatively low.

In contrast, since the late 1980s and early 1990s (the *late reform period*), the liberalization of domestic markets has reduced the distortions from domestic policies (as the market gradually has replaced the state as the primary mechanism for allocating resources and has become the basis for farmers' production and marketing decisions). At the same time, especially in the case of importable commodities, trade policy has been liberalized, with distortions from border measures falling substantially. As a result, we find that in recent years (that is, by the end of the late reform period), China's agriculture is much less distorted in two ways. First, the differences between international and domestic market prices have narrowed considerably for many commodities due to trade policy liberalization. Second, the elimination of domestic policy distortions increased farm prices for many commodities. Reductions in protection to nonagricultural tradables—a major element of the WTO accession negotiations—also appear to have reduced the costs imposed on the agricultural sector.

The main question, once the trade liberalization is established, then, shifts gears, and the focus of our analysis begins to try to understand how it could be—when there are many places in China that have experienced large falls in protection to the agricultural tariffs that they produce—that rural incomes still rose almost nationwide. In trying to explain this puzzle, we examine three sources of income increases that might help offset the fall in income brought on by trade liberalization. We explored the role of agricultural technology, the rise of markets, and the emergence of new subsidy and support policies.

In our analysis, we find that at the same time that trade liberalization policy was reducing returns to some products that had been receiving positive protection, a number of other elements were working to offset these effects. One was the reductions in taxation of other important commodities, such as rice. At the same time, investments in R&D, the fostering of markets and the new investment, and subsidy programs appear to have generated wide-ranging, positive income effects in rural China.

The implications of these findings are that, although trade policies may have had negative effects on incomes in certain parts of the agricultural community, the magnitude of these adverse impacts appears to have been widely overstated. This is partly because the usual way of assessing the impact of WTO commitments—comparisons of bound tariffs with prior applied tariffs—widely overstates the extent of liberalization required in China. Another reason that these adverse impacts have frequently been overstated is that the agricultural sector as a whole was negatively protected at the beginning of the period, and most of this taxation has been eliminated. Another important source of gains was the reduction in protection to some less-efficient import-competing sectors, which allowed farmers to increase the value of their output. There were also important dynamic benefits as new export activities emerged, and the cost to burden on agriculture of protection to nonagricultural sectors was reduced.

The reforms undertaken in China have included both trade policy reforms and complementary domestic reforms that have helped to create greater opportunities for rural people—a combination of policies widely seen as necessary if the greatest benefits are to be achieved. China's experience over the past quarter century appears to provide some important lessons both for the future and for policymakers grappling with similar challenges in other countries.

References

Anderson, K., M. Kurzweil, W. Martin, D. Sandri, and E. Valenzuela. 2008. Measuring distortions to agricultural incentives, revisited. *World Trade Review* 7 (4): 675–704.

Balat, J., and G. Porto. 2006. The WTO Doha Round, cotton sector dynamics, and poverty trends in Zambia. In *Poverty and the WTO: Impacts of the Doha Development Agenda,* ed. T. Hertel and L. A. Winters, 155–83. Basingstoke, UK: Palgrave Macmillan.

Bhattasali, D., S. Li, and W. Martin, eds. 2004. *China and the WTO: Accession, policy reform and poverty reduction strategies.* Washington, DC: World Bank and Oxford University Press.

Bi, X., J. Huang, and S. Rozelle. 2007. Modern supply chains, expansion of demand and the poor in China: The case of livestock. Working Paper, Center for Chinese Agricultural Policy, Institute of Geographical Sciences and Natural Resource Research, Chinese Academy of Sciences.

Carter, C. A., and A. Estrin. 2001. China's trade integration and impacts on factor markets. University of California, Davis, Working Paper.

Chen, S., and M. Ravallion. 2007. China's (uneven) progress against poverty. *Journal of Development Economics* 82:1–42.

de Brauw, A., and J. Giles. 2008. Migrant labor markets and the welfare of rural households in the developing world: Evidence from China. World Bank. Mimeograph.

de Brauw, A., J. Huang, and S. Rozelle. 2004. The sequencing of reforms in China's agricultural transition. *Economics of Transition* 12 (3): 427–66.

Fan, Z., T. Hertel, and Z. Wang. 2004. Implications of WTO accession for poverty in rural China. In *China and the WTO: Accession, policy reform, and poverty reduction strategies,* ed. D. Bhatasali, S. Li, and W. Martin. Washington, DC: World Bank and Oxford University Press.

Hu, R., K. Shi, Y. Cui, and J. Huang. 2007. Changes in China's agricultural research investment and its international comparison. *China's Soft Science* 194 (February): 53–58, 65.

Huang, J., and C. Chen. 1999. *Effects of trade liberalization on agriculture in China: Commodity and local agricultural studies.* United Nations, ESCAP CGPRT Centre, Bogor, Indonesia.

Huang, J., Y. Jun, Z. Xu, S. Rozelle, and N. Li. 2007. Agricultural trade liberalization and poverty in China. *China Economic Review* 18:244–65.

Huang, J., Y. Liu, W. Martin, and S. Rozelle. 2009. Changes in trade and domestic distortions affecting China's agriculture. *Food Policy* 34:407–16

Huang, J., and H. Ma. 2000. International comparison of agricultural prices. *International Trade* 10:20–24.

Huang, J., and S. Rozelle. 1996. Technological change: Rediscovering the engine of productivity growth in China's agricultural economy. *Journal of Development Economics* 49:337–69.

Huang, J., S. Rozelle, and M. Chang. 2004. The nature of distortions to agricultural incentives in China and implications of WTO accession. *World Bank Economic Review* 18 (1): 59–84.

Huang, J., S. Rozelle, W. Martin, and Y. Liu. 2009. Distortions to agricultural incentives in China. In *Distortions to Agricultural Incentives in Asia*, ed. K. Anderson and W. Martin. Washington, DC: World Bank. See www.worldbank.org/agdistortions.

Huang, J., S. Rozelle, C. Pray, and Q. Wang. 2002. Plant biotechnology in China. *Science* 295 (25): 674–77.

Ianchovichina, E., and W. Martin. 2004. Economic impacts of China's accession to the World Trade Organization. *World Bank Economic Review* 18 (1): 3–28.

Jin, S., H. Ma, J. Huang, R. Hu, and S. Rozelle. 2007. Productivity, efficiency and technical change: Measuring the performance of China's transforming agriculture. Paper presented at conference, Trends and Forces in International Agricultural Productivity Growth, Washington, DC.

Krueger, A., M. Schiff, and A. Valdés. 1991. *The political economy of agricultural pricing policy.* Baltimore: Johns Hopkins Press.

Lardy, N. 1983. *Agriculture in China's modern economic development.* Cambridge, UK: Cambridge University Press.

Lardy, N. 2001. *Integrating China into the global economy.* Washington, DC: Brookings Institution.

Li, S., F. Zhai, and Z. Wang. 1999. The global and domestic impact of China joining the World Trade Organization. Project Report, Development Research Center, the State Council, China. Beijing.

Lin, J. 1992. Rural reforms and agricultural growth in China. *American Economic Review* 82:34–51.

Liu, C., L. Zhang, R. Luo, and S. Rozelle. 2009. Infrastructure investment in rural China: Is quality being compromised during quantity expansion? *The China Journal* 61:105–29.

Luo, R., L. Zhang, J. Huang, and S. Rozelle. 2007a. Investing in rural China: Tracking China's commitment to modernization. Center for Chinese Agricultural Policy, Institute of Geographical Sciences and Natural Resource Research, Chinese Academy of Sciences, Working Paper.

Ma, H., A. Rae, J. Huang, and S. Rozelle. 2006. Enhancing productivity on suburban dairy farms in China. Stanford University, Freeman Spogli Institute for International Studies, Working Paper.

Martin, W., J. Huang, and S. Rozelle. 2006. Exchange rates and agricultural distortions in China's agriculture, 1981 to 2004. Working Paper. Washington, DC: World Bank.

National Development and Reform Commission (NDRC). 1995–2005. *China's price yearbook.* Beijing: NDRC.

National Statistical Bureau of China (NBSC). 1981–2006. *Statistical yearbook of China.* Beijing: China Statistics Press.

———. Various Years. *China yearbook of agricultural price survey.* Beijing: China Statistics Press.

Ni, H. 2007. Why are special products and the special safeguard mechanism essential to China? *Bridges* 11 (3): 3–5.

Park, A., H. Jin, S. Rozelle, and J. Huang. 2002. Market emergence and transition: Arbitrage, transition costs, and autarky in China's grain market. *American Journal of Agricultural Economics* 84 (1): 67–82.

Pray, C. E., S. Rozelle, and J. Huang. 1997. Can China's agricultural research system feed China? Rutgers University, Department of Agricultural Economics, Working Paper.

Rae, A. N., H. Ma, J. Huang, and S. Rozelle. 2006. Livestock in China: Commodity-specific total factor productivity decomposition using new panel data. *American Journal of Agricultural Economics* 88 (3): 680–95.

Rosen, D., J. Huang, and S. Rozelle. 2004. *Roots of competitiveness: China's evolving agriculture interests.* Policy Analysis in International Economics, vol. 72. Washington, DC: Institute for International Economics.

Rozelle, S., and J. Huang. 2003. China's maize economy: Supply, demand and trade. Report for the U.S. Grains Council. Beijing:

———. 2004. China's soybean economy: Supply, demand and trade. Report for the American Soybean Association. Beijing:

Rozelle, S., A. Park, J. Huang, and H. Jin. 2000. Bureaucrat to entrepreneur: The changing role of the state in China's transitional commodity economy. *Economic Development and Cultural Change* 48 (2): 227–52.

Schmidhuber, J. 2001. Changes in China's agricultural trade policy regime: Impacts on agricultural production, consumption, prices, and trade. In *China's agriculture in the international trading system,* 21–51. Paris: Organization for Economic Cooperation and Development.

Sicular, T. 1988a. Agricultural planning and pricing in the post-Mao period. *China Quarterly* 116:671–703.

———. 1988b. Plan and market in China's agricultural commerce. *Journal of Political Economy* 96 (2): 283–307.

———. 1995. Redefining state, plan, and market: China's reforms in agricultural commerce. *China Quarterly* 144:1020–46.

Sicular, T., Y. Ximing, B. Gustafsson, and S. Li. 2006. The urban-rural income gap and inequality in China. WIDER Research Paper no. 2006/135. Helsinki, Finland: World Institute for Development Economics Research.

Sicular, T., and Y. Zhao. 2004. Earnings and labor mobility in rural China: Implications for China's accession to the WTO. In *China and the WTO: Accession, policy reform, and poverty reduction strategies,* ed. D. Bhatasali, S. Li, and W. Martin. Washington, DC: World Bank and Oxford University Press.

Wang, H., X. Dong, J. Huang, T. Reardon, and S. Rozelle. 2007. Small traders and small farmers: The evolution of China's horticulture economy. Center for Chinese Agricultural Policy, Working Paper.

Wu, Y., J. Huang, and S. Rozelle. 2007. Modern supply chains, expansion of demand and the poor in China: The case of livestock. Center for Chinese Agricultural Policy, Institute of Geographical Sciences and Natural Resource Research, Chinese Academy of Sciences, Working Paper.

Zhao, Y. 1999. Leaving the countryside: Rural-to-urban migration decisions in China. *American Economic Review* 89 (2): 281–86.

Zhu, J., and W. Hong. 2007. Trade openness, domestic terms of trade, and welfare of agricultural producers in China. Paper presented to the summer symposium of the International Agricultural Trade Research Consortium, Beijing. http://aede.osu.edu/programs/Anderson/trade/37JingZhu.pdf.

Comment   Kym Anderson

In this chapter, the authors seek to resolve an apparent paradox: agricultural protection has been reduced in China, and yet the rural sector seems to have prospered, and rural poverty has fallen in all regions. According to Ravallion, Chen, and Sangruala (2007), the share of China's rural population living on less than $1 a day fell from 39 percent in 1993 to 22 percent by 2002.

Huang et al.'s explanation is also capable of resolving a related paradox: China's relatively low endowment of land per worker (below 30 percent of the global average) and rapid industrialization would lead one to expect its agricultural comparative advantage and net exports of farm products to have diminished over time, yet China has remained close to 100 percent self-sufficient in agricultural goods since the reforms began in the late 1970s.[1]

The resolution to both of these paradoxes lies mainly in reforms to price, trade, and fiscal policies affecting farmer incentives and net transfers to farm households in China. The authors report empirical results from their country case study contribution to a multicountry World Bank research project on agricultural price distortions (Huang et al. 2007), as well as qualitative information on some other recent policy changes, to support their claim. Their empirical evidence shows that the price of agricultural relative to nonagricultural goods had been severely depressed by price and trade policies as of the early 1980s, but the subsequent gradual removal of that antiagricultural policy bias stimulated farm production. True, there was some reduction in protection from import competition for certain crops, but that was more than offset by reductions in implicit taxation of agricultural exports. This phase-down in the antitrade bias of agricultural policies was part of a more general reduction in the dispersion of nominal rates of assistance (NRA) among the eleven farm products in the authors' case study: in the 1980s, their mean NRA was –46 percent, and their standard deviation 63 percent, whereas by 2000 to 2004, the mean was 1 percent, and the standard deviation 16 percent. That reduction in NRA dispersion allowed farmers previously producing goods protected from import competition to move from growing them to now-more-profitable crops.

The authors stress that many complementary domestic reforms coincided with reforms at the border to boost farm household incomes to generate

Kym Anderson is the George Gollin Professor of Economics at the University of Adelaide.

1. China's net exports of food and agricultural products as a share of the sum of farm exports and imports was 8 percent in the 1980s and 10 percent in the 1990s (Sandri, Valenzuela, and Anderson 2007). It fell to –16 percent in the period 2000 to 2004 but, as the authors indicate, that deficit was mainly because of the growth of cotton imports for the booming textile and clothing export industries.

rapid farm productivity growth and allow domestic production to keep up with the growth in domestic demand for many farm products. Indeed, exports of some farm products boomed, earning enough foreign currency to cover the increasing cost of imports of cotton and ingredients for livestock feed.

Notwithstanding the impressive rise in rural incomes and fall in rural poverty, there has been a steady increase in the ratio of urban to rural household income in China. That ratio fell from 2.5 to 1.8 between 1978 and 1983, but since 1985, it has risen steadily and has been above 3 in recent years, according to the *China Statistical Yearbook*. The authors list several recent attempts by the government to reduce that urban-rural income inequality, such as greater encouragement to investments in agricultural research and rural infrastructure, a decoupled subsidy to grain producers, and the elimination of school fees and agricultural taxes. Yet that inequality persists.

This raises the important question—not addressed in the chapter—as to what the government might do in the years ahead about the recent decline in self-sufficiency in farm products and the increase in urban-rural inequality. The first wave of Asian industrializers (Japan, and then Korea and Taiwan) chose to slow the growth of food import dependence and urban-rural inequality by raising their NRA for agriculture, such that their relative rate of assistance (RRA) became increasingly above the neutral zero level. Will China follow suit?

In the past, there has been a close association of RRAs with rising per capita income and falling agricultural comparative advantage (Anderson 2009, chapter 1). When the RRAs for Japan, Korea, and Taiwan are mapped against real per capita income, it is possible to superimpose on that same graph the RRAs for lower-income economies to see how they are tracking relative to the first industrializers. Figure 10C.1 does that for China and India and shows that their RRA trends of the past three decades are on the same upward trajectory as the richer Northeast Asians. That alone provides reason to expect the governments of China and other later industrializing economies to follow suit if other things were equal.

Might one expect different government behavior now, given that the earlier industrializers were not bound under the General Agreement on Tariffs and Trade (GATT) to keep down their agricultural protection? Had there been strict discipline on farm trade measures at the time Japan and Korea joined the GATT in 1955 and 1967, respectively, their NRAs may have been halted at less than 20 percent (figure 10C.2). At the time of China's accession to the World Trade Organization (WTO) in December 2001, its NRA was less than 5 percent according to the authors' study, or 7.3 percent for just import-competing agriculture. Its average bound import tariff commitment was about twice that (16 percent in 2005), but what matters most is China's out-of-quota bindings on the items whose imports are restricted by tariff rate quotas. The latter tariff bindings as of 2005 were 65 percent for

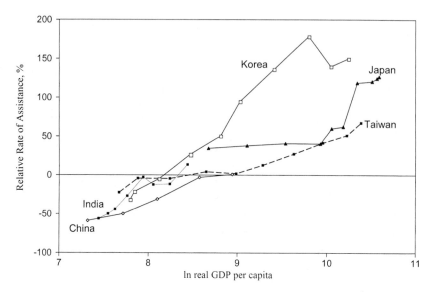

Fig. 10C.1   Relative rate of assistance and log of real per capita GDP, India and Northeast Asian focus economies, 1955 to 2005

Source: Anderson and Martin (2009, 75)

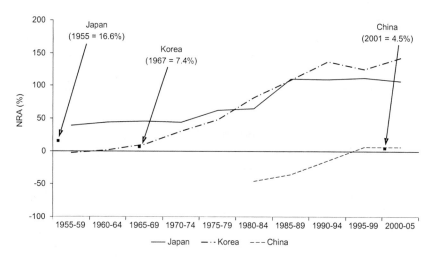

Fig. 10C.2   Nominal rate of assistance for Japan, Korea, and China and date of accession to GATT or WTO, 1955 to 2005 (percentage)

Source: Anderson and Martin (2009, 76).

grains, 50 percent for sugar, and 40 percent for cotton (see the authors' table 10.1). China also has bindings on farm product-specific domestic supports of 8.5 percent and can provide another 8.5 percent as non-product specific assistance if it so wishes—a total 17 percent NRA from domestic support measures alone, in addition to what is available through out-of-quota tariff protection. Clearly, the legal commitments China made on acceding to WTO are a long way from current levels of domestic and border support for its farmers and so are unlikely to constrain the government from raising agricultural support very much in the next decade or so. It thus remains to be seen whether the Chinese government is able to practice enough self-restraint to avoid following the agricultural protection growth path of earlier industrializing economies and to restrict any fiscal payments to investments with high social payoffs such as in rural infrastructure, rural education and health, and agricultural research.

References

Anderson, K., ed. 2009. *Distortions to agricultural incentives: A global perspective, 1955–2007.* London: Palgrave Macmillan.

Anderson, K., and W. Martin, eds. 2009. *Distortions to agricultural incentives in Asia.* Washington, DC: World Bank.

Huang, J., Y. Liu, W. Martin, and S. Rozelle. 2007. Distortions to agricultural incentives in China. Agricultural Distortions Working Paper no. 29. Washington, DC: World Bank, December. www.worldbank.org/agdistortions. Since published as chap. 3 (117–61) in Anderson and Martin (2009)

Ravallion, M., S. Chen, and P. Sangruala. 2007. New evidence on the urbanization of global poverty. Policy Research Working Paper no. 4199. Washington, DC: World Bank, April.

Sandri, D., E. Valenzuela, and K. Anderson. 2007. Economic and trade indicators for Asia. Agricultural Distortions Working Paper no. 20. Washington, DC: World Bank, December. www.worldbank.org/agdistortions.

Trade Growth, Production Fragmentation, and China's Environment

Judith M. Dean and Mary E. Lovely

11.1 Introduction

China often receives attention both for its rapidly growing trade and its serious environmental degradation. China's trade with the world has risen dramatically between 1995 and 2005. In current dollars, the value of China's exports plus imports rose from $280.9 billion in 1995 to $1422.1 billion in 2005—a growth of about 406 percent. While improvements have been made in water and air quality over the same period, China's Ministry of Environmental Protection (MEP) stated that "[t]he conflict between environment and development is becoming ever more prominent. Relative shortage of resources, a fragile ecological environment and insufficient environmental capacity are becoming critical problems hindering China's development" (MEP 2006).

Judith M. Dean is a senior international economist at the U.S. International Trade Commission (USITC). Mary E. Lovely is associate professor of economics at Syracuse University's Maxwell School of Citizenship and Public Affairs.

We thank Ming-Sun Poon (Library of Congress), Clifford Brown, Wendy Willis, and Robert Bauschspies (USITC Library) for their help in obtaining Chinese environmental data. We are also indebted to Andrew Gately (USITC) for translating tables from Chinese, and Russell Husen and Jesse Mora for assistance assembling data and generating graphs and tables. This chapter benefited from comments by Carol McAusland; Brent Haddad; and the participants in the University of Maryland, Department of Agriculture and Resource Economics seminar (2007); the University of California, Santa Cruz, International Economics Trade and Environment workshop (2007); the Midwest International Trade Meetings, University of Minnesota (2007); and the School of Advanced International Studies, Johns Hopkins University Economics seminar. We are also grateful to Robert Feenstra, Arik Levinson, and the other participants in the National Bureau of Economic Research (NBER) Conference on China's Growing Role in World Trade for helpful comments on a preliminary draft. The views expressed here are those of the authors. They do not necessarily represent the views of the USITC or the views of any of the individual Commissioners.

Some of the large literature on trade and environment lends credence to the idea that trade growth and environmental degradation are causally related. The environmental Kuznets curve literature suggests that low-income countries have relatively lenient environmental standards and, hence, a comparative advantage in pollution-intensive goods.[1] As a low-income country grows, environmental damage increases due to increased scale of production and a composition of output biased toward "dirty goods." However, higher incomes also generate pressure for more stringent environmental regulations. Because tighter regulations raise the cost of polluting and give producers incentives to find cleaner production techniques, this tends to reduce environmental damage.[2] For low-income countries, the scale and composition effects are thought to outweigh the technique effect, implying that the net effect of growth is detrimental to the environment. Because trade growth raises incomes, it, too, contributes to these scale, composition, and technique effects. Yet empirical evidence on the net effect of trade and environmental damage is mixed, with at least some studies (Dean 2002; Antweiler, Copeland, and Taylor 2001) finding evidence that the technique effect may be stronger than previously thought, leading to a net beneficial impact of trade growth on the environment.

China's integration with the world economy may not fit this conventional picture. Much of China's trade growth is attributable to the international fragmentation of production—the splitting of production processes into discrete sequential activities (fragments) that take place in different countries[3] (Chen et al. 2008; Ping 2005; Dean, Fung, and Wang 2008). China's trade statistics explicitly designate "processing imports" as imports of intermediate inputs to be used to produce products solely for export and "processing exports" as those exports that use these imported inputs.[4] This trade alone accounts for about 56 percent of the growth in China's exports and 41 percent of the growth in China's imports between 1995 and 2005. In addition, a large part of this trade is attributable to foreign-invested enterprises (FIEs).[5] In 2005, about 84 percent of China's processing exports and imports were carried out by FIEs.

1. The evidence on the existence of an environmental Kuznets curve is mixed and highly dependent upon time period, countries evaluated, and pollutants examined. Thus, there is no way to verify whether or not China is to the left or right of the turning point in the "inverted U." For surveys covering the broader literature on trade and environment, see Dean (2001) and Copeland and Taylor (2004).

2. In addition, some would argue that increased FDI would imply greater environmental degradation, as firms in pollution-intensive industries may move to avoid more stringent environmental regulations at home. See Dean, Lovely, and Wang (2009) for review of evidence and counterargument.

3. See Arndt and Kierzkowski (2001) for discussion of the causes of fragmentation.

4. Chinese trade statistics record two types of processing imports and exports: processing and assembly (where the foreigner retains ownership of imported inputs) and processing with imported inputs (where the importer acquires ownership of imported inputs).

5. Chinese trade statistics record several types of FIEs: fully-funded enterprises (i.e., wholly owned subsidiaries of foreign companies), equity joint ventures, and contractual joint ventures.

Trade arising from international production fragmentation could be cleaner than conventional trade. If highly fragmented industries (such as computers and other high-tech products) and the particular fragments within these products that China produces are relatively clean, then China's output and trade would shift toward cleaner goods as these activities expand. In addition, if the FIEs who carry out much of this trade in fragments produce using greener technologies than those used by domestic producers in China, production techniques within fragmented industries would become cleaner over time. In this way, both the composition and technique effects of trade growth may be favorable to China's environment.

This chapter explores these relationships using new evidence on the pollution content of Chinese trade. We first present evidence on the growth of trade and industrial emissions in China. Using official Chinese environmental data on air and water pollution from MEP, we find that industrial emissions of primary pollutants have slowed or fallen over the last decade while trade has grown. Across most industrial sectors, the pollution intensity of production has also fallen. We then explore trends in the pollution intensity of Chinese trade. Building on highly disaggregated trade data from China Customs, we report new evidence that the pollution intensity of Chinese exports has fallen dramatically from 1995 to 2004. We use a counterfactual exercise to show that this decrease in the pollution intensity of trade is due partly to a shift in the composition of trade toward cleaner goods, but also to a shift in production technique toward cleaner processes.

Finally, we explore the possibility that production fragmentation and processing trade may have played a role in making China's trade cleaner. Building on the framework provided by Copeland and Taylor (1994), we develop a reduced form model of the pollution intensity of trade, incorporating standard determinants of a country's production mix, such as factor proportions, income per capita, and trade policy. We then incorporate a fragmented export sector, building upon the work of Feenstra and Hanson (1996). The impact of fragmentation on the pollution intensity of China's exports and imports is estimated using data on four pollutants over a ten-year period. We find evidence consistent with the view that the increased role of processing trade and the extensive presence of FIEs have both contributed to reducing the pollution intensity of China's trade.

11.2   An Overview of China's Environmental Quality and Regulation

11.2.1   Environmental Quality

Descriptions of China invite superlatives, and this is certainly true of China's environmental problems. There are almost daily media reports of rivers and lakes poisoned by pollution and algal bloom, water tables dropping too low to meet basic needs, farmlands tainted by industrial pollution and fertilizers, and cities choking on smog.[6] With economic growth fore-casts exceeding 10 percent, the associated growth in industrial and municipal wastes, vehicle emissions, agricultural runoff, and deforestation have led observers to doubt the sustainability of China's development path. Indeed, as Naughton (2007, 503) notes, "The challenges of water availability, resil-ience of the natural environment, and atmospheric degradation and climate change are among the most serious that China confronts."

China's environmental problems are not the result of current emissions alone. The accumulation of past pollution; the ability of the air, land, and water to refresh itself; and changes in settlement patterns are all reflected in today's environment. Even if all economic activity were halted today, China would face serious "pollution problems" for years to come. When thinking about the effect of economic activity on the environment, therefore, it is important to distinguish between emissions, the "flow" of pollutants into the environment, and ambient quality, the "stock" of pollutants present at a specific point in time. Our analysis focuses on the former, while most news reports focus on the latter.

To put our discussion of trade and emissions (flows) into perspective, it is useful to review briefly trends in China's ambient quality (stocks). Despite widespread awareness of China's recurrent environmental crises, it is difficult to obtain consistent evidence on environmental quality. Repeated measures of ambient quality are available only through MEP, and even official reports reflect changing measurement methods and definitions over time, as Chi-na's environmental regulation and monitoring capability have improved. The data used in this study are drawn from official Chinese sources. There are many problems with official Chinese data, and environmental statistics are no exception. Nevertheless, there is no alternative set of data available. Moreover, these data provide systematic information to an area of research often dominated by anecdote.

Figure 11.1 provides summary data on the trend in water quality for China's seven major rivers drawn from MEP's annual *State of the Environ-ment* reports. From 2001 to 2005, there has been some improvement in water quality. The percentage of monitoring sections of the seven major rivers meeting a grade III quality standard or better rose from 30 percent to 40 percent, while the percentage considered to be highly polluted (grade V or worse than grade V) fell from 53 percent to 34 percent. These data suggest that China has succeeded in raising the quality of its extremely polluted water to a more moderately polluted level, but has made little progress in raising much of its water to the higher grade standards. These summary measures, though, hide substantial variation in water quality in

6. An excellent and informative example is the *New York Times* series, *Choking on Growth,* which reports on many aspects of China's environmental challenge. See http://www.nytimes.com/2007/08/26/world/asia/26china.html.

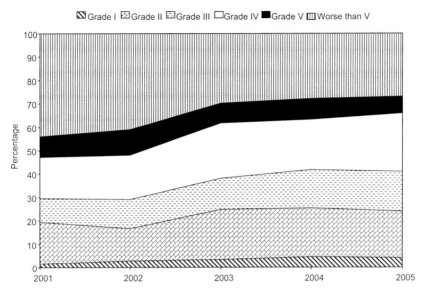

Fig. 11.1   Water quality: Seven major rivers
Source: Data from MEP, *Report on the State of the Environment,* various years. http://english
.mep.gov.cn/standards_reports/soe.
Note: Comparable data for earlier years are unavailable.

different segments of the rivers and in their tributaries. For example, the
mainstream of the Yellow River is considered to be only lightly polluted,
while most of its tributaries are heavily polluted (MEP 2007). Freshwater
lakes and reservoirs remain heavily polluted. In 2006, 48 percent of major
lakes and reservoirs were listed as worse than grade V, implying that they
are heavily polluted (MEP 2007). The most ubiquitous pollutant is readily
degradable organic materials from industry and households, with industry's share of these pollutants falling from 50 percent to 38 percent by 2005
(MEP 2007).

National survey data summarized by the World Bank (2001) suggest that
total emissions of major air pollutants (SO_2, soot, and dust) peaked in the
mid 1990s. As shown in figure 11.2, MEP reports that urban air quality
continued to improve between 2000 and 2005. The percentage of cities with
air quality rated grade II (up to standard) or better rose from 37 percent
to 52 percent during this period. Again, there are indications that most of
China's progress has been in reducing the extent of severe air pollution, as
the percentage of cities with air quality worse than grade III fell from 33
percent to 11 percent. Particulates are considered the most important pollutant affecting urban air quality, both in terms of frequency and health costs.
Particulate emissions are heaviest in China's largest cities, including Beijing
and Tianjin, due in part to the rapid growth of motor vehicle emissions in

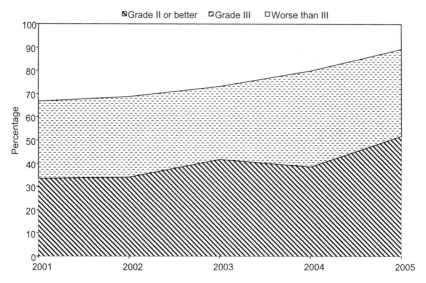

Fig. 11.2   Urban air quality

Source: Data from MEP, *Report on the State of the Environment,* various years. http://english .mep.gov.cn/standards_reports/soe/soe2006/200711/t2007/1105_112560.htm.
Note: Comparable data for earlier years are unavailable.

these areas. More than 80 percent of SO_2 and dust and most soot is attributed to industrial sources, which include coal-fired power plants.

11.2.2   Environmental Regulation and Policy

The Chinese government has long recognized the need for environmental protection. In 1989, a legislative base for environment protection was created by promulgation of the Environmental Protection Law. This law authorized the Environmental Protection Bureau of the State Council to set ambient standards and waste discharge and emission standards. In 1984, the bureau gained administrative independence as a separate office and its office staff size doubled. The bureau was renamed the National Environmental Protection Agency (NEPA) four years later, its staff size again doubled, and it was given direct links to the State Council. In recognition of the increasing importance placed upon environment in the overall development plan, NEPA was renamed the State Environmental Protection Agency and given ministerial rank in 1998. Despite this rank, SEPA did not have a seat in the State Council and remained less powerful than some other key ministries (OECD 2005), until it became the Ministry of Environmental Protection in 2008. It is considered to be underfunded and undermanned for the large portfolio it oversees.

The Ministry of Environmental Protection is responsible for developing policies and programs at the national level. In each province, Environmental Protection Bureaus (EPBs) oversee compliance with national and local environmental regulations. These local bureaus report to provincial administrators, which also oversee their funding. Recently, MEP has acquired some say in the selection of provincial EPB heads. The EPBs also exist at the prefecture, or municipal, and district or county levels. The EPBs report directly to upper-level environmental administrators as well as to the government of a geographic area. This reporting system is often cited as a source of conflict for local EPBs who may face interference from local leaders. Lower-level EPBs report to higher level EPBs, but the funding and supervision are provided by the province or lower-level administration (OECD 2005).

China has a well-developed regulatory system with over 2,000 laws related to environmental protection. During the 1990s, China gave increasing emphasis to prevention and shifted responsibility to polluters to pay for environmental damage. A key policy instrument in this shift was the introduction of a discharge fee system, with fees based on the concentration of effluents. These fees are applied to industrial emissions across China, with most revenue accruing from fees for discharges of wastewater and waste gases. This system has been criticized on a number of dimensions. It is widely believed that the fees are only a fraction of the social cost of pollution and that the fees do not encourage abatement. Local EPBs can also issue permits that limit the quantities and concentrations of pollutants in an enterprise's emissions, set deadlines for pollution control, and close plants deemed dependent on "backward" technology.

More recently, the criminal code has been revised to provide for criminal sanctions for egregious harm to the environment (OECD 2005). Environmental impact assessment has become routine for major economic projects and MEP and EPBs can suspend or delay projects that do not meet environmental standards. In 1992, the Chinese government removed a number of sectoral and regional restrictions on foreign direct investment (FDI) and decentralized approval (Lardy 1994). New rules introduced in 1995 prohibit foreign investment that involves dangerous, polluting, or wasteful processes (Henley, Kirkpatrick, and Wilde 1999).[7]

11.3   Trends in Chinese Industrial Emissions and Manufacturing Trade

11.3.1   Aggregate Trends

In this chapter, our interest is in the relationship between China's trade and China's environment, rather than the global environment. Hence, we focus on the primary pollutants that China uses to evaluate the condition of its own environment, rather than the greenhouse gases associated with

7. MEP also oversees a substantial program of pollution control, with 1.4 percent of GDP devoted to this purpose in 2003 (Naughton 2007). They also engage in scientific projects and international cooperative agreements promoting "leapfrogging" development, among other activities (MEP 2007).

global climate change. In the 10th Five-Year Plan (2001–2005), the Chinese government stated explicit goals for the reduction of its water pollution, as measured by chemical oxygen demand (COD) and its air pollution, as measured by sulfur dioxide (SO_2) and particulate matter, especially that generated by smoke and dust (OECD 2005). Chemical oxygen demand measures the mass concentration of oxygen consumed by chemical breakdown of organic and inorganic matter in water.[8] Chemical oxygen demand emissions account for the majority of industrial water pollution levies collected in China during this period. While emissions of other water pollutants are recorded in more recent years, they are generally positively correlated with COD. Industrial SO_2 emissions include the sulfur dioxide emitted from fuel burning and from the production processes on the premises of an enterprise. Industrial smoke (or soot) emissions include smoke emitted from fuel burning on the premises of an enterprise. Industrial dust emissions refer to the volume of dust suspended in the air and emitted by an enterprise's production processes.[9]

Figure 11.3 shows the trends in China's overall merchandise trade (billions of US\$ [2000]) and industrial emissions (billions of kilos) from 1995 to 2005. Trade data are Chinese official data obtained from China Customs. Industrial emissions data are from the *Chinese Environmental Yearbook* and *China Statistical Yearbook on Environment* (various issues). In Chinese official statistics, the industrial sector includes Mining, Manufacturing, and Production and Distribution of Electricity, Gas, and Water.[10] Emissions data prior to 1998 were recorded only for industrial enterprises at the "county level and above." After the "Investigation on Sources of Township Industrial Pollution," published in 1997, it was found that township and village industrial enterprises (TVIEs) were accounting for a growing percentage of emissions. Therefore, emissions data include these enterprises from 1998 onward. In figures 11.3 and 11.4, we have been able to include TVIE emissions for 1995 and for 1997. But the TVIE data are unavailable for 1996, so we treat 1996 as missing (indicated by the dashed lines).

The most remarkable trend in figure 11.3 is the dramatic and rapid increase in the value of China's merchandise exports plus imports over the period. By 2005, trade had increased nearly 300 percent in real terms over its 1995 value. During that same period, industrial emissions were decreasing. This decline is confirmed in the ten-year environmental review issued by MEP (2006) and is also noted by the World Trade Organization (WTO; 2006) and

8. *China Statistical Yearbook on Environment* (2006, 207).
9. *China Statistical Yearbook on Environment* (2006, 208).
10. Changes in Chinese industrial emissions should be fairly representative of air pollution emissions because industry accounts for at least 80 percent of SO_2, smoke, and dust emissions throughout the period. Chinese industrial water pollution emissions accounted for 60 percent of COD emissions at the start of the period. With emissions from households and services growing in importance, industry's share fell to only 40 percent by the end of the period.

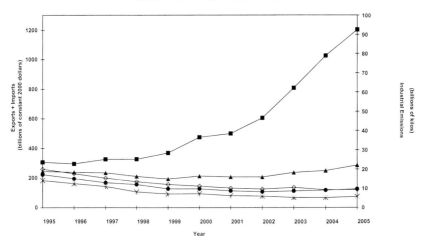

Fig. 11.3   China's trade and industrial emissions, 1995–2005

Source: Trade data are from China Customs. Industrial emissions data are from the *Chinese Environment Yearbook* and *China Statistical Yearbook on Environment* (various issues).

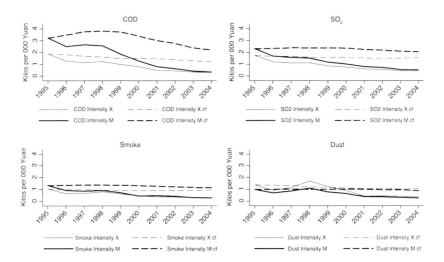

Fig. 11.4   The pollution intensity of China's trade, 1995–2004

Source: Data calculations by authors, as described in the text.

the OECD (2005). In 2005, annual industrial emissions of COD, smoke, and dust had declined to 56 percent, 46 percent, and 40 percent, respectively, of their levels in 1995. In contrast, industrial SO_2 emissions rose after 1999 and were 17.5 percent above 1995 levels by 2005.

11.3.2   Trends in the Composition of China's Trade

To understand what is driving these aggregate trends, we first examine trends in the composition of China's trade. Because data on emissions by industrial sectors are readily available, but data for agricultural or service sectors are not, we limit our analysis to manufacturing trade. In 2005, manufacturing trade accounted for 97 percent of Chinese exports and 83 percent of Chinese imports. Table 11.1 shows the shares of exports and imports in 1995 and 2004, by two-digit International Standard Industrial Classification (ISIC) sectors in manufacturing. The Chinese trade data were aggregated to Harmonized System (HS) (six-digit) and then converted to ISIC Revision 3 using the official Chinese concordance.

Even at this rather aggregated level, table 11.1 reveals some dramatic shifts in the sectoral composition of Chinese trade over this time period. In 1995, textiles and apparel accounted for the largest shares of Chinese exports to the world. These shares fell by about a third by 2004, while the export share of office and computing machinery grew by a factor of five, and that of communications equipment more than doubled. The largest shares of Chinese imports in 1995 were attributable to textiles and machinery. These shares fell by about 70 percent and 40 percent, respectively, by 2004, while import shares in office and computing machinery and in communications equipment more than doubled.

The sectoral shift in the composition of China's trade is interesting not only because it is dramatic, but because the same sectors have shown increases in both export and import shares. This suggests that much growth has taken place in sectors where production is internationally fragmented, resulting in two-way trade in "fragments" at varying stages of production. One rough indicator of the degree to which industries are internationally fragmented is the share of processing exports (imports) in each sector's total trade. Textile and apparel exports had substantial shares of processing exports across sectors in 1995, which fell somewhat by 2004. In contrast, office equipment and computing and communications equipment had extremely high shares of processing exports in 1995, and these shares remained high in 2004. Similarly, table 11.2 shows a decline in the share of processing imports in textiles and a contrasting rise in that share in communications equipment imports, though not in office and computing machinery imports. This evidence suggests that China's exports (and, to a lesser extent, imports) have become more concentrated in highly fragmented sectors and that the degree of fragmentation in some of these sectors has grown over time.

Table 11.1   The composition of China's trade, 1995 and 2004 (%)

ISIC Rev. 3 2-digit sector	Chinese manufacturing exports				Chinese manufacturing imports			
	Share of total manufacturing exports		Processing exports as a share of manufacturing exports		Share of total manufacturing imports		Processing imports as a share of manufacturing imports	
	1995	2004	1995	2004	1995	2004	1995	2004
15 Food products and beverages	5.5	2.6	24.4	31.0	4.9	2.4	45.2	26.2
16 Tobacco	0.7	0.0	26.6	2.9	0.3	0.0	0.3	0.3
17 Textiles	13.8	8.2	32.3	25.7	9.1	3.1	97.2	90.7
18 Wearing apparel	14.2	8.6	54.4	31.0	0.8	0.3	96.5	73.0
19 Leather shoes	7.3	4.1	72.7	47.0	1.9	0.8	98.6	85.9
20 Wood	1.5	1.0	14.8	19.4	1.0	0.5	44.4	59.9
21 Paper	0.6	0.4	42.3	59.8	2.5	1.7	66.1	38.2
22 Printing	0.1	0.1	79.5	54.3	0.0	0.0	55.0	35.2
23 Coke and petroleum	1.3	1.5	26.2	24.4	2.2	2.6	9.1	2.7
24 Chemicals	6.8	4.8	21.0	25.3	15.8	14.3	53.3	33.3
25 Rubber and plastics	2.7	2.7	71.7	62.7	1.8	1.7	83.0	56.1
26 Nonmetallic minerals	2.3	1.7	14.7	17.2	0.8	0.7	40.1	48.5
27 Basic metals	5.2	4.1	56.1	27.5	8.8	8.4	52.3	40.1
28 Fabricated metals	3.4	3.5	36.9	25.5	1.8	1.3	43.2	37.7
29 Machinery	4.7	7.2	45.7	48.2	20.7	12.8	3.8	7.8
30 Office and computing machinery	3.5	15.1	94.7	95.8	2.4	6.2	66.8	50.3
31 Electrical machinery	5.1	5.8	69.9	62.4	5.1	6.0	50.7	52.6
32 Communications equipment	7.8	15.7	85.6	86.0	10.4	23.0	59.8	71.9
33 Medical, precision, and optical instruments	2.9	3.0	80.5	76.2	3.6	8.6	42.8	57.0
34 Motor vehicles	1.4	2.1	73.6	59.8	2.5	3.3	4.2	2.1
35 Transport equipment	1.5	1.7	59.6	53.3	2.5	1.4	7.8	4.5
36 Furniture and other manufacturing	7.9	6.3	68.6	59.7	1.1	0.6	72.2	57.4

Source: China Customs and author calculations.

Note: ISIC = International Standard Industrial Classification.

Table 11.2   Pollution intensity of Chinese industrial output, 1995 and 2004

ISIC Rev. 3 2-digit sector	1995				2004			
	COD	SO$_2$	Smoke	Dust	COD	SO$_2$	Smoke	Dust
15 Food products and beverages	**11.47**	2.62	2.06	0.17	**1.59**	0.59	0.66	0.04
16 Tobacco	0.20	0.28	0.10	0.03	0.02	0.05	0.03	0.01
17 Textiles	1.05	1.48	0.81	0.03	0.73	0.70	0.27	0.03
18 Wearing apparel	0.61	0.63	0.35	0.01	0.44	0.35	0.17	0.02
19 Leather shoes	2.05	0.84	0.48	0.04	0.70	0.23	0.16	0.01
20 Wood	5.41	3.41	4.56	2.59	0.92	1.15	**1.38**	**0.58**
21 Paper	**67.36**	**6.89**	**4.66**	0.61	**6.95**	**1.86**	1.08	0.07
22 Printing	0.18	0.64	0.32	0.00	0.08	0.09	0.07	0.00
23 Coke and petroleum	0.79	2.85	1.67	1.15	0.08	0.85	0.58	0.19
24 Chemicals	3.19	4.17	2.29	0.58	0.67	1.13	0.54	0.16
25 Rubber and plastics	0.17	1.08	0.46	0.05	0.10	0.26	0.11	0.05
26 Nonmetallic minerals	0.35	**10.52**	**6.46**	**39.45**	0.14	**4.26**	**3.24**	**14.07**
27 Basic metals	0.81	5.33	2.10	**4.33**	0.12	1.26	0.50	**0.90**
28 Fabricated metals	0.12	1.47	0.74	0.18	0.08	0.32	0.14	0.10
29 Machinery	0.12	0.89	0.69	0.11	0.05	0.18	0.12	0.08
30 Office and computing machinery	0.08	0.34	0.22	0.01	0.03	0.03	0.03	0.01
31 Electrical machinery	0.14	0.84	0.50	1.23	0.02	0.16	0.12	0.41
32 Communications equipment	0.08	0.35	0.23	0.01	0.03	0.03	0.03	0.01
33 Medical, precision, and optical instruments	0.12	0.33	0.16	0.01	0.05	0.08	0.02	0.00
34 Motor vehicles	0.12	0.45	0.38	0.10	0.06	0.06	0.07	0.06
35 Transport equipment	0.12	0.43	0.37	0.10	0.06	0.06	0.07	0.06
36 Furniture and other manufacturing	0.37	0.55	0.50	0.95	0.12	0.28	0.19	0.34
40 Electricity, gas, steam, and hot water supply	1.48	**93.22**	**57.71**	0.47	0.25	**19.93**	**6.98**	0.17
41 Collection, purification, and distribution of water	12.33	2.79	1.67	0.45	2.08	0.92	0.34	0.00

Source: Chinese Environment Yearbook, *China Statistical Yearbook on Environment* (various issues), and author calculations.

Notes: Values are in kilos per thousand yuan output in 1995 yuan. COD = chemical oxygen demand; ISIC = International Standard Industrial Classification. Bold face indicates the three industries with the highest pollution intensity (for each pollutant, 1995 and 2004).

11.3.3 Trends in Industrial Pollution Intensity

To see the extent to which changes in production technology could be impacting emissions, we measure the pollution intensity of production by industry, from 1995 to 2004. We compiled data on emissions of the four pollutants at the industry level, as well as current value of output of the sampled enterprises, from the *Chinese Environmental Yearbooks* (Chinese editions). Pollution intensities were then calculated as emissions (kilos) per thousand yuan output (constant 1995 yuan) for thirty-three Chinese two-digit "divisions," including thirty manufacturing industries and three utilities, in the Chinese 2002 industrial classification.[11] These pollution intensities are shown in appendix table 11A.1. The appendix also provides a detailed explanation of these calculations and the treatment of missing or aggregated data. In table 11.2 we present these average water and air pollution intensities (in kilos per thousand yuan output [constant 1995 yuan]), mapped to the ISIC two-digit sectors, for 1995 and in 2004.[12] Pollution intensities for manufacturing (ISIC 15–36) and for utilities (ISIC 40–41) are included in the table.[13] In each year, the three sectors with the highest pollution intensities are shown in bold for each pollutant.[14]

Of the manufacturing industries, the major source of water pollution is production of paper and paper products. A few others—food products and beverages and wood products—show relatively high water pollution intensities, but these are far below that of the paper sector. Most industries show very low water pollution intensity. With respect to air pollution, nonmetallic minerals (which include cement) is by far the most SO_2-intensive and among

11. We measure pollution intensity as emissions relative to the value of output because the trade data are also measured in terms of value and our main concern is to measure the pollution intensity of the trade bundle. For some analyses of industrial pollution intensity, a measure of emissions per unit of value added might be preferable. We are unable to express pollution intensity relative to value added because value added data are not available at a sufficiently disaggregated level. A comparison of the two measures could reveal important, but unknown, differences. Because the emissions data are classified by economic activity, the numerator of these two measures should be similar as they are not affected by changes in the value of purchased intermediates used in the production process. However, the denominators will differ if an increase in purchased intermediates increases the value of output, thereby reducing pollution measured relative to total value but not relative to value added.

12. The official Chinese concordance maps the Chinese 2002 industrial classification at the four-digit level to ISIC Revision 3 at the four-digit level. Though some ISIC two-digit sectors correspond to a single Chinese two-digit "division," some correspond to either multiple Chinese divisions or to one division plus several four-digit lines from other divisions. Thus, the average pollution intensities for the ISIC two-digit sectors in table 11.2 generally represent a production-weighted average of the pollution intensity of multiple Chinese divisions. The production weights were constructed using Chinese gross industrial output data at the four-digit level from http://www.chinadataonline.org. Because not all sample years were available, weights were constructed using 2004 data.

13. ISIC 37 (recycling activities) is omitted. See appendix for discussion.

14. Because there are fewer ISIC two-digit sectors than Chinese divisions, there is some variation between the highest pollution intensities in table 11.2 and table 11A.1.

the top three in terms of smoke and dust. The other industries with high air pollution intensities include basic metals and paper (SO_2), paper and wood (smoke), and wood and basic metals (dust). But again these industries generally show much lower pollution intensities than nonmetallic minerals. Most industries, in fact, show very low air pollution intensities. The utilities as a group are highly polluting. The water utility is second only to paper production in water pollution intensity. The electricity and gas utilities are the dirtiest sectors overall in terms of SO_2 and smoke.[15]

Table 11.2 also reveals two interesting trends. The first is that across nearly all sectors, the pollution intensity of production has fallen over time. This is true for all four pollutants. Even the water and energy utilities show improvement over the period. Thus, there is some evidence of a shift toward cleaner industrial production techniques in China. The second trend is that China's trade does appear to be shifting toward cleaner sectors over time. Although trade in 1995 was not concentrated in the highest polluting sectors, textiles and leather products were somewhat high in terms of water pollution intensity and certainly not the lowest in terms of SO_2 and smoke intensity. Though these industries show cleaner production techniques by 2004, they remain significantly more polluting than office and computing machinery and communications equipment. The latter sectors' pollution intensities were low in 1995 and extremely low as of 2004.

The pollution intensities in table 11.2 include direct water and air emissions from production processes within each two-digit sector and indirect air emissions from fuel burning on enterprise premises. For a complete assessment of indirect emissions, we would ideally use an input-output (IO) table to capture emissions generated by (a) use of domestically produced intermediates in other two-digit ISIC sectors, and (b) use of energy and water purchased from utilities. However, two main issues impede such an assessment. First, goods exported under the processing regime use more imported intermediates—and, therefore, less domestically produced intermediates— than those exported under the normal regime. Thus, the IO table would have to distinguish imports of final goods from imports of intermediates and then distinguish imported intermediates used for processing exports from those used for normal exports. Second, indirect emissions from fuel burning on site are already included in our pollution intensities. Thus, IO coefficients reflecting energy demand would have to be adjusted to net out on-site supplies.

The official Chinese IO table does not address either of these issues. In recent work, Dean, Fung, and Wang (2008) and Koopman, Wang, and Wei (2008) provide an improved method for identifying imported intermedi-

15. The ISIC Revision 3 groups the electricity and fuel gas utilities into ISIC 40, and as a result, the dust intensity for ISIC 40 looks quite low. But fuel gas production and supply has the second highest dust intensity across Chinese divisions.

ates and for splitting the Chinese IO table between processing exports and normal exports for 123 sectors for 1997 and 2002.[16] In theory, this could be used to address the first issue discussed above for two years in our sample. However, because no separate data exist for the use of domestic intermediates in processing and normal exports (including energy and water), differences only emerge after rebalancing. There appear to be no data available to address the second issue. This is a critical drawback to any calculation of indirect emissions because this could lead to double-counting with respect to emissions from energy use, and table 11.2 shows that Chinese utilities are highly polluting industries. Therefore, in the present analysis, we use the pollution intensities in table 11.2 to assess changes in the pollution intensity of Chinese trade.

11.4   The Pollution Intensity of Chinese Trade

If the popular wisdom were correct, we would expect China's continuing trade liberalization, particularly after its 2001 WTO accession, to lead to increased specialization in "dirty goods" (Gardner 2008). This composition effect, along with increased scale of production, would be expected to worsen emissions and lead to "dirtier" trade than in earlier years (ceteris paribus). However, thus far we have presented at least superficial evidence that trade has shifted toward cleaner industries and that industrial production has become cleaner over time. In addition, this evidence suggests that production fragmentation may have played a role in these trends. In the evidence we present below, we find:

- Chinese exports are *less* water-pollution intensive and generally *less* air-pollution intensive than Chinese imports.
- *Both* Chinese exports and imports are becoming cleaner over time.
- The cleaner trends in exports and imports are driven by *both* composition and technique effects, with the latter being the strongest.
- Processing trade is indeed cleaner than ordinary trade.

To measure the pollution intensity of Chinese trade, we bring together the Chinese manufacturing pollution intensities discussed earlier and the Chinese trade data. Early studies of the pollution intensity of U.S. trade (Walter 1973; Robison 1988) did not have industrial emissions data so had to rely on estimates of environmental control costs (e.g., abatement capital and operating costs and research and development [R&D]) to calculate pollution intensity by industry. More recently, Ederington, Levinson, and Minier (2004) made use of U.S. industrial emissions data for a single year, and changes in the composition of exports and imports over time, to construct

---

16. Both papers include discussion of advances over earlier analyses by Chen et al. (2008) and Ping (2005).

changes in the pollution intensity of U.S. exports and imports. While this was a significant advance, the lack of time series emissions data confined the observed changes over time to composition effects. In a recent paper, Levinson (2009) uses several years of U.S. industrial emissions data to discern the relative importance of composition and technique effects in the pollution intensity of U.S. trade.

Here we use the annual Chinese pollution intensities across industries and annual trade data to calculate an export- or import-weighted average pollution intensity for aggregate exports (imports) for each of the eleven years in the sample (1995–2004). Using the official Chinese concordance, we map the Chinese pollution intensity for each Chinese division to the four-digit ISIC lines corresponding to that division.[17] This pollution intensity is then weighted by the share of manufacturing exports (imports) corresponding to that four-digit ISIC line, and summed to yield an export- or import-weighted average pollution intensity for each year.

Figure 11.4 shows that both exports and imports became steadily cleaner throughout the period. By 2004, the water pollution intensity of exports had fallen by about 84 percent, while that of imports had fallen by 89 percent, compared to 1995 levels. The drop in air pollution intensity was almost as dramatic, with export (import) SO_2 intensity falling by 75 percent (78 percent), smoke intensity by 75 percent (80 percent), and dust intensity by 73 percent (74 percent).[18] Interestingly, both Ederington, Levinson, and Minier (2004) and Levinson (2009) find evidence that U.S. exports and imports also have become cleaner over time.

Chinese exports also appear to be much cleaner than Chinese imports. In 1995, had Chinese imports been produced in China, they would have generated about 70 percent more COD emissions per thousand yuan than Chinese exports. This difference diminishes over time but remains throughout the period. Chinese exports are also less SO_2-intensive, and less smoke-intensive, than Chinese imports during 1995 to 2004, though these divergences are less dramatic than the water pollution case. Only if pollution intensity is measured with respect to dust emissions do we find Chinese exports dirtier than imports.

To understand the relative role of composition and technique effects in generating these trends in pollution intensity, we conduct a counterfactual experiment. We recalculate the pollution intensity of both aggregate exports and aggregate imports, assuming the pollution intensity of sectoral out-

17. In the very few cases where several Chinese divisions map to a single ISIC four-digit line, a production-weighted pollution intensity is assigned. As before, production weights are constructed from the 2004 Chinese four-digit level gross industrial output value data from China Data Online.

18. The peak in dust emissions intensity is largely due to the inclusion from 1998 onward of emissions from TVIEs. Because TVIE emissions data are unavailable at the sectoral level, the yearly industrial pollution intensities in 1995 to 1997 do not include TVIEs.

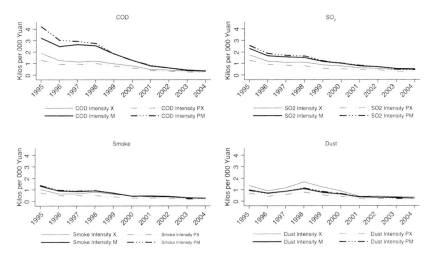

Fig. 11.5   The pollution intensity of China's overall trade and processing trade, 1995–2004

Source: Data calculations by authors, as described in the text.

put remained at its 1995 levels. These counterfactual pollution intensities, shown by the dashed lines in figure 11.5, represent the change in pollution intensity of exports (imports) if only the composition of traded products had changed over time.

For all four pollutants, figure 11.4 shows that changes in the composition of trade did imply both cleaner exports and imports. However, in every case, these composition effects account for a relatively small proportion of the observed changes in the pollution intensity of trade. This suggests that China's cleaner production techniques have been the most important force behind cleaner trade. It should be noted that with pollution intensity data only available at the Chinese two-digit level, the composition (technique) effect could be understated (overstated) in figure 11.4. A change in the composition of trade among activities *within* a division could lead to lower pollution intensity, but would be misattributed in our data to a technique effect.[19] While this is certainly possible, a closer look at the variation in the trade data suggests that within division changes in the composition of trade are not likely to be large enough to reverse the result. Interestingly, Levinson (2009) also finds evidence that technique effects are more important than composition effects in explaining the falling pollution intensity of U.S. trade.

Because table 11.1 shows a shift in the composition of China's trade toward highly fragmented manufacturing sectors, and because table 11.2

19. We are indebted to Arik Levinson for this observation.

suggests that these sectors are relatively low polluters, we examine more closely the pollution intensity of processing trade. Because the Chinese industrial pollution data are not differentiated by customs regime, the export- or import-weighted pollution intensities for processing trade differ from those for overall trade solely due to the composition of products traded under the processing regime. As figure 11.5 shows, many of the trends in the pollution intensities for overall trade are also true for processing trade. Processing exports appear to be cleaner than processing imports with respect to all pollutants. Processing exports and imports also both show downward trends in pollution intensity during the period. Counterfactual results (not shown) also suggest that, once again, composition effects are responsible for a small share of the decline in pollution intensity over time.

However, figure 11.5 also reveals that China's processing exports are cleaner than China's overall exports. The average COD, SO_2, and smoke intensities of processing exports are about 70 percent that of overall exports in 1995. The dust intensity of processing exports is even lower—only about 50 percent that of overall trade. Though some of these differences diminish over time, processing exports continue to have significantly lower pollution intensities than overall exports across all four pollutants throughout the period. This evidence is suggestive that the increase in China's processing exports has implied a composition effect that is favorable toward China's environment. This effect might be further magnified if the firms engaged in processing trade (largely foreign-invested firms) actually produce with cleaner techniques than average firms.

11.5   The Role of Fragmentation and FDI in Explaining the Pollution Intensity of Chinese Trade

To explore the role that production fragmentation and foreign investment play in the changes we observe in the pollution intensity of China's trade, we develop a model that embeds China into the global production network. Our model is tailored for the Chinese context in that it recognizes the magnitude of foreign investment and its effects on the composition of trade. The framework we use draws upon the structural model of pollution developed by Copeland and Taylor (1994) and the outsourcing model developed by Feenstra and Hanson (1996). We first consider the supply of pollution to identify the determinants of pollution regulation. Next, we examine the demand for pollution, first considering the pollution intensity of exports in a simple two-sector model without fragmented production and then adding a fragmented export sector. We use these models to explore the impact of foreign investment and trade liberalization on the pollution content of trade. Our goal is to derive several reduced form models of the determinants of the pollution intensity of Chinese trade, which we then test empirically.

11.5.1   Pollution Supply

We follow Copeland and Taylor (2003) in modeling the supply of pollution as the result of government behavior that maximizes the utility of a representative citizen:

$$V = u(R) - \gamma D.$$ (1)

Indirect utility is a function of real income, R, and the level of environmental damage, D. The government levies a pollution tax, τ, to induce the utility-maximizing level of damage, taking as given world prices, trade policy, and production possibilities. The gross national product (GNP) function gives the maximum value of national income as a function of domestic prices, the pollution tax rate, and vector of factor endowments. Consequently, real income for the representative citizen can be expressed as $R = G(p,\tau,v)/Lp$, where p is a price index, and L is the number of citizens.[20] Maximization of equation (1) yields the Samuelson rule for public good provision: the government sets the pollution tax equal to the sum of marginal damages across all citizens. Marginal damage measures the willingness to pay for reduced emissions, and it reflects the marginal rate of substitution between emissions and income. Given the indirect utility function (1), the pollution tax rate chosen is:

$$\tau = -L \frac{V_D}{V_I} = \frac{Lp\gamma}{u'(R')}$$ (2)

where the right-hand side gives the marginal damage from pollution.[21] Using equation (2), we express the endogenous pollution tax as $\tau(L, p, R)$.

11.5.2   Pollution Demand without Production Fragmentation

We begin with the simplest model of production and trade. This model serves as an alternative to a second model, presented below, that explicitly incorporates export processing with imported intermediate inputs. We consider a two-sector model of a small, open economy. China is endowed with capital and effective labor (E), which depends on the human capital of its labor force: $E = A(H)L$. The import-competing sector, M, uses effective labor and capital and it serves as numeraire. Each unit of M produced releases one unit of pollution emissions.

The export sector produces Good Y using effective labor and capital. Effective labor may also be used for abatement of the pollution emissions (D) created in the production process. Following Copeland and Taylor's

---

20. Pollution tax revenue is counted in G as a return to D, and it is assumed to be rebated to citizens lump sum.

21. Because we have adopted a specification in which the marginal disutility of pollution is constant, the pollution supply curve is horizontal. See Copeland and Taylor (2003) for further discussion and alternative specifications.

(2003) form for abatement, we may express the production function for Y treating emissions as an input:

$$Y = (E_Y^{1-\beta} D_Y^{\beta})^{\theta} K_Y^{1-\theta},$$

(3)

where $0 < \beta < 1$. The relative domestic price of Y is $p = \delta p^*$, where $1/\delta$ is a measure of trade frictions, and p^* is China's terms of trade. We use equation (3) to solve for the pollution intensity of export production, e_Y:

(4)
$$e_Y \equiv \frac{D_Y}{pY} = \frac{\beta\theta}{\tau}.$$

We use equation (4) to create our first estimating equation for the pollution intensity of Chinese exports. In doing so, we note that the pollution intensity given by equation (4) depends on the pollution intensity of China's export production, as measured by the term, β. As Copeland and Taylor (2003) discuss, differences across countries in factor abundance interact with regulatory differences to determine the pattern of trade. These considerations lead to an expression for the pollution intensity of Chinese exports of the form:

(5) $e_Y = e_Y(K, H, L, \tau) = e_Y(K, H, L, R, p^*, \delta).$

In this expression we have replaced the pollution tax rate with its determinants, based on equation (2). Thus, the pollution intensity of exports can be estimated as a function of China's factor endowments, its real income per capita, its terms of trade, and its trade frictions.

An increase in China's overall capital-labor ratio should raise the capital intensity of both the import-competing and export sectors. If pollution intensity rises with the capital intensity of production, we would expect China's capital-labor ratio to be positively related to the pollution intensity of both its exports and its imports.[22] Because an increase in real income raises the level of the pollution tax, we expect the pollution intensity of exports to fall as China's real income rises. The terms of trade and trade frictions have ambiguous effects on pollution intensity. Improved terms of trade imply an increase in real gross domestic product (GDP) and, hence, a higher domestic pollution tax, reducing e, but a higher relative price for exports raises the production value of factors used in abatement, raising e. If this latter consideration dominates, we would expect improved terms of trade and reduced trade frictions to raise the pollution intensity of China's exports.

11.5.3   Pollution Demand with Production Fragmentation

As an alternative to the simple two-sector model above, we consider a model with two export sectors. China is treated as a small economy rela-

---

22. It is common to assume that pollution intensity rises with the capital intensity of production. Copeland and Taylor (2003) provide some evidence for the case of SO_2.

tive to an advanced trading bloc (A). The first sector produces "ordinary" exports, those that are produced with domestic inputs, using the production technology given by equation (3). The "processing" sector produces a set of goods that are intermediate inputs for a single final good. This final good is costlessly assembled from a continuum of intermediate inputs, indexed by $z \in [0,1]$. Inputs are produced using effective labor, capital specific to the processing sector, and pollution discharge. Input production technology varies by the amount of labor used relative to the emissions created during production. We adopt a simple functional form for production technology of input z:

$$(6) \qquad x(z) = [E(z)^{1-\alpha(z)} D(z)^{\alpha(z)}]^{\theta} K(z)^{1-\theta}.$$

We also restrict $\alpha(z) \in [\underline{\alpha}(z), \overline{\alpha}(z)]$, $0 < \underline{\alpha} < \overline{\alpha} < 1$, and $0 < \theta < 1$. We assume that ordinary export production is more pollution-intensive than processing export production, implying that $\beta > \overline{\alpha}$.

Intermediate producers consider the price of labor, capital, and pollution discharge when choosing a production technique. The price of labor, w, measures the wage per effective labor unit, thereby accounting for labor quality differences across countries. The rental price of capital is given by r. If firms were unregulated, they would always choose to discharge as much as possible to economize on labor. However, China levies a pollution tax, τ, according to equation (2), and this tax is effective in the sense that firms abate some pollution. Given these factor prices, the firm's labor and discharge combination that satisfies cost minimization is:

$$(7) \qquad \frac{w}{\tau} = \left[\frac{1 - \alpha(z)}{\alpha(z)} \right] \frac{D(z)}{E(z)}.$$

Because equation (7) implies that the parameter $\alpha(z)$ determines how pollution discharge varies among intermediates producers, $\alpha(z)$ provides a measure of pollution intensity. We can order the intermediates in order of decreasing pollution intensity to obtain $\alpha'(z) < 0$.

To determine the pattern of trade between China and the advanced countries, we examine how unit production costs vary across intermediates. The unit cost of producing one unit of input x in country i is given by:

$$(8) \qquad c(w_i, \tau_i, r_i; z) = \kappa(z) w_i^{[1-\alpha(z)]\theta} \tau_i^{\alpha(z)\theta} r_i^{1-\theta},$$

where $\kappa(z)$ is an industry-specific constant. Input z is produced in an advanced country if $c(w_A, \tau_A, r_A; z) < c(w_C, \tau_C, r_C; z)$.

We assume that labor in the advanced bloc has high human capital levels and, thus, it is more productive than labor in China. The pollution tax levied in the advanced countries exceeds the rate set in China, such that $w_A/\tau_A < w_C/\tau_C$. Given these relative factor prices and assuming for the moment that rental rates are the same in both countries, input z would be produced in the advanced bloc if

$$(9) \qquad \omega \equiv \frac{w_A}{w_C} \leq \left(\frac{\tau_C}{\tau_A} \right)^{\alpha(z)/[1-\alpha(z)]} \equiv T(z).$$

With $\tau_A > \tau_C$ and $\alpha'(z) < 0$, $T(z)$ must be increasing in z. The advanced bloc's cost advantage increases as the pollution intensity of production decreases. For a given relative wage rate, ω, the $T(z)$ locus determines a critical industry z^* such that China has lower costs than the advanced bloc in the range of inputs indexed by $z \in [0, z^*)$, while the advanced bloc has lower costs in the range $z \in (z^*, 1]$.

Now we assume that the rental rate of capital is not the same in both countries and that instead, $r_A < r_C$. Because capital's cost share is the same across all goods, this rental differential lowers the cost of production in the advanced countries across the full range of intermediates. To consider an equilibrium with some trade in intermediates, we assume that despite its lower rental rate, the advanced bloc has a cost disadvantage for intermediates more pollution intensive than input z^*, defined as that input for which $c(w_A, \tau_A, r_A; z) = c(w_C, \tau_C, r_C; z)$. Figure 11.6 shows the minimum cost locus for China as CC and for the advanced bloc as AA.[23] While the slope of each locus depends on the underlying production functions, it can be shown that they are upward sloping.

The pollution intensity of this fragmented sector depends on which inputs China produces; that is, it depends on the value of z^*. Based on the production functions (6), total discharge from the X sector is

$$(10) \qquad D = \int_0^{z^*} D(z)dz = \frac{\theta}{\tau} \int_0^{z^*} \alpha(z)p(z)x(z)dz.$$

For simplicity, we assume that demand by the final good producer for each input is a constant share of total world expenditure and that, as a small country, China has a negligible impact on world income.[24] Using this assumption, $p(z)x(z) = \varphi(z)I^W$, in equation (10) leads to an expression for the pollution intensity of the fragmented sector:

$$(11) \qquad e_X = \int_0^{z^*} \frac{D(z)}{p(z)x(z)} \frac{p(z)x(z)}{\int_0^{z^*} p(z)x(z)dz}dz = \frac{\theta}{\tau \int_0^{z^*} p(z)x(z)dz} \int_0^{z^*} \alpha(z)\varphi(z)I^W dz$$

Equation (11) allows us to express the pollution intensity of the processing sector as a function of the capital share of export output $(1 - \theta)$, the pollution tax, τ, and the critical value, z^*. When the capital share of processing exports rises, the average pollution intensity of these exports falls. Similarly, when the pollution tax rises, the average pollution intensity of processing exports falls. Last, an increase in the critical value, z^*, reduces the average

---

23. Feenstra and Hanson (1996) introduce a similar diagram to illustrate the fragmentation of production between the United States and Mexico.

24. Copeland and Taylor (1994) also assume that budget shares are constant in their model, but they consider two countries large enough to affect international markets.

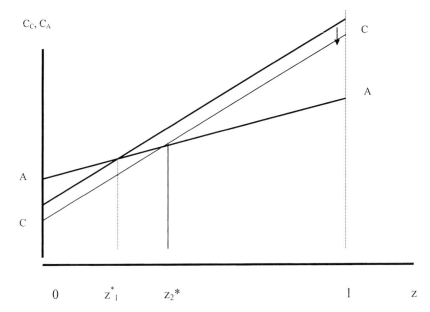

Fig. 11.6   FDI expands range of export processing activities performed in China

pollution intensity of the export processing sector because $\alpha(z)$ is a decreasing function of z. It is interesting also to note that an increase in z^* reduces the pollution intensity of the inputs imported from the advanced countries for processing. Thus, when the range of inputs produced in China expands, the pollution intensity of both processing exports and processing imports declines.

As discussed above, the critical value, z^* depends on the cost of intermediates production in China, $c(w_C, \tau_C, r_C; z)$. Therefore, z^* depends on all determinants of factor prices for the processing sector. These determinants are the terms of trade and the level of trade frictions, the determinants of the pollution tax rate, and all factor endowments. As discussed previously, foreign investment has been skewed toward those sectors that process and assembly imported intermediates. Therefore, we separate the capital stock into domestic (K^d) and foreign owned capital (K^f), allowing us to express the pollution intensity of the export processing sector as:

(12) $\qquad\qquad e_X = e_X(K^d, K^f, H, L, p^*, \delta, R).$

The pollution intensity of the whole export bundle is a weighted average of the pollution intensity of ordinary exports and the pollution intensity of processing exports. Using equation (5) to express the pollution intensity of ordinary exports and equation (12) to express the pollution intensity of processing exports and letting S_X denote the share of total exports that are processing exports, the pollution intensity of China's trade bundle is:

(13) $e = S_Y e_Y + S_X e_X = e_Y + S_X(e_X - e_Y) = e(K^d, K^f, H, L, p^*, \delta, R, S_X),$

where we have used the fact that $S_Y + S_X = 1$. Because we have assumed that $e_X < e_Y$, an increase in the processing share of exports obviously reduces overall export pollution intensity, ceteris paribus.

Foreign capital flows primarily to the export processing sector, reducing its cost of capital. Figure 11.6 can be used to illustrate the effect of this capital inflow on China's input competitiveness. At constant wages and pollution tax, the curve labeled CC shifts down, causing z^* to rise from z_1^* to z_2^*. With the pollution tax unchanged, there is no change in the pollution intensity of any intermediate. However, the capital inflow pulls labor into the processing sector, raising its share in exports. Moreover, because China now produces intermediates that are less pollution-intensive than any it produced before, the average pollution intensity of China's processing exports falls.[25] Likewise, the pollution intensity of China's processing imports falls because China now imports a narrower set of inputs, and this set is, on average, cleaner than before.

Foreign investment may reduce export pollution intensity through another channel, which we have not formally modeled, even if we hold the processing share of exports fixed. Foreign investment often involves the use of new capital equipment and new production techniques. In particular, investment from high-regulatory-standard countries may transfer new pollution control methods to the host country as investors use technology and techniques that they have developed within the context of stringent pollution regulation.[26] If foreign investors bring this sort of "technique effect" with them, the pollution intensity of China's exports should be negatively associated with the level of foreign capital, even when the share of processing exports is held constant.

11.6   Estimating the Determinants of the Pollution Intensity of China's Manufacturing Trade

How well does the previous model of production fragmentation and foreign investment explain the changes in the pollution intensity of Chinese exports and imports shown in figure 11.4? To find out, we begin with the simple model expressed in equation (5), in which there is no fragmentation, and FDI plays no distinct role. We then consider the model expressed

25. There will also be feedback effects, which we do not discuss here. First, increased foreign investment may raise domestic wages, but this wage effect cannot overturn the direct effect of foreign investment. Second, higher real per capita income implies a higher pollution tax, reinforcing the direct effect by further reducing pollution intensity.

26. This possibility is consistent with evidence presented in Dean, Lovely, and Wang (2009) on the location decisions of foreign investors. While provincial variation in pollution taxes influenced the location of Chinese investors, no effect was found for OECD investors.

in equation (13), which incorporates both ordinary and fragmented trade. Last, we allow for the endogeneity of fragmented trade and the explicit influence of foreign investment.

11.6.1   Econometric Specification

Because the pollution intensity of exports (imports) in figure 11.5 is linear in logs, equation (5) could be estimated by pooling the data on the four pollutants over the period 1995 to 2004 and adding pollutant-specific fixed effects and a linear time trend:

$$\ln e^j_{it} = \alpha_i + \beta_1 \ln K_{it} + \beta_2 \ln L_{it} + \beta_3 \ln p_{it} + \beta_4 \ln \delta_{it} + \beta_5 \ln R_{it}$$
$$+ \beta_6 \ln \text{trend}_{it} + \varepsilon_{it},$$

(where j is exports or imports, i is pollutant, and t is time). However, several difficulties arise with this approach. With this small sample of annual observations, the introduction of four additional variables (fixed effects and a trend) reduces the degrees of freedom substantially. In addition, recent literature suggests that there are many unresolved issues in the construction of reliable data on the Chinese capital stock.[27] Finally, some of the macroeconomic explanatory variables in the model may be nonstationary. An alternative approach that addresses all three concerns is to estimate a first-differenced specification of the model in equation (5):

$$(5')\quad \Delta \ln e^j_{it} = \gamma + \beta_1 \Delta \ln K_{it} + \beta_2 \Delta \ln L_{it} + \beta_3 \Delta \ln p_{it} + \beta_4 \Delta \ln \delta_{it}$$
$$+ \beta_5 \Delta \ln R_{it} + \eta_{it},$$

where Δ indicates first difference.

Equation $(5')$ is estimated using pooled data on COD, SO_2, smoke, and dust intensity of exports (imports) at the national level, from 1995 to 2004. After differencing, this yields a small panel of thirty-six observations. The estimation method is generalized least squares (GLS) with cross-section weights to correct for pollutant-specific heteroskedasticity. It might be reasonable to assume that the pollution intensity of trade responds differently across pollutants. Unfortunately, the limited sample size prevents us from using a varying coefficients model to explore this possibility. It might also be reasonable to assume that there is contemporaneous correlation across the pollutants in the sample. A change in the environmental regime, or a technological change that affects several pollutants simultaneously, could cause error terms to be correlated across pollutants in a given year. To address this issue, specifications of equation $(5')$ were also estimated using ordinary least squares (OLS) with panel-corrected cross-section standard errors (PCSE), which are robust to both cross-section heteroskedasticity and contemporaneous correlation. A comparison of the results allowed us to

27. See the discussion of published data, previous methods of measurement, and recent innovations by Holz (2006), and the response by Chow (2006).

assess the importance of contemporaneous correlation and the robustness of our results to an alternate estimation method. We found little difference in the results and so present only the GLS estimates.[28]

Most of the explanatory variables are constructed using data from the World Bank, *World Development Indicators,* 2007. Trends in the underlying data are shown in table 11.3. The log difference in the capital stock is proxied by gross capital formation (percent of GDP), while the log difference in the total labor force and in real GDP per capita are calculated directly from the data.[29] In this simple model, investment is not differentiated by source nor labor supply by skill level. The log difference in relative prices is proxied by the difference in China's net barter terms of trade, where the latter is defined as the ratio of the export price index to the import price index, measured relative to the base year 2000. The data used to calculate the log difference in tariffs are China's simple average most-favored-nation (MFN) tariffs (ad valorem equivalent) taken from the UNCTAD TRAINS database, via World Integrated Trade Solution (WITS).[30]

11.6.2   Estimating the Standard Model

Table 11.4 presents the results of estimation of equation (5′) for exports in column (1). These results support some of the predictions discussed previously. Ignoring the role of processing trade, an increase in the capital-labor ratio increases the pollution intensity of exports, suggesting that capital and pollution may be complements in production. Real GDP per capita—the proxy for stringency in environmental regulations—is negatively related to the pollution intensity of exports, though the impact is not significant. Trade liberalization appears to be favorable for China's environment. A fall in China's average tariff is associated with a fall in the pollution intensity of exports. Because China's tariffs actually fell by about 75 percent during this period, this suggests that trade reform may have contributed significantly to China's cleaner trade. In addition, China's entrance into the WTO in 2001 also seems to have been associated with a significant reduction in the pollution intensity of China's exports. Finally, though the impact of a change in the terms of trade is indeterminate in theory, here an improvement in the terms of trade is associated with increased pollution intensity of exports. The parallel results for the pollution intensity of imports are shown in table 11.5, column (1). While the results for trade barriers and entrance into the WTO are similar to that of exports, the results for other variables are much weaker.

---

28. Because of the small sample size, not all specifications could be estimated using PSCE. Results are available from the authors upon request.

29. Gross domestic product per capita is in constant 2000 U.S. dollars.

30. TRAINS has no Chinese tariff data for 1994 to 1995 or 2002. The simple average MFN tariff data for 1994 to 1995 (with no ad valorem equivalent [AVE] correction) was taken from Zhang, Zhang, and Wan (1998), and for 2002 (with no AVE correction) was taken from the WTO (2006).

Table 11.3   Trends in Chinese trade, investment, and growth

Year	Net barter terms of trade	Simple average tariff	Gross capital formation	FDI/GDP	Labor force growth	Processing exports (% of total exports)	Processing imports (% of total imports)	Growth of real GDP per capita
1995	101.9	35.9	39.3	4.9	1.1	49.5	44.2	9.26
1996	105.9	22.0	37.7	4.7	1.2	55.8	44.9	8.48
1997	110.2	16.7	36.0	4.6	1.1	54.5	49.3	7.87
1998	110.6	16.6	35.0	4.3	1.0	56.8	48.9	6.55
1999	104.1	16.3	34.2	3.6	1.1	56.3	44.0	6.38
2000	100.0	16.2	32.8	3.2	1.0	54.7	40.8	7.36
2001	100.9	15.2	34.2	3.3	1.0	54.4	38.3	7.25
2002	100.5	12.2	35.2	3.4	0.8	55.3	41.5	8.04
2003	97.3	10.5	37.8	3.3	0.9	55.4	39.7	8.91
2004	91.8	9.6	38.7	2.8	1.1	55.6	39.6	9.02

Sources: All data except the trade and tariff data are from the World Bank *World Development Indicators,* 2007. The trade data are from China Customs, and the tariff data are from the World Integrated Trade Solution (WITS).

Note: FDI = foreign direct investment; GDP = gross domestic product.

Table 11.4   The change in the pollution intensity of China's exports (variables in log difference unless otherwise noted)

	(1) Equation (5')		(2) Equation (13')		(3) Equation (13') IV		(4) Equation (13') IV		(5) Equation (13') IV	
	Coefficient	t-statistic[a]	Coefficient	t-statistic[a]	Coefficient	t-statistic[a]	Coefficient	t-statistic[a]	Coefficient	t-statistic[a]
Gross capital formation[b]	0.04**	2.03	0.05**	2.24	0.12***	2.68				
Domestic investment[b]							0.12***	4.34		
FDI[b]							-0.52***	-3.12		
Ratio of FDI to domestic investment[b]									-0.11***	-3.27
Ratio of skilled to unskilled labor[c]									-0.02***	-3.90
Labor force	-0.32	-1.61	-0.35*	-1.73	-0.54*	-1.75	0.29	1.13	-0.08	-1.33
Real GDP per capita	-0.01	-0.30	-0.04	-0.76	-0.18*	-1.80	-0.34***	-3.52	0.09***	6.00
Terms of trade[c]	0.04***	5.08	0.04***	4.94	0.04***	3.31	0.12***	5.12	1.24***	4.65
Average tariff	1.37***	5.05	1.23***	3.85	0.51	0.84	0.73***	2.40	-0.87***	-7.60
WTO dummy	-0.42***	-6.11	-0.42***	-5.92	-0.39***	-3.70	-0.83***	-5.91		
Processing exports share[c]			-0.01	-0.94	-0.08*	-2.15	-0.02**	-2.00	-0.03**	-2.25
Constant	-0.91**	-2.02	-1.11**	-2.25	-2.25**	-2.58	0.75	1.09	2.18**	2.67
No. of observations	36		36		36		36		36	
Weighted adjusted R^2[a]	0.65		0.65		0.36		0.74		0.74	
Weighted F-statistic[a]	11.71***		10.10***		12.26***		13.35***		15.73***	

Notes: Dependent variable is log difference of pollution intensity of exports. All regressions are generalized least squares with panel-specific weights to correct for pollutant-specific heteroskedasticity. FDI = foreign direct investment; GDP = gross domestic product; WTO = World Trade Organization.

[a]Eviews output gives weighted adjusted R^2 and F-statistics, where the weights adjust for the cross-section weights. Eviews also gives t-statistics rather than z-statistics.

[b]Expressed as share of GDP.

[c]Expressed as difference between value in period t and period $t-1$.

***Significant at the 1 percent level.

**Significant at the 5 percent level.

*Significant at the 10 percent level.

Table 11.5   The change in the pollution intensity of China's imports (variables in log difference unless otherwise noted)

	(1) Equation (5')		(2) Equation (13')		(3) Equation (13') IV		(4) Equation (13') IV		(5) Equation (13') IV	
	Coefficient	t-statistic[a]	Coefficient	t-statistic[a]	Coefficient	t-statistic[a]	Coefficient	t-statistic[a]	Coefficient	t-statistic[a]
Gross capital formation[b]	0.03	1.19	0.13***	3.34	0.16***	2.69				
Domestic investment[b]							0.14***	3.32		
FDI[b]							0.43	1.01		
Ratio of FDI to domestic investment (lagged)[b]									−0.21***	−2.37
Ratio of skilled to unskilled labor (lagged)[c]									0.13***	3.04
Labor force	−0.01	−0.06	−0.26	−1.13	−0.35	−1.32	−0.66	−1.08	−0.93**	−2.73
Real GDP per capita	0.01	0.16	−0.15**	−2.19	−0.21**	−2.02	−0.08	−0.67	0.05***	3.71
Terms of trade[c]	0.05***	4.42	0.06***	5.79	0.06***	5.12	0.03	0.63	−5.09**	−2.58
Average tariff	1.22***	3.62	1.19***	4.18	1.19***	4.05	1.38***	3.59	−2.62***	−3.32
WTO dummy	−0.32***	−3.71	−0.40***	−5.00	−0.43***	−4.40	−0.24	−0.98		
Processing imports share (lagged)[c]			−0.04***	−3.20	−0.06**	−2.38	−0.06**	−2.28	−0.03**	−2.13
Constant	−1.03	−1.85	−2.99***	−3.80	−3.63***	−3.01	−4.66***	−1.90	8.66**	2.61
No. of observations	36		36		36		36		32	
Weighted adjusted R^2[a]	0.39		0.52		0.49		0.51		0.48	
Weighted F-statistic[a]	4.77***		6.32***		4.76***		5.54***		5.11***	

Notes: Dependent variable is log difference of pollution intensity of imports. All regressions are generalized least squares with panel-specific weights to correct for pollutant-specific heteroskedasticity. FDI = foreign direct investment; GDP = gross domestic product; WTO = World Trade Organization.

[a]Eviews output gives weighted adjusted R^2 and F-statistics, where the weights adjust for the cross-section weights. Eviews also gives t-statistics rather than z-statistics.

[b]Expressed as share of GDP.

[c]Expressed as difference between value in period t and period $t − 1$.

11.6.3   Composition Effects and Fragmentation

Moving beyond the simple model, we incorporate both ordinary and fragmented exports, as in the reduced form model in equation (13). This model suggests that changes in overall pollution intensity will be explained not only by the changing pollution intensity of ordinary exports, as in equation (5′), but by growth in the share of fragmented exports and changes in that subsector's pollution intensity. The share of exports (imports) that are fragmented is proxied by the share of processing exports (imports) in total exports (imports). This variable is calculated directly from the trade data from China Customs; it includes both exports (imports) designated as processing and assembly, and those designated as processing with imported materials. We begin by treating the processing share as exogenous and simply add the change in this share to equation (5′) to form equation (13′).

$$(13') \quad \Delta \ln e_{it}^{j} = \gamma + \beta_1 \Delta \ln K_{it} + \beta_2 \Delta \ln L_{it} + \beta_3 \Delta \ln p_{it} + \beta_4 \Delta \ln \delta_{it}$$
$$+ \beta_5 \Delta \ln R_{it} + \beta_6 \Delta S_{X_{it}} + \upsilon_{it}$$

The results of estimating equation (13′) (column [2] of table 11.4) show weak support for the idea that increased fragmentation has reduced the pollution intensity of China's exports. An increase in the share of processing exports by a percentage point reduces the pollution intensity of China's exports by about 0.01 percent. The share of processing exports actually grew by about 6 percent during this time period, implying a larger impact than the small elasticity might suggest. However, in this specification, the estimate is not significant. The inclusion of the export processing share also strengthens the magnitude and significance of factor endowments and real GDP per capita in explaining the pollution intensity of exports over time. The parallel results for imports (table 11.5, column [2]) are even more striking. The impact of an increase in the lagged share of processing imports on the pollution intensity of China's imports is much larger and more significant (compare tables 11.4 and 11.5, column [2]). In addition, the inclusion of the lagged import processing share also dramatically strengthens the significance of all other explanatory variables (compare table 11.5, columns [1] and [2]).

However, the size of the fragmented sector is most likely endogenous. Clearly changes in trade frictions and factor endowments influence the size of the processing export share. Trade barriers on imports in highly fragmented sectors have fallen over this time period.[31] China's entrance into the WTO has also meant more favorable access for China's ordinary and fragmented

31. For example, the WTO (2006) reports that average tariffs on electronic and communications equipment imports fell with accession to the WTO. In April, 2003 China joined the WTO Information Technology Agreement, and 258 tariff lines at the HS eight-digit level became subject to zero tariffs. Import licenses and quotas on certain products have also been removed.

exports in other WTO members' markets. As discussed above, growth in foreign investment is predicted to raise the processing share of exports. Similarly, if export processing is more human-capital-intensive than ordinary export processing, growth in the relative supply of human capital will raise the share of resources devoted to export processing.

To account for this endogeneity, we reestimate equation (13') using instrumental variables. The instruments for growth in the processing export share include all other variables in the equation and the growth in the processing import share. Because by law, goods imported under the processing regime can only be used for production of processing exports, growth in the share of processing imports should be a good predictor of growth in the share of processing exports, while being uncorrelated with the dependent variable. The instrumented results (column [3] of table 11.4) now show much stronger evidence that growth in the share of fragmented exports leads to cleaner exports. The elasticity of pollution intensity with respect to processing export share is much larger and is now highly significant. The role of factor endowments in strengthened by the instrumental variable (IV) estimation and growth in real GDP per capita now significantly reduces the pollution intensity of exports.

Table 11.5, column (3) shows the IV estimation for imports. In this case, the instruments include all other variables in the equation and the share of processing exports lagged two periods. The IV estimates are generally larger than those that ignored endogeneity, but otherwise simply reinforce the role of fragmentation found in column (2).

11.6.4   Composition Effects, Technique Effects, and FDI

Thus far, we have not distinguished investment by source nor labor by skill. Yet FDI plays a crucial role in fragmented trade. As argued above, an increase in FDI flows should reduce pollution intensity by increasing the share of processing exports and by increasing the critical value, z^*. Domestic capital, in contrast, flows primarily to the import-competing and ordinary export sectors. Thus, an increase in domestically sourced investment pulls factors out of the export-processing sector, reducing the critical value z^*, and increasing the average pollution intensity of the export-processing sector.[32] Production shifts to the more highly polluting ordinary-export sector. Therefore, we expect that an increase in domestic investment raises the pollution intensity of China's exports.

An increase in the relative supply of human capital acts, in the model, like a decrease in the Chinese effective wage. A decrease in w shifts the CC line down in figure 11.6, allowing China to compete successfully in production of more human-capital-intensive intermediate inputs. Thus, an increase in

---

32. The CC line in figure 11.6 shifts up when labor is pulled out of the sector and wages rise.

Chinese human capital is predicted to reduce the pollution intensity of China's exports. An increase in unskilled labor, on the other hand, is predicted to have the opposite effect.

The last two columns of table 10.4 show evidence that is certainly suggestive of the important role that increased FDI and increased human capital play in making Chinese exports cleaner. In column (4) of table 11.4, we present results for the instrumented estimation of equation (13') again, but with investment split between domestically sourced investment and FDI. FDI (percent of GDP) is taken from the *World Development Indicators*.[33] Domestically-sourced investment (as a share of GDP) is calculated as the difference between gross capital formation and FDI. It is immediately evident that these two types of investment have opposite effects. As expected, increased FDI flows strongly reduce the pollution intensity of Chinese trade, while increased domestically sourced investment does the opposite. Because the effects of FDI flows on the size of the fragmented sector are captured via the IV estimation, the coefficient on the FDI variable actually suggests evidence of cleaner exports due to a change in composition *within* the fragmented sector (an increase in z^*). It may also suggest that foreign investors bring greener technologies than their local counterparts, implying an additional favorable technique effect. Parallel results for imports (table 11.5, column [4]) are much weaker and show no such role for FDI.

Because of the small sample size, we are unable to test for distinct roles of investment by source and labor by skill simultaneously. However, some evidence suggestive of the importance of both is shown in column (5) of table 11.4. In this final regression, we include the ratio of FDI to domestically sourced investment as well as growth in the ratio of skilled to unskilled labor. The latter is proxied by the share of the population with at least senior secondary education, relative to the illiterate share.[34] The results in column (5) of table 11.5 suggest that the pollution intensity of exports is strongly reduced by the relative growth of foreign investment and of skilled labor. This evidence is consistent with the notion that increased FDI flows expands the composition of fragmented exports to include cleaner intermediates and that more skill-intensive intermediates are cleaner. While the theory would suggest both these attributes should be true of imports as well, only the FDI results are borne out in table 11.5 (column [5]).[35]

---

33. These data closely parallel official Chinese data on utilized (or realized) FDI flows (percent GDP; see Annual FDI Statistics, www.fdi.gov.cn).

34. Data on shares of population aged > six years by educational attainment are from various issues of the China Statistical Yearbook. Data for the year 1995 are from Cao (2000, 4).

35. The results for the impact of the ratio of skilled to unskilled labor on the pollution intensity of imports appear to be highly sensitive to the lag chosen. More data are required to determine how illustrative they really are.

11.7   Global Engagement and the Environment

By all accounts, China's rapid economic growth over the past twenty years has been accompanied by severe environmental degradation. While much of this deterioration can be attributed to growth in domestic consumption, the extent to which China's environment has been sacrificed so that it can serve as "the world's factory" is an important economic and moral question. To begin to address this issue, this paper provides new evidence on trends in industrial pollution intensity, changes in the pollution intensity of Chinese trade, and the influence of foreign investment and production fragmentation on the pollution content of Chinese exports and imports. Contrary to the expectations of many commentators, we find that deeper global engagement has reduced the implicit environmental cost of Chinese income growth.

Using official Chinese environmental data on air and water pollution from MEP, we find that industrial emissions of primary pollutants have slowed or fallen over the last decade while trade has grown. Relative to 1995 levels, real manufacturing trade increased almost 300 percent by 2005, while annual industrial emissions of COD, smoke, and dust declined by 56 percent, 46 percent, and 40 percent. Industrial emissions of SO_2 rose only after 1999, but were 17.5 percent higher than 1995 levels by 2005. As noted by Naughton (2007, 495), the abatement of waste from large factories has been a relatively positive part of China's environmental record and the stabilization of waste while output has grown sharply represents a significant achievement in its development.

Using emissions data compiled from *Chinese Environment Yearbooks,* we present new evidence on the pollution intensity of Chinese industrial production. Tracking changes in these pollution intensities over time reveals surprising trends. Across all four pollutants, we find that the pollution intensity of almost all sectors has fallen since 1995. This finding suggests that China has benefited from a positive "technique effect," as emissions per real dollar of output have fallen across a wide range of industries. Suggestively, a review of trends in Chinese trade patterns reveals that China's trade appears to be shifting toward relatively cleaner sectors over time. In particular, the share of exports accounted for by textiles and leather products has fallen, while the share accounted for by office and computing and communications equipment has grown dramatically. These growth sectors are characterized by low air and water pollution intensities and by high shares of processing trade, indicating the substantial presence of two-way trade in production "fragments."

Linking the industrial pollution intensities to detailed trade statistics from China Customs yields a weighted average pollution intensity for China's manufacturing exports (imports) for each year in the period 1995 to 2005. Contrary to popular expectations, which emphasize the migration of dirty industries to poor nations, we find that Chinese exports are less water-pollution intensive and generally less air-pollution intensive than Chinese imports would be if produced domestically. Moreover, both Chinese exports and imports are becoming cleaner over time. Holding the pollution intensity of production constant in a counterfactual experiment, we find that changes in the composition of trade over the decade account for some of the trend toward cleaner trade, although a substantial share of the decline remains attributed to changes in production techniques. Finally, we find that processing trade is cleaner than ordinary trade.

The weight of this evidence suggests that the increased concentration of Chinese trade in highly fragmented industries has led to composition and technique effects that are favorable toward China's environment. Drawing on Copeland and Taylor (1994), we present a simple model of production and trade that leads to a reduced form equation for the pollution intensity of Chinese trade. Explicitly incorporating a role for fragmented trade yields a set of key determinants of the pollution intensity of trade: Chinese domestic factor endowments, foreign investment, the terms of trade, trade frictions, per capita real income, and the share of trade in fragmented sectors where this share is also influenced by the other key determinants. In theory, increased FDI inflows not only increase the size of the fragmented sector but also reduce its average pollution intensity.

Econometric evidence from instrumental variables estimation strongly supports the role of processing trade in explaining the drop in the pollution intensity of Chinese exports and imports over time. This suggests that there is indeed a favorable composition effect generated by the increased importance of fragmentation in Chinese trade. The evidence also suggests that, controlling for the size of processing exports, FDI inflows contribute to cleaner exports. This supports the idea that increased FDI may change the composition of the fragmented sector itself toward relatively cleaner intermediate goods and may also bring greener technology to the fragmented sector.

In the Five-Year Plan for 2006 to 2010, the Chinese authorities call for a reorientation of their economic growth model toward environmental sustainability. How China will achieve the dual goal of economic growth and reduced environmental degradation is far from clear. Trade and foreign investment has fueled much of China's trade boom, and so it is natural to ask whether China's unique brand of global engagement needs to be radically altered to move its development path in the desired direction. The new data analyzed in this paper suggests that, at least provisionally, the answer to this question is no. Industrial pollution intensity has already stabilized and, in many industries, has begun to decline. Looking specifically at the bundle of goods China trades with the world, we find that, contrary to what might have been expected, foreign investment and integration into global production networks has reduced the environmental cost of China's growth.

Appendix
Construction of the Pollution Intensities of Chinese Manufacturing Industries, 1995–2004

Data on emissions of COD, SO_2, smoke, and dust, as well as the current value of output of the sampled enterprises at the industry level, were compiled by the authors from the *Chinese Environmental Yearbooks* (Chinese editions) and the *China Statistical Yearbook on Environment* (dual language, 2000, 2005, and 2006). Emissions data are originally in tons and output in 1,000 current yuan. They are available by the two-digit "divisions" in the Chinese industrial classification system for the industrial sector, which includes Mining (six divisions); Manufacturing (thirty divisions); and Distribution of Electricity, Water, and Gas (three divisions). Pollution intensities were calculated as emissions (in kilos) per thousand real yuan (1995 yuan). Output was deflated using the manufacturing producer price index (*China Statistical Yearbook,* various issues). These pollution intensities are shown for Manufacturing and for the Distribution of Electricity, Water, and Gas by division (GB/T 4754-2002), in table 11A.1.

Change in Chinese Industrial Classifications

Prior to 2003, Chinese industrial data were classified using GB/T 4754-1994. From 2003 onward, industrial data are classified using GB/T 4754-2002. In both classifications, manufacturing has thirty two-digit "divisions." Using the official Chinese concordance, we compared the two classifications and found only two changes in manufacturing divisions.[36] First, the 1994 division 39 (weapons and ammunition mfg.) became part of 2002 division 36 (special equipment mfg.).[37] We address this change under aggregation issues in the following. Second, the 2002 division 43 (waste recycling) was added. This division was not part of manufacturing in the previous period. Therefore, we dropped it from the analysis.

Aggregation and Missing Data

In the published emissions and output data from 1995 to 2000, several divisions are aggregated together. Divisions 13 to 16 are grouped as "Food, Beverages and Tobacco," divisions 35 to 41 are grouped as "Machine, Electric Machinery & Electronic Equipment Mfg.," and divisions 44 to 46 are grouped as "Production and Supply of Electric Power, Gas, and Water." To disaggregate these grouped data, we first created corresponding groups for

---

36. The four-digit "classes" within each two-digit division remained essentially unchanged. There were fewer classes in total in the 2002 classification, largely due to merges of classes within the same division.

37. The remaining 2002 division codes were renumbered accordingly. Thus, 1994 division 40 corresponds to 2002 division 39, 1994 division 41 corresponds to 2002 division 40, and so on.

Table 11A.1   Pollution intensity of Chinese industrial output, 1995 and 2004, by industry (Chinese classification GB/T 4754-2002)

Division	1995				2004			
	COD	SO$_2$	Smoke	Dust	COD	SO$_2$	Smoke	Dust
13 Agricultural and sideline foods processing	13.30	2.43	2.29	0.23	1.87	0.55	0.77	0.06
14 Food production	7.65	2.47	1.09	0.08	1.10	0.62	0.38	0.02
15 Beverage production	9.57	3.38	2.40	0.07	1.26	0.72	0.61	0.02
16 Tobacco products processing	0.20	0.28	0.10	0.03	0.02	0.05	0.03	0.01
17 Textile industry	1.07	1.53	0.84	0.03	0.74	0.72	0.28	0.03
18 Clothes, shoes, and hat manufacture	0.31	0.56	0.31	0.01	0.33	0.29	0.14	0.02
19 Leather, furs, down, and related products	2.57	0.74	0.47	0.03	0.87	0.22	0.17	0.00
20 Timber processing, bamboo, cane, palm fiber, and straw products	6.08	3.83	5.12	2.91	1.02	1.28	1.55	0.64
21 Furniture manufacturing	0.94	1.07	1.25	0.54	0.14	0.22	0.16	0.01
22 Papermaking and paper products	70.02	7.08	4.80	0.63	7.22	1.90	1.11	0.07
23 Printing and record medium reproduction	0.18	0.64	0.32	0.00	0.08	0.09	0.07	0.00
24 Cultural, educational, and sports articles production					0.09	0.31	0.18	0.29
25 Petroleum processing, coking, and nuclear fuel processing	0.79	2.85	1.67	1.15	0.08	0.85	0.58	0.19
26 Raw chemical material and chemical products	3.07	5.08	2.77	0.78	0.65	1.34	0.66	0.22
27 Medical and pharmaceutical products	3.51	1.71	0.99	0.02	0.72	0.45	0.22	0.01
28 Chemical fiber	3.42	2.34	1.33	0.17	0.69	0.89	0.28	0.02
29 Rubber products	0.33	1.77	0.82	0.15	0.08	0.41	0.18	0.00
30 Plastic products	0.10	0.79	0.31	0.01	0.11	0.20	0.08	0.07
31 Nonmetal mineral products	0.36	10.73	6.59	40.26	0.14	4.33	3.29	14.29
32 Smelting and pressing of ferrous metals	1.05	4.63	2.25	5.56	0.14	0.98	0.47	1.05
33 Smelting and pressing of nonferrous metals	0.24	8.01	1.87	1.49	0.09	2.20	0.63	0.59
34 Metal products	0.11	1.02	0.65	0.07	0.08	0.17	0.09	0.05

35 Ordinary machinery manufacturing	0.11	0.97	0.78	0.13	0.06	0.22	0.14	0.09
36 Special equipment manufacturing	0.21	0.98	0.72	0.10	0.07	0.17	0.08	0.03
37 Transport equipment manufacturing	0.12	0.43	0.37	0.10	0.06	0.06	0.07	0.06
39 Electric machines and apparatuses manufacturing	0.13	0.54	0.31	0.02	0.02	0.04	0.03	0.02
40 Communications equipment, computer and other electronic equipment manufacturing	0.08	0.35	0.23	0.01	0.03	0.03	0.03	0.01
41 Instruments, meters, cultural and office machinery manufacture	0.11	0.24	0.08	0.00	0.05	0.07	0.01	0.00
42 Craftwork and other manufactures					0.09	0.13	0.08	0.09
43 Waste resources and old material recycling and processing					0.03	0.08	0.05	0.02
44 Electricity and heating production and supply	1.45	95.80	59.25	0.26	0.24	20.44	7.16	0.16
45 Fuel gas production and supply	2.47	9.69	7.77	7.20	0.75	1.84	0.80	0.52
46 Water production and supply	12.33	2.79	1.67	0.45	2.08	0.92	0.34	0.00

Notes: Values are in kilos per thousand yuan output in 1995 constant yuan. COD = chemical oxygen demand.

the years 2001 to 2004 by summing the appropriate division data. For each group, we calculated the average share of emissions of each pollutant attributable to each division within the group. We then applied these shares to the recorded group data in the earlier period. The group's annual emissions data from 1995 to 2000 for each pollutant was multiplied by the corresponding average share to derive the missing annual emissions data for each division within that group. We followed a similar procedure to derive the missing output data for each division within each group.

For example, during 2001 to 2004, Food Production (14) was responsible on average, for about 16 percent of annual COD emissions and about 17 percent of annual output of "Food, Beverages and Tobacco." Therefore, for each year during 1995 to 2000, 16 percent of the recorded COD emissions and 17 percent of the recorded output for that group were allocated to Food Production.

This method assumes that the 2001 to 2004 relative trends in emissions of each pollutant and in output across divisions within a group apply during the earlier period. This is certainly plausible. However, it could mask any radical changes in technique or in composition within a group that took place in a single year.

Emissions and output data for five divisions during the 1995 to 2000 period are missing: Clothes, Shoes and Hat Manufacture (18), Timber Processing, etc. (20), Furniture Manufacturing (21), Cultural, Educational and Sports Articles (24), and Craftwork and Other (42). To fill in the missing data for the first three, we paired each missing division with a related division for which complete data were available: (18) with (17) textiles; (20) with (22) papermaking and paper products; (21) with (22). For each pair, we calculated the average ratio of emissions of each pollutant for the missing division relative to the complete division during 2001 to 2004. These ratios were then applied to the recorded data for the complete division in the earlier period. For each year of 1995 to 2000, we multiplied the complete division's data by these average emissions ratios to derive the annual emissions data for the missing division in that pair. We then followed a similar procedure to derive the output data for the missing division.

For example, during 2001 to 2004, we found that the ratio of COD emissions for Clothes (18) relative to Textiles (17) averaged about 3.3 percent, while the ratio of SO_2 emissions averaged about 4.1 percent. Therefore, for each year during 1995 to 2000, we assigned values for division (18) COD and SO_2 emissions that were 3.3 percent and 4.1 percent, respectively, of the recorded data for division (17).

We were unable to find a related division to pair with (24) or (42). Therefore, these data are missing during 1995 to 2000.[38] These missing data essentially

---

38. These two divisions together account for only about 6 percent of manufacturing exports in 1995 and about 4 percent in 2000.

impact our estimates of the pollution intensity of ISIC 36 (Furniture and other manufacturing, not elsewhere specified). Division (24) maps almost exclusively to ISIC 36. The classes in division (42) map to several two-digit ISIC categories, but mostly to ISIC 36. These two divisions accounted for 76 percent (47 percent and 29 percent, respectively, of ISIC 36 exports in 1995, but declined in importance over the period. By 2000, they accounted for only 57 percent (45 percent and 12 percent, respectively), while furniture's share had roughly doubled (11 percent to 19 percent). Thus, while the pollution intensity of exports of ISIC 36 in our analysis during 1995 to 2000 is based nearly exclusively on the pollution intensity of furniture production, any bias this may introduce diminishes over these five years.[39]

Emissions from Township and Village-Level Enterprises (TVIEs)

Emissions data prior to 1998 were recorded only for industrial enterprises at the "county level and above." After the *Investigation on Sources of Township Industrial Pollution* (1997), it was found that township and village industrial enterprises (TVIEs) were accounting for a significant and growing percentage of emissions. Therefore, the emissions data included these enterprises from 1998 onward. Because TVIE emissions data are unavailable at the sectoral level, the yearly industrial pollution intensities in 1995 to 1997 do not include TVIEs. Thus, the values for 1995 in table 11A.1 and in table 11.2 are likely to be understated.

References

Arndt, Sven, and Henryk Kierzkowski. 2001. *Fragmentation.* Oxford, UK: Oxford University Press.

Antweiler, Werner, Brian R. Copeland, and M. Scott Taylor. 2001. Is free trade good for the environment? *American Economic Review* 91:877–908.

Cao, G.-Y. 2000. The future population of China: Prospects to 2045 by place of residence and by level of education. IR-00-026, IIASA, Austria. (http://www.iiasa.ac.at/Admin/PUB/Documents/IR-00-026.pdf).

Chen, Xikang, Leonard Cheng, K. C. Fung, and Lawrence Lau. 2008. The estimation of domestic value added and employment induced by exports: An application to Chinese exports to the US. In *China and Asia: Economic and financial interactions,* ed. Y. Cheung and K. Wong, 64–82. Oxford, UK: Routledge.

Chow, Gregory. 2006. New capital estimates for China: Comments. *China Economic Review* 17:186–92.

China Environment Yearbook. Various issues. Beijing: China Environmental Science Press.

China Statistical Yearbook. Various issues. Beijing: China Statistics Press.

---

39. The data for 2001 to 2004 in table 11A.1 suggest that this omission might bias the water pollution intensity of ISIC 36 upward, but its impact on air pollution intensity is unclear.

China Statistical Yearbook on Environment. 2006. Beijing: National Bureau of Statistics and Ministry of Environmental Protection.

Copeland, Brian R., and M. Scott Taylor. 1994. North-South trade and the environment. *Quarterly Journal of Economics* 109:755–87.

———. 2003. *Trade and the environment.* Princeton, NJ: Princeton University Press.

———. 2004. Trade, growth and the environment. *Journal of Economic Literature* 42:7–71.

Dean, Judith, ed. 2001. *International trade and the environment.* The International Library of Environmental Economics and Policy Series. Aldershot, UK: Ashgate.

Dean, Judith. 2002. Does trade liberalization harm the environment? A new test. *Canadian Journal of Economics* 34:819–42.

Dean, Judith, K. C. Fung, and Zhi Wang. 2008. How vertically specialized is Chinese trade? USITC Working Paper no. 2008-09D. Washington, DC: United States International Trade Commission.

Dean, Judith, Mary E. Lovely, and Hua Wang. 2009. Are foreign investors attracted to weak environmental regulations: Evaluating the evidence from China. *Journal of Development Economics* 90:1–13.

Ederington, Josh, Arik Levinson, and Jenny Minier. 2004. Trade liberalization and pollution havens. *Advances in Economic Analysis and Policy* 4 (6): 1–22.

Feenstra, Robert C., and Gordon H. Hanson. 1996. Foreign investment, outsourcing, and relative wages. In *Political economy of trade policy: Essays in honor of Jagdish Bhagwati,* ed. R. C. Feenstra, G. M. Grossman, and D. A. Irwin, 89–127. Cambridge, MA: MIT Press.

Gardner, Timothy. 2008. Rich world behind much of global pollution. *Reuters,* October 21. http://www.alertnet.org/thenews/newsdesk/N21532488.htm.

Henley, John, Colin Kirkpatrick, and Georgina Wilde. 1999. Foreign direct investment in China: Recent trends and current policy issues. *World Economy* 22: 223–43.

Holz, Carsten A. 2006. New capital estimates for China. *China Economic Review* 17:142–85.

Koopman, Robert, Zhi Wang, and Shang-Jin Wei. 2008. How much of Chinese exports are really made in China. NBER Working Paper no. 14109. Cambridge, MA: National Bureau of Economic Research.

Lardy, Nicholas R. 1994. *China in the world economy.* Washington, DC: Institute for International Economics.

Levinson, Arik. 2009. Technology, international trade, and pollution from U.S. manufacturing. *American Economic Review,* forthcoming.

Ministry of Environmental Protection (MEP). 2006. *Environmental protection in China 1996–2005.* Beijing: Information Office of the State Council of the People's Republic of China. http://www.china.org.cn/english/2006/Jun/170355.htm.

———. 2007. *Report on the state of the environment in China 2006.* Beijing: Information Office of the State Council of the People's Republic of China. http://english.mep.gov.cn/standards_reports/soe/soe2006/200711/t20071105_112560.htm.

Naughton, Barry. 2007. *The Chinese economy: Transitions and growth.* Cambridge, MA: MIT Press.

Organization for Economic Cooperation and Development (OECD). 2005. *Governance in China.* Paris: OECD.

Ping, Xin-Qiao. 2005. Vertical specialization, value added, and the US-China trade relationship. China Center for Economic Research Working Paper no. C2005005. Beijing: CCER.

Robison, H. David. 1988. Industrial pollution abatement: The impact on balance of trade. *Canadian Journal of Economics* 21:187–99.

Walter, Ingo. 1973. The pollution content of American trade. *Western Economic Journal,* 11:61–70.

World Bank. 2001. *China: Air, land, and water.* Washington, DC: World Bank.

World Trade Organization (WTO). 2006. *Trade policy review: People's Republic of China.* Geneva, Switzerland: WTO.

Zhang, Shuguang, Yansheng Zhang, and Zhongxin Wan. 1998. *The costs of protection in China.* Washington, DC: IIE.

Comment   Arik Levinson

Dean and Lovely's chapter makes an important and interesting contribution to our understanding of the relationship between international trade and pollution. Many observers argue that developed countries, such as the United States, have improved their environments in recent decades largely by outsourcing pollution-intensive production to developing countries, such as China.[1] If that is the case, U.S. imports and Chinese exports should be increasingly composed of pollution-intensive goods. Economists have now refuted that idea, from the U.S. perspective, by showing that the composition of U.S. imports has become less pollution-intensive over time, not more.[2] Dean and Lovely are the first I know of to examine the converse. They show that the composition of exports from China has been shifting toward cleaner goods, not dirtier.

The result nicely complements existing evidence from the U.S. perspective and is, therefore, both important and believable. However, the analysis contains two unavoidable biases that unfortunately work in favor of that result, making the composition of China's exports appear spuriously cleaner. Dean and Lovely acknowledge both biases clearly in their chapter and explain convincingly that they have exhausted all possibilities for ameliorating those biases given the available data. It is, therefore, worth taking a few moments here to demonstrate with the U.S. data just how large those biases can be.

The first bias involves industry aggregation. Dean and Lovely calculate emissions intensities (pollution per thousand yuan of output) for each of thirty-three sectors, listed in their appendix table 11A.1. They then conduct a counterfactual thought experiment, constructing the aggregate pollu-

Arik Levinson is an associate professor of economics at Georgetown University, and a research associate of the National Bureau of Economic Research.

1. See, for example, Jane Spencer, "Why China Could Blame Its CO2 on West," *Wall Street Journal,* November 12, 2007, A.2.

2. In addition to work cited by Dean and Lovely, see Kahn (2003), Cole (2004), and Gamper-Rabindran (2006).

tion intensity of Chinese exports, assuming each of the thirty-three sectors remained at its 1995 pollution intensity, but allowing the composition of exports among those thirty-three sectors to change over time. The results are the dashed lines in figure 11.5, which display how pollution caused by production of Chinese manufactured exports would have changed, holding the sector-specific pollution intensities constant, and allowing the composition of exports among the thirty-three sectors to change. The fact that the dashed lines slope down indicates that Chinese exports are increasingly composed of sectors with lower pollution intensities.

The industry aggregation bias arises because the thirty-three sectors are themselves heterogeneous. Sector 22, "papermaking and paper products," includes raw pulp manufacturing, which is extremely pollution-intensive, and envelope manufacturing, which is not. By holding the pollution-intensity of the entire paper sector constant, the dashed lines in figure 11.5 rule out any within-sector composition change. If the composition of industries within each of the thirty-three sectors has shifted toward dirtier goods (more raw pulp and fewer envelopes), Dean and Lovely's calculation will overstate the degree to which Chinese export composition has become cleaner.

To get a feel for the magnitude of this bias, I apply their analysis to data on U.S. imports and sulfur dioxide (SO_2) emissions. The bottom (dashed) line in figure 11C.1 depicts the pollution intensity of U.S. imports from non-Organization for Economic Cooperation and Development (OECD) countries. It is calculated by holding constant the pollution intensities of each of the eighty-six four-digit North American Industry Classification System (NAICS) industry codes at their 1997 levels and calculating the aggregate pollution intensity of imports. The dashed line in my figure 11C.1 is analogous to the dashed line in Dean and Lovely's figure 11.5 (though my line uses eighty-six sectors while theirs uses thirty-three, and mine plots U.S. manufactured imports from all non-OECD countries, while theirs plots all Chinese manufactured exports). I then reconstruct the same line using the 469 six-digit NAICS industry codes. Paper manufacturing, for example, has eighteen different six-digit industry codes. This new line is plotted as the middle (solid) line in figure 11C.1. It lies above the dashed line, indicating that using the more aggregate industry definitions (eighty-six four-digit NAICS codes) exaggerates the composition change of U.S. imports toward cleaner goods. It also suggests that aggregating trade into even fewer sectors, as Dean and Lovely do, may exaggerate that composition change even more if the within-sector composition of Chinese exports has shifted toward pollution-intensive industries.

The second bias involves intermediate goods. When China exports a good, part of the pollution comes directly from the industry that manufactured it. But part also comes from the industries that manufacture the inputs to that good, and the inputs to those inputs, and so on. Look, for example, at Dean and Lovely's table 11.1. Chinese exports of basic metals (sector 27) declined

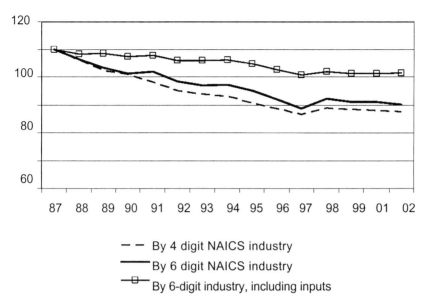

Fig. 11C.1   Pollution (SO$_2$) intensity of U.S. imports from non-Organization for Economic Cooperation and Development (OECD) countries, 1987–2002

from 5.2 to 4.1 percent of exports, while at the same time motor vehicles (sector 34) rose from 1.4 to 2.1 percent of exports. Because basic metals production is more pollution-intensive than motor vehicle manufacturing, this change represents a composition shift toward exporting cleaner industries. But motor vehicles use fabricated metals as an input, and fabricated metals use basic metals as an input. So exporting more cars does not necessarily reduce China's emissions. The problem here is that the emission intensities ignore pollution from intermediate inputs. What we need is a *total* emissions coefficient that includes pollution from the direct manufacture of each good, the pollution from manufacturing that good's intermediate inputs, the pollution from manufacturing inputs to those inputs, and so on.

In figure 11C.1, I recreate the Dean and Lovely thought experiment, from the perspective of U.S. imports, using total emissions coefficients, including all intermediate manufactured inputs.[3] The top line plots the average emissions intensity of U.S. imports from non-OECD countries, holding constant the emissions intensity of each six-digit NAICS industry code at its 1997 level, but including emissions caused by manufactured inputs to those industries. The top line slopes down much less steeply than the middle line, which ignores intermediate inputs. Importing relatively more cars does not make import composition appear as clean once we account for the steel,

3. Details of this calculation can be found in Levinson (2007).

rubber, and glass that go into those cars. Ignoring those intermediate inputs exaggerates the composition change of U.S. imports toward cleaner goods. And, figure 11C.1 also suggests that ignoring intermediate inputs exaggerates the composition change of Chinese exports documented in Dean and Lovely's figure 11.5.

Figure 11C.1 presents a version of Dean and Lovely's analysis using data on U.S. imports, where it is possible to combat both biases. It demonstrates that, at least for the case of U.S. imports, the two biases exaggerate the composition change. But the biases do not overturn the basic result, that the composition of U.S. imports has become cleaner in recent decades. Because the Dean and Lovely analysis is essentially the converse of this U.S. analysis (Chinese exports rather than U.S. imports), their result also seems likely to survive the two biases. We will never know for sure, however, until somebody constructs emissions coefficients for a finer disaggregation of Chinese industries and input-output tables that can be used to construct emissions coefficients that account for intermediate inputs.

References

Cole, Matthew A. 2004. U.S. environmental load displacement: Examining consumption, regulations and the role of NAFTA. *Ecological Economics* 48 (4): 439–50.
Gamper-Rabindran, S. 2006. NAFTA and the environment: What can the data tell us? *Economic Development and Cultural Change* 54:605–33.
Kahn, Matthew E. 2003. The geography of U.S. pollution intensive trade: Evidence from 1959 to 1994. *Regional Science and Urban Economics* 33 (4): 383–400.
Levinson, Arik. 2007. Technology, international trade, and pollution from U.S. manufacturing. NBER Working Paper no. 13616. Cambridge, MA: National Bureau of Economic Research.

IV

Foreign Investment and Trade

Please Pass the Catch-Up
The Relative Performance of Chinese and Foreign Firms in Chinese Exports

Bruce A. Blonigen and Alyson C. Ma

12.1 Introduction

The phenomenal growth in Chinese trade with the rest of the world since the opening of its markets in the 1980s is well documented. Recent attention has begun to examine the sources of such growth, particularly the concomitant growth of foreign firm presence in China and their use of China as a low-cost export platform. Whalley and Xin (2006) document that the foreign-invested firms' (FIEs) share of Chinese exports has risen from around 10 percent in 1990 to almost 60 percent in 2004 (figure 4). The Chinese experience in this regard is unique in that a substantial portion of FIE presence is by investors from Hong Kong, Macau, and Taiwan—regions that are considered politically separate to some degree, but are populated with ethnic Chinese who have strong connections to mainland China. However, the share of FIE from other countries is significant and growing over time.

More broadly, the Chinese situation is also unique in its mixture of markets and state-controlled portions of the economy. Openness to market forces has been allowed in a stepwise fashion by the government since 1980, with successive new policy announcements, presumably informed by prior experience. With respect to foreign direct investment (FDI), market openness really

Bruce A. Blonigen is the Knight Professor of Social Science at the University of Oregon, and a research associate of the National Bureau of Economic Research. Alyson C. Ma is an assistant professor of economics at the University of San Diego.

The authors would like to thank Robert Feenstra, Raymond Robertson, Shang-Jin Wei, and participants of a seminar at the California State University, Sonoma, and the National Bureau of Economic Research (NBER) conferences connected with this book for helpful comments and suggestions. We also thank Helen Naughton and Laura Kerr-Valentic for excellent research assistance. Any remaining errors are our own.

began with the creation of special economic zones (SEZs) in Guangdong and Fujian provinces in 1979 that allowed FIEs for the first time, charging such firms a profit tax lower than that applied to domestic firms. Through the 1980s, the number of these government-policy zones increased substantially, and by 1991, many of the restrictions limiting FIEs to SEZs were lifted. Nevertheless, there continues to be substantial government oversight with respect to FDI in that all new FIE projects require approval from the central government and regional governments. In addition, FIEs are often subject to performance requirements regarding export percentages, local content, and technology transfer. In 1997, the Chinese government published the *Catalogue for the Guidance of Foreign Investment Industries,* which provided explicit information on which sectors it encourages, restricts, or prohibits FDI. Tax policies toward FIEs has changed over time as well, with initially lower tax rates for FIEs to recent elimination of such special treatment in accordance with China's accession to the World Trade Organization (WTO), which specifies "national treatment" of tax policies.[1]

There are a couple features of the Chinese government's policy objectives toward FIEs that will be important for our analysis and that have been deemed important by previous literature as well. The first is the Chinese government's concern with the negative competition effects of FIEs on state-owned enterprises (SOEs) and its intention to limit domestic access to FIEs. The first SEZs were purposely chosen to be in regions that had little industrial (and, hence, SOE presence). Branstetter and Feenstra (2002) use provincial data on FIE presence from 1984 through 1995 to estimate that the Chinese government's FIE policies are inherently weighting the welfare of the SOEs four to seven times larger than consumer welfare. In addition, wholly-owned FIEs are almost always subject to minimum export targets and local content requirements in order to limit their domestic sales but keep their domestic purchases high. Nevertheless, the share of SOEs in the Chinese economy and its exports have been falling significantly as the share of FIEs and, more recently, private firms has increased.

A second Chinese policy objective with respect to FDI is facilitation of technology transfer from FIEs to domestic firms. Technology transfer agreements are often an implicit quid pro quo necessary for approval of an FIE project and are explicitly necessary to get approval of an FIE project that will also have access to the domestic market (Rosen 1999). The clear intent is to improve the Chinese's own productive capabilities allowing them to fully appropriate the profits from their manufactures of technological goods and increasing their long-run growth potential. The risk is that such policies are discouraging FDI in these sectors and, thus, causing China to miss out on the type of technological spillovers that would occur naturally.

---

1. More detailed discussion of these policies and policy changes are discussed by Li and Li (1999), Rosen (1999), and Graham (2004).

The evidence on the net effect of such technology transfer policies is far from known, with only a bit of evidence to date. For example, the Chinese government has required foreign automakers to partner with domestic producers, and Shanghai Automotive recently announced plans to start up its own factory to produce a luxury sedan based on plans purchased from Rover after jointly producing autos in China with General Motors and Volkswagen for many years. Whether Shanghai Automotive will be successful in this independent venture is clearly uncertain. Chen and Swenson (2006) and Hale and Long (forthcoming) provide the first careful evidence on productivity spillovers from foreign firms to domestic ones in China. Both find evidence for such spillovers, but for very limited groups of Chinese firms. Chen and Swenson (2006) find evidence for positive own-industry productivity spillovers for private domestic firms in China (which are still a fairly small portion of the Chinese economy), while Hale and Long (forthcoming) find that such spillovers are only positive for the most technologically advanced Chinese firms.

The extent to which Chinese firms are able to develop their own productive capabilities and transition from state-controlled firms to private, market-oriented firms is extremely important. Whalley and Xin (2006) undertake a growth accounting exercise that finds that while the employment share of FIEs is only 3 percent, they account for over 20 percent of the Chinese economy and around 40 percent of its recent growth. Their conclusion is that the sustainability of China's export growth and, indeed, its overall gross domestic product (GDP) growth is suspect if inward FDI flows plateau. This would be especially true if productivity spillovers are limited. This point also relates to recent analysis by Rodrik (2006), which shows that the composition of Chinese exports is much closer to that of a developed economy than other developing economies and that this "advanced" composition of China's export basket is correlated with higher long-run growth potential.[2] However, the extent to which FIEs are behind such compositional differences, as well as spillover potential, clearly affects this assertion. Wang and Wei (chapter 2 in this volume) analyze this further by examining the factors affecting the evolution of Chinese exports vis-à-vis the rest of the world. In contrast, our focus is on the internal comparison of how Chinese firms have fared relative to foreign-owned firms, with an eye toward understanding how much Chinese firms are "catching up" and the extent to which Chinese policies have facilitated a "catch-up" effect.

In summary, foreign investment and exports by foreign-owned firms have become quite important to the Chinese economy. At the same time, the Chinese government has been quite active in trying to "manage" foreign investment into China and, particularly, to encourage technology transfer

---

2. Schott (forthcoming) points out that the unit values of the Chinese goods in the more "advanced" products are much lower than for developed economies.

so that their own Chinese-owned firms can "catch up" in their technological know-how.

This chapter examines these issues by first presenting a model of potential foreign investment into a vertically differentiated industry, with a foreign firm producing a higher quality product than its Chinese rival. The two-period model begins with a foreign firm deciding whether to locate production into China, knowing that foreign investment into China will lower its production costs but may lead to greater technology transfer due to closer proximity to the Chinese firm. The model generates a number of predictions for relative market shares and prices (unit values) charged by the two firms. We also generate predictions about how Chinese government policies toward FDI will affect these patterns as well. We then examine these hypotheses using detailed data on Chinese exports by type of firm (wholly-owned foreign-invested firms, SOEs, joint ventures, etc.) to analyze the evolution of Chinese export market shares and unit values over time during our sample period of 1997 to 2005.

The remainder of the chapter is organized as follows. Section 12.2 provides the literature review, while section 12.3 presents a model of foreign investment into China. We briefly discuss the descriptive analysis of exports and unit values over time in section 12.4. Section 12.5 offers the empirical analyses, and section 12.6 concludes.

12.2   Literature Review

A significant portion of the previous academic literature on export activities of China and the role of FIEs has concerned itself with ownership issues. Feenstra and Hanson (2004) and Feenstra, Hanson, and Lin (2004) examine the prominent role of Hong Kong investors as intermediaries in China's trade to the rest of the world. They find that Hong Kong's reexports of Chinese products involve an average of around 25 percent markups, which are even larger for differentiated products and allow for price discrimination across different destinations. They also develop a discrete choice model of the decision whether to use Hong Kong as an intermediary for trade. Their empirical analysis based on this model estimates that the benefits of using Hong Kong intermediaries are equivalent to 16 percent of the value of the product, on average. This is evidence that Hong Kong traders have significant informational advantages over traders and investors from other countries.

A related literature has examined the type of FIE chosen by all foreign investors in China. Initially, the Chinese government only allowed joint ventures, not wholly-owned FIEs. In addition, exports receive different Customs treatment depending on whether imported inputs are supplied by the foreign party. Feenstra and Hanson (2005) develop a property-rights model to explain when the foreign party will own the plant or make input decisions, and when such ownership and input decisions will be made by the Chinese party. Their model and empirical analysis finds that foreign owners will be more likely to cede control over input decisions when the value added in processing those inputs is higher (such as for more–technologically advanced products) and when contracts are easier to write. A complementary study by Feenstra and Spencer (2005) develops a model to understand the economic forces that determine whether foreign firms outsource intermediate inputs through pure external transactions, through contractual arrangements, or through their own foreign affiliates. They use data on Chinese export behavior by these various types of arrangements to verify their model's predictions that the variety of exported intermediate inputs from foreign affiliates and contractual arrangements increases more relative to "ordinary" exports the lower the (internal) transport costs within China.

There is a very recent empirical literature that has begun to examine export behavior and productivity spillovers using a 2001 World Bank survey of 1,500 firms across five major Chinese cities. Hale and Long (forthcoming) estimate productivity spillovers from foreign to domestic firms in the same industry and city using these data and find evidence for such effects only for the most technologically advanced Chinese firms. Further investigation finds that a significant part of this effect is due to these firms' higher share of managers with foreign-firm experience, suggesting that spillovers are occurring through labor mobility.[3] Park et al. (forthcoming) use the Asian financial crisis as a natural experiment to examine whether exporting affects productivity of the foreign firms in the sample.[4] Variation in export destinations and their currency devaluation with the crisis is used to identify the effect of exporting experience on firms' productivity. The study estimates that such "learning-by-exporting" effects are significant for firms exporting to developed countries but not those exporting via Hong Kong or directly to less-developed countries. A final paper that uses these World Bank survey data, and which is perhaps closest in topic to this chapter, is Brambilla (forthcoming). This study presents a model that connects experience and productivity to firms' ability to develop new product varieties. She finds that foreign firms in the sample introduce about twice as many new varieties as domestic ones and, consistent with the model's predictions, a significant portion of this is due to productivity differences.

The papers we have surveyed to this point are mainly microeconomic and relatively static in their analysis, using detailed firm- or product-level data

3. Chen and Swenson (2006) also examine productivity spillovers from foreign firms to domestic ones in China but use the same data set we examine in this study. While this data set is not firm-level data per se, it has trade data by type of firm and city code for later years of the sample. Their productivity spillover analysis finds that the export presence of foreign firms in the same city and sector is correlated with an increased variety of exported product codes and higher unit values for private Chinese firms.

4. They can only examine the foreign firms, as domestic Chinese firms do not report their export destinations, which is key for the study to identify firm-specific exchange rate shocks.

to document patterns of firm organization and performance for a given period of time. A number of papers have taken a broader view of Chinese exporting patterns. For our purposes, we focus on Rodrik (2006) and Schott (forthcoming). Rodrik (2006) compares the composition of China's exports and finds that it is much closer to that of Organization for Economic Cooperation and Development (OECD) countries than its level of per capita income would suggest. This bodes well for China in that a related paper by Hausmann, Hwang, and Rodrik (2007) finds a strong correlation between the sophistication of a country's export basket and its economic growth. Schott (forthcoming) verifies this increasing sophistication of the export bundle in terms of the types of products exported by China, but finds that its "exports sell at a substantial discount relative to its level of GDP and the exports emanating from the OECD." Neither paper examines the role of FIEs in these export patterns. Yet Whalley and Xin's (2006) analysis suggests that FIEs account for the majority of exports from China and find that overall growth of the Chinese economy is quite dependent on the highly productive FIEs in their economy.

12.3   A Model of Foreign Investment into China

In this section, we present a simple model to motivate what one may expect to happen to FDI decisions by foreign firms into China, technology transfer from foreign firms to Chinese ones, and the ultimate impact on the share of Chinese exports by foreign firms.

12.3.1   Producers

We employ a partial equilibrium setup, with one foreign firm and one domestic Chinese firm producing a good. For convenience, we assume away demand in the Chinese market so that both firms only supply consumers in the foreign country. Thus, prior to any FDI decision by the foreign firm, the Chinese firm is the sole source of Chinese exports of the good to the foreign country.

There is vertical differentiation of the good supplied by the two firms, with the foreign firm producing a higher quality good with quality level K_F, and the Chinese firm producing with a lower quality level K_{CH}; that is, $K_F > K_{CH}$.[5] Variable production costs are lower for any firm located in the Chinese market, with an assumed zero constant marginal cost of production in China and a marginal cost of $c > 0$ in the foreign market. Thus, FDI into the Chinese market is attractive to the foreign firm due to the lower costs of production. However, we also assume that technology transfer may occur between the firms if the foreign firm locates in the Chinese market. This technology transfers raises the quality (K_{CH}) of the low-quality Chinese

---

5. We assume away fixed costs of production for convenience.

producer, but comes at a cost. For convenience, we assume that technology transfer is zero if the foreign firm does not locate production in the Chinese market.[6] Because of this difference, the foreign firm has incentives to not locate production in the Chinese market, everything else equal.

12.3.2 Consumers

Consumers have identical preferences for goods but vary in their income levels. We assume that income levels are distributed uniformly over the unit interval, where h indexes the consumer with income of h. Consumers may purchase the good from either the foreign or domestic producer or choose not to purchase. If they do not purchase the good, they receive a level of utility equal to $U_0 h$, where $U_0 > 0$. If they purchase the good from a supplier, they receive utility of $U(K_i)(h - p_i)$, where p is the price charged by the supplier, and $i = CH, F$. We make the natural assumption that $U(.)$ is increasing in K so that higher quality means higher utility. We also restrict $U(K) > U_0$ for all K so that all consumers would prefer to purchase a product (regardless of its quality) if its price is zero.

With this setup, we can now solve for the demand function for each firm in the following way. Given the parameter space we consider (particularly our restrictions on marginal cost in the preceding), the high-quality firm will always charge a higher price than the low-quality firm in equilibrium ($p_F > p_{CH}$). Thus, demand along the unit interval of consumers can be divided into the sections shown in figure 12.1, with the highest-income consumers choosing the high-quality variety and lower-income consumers choosing the low-quality variety or possibly not purchasing the good. This gives us two cutoff income levels: h_F designates the consumer indifferent to purchasing either the high- or low-quality variety, while h_{CH} designates the consumer indifferent between purchasing the low-quality variety or not purchasing the good. Formally, the following expression of indifference obtains for the consumer at h_F:

(1) $$U(K_F)(h_F - p_F) = U(K_{CH})(h_F - p_{CH}).$$

Letting x denote $U(K_F)$ and y denote $U(K_{CH})$, we can easily derive the following expression for h_F:

(2) $$h_F = \frac{(x\, p_F - y\, p_{CH})}{(x - y)}.$$

In similar fashion, h_{CH} can be solved as:

(3) $$h_{CH} = \frac{(y\, p_{CH})}{(y - U_0)}.$$

---

6. This keeps the model simple but captures the idea that it is easier for technology to transfer when firms are geographically closer.

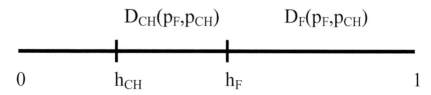

Fig. 12.1   **Firm demands and cutoff points along the distribution of consumers**

General expressions of demand for each firm are then easily derived as:

(4)
$$D_F(p_F, p_{CH}) = 1 - h_F = 1 - \frac{(x\,p_F - y\,p_{CH})}{(x - y)},$$

and

(5)
$$D_{CH}(p_F, p_{CH}) = h_F - h_{CH} = \frac{(x\,p_F - y\,p_{CH})}{(x - y)} - \frac{(y\,p_{CH})}{(y\,U_0)}.$$

12.3.3   Timing of Decisions

We assume that the foreign firm is initially producing a high-quality variety in the foreign country with per-unit costs of c, while the Chinese firm is producing a low-quality variety in the domestic Chinese market with per-unit costs of 0. In period 1, the foreign firm first decides whether to invest into China. If they locate into China, their per-unit production costs are immediately reduced to 0. Then both firms choose their prices simultaneously to compete for consumers.

If the foreign firm locates into China in the first period, then in period 2 the Chinese firm decides how much to invest in transferring technology from the foreign firm. In particular, we assume that the Chinese firm chooses a $\lambda \in [0,1]$ that leaves it with a new quality level $K_{Tech} = (1 - \lambda) K_{CH} + \lambda K_F$. The Chinese firm may choose to not engage in technology transfer activities ($\lambda = 0$), which would leave it with its original level of quality, K_{CH}. The associated level of consumer utility connected with this new level of quality is $U(K_{Tech})$. Costs of technology transfer are increasing in λ, via a quadratic function, $C_{Tech}(\lambda) = \theta \lambda^2$. Once a level of technology transfer is chosen, indexed by λ, then the firms compete in prices again. If the foreign firm did not locate in the foreign market, the firms compete in prices under the same conditions as in the first period with no foreign firm relocation. Profits for each firm in each period take the general form of $\Pi_i^t(p_{CH}^t, p_F^t, K_{CH}, K_F, \lambda, c)$, where t denotes the period-subgame combination.

12.3.4   Solving for Equilibrium

We solve for the subgame-perfect equilibrium of the model in the usual fashion by solving backward beginning with period 2 of our model. In period 2, there are two possible subgames—one where the foreign firm did not locate in China and, thus, technology transfer did not occur (which we denote as $2N$) and one where the foreign firm located in China and technology transfer has potentially occurred to the Chinese firm (which we denote as subgame $2T$). In subgame $2N$, the foreign firm does not locate production into China and continues to have a cost disadvantage (i.e., $c > 0$), but no technology transfer occurs ($\lambda = 0$). In this case, we denote the respective Nash equilibrium profits of the foreign and Chinese firms as:

$$(6) \qquad \Pi_{CH}^{2N} \equiv \Pi_{CH}(p_{CH}^{2N}, p_F^{2N}, K_{CH}, K_F, 0, c)$$

$$(7) \qquad \Pi_F^{2N} \equiv \Pi_F(p_{CH}^{2N}, p_F^{2N}, K_{CH}, K_F, 0, c),$$

where p_{CH}^{2N} p_F^{2N} are the optimally chosen prices by the Chinese and foreign firm, respectively. These equilibrium prices and profits will be identical to those in period 1 when the foreign firm does not relocate to China (denoted subgame $1N$).

The more interesting and relevant case for our purposes is subgame $2T$, where the foreign firm has located into China and reduced its production costs from c to 0, but the Chinese firm has the ability to increase its quality from K_{CH} to K_{Tech} through technology transfer. Given costs, qualities, and optimally chosen technology transfer, the firms simultaneously choose their own price to maximize profits. We denote the respective Nash equilibrium profits of the foreign and Chinese firms in this subgame as:

$$(8) \qquad \Pi_{CH}^{2T} \equiv \Pi_{CH}(p_{CH}^{2T}, p_F^{2T}, K_{CH}, K_F, \lambda, c)$$

$$(9) \qquad \Pi_F^{2T} \equiv \Pi_F(p_{CH}^{2T}, p_F^{2T}, K_{CH}, K_F, \lambda, c),$$

where p_{CH}^{2T}, p_F^{2T} and are the optimally chosen prices by the Chinese and foreign firm, respectively, and λ is the optimal degree of technology transfer chosen by the Chinese firm. From this, we get Propositions 1a and 1b:

PROPOSITION 1a. *The ratio of the foreign firm's equilibrium price to the Chinese firm's equilibrium price is decreasing in the amount of technology transfer. (See appendix for proof.)*

PROPOSITION 1b. *The ratio of the foreign firm's market share to the Chinese firm's market share in equilibrium is decreasing in the amount of technology transfer. (See appendix for proof.)*

The results in propositions 1a and 1b are quite intuitive. It is easy to show in the model that a higher quality firm will charge a higher price. Thus, as technology transfer leads to the quality of the two firms converging, the equilibrium prices charged by the firms also converge. An increase in technology also allows the low-quality firm to "steal" market share away from the high-quality firm even though the high-quality firm will optimally respond by lowering its equilibrium price some.

Now we turn to the Chinese firm's optimal technology transfer decision as represented by their choice of λ prior to the market competition in period 2.

The Chinese firm's problem is to choose λ to maximize second-stage profits net of technology transfer costs:

$$(10) \qquad \operatorname*{Max}_{\lambda} \Pi_{CH}^{Net} \equiv \Pi_{CH}^{2T} (p_{CH}^{2T}, p_{F}^{2T}, K_{CH}, K_{F}, \lambda, 0) - \theta\lambda^2$$

From this optimization problem, we can derive:

PROPOSITION 2. *The level of technology transfer chosen by the Chinese firm is decreasing in the cost or difficulty of such transfer (θ). (See appendix for proof.)*

This leads to the following corollaries:

COROLLARY 3a. *The greater the cost of technology transfer, the less the Chinese firm's equilibrium price moves closer to the foreign firm's equilibrium price for the case where the foreign firm locates in China. (See appendix for proof.)*

COROLLARY 3b. *The greater the cost of technology transfer, the higher the ratio of the foreign firm's market share to the Chinese firm's market share in equilibrium for the case where the foreign firm locates in China. (See appendix for proof.)*

Corollaries 3a and 3b are a primary focus for our empirical work in the following, where we examine how the relative prices and export market shares of the Chinese and foreign firms evolve after FDI into China. In particular, our hypotheses stemming from these corollaries is that factors that make technology transfer more costly/difficult mitigates positive spillover effects from foreign firm presence to the Chinese firms. In the case of prices, more costly or difficult technology transfer means that Chinese firms' export prices do not catch up to foreign firm export prices for the same good very quickly or at all. In the case of market shares, more costly or difficult technology transfer means that Chinese firms' relative export market share will increase less or even decline with foreign firm presence.

Finally, we solve the first-period of the model. If the foreign firm does not locate in China (subgame $1N$), then equilibrium prices and profits are identical to those in subgame $2N$ described in the preceding. If the foreign firm locates in the Chinese market, production costs are lowered, but technology transfer has not yet occurred. Equilibrium profits in this subgame (denoted subgame $1L$) are:

$$(11) \qquad \Pi_{CH}^{1L} \equiv \Pi_{CH} (p_{CH}^{1L}, p_{F}^{1L}, K_{CH}, K_{F}, 0, 0)$$

$$(12) \qquad \Pi_{F}^{1L} \equiv \Pi_{F} (p_{CH}^{1L}, p_{F}^{1L}, K_{CH}, K_{F}, 0, 0),$$

where p_{CH}^{1L}, p_{F}^{1L} are the optimally chosen prices by the Chinese and foreign firm in this subgame. It's easy to show the following relationships between equilibrium profits for the foreign firm:

(13) $$\Pi_F^{1L} > \Pi_F^{1N} \equiv \Pi_F^{2N} \text{ and}$$

(14) $$\Pi_F^{2T} \leq \Pi_F^{2N}.$$

This leads us to an analysis of the foreign firm's initial decision whether to engage in FDI by locating in China. Assuming a one-time fixed cost of FDI, which we denote as F, the foreign firm decides to locate to China if:

(15) $$\Pi_F^{1L} + \Pi_F^{2T} - F > \Pi_F^{1N} + \Pi_F^{2N}.$$

This leads to:

PROPOSITION 4. *The FDI decision by the foreign firm into China is more likely (a) the greater the cost savings, and (b) the greater the cost or difficulty of technology transfer. (See appendix for proof.)*

While our empirical work in the following does not examine data on FDI into China, Proposition 4 highlights that FDI is endogenous with the ability of Chinese firms to transfer technology from the foreign firm. When technology transfer is made relatively easy by the FDI, the foreign firm is less likely to locate in China. This selection issue suggests that we may only observe FDI into industries where technology transfer is difficult or costly. Thus, we may find little evidence of convergence of relative export prices and increases in Chinese market share after FDI increases in an industry. Our empirical analysis will account for this potential endogeneity bias.

12.3.5 Role of Government Policies

The Chinese government has active policies to encourage or restrict FDI into certain industries or products. A simple way to examine the impact of these policies in the model is to think of these policies as either lowering or raising the fixed costs of FDI (F). Encouragement of FDI (lowering of F) would obviously lead to the condition in equation (15) being more likely satisfied, increasing the probability of FDI. The immediate effect would be to increase the foreign firm market share (from zero when no FDI takes place). However, the foreign firms that did not engage in FDI in the first place were ones for which technology transfer would be more significant or production cost decreases from locating to China is less significant. If the encouragement policy selects a foreign firm into China that otherwise would have stayed out because of technology transfer concerns, then by Proposition 1a and 1b, we may expect the encourage policy to lead to a greater decrease in the ratio of foreign-to-Chinese market shares and unit values over time.

Of course, all of these effects stemming from a policy of encouraging FDI would be the exact opposite with a Chinese government policy of restricting FDI, if such restrictions simply increase the costs of FDI. However, in many cases, Chinese restrictions on FDI involve requiring foreign firms to partner with a Chinese firm or arrange for technology transfer. A prominent example of this is the automobile industry. This restriction can easily be modeled as a lowering of technology transfer costs (θ) in our model, which by corollaries 3a and 3b would make the ratio of foreign-to-Chinese market shares and unit values decrease in the second period, ceteris paribus. However, both the higher fixed costs of FDI and greater technology transfer makes it less likely that the foreign firm would enter.

12.3.6   Ownership Structure

For simplicity, we do not consider alternative forms of FDI ownership structure in our model. However, the data we explore in the following have considerable information on the amounts of activity from both joint venture and wholly-owned foreign firms. Joint venture activity presumably facilitates greater technology transfer (i.e., lower costs of transfer for the Chinese firm). A foreign firm could conceivably be interested in pursuing a joint venture, nevertheless, if it lowered its fixed costs of FDI or provided an even greater reduction in production costs. This would lead to a positive selection effect, making it more likely that a foreign firm will invest in China despite technology transfer concerns. Thus, while we have not modeled a foreign firm's decision of ownership structure, this discussion suggests that when a foreign firm does choose to engage in a joint venture, we should expect a greater decrease in relative foreign-to-Chinese market shares and unit values over time than in the case where the foreign firm chooses to be an independent, wholly-owned foreign firm.

12.4   A Brief Descriptive Analysis of Exports and Unit Values over Time

Before examining our hypotheses, we briefly describe and look at some general trends in the primary data set on Chinese exports we use for our analysis. These Chinese trade data span the years from 1995 to 2005 and were made available through the Customs General Administration of the People's Republic of China, as part of the project described in Feenstra et al. (1998). Our data set includes both ordinary and processing trade. An important feature of the data is that it disaggregates export trade activity by the type of firm, namely, foreign-invested enterprises (FIEs), state-owned enterprises (SOEs), contractual joint ventures (CJVs), equity joint ventures (EJVs), collectively owned enterprises (COEs), and privately owned enterprises (POEs). Foreign-invested firms are firms wholly-owned by foreign funded firms and overseas Chinese companies. State-owned enterprises are the traditional noncorporation economic units, where the entire assets are owned by the state. Collectively owned enterprises are collectively owned economic units, including township and village firms. Privately owned enterprises are economic units owned by private, domestic Chinese individuals. Finally, CJVs are joint ventures between Chinese corporations and foreign partners, where profits and risks are shared in accordance with their agree-

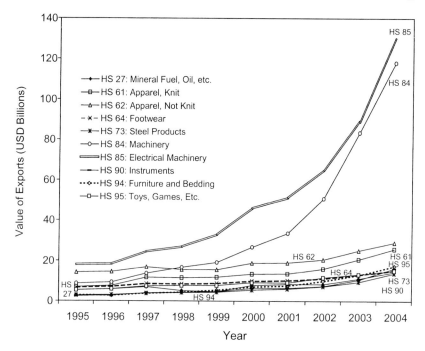

Fig. 12.2   Chinese exports by top industries at two-digit HS Level, 1995–2004

ments, whereas EJVs are joint ventures where profits and risks are shared in accordance with the percentage of shareholdings, and the foreign entity may not own more than 50 percent of the venture. These distinctions will allow us to understand the various and changing role of foreign and domestic firms in Chinese exporting patterns.

Figure 12.2 provides the value of exports over time for the top ten industries at the two-digit Harmonized System (HS) level.[7] Machinery (HS 84) and Electrical Machinery (HS 85) clearly represent the largest exporting sectors in China and have been a primary driving force in the growth of Chinese exports over this period. These two sectors are followed by the two main apparel sectors (HS 61 and 62), the Furniture and Bedding sector (HS 94) and the Toys and Games sector (HS 95). Figure 12.3 shows the export shares of all Chinese exports for years 1995, 2000, and 2005 by firm types. Although the share of SOE exports in 1995 is the largest, the value of exports by SOE has been significantly decreasing relative to the other firm types over the years. In place of the declining SOE export shares is the rise in exports by FIEs, EJVs, COEs, and POEs. Most significant is the relatively large increase in export shares by POEs from 2000 to 2005. For purposes of our

7. We use the end-of-sample 2004 rankings of export shares to determine the top ten sectors.

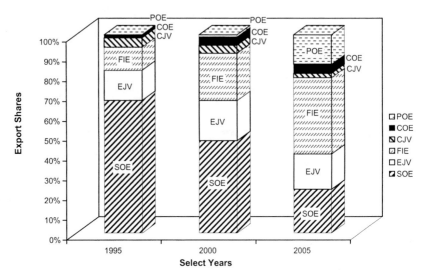

Fig. 12.3   Export shares of all Chinese exports, selected years

analysis, we will primarily separate our data into two groups, which we call the foreign firms, consisting of the CJVs, EJVs, and FIEs, and the Chinese firms, consisting of the COEs, POEs, and SOEs.

12.5   Empirical Analysis

12.5.1   Specification

We now turn to a statistical analysis of relative market shares and unit values for foreign and Chinese exports from 1997 through 2005. Our focus is the changes over time in these relative foreign-to-Chinese measures and how various factors, as suggested by our model, affect these dynamic patterns. Our estimation strategy is quite simple, with our empirical models specified as the following:

$$(16) \quad FS_{jt} = \alpha + \sum_{t=1998}^{2005} \beta_t YD_t + \sum_{m=1}^{M} \sum_{t=1998}^{2005} \gamma_{tm} (YD_t \times Z_j^m) + \psi_j + \varepsilon_{jt}$$

$$(17) \quad \ln UV_{jt}^F - \ln UV_{jt}^{CH} = \alpha + \sum_{t=1998}^{2005} \beta_t YD_t + \sum_{m=1}^{M} \sum_{t=1998}^{2005} \gamma_{tm} (YD_t \times Z_j^m)$$
$$+ \psi_j + \varepsilon_{jt},$$

where FS_{jt} is the foreign firm's share of Chinese exports for a given six-digit HS (HS6) product code j and year t; UV_{jt}^F and UV_{jt}^{CH} are Chinese export unit values for the foreign and Chinese firms for the HS6 product code j

and year t, respectively; YD_t are year dummy variables; Z_j^m are a set of M variables representing product attributes or policy variables that are hypothesized to affect technology transfer and market competition between the Chinese and foreign firms; ψ_j are the HS6 product fixed effects, and ε_{jt} is an assumed white-noise random error term.

Given the specification of the dependent variable in equation (16), the coefficients on our year dummies in our "export market share regressions" show the *percentage point* difference in the foreign market share from our base year, 1997.[8] For the "unit value difference regressions" in equation (17), the year dummy coefficients capture the *percentage* difference from the base year, 1997. A key focus is also on the double-summation term in each equation, which represents sets of year-dummy interactions with our focus variables related to our model's hypotheses. We describe these factors that comprise Z_j^m next.

Our theoretical model in section 12.3 suggests three types of factors that may affect the evolution of our dependent variables: (a) cost of technology transfer, (b) government policies, and (c) ownership structure. Measures of technology transfer costs are difficult to observe, so we rely on two proxies: (a) product differentiation and (b) research and development (R&D) intensity. Our hypotheses are that sectors with higher R&D intensity and product differentiation will be ones for which technology transfer is more costly for the Chinese firm. Thus, by corollaries 3a and 3b, these factors should be associated with lower declines in relative foreign-to-Chinese market shares and unit values. The R&D intensity, defined as the number of R&D scientists and engineers per 1,000 employees in R&D-performing companies, is from the National Science Foundation's *Research and Development in Industry* (various years). The identification of differentiated goods comes from Rauch (1999).

With respect to government policies, we focus on official lists from the Chinese government indicating in which sectors they are encouraging or restricting FDI. Information on industries that the Chinese government encourages, restricts, or prohibits comes from the *Catalogue for the Guidance of Foreign Investment Industries,* first published by the Chinese government in 1997 and significantly updated in 2002. The listed industries and products are not identified with any formal industrial classification system. We use key words in the industry/product description for both the 1997 and 2002 lists to search for associated HS codes using the U.S. International Trade Commission (USITC) tariff database search engine, available at http://dataweb.usitc.gov/scripts/tariff2003.asp. As discussed in section 12.3, our model predicts that encouragement of FDI will increase the relative foreign firm's share of exports but may accentuate technology transfer, leading to a greater decrease

8. We exclude the first year (1997) of our year-dummy variables and sets of year-dummy interactions to avoid perfect multicollinearity with our constant.

in the unit value relative to domestic firms. On the other hand, restrictions on FDI should lead to greater decreases in both the foreign firm's export share and relative unit value.

Likewise, as discussed in section 12.3, we would expect to see greater decreases in both the foreign firm's export share and relative unit value for joint ventures (where the foreign firm is working in close connection with a Chinese partner) than with a wholly-owned (and independent) FIE. Because these are not product-level attributes or policies, we do not empirically assess this impact through interactions with year dummies in our full sample. Rather, we will address these hypotheses by examining our estimates when we reconstruct our dependent variables in terms of only FIE or only joint venture transactions, respectively.

Before turning to our results, it is important to note that our hypotheses come from a model of one-time competition between a single foreign firm and a single Chinese firm. In reality, of course, there are likely many foreign and Chinese firms for even a given HS6 product, and there has been ongoing FDI into China over our sample period. This most obviously affects our foreign export share variable, where continual FDI can lead us to see increasing foreign export shares, even if significant technology transfer is taking place. Likewise, unit value gaps may increase over time if foreign firms are locating ever more sophisticated products into China. Ideally, one would like to control for the relative entry rates of domestic and foreign firms by HS6 product categories. But no such data exist.

However, there are a number of important points in regard to this issue. First, both the ratio of FDI stock in China relative to GDP and the ratio of annual net FDI inflows to gross domestic capital formation in the Chinese economy have been fairly constant since the early 1990s, as shown in figure 12.4. In fact, both ratios have actually fallen some over our sample period from 1997 to 2005. This argues against an upward-trending bias of foreign export share in our sample from greater growth in foreign capital than domestic Chinese capital. However, to the extent that one still thinks such bias may exist, it only modifies our connection to our model's hypothesis in the sense that a factor that would lead to *greater declines* in foreign market share in our pure theoretical model simply translates into *smaller increases* in foreign market share in a world where foreign market shares are generally increasing over time due to other reasons. Finally, at the end of our empirical section, we regress unit value gaps not only on year dummies, but also on lagged foreign market share to control for the dynamic changes in FDI patterns explicitly and more clearly identify any net technology transfer effect.

12.5.2   Base Results

Columns (1) and (2) of table 12.1 provide our results when we estimate our foreign firms' export share specification (equation [16]), first without

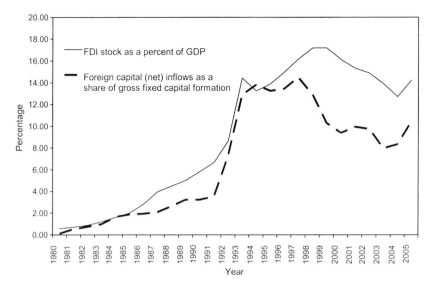

Fig. 12.4   FDI in China relative to domestic output and capital formation, 1980–2005

Sources: FDI stock data come from UNCTAD's *World Investment Report,* various issues; and GDP, net foreign capital inflow, and gross fixed capital formation data from the World Bank's *World Development Indicators.*

interactions between the year dummies and the set of Z_j^m variables, and then with these year-dummy interactions. Likewise, columns (3) and (4) of table 12.1 provide analogous results for our unit value differences specification (equation [17]). Statistical significance of these regressions is generally quite good with R^2-statistics over 0.8 in the foreign share equations and over 0.6 in the unit value differences equations. Most of the variation in the data is explained by the HS6 product fixed effects.

Our coefficients on the year dummy variables in columns (1) and (3) of table 12.1 show us how our dependent variables are changing, on average, across our sample and over time. Surprisingly, these estimates provide evidence that domestic Chinese firms are "falling behind," rather than "catching up" to, foreign firms. In our foreign firms' export share equation (column [1]), these estimates suggest that the share of foreign firms responsible for Chinese exports has been increasing over our sample for the average HS6 product. By 2005, the average foreign firm export share in an HS6 product climbed 4.9 percentage points from its level in 1997 of 50.6 percent. The coefficients on the year dummy terms in the unit value difference estimates (column [3]) also suggest significant "falling behind" by domestic Chinese firms, with unit value differences 9.5 percent higher at the end of our sample in 2005 than the first year of the sample, 1997. Interestingly, the relative differences in unit values had grown by over 13 percent from 1997 to 2003,

Table 12.1   **National annual changes in relative market shares and unit values of
Chinese exports (1997–2005)**

	Relative market shares		Relative unit values	
	(1)	(2)	(3)	(4)
Year 1998	0.012	0.017	0.017	–0.067
	(0.009)	(0.028)	(0.028)	(0.076)
Year 1999	0.009	0.026	0.057***	–0.041
	(0.009)	(0.027)	(0.023)	(0.058)
Year 2000	0.018**	0.046**	0.113***	–0.028
	(0.008)	(0.023)	(0.023)	(0.050)
Year 2001	0.027***	0.058***	0.117***	–0.037
	(0.008)	(0.022)	(0.025)	(0.050)
Year 2002	0.029***	0.064***	0.112***	0.025
	(0.008)	(0.022)	(0.026)	(0.054)
Year 2003	0.035***	0.069***	0.138***	–0.063
	(0.007)	(0.021)	(0.025)	(0.054)
Year 2004	0.044***	0.073***	0.093***	–0.032
	(0.007)	(0.021)	(0.026)	(0.053)
Year 2005	0.049***	0.081***	0.095***	0.007
	(0.008)	(0.022)	(0.026)	(0.051)
Year 1998 • Differentiated		–0.005		0.044
		(0.027)		(0.060)
Year 1999 • Differentiated		–0.020		0.076
		(0.023)		(0.049)
Year 2000 • Differentiated		–0.034		0.102**
		(0.022)		(0.048)
Year 2001 • Differentiated		–0.037*		0.161***
		(0.021)		(0.051)
Year 2002 • Differentiated		–0.049***		0.090*
		(0.021)		(0.054)
Year 2003 • Differentiated		–0.052***		0.151***
		(0.021)		(0.054)
Year 2004 • Differentiated		–0.047***		0.131***
		(0.021)		(0.053)
Year 2005 • Differentiated		–0.048***		0.151***
		(0.022)		(0.051)
Year 1998 • R&D intensity		–0.0003		0.002
		(0.0003)		(0.001)
Year 1999 • R&D intensity		–0.0002		0.001
		(0.0004)		(0.001)
Year 2000 • R&D intensity		–0.0002		0.002**
		(0.0002)		(0.028)
Year 2001 • R&D intensity		–0.0002		0.001
		(0.0002)		(0.001)
Year 2002 • R&D intensity		–0.0001		0.001
		(0.0002)		(0.001)
Year 2003 • R&D intensity		0.00004		0.002**
		(0.0002)		(0.001)
Year 2004 • R&D intensity		0.0000003		0.0004
		(0.0002)		(0.001)
Year 2005 • R&D intensity		–0.00005		–0.0004
		(0.0002)		(0.001)

Table 12.1 (continued)

	Relative market shares		Relative unit values	
	(1)	(2)	(3)	(4)
Year 1998 • Encouraged FDI		0.033		0.136
		(0.024)		(0.098)
Year 1999 • Encouraged FDI		0.032		0.124**
		(0.026)		(0.063)
Year 2000 • Encouraged FDI		0.036**		0.090
		(0.017)		(0.061)
Year 2001 • Encouraged FDI		0.031**		0.057
		(0.014)		(0.074)
Year 2002 • Encouraged FDI		0.024**		−0.048
		(0.011)		(0.053)
Year 2003 • Encouraged FDI		0.018*		0.040
		(0.011)		(0.051)
Year 2004 • Encouraged FDI		0.024**		0.045
		(0.010)		(0.053)
Year 2005 • Encouraged FDI		0.027**		0.045
		(0.012)		(0.051)
Year 1998 • Restricted FDI		0.035**		−0.204***
		(0.018)		(0.071)
Year 1999 • Restricted FDI		0.037**		−0.134**
		(0.017)		(0.064)
Year 2000 • Restricted FDI		0.019		−0.151*
		(0.013)		(0.089)
Year 2001 • Restricted FDI		0.015		−0.106
		(0.013)		(0.071)
Year 2002 • Restricted FDI		0.004		−0.082
		(0.017)		(0.056)
Year 2003 • Restricted FDI		−0.005		−0.070
		(0.016)		(0.057)
Year 2004 • Restricted FDI		0.007		−0.037
		(0.014)		(0.078)
Year 2005 • Restricted FDI		0.002		−0.133**
		(0.014)		(0.066)
Constant	0.506***	0.505***	0.318***	0.306***
	(0.007)	(0.007)	(0.018)	(0.022)
Province dummies	No	No	No	No
HS6 dummies	Yes	Yes	Yes	Yes
No. of observations	116,854	116,854	86,443	86,443
F-test	10.91	3.11	7.09	3.60
Prob $> F$	0.0000	0.0000	0.0000	0.0000
R^2	0.8382	0.8390	0.6011	0.6069
Root MSE	0.1274	0.1271	0.4069	0.4040

Notes: Weighted by value of total exports in 6-digit Harmonized System (HS6) sector. Robust standard errors are in parentheses. Winsorize bottom 5 percent and top 5 percent of sample. MSE = mean square error.

***Significant at the 1 percent level.

**Significant at the 5 percent level.

*Significant at the 10 percent level.

but then fell to just 9.5 percent greater than 1997 by 2005. This may be evidence of catching up over the 2003 to 2005 period, but, nevertheless, the broad trends suggest Chinese firms losing export share and relative sophistication (i.e., unit values) over the period.

We next turn to examination of estimates connected with our year-dummy variable interactions with the set of Z_j^m variables, which are connected to our model's hypotheses. These are shown in the specifications in columns (2) and (4) of table 12.1. The coefficients on the interaction terms show the *marginal* difference in the yearly effect for the associated Z_j^m variable. To get the total annual change in the dependent variable for an HS6 product with the associated Z_j^m attribute, one must add up these marginal difference coefficients from the appropriate interaction terms with the year-dummy coefficients.

We have two proxies for ease of technology transfer in our set of Z_j^k variables: product differentiation and R&D intensity. Our estimates do not suggest that higher R&D intensity has any differential effect on the evolution of foreign export share or unit value differences from other products in our sample. However, there are significant differences between differentiated and undifferentiated products. Consistent with corollary 3b, we find strong evidence that foreign unit values have increased significantly more over our sample for differentiated goods, where technology transfer is presumed more difficult, than undifferentiated ones. The gain in the foreign firms' unit values for differentiated products has increased more than 10 percentage points over the gains shown in undifferentiated products. Thus, Chinese firms appear to be falling behind even faster for these products. However, counter to corollary 3a, we actually find that the foreign firms' share in Chinese exports actually increases less for differentiated products than for undifferentiated products. Thus, the data suggest that Chinese-owned firms maintain their market share of exports as they fall quickly in terms of sophistication (as proxied by unit values) relative to the FOEs in differentiated products.

Our set of Z_j^m variables also includes two Chinese government policies directed at FDI into various HS products: encouragement and restrictions. According to our discussion in section 12.3.5, policies encouraging FDI are expected to increase the export share of foreign firms and also make catching up by Chinese firms more likely (that is, a decline in the unit value differences). While our estimates show that the export shares of foreign firms grow significantly more over time in our sample for "encouraged" HS6 products, there are no differences for these "encouraged" sectors in terms of their changes in relative unit values. In other words, it does not lead to greater catching up by domestic-owned Chinese firms. For "restricted" sectors, we would expect lower shares of foreign firms in Chinese exports, but greater catching up. We find no statistical effect on the evolution of foreign firms' share of Chinese exports. However, we do find that unit value differences were significantly lower for these restricted sectors for a number of years in sample, especially prior to 2000. This may suggest that Chinese government

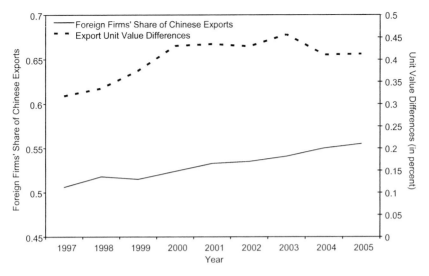

Fig. 12.5   Foreign firms' share of Chinese exports and export unit values relative to Chinese-owned firms, 1997–2005: Sample average

restrictions on technology sharing for these sectors decreased or became less effective over time.

Figure 12.5 through 12.9 provide a visual summary of our coefficient estimates. Figure 12.5 displays the evolution of foreign firms' share of Chinese exports and the relative difference in foreign versus domestic-owned Chinese firms' export unit values based on our estimates for the general sample. Figures 12.6 through 12.9 show evolution of these same variables for products with Z_j^m attributes (e.g., differentiated products in figure 12.6). These come from our estimates in columns (2) and (4) of table 12.1.

In summary of these base results, we largely find no evidence for catching up by Chinese firms based on the evolution of unit value differences and even significant falling behind in the case of differentiated goods. There is also a general increase in foreign firms' share of Chinese exports over the 1997 to 2005 period, which is even larger in "encouraged" sectors, but actually smaller for differentiated goods.

12.5.3   Controlling for Potential Cost Differences— Provincial-Level Data

Our theoretical model assumes identical cost conditions for foreign- and domestic-owned firms in China. However, foreign and domestic firms within an HS6 product category may be in quite different locations, particularly because we know that Chinese policy (especially in earlier years) only allowed foreign investment in certain regions of China. Thus, one may wonder if our results in the preceding are driven by differences in evolving costs conditions

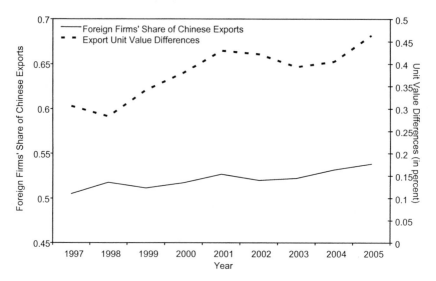

Fig. 12.6   Foreign firms' share of Chinese exports and export unit values relative to Chinese-owned firms, 1997–2005: Differentiated Products

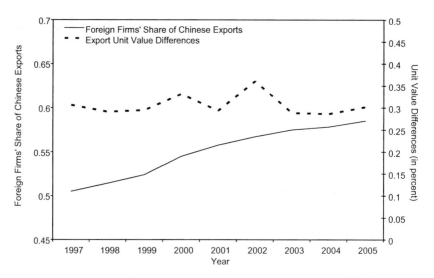

Fig. 12.7   Foreign firms' share of Chinese exports and export unit values relative to Chinese-owned firms, 1997–2005: High R&D products

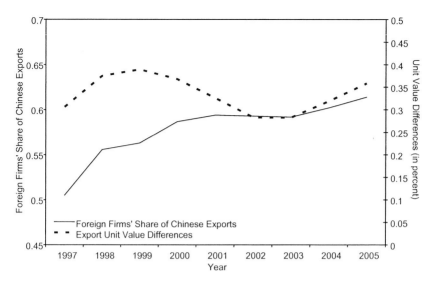

Fig. 12.8   Foreign firms' share of Chinese exports and export unit values relative to Chinese-owned firms, 1997–2005: Encouraged products

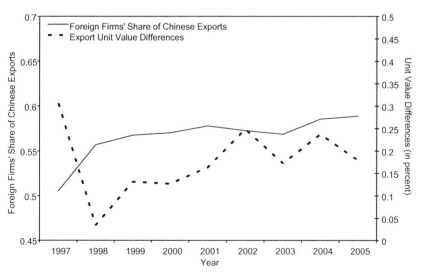

Fig. 12.9   Foreign firms' share of Chinese exports and export unit values relative to Chinese-owned firms, 1997–2005: Restricted products

across the differing locations foreign- and domestic-owned firms in China. Controlling for such cost differences is also hopefully helpful in assigning any differences and changes in relative unit values as due to product quality or sophistication factors.

To address this, we next disaggregate our sample of observations to the level of province-product-year observations and reestimate equations (16) and (17). This increases our sample size by an order of magnitude. Our dependent variables now compare relative export shares and unit values for foreign and domestic firms within the same HS *and province.* We also include provincial fixed effects, which will control for any other unobserved time-invariant provincial fixed effects (such as relatively fixed differences in province-specific encouragement of FDI).

Table 12.2 presents our results for this province-level sample in analogous fashion to table 12.1. (Figures 12.10 through 12.14 show our the effects visually in analogous fashion to figures 12.5 through 12.9.) There is much more variance in these data, resulting in lower, but still respectable, R^2-statistics (over 0.60 in the foreign export share equations and over 0.30 in the unit value differences equations). Surprisingly, we get qualitatively identical results to our estimates in the previous section. The share of foreign firms in Chinese exports increases significantly over time, and there is no significant change in relative unit values. As before, foreign firms in "encouraged" sectors see even larger-than-average increases in export shares, while firms in differentiated product sectors see much smaller increases in export shares.

12.5.4   Ownership Structures

As discussed in section 12.3.6, we expect to find that the foreign-firm export market share and unit value difference both decrease for joint ventures relative to FIEs. To examine these hypotheses we reconstruct our dependent variables, first in terms of joint ventures relative to domestic Chinese firms, then in terms of FIEs relative to domestic Chinese firms, and then we reestimate equations (16) and (17). We estimate these models using province-level data and include province fixed effects. Our estimates indicate that the share of FIEs in Chinese exports rising quite significantly (over 10 percentage points) over our sample period, while the share of joint ventures in Chinese exports does not change over time in any statistically significant manner. This is in line with our hypotheses. With respect to unit value differences, both FIEs and joint ventures export unit values do not change over time. Thus, for both types of foreign-owned firms, there is no evidence of catching up by domestic-owned Chinese firms, even for joint ventures where we would most expect to see such effects. We don't report these results here for the sake of space, but they are available from the authors upon request.

Table 12.2 Provincial annual changes in relative market shares and unit values of Chinese exports (1997–2005)

	Relative market shares		Relative unit values	
	(1)	(2)	(3)	(4)
Year 1998	0.012*	0.017	0.031	0.014
	(0.007)	(0.020)	(0.021)	(0.053)
Year 1999	0.009	0.020	0.069***	−0.054
	(0.007)	(0.019)	(0.025)	(0.075)
Year 2000	0.018***	0.042**	0.101***	0.057
	(0.007)	(0.021)	(0.022)	(0.058)
Year 2001	0.027***	0.051***	0.090***	−0.023
	(0.007)	(0.019)	(0.020)	(0.051)
Year 2002	0.029***	0.057***	0.119***	−0.013
	(0.007)	(0.017)	(0.022)	(0.061)
Year 2003	0.035***	0.061***	0.157***	0.006
	(0.007)	(0.017)	(0.025)	(0.066)
Year 2004	0.044***	0.063***	0.111***	0.002
	(0.007)	(0.017)	(0.025)	(0.061)
Year 2005	0.049***	0.070***	0.150***	−0.001
	(0.006)	(0.018)	(0.026)	(0.061)
Year 1998 • Differentiated		−0.005		−0.017
		(0.019)		(0.043)
Year 1999 • Differentiated		−0.018		0.013
		(0.017)		(0.044)
Year 2000 • Differentiated		−0.034**		0.005
		(0.019)		(0.046)
Year 2001 • Differentiated		−0.035**		0.112***
		(0.018)		(0.042)
Year 2002 • Differentiated		−0.046***		0.081
		(0.016)		(0.050)
Year 2003 • Differentiated		−0.046***		0.118***
		(0.016)		(0.052)
Year 2004 • Differentiated		−0.039***		0.137***
		(0.016)		(0.051)
Year 2005 • Differentiated		−0.038**		0.201***
		(0.017)		(0.048)
Year 1998 • R&D intensity		−0.0003		0.001
		(0.0002)		(0.001)
Year 1999 • R&D intensity		−0.0002		0.003
		(0.0003)		(0.002)
Year 2000 • R&D intensity		−0.0002		0.001
		(0.0002)		(0.001)
Year 2001 • R&D intensity		−0.0002		0.001
		(0.0002)		(0.001)
Year 2002 • R&D intensity		−0.0001		0.002
		(0.0002)		(0.001)
Year 2003 • R&D intensity		0.00002		0.001
		(0.0002)		(0.001)
Year 2004 • R&D intensity		−0.00002		0.0002
		(0.0002)		(0.001)

(*continued*)

Table 12.2 (continued)

	Relative market shares		Relative unit values	
	(1)	(2)	(3)	(4)
Year 2005 • R&D intensity		−0.0001		−0.0002
		(0.0002)		(0.001)
Year 1998 • Encouraged FDI		0.040**		0.089
		(0.020)		(0.065)
Year 1999 • Encouraged FDI		0.036**		0.176***
		(0.019)		(0.071)
Year 2000 • Encouraged FDI		0.036***		0.188***
		(0.015)		(0.066)
Year 2001 • Encouraged FDI		0.033***		0.105
		(0.014)		(0.065)
Year 2002 • Encouraged FDI		0.024**		−0.006
		(0.012)		(0.051)
Year 2003 • Encouraged FDI		0.021**		0.073
		(0.012)		(0.049)
Year 2004 • Encouraged FDI		0.025***		−0.0005
		(0.011)		(0.047)
Year 2005 • Encouraged FDI		0.028***		0.042
		(0.012)		(0.048)
Year 1998 • Restricted FDI		0.027*		−0.158**
		(0.015)		(0.073)
Year 1999 • Restricted FDI		0.032**		−0.116**
		(0.015)		(0.058)
Year 2000 • Restricted FDI		0.015		−0.185***
		(0.013)		(0.063)
Year 2001 • Restricted FDI		0.007		−0.107
		(0.013)		(0.068)
Year 2002 • Restricted FDI		−0.007		−0.011
		(0.018)		(0.071)
Year 2003 • Restricted FDI		−0.012		−0.170***
		(0.020)		(0.065)
Year 2004 • Restricted FDI		−0.0001		0.008
		(0.016)		(0.077)
Year 2005 • Restricted FDI		−0.002		−0.050
		(0.018)		(0.073)
Constant	0.506***	0.316***	0.279***	0.138
	(0.006)	(0.016)	(0.017)	(0.103)
Province dummies	No	Yes	No	Yes
HS6 dummies	Yes	Yes	Yes	Yes
No. of observations	1,125,254	1,125,254	329,231	329,231
F-test	9.93	92.95	10.38	8.41
Prob > F	0.0000	0.0000	0.0000	0.0000
R^2	0.6060	0.6510	0.3166	0.3176
Root MSE	0.2292	0.2157	0.5628	0.5584

Notes: See table 12.1.
***Significant at the 1 percent level.
**Significant at the 5 percent level.
*Significant at the 10 percent level.

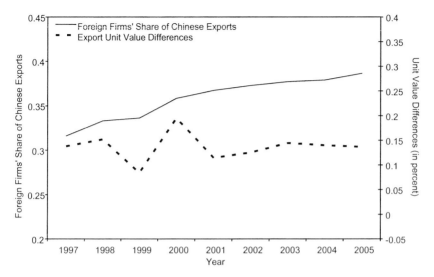

Fig. 12.10   Foreign firms' share of Chinese exports and export unit values relative to Chinese-owned firms, 1997–2005: Sample average with provincial-level data

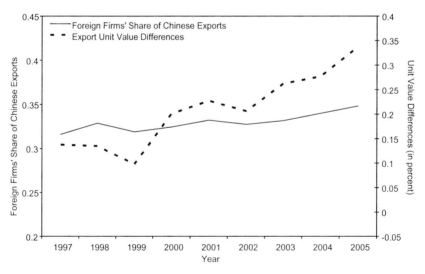

Fig. 12.11   Foreign firms' share of Chinese exports and export unit values relative to Chinese-owned firms, 1997–2005: Differentiated products with provincial-level data

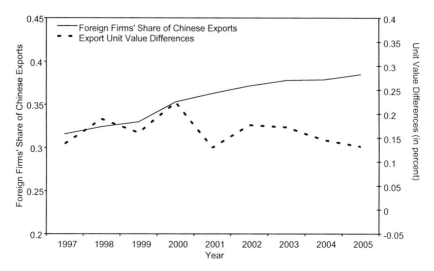

Fig. 12.12   Foreign firms' share of Chinese exports and export unit values relative to Chinese-owned firms, 1997–2005: High R&D products with provincial-level data

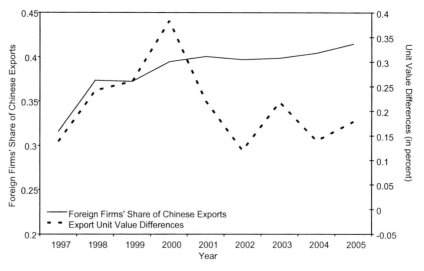

Fig. 12.13   Foreign firms' share of Chinese exports and export unit values relative to Chinese-owned firms, 1997–2005: Encouraged products with provincial-level data

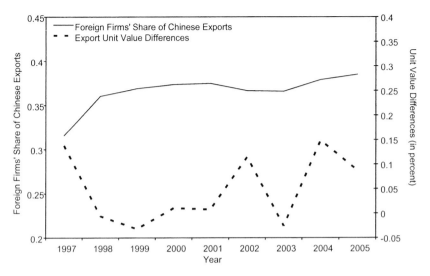

Fig. 12.14   Foreign firms' share of Chinese exports and export unit values relative to Chinese-owned firms, 1997–2005: Restricted products with provincial-level data

12.5.5   Exploring Other Subsamples

We also examined whether evolution of foreign firms' share of exports or relative export unit values varies for some notable subsamples of our data.[9] First, one may suspect that catching-up effects may differ for exports to markets that are industrialized than for developing economies. This may be particularly true in that the foreign-owned firms that export to industrialized countries from China are likely to be from these same industrialized countries, and thus more technologically advanced. However, when we sample only observations of Chinese exports to the United States, Japan, and the European Union (EU), we get qualitatively identical results as those with the full sample.

We also estimated separate results for the machinery (HS84) and electrical machinery (HS85) sectors because these two sectors are easily the top two in terms of Chinese exports—see figure 12.2. Both the electrical and machinery sectors yield qualitatively similar results to our full sample, with a couple of notable exceptions. First, in the machinery results, restricted sectors show foreign firms gaining significantly more than export share over our sample than other HS6 products in the machinery sector and also show some relatively small catching up effects for differentiated machinery products. In contrast, there are fairly large "falling behind" effects for Chinese firms in the electrical machinery sectors. These results highlight the potential for

9. Results in this section are also not reported for sake of brevity but are available from authors upon request.

exploring sectoral heterogeneity in future analyses, though we caution that smaller sample sizes certainly lower precision of estimates.

12.5.6   Is Increasing FDI Masking "Catch-Up" Effects?

As discussed earlier, a potential concern with our estimates is the possibility of increasing FDI activity over time. Obviously an increase of FDI into China of export-oriented foreign firms could be a driving force in the increase in foreign firm export market shares, thus masking any catch-up effects. Likewise, if these new foreign firms are locating products in China that are increasingly more sophisticated, this could be behind the rising gap in foreign-to-Chinese relative unit values as well. As discussed, the aggregate trends shown in figure 12.4 argue against this scenario of faster growing foreign firm formation or entry. However, in this section, we explore this issue in one final manner. While we do not have data on FDI by industries into China over time (much less at the HS6 product level), we can use prior foreign market share in an HS6 product as a proxy for previous FDI. Thus, we estimate the following specification:

$$(18) \quad \ln UV_{jt}^F - \ln UV_{jt}^{CH} = \alpha + \theta_1 FS_{jt} + \theta_2 LagFS_{jt} + \psi_j + \nu_t + \varepsilon_{jt},$$

where FS_{jt} and $LagFS_{jt}$ are terms that control for current and previous (lagged) foreign firms' export share in a HS6 product, while ψ_j and ν_t control for HS6 product fixed effects and year fixed effects, respectively.[10] There are a number of ways in which we could specify the lagged foreign firm export share term, but we chose to construct it as a moving average of the previous three years of the foreign market share (FS_{jt}) in a given HS6 product j.[11] Our focus will be on the coefficient estimates for FS_{jt} and $LagFS_{jt}$ in this analysis, not those for the year dummies. If foreign firms are continuously bringing into China production of evermore-sophisticated products, we would expect a positive coefficient on current foreign firm export share (FS_{jt}), but if there is catching up by domestic Chinese firms due to technology transfer from foreign firms, then we would expect a negative coefficient on prior foreign-firm export share ($LagFS_{jt}$).

Column (1) of table 12.3 provides our results from estimating equation (18). There is a significant and large coefficient on current FDI export share, suggesting that new FDI brings in more-sophisticated products for production and export from China. There is also a statistically insignificant coefficient on lagged FDI export share, which is consistent with our other findings that the Chinese firms are not gaining technology from foreign firms and then catching up over time, on average.

---

10. We do not estimate a similar foreign market share equation due to more serious endogeneity concerns adding lagged foreign market share terms in that setting.

11. We also tried putting in separate lags of Fshare going back up to four years but found that standard errors for our coefficients were often quite high due to multicollinearity amongst the lagged terms.

Table 12.3   Changes in relative unit values of Chinese exports with lagged foreign market share (2000–2005)

	Benchmark		Foreign-invested enterprises		Joint ventures	
	(1)	(2)	(3)	(4)	(5)	(6)
FS	0.403***	0.036	0.129***	0.141	0.029	−0.100**
	(0.024)	(0.075)	(0.045)	(0.088)	(0.045)	(0.052)
LagFS	−0.060	−0.178	−0.024	−0.112	−0.130**	−0.019
	(0.046)	(0.113)	(0.059)	(0.150)	(0.059)	(0.134)
FS •		0.375***		0.260***		0.060
Differentiated		(0.050)		(0.077)		(0.052)
LagFS •		0.074		0.166		0.059
Differentiated		(0.107)		(0.151)		(0.143)
FS • R&D		0.002		−0.004***		0.003**
intensity		(0.002)		(0.001)		(0.001)
LagFS • R&D		−0.0001		0.0002		−0.004***
intensity		(0.001)		(0.001)		(0.002)
FS • Encouraged		0.069		0.104		−0.143**
		(0.056)		(0.067)		(0.067)
LagFS •		0.190**		−0.166		0.172
Encouraged		(0.096)		(0.115)		(0.122)
FS • Restricted		−0.312***		−0.532***		−0.230***
		(0.072)		(0.107)		(0.080)
LagFS •		−0.025		0.011		0.059
Restricted		(0.087)		(0.120)		(0.162)
Constant	0.404***	0.314***	0.504***	−0.552	0.193	0.206*
	(0.082)	(0.105)	(0.097)	(0.108)	(0.118)	(0.118)
Provincial						
dummies	Yes	Yes	Yes	Yes	Yes	Yes
Year dummies	Yes	Yes	Yes	Yes	Yes	Yes
HS6 dummies	Yes	Yes	Yes	Yes	Yes	Yes
No. of						
observations	198,414	198,414	198,422	198,422	226,466	226,466
F-test	16.29	17.39	7.80	9.16	10.26	9.80
Prob > F	0.0000	0.0000	0.0000	0.0000	0.0000	0.0000
R^2	0.3682	0.3743	0.3544	0.3640	0.4077	0.4113
Root MSE	0.4807	0.4784	0.4859	0.4823	0.5330	0.5314

Notes: Weighted by value of total exports in a 6-digit Harmonized System (HS6) sector. Robust standard errors in parentheses. Winsorize bottom 5 percent and top 5 percent of sample. Lags created using a three-year moving average.

MSE = mean square error; FS = foreign enterprises' share of Chinese exports.

***Significant at the 1 percent level.

**Significant at the 5 percent level.

*Significant at the 10 percent level.

In column (2) of table 12.3, we interact our variables proxying for costly technology transfer (product differentiation and R&D intensity) and Chinese government policies (encourage and restrict) with our current and lagged foreign export share variables. These results show a couple effects of note. First, the introduction of increasingly sophisticated products is primarily coming in the differentiated product sectors, as seen by the large positive coefficient on current foreign export share interacted with a differentiated product dummy. On the other hand, the restricted sector shows a large negative coefficient on current foreign export share, suggesting that the restrictions are leading to introduction of much-less-sophisticated products in these sectors. The effects of lagged foreign export share continue to be statistically insignificant, indicating no evidence of catching up by Chinese firms.

Finally, columns (3) through (6) in table 12.3 show results when we run the same specifications defining foreign firms first as only wholly-owned FIEs, and then as only joint ventures. While again, there is no evidence of catching up for the FIEs, we estimate a 13 percent catch up in relative unit values for Chinese firms from the previous three years of foreign joint venture firm export activity. This is consistent with our hypotheses that technology transfer to Chinese firms is more likely when partnering with a foreign firm in a joint venture than from wholly-owned FIEs in their own sector.

12.6   Conclusion

Facilitating technology transfer to allow domestic firms to catch up to foreign firms invested in their country is an obvious goal of the Chinese government in the policies they have regarding FDI. Recent literature has documented the high level of sophistication of Chinese exports for a country at its general level of development. An important question is whether this is simply driven by the foreign firms in China or whether Chinese firms are also gaining greater sophistication from this foreign presence. The answer to this question has significant implications for China's long-term growth potential.

We explore the extent to which Chinese firms may gain sophistication relative to foreign firms present in China (i.e., catching up) by first building a model of market competition between foreign and domestic firms where products are vertically differentiated, but Chinese firms can close the quality gap in products through technology transfer. We term this effect "catching up" by the Chinese firms. We then estimate the catching up by Chinese firms (and related hypotheses) using detailed Chinese export data that separately reports exports from foreign and Chinese firms. The general patterns over our time period, 1997 to 2005, run exactly counter to what one would expect if Chinese firms were catching up—foreign firm's share of exports by product category and foreign unit values relative to Chinese unit values are increasing over time, not decreasing. We see these patterns despite the fact that FDI into China as a percent of GDP has not increased since before our sample. These results are quite robust to a number of specifications and varying samples of our data, though a final specification examining how previous foreign market share affects current unit value gaps finds only modest catching up for Chinese domestic firms from joint venture activity.

Appendix

This appendix provides proofs for the results in the propositions and corollaries presented in the theory section of the paper. Throughout, we simplify notation by letting x denote $U(K_F)$, y denote $U(K_{CH})$, and x_{Tech} denote $U(K_{\text{Tech}})$, recalling that $K_{\text{Tech}} = (1 - \lambda)K_{CH} + \lambda K_F$.

PROOF OF PROPOSITION 1a. Solving for Nash Equilibrium prices in period 2 after the foreign firm has located to China and technology transfer has taken place (subgame $2T$), one can then construct expressions for demands for each firm in terms of parameters as:

(A1)
$$D_F^{2T} = \frac{2(x - x_{\text{Tech}})}{(4x - 3U_0 - x_{\text{Tech}})},$$

(A2)
$$D_{CH}^{2T} = \frac{(x - U_0)}{(4x - 3U_0 - x_{\text{Tech}})}.$$

Thus, the ratio of foreign-to-Chinese demands is:

(A3)
$$\Theta^{2T} \equiv \frac{D_F^{2T}}{D_{CH}^{2T}} = \frac{2(x - x_{\text{Tech}})}{(x - U_0)}.$$

Then, the effect of technology transfer on this ratio is the following:

(A4)
$$\frac{\partial \Theta^{2T}}{\partial \lambda} = \frac{\partial \Theta^{2T}}{\partial x_{\text{Tech}}} \frac{\partial x_{\text{Tech}}}{\partial \lambda} = -2(x - U_0) < 0$$

QED

PROOF OF PROPOSITION 1b. Solving for Nash equilibrium prices in period 2 after the foreign firm has located to China and technology transfer has taken place (subgame $2T$), we obtain:

(A5)
$$p_F^{2T} = \frac{[2(x - U_0)(x - x_{\text{Tech}})]}{[x(4x - 3U_0 - x_{\text{Tech}})]},$$

(A6)
$$p_{CH}^{2T} = \frac{[(x_{\text{Tech}} - U_0)(x - x_{\text{Tech}})]}{[x_{\text{Tech}}(4x - 3U_0 - x_{\text{Tech}})]}.$$

Thus, the ratio of foreign-to-Chinese prices is:

(A7)
$$\Omega^{2T} = \frac{p_F^{2T}}{p_{CH}^{2T}} = \frac{[2x_{\text{Tech}}(x - U_0)]}{[x(x_{\text{Tech}} - U_0)]}$$

Then the effect of technology transfer on this ratio is the following:

(A8)
$$\frac{\partial\Omega^{2T}}{\partial\lambda} = \frac{\partial\Omega^{2T}}{\partial x_{\text{Tech}}}\frac{\partial x_{\text{Tech}}}{\partial\lambda}$$

$$= \left[\frac{2(x - U_0)}{x(x_{\text{Tech}} - U_0)}\right]\left[1 - \frac{x_{\text{Tech}}}{(x_{\text{Tech}} - U_0)}\right](K_F - K_{CH})$$

Given the parameter values and assumed relationships presented in the text, this is easily signed as negative. QED

PROOF OF PROPOSITION 2. We assume that optimal second-period prices and demands are known functions of parameters for the Chinese firm when choosing the optimal λ. Then, provided second-order sufficient conditions hold for profit maximization in equation (10), we can write and sign the relevant comparative static as follows:

(A9)
$$\frac{\partial\lambda^*}{\partial\theta} = \frac{-(\partial\Pi_{CH}^{2T} / \partial\lambda\partial\theta)}{\partial\Pi_{CH}^{2T} / \partial\lambda\partial\lambda} = \frac{2\lambda}{\partial\Pi_{CH}^{2T} / \partial\lambda\partial\lambda} < 0.$$

QED

PROOF OF COROLLARIES 3a AND 3b. Using notation for relative price and unit values in the preceding, we can derive the following expressions:

(A10)
$$\frac{\partial\Theta^{2T}}{\partial\lambda} = \frac{\partial\Theta^{2T}}{\partial\lambda}\frac{\partial\lambda}{\partial\theta} \text{ and } \frac{\partial\Omega^{2T}}{\partial\lambda} = \frac{\partial\Omega^{2T}}{\partial\lambda}\frac{\partial\lambda}{\partial\theta}.$$

By the relationships established in propositions 1a, 1b, and 2, relative foreign demand and unit values are then increasing in θ. QED

PROOF OF PROPOSITION 4. Π_F^{1N} and Π_F^{2N} are decreasing in c, while c is a nonvarying parameter in Π_F^{1L} and Π_F^{2T}. Thus, by the envelope theorem, an increase in c (i.e., greater cost savings when the firm locates in China) lowers the right-hand side of equation (9) in the text and makes FDI more likely. Likewise, the technology cost variable, θ, is only an argument in Π_F^{2T} on the left-hand side of equation (9). By the envelope theorem, Π_F^{2T} is increasing in θ, thus making FDI more likely. QED

References

Brambilla, Irene. Forthcoming. Multinationals, technology, and the introduction of new goods. NBER Working Paper no. 12217. *Journal of International Economics.*

Branstetter, Lee G., and Robert C. Feenstra. 2002. Trade and foreign direct investment in China: A political economy approach. *Journal of International Economics* 58 (2): 335–58.

Chen, Huiya, and Deborah L. Swenson. 2006. Multinational firms and new Chinese export transactions. University of California, Davis. Mimeograph.

Feenstra, Robert C., Wen Hai, Wing T. Woo, and Shunli Yao. 1998. The U.S.-China bilateral trade balance: Its size and determinants. NBER Working Paper no. 6598. Cambridge, MA: National Bureau of Economic Research.

Feenstra, Robert C., and Gordon H. Hanson. 2004. Intermediaries in entrepot trade: Hong Kong re-exports of Chinese goods. *Journal of Economics and Management Strategy* 13 (1, special issue): 3–35.

———. 2005. Ownership and control in outsourcing to China: Estimating the property-rights theory of the firm. *Quarterly Journal of Economics* 120 (2): 729–61.

Feenstra, Robert C., Gordon H. Hanson, and Songhua Lin. 2004. The value of information in international trade: Gains to outsourcing through Hong Kong. *Advances in Economic Analysis and Policy* 4 (1): 1–35.

Feenstra, Robert C., and Barbara J. Spencer. 2005. Contractual versus generic outsourcing: The role of proximity. NBER Working Paper no. 11885. Cambridge, MA: National Bureau of Economic Research.

Graham, Edward M. 2004. Do export processing zones attract FDI and its benefits? The experience from China. *International Economics and Economic Policy* 1 (1): 87–103.

Hale, Galina, and Cheryl Long. Forthcoming. What determines technological spillovers of foreign direct investment: Evidence from China. *Pacific Economic Review.*

Hausmann, Ricardo, Jason Hwang, and Dani Rodrik. 2007. What you export matters. *Journal of Economic Growth* 12 (1): 1–25.

Li, Feng, and Jing Li. 1999. *Foreign investment in China.* New York: St. Martin's.

Park, Albert, Dean Yang, Xinsheng Shi, and Yaun Jiang. Forthcoming. Exporting and firm performance: Chinese exporters and the Asian financial crisis. *Review of Economics and Statistics.*

Rauch, James E. 1999. Networks versus markets in international trade. *Journal of International Economics* 48 (1): 7–35.

Rodrik, Dani. 2006. What's so special about China's exports? NBER Working Paper no. 11947. Cambridge, MA: National Bureau of Economic Research.

Rosen, Daniel H. 1999. *Behind the open door: Foreign firms in the Chinese marketplace.* Washington, DC: Institute for International Economics.

Schott, Peter K. Forthcoming. The relative sophistication of Chinese exports. NBER Working Paper no. 12173. *Economic Policy.*

Whalley, John, and Xian Xin. 2006. China's FDI and non-FDI economies and the sustainability of future high Chinese growth. NBER Working Paper no. 12249. Cambridge, MA: National Bureau of Economic Research.

Comment   Raymond Robertson

Like many developing countries in the 1990s, China pursued export-led market liberalization with the intention of fostering development. China seems to stand out in several important dimensions, including the share of exports in manufacturing and the kinds of products that China exports. Several papers have documented that China's exports are more on the "high end" of

Raymond Robertson is professor of economics at Macalester College.

the product spectrum when comparing across industries, but possibly in the "low end" of the product spectrum when comparing within industries. Other papers, including this one by Blonigen and Ma, document the important role that foreign firms are playing in China's remarkable export growth.

In this context, Blonigen and Ma's chapter makes several important contributions. The chapter's focus on Chinese firms' performance relative to foreign firms certainly gets at the heart of a critical question: what are the benefits of China's FDI-driven export-led growth policies for domestic (Chinese) firms? The answer to this question would tell us a great deal about the long-run prospects of China's growth.

This chapter addresses this question with a model of location choice to identify the key factors that would affect the relative performance of Chinese firms: the more difficult it is to transfer technology from foreign to domestic firms, the less Chinese firms will catch up to foreign firms in terms of market share and unit values. Furthermore, government policies to encourage investment should help domestic firms catch up, holding the cost of technology transfer constant.

The model generates several straightforward predictions that are then taken to a relatively new data set of sector- and region-specific exports that are disaggregated into six groups based on firm ownership: state-owned enterprises (SOEs), foreign-invested enterprises (FIEs), contractual and equity joint ventures, collectively owned enterprises (COEs), and privately owned enterprises (POEs). The main emphasis is to compare the performance of the domestic firms to the foreign firms. The performance criteria are the shares of total exports of foreign and domestic firms and the ratio of unit values of foreign and domestic firms. The data cover the 1995 to 2005 period.

As the reader is probably aware, Blonigen and Ma's main result (which seems to be quite robust) is that there is little, if any, evidence of "catch up" of domestic firms. If anything, domestic firms seem to be losing export shares (in most cases) to foreign firms and have experienced falling relative unit values.

This chapter does an excellent job of clearly presenting a useful model and clear empirical results. As with any valuable contribution, there are several implications for future research that seem to follow from this chapter. The lack of evidence of catch-up seems to raise the question about the relative success of the government's policy. Indeed, if the criteria used to motivate the liberalization policies was to enable domestic firms to compete with foreign firms in export markets (in terms of export market share and unit values), the results of this chapter suggest that this policy has not been successful. An alternative hypothesis, however, is that these are actually not the relevant criteria.

Assuming alternative criteria could generate predictions that are consistent with the empirical results. Two possibilities come to mind: establishing and fostering the private sector. One policy that may be relevant for the analysis is privatization. Privatization policies may signal intent to establish a private sector and in the process may affect the relative export shares and unit values of domestic firms. The number of SOEs fell from 114,000 in 1996 to 34,000 in 2003. Half of this decline was due to privatization. The characteristics of firms that were privatized, and when they were privatized, could easily have affected the measures highlighted in this paper. Furthermore, in 2002, the 16th Party Congress opened SOE privatization to foreign investment, which could have had a distinct impact on the share of exports by foreign and domestic firms. Until firm-level data are available, however, these questions remain on the agenda for future research.

More at the heart of the chapter's analysis, however, lies the relationship between technology transfer and catch-up. Productivity spillovers seem to be limited in China and other developing countries. Blonigan and Ma review the literature of technology spillovers for foreign firms in China, which suggests that there is very limited evidence of technology spillovers. They do not review the literature of technology spillovers in other developing countries, but these papers tend to find similar results.[1] Overall, then, it is not surprising that the influx of foreign firms has not led to significant spillovers and catch-up. On the other hand, any positive technology transfer should have generated evidence of catch-up. The results, therefore, do not seem consistent with the model.

The model's underlying assumption (and, therefore, the underlying assumption of the paper) is that foreign firms and domestic firms are both competing in final goods in the export market. Under this assumption, foreign firms and domestic firms are competitors and their products are substitutes. An alternative approach would be to allow for the possibility that domestic and foreign firms are complements. Allowing for an endogenous choice of vertical specialization would allow for this possibility and, I would argue, would better fit the empirical results.

Imagine that prior to entry of foreign firms, domestic firms produce intermediate and final goods, and that final goods have higher unit values than intermediate goods. Prior to entry, domestic firms would be the only exporters (and thus have export shares of 100 percent) and would have relatively high unit values. Furthermore, assume that the entry of foreign firms creates the possibility of vertical specialization. Given the foreign firms' technological superiority, they might have a comparative advantage in final goods, giving domestic firms the comparative advantage in intermediate goods.

Given the comparative advantage of the arriving foreign firms, the relative price of final goods falls for domestic firms when foreign firms enter,

1. For, example, see Rossitza B. Wooster and David S. Diebel, Productivity Spillovers from Foreign Direct Investment in Developing Countries: A Meta-Regression Analysis, http://ssrn.com/abstract=898400 (2006). This paper conducts a meta-analysis of thirty-two studies and finds very weak evidence of productivity spillovers.

inducing a change in their production into intermediate goods. These intermediate goods might be sold to the foreign firms in China or exported as intermediate inputs (say, to Taiwan, Indonesia, or other countries). In other words, the arrival of foreign firms may push domestic firms to a lower stage in a vertically integrated production process, possibly through outsourcing relationships with the arriving foreign firms.

This simplistic vertical integration model has several predictions for unit values and export shares. First, under the assumption that intermediate goods have lower unit values than final goods, the observed unit values of the domestic firms should fall when compared to the foreign firms. Second, because final goods are exported, this model predicts that the foreign firms' market share should be increasing as foreign firms enter the market. Note that this does not mean that the production of the domestic firms is not increasingly exported. The production of the domestic firms is exported as part of the final goods but is not measured separately.

The basic results of the model seem consistent with these predictions: the entrance of foreign firms coincides with rising, not falling, foreign export shares and rising, not falling, relative unit values. If differentiated products are more likely to be characterized by outsourcing, the differentiated results are also consistent with the vertical integration model. In particular, the empirical results suggest rising export shares but falling unit values for domestic firms in differentiated industries. Again, if differentiated products are more likely to be characterized by outsourcing relationships, one might expect that falling prices and rising export shares would be found in differentiated products as domestic firms increased their production and export of intermediate inputs.

If the vertical specialization model has merit, it might suggest that other criteria for judging the "success" of China's FDI-driven export-led growth policy might be relevant. For example, it may take more than ten years for Chinese firms to move up the quality ladder and be able to export final goods that would compete with foreign firms. In the meantime, the success of the Chinese policy might be gauged by changes in employment and production, rather than exports, and wages paid by the Chinese firms. The vertical specialization model predicts that the influx of foreign firms increases the demand for Chinese production, while the competition model predicts the opposite.

This important paper raises the question of whether Chinese firms have been catching up to foreign firms in terms of export shares and unit values. The results suggest that, in general, they have not. Does this imply a lack of success of Chinese policies? The results of this chapter are consistent with the idea that the policies may have been successful along alternative lines, leaving open several possible avenues for future research.

13

Facts and Fallacies
about U.S. FDI in China

Lee Branstetter and C. Fritz Foley

Everything you hear about China is true. But none of it is
accurate.
—Dr. John Frankenstein, Research Associate, Weatherhead
East Asian Institute, Columbia University

In the late 1970s, China began to adopt economic policies that were more
market oriented than policies it had pursued in the past, and this shift has
been very successful in promoting economic growth.[1] Rising levels of industrial output have been accompanied by increases in foreign direct investment
(FDI) inflows, leading many to conclude that FDI has played an important
role in China's success. Since China's official entry to the World Trade Organization (WTO) in 2001, China's economy has continued to expand rapidly,
FDI inflows have continued on a large scale, and China's role in world trade
has continued to increase.

These developments have heightened American public interest in China.
Numerous recent books seek to explain the Chinese economy to the general
reader, and the popular press has expanded its coverage of Chinese economic developments. Despite this growing level of information, however,
significant misconceptions continue to cloud the popular understanding of
the role of foreign firms in China, and, particularly, the role of U.S.-based
multinationals. Some of these misconceptions have even taken root in the

Lee Branstetter is an associate professor of economics and public policy at Carnegie Mellon
University, and a research associate of the National Bureau of Economic Research. C. Fritz
Foley is an associate professor in the finance unit at Harvard Business School, and a faculty
research fellow of the National Bureau of Economic Research.

The authors thank Robert Feenstra, Nicholas Lardy, Shang-Jin Wei, Stephen Yeaple, and
Bill Zeile for helpful comments and suggestions. Some sections of the paper draw upon earlier
work by the authors, especially Branstetter and Lardy (2006, 2008). The statistical analysis of
unpublished data on U.S. multinational companies reported in this study was conducted at the
U.S. Bureau of Economic Analysis under arrangements that maintained legal confidentiality
requirements. Views expressed are those of the authors and do not necessarily reflect those of
the Bureau of Economic Analysis.

1. For extensive descriptions of the history of Chinese policy with respect to FDI, please see
Branstetter and Lardy (2006, 2008), Lardy (2002), and Naughton (1996).

thinking of professional economists who are outside the small community of China specialists.

In the late 1990s, when popular and professional interest in the general phenomenon of expanding FDI was increasing, Robert Feenstra (1999) wrote a useful article called "Facts and Fallacies about Foreign Direct Investment." The article corrected a number of widely misconceptions about the subject. Inspired by his title as well as his approach, we seek to dispel four widely held beliefs about U.S. affiliate activity in China by using the most recent available data.

13.1   Fallacy Number 1: U.S. FDI in China Is Large

The attention paid to China and its economic engagement with the rest of the world has led many to conclude that it is a leading destination of U.S. FDI. Casual observers believe that China's abundance of labor, high growth rates, and huge consumer markets attract large amounts of U.S. FDI. This view is even held by many corporate executives. A 2004 A. T. Kearney study found that China was perceived as the most favored location for FDI. The amount of capital flowing to China from the United States in the form of FDI is thought to be sufficient to have a large effect on Chinese capital formation. However, data collected by Chinese statistical agencies indicate that U.S. FDI is a small component of total FDI in China, and data collected by U.S. agencies show that American firms' investment in China is a small, albeit quickly growing, part of their total investment abroad.[2]

Statistics from the Ministry of Commerce of the People's Republic of China track investment by approved foreign-invested enterprises (FIEs) on an annual basis. Figure 13.1 breaks down this growth in investment by the nationality of the foreign owner or partial owner of the FIE.[3] Prior to 1989, FDI inflows were limited and dominated by Hong Kong and Taiwan-based investors seeking to exploit opportunities in China's special economic zones.

After the international unease generated by the Tiananmen Incident dissipated, there was a sharp increase in FDI inflows and a pronounced diversification in its sources. It was in these years that Western countries and Japan began to enter the Chinese market in earnest. However, despite the

2. We are certainly not the first observers to point this out. As an earlier FDI boom in China was cresting, Wei (2000b) argued that the levels were small given China's size.

3. Because of official restrictions on direct Taiwanese investment in the mainland, some Taiwanese FDI gets routed through Hong Kong or through "tax haven" nations such as the Cayman Islands. Such tax haven jurisdictions are a prominent component of the "other nations" category shown in figure 13.1. Some advanced countries also preferred to invest in China through Hong Kong-based subsidiaries, further exaggerating the apparent role played by Hong Kong. Finally, it is widely speculated that as much as one-quarter of the FDI originating in Hong Kong consists of Chinese entrepreneurs investing through Hong Kong shell companies in order to qualify as FIEs for tax and other benefits.

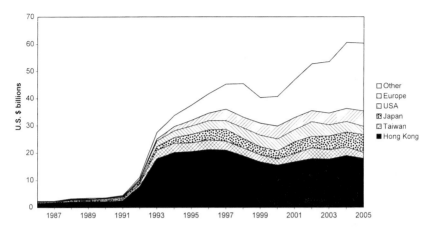

Fig. 13.1   FDI by source country
Source: China Statistical Yearbook, various issues

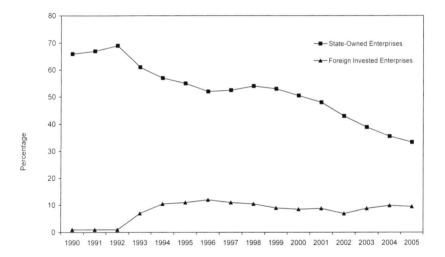

Fig. 13.2   Fixed asset investment by organizational form
Source: Data on the fraction of fixed asset investment undertaken by state-owned enterprises and foreign-invested enterprises are taken from the *China Statistical Yearbook,* various issues.

growth, the role of American firms in these inflows has been and remains relatively modest.

It is worth noting that even overall levels of FIE investment are modest. As indicated in figure 13.2, the share of fixed asset investment performed by FIEs grew from near 0 percent to over 10 percent in the mid-1990s, then fell slightly to the high single digits where it remains in the mid-2000s. Foreign-invested enterprises accounted for less than 5 percent of urban employment in China in the middle of the current decade.

Consideration of these facts provide an interesting perspective on the work of Dooley, Folkerts-Landau, and Garber (2003, 2004a,b). These papers argue that Asian developing countries, including China, suffer from severe deficiencies in their financial systems that undermine the efficient allocation of domestic savings. As a consequence, these countries export capital to the United States, and this capital is then reinvested in Asian developing countries, including China, through multinational firms in the form of FDI. This type of investment is allocated in a relatively efficient manner, and it generates industrial expansion in export-related sectors and absorption of excess labor. Ju and Wei (2007) present a model that illustrates how financial market imperfections in a developing country could generate capital exports to countries with better-developed financial markets and substantial inflows of FDI from those countries, even when there is free trade in goods that gives rise to a current account surplus.

However, the facts suggest that FDI in China does not exactly play the role assigned to it in this stream of research. Foreign-invested enterprises account for relatively little investment or employment generation in contemporary China, and American investment is but a minor component of that small contribution. As described in the following section, American FDI is focused on the domestic market rather than exports back to the United States, and U.S. affiliates tap Chinese sources of funds to finance their activities. The largest share of FDI inflows appear to come from other Asian countries whose own financial systems exhibit varying levels of development.

Just as American firms collectively account for a relatively small component of FDI in China, American investment in China accounts for a relatively small portion of total U.S. multinational activity around the world. Table 13.1 shows 2004 total assets, sales, and employment of U.S. affiliates in China and in four regions that are the major destinations of U.S. FDI. China's share of U.S. multinational enterprise (MNE) total affiliate sales and assets were 1.9 percent and 0.7 percent, respectively, in 2004. Although the compound annual growth rate of U.S. MNE sales in China over the 1982 to 2004 period exceeds 40 percent, this rapid growth has proceeded from a small base, and it has taken place in a context of growing multinational activity worldwide.[4] Chinese affiliates comprise 4.5 percent of U.S. total affiliate employment, which is a larger share than their share of assets and sales, suggesting that work performed in China is relatively labor-intensive.[5]

---

4. The reported profits of U.S. affiliates in China have also grown rapidly, especially in recent years. Between the 1999 and 2004 benchmark surveys, net income grew nearly sevenfold. However, net income from Chinese affiliates only accounts for about 2 percent of the global net income of U.S. affiliates worldwide.

5. These employment figures need to be placed in some context. The total Chinese urban workforce in 2005 was 273 million persons. Foreign-invested enterprises from all source countries collectively employed about 12.4 million persons, less than 5 percent of the total. Clearly, U.S. firms' contribution to employment in China is vanishingly small.

Table 13.1   **Measures of U.S. multinational affiliate activity in 2004**

	No. of affiliates	Sales	Assets	Employment
China	688	71,721	63,783	455
Europe	12,367	1,909,697	5,376,372	4,291
Canada	1,839	442,607	634,677	1,092
Latin America and other				
Western Hemisphere	3,693	417,185	1,208,716	1,936
Asia and Pacific	5,093	886,596	1,362,061	2,396
Total affiliate activity	23,928	3,768,733	8,757,063	10,028

Notes: These data are drawn from preliminary published results of BEA's 2004 Benchmark Survey of U.S. Direct Investment Abroad. They cover all nonbank affiliates of nonbank U.S. parents. Sales and assets are in millions of U.S. dollars; employment is in thousands.

As the data in table 13.1 illustrates, most U.S. MNE activity takes place in other developed countries like Canada and countries in Europe.

Although the data from both Chinese and U.S. sources indicate levels of FDI that are smaller than the popular press suggests, there are significant discrepancies between data from these sources. The most comparable data sets attempt to provide measures of FDI flows as opposed to measures of MNE operating activity. Table 13.2 presents estimates of U.S. FDI outflows to China produced by the Bureau of Economic Analysis (BEA) and Chinese Ministry of Commerce estimates of U.S. FDI inflows into China from the United States over the 1994 to 2005 period. In each year, Chinese Ministry of Commerce estimates exceed the BEA estimates, often by a factor of more than 2.

A number of measurement issues could be important in explaining this discrepancy. First, the Ministry of Commerce reports measures of "actually utilized investment" by FIEs, and these measures may include investment that is financed by capital flows from the foreign parent as well as investment that is financed through local sources, including borrowing from local banks.[6] Foreign-invested enterprises are surveyed regarding their investments. If the surveys do not precisely capture differences between investment financed by retained earnings, capital transfers from the parent, investment funds provided by a local partner, and investment financed by local borrowing, this could result in official Chinese FDI flow measures that are larger than the corresponding U.S. measures. When individual investment projects rely on investment from multiple sources, correct attribution could be difficult, generating such measurement problems. While we cannot point to firm evidence quantifying the existence of this particular source of measurement

---

6. We are extremely grateful to Nicholas Lardy for a series of detailed discussions that clarified our understanding of Chinese statistics on FDI, including the degree to which it may reflect investment financed by local borrowing.

Table 13.2		U.S. and Chinese estimates of foreign direct investment (FDI) flows from the United States to China

	U.S. data	Chinese data
1994	1,232	2,491
1995	261	3,084
1996	933	3,444
1997	1,250	3,461
1998	1,497	3,989
1999	1,947	4,216
2000	1,817	4,384
2001	1,912	4,433
2002	875	5,424
2003	1,273	4,199
2004	3,670	3,941
2005	1,613	3,061

Notes: This table presents data on aggregate annual FDI flows from the United States to China. The U.S. data are taken from U.S. Bureau of Economic Analysis publications. These data are compared with the data reported by the Chinese Ministry of Commerce on investment by foreign firms with U.S. parents for the same years; the Chinese data are taken from various years of the *China Statistical Yearbook.* Both series are reported in millions of U.S. current dollars at prevailing exchange rates.

error, U.S. data on the financing patterns of U.S. affiliates in China suggests that it could play a role.

Table 13.3 provides some indication of how important local sources of capital are for foreign firms in China. In 2004, only 70 percent of U.S. affiliates based in China were wholly owned. Joint ventures often involve a local partner who provides equity capital as well as other inputs, and these types of organizational forms are more prevalent in China than in the other regions displayed in the table. Slightly more than one half of the assets of U.S. affiliates based in China are financed with debt, and 61 percent of this debt is provided by local sources. The widely documented shortcomings of Chinese financial markets make it surprising that Chinese lenders would figure so prominently.[7] However, given the hazards attending other classes of borrowers, the local subsidiaries of foreign multinationals can be seen as relatively creditworthy borrowers, ultimately backed by deep-pocketed foreign parents, and in possession of brand name and technological advantages over potential domestic competitors. Loans from the parent are 19 percent of total debt. While this share exceeds shares of intrafirm debt elsewhere around the world, it is still fairly small.[8] If funds obtained locally are counted

---

7. Scholarship critical of the efficiency of Chinese financial institutions includes Lardy (1998), Tsai (2002), and Branstetter (2007), among many other sources.

8. Desai, Foley, and Hines (2004a) document that multinationals tend to make extensive use of parent provided capital in countries with poor financial development, and Antràs, Desai, and Foley (2007) provide a theoretical explanation for why this would be the case. This regularity does not seem to be prevalent in China.

Table 13.3   External finance of affiliates in 2004

	Share of affiliates that are wholly owned (%)	Total external finance	Owners equity excluding retained earnings and translation adjustments	Total current liabilities and long-term debt	Share of total current liabilities and long-term debt owed to parents (%)	Share of total current liabilities and long-term debt owed to local persons (%)	Share of total current liabilities and long-term debt owed to other persons (%)
China	70	42,634	17,026	25,609	19	61	20
Europe	89	4,036,186	1,469,373	2,566,813	14	46	40
Canada	90	425,659	136,922	288,737	14	74	12
Latin America and other Western Hemisphere	81	816,610	413,788	402,822	17	40	43
Asia and Pacific	78	746,650	227,323	519,328	12	61	28
Total affiliate activity	85	6,113,840	2,285,402	3,828,438	14	49	36

Notes: These data are drawn from preliminary published results of BEA's 2004 Benchmark Survey of U.S. Direct Investment Abroad. The data on the use of whole ownership covers all nonbank affiliates of nonbank affiliates of U.S. parents, and the data on patterns in external financing only cover majority-owned nonbank affiliates of nonbank U.S. parents. Total external finance, total current liabilities and long-term debt, and owners equity excluding retained earnings and translation adjustments are measured in millions of U.S. dollars.

when computing FDI flows from the United States to China in the Chinese data but not the U.S. data, the official Chinese statistics can be viewed as overstating the contribution of U.S. firms to Chinese investment.

A second factor that might contribute to the discrepancy concerns how source countries are determined in FDI flow data. In the U.S. data, any capital flow from the parent company to an affiliate in China through a holding company located in a third country is captured as a outflow from the United States to the third country, not from the United States to China. The exact procedures followed by Chinese statistical authorities are not clear, and it is possible that data collectors use information about the ultimate nationality of foreign investors to classify some of the FDI routed through tax haven holding companies according to the nationality of the ultimate parent. The fact that Chinese official statistics continue to measure large inflows from tax haven jurisdictions suggests that this is unlikely to explain much of the discrepancy, but it could conceivably explain some.

Differences in measured FDI inflows could also be a consequence of other deviations between Chinese and international statistical practice. The view that much of the discrepancy lies in differences in statistical practice was strengthened recently by massive revisions of the Chinese government's own official estimates of the net inward FDI stock. Beginning in 2005, the Ministry of Commerce released revised estimates of China's net FDI stock that reduced its size by a half. Previous estimates of the stock had been based on accumulated inflows, and these data may not have captured reductions in FDI capital provided by foreigners. The new, revised FDI stock measures are not broken down by source country, but the magnitude of this revision amounts to an admission that the previously reported figures were far too high and suggests that the true level of FDI may lie closer to that indicated by U.S. data.[9] Given this, and the extent to which, even in the Chinese data, U.S. FDI is a relatively small component of cumulated total inflows, we are quite confident in our conclusions regarding the relative size of U.S. FDI in China.

In order to explore why U.S. FDI in China appears to be small, we run gravity specifications to explain levels of U.S. MNE activity by country.[10] In these tests, we use confidential data from BEA's 2004 Benchmark Survey of U.S. Direct Investment Abroad on the operations of majority-owned nonbank affiliates of nonbank U.S. parents, which we aggregate to the country level.[11] We employ three different measures of U.S. MNE activity as dependant variables, the log of affiliate sales, the log of affiliate assets, and the log

9. The United Nations Conference on Trade and Development (UNCTAD) issued a briefing pointing out this and other issues regarding Chinese FDI data and the challenges involved in comparing Chinese FDI statistics with those of other sources. See UNCTAD (2007).

10. We thank Shang-Jin Wei and Robert Feenstra for suggesting that we explore this question.

11. For a detailed explanation of these data, see Mataloni (1995).

of affiliate employment compensation. Our baseline specification controls for geographic distance from the United States and the log of gross domestic product (GDP; measured at market exchange rates). It also includes a China dummy that is equal to 1 for China and zero for other countries. If the coefficient on the China dummy is negative, this would indicate that measures of U.S. MNE activity in China are lower in China than a simple gravity specification would suggest they should be.

Once we have estimates from this baseline specification, we include other country characteristics that could explain the extent to which U.S. MNEs engage in activity in China. Given the potential importance of taxes and corruption noted by Desai, Foley, and Hines (2004b) and Wei (2000a), we include a measure of each country's corporate income tax rate and the corruption index taken from the International Country Risk Guide (ICRG) political risk data set. In order to control for factors related to levels of wealth and economic development more generally, we also include the log of GDP per capita (measured at market exchange rates). Descriptive statistics for the data used in the analysis presented in table 13.5, as well as the analysis presented in table 13.7, appear in table 13.4.

The results of the gravity specifications appear in table 13.5. The dependent variable used in columns (1) to (4) is the log of affiliate sales, in (5) to (8) is the log of affiliate assets, and in (9) to (12) is the log of affiliate employment compensation.[12] Our baseline specifications appear in columns (1), (5), and (9). In each of these, the coefficient on the log of distance is negative and significant, and the coefficient on the log of GDP is positive and significant. These findings are consistent with previous work and indicate that U.S. MNEs engage in more activity in larger countries that are closer to the United States.

In each of the baseline specifications, the coefficient on the China dummy is negative and significant. In interpreting these results, it is important to keep in mind that China is a large country that is located a considerable distance from the United States. The log of GDP for China is about 2 standard deviations above the mean value in the sample, and the log of distance from the United States is about 1 standard deviation above the mean. Therefore, China's size implies that it should attract a significant amount of foreign investment, and its location tempers this implication. The estimated China dummy coefficients point out that levels of U.S. MNE activity in China are lower than would be predicted by a simple model in which levels of MNE activity vary with distance and country size.

The specifications in columns (2), (6), and (10) of table 13.5 include measures of corporate tax rates. This variable is not significant in these specifications, and its inclusion does not change the negative coefficient on the

---

12. We analyze employment compensation instead of employment because differences in labor productivity make it difficult to compare levels of employment across countries.

Table 13.4   Descriptive statistics

	Mean	Median	Standard deviation
Log of affiliate sales	14.8417	14.7465	2.5201
Log of affiliate assets	15.2026	15.2270	2.7386
Log of affiliate employment compensation	12.1616	12.1126	2.7121
Log of affiliate sales outside host country	12.4630	13.4019	4.7275
Share of sales to countries other than host country and the U.S.	0.2719	0.2105	0.2390
Share of sales to the U.S.	0.0785	0.0290	0.1250
Log of distance	8.4632	8.4972	0.5089
Log of GDP	24.3406	23.8887	1.8934
Country tax rate	0.2143	0.2354	0.1319
Corruption index	2.5636	2.4792	1.1395
Log of GDP per capita	8.0364	8.0819	1.5652

Notes: This table presents descriptive statistics for variables used in the analysis of 2004 U.S. multinational affiliate activity aggregated to the country level. Sales, assets, and employment compensation are measured in thousands of U.S. dollars. The log of distance is the log of distance between U.S. and affiliate host-country capital cities measured in miles. The log of GDP and the log of GDP per capita measure host-country gross domestic product and gross domestic product per capita, respectively, and these variables are drawn from the World Bank's *World Development Indicators.* The country tax rate is a measure of the median effective corporate tax rate paid by U.S. multinationals in a host country. The corruption index is an index of corruption that ranges from 0 to 6, with lower numbers indicating higher levels of corruption, and it is taken from the International Country Risk Guide political risk data.

China dummy very much. Controlling for corruption, as in columns (3), (7), and (11), reduces the magnitude and significance of the China dummy. This dummy becomes insignificant although still negative in column (3) and marginally significant in column (11), while the coefficient on the corruption index is positive and significant. China has a corruption index of 2 on a scale of 0 to 6, where higher numbers imply lower levels of corruption. These results suggest that China's low level of U.S. MNE activity is at least in part a consequence of corruption or a factor that is correlated with corruption.[13] The specifications presented in columns (4), (8), and (12) also include the log of GDP per capita. Once this variable is included, the coefficient on the China dummy is no longer significant. These results indicate that U.S. MNE activity is actually not lower than one would expect if one accounts for the fact that per capita income is low in China and corruption is high.

While caution is surely warranted in using regression coefficients derived from cross-sectional evidence to make predictions about the evolution of economic variables over time, it is interesting to consider what our regression coefficients imply about the future of U.S. FDI in China. Given its rapid rate of current economic growth, it is likely that per capita income

13. This finding confirms earlier work by Wei (2000a) pointing to the negative impact of Chinese corruption on FDI inflows.

Table 13.5   Levels of affiliate activity

	Log of affiliate sales				Log of affiliate assets				Log of affiliate employment compensation			
	(1)	(2)	(3)	(4)	(5)	(6)	(7)	(8)	(9)	(10)	(11)	(12)
Constant	-5.2715	-5.3051	-5.1289	-5.2290	-6.6216	-6.4111	-6.1649	-6.3221	-8.8940	-8.8730	-8.5979	-8.7062
	(2.5952)	(2.6137)	(2.5348)	(2.5886)	(2.7525)	(2.7103)	(2.5884)	(2.6119)	(2.8202)	(2.8286)	(2.6407)	(2.7182)
China dummy	-0.7304	-0.6996	-0.3181	0.1592	-1.4867	-1.6798	-1.1471	-0.3979	-1.2344	-1.2537	-0.6584	-0.1420
	(0.3040)	(0.3645)	(0.4006)	(0.5909)	(0.3132)	(0.3640)	(0.3537)	(0.5044)	(0.3161)	(0.3659)	(0.3706)	(0.5350)
Log of distance	-0.8477	-0.8471	-0.7660	-0.7026	-0.8491	-0.8530	-0.7398	-0.6402	-1.0653	-1.0657	-0.9392	-0.8706
	(0.1919)	(0.1924)	(0.1870)	(0.1722)	(0.2230)	(0.2226)	(0.2200)	(0.1961)	(0.2126)	(0.2129)	(0.2053)	(0.1919)
Log of GDP	1.1213	1.1206	1.0558	0.9757	1.1924	1.1970	1.1066	0.9807	1.2359	1.2364	1.1353	1.0485
	(0.0717)	(0.0723)	(0.0792)	(0.0921)	(0.0818)	(0.0792)	(0.0834)	(0.0902)	(0.0798)	(0.0798)	(0.0809)	(0.0851)
Country tax rate		0.2148	0.2722	0.9495		-1.3462	-1.2660	-0.2028		-0.1345	-0.0449	0.6879
		(1.0890)	(1.0641)	(1.4285)		(1.2924)	(1.2308)	(1.4796)		(1.1550)	(1.0928)	(1.4394)
Corruption index			0.2725	0.1294			0.3806	0.1560			0.4253	0.2705
			(0.1118)	(0.1416)			(0.1351)	(0.1714)			(0.1025)	(0.1486)
Log of GDP per capita				0.2155				0.3382				0.2331
				(0.1690)				(0.1719)				(0.1692)
No. of observations	116	116	116	116	116	116	116	116	116	116	116	116
R^2	0.7260	0.7261	0.7387	0.7445	0.6871	0.6913	0.7121	0.7243	0.7665	0.7666	0.7931	0.7990

Notes: This table presents results of specifications explaining measures of 2004 affiliate activity aggregated to the country level. The dependant variable in the specifications presented in columns (1)–(4) is the Log of affiliate sales, and it is the Log of affiliate assets and the Log of affiliate employment compensation in the specifications presented in columns (5)–(8) and (9)–(12), respectively. Sales, assets, and employment compensation are measured in thousands of U.S. dollars. The China dummy is equal to one for China and zero for other countries. The Log of distance is the log of distance between United States and affiliate host-country capital cities measured in miles. The Log of GDP and the Log of GDP per capita measure host-country gross domestic product and gross domestic product per capita, respectively, and these variables are drawn from the World Bank's *World Development Indicators.* The Country tax rate is a measure of the median effective corporate tax rate paid by U.S. multinationals in a host country. The Corruption index is an index of corruption that ranges from 0 to 6, with lower numbers indicating higher levels of corruption, and it is taken from the International Country Risk Guide political risk data. Heteroskedasticity-consistent standard errors are presented in parentheses.

and aggregate GDP in China will rise sharply over the next ten years. If the overall Chinese economy were to maintain growth rates of 10 percent per year over the next decade, the combined effects of the estimated coefficients on GDP and GDP per capita would predict that U.S. affiliate sales in China would more than triple.[14]

13.2   Fallacy Number 2: U.S. FDI in China Is Export-Oriented

As the U.S.-China trade deficit has grown in recent years, a number of commentators have suggested that it has been driven by U.S. purchases of goods produced by U.S. affiliates in China.[15] For example, in a 2000 briefing paper for the Economic Policy Institute, James Burke wrote, "The activities of U.S. multinational firms, together with China's protectionist trade policies, have had a significant role in increasing the U.S. trade deficit with China."[16]

Foreign firms in China have indeed played an increasingly dominant role in China's trade. Figure 13.3 shows the role of foreign firms in Chinese imports and exports, respectively. In a period in which Chinese exports and imports have been growing rapidly, these shares have been rising. By 2000, the share of FIEs in Chinese exports had reached more than 50 percent, and it continued to expand. Clearly, FIEs have accounted for a disproportionately large share of export growth during the years in which China has come to loom so large in world trade.

What role do U.S. affiliates play in this incredible surge of export growth? Almost none. Table 13.6 presents statistics on the extent to which U.S. affiliates in China sell their goods to customers located in the United States and the extent to which they trade with the United States. The data illustrate that in 2004, about $39.7 billion of local affiliate sales were directed to the local market, and only $3.7 billion were directed to the U.S. market. The growth in exports from Chinese affiliates to the United States and to third countries has been explosive, but their scale remains small. In 2004, U.S. exports to affiliates in China and U.S. imports from affiliates in China comprised less than 5 percent of affiliate sales. These facts are not consistent with the hypothesis that U.S. affiliates operating in China are contributing to the large U.S. trade deficit by producing there and selling back to the

---

14. The work of Dooley, Folkerts-Landau, and Garber (2003, 2004a,b) and Ju and Wei (2007) assigns an important role to Chinese financial imperfections in generating capital outflows and FDI inflows. While severe imperfections remain in Chinese financial markets, many indicators show marked signs of improvement over the past decade. This has not been associated with a decline in measured FDI inflows—in fact, FDI inflows have expanded substantially in absolute terms, possibly suggesting the dominating effects of gravity factors rather than financial imperfection.

15. Earlier versions of the Dooley, Folkerts-Landau, and Garber (2003) hypothesis assigned an important role to U.S. investment in affiliates' export production.

16. See Burke (2000).

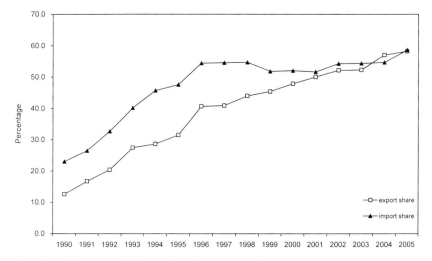

Fig. 13.3   The role of FIEs in China's exports and imports

Source: Data measure the share of export value and import value accounted by foreign-invested enterprises. Data are taken from the *China Statistical Yearbook,* various issues

United States. Intrafirm trade by U.S. multinationals does not loom nearly as large in intermediating U.S.-China trade as the overall role of FIEs in Chinese trade might suggest. In fact, a comparison of the total exports to and imports from China ascribed to U.S. multinationals seems rather small in comparison to the magnitudes of bilateral trade flows in 2004. Total U.S. imports from China were $196.7 billion, and total U.S. exports were $34.7 billion.[17] U.S. imports and exports between U.S. affiliates in China and their U.S. parents were $2.6 billion and $2.5 billion, respectively.

What is true of U.S. multinationals seems broadly true of multinationals from other Western countries. Every year, the Chinese Ministry of Commerce publishes a list of the top 200 largest mainland Chinese firms by export value. The 200 firms included in the 2005 list accounted for one-third of total mainland exports in that year, providing a useful, if incomplete, sample of important exporting firms of all nationalities. Inspection of this list suggests that the total share of U.S., European, and Japanese multinationals in the exports of the top 200 is only 11 percent.[18] The majority of firms in this list are indeed foreign invested, but the foreigners hail from Taiwan, Hong Kong, and South Korea. Like American firms, the leading European multinationals in China appear to be focused primarily on the

17. These figures were obtained from the U.S. Census Bureau Web site at http://www.census .gov/foreign-trade/balance/c5700.html#2004. In 1999, U.S. exports to China totaled about $13 billion, and imports from China were almost $82 billion.

18. See Anderson (2006), from whom the statistics in this paragraph and the next are taken. The language here closely follows his.

Table 13.6   Affiliate sales, by destination and trade activity

	1989	1994	1999	2004
U.S. multinational affiliate sales				
Sales to the United States	1	219	2,703	3,694
Local sales	242	2,520	14,306	39,719
Sales to other foreign countries	13	486	3,371	11,293
U.S. exports of goods to affiliates				
Total	39	371	3,103	2,974
Shipped by U.S. parents	35	288	2,529	2,541
Shipped by unaffiliated U.S. persons	4	83	574	433
U.S. imports of goods shipped by affiliates				
Total	1	448	2,640	3,188
Shipped to U.S. parents	1	403	1,778	2,640
Shipped to unaffiliated U.S. persons	n.a.	45	862	548

Notes: These data are drawn from published results of BEA's benchmark surveys of U.S. direct investment abroad for 1989, 1994, 1999, and 2004. The data only cover majority-owned nonbank Chinese affiliates of nonbank U.S. parents. Sales, exports, and imports are measured in millions of U.S. dollars. n.a. indicates that the value is not available.

domestic market, not exports. The Chinese export miracle largely reflects the activity of the foreign affiliates of firms based in Asia's other newly industrialized countries.

The role played by Japanese firms in Chinese exports appears to lie somewhere in between the roles played by Western firms and firms headquartered in developing countries in Asia. Ahn, Fukao, and Ito (2007) have used Japanese data and South Korean data to undertake an extensive study of the role played by these firms' affiliates in regional trade flows. Because many Japanese firms route their exports through Hong Kong, these authors aggregate Chinese and Hong Kong trade statistics. They find that the exports of Japanese firms' Chinese affiliates collectively account for nearly 41 percent of total Chinese/Hong Kong exports to Japan. Likewise, about 30 percent of total Japanese exports to China go to the Chinese affiliates of Japanese firms. The relatively greater role of Japanese affiliates in mediating Japan-China trade is likely to be related to geographic proximity and history. China is the closest major economy to Japan, and many Japanese companies were quite active in parts of China prior to the end of World War II.

The limited role played by U.S. firms in mediating U.S.-China trade is surprising given the extent to which large U.S. retail chains distribute Chinese goods. According to some estimates, Wal-Mart accounts for almost $20 billion of Chinese exports to the United States. However, Wal-Mart and other large-scale U.S. retailers typically procure their goods from China-based export-oriented manufacturing plants that are not U.S.-owned to any significant degree.[19] They tend to purchase from the same Taiwanese, Hong

19. See Anderson (2006).

Kong, and Korean firms they sourced from a decade or two ago, except that the final production is now based in mainland China.

In order to explore in more detail if U.S. affiliates based in China are more focused on serving the local market than one should expect, we again make use of gravity specifications. In table 13.7, we report results of tests that are identical to those presented in table 13.5 except that dependant variables measure the extent to which U.S. affiliates based in different countries focus on serving markets outside of their host country. These tests use data aggregated to the country level for the year 2004.

The dependent variable used in columns (1) to (4) of table 13.7 is the log of affiliate sales to persons outside the affiliate's host country; in (5) to (8) it is the share of affiliate sales to persons outside the host country and the United States, and in (9) to (12) it is the share of affiliate sales to persons in the United States. Our baseline specifications are given in columns (1), (5), and (9), and these include the log of distance from the United States, host-country GDP, and a China dummy as controls. The coefficient on the China dummy in column (1) is negative and marginally significant; it is negative and significant in column (5), but it is positive and insignificant in column (9). The negative coefficients on the China dummy in specifications explaining the log of affiliate sales outside the host country and the share of sales to countries other than the host country and the United States could be misleading if third-country markets were inconvenient to serve from China. However, Japan, South Korea, and Taiwan are all large markets that are reasonably close by. Taken together, there is only some evidence that U.S. affiliates in China are less focused on serving consumers outside their host country than are U.S. affiliates elsewhere. In fact, the share of sales to persons in the United States is not lower than one would expect once country size and distance from the United States are taken into account.

Levels of sales to countries other than the host country are higher for affiliates located closer to the United States and for affiliates in larger countries. Shares of sales to persons in the United States are higher for affiliates located closer to the United States, but distance from the United States does not, perhaps unsurprisingly, affect the share of sales to persons in countries other than host countries and the United States. The log of GDP is also not significant in explaining shares of sales to the United States or countries other than the host country and the United States.

Adding corporate tax rates to our specifications reduces the coefficients on the China dummy. The negative coefficients on this dummy presented in columns (2) and (6) of table 13.7 are both statistically significant. The negative coefficients on host-country tax rates imply that sales to persons outside the host country are higher in low tax countries. Tax rates faced by multinationals are relatively low in China. Therefore, accounting for corporate tax rates would lead one to predict that affiliates based in China should be more focused on serving markets outside of China. When we add the corruption index to the specifications, the coefficients on this variable are positive and

Table 13.7   **Affiliates sales, by location**

	Log of affiliate sales outside host country				Share of sales to countries other than host country and the United States				Share of sales to the United States			
	(1)	(2)	(3)	(4)	(5)	(6)	(7)	(8)	(9)	(10)	(11)	(12)
Constant	-13.6344	-12.9538	-12.5654	-12.8197	-0.0849	-0.0289	0.0008	-0.0267	0.6123	0.6360	0.6305	0.6289
	(7.6975)	(7.1763)	(6.9449)	(6.9341)	(0.3983)	(0.3913)	(0.3800)	(0.3683)	(0.3165)	(0.3100)	(0.3128)	(0.3137)
China dummy	-1.2602	-1.8846	-1.0439	0.1684	-0.0826	-0.1340	-0.0698	0.0611	0.0304	0.0087	-0.0030	0.0046
	(0.7222)	(0.9812)	(1.0882)	(1.3090)	(0.0419)	(0.0515)	(0.0619)	(0.0885)	(0.0299)	(0.0262)	(0.0300)	(0.0457)
Log of distance	-1.3042	-1.3168	-1.1381	-0.9769	0.0567	0.0557	0.0693	0.0867	-0.0485	-0.0490	-0.0515	-0.0505
	(0.6683)	(0.6549)	(0.6483)	(0.6390)	(0.0338)	(0.0346)	(0.0326)	(0.0320)	(0.0213)	(0.0212)	(0.0217)	(0.0215)
Log of GDP	1.5261	1.5410	1.3983	1.1947	-0.0050	-0.0038	-0.0147	-0.0367	-0.0051	-0.0045	-0.0025	-0.0038
	(0.2061)	(0.2017)	(0.2124)	(0.2380)	(0.0111)	(0.0106)	(0.0121)	(0.0172)	(0.0080)	(0.0074)	(0.0080)	(0.0096)
Country tax rate		-4.3521	-4.2255	-2.5052		-0.3585	-0.3489	-0.1631		-0.1511	-0.1529	-0.1421
		(3.2355)	(3.3056)	(3.3893)		(0.1911)	(0.1871)	(0.1986)		(0.1114)	(0.1113)	(0.1302)
Corruption index			0.6006	0.2372			0.0459	0.0067			-0.0084	-0.0107
			(0.2663)	(0.4416)			(0.0229)	(0.0253)			(0.0076)	(0.0140)
Log of GDP per capita				0.5473				0.0591				0.0034
				(0.4405)				(0.0269)				(0.0156)
No. of observations	116	116	116	116	116	116	116	116	116	116	116	116
R^2	0.3852	0.3997	0.4172	0.4278	0.0169	0.0557	0.0954	0.1441	0.0448	0.0699	0.0748	0.0754

Notes: This table presents results of specifications explaining measures of 2004 affiliate sales aggregated to the country level. The dependant variable in the specifications presented in columns (1)–(4) is the log of affiliate sales outside of the host country, and it is the share of affiliate sales to countries other than the host country and the United States in columns (5)–(8) and (9)–(12). Sales are measured in thousands of U.S. dollars. The China dummy is equal to one for China and zero for other countries. The Log of distance is the log of the distance between U.S. and affiliate host-country capital cities measured in miles. The Log of GDP and the Log of GDP per capita measure host-country gross domestic product and gross domestic product per capita, respectively, and these variables are drawn from the World Bank's *World Development Indicators*. The Country tax rate is a measure of the median effective corporate tax rate paid by U.S. multinationals in a host country. The Corruption index is an index of corruption that ranges from 0 to 6, with lower numbers indicating higher levels of corruption, and it is taken from the International Country Risk Guide political risk data. Heteroskedasticity-consistent standard errors are presented in parentheses.

significant in columns (3) and (7), indicating that affiliates in countries with less corruption sell more output outside the host country. Once this variable is included, none of the coefficients on the China dummy are significant. The specifications presented in columns (4), (8), and (12) also include a control for the log of GDP per capita. In each of these specifications, the coefficient on the China dummy is positive, although these coefficients are not significant. These results suggest that once one accounts for levels of corruption and country wealth, as well as tax rates, distance, and country size, U.S. affiliates in China are not less export oriented than affiliates based in other countries.

13.3   Fallacy Number 3: U.S. Multinational Investment in China Displaces Investment Elsewhere

U.S. workers often express concerns about increased competition from workers located in countries like China. Given the vast supply of labor in China, the low costs of production, and the alleged existence of technologically skilled workers, few employees outside of China feel secure. In the extreme, these concerns would predict that increased activity in China by U.S. multinationals would displace activities that had been performed elsewhere.

The results of the previous sections suggest these concerns may be misplaced. As we have already demonstrated, levels of U.S. affiliate activity in China are modest. Furthermore, these affiliates have been and remain focused on the Chinese market. Given this, one would not expect increased activity in China to displace activity in other countries to a significant degree. However, we can approach this question much more directly. Using the BEA data, it is possible to see if multinationals that expand employment in China cut it at home or among their other affiliates. The data presented in table 13.8 address this issue by providing number counts of incidents in which firms that increase or decrease employment in China increase or decrease employment in other locations. The data include observations computed using firm-level data from the 1989, 1994, 1999, and 2004 benchmark survey results, so there are three periods over which increases and decreases are considered, the 1989 to 1994, 1994 to 1999, and 1999 to 2004 periods. Entries into China by existing multinationals are counted as increases in employment in China, and exits from China are counted as decreases.

The data in the top panel reflect the growth in employment that has taken place among Chinese affiliates of U.S. multinationals. It also points out that firms that expand in China are almost as likely to expand employment domestically as they are to cut it. This evidence is not what one would expect if growth in China were strictly displacing activity in the United States. The bottom panel displays similar data, but instead of considering the trade-off between activity in China and activity in the United States, it considers the trade-off between activity in China and activity among other affiliates. It

Table 13.8   **Changes in affiliate employment in China and changes in firm employment elsewhere**

		Change in domestic employment		Change in employment among other affiliates	
		Increase	Decrease	Increase	Decrease
Change in employment in China	Increase	203	213	316	155
	Decrease	27	74	42	84

Notes: This table present number counts of the incidents in which changes in a firm's employment in China are associated with changes in the firm's employment in the United States and among its other affiliates. Changes are measured over three distinct time periods, 1989–1994, 1994–1999, and 1999–2004.

appears that firms that are increasing employment in China are increasing, and not decreasing, it elsewhere. Although somewhat crude, these statistics suggest that at least extreme notions that would give rise to concerns of multinational employees in the United States and elsewhere in the world are unfounded.

13.4   Fallacy Number 4: U.S. Multinationals Are Aggressively Exploiting China's Growing Technological Prowess

In the United States, China is often perceived as being an emerging technological superpower. Industrialists, economists, and policymakers believe that China is becoming an attractive location to perform innovative activity. In 2003, Intel chief executive officer (CEO) Craig Barrett identified China's rising technological strength as constituting a competitive threat to U.S.-based high-technology industries.[20] Harvard economist Richard Freeman (2006) has outlined the potential consequences of the globalization of the science and engineering workforce for America's historical pattern of comparative advantage in high-technology industries. Freeman points to the striking rise in the number of multinational research and development (R&D) centers in China—more than 700 by the end of 2004—and argues that this is only the harbinger of greater reallocation yet to come.[21] Puga and Trefler (2005) point to the rise of R&D activity in China and declare that the economics profession should "wake up and smell the ginseng!" In its 2005 annual survey of global FDI trends, the *World Investment Report* produced by UNCTAD highlighted the internationalization of R&D and singled out

20. This speech by Barrett was widely noted at the time. See http://money.cnn.com/2003/10/03/technology/barrett/index.htm.
21. See also the discussion of this trend in the 2005 *World Investment Report* published by UNCTAD.

the growth of foreign R&D centers in China as a development of particular significance. Management scholar Minyuan Zhao (2004) has studied the patents generated by these centers for clues as to how American multinationals have apparently learned to engage in large-scale, sophisticated R&D in a national context with notoriously weak intellectual property rights.

Proponents of the view that China is quickly emerging as a favorable location for high-tech activity often point to evidence on the growing sophistication of China's exports as proof of their claims. Schott (2008), for example, finds that over time Chinese exports exhibit rising sophistication relative to countries with similar aggregate endowments.[22] Rodrik (2006) finds an unusually high degree of technological sophistication in China's export pattern. Cui and Syed (2007) suggest that recent changes in China's trade patterns indicate that it is rapidly becoming a surprisingly mature economy. Preeg (2004), a researcher with the Manufacturers Alliance, charges that China's emergence as a major supplier of information technology, communication, and electronic products poses a major challenge to U.S. commercial and security interests.

Several considerations suggest these views are overblown. First, the extent of innovative activity performed in China by U.S. multinationals is surprisingly modest. Table 13.9 provides 2004 data on expenditures for R&D performed by U.S. affiliates in China, U.S. affiliates based in other regions, and the U.S.-based parent operations of U.S. MNEs. Only $622 million was spent by U.S. MNEs on R&D in China, an amount that is about three-tenths of 1 percent of the total R&D undertaken globally by U.S. MNEs.[23] Nearly 85 percent of R&D performed by U.S. multinationals in 2004 was performed by the U.S.-based parent company. Less than 13 percent of the $4.9 billion of the R&D that U.S. multinationals performed in the Asia and Pacific region was performed in China.

U.S. patent data also indicate that China's innovative capability is more limited than some have suggested and that U.S. firms are not performing very much innovative activity there. Anyone seeking to protect intellectual property within the borders of the United States must apply for patent protection from the U.S. Patent and Trademark Office (U.S. PTO). Given the importance of the U.S. economy to the world in general and to China in particular, it is reasonable to regard patents taken out by China-based inventors in the United States as a useful indicator of inventive activity. The CASSIS CD-ROM produced by the U.S. PTO provides information about U.S. patents, and we use the December 2006 version to produce figure 13.4.

22. However, Schott (2008) qualifies this finding by documenting a decline in the prices of Chinese exports relative to Organization for Economic Cooperation and Development (OECD) exports of similar products.
23. This fraction takes as its denominator the sum of expenditures on R&D preformed by the U.S. parent and the R&D expenditures performed by all affiliates of U.S. firms in all countries.

Table 13.9   U.S. multinational enterprise research and development expenditures

	2004
China	622
Europe	18,148
Canada	2,702
Latin America and other Western Hemisphere	882
Asia and Pacific	4,934
Total affiliate activity	27,529
Parent activity	152,384

These data are drawn from the preliminary published results of the 2004 BEA Survey of U.S. Direct Investment Abroad. The affiliate data only cover majority-owned nonbank affiliates of nonbank parents, and the parent activity measure covers all nonbank parents of nonbank affiliates. Research and development expenditures are measured in millions of U.S. dollars.

Figure 13.4 tracks China-generated patents in various categories over time. The dramatic growth in patenting over time is evident in this graph, but levels of patenting activity remain low. From the beginning of 2000 to the end of 2006, the U.S. PTO granted 3,447 patents to inventors based in China or teams of inventors that included at least one member with a Chinese address. Over the same period, inventors with ties to Japan received nearly 241,000 patents, inventors with ties to Taiwan received over 39,000 patents, and inventors with ties to Israel received over 8,000 patents.

It is informative to break out patents generated in China into patents in which all listed inventors at the time of invention were based in China and also to break out patents that were assigned to U.S. corporate entities. As figure 13.4 indicates, a large and growing fraction of patents with Chinese inventors reflect collaborative work with inventors located elsewhere.[24] U.S. corporate entities appear to be associated with fewer than 1,000 granted patents, and only a relatively small percentage of China-generated patents assigned to U.S. multinationals reflect the inventive input of a purely Chinese team of inventors. This could indicate a deliberate attempt on the part of U.S. R&D centers in China to conduct research that only has value when combined with a complementary research input from the United States or from another relatively advanced country. Zhao (2006) describes this strategy as a way for U.S.-based multinationals to cope with the poor intellectual property rights regime in China. Another interpretation is that Chinese scientists and engineers, despite impressive levels of raw talent and basic skills, find it difficult to innovate effectively at the technological frontier on

24. Nearly 40 percent of China-generated U.S. patents identify inventors based in at least one other country. In contrast, nearly 90 percent of U.S. patents granted to U.S. firms in the last three years are generated by inventors based solely in the United States, and a similar percentage of Japan-generated U.S. patents represent the product of only Japanese inventors.

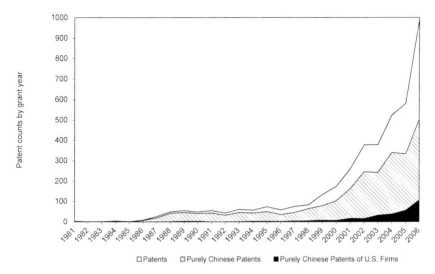

Fig. 13.4   China-generated U.S. patents, 1981–2006

Source: Data are taken from the U.S. Patent and Trademark Office CASSIS CD-ROM database, December 2006 version.

Notes: China-generated U.S. patents are U.S. utility patents for which at least one listed inventor was resident in China at the time of patent application. Purely Chinese patents are those patents for which all listed inventors have addresses in the People's Republic of China. Purely Chinese patents of U.S. firms are "purely Chinese" patents assigned to a U.S. corporate entity.

their own and often require the input of R&D managers and experts based elsewhere in the world to go beyond the existing state of the art.

It is also possible to use the U.S. PTO data to assess the importance of China, relative to other countries, in generating patents for U.S. firms and to examine which firms do have inventors based in China. There are 120 U.S. corporate assignees who have been granted at least two patents for which at least one inventor was based in China. The Chinese patents of these firms comprise only slightly more than 1 percent of the annual patenting activity of these firms in 2006.[25]

By far, the leading U.S. firm, in terms of China-generated patents, is Microsoft. Table 13.10 lists the top ten corporate assignees in terms of China-generated U.S. patents. Microsoft has nearly three times as many

25. One can combine the patent data with the R&D data to generate crude estimates of the patents per R&D dollar generated by U.S. affiliate R&D spending in China and compare that to the patents per R&D dollar generated by R&D spending by the parent firm in the United States. According to our estimates, the ratio of U.S. patents per R&D dollar in China is less than half this ratio in the United States. This difference is consistent with the view that the R&D conducted in Chinese affiliates tends to be more focused on modification of the parent firm's technology for the Chinese market or the development of technology specifically for that market than it is on the kind of fundamental, strategically sensitive research conducted in the parents' own labs.

Table 13.10   Top ten generators of U.S. patents in China

Rank	Firm name	Nationality	Number of patents
1	Hon Hai/Foxconn	Taiwan	644
2	Microsoft Corporation	United States	151
3	Inventec Corporation	Taiwan	94
4	China Petrochemical	Taiwan	79
5	SAE Magnetics	Japan	39
5	China Petroleum and Chemical Company	China	39
6	Huawei Technologies	China	34
7	IBM	United States	33
7	Winbond Electronics	Taiwan	33
8	Intel	United States	30
9	United Microelectronics	Taiwan	27
10	Proctor and Gamble	United States	24

Notes: This table ranks firms based on the number of U.S. patents they generated through 2006, which include at least one inventor with a mainland Chinese address. Patents are allocated to firms on the basis of the assignee name that exists in U.S. patent records. Data are taken from the December 2006 version of the CASSIS CD-ROM supplied by the U.S. Patent and Trademark Office. Hon Hai Precision Industries takes out U.S. patents under its official name and under its English trade name, Foxconn. The reported numbers reflect the sum of these patents. The numbers for Inventec Corporation represent the sum of patents taken out under the names of various subsidiaries. SAE Magnetics is a wholly-owned subsidiary of TDK, a Japanese multinational.

China-generated patents as IBM and Intel. After years of fractious relationships with the Chinese government, Microsoft sought to cultivate more harmonious ties with key government officials by opening multiple research centers in the People's Republic of China (PRC).[26] Microsoft lavished rather large sums of money on these facilities and sought to attract high-profile researchers to them, an effort described at length in a recent book by Buderi and Huang (2006), *Guanxi (The Art of Relationships)*. Senior Microsoft executives, including former CEO Bill Gates, have regularly reiterated their commitment to conducting world-class research in China at the very frontier of software technology. In the context of that public commitment, it is interesting to note that Microsoft's China-generated patents amount to less than 4 percent of its total cumulative patents to date.[27] If we restrict ourselves to patents with solely Chinese inventor teams, this fraction drops to about 1.5 percent.

26. An interesting account of Microsoft's early missteps in the PRC is provided by Khanna (1997). Poor relationships with the central government of the PRC ensured that rates of piracy of Microsoft products in China remained among the highest in the world for years.

27. In private conversations with the authors, some U.S. corporate managers have referred to the R&D centers opened by their firms in China as "PR&D" centers—that is, they were as much about public relations efforts directed at a mainland regime reluctant to enforce intellectual property rights as they were about "real" research and development.

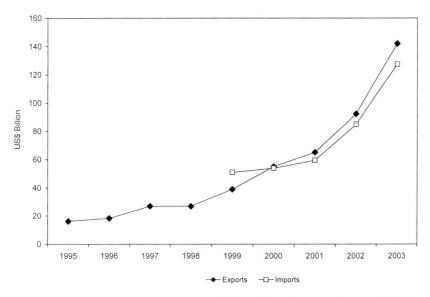

Fig. 13.5   China's trade in electronics and information industry products, 1995–2003

Source: Original data come from China Customs Statistics and the Chinese Ministry of Information Industries (MII). The authors wish to thank Nicholas Lardy for provision of these data. A similar figure is presented in Branstetter and Lardy (2008).

Interestingly, the leading patent-generating firm in China, with more than four times Microsoft's cumulated patent stock and a commanding lead over any indigenous mainland Chinese firm, is the Taiwanese contract manufacturing firm, *Hon Hai,* also known by its English trade name, Foxconn. Hon Hai is one of five Taiwanese manufacturing firms to appear on this top ten list. As is the case with export-oriented manufacturing, it appears the Taiwanese firms are more aggressively exploiting the opportunities to conduct research in China than are their U.S. counterparts.

Although the amount of innovative activity performed in China is lower than it is often perceived to be, the types of goods China exports are fairly technologically advanced. This has posed a puzzle to some economists. However, China is able to export huge quantities of high-tech goods only because it imports most of the high value added parts and components that go into these goods.[28] Figure 13.5 displays the level of Chinese exports and imports in electronic and information industry products. The domestic value added component of the value of exported electronic and information

28. This section of the text reflects the influence of Nicholas Lardy's writings on this subject. Some of the facts and figures in the following paragraphs reproduce points made in Lardy's presentations and in Branstetter and Lardy (2006, 2008).

technology products, while growing, remains quite low.[29] Even in the most recent years for which data are available, more than 70 percent of the value of these exports is comprised of imported inputs.[30]

While U.S. multinationals, with a few exceptions, do not play a major role in Chinese exports of high-tech goods, we also see in U.S. affiliate data a strong correlation in high-tech industries between imports from the parent and sales. Regression analyses of affiliate sales on measures of imported intermediates from the parent show a dramatically stronger connection for more R&D intensive industries, underscoring the relatively higher dependence of such activity in China on key inputs from the parent. Taken together, levels of R&D conducted in China, the amount of patenting associated with innovation based in China, and the low Chinese value added in high-tech Chinese exports suggest that China is far from becoming a technological superpower that will be home to a large share of U.S. MNE innovative activity.

13.5   Conclusions

The emergence of China as an important trading economy has been one of the most significant economic developments of our time, and it has captured the attention of the popular press. Understanding the economic changes in China while they are occurring is challenging, and several misconceptions about the role played by different factors, especially the role played by U.S. FDI, have become widely held. In this paper, we attempt to address four commonly held views that we believe do not reflect an informed interpretation of available data. These relate to the size of U.S. FDI in China, the degree to which it is export oriented, the extent to which it displaces U.S. multinational activity elsewhere, and the amount of innovative activity that is associated with it.

Despite the size of the Chinese economy and its rapid growth, the scale of U.S. affiliate activity there remains modest. U.S. affiliates based in China account for less than 2 percent of total U.S. affiliate sales, they contribute relatively little to aggregate Chinese investment, and they play a surprisingly small role in mediating the expansion of U.S.-China trade. Partly because of their focus on the domestic market and partly because of the small scale of their operations, U.S. affiliates in China do not appear to have significantly displaced investment elsewhere as they have increased the scale and scope of their operations in China.

29. An entertaining specific example of this is provided by Linden, Kraemer, and Dedrick (2007), who break down the production process for an Apple iPod, all of which are assembled in and exported from China. The authors' careful, if incomplete, cost accounting suggests that Chinese value added represents at most a few dollars of the roughly $150 factory cost for the typical iPod.

30. In light manufacturing, in contrast, domestic content accounts for nearly 70 percent of the value of exports. See Anderson (2007) for a useful review of the most recent data.

The limited level of U.S. affiliate activity in China does not indicate an unusual degree of aversion to China on the part of U.S. investing firms. Rather, it reflects the fact that most U.S. affiliate activity takes place in countries that are not only large, but also that are geographically proximate to the United States, that have low levels of corruption, and that are wealthy. Controlling for GDP, distance, tax rates, corruption, and GDP per capita, U.S. MNE activity in China and the extent to which U.S. affiliates in China sell goods to the United States and other countries besides China are neither especially low, nor especially high.

Despite widespread interest in the possible emergence of China as a center of technological innovation, U.S. affiliates conduct relatively little R&D in the country, and affiliate activity in technology-intensive industries appears to remain quite dependent on the supporting activities of the parent firm. China's ability to innovate, as evidenced by numbers of U.S. patents with at least one China-based inventor, remains well behind the much more developed capabilities of other East Asian countries like Japan, Taiwan, and South Korea. The picture traced out by rapid changes in the structure of Chinese exports of an emerging technological superpower belies a more modest reality. China's exports of high-technology goods are still quite dependent on imported components, technology, and expertise.

Rapid growth of Chinese aggregate GDP, income per capita, and human capital is likely to motivate U.S. firms to continue to expand their base of activity there. Given that current levels of activity are much smaller than levels of activity elsewhere, the relative scale of affiliate activity in China is likely to remain modest for many years to come. However, if the pace of progress persists, some of today's fallacies about U.S. FDI in China are likely to become facts.

References

Ahn, S., K. Fukao, and K. Ito. 2007. Outsourcing in East Asia and its impact on the Japanese and South Korean labor markets. Hitotsubashi University, Institute of Economic Research, Working Paper.

Anderson, J., 2006. What happened to the MNCs? UBS Investment Research: Asia Focus, September 29, 2006.

———. 2007. To boldly go where no country has gone before? UBS Investment Research: Asia Focus, July 6, 2007.

Antràs, P., M. Desai, and F. Foley. 2007. Multinational firms, FDI flows, and imperfect capital markets. NBER Working Paper no. 12855. Cambridge, MA: National Bureau of Economic Research.

Branstetter, L. 2007. China's financial markets: An overview. In *China at the crossroads: Capital markets and foreign exchange policies for the next decade,* ed. C. Calomiris. New York: Columbia University Press.

Branstetter, L., and N. Lardy. 2006. China's embrace of globalization. NBER Working Paper no. 12373. Cambridge, MA: National Bureau of Economic Research.
———. 2008. China's embrace of globalization. In *China's great economic transformation,* ed. L. Brandt and T. Rawski. New York: Cambridge University Press.
Buderi, R., and G. Huang. 2006. *Guanxi (the art of relationships): Microsoft, China, and Bill Gates' plan to win the road ahead.* New York: Simon & Schuster.
Burke, J. 2000. U.S. investment in China worsens deficit. Economic Policy Institute, Briefing Paper.
Cui, L., and M. Syed. 2007. Is China changing its stripes? The shifting structure of China's external trade and its implications. Paper presented at the International Monetary Fund conference on Global Implications of China's Trade, Investment, and Growth.
Desai, M., C. Foley, and J. Hines. 2004a. A multinational perspective on capital structure choice and internal capital markets. *Journal of Finance* 59 (6): 2451–88.
———. 2004b. Foreign direct investment in a world of multiple taxes. *Journal of Public Economics* 88 (12): 2727–44.
Dooley, M. P., D. Folkerts-Landau, and P. M. Garber. 2003. An essay on the revised Bretton Woods system. NBER Working Paper no. 9971. Cambridge, MA: National Bureau of Economic Research.
———. 2004a. Direct investment, rising real wages, and the absorption of excess labor in the periphery. NBER Working Paper no. 10626. Cambridge, MA: National Bureau of Economic Research.
———. 2004b. The U.S. current account deficit and economic development: Collateral for a total return swap. NBER Working Paper no. 10727. Cambridge, MA: National Bureau of Economic Research.
Feenstra, R. 1999. Facts and fallacies about foreign direct investment. In *International capital flows,* ed. M. Feldstein, 331–50. Chicago: University of Chicago Press.
Freeman, R. 2006. Does globalization of the scientific/engineering workforce threaten U.S. economic leadership. In *Innovation policy and the economy.* Vol. 6, ed. A. Jaffe, J. Lerner, and S. Stern. Cambridge, MA: MIT Press.
Ju, J., and S.-J. Wei. 2007. A solution to two paradoxes of international capital flows. Columbia Business School, Working Paper.
Khanna, T. 1997. Microsoft in the People's Republic of China. Harvard Business School Case Study.
Lardy, N. 1998. *China's unfinished economic revolution.* Washington, DC: Brookings Institution.
———. 2002. *Integrating China into the global economy.* Washington, DC: Brookings Institution.
Linden, G., K. Kraemer, and J. Dedrick. 2007. Who captures value in a global innovation system? The case of Apple's iPod. University of California, Irvine, Personal Computer Industry Center, Working Paper.
Mataloni, Raymond. 1995. A guide to BEA statistics on U.S. multinational companies. *Survey of Current Business* 75:38–53.
Naughton, B. 1996. China's emergence and prospects as a trading nation. *Brookings Papers on Economic Activity,* Issue no. 2:273–343. Washington, DC: Brookings Institution.
Preeg, E. 2004. *The threatened U.S. competitive lead in advanced technology products (ATP).* Washington, DC: Manufacturers Alliance/MAPI.
Puga, D., and D. Trefler. 2005. Wake up and smell the ginseng: The rise of incremental innovation in low-wage countries. NBER Working Paper no. 11571. Cambridge, MA: National Bureau of Economic Research.

Rodrik, D. 2006. What's so special about China's exports? NBER Working Paper no. 11947. Cambridge, MA: National Bureau of Economic Research.

Schott, P. 2008. The relative sophistication of Chinese exports. *Economic Policy* 53:5–49.

Tsai, K. 2002. *Back-alley banking: Private entrepreneurs in China.* Ithaca, NY: Cornell University Press.

United Nations Conference on Trade and Development (UNCTAD). 2005. *World investment report 2005: Transnational corporations and the internationalization of R&D.* New York: United Nations.

———. 2007. *UNCTAD investment brief no. 2, 2007, rising FDI into China: The facts behind the numbers.* http://www.unctad.org/en/docs/iteiiamisc20075_ed.pf/.

Wei, S.-J. 2000a. Local corruption and global capital flows. *Brookings Papers on Economic Activity,* Issue no. 2: Washington, DC: Brookings Institution.

———. 2000b. Why does China attract so little foreign direct investment. In *The role of foreign direct investment in East Asian economic development,* ed. T. Ito and A. Krueger. Chicago: University of Chicago Press.

Zhao, M. 2006. Conducting R&D in countries with weak intellectual property rights protection. *Management Science* 52:1185–99.

Comment   Stephen Yeaple

The foreign activities of American corporations have long been a source of concern to both the American public and to American policymakers. The list of potential concerns is long. Does the expansion of foreign production capabilities abroad threaten the availability of jobs that have traditionally been filled by American citizens? Does the transfer of technologies by American corporations to their foreign affiliates result in the loss of American competitiveness in key industries? What impact does multinational activity have on the balance of payments of the United States? It is concerns such as these that have motivated the careful collection of data by the U.S. Bureau of Economic Analysis (BEA) over the last several decades the on the foreign activities of American multinationals. More recently, these traditional concerns about the foreign activities of U.S. multinational enterprises (MNEs) on the U.S. economy have been magnified by the rapid expansion of economic activity in China.

In this chapter, Professors Bramstetter and Foley argue that assertions frequently made by commentators with respect to the activities of U.S. MNEs in China are false. These assertions essentially are of two types. According to the first, the activities of U.S. MNEs have had a substantial impact on Chinese economic development and its integration into the international trading system. According to the second, the activities of U.S. MNEs in China

Stephen Yeaple is an associate professor of economics at the Pennsylvania State University, and a research associate of the National Bureau of Economic Research.

have resulted in a substantial diversion of economic activity away from the United States and from other countries that host affiliates of U.S. MNEs. Unfortunately, there is no direct way to falsify these assertions because we cannot observe the counterfactual state of the world in which U.S. MNEs cannot invest in China. Instead, Professors Bramstetter and Foley ask whether the magnitude of activity of U.S. MNEs in China is consistent with an important impact on the global structure of economic activity.

The recurring message throughout the paper is that the magnitude of U.S. multinational activity into China is quite limited in size and scope. First, compared to U.S. multinational activity in traditional hosts, such as Canada, Mexico, and the European Union, the activity at the Chinese affiliates of U.S. corporations does not appear unduly large and so is unlikely to have had an unusually large impact on Chinese economic development. Second, this activity appears primarily geared toward the Chinese market rather than toward serving the American market and so is unlikely to have displaced much economic activity in other countries. Third, there is no direct evidence that American firms that increase employment in China reduce employment elsewhere, which further reduces the concern that U.S. foreign direct investment (FDI) in China diverts economic activity from elsewhere. Finally, American research and development (R&D) does not yet appear to be in the process of being offshored to China.

The sober assessment of U.S. multinational activity in China provided by the authors is well taken. If the popular view is that U.S. multinational activity is "large" in the sense that it dwarfs all U.S. multinational activity elsewhere, then the popular view is mistaken. However, "large" is not a very precise term, and an alternative reading is that U.S. multinational activity is reasonably substantial at least according to some metrics. Hence, it may be premature to conclude that U.S. FDI in China has been of little importance to the Chinese economy or to the economies of other countries.

Consider one particular metric of the size of U.S. MNE activity in China: the magnitude of employment at the Chinese affiliates of U.S. firms relative to employment at majority-owned manufacturing affiliates located in different countries. Table 13C.1 reports employment statistics from the BEA for U.S. affiliates for the seven host countries in which U.S. MNEs are the most active. Table 13C.1 shows the name of the host country and the aggregate manufacturing employment at U.S. affiliates by host country. The countries are listed in order of the size of employment. As the table reveals, China is the fifth largest according to this metric and second largest among middle-income countries. Whether U.S. FDI in China is "small" depends on your frame of reference. Surely, U.S. MNEs have a larger impact on the economy of Mexico than on the economy of China, but relative to most countries, it is not clear that the impact of U.S. MNE activity is unusually small.

Even if one were to conclude that the aggregate employment of U.S. manufacturing affiliates in China is small, China may still be "large" in specific industrial categories. Table 13C.2 reports the host country employment

Table 13C.1   **Employment of majority-owned foreign affiliates of U.S. multinational enterprises in 2004 (manufacturing)**

Country	Manufacturing (in thousands)
Mexico	526.0
Canada	405.3
United Kingdom	368.7
Germany	364.8
China	275.8
Brazil	249.7
France	237.9

Table 13C.2   **Employment of majority-owned foreign affiliates of U.S. multinational enterprises in 2004 (computers and electronics)**

Country	Computers and electronic products (in thousands)
China	98.3
Mexico	78.5
Malaysia	63.2
Singapore	39.6
Canada	38.0
United Kingdom	29.2
Germany	28.5

of U.S. affiliates in the computer and electronic product industries. In this particular industry, employment by U.S. affiliates in China is larger than in any other host country. Again, the question of whether in an absolute sense Chinese employment is large can be debated, but relative to other countries, it is not small.

That China is relatively large in terms of manufacturing employment in 2004 is all the more impressive given how small China was a decade ago. Since 1994, employment at the Chinese affiliates of U.S. companies has grown 390 percent, which is by far the fastest of any major destination country! Much of this growth can be thought of as a stock adjustment from very low levels of employment in the mid-1990s to a level consistent with the size of the Chinese economy by the turn of the century.

Figure 13C.1 illustrates the difference between the actual level of manufacturing employment (in logarithms) at U.S. affiliates and the level predicted by a simple gravity equation. The figure reveals that U.S. multinational activity into China in 1994 was far below the level expected for a country of China's size. By 1999, the gap between actual and predicted disappears, and there is little deviation thereafter. Keep in mind, however, that the Chinese economy has grown very rapidly over the last four years, and employment growth has kept apace. The stock adjustment of the late 1990s may well have

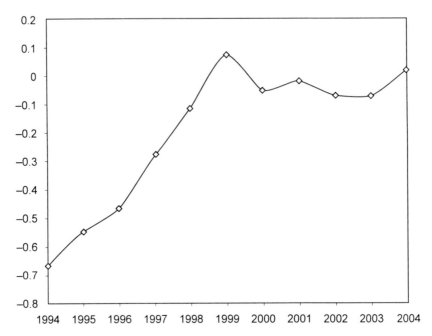

Fig. 13C.1   The difference between actual and predicted log employment at U.S.-owned Chinese affiliates

inflated perceptions about the size of U.S. FDI into China, but given the rapid growth of the Chinese economy, it would still seem to be safe to say that this expansion has been "large."

Assessing whether the rapid growth of employment at Chinese affiliates over the last decade has proven disruptive to other developing countries is a tricky exercise. Certainly the perception that China is a threat is strong in other middle-income countries such as Mexico. It is worth noting in the case of Mexico, that between 2000 and 2004, when the employment of U.S.-owned Chinese manufacturing affiliates expanded from approximately 193,000 to roughly 276,000, the employment of the Mexican manufacturing affiliates of U.S. firms contracted from about 642,000 to 526,000. Other examples of contraction can be found as well: employment at U.S. manufacturing affiliates in Malaysia contracted from 108,000 in 2000 to 82,000 in 2004. Whether there is any direct link between these facts cannot be substantiated using the publicly available BEA data, but the fact that employment has fallen over this period in other major middle-income countries makes the rapid growth in China all the more impressive.[1]

An important point made by Professors Bramstetter and Foley is that very

1. It would be worthwhile to apply the analysis used to create table 13.8 in Branstetter and Foley to individual countries.

little of what is produced by U.S. affiliates in China is exported directly back to the United States and so is unlikely to have directly resulted in substantial American job loss. As is frequently the case in large countries, U.S. affiliates appear to serve primarily the host-country market. One interesting fact that would be useful to explore further is the sales category, "exports to third countries." While the value of total sales of U.S. affiliates grew 168 percent between 1999 and 2004, the value of exports to third countries has grown 235 percent. This suggests that U.S.-owned affiliates operating in China are increasingly integrated into Asian production networks. To the extent that these production networks ultimately result in exports to the United States, it may be a bit premature to argue that U.S. FDI in China has had very little direct effect on the U.S. economy simply because the volume of direct exports is low.

Perhaps the strongest point made by Bramstetter and Foley concerns the R&D conducted by U.S. multinationals in China. Here, the hype in the popular press appears to be the most out of touch with the facts as presented in the chapter. It may be a long time before U.S. multinationals can be accurately accused of offshoring technology development to China, and so American prowess in R&D does not appear to be undermined directly by the technology sourcing of American MNEs. It should be pointed out, however, that this does not mean that American FDI in China has not had an impact on Chinese productivity: technology spillovers and agglomeration benefits through upstream suppliers are alternative channels through which U.S. FDI could affect the relative productivity of Chinese firms.

In conclusion, as Professors Bramstetter and Foley argue, it is easy to overstate the size and activity of U.S. MNEs in China. Public perceptions of the role of U.S. firms in offshoring production to China may well be out of line with reality and so overstate the economic importance of U.S. MNE activity in Chinese economic development. As the authors convincingly demonstrate, relative to a "gravity equation" benchmark, the level of U.S. multinational activity in China is unexceptional. Further, to the extent that multinationals play an important role in Chinese economic development, it is probably multinationals originating from other Asian countries such as Korea and Japan that have had the largest impact.

China is an exceptional country, however, in terms of its size and in terms of its breakneck speed of economic growth. It would be hard to argue that events in China have not had wide-ranging economic ramifications throughout the world. Indeed, the growth of employment at U.S. multinationals in China has been exceptionally fast even as it has fallen in other major middle-income host countries. It is premature, therefore, to conclude that the ability of U.S. firms to invest in China has not resulted in a diversion of economic activity, particularly in the case of certain industries, such as computers and electronics, and in the case of particular alternative host countries, such as Mexico and Malaysia.

14

China's Outward
Foreign Direct Investment

Leonard K. Cheng and Zihui Ma

14.1 Introduction

China has achieved remarkable success in attracting foreign direct investment (FDI) since the early 1990s. It became the largest recipient of FDI among developing economies for the first time in 1993 and then became one of the top three recipients of FDI in the world in 2003 to 2005 and number four in 2006 based on preliminary estimates.[1] Perhaps as a reflection of this success, there are many papers written on the various aspects of China's

Leonard K. Cheng is a Chair Professor of economics and Dean of Business and Management at the Hong Kong University of Science and Technology. Zihui Ma is a lecturer of international economics at Renmin University of China.

We would like to thank Lee Branstetter, Robert Feenstra, Martin Feldstein, Nicholas Lardy, Shang-Jin Wei, and other participants of the National Bureau of Economic Research's conference on China's Growing Role in World Trade for their encouragement and suggestions. We would also like to thank Bih Jane Liu, Chao-Cheng Mai, and participants at a conference on Studies of China's Mode of Economic Development held at Academia Sinica in Taipei on June 28–29, 2007, and to seminar participants at the Indian Statistical Institute for their comments on earlier drafts of this chapter. Finally, we are grateful to Mayumi Fukumoto for her assistance in providing Japan's foreign direct investment (FDI) data, and to Jae Nahm for his assistance in providing South Korea's FDI data.

1. According to UNCTAD's *World Investment Report 2004* (annex table B.1, 367 and 370), in 2003, China's inward FDI of US$53.5 billion ranked number one, before both France (US$47 billion) and the United States (US$29.8 billion), the second and third largest recipients of FDI in that year. However, in the *World Investment Report 2005* (annex table B.1, 303), the U.S. figure for 2003 was revised to become US$56.8 billion, implying that China would rank number two in that year after the United States. In 2004, China's inward FDI (US$60.6 billion) ranked number three after the United States (US$95.9 billion) and the United Kingdom (US$78.4 billion). According to UNCTAD Investment Brief Number 1 2007, China was ranked number two (after the United States) in 2004, number three (after the United Kingdom and the United States) in 2005, and number four (after the United States, the United Kingdom, and France) in 2006. The 2006 data were preliminary estimates.)

inward FDI. In contrast, China's outward FDI up to now is small and, thus, not as much systematic research has been carried out.

Nevertheless, as China is rapidly integrating with the global economy, its outward FDI has picked up in recent years. More important, perhaps, several major acquisition efforts have brought media attention to China as a source of FDI. Among them, Lenovo's acquisition of IBM PC announced in December 2004 could arguably be the most eye-catching example of these efforts. The other highly visible cases included the electronic appliance manufacturer TCL's acquisition of France's Thomson Electronics in 2004, white-goods manufacturer Haier's building of plants in the United States since the late 1990s, China's third-largest oil producer China National Offshore Oil Corporation's (CNOOC) failed attempt to acquire U.S. oil company UNOCAL in 2005, and Nanjing Automotive's success in acquiring the United Kingdom's MG Rover Group in 2005.[2] The energy crunch in 2006 also witnessed numerous stories about China's effort to invest in oil companies in the world, in particular in Russia, Central Asia, and Africa, giving an impression that resource grabbing was a key driving force behind China's outward FDI.

14.1.1   Background

A description of China's outward FDI from 1979 to 1996 can be found in Cai (1999). The country's annual FDI outflow grew from virtually zero in 1979, when China embarked upon its open-door policy, to US$628 million in 1985, and to US$913 million in 1991, before shooting up to US$4 billion in 1992, the year in which China's paramount leader Deng Xiaoping made an important tour to South China to reaffirm China's commitment to its reform and open-door policy in the aftermath of the Tiananmen crackdown in 1989.

By the end of 1996, China's total stock of FDI outflows was over US$18 billion. It surpassed South Korea (US$13.8 billion) and Brazil (US$7.4 billion) to move up to the number four position among developing economies, behind Hong Kong (US$112 billion), Singapore (US$37 billion), and Taiwan (US$27 billion; Cai, 1999, 861).

In the period of 1979 to 1993, almost two-thirds of China's FDI was made in Asia, including 61 percent in Hong Kong and Macau. The other regions in descending order were North America (15 percent), Oceania (8 percent), Central and Eastern Europe (5 percent), Africa (2 percent), Latin America (2 percent), and Western Europe (2 percent; Cai 1999, p. 864). Nearly 60 percent of China's FDI up to 1994 was in the services sector, mainly to service and promote its exports. The remaining FDI was in natural resources

---

2. Even though Shanghai Automotive started to have some cooperative arrangements with MG Rover involving intellectual property rights, in the end, the British automaker was sold to Nanjing Automotive after the former went into bankruptcy (http://www.zydg.net/magazine/article/1671-4725/2005/16/222961.html).

(25 percent) and manufacturing (15 percent, mainly in textiles and clothing and other labor-intensive industries, located primarily in Africa, Asia, and the Pacific.

The FDI statistics used by Cai were provided by the United Nations Conference on Trade and Development (UNCTAD) and collected by the International Monetary Fund (IMF) based on balance-of-payments accounting. Relative to the UNCTAD statistics, outward FDI statistics provided occasionally by the Ministry of Commerce (MOFCOM) and its predecessor MOFTEC up to 2002 represented serious underestimates.[3] Among other things, MOFCOM excluded investment projects not screened and approved by relevant government agencies and did not include investment made after the projects' initial approval, such as the plough back of retained earnings. However, as part of China's policy of encouraging its firms to go overseas, from 2002 onward, MOFCOM's FDI statistics have been collected in accordance with Organization for Economic Cooperation and Development (OECD) definitions and IMF's balance-of-payments guidelines. Thus, if there were still discrepancies between MOFCOM and UNCTAD's FDI statistics, the discrepancies from 2003 onward should be smaller than before.

Hong and Sun (2004), also using UNCTAD's FDI statistics, reported that the stock of China's outward FDI reached about US$36 billion by end the of 2002, ranked number six among 118 developing economies. They found that the growth of China's aggregate FDI outflows during 1988 to 2002 were quite similar to those of South Korea during the same period and to Japan's outflows in the period of 1968 to 1982. The sector composition of China's FDI, with 40 to 50 percent of shares in the nontrade category, was similar to that of South Korea in the 1980s and that of Japan in the 1960s and 1970s.

Hong and Sun found that the motives, destination, financing, and mode of entry of Chinese investors had undergone changes in the 1990s. For example, even though natural resources were still an important motive, in the late 1990s, increasingly more Chinese firms used FDI to acquire advanced foreign technologies and managerial skills, which had the effect of increasing their investment in the United States. Also, from 1992 to 2001, Chinese firms increasingly exploited and further developed their comparative advantages in Asia, Africa, and Latin America. In 1997 to 2001, Africa, with a share of 24.1 percent, became the second largest regional destination of Chinese FDI outflows, only after Asia. Since the mid-1990s, more and more Chinese firms used listing in overseas stock markets (Hong Kong and New York) to raise equity capital and to enhance their international reputation. What they found most striking, however, was that mergers and acquisitions gradually became the main form of investing overseas.

---

3. As indicated in Cai (1999, 857), some argued that the actual stock of FDI outflows from the beginning of China's open-door policy to the late 1990s were between US$80 billion and US$100 billion, even though only US$15 billion was officially approved.

14.1.2   Related Literature

Because China is a developing economy and until the last few years had been generally short of capital and foreign exchange, its outward FDI requires some explanations. Cai (1999) identified four motives for Chinese FDI: (a) market; (b) natural resources; (c) technology and managerial skills; and (d) financial capital. These motives were later augmented by other researchers. For instance, Deng (2004) identified two additional motives: (e) strategic assets (e.g., brands, marketing networks), and (f) diversification. Clearly, because China was itself a low-cost production base, cost minimization was not a major motivation of Chinese FDI overseas.

Alternative routes taken by China and its national firms to acquire the preceding assets and resources have received attention in fields of international business and politics. For example, Child and Rodrigues (2005), on the basis of case studies, examined the pros and cons of three alternative routes taken by Chinese firms in seeking technological and brand assets: (a) acting as an original equipment manufacturing (OEM) firm and forming joint ventures with foreign firms; (b) mergers with and acquisitions of foreign firms; and (c) organic international expansion (i.e., green field investment overseas).

As a world factory, China will become increasingly more dependent on the global supply of raw materials and energy, and China's FDI in natural resources seems to have captured the world's imagination. There were many reports of billion dollar deals in 2006 and 2007 involving oil-producing African countries (e.g., Taylor 2009), central Asian countries (e.g., *International Herald Tribune,* October 27, 2006), and elsewhere. This impression of foreign investment activities in natural resources indeed found support in the FDI statistics, which shows that China made US\$8.54 billion in 2006 in "mining, quarrying, and petroleum," accounting for 40.4 percent of the country's total FDI in that year.[4] However, the gap between official statistics and figures found in news reports appears to be big.

---

4. The figures quoted in news reports would not necessarily result in official FDI statistics because the former often included the total value of planned investment over many years into the future, and some of the planned investment might not take place as planned. Let's use two examples to compare the FDI statistics as reported in the 2005 Statistical Bulletin issued by China's Ministry of Commerce against the statistics quoted in the newspaper reports. As an example, the total stock of Chinese FDI in Algeria by the end of 2005 as reported in the Bulletin was US\$171 million, much less than the value of a single deal involving China National Petroleum Corporation (CNPC) as reported in Taylor (2009, 45): "In 2003 CNPC purchased a number of Algerian refineries for \$350 million and signed a deal to explore for oil in two blocks." What could be the explanations of the big difference in FDI statistics besides misreporting on either side or on both sides? Did CNPC take a long time to implement its deal so that by the end of 2005 only a fraction of the transacted amount was actually invested? Or did CNPC sell part or all of its interests before the end of 2005? Or was part or all of the investment considered portfolio investment and, thus, not included as direct investment? As another example, according to Taylor (2009, 50), China's investment in Sudan was estimated at \$4 billion. However, by the end of 2005, China's official statistics showed only a stock of US\$352 million, which was even less than Taylor's report of US\$600 million that Sinopec and CNPC jointly paid in November 2005 for drilling rights to an oilfield in the country.

As a reflection of Chinese effort to secure the supply of raw materials and energy for its national economy, there is a literature on "resource diplomacy," which was, according to Zweig (2006, 2), defined as "diplomatic activity designed to enhance a nation's access to resources and its energy security." While the first and foremost resource sought after by China is oil, the country is also in great demand for other minerals such as copper, bauxite, uranium, aluminum, manganese, iron ore, and so on (see, e.g., Taylor 2009, 37).[5] As pointed out by Taylor, "the strategy chosen is basically to acquire foreign energy resources via long-term contracts as well as purchasing overseas assets in the energy industry" (37). These strategic choices also apply to other key natural resources. After a systematic analysis of China's FDI statistics, we shall highlight its investment in the energy sector.

Using statistics on approved outward FDI as published in the *Almanac of China's Foreign Economic Relations and Trade* from 1991 to 2005, Cheung and Qian (2007) found that, consistent with the earlier literature, China's investment was motivated by both market-seeking and resource-seeking. However, they did not find substantial evidence that its investment in African and oil-producing countries was mainly for their natural resources. In addition, they found that China's international reserves and exports to developing countries tended to promote FDI; the latter finding suggests that some investment in developing countries could be either for the purpose of facilitating or complementing exports.

Researchers in the fields of international business and politics recognize the importance of the role of the Chinese government in China's outward FDI. This point would not be hard to appreciate because, as we shall see in the following, until now the lion's share of China's outward FDI has been made by firms that have close relationships to various levels of government. Moreover, overseas investment by Chinese private firms requires government approval. Partly as a result of the perceived need to secure key natural resources and technologies through ownership, and partly due to the awareness that Chinese firms must compete in the global arena when foreign firms intensify their entry into the domestic market, China started to initiate a policy to encourage its national firms to "go overseas" in 2001. The government not only relaxed the approval process of outward FDI, but also provided incentives for FDI in target industries and recipient countries. This policy shift toward outward FDI will be further discussed in the following.

Stimulated by international attention on some successes and failed attempts of buyout by Chinese multinational firms, Antkiewicz and Whalley (2006) discussed three policy issues about cross-border mergers and acquisitions. They were (a) government subsidization of cross-border mergers and acquisitions; (b) transparency of the acquiring firms; and (c) national

---

5. According to Taylor (2009, 39), China surpassed Japan in 2003 to become the world's second largest user of oil products after the U.S.

security concerns of OECD countries whose firms are the targets of foreign buyouts.

The purpose of this paper is fourfold: (a) to provide a brief introduction to China's "go overseas" policy; (b) to provide a systematic analysis of the size and composition of China's outward FDI in 2003 to 2006, the period over which such data are available from China's Ministry of Commerce; (c) to uncover the determinants of the amounts of China's outward FDI to the host economies, and (d) to shed light on China's past and future outward FDI by analyzing the determinants of the amounts of the outward FDI of the world's source economies and those of Japan and South Korea to yield an East Asian perspective.

The paper is organized as follows. The next section describes China's "go overseas" policy first proclaimed in 2001, to be followed by section 14.3, which analyzes the pattern of China's outward FDI in 2003 to 2006, including the total amounts, sector composition, geographical distribution, and the identity of investing firms. Section 14.4 discusses China's foreign investment in the energy sector, while section 14.5 attempts to uncover the determinants of the amounts of China's outward FDI in the host economies with the help of gravity equation regression analysis. Section 14.6 examines the determinants of the total amounts of outward FDI of the world's source economies, with a particular focus on Japan and South Korea's experience, to shed light on China's past and future FDI. Section 14.7 compares China sector composition and geographical distribution of FDI against those of Japan and South Korea. The final section summarizes and indicates directions for further research.

14.2   China's "Go Overseas" Policy toward Outward FDI

The Chinese government first proposed Chinese firms to "go overseas" ("zouchuqu" literally means "go out" but may be taken to mean "go global" as some authors have done) in 2001 in its 10th Five-Year plan. In the sixth national congress of the China Communist Party (CCP) in 2002, President Jiang Zeming proclaimed the go overseas policy, which covers FDI, the undertaking of foreign construction and engineering projects, and the export of Chinese employment or labor services. Due to lack of publicly available information, however, it is difficult to provide a complete catalogue of specific measures that have been introduced under the go overseas policy. It is known that in the initial stage of the policy's introduction, policy measures were mainly in the form of relaxation of restrictions on investment overseas, including the vetting and approval of such investment, plus some minor financial support.

In January 2004, the Ministry of Commerce, the Ministry of Finance, and the State Administration of Foreign Exchange promulgated a series of measures that aimed to promote Chinese investment overseas in goods processing (including export processing). Among other things, the vetting and approval of investment of US$3 million or less were delegated to provincial level government agencies, while project proposal and feasibility study no longer required approval. In addition, a "Central Foreign Trade Development Fund" of RMB2.3 billion was set up to support investment in overseas processing activities, and both the scope and proportion of interest payment subsidy were increased. For nonfinance, nonprocessing FDI, the approval of foreign investment projects was delegated to local authorities at twelve coastal Chinese cities.

In addition to policies in support of FDI, funds were also set up to support Chinese firms in bidding for foreign construction or engineering projects, in the form of subsidy for project finance and insurance.

To promote Chinese firms to go overseas, a wide variety of services was provided by the government, ranging from promoting national firms during official visits by government officials and state leaders, to incorporating business negotiations into intergovernmental cooperation frameworks, to building databases on investment environment and opportunities in specific host countries, to providing consultancy services to Chinese firms that consider overseas investment.[6] Furthermore, in addition to the central government and its overseas offices, local governments were also involved in supporting investment overseas. Government agencies worked closely with investing firms and industry associations to promote the investing firms' interests. Both policy banks and commercial banks were involved in assisting the finance of overseas activities, including FDI.

A regular mechanism was set up by the Ministry of Commerce in association with All-China Federation of Industry and Commerce as early as May 2004 to encourage private firms to go overseas, and a draft document that surfaced in 2006 called for stronger support for non-state-owned firms in the areas of taxation, finance, foreign exchange, and insurance. An example was the facilitation of obtaining finance from the global capital market, including listing in overseas stock markets, debt issuing, project finance, and guarantee for overseas subsidiaries.

Despite the government's early effort to encourage non-state-owned firms to go overseas, the policy measures effectiveness was unclear. Some private Chinese firms felt that by 2006, government restrictions on their going overseas were largely gone, but they had not seen any helping hand yet. Government officials in the Ministry of Commerce felt that there were already many policy measures to assist the private firms (such as interest subsidies and deductibility of the cost of feasibility studies in the case of natural resource development), but the firms did not utilize them due to lack of information. According to some researchers in the government, while there were many

---

6. The Ministry of Commerce compiled a list of countries suitable for investment in textile and consumer electronics as early as January 2004.

such promotional measures, their effectiveness was limited. It is interesting that the same researchers also questioned the rationale for subsidizing outward FDI with taxpayers' money.

Other private firms felt that they were not free to make quick investment decisions in a rapidly changing world economy. They complained that the investment facilitating measures were unclear and the approval of overseas investment project proposals still took a long time. Instead of going through successive levels of the Ministry of Commerce, then to the Commission on Development and Reform, and finally to the State Administration of Foreign Exchange, Chinese private firms wanted to have a one-stop shop to get all the required approvals. Some other private firms complained that, on the one hand, they were unable to obtain long-term loans from policy banks due to quotas on total lending and, on the other hand, commercial banks were not willing to take any risk in longer-term lending. Obtaining finance overseas with domestic collateral was not permitted by the Chinese government, but some private firms did it illegally anyway.

In 2006, China started to explore the idea of setting up "overseas China economic and trade cooperation zones" in host countries. These zones were perceived to serve several purposes: (a) to expand exports through the host economies that satisfy rules of origin in order to lessen bilateral trade frictions caused by rapid increase in Chinese exports; (b) to develop Chinese firms and to build Chinese brands in the global market place; (c) to reduce the country's bursting foreign reserves, and (d) to provide employment in host countries, thus contributing to the host economies and bilateral relations.

The reason for encouraging Chinese firms to invest in these zones rather than in other locations in the host countries is that Chinese firms would be more effective when they go overseas in groups, rather than as individual firms. That way, they will be able to support each other and to enjoy better support by host governments. In addition, the terms of agreement reached between host governments and Chinese investing firms will be firmed up as part of the bilateral investment agreements between the Chinese and host governments.

The hosts for these zones are chosen mostly on the basis of good bilateral relations, political stability, and comparative advantages. The host countries include North Korea, Russia, Kazakstan, Nigeria, and Pakistan. China envisions building fifty or so zones in the near future. By the end of November 2007, eight zones were approved, and one was officially established. Each approved zone may get RMB200 to 300 million of fiscal support and up to RMB2 billion of medium- to long-term loans. The following are examples of such zones:[7]

---

7. The information is taken from an article posted at http://mnc.people.com.cn/GB/54824/5127355.html.

1. Haier-Ruba Economic and Trade Cooperation Zone in Pakistan: Officially established in November 2006, this is an industrial park mainly for the production of consumer electronics;

2. Ussuriysk Economic and Trade Cooperation Zone in Russia: Officially approved in October 2006, it focuses mainly on lumber, textiles, and logistics.

3. Lake Tai International Economic Cooperation Zone in Cambodia: It is mainly a regional trade center for distribution of goods produced in China's Jiangsu Province.

4. China Nonferrous Metal Group to invest in nonferrous mines in Zambia, especially in the Chambishi copper mine.

5. Transbaikai Economic and Trade Cooperation Zone in the area of Transbaikai, Chita, on the China-Russia border: It is mainly for industrial processing and cross-border trade.

14.3 Patterns of China's Recent Outward FDI

From this point onward, we shall omit the adjective "outward" if the meaning of FDI is clear without it. In this section, we first present China's aggregate annual FDI flow from 1982 to 2006 and its global shares in aggregate flows and stocks from 2002 to 2006. After that, we shall examine the sector composition and geographical distribution of China's FDI flows and stocks, to be followed by an analysis of the organizational background of the Chinese investors. Note that the difference between the FDI stocks (measured as of end of year) of two successive years is not necessarily equal to the FDI flow of the later year, as one might expect, due to reasons such as revaluations of the stock of investment.

14.3.1 Amounts and Global Shares

By the end of 2006, more than 5,000 Chinese firms had established nearly 10,000 overseas subsidiaries, joint ventures, and representative offices in 172 countries (regions) around the world.[8] The flow of China's FDI from 1990 to 2006 is depicted in figure 14.1, where the data from 1982 to 2001 were based on UNCTAD's *World Investment Reports*, while data from 2002 were provided by MOFCOM based on international definitions and data collection methods. Note that statistics for FDI in financial industries in 2002 to 2005 was not available. To maintain consistency, the total FDI for 2006 shown in the figure excluded FDI in financial industries, whose statistics became available for the first time in that year.

In 2006, China's total FDI flow amounted to US$21.16 billion, 24.4 percent of which was made up of new equity investment, and 31.4 percent of

---

8. In terms of the number of FIEs, by the end of 2006, 95 percent of them were subsidiaries and representative offices, while joint ventures accounted for only 5 percent.

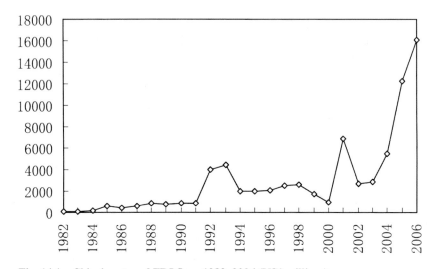

Fig. 14.1   China's outward FDI flow: 1982–2006 (US$ millions)

Source: Ministry of Commerce, China (2006, 2007). Data for 1982–2001 are based on various issues of UNCTAD's *World Investment Report,* whereas data for 2002–2006 were compiled by the ministry.

which was made up of reinvestment of current profits. From a different angle, 39 percent of the total FDI took the form of merger of acquisition (M&A), and 35.4 percent of FDI in financial industries took the form of M&A. In addition, about half of the nonfinance FDI was in the form of loans extended by parent companies in China to its overseas units.

In 2002 to 2005, statistics for FDI in financial industries such as banking and insurance was not included due to lack of data, so the total amounts of shown in the figure were underestimates of China's actual FDI. In 2006, when statistics on FDI in financial industries became available for the first time, such FDI accounted for about one-sixth of the flow in that year and the stock at the end of the same year.[9] If the shares of financial industries in China's total FDI flow and stock in 2006 were indicative of their importance in earlier years, then the statistics from 2002 to 2005 should be adjusted upward by about 17 percent.

China's FDI flow in nonfinance industries, on average, grew by 59.5 percent per annum (compound) between 2002 and 2006; its FDI stocks in the nonfinance industries, on average, grew by 34.5 percent per annum

---

9. By the end of 2006, Chinese state-owned commercial banks established a total of forty-seven branches, thirty-one subsidiaries, and twelve representative offices in twenty-nine countries and regions, including the United States, Japan, and the United Kingdom. The banking industry accounted for the lion's share of that year's FDI in the financial industries: 71 percent of flow and 79 percent of stock; insurance, second in place, accounted for 5 percent of the stock.

Table 14.1   China's outward foreign direct investment (FDI) flows and stocks in relation to the world's total FDI flows and stocks

	2002	2003	2004	2005	2006
China's outward FDI flow					
(U.S.$ billions)	2.7	2.85	5.5	12.26	21.16
World's total FDI flow					
(U.S.$ billions)	540.7	560.1	877.3	837.2	1215.8
Global share (%)	0.50	0.51	0.63	1.46	1.74
China's outward FDI stock					
(U.S.$ billions)	22.9	33.2	44.8	57.2	90.63
World's total FDI stock					
(U.S.$ billions)	7,433.9	8,779.5	10,151.8	10,578.8	12,474.3
Global share (%)	0.31	0.38	0.44	0.54	0.73

Notes: Stocks were measured at the end of each calendar year. The FDI flow and stock figures for 2003–2005 were underestimates of China's actual outward FDI flows and stocks because before 2006, FDI in financial industries were not included. In 2006, when data became available, FDI in financial industries accounted for about one-sixth of China's total FDI flow and stock in 2006. The global shares of China's FDI flows and stocks reported in this table are slightly different from those reported in the Ministry of Commerce's Statistical Bulletins, where the shares were calculated as percentages of China's flows and stock in the world's total FDI flows and stocks of the preceding (instead of the same) years.

(compound). Despite such rapid growth, its shares of the world's total FDI remained very small. As shown in table 14.1, China's FDI flow in 2006 accounted for about 1.74 percent of the world's total FDI flow and 0.73 percent of the world's total FDI stock. The figures in the earlier years were even smaller, and any adjustment to account for FDI in financial industries would not have made any significant difference.

When compared against the 2006 FDI statistics of other countries, the amounts of China's FDI flow and stock in 2006 would rank number seventeen and number twenty-four, respectively. Not only the world's major industrial economies such as the United States, the United Kingdom, and France, but also some of the small developed economies and major developing economies had more FDI than China. As examples of the latter, China's FDI flow in 2006 (US$21.16 billion) was below that of Hong Kong (US$43.5 billion), Sweden (US$24.6 billion), and Holland (US$22.7 billion) in the same year. Its FDI stock in 2006 (US$90.63 billion) was below that of Holland, Australia, Ireland, Denmark, Hong Kong, Singapore, and Russia.

Nevertheless, given the expectation that China's FDI flows in the future will continue to grow rapidly relative to other source economies, it would be reasonable to expect China's rankings to continue to move up further.

14.3.2   Sector Composition

China's FDI flows and stocks in 2003 to 2006 by sector are shown in table 14.2. In 2006, 53.8 percent of China's FDI flow went into the services

Table 14.2   Values and shares of China's outward foreign direct investment (FDI), by sector

	Flow				Stock			
	2003	2004	2005	2006	2003	2004	2005	2006
Agriculture, forestry, husbandry, and fishery								
Value (U.S.$ millions)	85.5	288.66	105.36	185.04	332	834.23	511.62	816.70
Share (%)	3	5.25	0.86	0.87	1	1.86	0.89	0.90
Mining and petroleum								
Value (U.S.$ millions)	1,380	1,800.2	1,675.22	8,539.51	5,900	5,951.37	8,651.61	1,7901.6
Share (%)	48.4	32.74	13.66	40.35	18	13.29	15.12	19.75
Manufacturing								
Value (U.S.$ millions)	620	755.55	2,280.4	906.61	2,070	4,539.07	5,770.29	7,529.62
Share (%)	21.8	13.74	18.60	4.28	6.2	10.14	10.09	8.31
Services								
Value (U.S.$ millions)	763.8	2,643.4	8,198.58	11,377.6	24,833	33,470.9	42,280	62,335.9
Share (%)	26.8	48.08	66.87	53.77	74.8	74.75	73.91	68.8
Business services								
Value (U.S.$ millions)	280	749.31	4,941.59	4,521.66	1,992	16,445.5	16,553.6	19,463.6
Share (%)	9.8	13.63	40.30	21.37	6	36.73	28.94	21.48
Finance								
Value (U.S.$ millions)	n.a.	n.a.	n.a.	3,530	n.a.	n.a.	n.a.	15,610
Share (%)	n.a.	n.a.	n.a.	16.78	n.a.	n.a.	n.a.	17.22
Wholesale and retail								
Value (U.S.$ millions)	360	799.69	2,260.12	1,113.91	6,530	7,843.27	11,417.9	12,955.2
Share (%)	12.6	14.55	18.43	5.26	19.7	17.52	19.96	14.29
Transportation and storage								
Value (U.S.$ millions)	85.5	828.66	576.79	1,376.39	1,992	4,580.55	7,082.97	7,568.19
Share (%)	3	15.07	4.70	6.5	6	10.23	12.38	8.35

Sources: Ministry of Commerce, China (2004–2007), *World Investment Report* (2006, 2007).

Notes: The sector shares for 2003–2005 are not directly comparable with those for 2006 because data for FDI flows and stocks in finance for 2003–2005 were not available. Moreover, the 2003 figures are subject to rounding errors because the values by sector were not explicitly provided in the *2003 Statistical Bulletin of China's Outward Foreign Direct Investment*, but calculated by the authors from the sector percentages and aggregate FDI figures.

n.a. = not available.

industries; 40.4 percent went into mining and petroleum; and a miniscule 4.3 percent went into manufacturing.[10] Within the services sector, 21.4 percent went into business services, 16.8 percent into finance, 6.5 percent into transportation and storage (mainly marine transportation), and 5.3 percent into wholesale and retail (mainly imports and exports).

By the end of 2006, business services accounted for the largest share of China's outward FDI stock (21.5 percent), to be followed by mining and petroleum (19.8 percent), finance (17.2 percent), wholesale and retail (14.3 percent), transportation and storage (8.4 percent), and manufacturing (8.3 percent).

Due to the inclusion of finance for the first time in 2006, the shares of most of the other industries in 2006 inevitably fell from their 2005 levels. It is interesting to note that the total shares of the services sector in total FDI stock varied from the over 70 percent in 2003 to 2005 to close to 69 percent in 2006, signifying the predominant importance of the sector in China's FDI.

14.3.3   Geographical Distribution

In 2006, China's FDI flowed into 172 countries and regions spread over all continents except the Antarctica. Tables 14.3 and 14.4 show the geographical distributions of China's nonfinance FDI flows and stocks, respectively. In 2006, 48.0 percent of China's FDI flow was destined for Latin America, which exceeded the share of Asia, a new development that began in 2005. The bulk of China's investment in Latin America was made in two tax havens there: Cayman Islands and British Virgin Islands; the other well-known tax haven, the Bahamas, played a much smaller role. Investment in these and other tax havens typically results in reinvestment in other host economies, including China itself.

Until 2004, Asian economies accounted for more than half of China's investment flows. However, the share of Asia declined to 35.7 percent and 43.5 percent in 2005 and 2006, respectively, as investment shifted to Latin America. Despite this recent slow down, however, Asia still accounted for 64 percent of the total stock of China's FDI by the end of 2006, with 88 percent of it going to Hong Kong. Clearly, China's substantial FDI flows to Latin America were a relatively recent phenomenon.

The other regions in the world were not important destinations for China's FDI at all. In every year from 2003 to 2006, together they accounted for less than 10 percent of China's total flows and total stocks. Africa was slightly ahead of Europe in some years, but Europe was ahead of Africa in other years, and both accounted for more Chinese FDI than North America, whereas Oceania came in last. By the end of 2006, the shares of Africa,

---

10. This is mainly telecom equipment, computers and other electronic equipment, textile, electro-mechanical manufacture, transportation equipment, lumber processing, nonferrous metal, and so on.

Table 14.3   **Values and shares of China's nonfinance foreign direct investment (FDI) flows, by region**

	2003	2004	2005	2006
Values of China's outward FDI flows (U.S.$ millions)				
Asia	1,498.95	3,000.27	4,374.64	7,663.25
Africa	74.79	317.42	391.68	519.86
Europe	151.14	170.92	505.02	597.71
Latin America	1,038.15	1,762.72	6,466.16	8,468.74
North America	57.74	126.49	320.84	258.05
Oceania	33.88	120.15	202.83	126.36
Share of China's outward FDI flows (%)				
Asia	52.51	54.57	35.68	43.46
Africa	2.62	5.77	3.19	2.95
Europe	5.29	3.11	4.12	3.39
Latin America	36.37	32.06	52.74	48.03
North America	2.02	2.30	2.62	1.46
Oceania	1.19	2.19	1.65	0.72
Relative ratio of China's outward FDI flows				
Asia	2.37	2.25	1.56	2.12
Africa	0.79	2.38	1.02	1.08
Europe	0.10	0.09	0.07	0.07
Latin America	4.59	2.52	6.60	7.49
North America	0.18	0.11	0.20	0.08
Oceania	0.62	0.41	−0.47	0.29

Sources: China's data from Ministry of Commerce, China (2004–2007); world's data from UNCTAD's FDI database.

Notes: Share of China's outward FDI flow to region = China's outward FDI flow to region/ China's aggregate outward FDI flow. Relative ratio of China's outward FDI flow = share of China's outward FDI flow to region/share of world's FDI flow to region. The world's outward FDI to Oceania in 2005 was negative.

Europe, North America, and Oceania in China's total nonfinance FDI stock were 3.4 percent, 3.0 percent, 2.1 percent, and 1.3 percent, respectively.

When compared with the shares of the world's aggregate FDI flows to different regions, tables 14.3 and 14.4 show that the shares of China's FDI flows to Asia and Latin America were significantly higher than those of the world's, and its shares to Europe, North America, and Oceania were very low. In contrast, its share to Africa was more or less average, so the recent Chinese initiative to expand its economic role on the dark continent has yet to appear to the latter's future FDI figures.

The top ten recipients of China's FDI stock by the end of 2006 in descending order were Hong Kong, Cayman Islands, British Virgin Islands, the United States, South Korea, Russia, Australia, Macau, Sudan, and Germany. Immediately after them were Singapore, Mongolia, Kazakstan, Saudi Arabia, Zambia, Vietnam, Algeria, Thailand, Indonesia, and Japan. In

Table 14.4   **Values and shares of China's outward nonfinance foreign direct investment (FDI) stocks, by region**

	2003	2004	2005	2006
Values of China's outward FDI stocks (U.S.$ millions)				
Asia	26,559.39	33,409.53	40,629.04	47,978.04
Africa	491.22	899.55	1,595.25	2,556.82
Europe	531.52	746.66	1,598.19	2,269.82
Latin America	4,619.34	8,268.37	11,469.62	19,694.37
North America	548.49	909.21	1,263.24	1,587.02
Oceania	472.26	543.94	650.28	939.48
Share of China's outward FDI stocks (%)				
Asia	79.94	74.61	71.02	63.95
Africa	1.48	2.01	2.79	3.41
Europe	1.60	1.67	2.79	3.03
Latin America	13.90	18.47	20.05	26.25
North America	1.65	2.03	2.21	2.12
Oceania	1.42	1.21	1.14	1.25
Relative ratios of China's outward FDI stocks				
Asia	5.16	4.91	4.28	3.69
Africa	0.60	0.80	1.03	1.30
Europe	0.03	0.03	0.06	0.06
Latin America	1.83	2.47	2.47	3.47
North America	0.08	0.10	0.11	0.11
Oceania	0.47	0.37	0.44	0.48

Sources: China's data from Ministry of Commerce, China (2006); world's data from UNCTAD's FDI database.

Notes: Share of China's outward FDI stock to region = China's outward FDI stock to region/ China's aggregate outward FDI stock. Relative ratio of China's outward FDI to region = share of China's outward FDI stock to region/share of world's FDI stock to region.

terms of FDI flows in 2006, the top ten recipients in descending order were Cayman Islands, Hong Kong, British Virgin Islands, Russia, the United States, Singapore, Saudi Arabia, Algeria, and Zambia. Immediately after them were Mongolia, Germany, Nigeria, Iran, Indonesia, Sudan, Vietnam, Kazakstan, South Africa, and Japan.

Both lists were indicative of the role of natural resources in attracting Chinese FDI to Africa, central Asia, Southeast Asia, and Australia.

Given that 86.8 percent of China's total FDI flows in 2006 was made in three tax havens (namely, Hong Kong, Cayman Islands, and British Virgin Islands), and at least 80 percent and 78 percent of its FDI flow in 2005 and 2004 were made in them, respectively, the true breakdown of the destination of China's FDI was largely unknown. Our attempts to obtain information about China's actual investment destinations from news databases and the annual reports of publicly listed Chinese companies, unfortunately, proved to be unsuccessful.

14.3.4 Identity of Chinese Investors

The bulk of China's FDI was made by the country's state-owned enterprises (SOEs), in particular, those large multinational companies that were administered by the Central Government's ministries and agencies. The shares of FDI flows in 2003 to 2006 made by SOEs under the Central Government were 73.5 percent, 82.3 percent, 83.2 percent, and 86.4 percent, respectively. Their shares of FDI stocks by the end of 2004 to 2006 were 85.5 percent, 83.5 percent, and 82.1 percent, respectively. The remaining shares of FDI flows and stocks were made by SOEs administered by regional governments and non-SOEs that are owned collectively and privately.[11] The private firms' share of FDI was miniscule; in 2004, private firms in China accounted for 1.5 percent of the country's total FDI flow, and by the end of 2006 their share of China's total FDI stock was 1 percent.

At the end of 2004, the thirty Chinese multinational companies with the largest stocks of FDI accounted for 80.4 percent of China's total nonfinance FDI stock. Over twenty of them were SOEs administered by the Central Government. The remainder included the listed companies Lenovo, TCL, Beida Jade Bird,[12] and other listed companies that are owned by the regional governments of Beijing, Shanghai, and Guangdong.[13]

14.4 China's FDI in the Energy Sector

Despite frequent news reports on China's FDI in the energy sector, no systematic data are available in the public domain. As pointed out in the preceding, China's go overseas policy covers not only outward FDI, but also the undertaking of overseas construction and engineering projects as well as the export of labor services. China's energy policy as stated in the 11th Five-Year plan (2006–2010) was to develop domestic supply as the primary means of meeting domestic demand, and to supplement that supply by tapping foreign sources of energy. To secure the foreign supply of oil, gas, and other forms of energy, China has relied on both long-term contracts and FDI. In some cases, these contracts may go beyond the purchase and sale of oil and gas. For example, in an agreement reached in 2004, China swapped its construction projects for Brazil's oil.[14]

---

11. In China, the provincial-level regions include provinces, provincial-level autonomous regions, and provincial-level municipalities directly administered under the central government.

12. In the 2006 list, Huawei and Haier replaced TCL and Beijing Jade Bird on the top thirty list.

13. For example, GDH Limited and Shum Yip Holdings Company Limited are from Guangdong, whereas Shanghai Automotive Industry Corporation and Shanghai Baosteel Group Corporation are from Shanghai.

14. This agreement was reached in May 2004 when Brazil's president Lula visited China. Under the agreement, China was to invest US$1 billion in a port facilities in return for Brazil's iron ore, oil, bauxite, and other raw materials of equal total value.

China's three biggest oil companies in descending order are China National Petroleum Corporation (CNPC), China Chemical and Petroleum Corporation (Sinopec), and China National Offshore Oil Corporation (CNOOC).[15] In terms of the importance of overseas operations, the order is CNPC, CNOOC, and Sinopec.

China National Petroleum Corporation started its overseas ventures in 1995. A decade later, it had four production bases in North Africa (mainly Sudan); Central Asia (mainly Kazakstan); South America (mainly Venezuela); and Asia and Australia, with annual target production of 35 million tons. In 2006 it had sixty-five cooperative projects in twenty-five countries, producing 54 million tons of oil (of which 28 million tons went to the company) and 5.7 billion cubic meters of natural gas (of which 3.5 billion cubic meters went to the company).

In 2002, CNOOC acquired three oil/gas fields in Australia and Indonesia at the cost of US$1.2 billion, including offshore oil fields in Indonesia that were acquired from Spain's Repsol-YPE; the latter oil fields yielded 5.4 million tons of oil for the company. In 2006, it expanded its operations in Africa by acquiring a Nigerian tract at a cost of US$2.068 billion and signed an agreement with Kenya for the largest area ever obtained from its overseas agreements. In that year, it also reached an agreement with Vietnam to jointly develop oil in the South China Sea, received permission to participate in the second largest gas field in Iran, and acquired a 25 percent stake in four offshore exploration tracts in Australia.

Sinopec established its international subsidiary Sinopec International Petroleum Exploration and Production (SIPC) in 2001 for the purpose of going overseas. By 2005, it had oil and gas projects in Iran, Saudi Arabia, Libya, Angola, Congo, Gabon, Kazakstan, Yemen, and Ecuador. In that year, it signed a joint venture agreement with the Russian oil company Rosneft to explore and develop oil and gas, the first of its kind involving a Russian oil company and China's three major oil companies. It also had activities in Australia and Indonesia. In 2006, it signed an agreement with Rosneft on a framework of strategic cooperation and joined forces with India's Oil and Natural Gas Corporation (ONGC) to acquire a Columbian oil company.

An interview with some businessmen in Beijing has revealed that they were not aware of any government policies explicitly implemented to support Chinese firms in the energy sector to go overseas, but they could see three advantages the energy firms enjoy with regard to outward FDI. First, they have cooperated with foreign partners for a long time, so they are much more familiar with foreign countries than nonenergy firms. Second, they are SOEs (state-owned enterprises), so they enjoy preferential policies that are specific to SOEs. Third, the energy firms they buy are good collateral

15. The ratios of their market capitalization in 2007 were about 5:2:1.

for loans, so banks are willing to finance their M&A activities overseas. Separately, Sinosure (China Export and Credit Insurance Corporation) has provided insurance to Chinese oil companies big and small in the areas of equity investment, debt financing, and working capital loans.

To support Chinese oil companies going overseas, the Chinese government has considered setting up a foreign exchange fund to facilitate the acquisition of and merger with foreign oil companies. However, whether this should be done remains controversial.

14.5   Determinants of China's Outward FDI Flows and Stocks: A Gravity Model Analysis

The China Ministry of Commerce (2007) has released data on the FDI flows and stocks by destination in 2003 to 2006. There were 151 host economies in the sample for FDI flows and 172 host economies in the sample for FDI stocks. However, due to lack of macroeconomic data for many of these economies for some years, we are forced to use two substantially smaller subsamples, namely, a subsample of 90 to 98 host economies for flows and a subsample of 125 to 150 host economies for stocks, depending on the choice of our explanatory variables and their data availability. The gravity equation to be estimated for the purpose of uncovering the determinants of China's outward FDI is as follows:[16]

$$\log(\text{FDI}_{i,t}) = \alpha + \beta_1 \cdot \log(\text{GDP}_{i,t}) + \beta_2 \cdot \log(\text{PGDP}_{i,t}) + \beta_3 \cdot \log(\text{dist}_i) + \beta_4 \cdot \text{ChineseLang}_i + \beta_5 \cdot \text{Border}_i + \beta_6 \cdot \text{Landlock}_i + \beta_7 \cdot \text{Island}_i + \beta_8 \cdot \text{Dummy}_t,$$

where FDI_{it} stands for China's FDI flow to (or FDI stock in) economy i in year t, GDP_{it} and PGDP_{it} stand for the host economy's real GDP and real per capita GDP, respectively;[17] dist_i stands for the distance between the economy's capital and Beijing, ChineseLang_i is a dummy variable for the use of the Chinese language, Border_i stands for its sharing a common border with China, Landlock_i indicates that it is a landlocked economy, and Island_i indicates that it is an island economy.

Because FDI that goes into tax havens and offshore financial centers will typically be invested elsewhere, these host economies are not the ultimate destination of the FDI. In order to avoid the influence of FDI that went to tax havens and offshore financial centers, we carried out the estimation

16. In theory, China's exports to its host economies could be a factor in its outward FDI to them. However, the coefficient of correlation between them was rather small. The coefficient of correlation between China's annual exports and FDI flow in 2003 to 2006 ranged from 0.3 to 0.5; that between China's annual exports and year end FDI stock ranged from 0.53 to 0.55 during the same period. Due to these results, we have decided not to include China's exports as an explanatory variable in the regression equation.

17. The estimation results are qualitatively similar whether the GDP of host economies was measured in nominal or real terms.

Table 14.5   Regression results for recipient economies of China's outward foreign direct investment (FDI) flows (2003–2006)

	Full sample	Tax haven economies (OECD list) excluded	Offshore financial center economies (IMF list) excluded[a]
log(GDP)	0.34782***	0.37272***	0.35160***
	(0.06634)	(0.07164)	(0.07252)
log(PGDP)	–0.07953	–0.09717	–0.07004
	(0.10504)	(0.10908)	(0.11214)
log(dist)	–0.33384	–0.43786**	–0.45020**
	(0.21989)	(0.21883)	(0.21889)
ChineseLang	4.21955***	4.26286***	
	(0.77379)	(0.76620)	
Border	1.12032***	0.98454**	0.83061**
	(0.39081)	(0.38849)	(0.39380)
Landlock	–0.59648**	–0.57681**	–0.53456*
	(0.27200)	(0.26986)	(0.27474)
Island	–0.19364	–0.35730	–0.37500
	(0.30334)	(0.31798)	(0.35283)
R^2	0.3087	0.3212	0.2364
No. of observations	392	375	362

Notes: Standard deviations are in parentheses. OECD = Organization for Economic Cooperation and Development.

[a]Because Hong Kong, Macau, and Singapore appeared on the International Monetary Fund (IMF) list, and Taiwan had no FDI from China, the ChineseLang dummy became irrelevant for the sample that excluded offshore financial center economies.

***Significant at the 1 percent level.
**Significant at the 5 percent level.
*Significant at the 10 percent level.

of the gravity equation first by using the full sample and then by excluding them. Because there are many country lists of tax havens and offshore financial centers, we adopt the two most widely used lists, namely, the tax haven list issued by the OECD in 2000,[18] and the offshore financial center list issued by the IMF in 2006.[19]

The estimation results of the gravity equation (except those for the time dummies) for FDI flows are reported in table 14.5, and those for FDI stocks are reported in table 14.6. It should be pointed out that the real GDP data for the entire period were taken from IMF's *World Economy Outlook,* and

18. The OECD report listed thirty-five countries/regions as tax havens: Andorra, Anguilla, Antigua and Barbuda, Aruba, Bahamas, Bahrain, Barbados, Belize, British Virgin Islands, Cook Islands, Dominica, Gibraltar, Grenada, Guernsey/Sark/Alderney, Isle of Man, Jersey, Liberia, Liechtenstein, Maldives, Marshall Islands, Monaco, Montserrat, Nauru, The Netherlands Antilles, Niue, Panama, Samoa, Seychelles, St Lucia, St. Christopher and Nevis, St. Vincent and the Grenadines, Tonga, Turks and Caicos, U.S. Virgin Islands, and Vanuatu.

19. The IMF report listed forty-six countries/regions as offshore financial centers: Bahrain, Andorra, Aruba, Hong Kong Special Administrative Region (SAR), Belize, Anguilla,

Table 14.6   **Regression results for recipient economies of China's outward foreign direct investment (FDI) stocks (2003–2006)**

	Full sample	Tax haven countries (OECD list) excluded	Offshore financial center countries (IMF list) excluded[a]
log(GDP)	0.62499***	0.70896***	0.67533***
	(0.05363)	(0.06023)	(0.05803)
log(PGDP)	–0.56010***	–0.64311***	–0.62610***
	(0.08950)	(0.09454)	(0.09419)
log(dist)	0.06776	–0.09136	–0.10108
	(0.20567)	(0.20979)	(0.20340)
ChineseLang	4.39037***	4.61002***	
	(0.69751)	(0.69994)	
Border	1.28780***	1.01828***	0.74908**
	(0.36532)	(0.37049)	(0.36717)
Landlock	–0.82442***	–0.76846***	–0.79178***
	(0.22817)	(0.22929)	(0.22735)
Island	0.21579	–0.18572	0.01671
	(0.25107)	(0.27686)	(0.29391)
R^2	0.3515	0.3604	0.3087
No. of observations	563	519	500

Note: See table 14.5 notes.

[a]Because Hong Kong, Macau, and Singapore appeared on the International Monetary Fund (IMF) list, and Taiwan had no FDI from China, the ChineseLang dummy became irrelevant for the sample that excluded offshore financial center economies.

***Significant at the 1 percent level.

**Significant at the 5 percent level.

similar estimation results were obtained when the real GDP data for 2003 and 2004 were substituted with real GDP data from the Penn World Tables, which do not have data for 2005 and 2006.

The results in table 14.5 reveal that, as expected, the host economies' GDP had a positive impact, whereas their respective distances from China had a negative impact on attracting China's FDI.[20] The landlocked economies seemed to be at a disadvantage in attracting Chinese FDI, while sharing a common border with China (which included some landlocked economies) was a positive factor in attracting China's FDI. While the use of the Chinese language had a positive impact on China's FDI, there were only four such

---

Grenada, Ireland, Bermuda, Antigua and Barbuda, Lebanon, Luxembourg, Cayman Islands, Bahamas, Malaysia (Labuan), Malta, Cyprus, Barbados, Marshall Islands, Switzerland, Gibraltar, British Virgin Islands, Nauru, Guernsey, Cook Islands, Turks and Caicos Islands, Isle of Man, Costa Rica, Jersey, Dominica, Macao SAR, Liechtenstein, Mauritius, The Netherlands Antilles, Monaco, Niue, Montserrat, Palau, Samoa, Panama, Seychelles, St. Kitts and Nevis, Singapore, St. Lucia, St. Vincent and the Grenadines, and Vanuatu.

20. But the coefficient for the GDP variable was not statistically significant when the full sample was used, that is, when the influence of tax havens was not controlled for.

economies in the world.[21] As in other studies, the language variable served to capture the impact of common culture and custom, and in the case of Hong Kong and Macau, it probably also captured their political affiliation with China. The host economy's per capita GDP and its being an island had no impact at all.

The estimation results about China's FDI stocks as contained in table 14.6 are similar to those contained in table 14.5, with two exceptions: first, real per capita GDP had a significantly negative impact, suggesting that, in the past, China's FDI tended to be negatively correlated with the level of development of the host economies; second, the distance ceased to have any significant impact on China's FDI. To the extent that FDI flows are more volatile than stocks, one could argue on theoretical grounds that the gravity model has greater validity for stocks than for flows and, thus, has greater explanatory power.[22] Hence, the negative relationship between China's FDI and the real per capita GDP of the host economies should not be ignored. Nevertheless, the determinants of China's FDI as revealed in tables 14.5 and 14.6 should be interpreted with caution because a predominant share of the FDI was invested in the world's tax havens, implying the investment's ultimate destination is to a large extent unknown.

14.6 Determinants of the Outward FDI of the World's Source Economies: Benchmarks for China

On the one hand, because there was a structural change in China's outward FDI in recent years (e.g., less restrictions due to increased supply of foreign reserves, more liberal approval processes, government encouragement, etc.), its past FDI flows from the 1980s would tend to underestimate China's future investment flows. On the other hand, the number of observations from 2003 to 2006 is too small to make any estimation reliable. An alternative approach is to use the experiences of the world's source economies at various stages of economic development over a reasonably long period of time to explore the determinants of China's outward FDI. Still another approach is to use the experiences of Japan and South Korea, two East Asian economies that are more advanced than China in their stages of economic development and their overseas investment, as benchmarks for China's past and future FDI.

A question is whether the experience with FDI far in the past is good for predicting investment behavior in the future because FDI has become increasingly more important in an increasingly globalized world economy.

21. Outside China, the Chinese language is used in Hong Kong, Macao, Singapore, and Taiwan. However, China's outward FDI in Taiwan was zero due to policy restrictions on the part of Taiwan's government.
22. When the two regression equations use the same set of explanatory variables, the R^2 for stocks is indeed greater than that for flows.

The experience of Japan, South Korea, and other leading investor countries in the world might fail to capture the dynamics of China's future FDI. Another question is whether the experience of the world's economies is relevant to China's FDI in view of the fact that the key Chinese investors are closely related to various levels of government.

We have no good answers to these two questions. We do not know if the key Chinese investors' relationships with their governments will lead them to make more or less FDI than if they were privately owned, and we believe that the world's experience with FDI may contain useful hints about China's future aggregate FDI. In any event, we believe that having some bases of benchmarking would seem better than having none at all.

14.6.1   Determinants of FDI Flows for 211 Source Economies

We use a sample of 211 source economies that had the relevant macroeconomic statistics during 1980 to 2005. More specifically, the equation for outward FDI is as the following:

$$\log (F_{i,t}) = \beta_1 \cdot \log (GDP_{i,t}) + \beta_2 \cdot \log (PGDP_{i,t}) + \beta_3 \cdot \log (FR_{i,t})$$
$$+ \beta_4 \cdot Open_{i,t} + \beta_5 \cdot Dep_{i,t} + \beta_6 \cdot WTH_{i,t} + \beta_6 \cdot t + C,$$

where $F_{i,t}$ is source economy i's outward FDI flow or stock at time t, $GDP_{i,t}$ and $PGDP_{i,t}$ are the economy's real GDP (constant prices: chain series) and real per capita GDP,[23] $FR_{i,t}$ stands for its foreign reserves, Open stands for its degree of openness (which is represented by "trade openness," $TOpen$ = total trade/GDP,[24] or "financial openness," $FOpen$ = inward FDI flow/GDP)[25], $Dep_{i,t} = \log (Exch_{i,t}) - \log (Exch_{i,t-1})$ measures the rate of depreciation of country i's currency, or the difference between the current period log value of exchange rate (the number of local currency per U.S. dollar) and that of the previous period, C is a constant, and WTH_i stands for a dummy variable associated with the status of tax heaven or offshore financial center but weighted by its relative importance in attracting FDI (i.e., its inward FDI divided by the world's total inward FDI). The variables $F_{i,t}$, $FR_{i,t}$, exports, and imports are adjusted with the U.S. Consumer Price Index (CPI) index with 2000 as the base year.[26]

The estimation results are reported in table 14.7.[27] They indicate that

---

23. Data on real GDP before 2004 are obtained from PWT6.2 and that after 2005 from the World Bank's *World Development Indicators* (*WDI*), while data on population are obtained from *WDI*.

24. The total trade-GDP ratio of an economy is given by the ratio of the nominal value of the sum of its exports and imports to its nominal GDP.

25. The inward FDI flow-GDP ratio of an economy is given by the ratio of the nominal value of inward FDI flow to its nominal GDP.

26. Data on foreign reserves, exports, imports, and U.S. CPI are obtained from the World Bank's *World Development Indicators* and IMF's IFS statistics, and data on outward FDI flows are obtained from the UNCTAD's FDI database

27. Here we only report the results when $TOpen$ is used as explanatory variable. The results with $FOpen$ as an explanatory variable are similar.

Table 14.7   **Regression results for source economies' outward foreign direct investment flows and stocks (1980–2005)**

	Flows		Stocks	
	(1)	(2)	(3)	(4)
log(GDP)	0.91625***	0.89516***	0.99006***	0.95071***
	(0.05672)	(0.05724)	(0.04342)	(0.04340)
log(PGDP)	1.18505***	1.22769***	1.06723***	1.12771***
	(0.06636)	(0.06713)	(0.04991)	(0.049990)
log(FR)	0.14962***	0.11780**	0.04900	0.01887
	(0.04955)	(0.04977)	(0.03825)	(0.03800)
TOpen	0.56185***	0.25752*	0.310***	–0.18991*
	(0.12659)	(0.15622)	(0.097993)	(0.11861)
Dep	–0.70089***	–0.71483***	–0.30845***	–0.31888***
	(0.12670)	(0.12701)	(0.09844)	(0.09763)
t	0.02066***	0.02217***	0.05892***	0.06201***
	(0.00799)	(0.00805)	(0.00593)	(0.00590)
WTH (OECD)	808.28124***		488.99461***	
	(156.46368)		(111.13303)	
WTH (IMF)		67.63911***		103.64531***
		(17.11093)		(13.45273)
R^2	0.6128	0.6108	0.6804	0.6856
No. of observations	2,088	2,088	2,411	2,411

Notes: Standard deviations are in parentheses. OECD = Organization for Economic Cooperation and Development; IMF = International Monetary Fund.
***Significant at the 1 percent level.
**Significant at the 5 percent level.
*Significant at the 10 percent level.

both real GDP and real per capita GDP had a significantly positive impact, whereas currency depreciation had a significantly negative impact on the source economies' outward FDI flows (equivalently, currency revaluation had a positive impact on outward FDI). The coefficients for the GDP variables were similar in magnitude regardless of whether the OECD list of tax havens or the IMF list of offshore financial centers was used. It is interesting that the coefficient of real GDP was slightly below unity, but that for per capita real GDP was slightly above unity, with the latter suggesting that the stage of economic development appeared to be an even more important determinant of FDI outflows than the size of the source economies.

As expected, the coefficient of foreign reserves was positive. However, it was statistically significant only for FDI flows. The coefficient of openness was significantly positive for FDI flows, but surprisingly, the coefficient for FDI stocks was negative at the 10 percent significance level when the IMF list of offshore financial centers was used. The coefficients of the tax haven dummy variable WTH_i, while significantly positive, had substantially different sizes depending on the list of tax havens.

After controlling for real GDP, real per capita GDP, foreign reserves, openness, currency depreciation, and tax haven status, there remained a significantly positive time trend for both FDI flow and stock, which supports the hypothesis that FDI becomes increasingly important over time for all economies.

In view of the pressure generated by China's bursting foreign reserves (US$1.9 trillion by November 2008) on its money supply and its exchange rate, it had been China's official policy to encourage foreign reserves to leave the country until the onset of the global financial and economic crisis of 2008: "To open the flood gate," according to the official policy speak. As a result of this new policy, there will be a significant increase in both outward direct investment and portfolio investment. So far, there are two major channels of "flood letting": (a) overseas investment by qualified domestic institutional investors (QDII) to initially invest in Hong Kong but ultimately in the entire world; (b) overseas investment by a state-owned foreign investment arm called China Investment Corporation (CIC), whose initial investment fund was US$200 billion.[28] China announced in August 2007 that individual Chinese citizens would be allowed to invest any amount overseas via Tianjin's Seashore New Zone and other cities. This policy, popularly dubbed "Hong Kong Stocks through Train" that was expected to be extended to investment in the rest of the world over time, was later aborted due to internal conflicts of interest and concerns about national financial security, such as uncontrolled capital flight and further weakening of a collapsed Chinese stock market.

With the onset of the biggest financial and economic crisis since the Great Depression in the 1930s and serious losses by CIC, however, Chinese firms started to reassess their foreign investment strategies. Whether this will have a permanent major negative impact on China's outward FDI remains to be seen.

14.6.2   Determinants of Japan and South Korea's Aggregate FDI

Japan and Korea are China's two significant East Asian neighbors that have gone through stages of economic development that China is expected to go through in the future. In terms of per capita real GDP, China's present development stage is similar to Japan's in the 1960s and Korea's in the 1980s.[29] Thus, Japan and South Korea's experiences with outward FDI could be indicative of the development of China's future FDI. In section 14.1, we noted that Hong and Sun (2004), by comparing growth trends, found that

28. Even before the investment company was officially established, China invested US$3 billion in the Blackstone Group, a private equity firm, in May 2007. After the subprime debacle that hurt many major investment banks, the company invested US$5 billion in Morgan Stanley for a 9.9 percent stake.

29. According to PWT6.2, in 2004 China's real per capita GDP (at Laspeyres constant prices) was US$ 5,333, which was close to that of Japan in 1962 (US$ 5,550) and of Korea in 1983 (US$ 5,457).

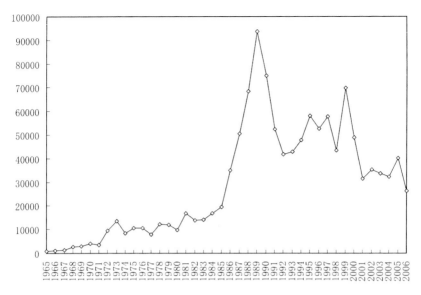

Fig. 14.2   Japan's outward FDI flow (US$ millions at 2000 constant price), 1965–2006

Sources: Japan External Trade Organization (JETRO) and International Financial Statistics (IFS).

China's aggregate FDI outflows during 1988 to 2002 were quite similar to those of South Korea during the same period and to those of Japan in 1968 to 1982. Instead of directly comparing growth trends, in this section, we shall match China's stages of economic development as measured by per capita real GDP with those of South Korea and Japan.

Figures 14.2 and 14.3 depict, respectively, Japan's aggregate outward FDI flow from 1965 to 2006 and Korea's aggregate outward FDI flow from 1980 to 2006. From these figures, we observe that each country experienced two high growth periods of outward FDI flow. From 1967 to 1973, Japan's FDI flow increased by about 855 percent (which translated into a compound average rate of growth of 45.6 percent per annum), and from 1985 to 1989 its flow increased by about 380 percent (which translated into a compound average rate of growth of 48.0 percent per annum). Similarly, from 1989 to 1996, Korea's outward FDI flow increased by about 517 percent (which translated into a compound average rate of growth of 29.7 percent per annum), and from 2003 to 2006, its flow increased by about 141 percent (which translated into a compound average rate of growth of 34.1 percent per annum). Interestingly, Japan's real per capita GDP (measured at Laspeyres constant prices) in 1968, 1973, and 1985 was US$ 9,286; US$ 13,359; and US$ 17,434, respectively, and Korea's real per capita GDP (at Laspeyres constant prices) in 1989, 1996, and 2003 were US$ 8,689;

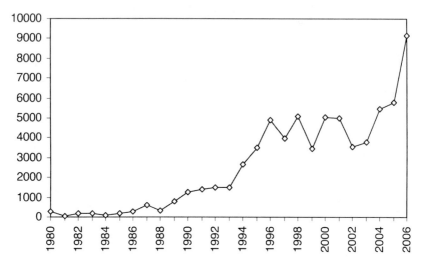

Fig. 14.3   Korea's outward FDI flow (US$ millions at 2000 constant price), 1980–2006

Sources: Korea Eximbank and IFS; FDI figures were deflated by U.S. CPI.

Note: The figure for 1980 stands for the cumulated outward FDI flows up to 1980.

US$ 14,115; and US$ 17,595, respectively. For these two countries, US$ 8,300; US$ 14,200; and US$ 17,000 appeared to be three watersheds of outward FDI.

A simplistic idea is that when China's real GDP reaches these critical levels, its FDI may grow at comparable rates. However, because China has greater income disparity, and that outward FDI tends to originate mostly from the more advanced Chinese regions, even if Japan and Korea's experiences were to be repeated in China, the watersheds may occur at lower levels of real per capita GDP. Moreover, as the extent of globalization in the twenty-first century is greater than that in the 1970s as well as the 1990s, China's FDI may exceed those of Japan and South Korea for the same level of real per capita GDP.

As demonstrated in table 14.7, real GDP and real per capita GDP, foreign reserves, openness, and currency appreciation had a significantly positive impact on the amount of outward FDI. An examination of the relationship between the exchange rate of the Korean won and Korea's outward FDI shows weak correlation between them. In the case of Japan, its first period of rapid growth of outward FDI began in 1968, two years before the yen's appreciation in 1970. Its second period of rapid growth in FDI began in 1986, in the same year of the beginning of currency appreciation, but its FDI started to decrease in 1989 even though the yen reached its highest value in 1995. Thus, it would seem reasonable not to include currency depreciation as an explanatory variable.

Table 14.8	Regression results of the outward foreign direct investment flows of Japan (1965–2004) and Korea (1981–2004)	
	log(GDP)	2.62109
		(0.31818)***
	l_1 (PGDP)	0.42293
		(0.25037)*
	l_2 (PGDP)	0.22870
		(0.35259)
	l_3 (PGDP)	0.29950
		(0.45017)
	R^2	0.9948
	No. of observations	64

Note: Standard deviations are in parentheses.
***Significant at the 1 percent level.
*Significant at the 10 percent level.

When the explanatory variables foreign reserves and openness were included in estimating the determinants of Japanese and South Korean FDI flows, the estimation results became unstable, perhaps due to the small sample size and the strong correlation among some of the explanatory variables. Thus, these two variables are excluded. That is, we include only real GDP and real per capita GDP as the regressors. To capture the upward jumps in Japan and Korea's outward FDI flows at the critical levels of economic development, we need a model in which the coefficient of real per capita GDP depends on which of the following four development levels the investing country found itself: (0) less than US$ 8,500; (1) between US$ 8,501 and US$ 14,200; (2) between US$ 14,201 and US$ 17,000; and (3) greater than US$ 17,001. More specifically, we estimate the following regression model with Japan and Korea's FDI flow data:[30]

$$\log (F_{i,t}) = \beta_1 \log (GDP_{i,t}) + \gamma_i + \alpha_1 \cdot l_1 (PGDP_{i,t}) + \alpha_2 \cdot l_2 (PGDP_{i,t}) + \alpha_3 \cdot l_3 (PGDP_{i,t}),$$

where $F_{i,t}$ is the country i's FDI flow (measured at constant price) in time t, $GDP_{i,t}$ is its real GDP (constant prices: chain series) in time t, γ_i captures country i's fixed effects, $l_i(PGDP_{i,t})$ is the dummy variable for development level l.

The estimation results are given in table 14.8, which shows that the coefficient for real GDP was significantly positive, capturing not only the fact that Japan as a bigger country than Korea also invested more than Korea, but also that both countries invested more as they grew bigger, hold-

---

30. Japan's FDI stock statistics before 1980 are unavailable, making estimation of a similar model in FDI stock impossible. The UNCTAD database contains both flow and stock data from 1980, whereas data obtained from the Japan External Trade Organization (JETRO) contains only flow data beginning in 1965.

ing real per capita GDP as given. Among the three dummy variables, only that for development level 1 was significantly positive, implying that reaching the per capita real GDP of US$ 8,500 had a statistically significantly positive impact on FDI flows.

If the determinants of outward FDI uncovered in the preceding sections are regarded as reliable, then they may be used as two different benchmarks with which to forecast the amount of Chinese FDI outflows in future years by incorporating the forecasts of China's explanatory variables. As stated in the preceding, it remains to be seen to whether the 2008 global financial and economic crisis led to a significant regime change for China's outward FDI.

14.7   Host Economies, Sector Composition, and Geographical Distribution: A Comparison of China against Japan and South Korea

We first analyze the determinants of the amounts of South Korea (1981–2006) and Japan's (1965–2004) FDI flows to their different host economies and compare them with the results for Chinese FDI as contained in table 14.5. The regression results for the gravity equation for South Korea and Japan are shown in tables 14.9 and 14.10, respectively, with the coefficients for time dummies omitted. The common border variable was included for neither South Korea (which had common border only with North Korea, an adver-

Table 14.9   **Regression results for recipient economies of South Korea's outward foreign direct investment (FDI) flows (1981–2006)**

	Full sample	Tax haven economies (OECD list) excluded	Offshore financial center economies (IMF list) excluded[a]
log(GDP)	0.62371***	0.67150***	0.73981***
	(0.03920)	(0.04056)	(0.04269)
log(PGDP)	−0.01846	−0.04520	−0.15548**
	(0.06349)	(0.06353)	(0.06894)
log(dist)	−0.46704***	−0.50343***	−0.30681***
	(0.08717)	(0.08694)	(0.09096)
Landlock	−0.21794	−0.09816	0.16090
	(0.19516)	(0.19557)	(0.20581)
Island	0.16547	0.25192	0.42101**
	(0.15574)	(0.15636)	(0.16746)
R^2	0.2871	0.3033	0.3157
No. of observations	1,334	1,305	1,195

Note: See table 14.5 notes.

[a]Because Hong Kong, Macau, and Singapore appeared on the International Monetary Fund (IMF) list, and Taiwan had no FDI from China, the ChineseLang dummy became irrelevant for the sample that excluded offshore financial center economies.

***Significant at the 1 percent level.

**Significant at the 5 percent level.

Table 14.10   Regression results for recipient economies of Japan's outward foreign direct investment (FDI) flows (1965–2004)

	Full sample	Tax haven economies (OECD list) excluded	Offshore financial center economies (IMF list) excluded[a]
log(GDP)	0.51785***	0.81830***	0.70191***
	(0.02779)	(0.02870)	(0.03248)
log(PGDP)	0.32544***	0.50903***	0.09119*
	(0.04746)	(0.04376)	(0.05180)
log(dist)	−0.57466***	−0.82535***	−0.41346***
	(0.08402)	(0.07441)	(0.08847)
Landlock	−0.09821	0.69567***	−0.32926*
	(0.15794)	(0.14201)	(0.18778)
Island	0.73837***	1.21364***	0.85247***
	(0.11771)	(0.10806)	(0.13322)
R^2	0.2766	0.4515	0.3387
No. of observations	2,014	1,860	1,663

Note: See table 14.5 notes.

[a]Because Hong Kong, Macau, and Singapore appeared on the International Monetary Fund (IMF) list, and Taiwan had no FDI from China, the ChineseLang dummy became irrelevant for the sample that excluded offshore financial center economies.

***Significant at the 1 percent level.

*Significant at the 10 percent level.

sary during much of this period), nor Japan (which is an island economy that does not share any common border with any other country).

The results for China, South Korea, and Japan are similar in that their coefficients for GDP and distance had the same signs. The coefficient of per capita GDP was negative for both China and South Korea, but positive for Japan, probably reflecting the fact that Japan was a more advanced economy than both China and South Korea in the sample periods. Being a landlocked host economy was a disadvantage in attracting Chinese and Japanese FDI but not South Korean FDI.[31] Finally, being an island economy had a significantly positive impact on attracting Japanese FDI, a less significantly positive impact on attracting South Korean FDI, and no impact on Chinese FDI.

Next, let's examine the sector composition of Japan and South Korea's FDI flows. Figures 14.4 and 14.5 illustrate the percentages of Japan and South Korea's outward FDI flows in different sectors, respectively. Before 1982, the mining sector was an important target of Japan's FDI, averaging about 20 percent. After that year, the sector's share fell to below 5 percent. South Korea's experience around 1990 was similar: before 1989, the share of investment in the mining sector was more than 10 percent, but it fell to

31. Japan made significant investment in Taiwan, Indonesia, and The Philippines.

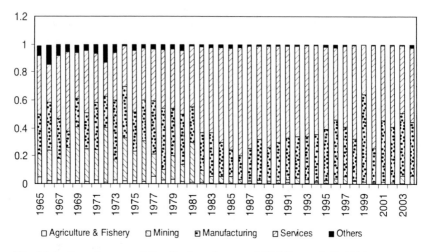

Fig. 14.4   Japan's sectoral distribution of outward FDI flows: 1965–2004
Source: JETRO.

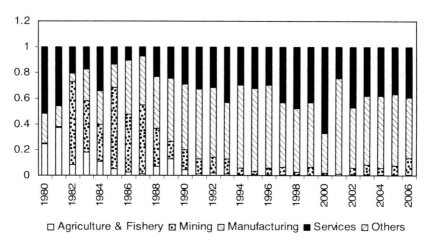

Fig. 14.5   Korea's sectoral distribution of outward FDI flow: 1980–2006
Source: Korea Eximbank.
Note: The figures for 1980 refer to cumulated outward FDI flows up to 1980.

about 5 percent by 1994. In contrast, the two countries' shares of investment in the services sector grew gradually over time. After 2000, Japan's share of investment in the services sector was about 50 percent, whereas South Korea's share was about 40 percent.

Notice that the decline of Japan's FDI in the mining sector occurred in its development stage 2 as defined in the previous section, whereas the decline of South Korea's FDI in the same sector occurred right from the beginning of its development stage 1. Also, South Korea's high share of FDI in the services sector occurred in its development stage 2, whereas Japan's high share of FDI in the same sector occurred long after it entered its development stage 3. That is to say, South Korea's sector composition followed similar changes as Japan's, but the pace of change was much faster, implying that there seemed to be less similarity in the two countries' evolution of their sector composition than in the evolution in their aggregate FDI outflows. A possible explanation is that South Korea's real per capita GDP reached Japan's level twenty years later, and the more globalized world economy by then could have required or permitted greater foreign investment in the services industries.

Let us compare China's sector composition of FDI flow with those of Japan and South Korea. In the following figures, we assume that investment in financial industries was one-sixth of the total FDI flows and stocks in 2003 to 2005, more or less the ratio observed in 2006. On this assumption, during 2003 to 2006, China's average share of investment in the mining sector was 29.8 percent, which was higher than Japan and South Korea's historically high shares. Because China's present stage of economic development is similar to that of Japan in the 1960s and South Korea in the 1980s, China's investment in this sector may continue to grow until China's real per capita GDP reaches the range of US$ 10,000.[32] The average share of China's investment in the manufacturing sector during 2003 to 2006 was 12.4 percent, less than Japan in the 1960s and South Korea in the 1980s. Thus, its share in investment in the manufacturing sector may grow further.

Making the same assumption about the shares of FDI in finance during 2003 to 2005, we see that China's investment in the services sector during 2003 to 2006 averaged at 55.5 percent, which was significantly higher than that of Japan and South Korea in the 2000s. Judged against the experiences of Japan and South Korea, it seems curious why China's investment share in the services sector was so high, even after account is taken of the fact that the world economy in the twenty-first century was more services-oriented than in the last century. One may speculate that it was a result of China's capital control policy, which induced Chinese firms to invest in offshore financial centers before they were reinvested elsewhere in other nonservice-related sectors (including "round-tripping" FDI back to China). Perhaps the fact that most of the Chinese investors were SOEs was another reason because they might have an incentive to hide their identity and destination of investment through companies set up in the tax havens. If Japan and South Korea's sector compositions in outward FDI had predictive value for China's, however, then China's investment share in the services sector may decline over time in response to China's increasing liberalization of its capital accounts and as a result of increases in the shares of mining and manufacturing.

32. This may occur in the early 2010s.

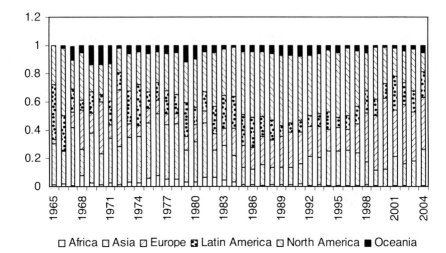

□ Africa □ Asia ◪ Europe ◩ Latin America □ North America ■ Oceania

Fig. 14.6   Japan's regional distribution of outward FDI flow: 1965–2004
Source: JETRO.

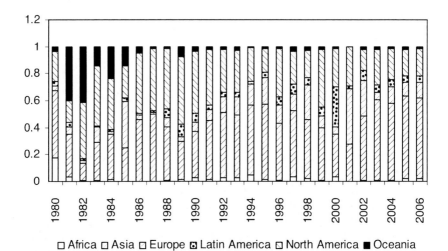

□ Africa □ Asia □ Europe ◙ Latin America □ North America ■ Oceania

Fig. 14.7   Korea's regional distribution of outward FDI flow: 1980–2006
Source: Korea Eximbank.
Note: The figures for 1980 refer to cumulated outward FDI flows up to 1980.

Figures 14.6 and 14.7 depict the shares of Japan and South Korea's FDI flow to different regions. A comparison of these figures against those for China contained in table 14.3 indicates that the share of China's outward FDI flow to Asia in 2003 to 2005 was broadly similar to those of Japan in 1960s and South Korea in 1980s. However, China's shares of investment flows to Europe and North America in the same years were much lower than those of Japan and South Korea's in their respective comparable periods. In contrast, China's share of investment flow to Latin America was abnormally higher than Japan and South Korea's due to China's huge investment in tax havens in Latin America.

Japan's average FDI share in Africa from 1965 to 1985 was 3.6 percent, equal to that of China during 2003 to 2006. However, Japan's share declined significantly after 1985 and reached a negligible 0.3 percent by 2004. Compared with Japan, South Korea's FDI share in Africa was relatively low in the entire period. During 1990 to 1998, its average share was about 2.3 percent. Its African share began to decrease after 1998, and by 2004, it dropped to 0.85 percent, which was less than China's current share. Given Africa's much greater political importance to China than to Japan and South Korea, China's future African shares could easily be much higher than the current shares of Japan and South Korea.

14.8   Summary and Direction of Further Research

In this paper, after briefly describing China's "go overseas" policy, we have provided a systematic analysis of the size and composition of China's outward FDI in 2003 to 2006, using data provided by China's Ministry of Commerce. In addition, we made an attempt to uncover the determinants of the direction and amount of China's outward FDI and briefly described China's foreign direct investment and other forms of overseas cooperation in the energy sector. Finally, we also attempted to understand the determinants of the world's source economies' outward FDI and, in particular, those of Japan and South Korea, in order to provide benchmarks for China's past and future outward FDI.

Our empirical analysis of the destination of China's FDI reveals that the real GDP of host economies had a positive impact on the amounts of Chinese FDI flows to and FDI stocks in them. Their real per capita GDP had no impact on FDI flows but a negative impact on FDI stocks. Their distance from China, sharing a common border and speaking the same language, had the expected impact. The empirical analysis of the world's source economies reveals that real GDP, real per capita GDP, foreign reserves, currency appreciation, and time trend all had a significantly positive impact on their aggregate outward FDI flows and stocks.

One direction of further research is the use of the experience of the world's leading source economies, in particular Japan, South Korea, and major emerging economies such as Brazil, Russia, and India to forecast China's outward FDI in the future.

References

Antkiewicz, Agata, and John Whalley. 2006. Recent Chinese buyout activity and the implications for global architecture. NBER Working Paper no. 12072. Cambridge, MA: National Bureau of Economic Research, March.

Cai, Kevin G. 1999. Outward foreign direct investment: A novel dimension of China's integration into the regional and global economy. *China Quarterly* 160:856–80.

Cheung, Yin-Wong, and Xing Wang Qian. 2009. Empirics of China's outward direct investment. *Pacific Economic Review* 14 (3): 312–41.

Child, John, and Suzana B. Rodrigues. 2005. The internationalization of Chinese firms: A case for theoretical extension? *Management and Organization Review* 1 (3): 381–410.

Deng, Ping. 2004. Outward investment by Chinese MNCs: Motivations and implications. *Business Horizons* 47 (3): 8–16.

Hong, Eunsuk, and Laixiang Sun. 2004. Go overseas via direct investment: Internationalization strategy of Chinese corporations in a comparative prism. Working Paper. University of London, Centre for Financial and Management Studies. School of Oriental and African Studies.

Ministry of Commerce. 2004–07. *Statistical bulletin of China's outward foreign direct investment 2003–2006* (in Chinese). Beijing: Ministry of Commerce.

Taylor, Ian. 2009. *China's new role in Africa*, 37–63. Boulder, Colorado: Lynne Rienner.

Zweig, David. 2006. "Resource Diplomacy" under hegemony: The sources of Sino-American competition in the 21st century? Working Paper no. 18. Center on China's Transnational Relations, Hong Kong University of Science and Technology, Hong Kong.

Comment   Nicholas Lardy

The analysis of Leonard K. Cheng and Zihui Ma is an important addition to our understanding of the nature of China's outbound foreign direct investment (FDI). While outbound FDI from China has grown substantially in recent years, it remains far smaller than inward investment flows, and most of the existing literature focuses on the latter.

One strength of the analysis of Cheng and Ma is that it relies on FDI data that are compiled in accordance with Organization for Economic Cooperation and Development (OECD) definitions and International Monetary Fund (IMF) balance of payments guidelines. This is a much more realistic approach than the all too prevalent practice of relying on a compilation of press reports. Press accounts fail to differentiate between proposed projects and actual flows, fail to recognize that flows for those projects that are undertaken frequently occur over a period of years, and fail to differentiate between projects financed with Chinese direct investment from those financed with loans from Chinese financial institutions.

Nicholas Lardy is a senior fellow at the Peterson Institute for International Economics.

Cheng and Ma use a gravity model to estimate the determinants of China's FDI outflows, finding that they are significantly related to the host economies' gross domestic product (GDP) and negatively related to distance from China. They report results also for a large universe of countries with outbound FDI, finding that in addition to GDP and per capita GDP in the host country, that the level of reserves, openness (measured by the ratio of trade or inward FDI flow to GDP), and currency appreciation in the investing country all are also significant in explaining outward FDI flows. In a closer examination of outbound FDI from Japan and South Korea, they find discontinuous upward jumps in FDI outflows as these economies achieved critical thresholds of per capita GDP.

The authors are wisely cautious in trying to extrapolate the implications of these findings for the future levels of FDI outflows from China. China's outflows could easily exceed those of their East Asian neighbors for at least two reasons. First, the level of China's foreign exchange reserves is much larger, and these large reserves have been achieved at a much earlier stage of economic development than was the case, for example, in Japan. Thus, there is at least the potential for much larger outbound FDI in the case of China.

Second, compared to its East Asian neighbors, China has been much more open in terms of foreign investment. To date, the most successful outbound investors in China are firms that have first competed successfully with foreign firms in China's domestic market and then later invested or made acquisitions abroad. Legend (now called Lenovo) may be the best example. Legend, which was founded in the mid-1980s, initially was a distributor of foreign brands of personal computers (PCs). It began producing PCs in 1990 when the market leaders in China were all foreign firms. Compaq, IBM, HP, and Digital Equipment were ranked one to four, respectively. But in less than a decade, in 1997, Legend had become the market leader, and by 2000 it controlled 31 percent of domestic market. In contrast, the combined market share of all foreign brands had fallen to only 15 percent. Only a few years later, Legend purchased the PC business of IBM. At the time, that transaction was one of the largest Chinese cases of outbound FDI.

The story is similar for the Chinese firm Huawei. Initially, it competed in the telephone switching equipment market against both imports and the output of Chinese joint ventures involving Siemens (Beijing International Switching Systems Corporation) and Alcatel (Shanghai Bell) and pure foreign suppliers, such as Lucent. Joint ventures and imports had 95 percent market share in 1995. But Huawei became successful competitor, and its market share rose to 18 percent and 35 percent in 1998 and 2000, respectively. Huawei then began to sell its products abroad and, shortly later, started to invest abroad.

Perhaps more Chinese brands will emerge as successful global players at an earlier stage of economic development than was the case in Korea and

Japan because China's massively larger amounts of inward foreign investment have made the domestic environment more competitive than was the case in Korea and Japan. Joint venture production in China now accounts for more than 25 percent of manufactured goods output, many times the level in Japan and South Korea in the 1960s and 1980s, respectively.

Contributors

Joshua Aizenman
Department of Economics
Engineering 2
University of California, Santa Cruz
1156 High Street
Santa Cruz, CA 95064

Mary Amiti
International Research
Federal Reserve Bank of New York
33 Liberty Street
New York, NY 10045

Kym Anderson
School of Economics and Centre for
International Economic Studies
University of Adelaide
Adelaide SA 5005, Australia

Bruce A. Blonigen
Department of Economics
University of Oregon
Eugene, OR 97403

Chad P. Bown
Department of Economics
MS 021
Brandeis University
PO Box 549110
Waltham, MA 02454-9110

Irene Brambilla
Department of Economics
37 Hillhouse
Yale University
P.O. Box 208264
New Haven, CT 06520-8264

Lee Branstetter
H. John Heinz III School of Public
Policy and Management
and Department of Social and
Decision Sciences
2504B Hamburg Hall
Carnegie Mellon University
Pittsburgh, PA 15213

Christian Broda
Graduate School of Business
University of Chicago
5807 South Woodlawn Avenue
Chicago, IL 60637

Leonard K. Cheng
School of Business and Management
Hong Kong University of Science and
Technology
Clear Water Bay
Kowloon, Hong Kong

Yin-Wong Cheung
Department of Economics
Engineering 2
University of California, Santa Cruz
1156 High Street
Santa Cruz, CA 95064

Menzie D. Chinn
Robert M. La Follette School of Public
    Affairs
and Department of Economics
University of Wisconsin
1180 Observatory Drive
Madison, WI 53706-1393

Judith M. Dean
Research Division, Office of
    Economics
United States International Trade
    Commission
500 E. Street SW
Washington, DC 20436

Haiyan Deng
The Conference Board
845 Third Avenue
New York, NY 10022-6679

Michael Dooley
Department of Economics
Engineering 2
University of California, Santa Cruz
1156 High Street
Santa Cruz, CA 95064

Robert C. Feenstra
Department of Economics
University of California, Davis
One Shields Avenue
Davis, CA 95616

C. Fritz Foley
Baker Hall 235
Harvard Business School
Soldiers Field Road
Boston, MA 02163

Joseph Francois
Department of Economics
Johannes Kepler University Linz
Altenbergerstrasse 69
A - 4040 Linz, Austria

Jeffrey Frankel
Kennedy School of Government
Harvard University
79 JFK Street
Cambridge, MA 02138

Caroline Freund
Research Department
The World Bank
1818 H Street, NW
Washington, DC 20433

Eiji Fujii
Graduate School of Systems and
    Information Engineering
University of Tsukuba
Tennodai 1-1-1, Tsukuba
Ibaraki, Japan

Galina Hale
Economic Research
Federal Reserve Bank of San Francisco
101 Mark Street, MS 1130
San Francisco, CA 94105

Gordon H. Hanson
IR/PS 0519
University of California, San Diego
9500 Gilman Drive
La Jolla, CA 92093-0519

James Harrigan
Department of Economics
University of Virginia
P.O. Box 400182
Charlottesville, VA 22904-4182

Chang Hong
Department of Economics
Clark University
950 Main Street
Worcester, MA 01610-1477

Jikun Huang
Center for Chinese Agricultural Policy
11 A Datun Road
Chaoyang District
Beijing 100101, China

Amit K. Khandelwal
Finance and Economics Division
Columbia Business School
Uris Hall 606
3022 Broadway
New York, NY 10027

Nicholas Lardy
Peterson Institute for International
    Economics
1750 Massachusetts Avenue, NW
Washington, DC 20036

Arik Levinson
Department of Economics, ICC 571
Georgetown University
3700 O Street NW
Washington, DC 20057

Yu Liu
Economic Forecasting Department
    State Information Center (SIC)
No. 58, Sanlihe Road
Xicheng District
Beijing 100045, P.R. China

Mary E. Lovely
Department of Economics
Maxwell School of Citizenship and
    Public Affairs
Syracuse University
Syracuse, NY 13244-1090

Alyson C. Ma
School of Business Administration
University of San Diego
San Diego, CA, 92110

Zihui Ma
School of Economics
Renmin University of China
Beijing, 100872 P.R. China

Will Martin
Development Research Group, Trade
The World Bank, MC3-303
1818 H Street NW
Washington, DC 20433

Thomas J. Prusa
Department of Economics
New Jersey Hall
Rutgers University
75 Hamilton Street
New Brunswick, NJ 08901-1248

Raymond Robertson
Department of Economics
Macalester College
1600 Grand Avenue
St. Paul, MN 55105

Scott Rozelle
Shorenstein APARC
Encina Hall East, E301
Stanford University
Stanford, CA 94305-6055

Peter K. Schott
Yale School of Management
135 Prospect Street
New Haven, CT 06520-8200

Shang-Jin Wei
Graduate School of Business
Columbia University
Uris Hall 619
3022 Broadway
New York, NY 10027

David E. Weinstein
Department of Economics, MC 3308
Columbia University
420 W. 118th Street
New York, NY 10027

Zhi Wang
Research Division, Office of
    Economics
United States International Trade
    Commission
Room 603F
500 E Street SW
Washington, DC 20436

Chong Xiang
Department of Economics
Purdue University
403 West State Street
West Lafayette IN 47907-2056

Bin Xu
Department of Economics and
    Decision Sciences
China Europe International Business
    School (CEIBS)
699 Hongfeng Road
Pudong, Shanghai 201206, China

Stephen Yeaple
Department of Economics
The Pennsylvania State University
520 Kern Building
University Park, PA 16802-3306

Author Index

Subject Index

Page numbers followed by f *or* t *refer to figures or tables, respectively.*